The Presidency
and the Political System

The Presidency
and the Political System

FOURTH EDITION

Michael Nelson, *Editor*

Rhodes College

A Division of Congressional Quarterly Inc.
Washington, D.C.

Book design: Joyce Kachergis, Kachergis Book Design, Pittsboro, North Carolina.

Cover Images and Credits

1		2
3	4	
5		6
7	8	
9		10
11	12	
13	14	
15	16	

1. Dwight D. Eisenhower, Dwight D. Eisenhower Library
2. William Howard Taft tosses first baseball, 1910, Library of Congress
3. Abraham Lincoln with compatriots, Library of Congress
4. Lyndon B. Johnson with Senate leaders, courtesy Lyndon Baines Johnson Library
5. Bill Clinton and Al Gore with congressional leaders, Associated Press
6. George Washington's inaugural address, 1789, mezzotint by H. S. Sadd.
7. Woodrow Wilson addresses Congress, 1916, Library of Congress
8. President Bush promotes House health care legislation, Michael Jenkins
9. Theodore Roosevelt with leaders after Russo-Japanese War, Theodore Roosevelt Collection, Harvard College Library
10. Richard Nixon with Chinese officials at the Great Wall of China, Nixon Project / National Archives
11. John F. Kennedy at joint session of Congress, photo # St-C7-2-63 in the John F. Kennedy Library
12. *Air Force One,* The White House
13. Jimmy Carter in Oval Office, The White House
14. Ulysses S. Grant, Library of Congress
15. Ronald and Nancy Reagan at Camp David, Bill Fitz-Patrick, The White House
16. Franklin D. Roosevelt at press conference, Library of Congress

Copyright © 1995 Congressional Quarterly Inc.
1414 22nd Street, N.W., Washington, D.C. 20037

Printed in the United States of America

Library of Congress Cataloging-in-Publication Data

The Presidency and the political system / Michael Nelson, editor.— 4th ed.
    p. cm.
    Includes bibliographical references and index.
    ISBN 0-87187-786-4 (hard) : —ISBN 0-87187-788-0 (soft) :
    1. Presidents—United States. I. Nelson. Michael, 1949–
JK516.P639   1994
353.03'13—dc20
                                          94-22207
                                            CIP

To my beloved wife, Linda.

She opens her mouth with wisdom,
and the teaching of kindness is on her tongue. . . .
Her children rise up and call her blessed;
her husband also, and he praises her.

PROVERBS 31:26, 28

Contents

Preface

Political scientists commonly draw a useful distinction between the *presidency*—the more than two-centuries-old office that was created by the Constitutional Convention in 1787—and the *president*—the person who at any moment occupies the office. Manifold changes have occurred in both the person and the office since the third edition of this book was published in 1990. As a result of the 1992 elections, Bill Clinton has succeeded George Bush in the White House, bringing to a close the twelve-year reign of Republican presidents and restoring unified party government to Washington. The cold war has ended—a historic triumph for the United States that has had uncertain effects on the role of the presidency in national and international affairs. Elements of the political system that interact with the president and the presidency have developed along sometimes continuing, sometimes new lines: the media, the political parties, interest groups, Congress, the Supreme Court, the others.

Parallel with events, the fourth edition of this book marks a significant change from previous editions. To be sure, I have preserved—and the authors have updated, often substantially—many of the chapters that scholars have singled out for special praise in their reviews and letters. Jeffrey K. Tulis on the rhetorical presidency, Stephen Skowronek on political time, Paul J. Quirk on presidential competence, John P. Burke on the institutional presidency, Bert A. Rockman on comparative executives, John H. Aldrich and Thomas Weko on electoral "frames," Bruce Miroff on presidential "spectacles," Sidney M. Milkis on political parties, Benjamin Ginsberg and Martin Shefter on interest groups, Joseph A. Pika III on the vice presidency, and Michael Nelson on the psychological presidency—they are all still here.

The other half of the book is entirely new—new *authors* (such as Terry M. Moe, Lyn Ragsdale, Mark A. Peterson, Bruce Buchanan, Timothy C. Cook, John Anthony Maltese, Walter R. Mebane, Jr., and Bartholomew H. Sparrow) and some new *topics* (such as policy making in conditions of divided government and the presidency in the post–cold war world). But the new chapters rise to the standard set by the old. Each reports the results of important new research about or interpretations of the presidency. Each takes full account of recent events and of recent additions to the literature of political science. Each has been written expressly for this book.

I do not agree with everything that every author has to say, nor will any reader. But together they have written a collection of essays whose readability is fully matched by its intellectual substance. Through three editions, this book has been widely assigned in courses and widely cited and reviewed in scholarly journals. Students may be assured of receiving the widest possible understanding of the presidency.

A number of people—the contributors first among them—have worked to bring this book to fruition. Susan Sullivan and Jean Woy, formerly of Congressional Quarterly, and Erwin C. Hargrove of Vanderbilt University helped me to think through the themes and organization of the first edition, and Barbara de Boinville served as a capable and gracious editor. Joanne Daniels, Nola Healy Lynch, and Tracy White contributed mightily to the second edition, as did Nancy Lammers, Kristen Carpenter Stoever, and Ann O'Malley to the third edition. For this fourth edition, I thank Brenda Carter, Michelle Sobel, and, especially, Joanne S. Ainsworth, who worked hard and well in various and manifold ways to help produce a version of this book that I hope will be even better received than its predecessors.

Michael Nelson

Contributors

JOHN H. ALDRICH is political science professor and department chair at Duke University. He is author of *Before the Convention* (1980) and coauthor of the *Change and Continuity in Elections* series, including the most recent *Change and Continuity in the 1992 Elections* (1994). His book, *Why Parties?* (forthcoming), examines American political parties. He has written numerous articles on American politics and elections and currently is researching the founding period and other topics related to democracy in America.

BRUCE BUCHANAN is professor of government at the University of Texas at Austin. He is author of *The Presidential Experience* (1978), *The Citizens' Presidency* (1987), and *Electing a President* (1991). He was executive director of the Markle Commission on the Media and the Electorate during the 1988 presidential campaign and was research director for the Markle Foundation's 1992 presidential election study. He has written articles on presidential campaigns, White House organization, and public policy. He currently is working on a comparative study of the 1988 and 1992 presidential elections.

JOHN P. BURKE teaches political science at the University of Vermont. He is author of *The Institutional Presidency* (1992) and *Bureaucratic Responsibility* (1986). He is coauthor of *How Presidents Test Reality: Decisions on Vietnam, 1954 and 1965* (1989) and *Advising Ike: The Memoirs of Attorney General Herbert Brownell* (1993).

TIMOTHY E. COOK is professor of political science at Williams College. An American Political Science Association congressional fellow and a guest scholar at the Brookings Institution from 1984 to 1985, he also has been a visiting professor at the Kennedy School of Government at Harvard and will be a visiting professor at Yale in the spring of 1995. He is author of *Making Laws and Making News: Media Strategies in the U.S. House of Representatives* (1989). He currently is working on a project that explores what it means to conceive of the news media as a political institution and on a four-site study of the interactions among news media, candidates, and citizens in the 1992 presidential election.

BENJAMIN GINSBERG teaches political science at Johns Hopkins University. He is author of *The Consequences of Consent* (1982), *The Captive Public* (1986), and *The Fatal Embrace* (1993). He is coauthor of *Poliscide* (1976), *American Government: Freedom and Power* (1990), *Politics by Other Means* (1990), and *Democrats Return to Power* (1994) and coeditor of *Do Elections Matter?* (1986) and *Readings and Cases in American Government* (1992). He has written many articles for *American Political Science Review*, *Political Science Quarterly*, *American Journal of Political Science*, and the *Washington Post*, among other publications.

JOHN ANTHONY MALTESE is assistant professor of political science at the University of Georgia. He is author of *Spin Control: The White House Office of Communications and the Management of Presidential News* (1992, 1994) and coauthor of *Selecting the President* (1992). He also has published articles and book chapters on judicial selection, the presidency, and White House communications; and he has contributed essays to the *CQ Guide to the Presidency* (1989), *The Oxford Companion to the Supreme Court* (1992), and *The Encyclopedia of the American Presidency* (1994). He currently is writing a book on the Supreme Court appointment process.

WALTER R. MEBANE, JR. teaches government at Cornell University. He has published articles on American social welfare, elections, local government fiscal activity, and methodology in *American Political Science Review* and *Political Analysis*. His current research concerns pork barrel politics in presidential and congressional elections, public opinion and public choice, and model specification selection methods.

SIDNEY M. MILKIS teaches politics and is a research associate with the Gordon Public Policy Center at Brandeis University. His articles on the presidency and political parties have appeared in *Political Science Quarterly*, *PS*, and *Administration and Society*, as well as in several edited volumes. He is author of *The President and the Parties: The Transformation of the American Party System Since the New Deal* (1993) and coauthor of *Remaking American Politics*

(1989), *The Politics of Regulatory Change: A Tale of Two Agencies* (1989), and *The American Presidency: Origins and Development, 1776–1993*, 2d ed. (1994).

BRUCE MIROFF teaches political science at the State University of New York at Albany. He is author of *Pragmatic Illusions: The Presidential Politics of John F. Kennedy* (1976) and *Icons of Democracy: American Leaders as Heroes, Aristocrats, Dissenters, and Democrats* (1993). He also has written numerous articles on the presidency and political leadership.

TERRY M. MOE is professor of political science at Stanford University and senior fellow at the Hoover Institution. He is author of *The Organization of Interests* (1980) and coauthor of *Politics, Markets, and America's Schools* (1990). He has written extensively on American political institutions and organization theory, with special attention to public bureaucracy, the presidency, and interest groups.

MICHAEL NELSON is professor of political science at Rhodes College. His articles have appeared in the *Journal of Politics, Political Science Quarterly, Public Interest*, and numerous other publications; more than forty have been anthologized in works of political science and English composition. His books include *Presidents, Politics, and Policy* (1984), *A Heartbeat Away* (1988), *The Elections of 1992* (1993), and *The American Presidency: Origins and Development, 1776–1993* (1994).

BRUCE NESMITH is assistant professor of political science at Coe College. He teaches courses on American political institutions, as well as on religion and U.S. politics. He is author of *The New Republican Coalition: The Reagan Campaigns and White Evangelicals* (forthcoming).

MARK A. PETERSON is associate professor in the Graduate School of Public and International Affairs and the Department of Political Science at the University of Pittsburgh. He is author of *Legislating Together: The White House and Capitol Hill from Eisenhower to Reagan* (1990). His work on American national institutions also has appeared in the *American Political Science Review*, in the *British Journal of Political Science*, and in edited volumes. He is editor of the *Journal of Health Politics, Policy and Law*. Named American Political Science Association congressional fellow (1990–1991), he served as a legislative assistant in the U.S. Senate. He currently is researching health care policy making at the national level.

JOSEPH A. PIKA is professor of political science and department chair at the University of Delaware. He is coauthor of *The Politics of the Presidency*, 3d ed. (1994) and of *The Presidential Contest*, 4th ed. (1992). His published work in collections and journals, including *Political Science Quarterly*, *Presidential Studies Quarterly*, and *Congress and the Presidency*, deals with White House staffing, presidential relations with Congress and with interest groups, and presidency research as a field of study. His ongoing research projects include presidential management and relations between the White House and interest groups. He served as executive director of the Delaware Commission on Government Reorganization and Effectiveness in 1993.

PAUL J. QUIRK is professor in the Department of Political Science and the Institute of Government and Public Affairs at the University of Illinois at Urbana–Champaign. He teaches courses on the presidency, political institutions, and public policy formation. He is author of *Industry Influence in Federal Regulatory Agencies* (1981) and coauthor of *The Politics of Deregulation* (1985). He and Bruce Nesmith currently are writing a book to be titled *The Presidency, Congress, and the Performance of Government*.

LYN RAGSDALE is professor of political science at the University of Arizona. She is author of *Presidential Politics* (1993) and *Vital Statistics on the Presidency* (1994) and coauthor of *The Elusive Executive* (1988). She also has written numerous articles, which have appeared in journals such as the *American Political Science Review*, *American Journal of Political Science*, *Journal of Politics*, and *Legislative Studies Quarterly*. She currently is working on a project that explores the institutionalization of the presidency from 1924 to 1992.

BERT A. ROCKMAN is professor of political science at the University of Pittsburgh, where he also is research professor at the University Center for International Studies. He is also a nonresident senior fellow at the Brookings Institution. Author of *The Leadership Question: The Presidency and the American System* (1984) and coauthor of *Bureaucrats and Politicians in Western Democracies* (1981), he most recently has coedited *Do Institutions Matter? Governing Capabilities in the United States and Abroad* (1993) and *Researching the Presidency: Vital Questions, New Approaches* (1993). His present research focuses on executive and political change in Washington, on the role of institutions in policy making, and on foreign policy decision making.

MARTIN SHEFTER is professor of political science at Cornell University. He is author of *Political Parties and the State* (1994) and *Political Crisis/Fiscal Crisis: The Collapse and Revival of New York City* (1992); he cowrote *Politics by Other Means* (1990) with Benjamin Ginsberg. He is editor of *Capital of the American Century: The National and International Influence of New York City* (1993).

STEPHEN SKOWRONEK is professor of political science at Yale University. He is author of *Building a New American State: The Expansion of National Administrative Capacities, 1877–1920* (1982) and of *The Policies Presidents Make: Leadership from John Adams to George Bush* (1993). He is also managing editor of *Studies in American Political Development*.

BARTHOLOMEW H. SPARROW teaches government at the University of Texas at Austin. He is author of *From the Outside In: The Effects of World War II on the American State* (forthcoming), which, as a dissertation, won the 1992 Leonard D. White Award of the American Political Science Association. His current research focuses on the news media as a political institution and on the relationship between changes in the international system and the development of U.S. political institutions.

JEFFREY K. TULIS teaches political science at the University of Texas at Austin. He is author of *The Rhetorical Presidency* (1987), coauthor of *The Presidency in the Constitutional Order* (1981), and coeditor of *The Johns Hopkins Series in Constitutional Thought*. He currently is writing a book on the institutional deference among president, Congress, and court.

THOMAS WEKO is assistant professor at the University of Puget Sound. He is author of *Taming the Administrative State: The Evolution of the Modern White House Personnel Office* (1994).

Part I Approaches to the Presidency

1 Evaluating the Presidency

Michael Nelson

First impressions are important in politics. Numerous studies of political socialization have found that long before children have any real knowledge of what the federal government actually does, they already think of the president in terms of almost limitless power and goodness. In this chapter, Michael Nelson uncovers powerful traces of these first impressions in the later impressions of politically aware adults. Presidential scholars, White House correspondents, average citizens, members of Congress, and civil servants working in the federal bureaucracy—each of these important constituencies may seem at first blush to hold attitudes that are detrimental to presidential power. Closer inspection, however, reveals that each group's surface judgments overlie more fundamental orientations toward politics that exalt presidential power.

The November 1, 1948, issue of *Life* magazine is a collector's item because of a picture on page 37 that is captioned, "The next president travels by ferry over the broad waters of San Francisco bay." (The picture is of Thomas E. Dewey.) Of greater significance, however, is an article that begins on page 65, called "Historians Rate U.S. Presidents." It was written by Professor Arthur M. Schlesinger, Sr., who had called on fifty-five of his fellow historians to grade each president as either "great," "near great," "average," "below average," or a "failure," then tallied up the results. Abraham Lincoln, George Washington, Franklin D. Roosevelt, Woodrow Wilson, and Andrew Jackson scored as great presidents, Ulysses S. Grant and Warren G. Harding were rated as failures, and the rest fell in between.

As interesting as the Schlesinger evaluations and their many imitators are, the important lessons may be more about the judges than their judgments, more about the presidency than about the presidents. What standards do scholars use to evaluate presidents? What image of the presidency do they measure the Lincolns and Hardings, the Reagans and Clintons, against? What standards for evaluation do other important judges of the presidency use: journalists, citizens, members of Congress, bureaucrats?

Answering these questions can tell us a lot, not only about the presidency's evaluators, but also about the presidency itself.[1] Presidents, after all, want the "verdict of history" that scholars eventually render to be favorable. In the short run, they need to win the support of journalists, the mass public, and congressional and bureaucratic officeholders if they are to succeed. To do so, presidents must understand the standards of evaluation that these groups apply to them.

Scholars: Strength amid Confusion

Schlesinger followed his 1948 survey of historians with another in 1962. The results were strikingly similar: the same pair of "failures" and, with the single exception of Jackson, the same set of "greats." More important, so were the twin standards that historians in the late 1940s and early 1960s appeared to measure presidents against: strength and the desire to be strong. "Washington apart," Schlesinger wrote, "none of [the great presidents] waited for the office to seek the man; they pursued it with all their might and main." Once in office, their greatness was established because "every one of [them] left the Executive branch stronger and more influential than he found it." When dealing with Congress, they knew "when to reason and to browbeat, to bargain and stand firm, . . . and when all else failed, they appealed over the heads of the lawmakers to the people." Nor did the great presidents shy away from confrontations with the Supreme Court. They were, to be sure, inattentive to administration of the bureaucracy, but this freed them, according to Schlesinger, for the more important tasks of "moral leadership."[2] A 1968 survey by Gary Maranell not only confirmed Schlesinger's conclusion that "strength" and "activeness" were important criteria in the historians' model of the presidency but also found that "idealism" and "flexibility" were not.[3]

The historians' model was very much like that of the other group of scholars who write and talk about the presidency, political scientists.[4] Their view in the 1950s and 1960s was summed up nicely in the title of an article by Thomas Cronin: "Superman: Our Textbook President."[5] After reviewing dozens of political science textbooks written in those two decades, Cronin found that political scientists characterized the presidency as both omnipotent and benevolent. The idea that strength and goodness go hand in hand shone through, for example, in James MacGregor Burns's assessment that "the stronger we make the Presidency, the more we strengthen democratic procedures."[6] It also animated the most influential book on the presidency of this period, *Presidential Power*. "A president's success" in maximizing power, wrote its author, Richard Neustadt, "serves objectives far beyond his own and his party's. . . . Presidential influence contributes to the energy of the government and to the viability of public policy. . . . What is good for the country is good for the president, and *vice versa*."[7]

Underlying the political scientists' model was a quasi-religious awe of the presidency. Clinton Rossiter began his book *The American Presidency* by confessing his "feeling of veneration, if not exactly reverence, for the authority and dignity of the presidency." He described Lincoln as "the martyred Christ of democracy's passion play" and quoted favorably the "splendid judgment" of the Englishman John Bright in 1861 that

there is nothing more worthy of reverence and obedience, and nothing more sacred, than the authority of the freely chosen magistrate of a great and free people; and if there be on earth and amongst men any right divine to govern, surely it rests with a ruler so chosen and so appointed.[8]

Herman Finer was equally reverent, although in a polytheistic way. Finer characterized the presidency not only as "the incarnation of the American people in a sacrament resembling that in which the wafer and the wine are seen to be the body and blood of Christ" but also as "belong[ing] rightfully to the offspring of a titan and Minerva husbanded by Mars."[9]

Thus, strength and the desire to be strong, power and virtue, omnipotence and benevolence, all were tied in with each other in what may be called (only half-facetiously) the "Savior" model of the presidency. According to the model's underlying rationale, the president is the chief guardian of the national interest, not only in foreign policy (because no one else can speak and act for the nation), but also in domestic affairs because of the pluralistic structure of government and society. Members of Congress cater to wealthy and influential interests within their constituencies, it was argued, but the president can mobilize the unorganized and inarticulate and speak for national majorities against special interest groups.

Clearly, scholars' normative preference for presidential strength in the 1950s and 1960s had more to it than their value judgments about the proper distribution of power among the branches of government. It was rooted in their liberal policy preferences as well. Democratic historians outnumbered Republicans by two to one in the Schlesinger samples, for example. One of the reasons they found the strength of the presidents they labeled "great" so appealing was that, as Schlesinger put it, each of these presidents "took the side of liberal-

be less important than coverage itself. Simply by dwelling on the presidency, the media reinforce images of its strength and importance.[40] Finally, reporters tend to look at government through the lens of electoral politics. They often describe relations between the presidency and other policy-making institutions, especially Congress, in terms of victories and defeats for the president. This, too, reinforces the notion that strong presidents who dominate the system are good presidents.

Citizens: Strength amid Contradiction

The American presidency combines the roles of chief of government and chief of state. As chief of government, the president is called on to act as a partisan political leader, in the manner of the British prime minister. As chief of state, the president is the equivalent of the British monarch: the ceremonial leader of the nation and the living symbol of its unity.

Because the presidency embodies both roles, the general public tends to evaluate presidents by standards that seem contradictory. According to Cronin, Americans want the president to be "gentle and decent but forceful and decisive," "inspirational but 'don't promise more than you can deliver,'" "open and caring but courageous and independent," a "common man who gives an uncommon performance," and a "national unifier-national divider."[41] George Edwards suggests several similar sets of contradictory public expectations about presidential style, including "leadership vs. responsiveness," "statesman vs. politician," and "empathy vs. uniqueness."[42] Most of these are really one: Americans want the president to be a chief of state who represents the things that unite them *and* a chief of government who will lead and thus divide them.

Expectations of presidential policy making also seem to be contradictory. On the one hand, the public expects the president to reduce unemployment, cut the cost of government, increase government efficiency, deal effectively with foreign policy, and strengthen national defense. In a survey taken shortly after Carter's election in 1976, 59 to 81 percent of the respondents, depending on the policy in question, said they expected these accomplishments. The comparable figures following Reagan's 1980 election ranged from 69 to 89 percent. Similarly high expectations arose after Clinton was elected in 1992.[43]

Yet the conventional wisdom among scholars is that the public would also prefer that Congress—the other, constitutionally equal branch it elects—dominate the presidency in the policy-making process. After reviewing a wide variety of poll data from as far back as 1936, Hazel Erskine concluded: "Whenever given a choice between congressional vs. presidential decision-making, the people tend to trust Congress over the chief executive. Whether the issue pertains to specific domestic or military matters, or to authority in general, seems immaterial."[44] Donald Devine agreed: "The American people believe . . . that the Congress should be supreme." He cited as evidence the 61 to 17 percent margin by which they chose Congress in response to this 1958 Survey Research Center question: "Some people say that the president is in the best position to see what the country needs. Other people think the president may have some good ideas about what the country needs but it is up to Congress to decide what ought to be done. How do you feel about it?"[45] A 1979 Gallup poll question that asked whether Congress or the president "ought to have major responsibility" in three policy areas found that Congress was preferred for energy policy and the economy and the president only for foreign policy.[46]

In apparent contradiction of their high expectations of presidential performance, then, Americans are *philosophical congressionalists*. But in truth, all this means is that when pollsters ask abstract, theoretical questions, the public tends to side with Congress against the president. (It is hard to imagine that questions about the proper balance of power between the branches come up very often in ordinary discussions.)[47] When one looks at evidence about attitudes and feelings that bear more directly on political behavior, the balance shifts. The American public, like American scholars and journalists, wants and admires strength in the presidency.

One finds first that Americans are *operational presidentialists*. Whatever they may say about proper institutional roles in theory, the presidents they like are the ones who take the lead and the Congresses they like are the ones that follow. Stephen Wayne provides evidence for the first half of this proposition in his report on a survey that asked people what qualities they admired most in their favorite president. "Strong" led the list by far; "forceful," "ability to get things done," and "decisive" ranked third, fifth, and seventh, respectively. "Concern for the average citizen," "honest," and "had confidence of people" were the only oft-mentioned qualities that were not clear synonyms for strength.[48] As for Congress, the only times that a majority of the respondents have rated its performance as either "excellent" or "pretty good" in more than two decades of Harris surveys were in the mid-1960s, the years in which Congress was most responsive to strong presidential leadership, and the mid-1980s, when, according to Roger Davidson and Walter Oleszek, "satisfaction with President Ronald Reagan's leadership carried over into optimism and confidence in other sectors of the federal government."[49]

Americans can also be described as *emotional presidentialists*. Almost all of their political heroes from the past are presidents;[50] when candidates run for president, they promise to be like the best of their predecessors. (In contrast, members of Congress—the "only distinctly native American criminal class," in Mark Twain's jest—serve in political folklore as the butt of jokes. Congressional aspirants tend to "run *for* Congress by running *against* Congress.")[51] Heroic feelings about the presidency show up most dramatically when a president dies. Surveys taken shortly after President Kennedy's assassination found Americans to be displaying symptoms of grief that otherwise appear only at the death of a close friend or relative. They "didn't feel like eating" (43 percent), were "nervous and tense" (68 percent), and felt "dazed and numb" (57 percent).[52] They also feared, for a short time at least, that the Republic was in danger.[53] Similar emotional outpourings seem to have accompanied the deaths in office of all presidents, whether by assassination or natural causes and whether they were popular or not. In Great Britain, it is the monarch's death that occasions such deep emotions, not the death of the prime minister, the chief of government.[54]

The public's emotional attachment to the presidency has implications of its own for strong leadership. The honeymoon that a new president enjoys with the people at the start of the term is, in a sense, an affirmation of faith in the office. New and reelected presidents almost always receive the early approval of millions of citizens who had voted against them, and most presidents are able to keep their public approval ratings at near-honeymoon levels for a year or more. As we will see, popularity with the voters is quite helpful to presidential leadership of Congress.

Presidents can also trade on the public's emotional support for the office in foreign affairs. Citizens will "rally 'round the flag" in the form of their chief of state in all sorts of international circumstances.[55] According to a study by Jong Lee, wars and military crises head the list of support-inspiring events, followed by new foreign policy initiatives, peace efforts, and summit conferences.[56] Nixon's approval rating in the Gallup poll went up 12 percentage points after his October 1969 "Vietnamization" speech, Ford's jumped 11 points after he "rescued" the merchant ship *Mayaguez*, and Carter added 12 points to his rating as a result of the Camp David summit that brought Israel and Egypt together. Reagan enjoyed a number of such boosts: from 45 to 53 percent after the Grenada invasion in 1983 and from 62 to 68 percent after the 1986 bombing of Libya, for example. In early 1991, Bush's approval rating soared higher (89 percent) than any president's in history after the U.S. victory against Iraq in the Gulf War.

Rossiter sums up the symbolic and political importance of the presidency:

No president can fail to realize that all his powers are invigorated, indeed are given a new dimension of authority, because he is the symbol of our sovereignty, continuity, and grandeur. When he asks a senator to lunch in order to enlist support for a pet project, ... when he orders a general to cease caviling or else be removed from his command, the senator and ... the general are well aware—especially if the scene is laid in the White House—that they are dealing with no ordinary head of government.[57]

The evaluators of the presidency to whom Rossiter refers, of course, are not outside of government but are fellow officeholders. Like scholars, journalists, and the general public, members of Congress and bureaucrats evaluate the presidency in ways that are superficially detrimental to presidential leadership, yet their underlying attitudes offer support for strong presidents.

Members of Congress: Strength amid Constituency-Centeredness

Whether animated by a selfish urge to do well or a generous desire to do good, the modern member of Congress wants to be reelected.[58] As Richard Fenno explains, "For most members of Congress most of the time, [the] electoral goal is primary. It is the prerequisite for a congressional career and, hence, for the pursuit of other member goals."[59] From 1946 to 1992, an average of more than 90 percent of all representatives sought another term in each election, as did approximately 85 percent of all senators.[60]

To be reelected, of course, members must please their constituents, a task best accomplished by working in Congress to advance local interests as defined by local people. A 1977 Harris survey conducted for the House Commission on Administrative Review asked respondents whether they thought their representative should be primarily concerned with looking after the needs and interests of "his own district" or "the nation as a whole." They chose "own district" by a margin of 57 to 34 percent. About twice as many voters in a 1978 survey said that when a legislator sees a conflict between "what the voters think best" and "what he thinks best," he should obey the voters. More recent studies confirm these findings.[61]

Personal ambition and constituents' demands powerfully influence how members of Congress behave in office. Most channel their energy and resources into activities that translate readily into votes. This creates an anomaly: although Congress's main constitutional task is to legislate in the national interest, most of the activities that produce votes for members are nonlegislative, primarily "pork-barreling" and casework.[62] (Pork-barreling involves getting federal grant and project money for their home states and districts; casework is handling constituents' complaints about their personal experiences with the federal bureaucracy.) David Mayhew adds "advertising" to the list of leading congressional activities: newsletters or questionnaires mailed home, personal visits, and similar efforts "to create a favorable image but in messages having little or no issue content."[63]

What time is left for legislative activity generally is spent in two reelection-oriented ways. First, members propose laws that sound pleasing to the voters. This takes little effort but enables them to gain publicity in local media and to answer almost any constituent's inquiry about policy or legislation with: "I introduced (or cosponsored) a bill on that very subject." Almost every member of Congress, for example, introduced or cosponsored a health care reform bill in 1994. At the same time, it commits them to none of the difficult, time-consuming, and largely invisible activities needed to get legislation over the hurdles of subcommittee, committee, and floor passage in each house.

Second, legislators work very hard on those few areas of lawmaking that are of particular interest to the local constituency and to large campaign contributors. For example, the senators from a farm state can be certain that their effectiveness, not just their rhetoric, on agricultural issues will be monitored closely by opinion leaders back home. This explains why, for example, farm-state members dominate the Agriculture committees in both houses, westerners dominate the Interior and Insular Affairs Committee in the House and the Environment and Public Works Committee in the Senate, and coastal-state representatives dominate the House Merchant Marine and Fisheries Committee.[64] Once on these committees, members often enter into mutually beneficial relationships with the interest groups and executive agencies in their policy "subgovernment." By supporting programs that interest groups favor, legislators obtain campaign funding and other electoral benefits. From agencies they receive special consideration for their constituents and influence over the distribution of patronage and contracts in return for generous appropriations and loose statutory reins.

Not surprisingly, representatives and senators also evaluate the presidency according to constituency-based criteria. To presidents who have an extensive legislative agenda, this can seem very discouraging. Their difficulty in moving bills through a constitutionally bicameral legislature is compounded by Congress's culture of constituency service, which distracts members from serious legislative activity into the more electorally rewarding business of pork-barreling, casework, and advertising. Successful presidential leadership also requires that members direct their attention to national concerns. But congressional ambition is such that local issues, or the local effects of national issues, usually come first. Finally, most presidential initiatives call for legislative alteration of the status quo. Such proposals often conflict with the general satisfaction that each component of the various subgovernments, including the congressional committees and subcommittees, has with existing arrangements.

Nevertheless, in other, perhaps more important, ways, Congress's constituency-centered culture enhances rather than inhibits presidential strength. These are: the power to initiate, the power of popularity, and power in foreign policy.

Power to Initiate

During the past century, the public has placed ever greater demands for action on the federal government, most of which have required the passage of new legislation. To satisfy each of these demands, Congress as an institution has had to move through the long, tortuous, and largely subterranean process of developing programs and steering them past its own internal obstacles to action. Representatives and senators naturally have wanted the legislative process to work, but as noted earlier, the pursuit of reelection takes them mainly into nonlegislative areas of activity.

Again and again since 1932, members of Congress have found their way out of this dilemma by turning to the presidency. Not only did Congress give Franklin Roosevelt a virtual blank check to deal with the Great Depression as he saw fit—in the fabled first hundred days, it passed more than a dozen pieces of Roosevelt-spawned legislation—it also authorized actions that allowed the president to institutionalize the role of policy initiator. The Bureau of the Budget was transferred from the Treasury Department to a newly created Executive Office of the President and empowered to screen all departmental proposals for legislation before Congress could see them. In addition, the president was authorized to hire a personal political staff, largely for the purpose of developing and selling legislation to Congress.

In succeeding administrations, these trends continued. The Employment Act of 1946 called on the president (with the aid of the new Council of

Economic Advisers) to monitor the economy and recommend corrective legislation in times of economic distress. Similar congressional requests for presidential initiative were included in the Manpower Development and Training Act of 1962, the Housing and Urban Development Act of 1968, the National Environmental Policy Act of 1969, and several other acts. When President Eisenhower, deferring to what he assumed would be Congress's preference, did not submit a legislative program in 1953, senators and representatives of both parties complained; since then, every president has used the annual State of the Union address in effect to establish Congress's policy agenda for the year. Remarkably, when Congress wanted to express its deep dissatisfaction with President Nixon's economic policies in 1971, it passed a law that forced on him the power to impose wage and price controls on the entire economy. Congress sometimes demands strength from the president even when the president does not want to act strongly.

Power of Popularity

The power to initiate legislation that members of Congress have ceded to the presidency in the interests of their own reelection is formidable in itself, but what of the power to actually get laws passed? Again, the constituency-centered culture of Congress can work to the advantage of presidential strength. The same congressional preoccupation with reelection that has led members to try to insulate their relationship with the voters from national political forces has also made them extremely sensitive to any national forces that might cost them votes. In particular, when legislators think that the president's support among voters is high, they are more likely to follow presidential leadership.[65]

Perceptions of presidential popularity may grow out of a landslide election victory that is accompanied by unusually large gains for the president's party in Congress. (Gains of thirty to forty seats are large enough to seem unusual nowadays; until recently, they were quite ordinary.) Such gains are invariably attributed, accurately or not, to the president's coattails or to a mandate shared with Congress. Either way, the election creates a heightened disposition among legislators of both congressional parties to support the president's legislative agenda: copartisans because they want to ride the bandwagon, electorally vulnerable members of the opposition party because they want to avoid being flattened by it. Such was the case following the landslide elections of Johnson in 1964, whose party gained thirty-seven seats in the House, and Reagan in 1980, when Republicans won thirty-three new seats in the House and took control of the Senate with a gain of twelve seats.

The obsession with reelection that governs legislators' reactions to election results causes them to respond in a similar manner to indexes of presidential popularity during a president's term. Because reelection-oriented members of Congress "are hypersensitive to anticipated constituent reaction" to their actions, it is not surprising that the amount of support Congress gives to a president's legislative agenda is related to some extent to the Gallup approval rating.[66] Most presidents, of course, enjoy a honeymoon period of high voter approval at the start of the term. (Clinton squandered his by bogging down quickly in the highly controversial issue of gays and lesbians in the military.) Broadly speaking, among recent presidents, Eisenhower, Kennedy, and Reagan maintained their initial popularity throughout their terms, Johnson and Nixon kept theirs for the first two years, and Carter and Bush held their ground in the polls for at least the first year. Even after their approval ratings declined, all but Johnson were able to revive their initial popularity, at least for short periods.[67] And Johnson and Reagan held on long enough to get their particularly dramatic legislative programs through Congress virtually intact, Johnson in 1964 and 1965 and Reagan in 1981.

Power in Foreign Policy

Congress's constituency-centered culture also encourages presidential strength in foreign policy, although to a lesser extent now than in the past. Historically, Congress has been assertive only on the foreign policy issues that concern voters the most, especially unpopular wars and issues that have a clear domestic politics coloration: foreign trade; support for nations such as Israel and Greece (and hostility to nations, such as South Africa in the 1980s) that have vocal and well-organized ethnic lobbies in this country; and the like. Until the cold war ended in the early 1990s, these issues were overshadowed by the worldwide conflict between the United States and the Soviet Union. Since the cold war ended, they have become more prominent. For members of Congress to pursue an interest in foreign policy much further than their constituents' interests is to tempt electoral fate. Between 1970 and 1984, three consecutive Senate Foreign Relations Committee chairs were defeated in reelection bids by opponents who charged that they cared more about world politics than about local concerns.

Bureaucrats: Strength amid Careerism

Career civil servants may seem to be the group whose favorable evaluations presidents need the least. In civics book theory, they are part of the president's executive chain of command and perform purely administrative, not policy-making, functions. In practice, however, Congress and the courts, not just the chief executive, have a rightful say over what bureaucrats do. And in modern society, bureaucracy increasingly involves those who implement policy in the making of it.

Like members of Congress, career civil servants, who represent virtually 99 percent of the federal work force, often are motivated by self-interest. "The prime commitments of civil servants," writes Erwin Hargrove, "are to their career, agency, and program. The markers of success are autonomy for their bureaus and expansion of budgets."[68] Such self-interested commitments make life difficult for the remaining few: the departmental secretaries, under secretaries, assistant secretaries, and other political executives whom the president appoints to manage the bureaucracy in pursuit of the administration's policies.

The stance of both presidents and their political executives toward the career bureaucrats, observes James Fesler, includes "an assumption that the bureaucracy is swollen, a doubt of careerists' competence, and an expectation of their unresponsiveness to the administration."[69] This view of the unresponsive bureaucrat seemed to be validated by Joel Aberbach and Bert Rockman in their 1970 study of the political beliefs of high-ranking civil servants in several social service agencies.[70] Large majorities of the supergrade bureaucrats whom they interviewed disapproved of President Nixon's policies to reduce the social agencies' programs and budgets. This was especially true of the 47 percent who were Democrats, but the bulk of the 36 percent who were independents also opposed the president. These data seemed so supportive of the stereotype of the self-interested bureaucrat resisting the policies of the elected president that Nixon actually quoted the authors' conclusion in his memoirs: "Our findings . . . pointedly portray a social service bureaucracy dominated by administrators hostile to many of the directions pursued by the Nixon administration in the realm of social policy."[71]

But far from proving Nixon's point, Aberbach and Rockman actually laid the groundwork for a later study that appears to have refuted it. In 1976 Richard Cole and David Caputo conducted a similar survey and discovered that most supergrade bureaucrats, including Democrats and especially independents, by then supported Nixon's policies. "We find the 'pull' of the presidency to be very strong," Cole and Caputo concluded.[72]

What accounts for the apparent willingness of career bureaucrats to respond to strong presidential leadership? In part, the stereotype of bureaucratic self-interest has been overdrawn. As Fesler notes, most careerists feel obliged "to serve loyally the people's choice as president. Because senior careerists have been through several changes in administration, this is a well-internalized commitment."[73] Presumably, the stronger a president's leadership, the easier it is for loyal bureaucrats to follow.

A more important explanation may be the apparent harmony of self-interest between career bureaucrats and strong presidents. Cole and Caputo report that the Nixon administration played an unusually purposeful and active role in the job-promotion process within the upper reaches of the civil service. Civil servants sympathetic to the administration's policies were favored. This group included Republicans, of course, but also many independents and some Democrats who recognized that the administration meant business and therefore adapted their views to further their own careers.

Nixon's successors enjoy even greater resources for influencing the bureaucracy than he did. The Civil Service Reform Act of 1978, which was passed at the request of President Carter, created a 7,000-member corps of senior civil servants—the Senior Executive Service—whom the president may transfer or demote more easily than in the past. Reagan, according to Terry Moe, made "explicitly political use of the Senior Executive Service, usually by removing career officials from important slots and filling them with partisans. He also used reductions in force as a legal means of eliminating whole bureaucratic units staffed by careerists."[74] Subsequent presidents have followed suit.

In sum, the civics books are not entirely wrong. Some bureaucrats follow the ethic of loyal service to the president because they believe in it. Others will follow when promotions are based on faithful obedience to the president. In either event the result is the same: "Senior bureaucrats, like Supreme Court justices, 'follow the election returns.'"[75]

Summary and Conclusion

Presidential scholarship in recent years has been marked by a bewildering succession of new models of the presidency, each the product of an admixture of empirical and normative assessments, each constructed in hasty overreaction to the most recent president. Journalists' coverage of the presidency has been tinged by a Vietnam- and Watergate-induced cynicism whose real source may be the status frustration of the modern White House press corps. Citizens pin all their hopes for chief-of-state-like symbolic leadership and chief-of-government-like political leadership on one office, the presidency. Members of Congress view the White House through constituency-colored lenses, judging the presidency by the narrow standard of personal reelection ambitions. Tenured civil servants, whose working life is committed to the bureaucracy, also evaluate the presidency in terms of their own careers.

Each of these judgments, although true in part, is superficial. Underlying the scholars' confusion is an implicit appreciation that significant policy change, whatever its ideological direction, requires a strong president. The career needs and worldviews of journalists lead them, too, to exalt presidential strength. Citizens apparently want to have the contradictions in their expectations resolved through presidential actions that are strong but appear to be unifying. Legislators and bureaucrats realize, albeit reluctantly at times, that their career interests can be served by strong presidential initiatives.

On the whole, the underlying admiration for and celebration of presidential strength by scholars, journalists, citizens, members of Congress, and career bureaucrats should be a source of comfort to presidents and to all who have fretted in recent years about a decline in the authority of the presidency. But two cautionary notes need to be sounded.

First, strength means different things to different people. Scholarly celebrants of a strong presidency have traditionally dismissed the president's administrative duties as distractions from the real tasks of moral and political leadership. Yet many bureaucrats will respond to strong presidential initiatives only when they seem likely to influence their own careers. Similarly, although the public tends to respond enthusiastically to strong presidential action of a unifying kind, journalists write most approvingly when a president defeats the political opposition.

Second, the urge that presidents may feel to impress audiences both present and future as a strong—and hence "great"—leader may lead them to behave in ways that disserve themselves, the government, and the nation. "For fear of being found out and downgraded," writes Nelson Polsby, "there is the temptation to hoard credit rather than share it . . . [and] to export responsibility away from the White House for the honest shortfalls of programs, thus transmitting to the government at large an expectation that loyalty upward will be rewarded with disloyalty down." The final and most dangerous temptation is "to offer false hopes and to proclaim spurious accomplishments to the public at large."[76]

The complete lesson for presidents who wish to exert strong leadership, then, is that they need not worry about threats from the rest of the political system. Their problems really begin only when the concern for appearing strong distracts them from the business of the presidency.

Notes

1. Some of the themes in this chapter are discussed in more detail in Erwin C. Hargrove and Michael Nelson, *Presidents, Politics, and Policy* (New York: Knopf, 1984).

2. Arthur Schlesinger, "Our Presidents: A Rating by 75 Historians," *New York Times Magazine*, July 29, 1962, 12ff.

3. Gary Maranell, "The Evaluation of Presidents: An Extension of the Schlesinger Polls," *Journal of American History* 57 (June 1970): 104–113.

4. A study of how social scientists rated presidents from Franklin D. Roosevelt through Richard M. Nixon found economists' rankings to be similar to those of political scientists and historians. Malcolm B. Parsons, "The Presidential Rating Game," in *The Future of the American Presidency*, ed. Charles Dunn (Morristown, N.J.: General Learning Press, 1975), 66–91.

5. Thomas Cronin, "Superman: Our Textbook President," *Washington Monthly*, October 1970, 47–54.

6. James MacGregor Burns, *Presidential Government: The Crucible of Leadership* (Boston: Houghton Mifflin, 1965), 330.

7. Richard Neustadt, *Presidential Power: The Politics of Leadership* (New York: Wiley, 1960). The theme of Neustadt's book is that, although presidents can do little by direct command, they can and should wield great power through skillful bargaining and persuasion.

8. Clinton Rossiter, *The American Presidency* (New York: Harcourt, Brace and World, 1960), 15–16, 108.

9. Herman Finer, *The Presidency* (Chicago: University of Chicago Press, 1960), 111, 119.

10. Schlesinger, "Our Presidents," 40.

11. William Andrews, "The Presidency, Congress, and Constitutional Theory," in *Perspectives on the Presidency*, ed. Aaron Wildavsky (Boston: Little, Brown, 1975), 38. For further evidence of partisan and ideological bias in scholarly assessments of the presidency, see Parsons, "The Presidential Rating Game," and, more recently, Christopher J. Bosso, "Congressional and Presidential Scholars: Some Basic Traits," *PS: Political Science and Politics* 22 (December 1989): 839–848.

12. Arthur M. Schlesinger, Jr., *A Thousand Days* (Boston: Houghton Mifflin, 1965), 677; and Schlesinger, Jr., *The Imperial Presidency* (Boston: Houghton Mifflin, 1973).

13. Marcus Cunliffe, "A Defective Institution?" *Commentary*, February 1968, 28.

14. Nelson Polsby, "Against Presidential Greatness," *Commentary*, January 1977, 63.

15. James David Barber, *The Presidential Character* (Englewood Cliffs, N.J.: Prentice-Hall, 1972).

16. Thomas Cronin, *The State of the Presidency* (Boston: Little, Brown, 1975), 138.

17. George Reedy, *The Twilight of the Presidency* (New York: New American Library, 1970), chap. 1. See also Bruce Buchanan, *The Presidential Experience* (Englewood Cliffs, N.J.: Prentice-Hall, 1978); and Irving Janis, *Victims of GroupThink* (Boston: Houghton Mifflin, 1972).

18. Gerald Ford, "Imperiled, Not Imperial," *Time*, November 10, 1980, 30–31; and Thomas Franck, ed., *The Tethered Presidency* (New York: New York University Press, 1981).

19. Aaron Wildavsky, "The Past and Future Presidency," *Public Interest* 41 (Fall 1975): 56–76.

20. Godfrey Hodgson, *All Things to All Men* (New York: Simon and Schuster, 1980), 239.

21. A fourth, Seraph, model of the presidency as an institution that is and should be weak, has never dominated presidential scholarship. But it has its adherents. See, for example, Fred Greenstein, "Change and Continuity in the Modern Presidency," in *The New American Political System*, ed. Anthony King (Washington, D.C.: American Enterprise Institute for Public Policy Research, 1978); and Peter Woll and Rochelle Jones, "The Bureaucracy as a Check upon the President," *Bureaucrat* 3 (April 1974): 8–20.

22. Barber, *Presidential Character*, chap. 13; Schlesinger, Jr., *The Imperial Presidency*, chap. 11; Robert K. Murray and Tim H. Blessing, *Greatness in the White House* (University Park: Pennsylvania State University Press, 1988), 16; and Fred I. Greenstein, *The Hidden-Hand Presidency: Eisenhower as Leader* (New York: Basic Books, 1982).

23. Pre-Vietnam and Watergate press attitudes are described in Tom Wicker, "News Management from the Small Town to the White House," *Washington Monthly*, January 1978, 19–26.

24. Stephen Hess, *The Washington Reporters* (Washington, D.C.: Brookings Institution, 1981), 78.

25. Quoted in Michael Baruch Grossman and Martha Joynt Kumar, *Portraying the President: The White House and the News Media* (Baltimore: Johns Hopkins University Press, 1981), 131.

26. Ibid., 206–207.

27. Hess, *Washington Reporters*, 49; Stewart Alsop, *The Center* (New York: Popular Library, 1968), 161.

28. Quoted in Grossman and Kumar, *Portraying the President*, 183.

29. Ibid., 43.

30. Ibid., 36.

31. Ibid., 301.

32. Ibid., chap. 10.

33. Ibid., 232–238; Mark Hertsgaard, *On Bended Knee: The Press and the Reagan Presidency* (New York: Farrar, Straus, and Giroux, 1988).

34. Quoted in David Paletz and Robert Entman, *Media Power Politics* (New York: Free Press, 1981), 57.

35. Quoted in Grossman and Kumar, *Portraying the President*, 33.

36. Ibid., 182.

37. Paletz and Entman, *Media Power Politics*, 55.

38. Elmer Cornwell, "Presidential News: The Expanding Public Image," *Journalism Quarterly* 36 (Summer 1959): 282; and Alan Balutis, "The Presidency and the Press: The Expanding Public Image," *Presidential Studies Quarterly* 7 (Fall 1977).

39. Doris Graber, *Mass Media and American Politics*, 4th ed. (Washington, D.C.: CQ Press, 1993), 290.

40. Bruce Miroff, "Monopolizing the Public Space: The President as a Problem for Democratic Politics," in *Rethinking the Presidency*, ed. Thomas Cronin (Boston: Little, Brown, 1982), 218–232.

41. Thomas Cronin, "The Presidency and Its Paradoxes," in *The Presidency Reappraised*, 2d ed., ed. Thomas Cronin and Rexford Tugwell (New York: Praeger, 1977), 69–85.

42. George C. Edwards III, *The Public Presidency* (New York: St. Martin's, 1983), 196–198.

43. "Early Expectations: Comparing Chief Executives," *Public Opinion* (February/ March 1981): 39; George C. Edwards III and Stephen J. Wayne, *Presidential Leadership*, 2d ed. (New York: St. Martin's Press, 1990), 98.

44. Hazel Erskine, "The Polls: Presidential Power," *Public Opinion Quarterly* 37 (Fall 1973): 488.

45. Donald Devine, *The Political Culture of the United States* (Boston: Little, Brown, 1972), 158.

46. Thomas Cronin, "A Resurgent Congress and the Imperial Presidency," *Political Science Quarterly* 95 (Summer 1980): 211.

47. Richard Fenno, Jr., *Home Style: House Members in Their Districts* (Boston: Little, Brown, 1978), 245. According to Fenno: "Most citizens find it hard or impossible to think about Congress as an institution. They answer questions about it; but they cannot conceptualize it as a collectivity."

48. Stephen Wayne, "Great Expectations: What People Want from Presidents," in *Rethinking the Presidency*, 192–195.

49. Roger Davidson and Walter Oleszek, *Congress and Its Members*, 3d ed. (Washington, D.C.: CQ Press, 1990), 422.

50. Devine, *The Political Culture*, 128.

51. Fenno, *Home Style*, 168.

52. Paul Sheatsley and Jacob Feldman, "The Assassination of President Kennedy: Public Reactions," *Public Opinion Quarterly* 28 (Summer 1964): 197–202.

53. Ibid., 197.

54. Sebastian de Grazia, *The Political Community* (Chicago: University of Chicago Press, 1948), 112–115.

55. John Mueller, *War, Presidents, and Public Opinion* (New York: Wiley, 1973), 69–74, 122–140.

56. Jong R. Lee, "Rally Round the Flag: Foreign Policy Events and Presidential Popularity," *Presidential Studies Quarterly* 7 (Fall 1977): 255.

57. Rossiter, *The American Presidency*, 16–17.

58. See Morris Fiorina, *Congress: Keystone of the Washington Establishment* (New Haven: Yale University Press, 1977), 41–49; and David Mayhew, *Congress: The Electoral Connection* (New Haven: Yale University Press, 1974).

59. Fenno, *Home Style*, 31.

60. Calculated from data presented in Harold W. Stanley and Richard G. Niemi, eds., *Vital Statistics on American Politics*, 2d ed. (Washington, D.C.: CQ Press, 1990), 186–187. In that same period, more than 90 percent of the representatives and nearly 80 percent of the senators who ran were reelected.

61. Morris Fiorina, "Congressmen and Their Constituents: 1958 and 1978," in *The United States Congress*, ed. Dennis Hale (Chestnut Hill, Mass.: Boston College, 1982), 39; Davidson and Oleszek, *Congress and Its Members*, chaps. 4–5.

62. Fiorina, *Congress*, 41–49.

63. Mayhew, *Congress*, 49.

64. Kenneth A. Shepsle, *The Giant Jigsaw Puzzle: Democratic Committee Assignments in the Modern House* (Chicago: University of Chicago Press, 1978); Roger Davidson, *The Role of the Congressman* (New York: Pegasus, 1968), 121.

65. For a study of the complex relationship between presidential popularity and legislative success, see Mark A. Peterson, *Legislating Together: The White House and Capitol from Eisenhower to Reagan* (Cambridge: Harvard University Press, 1990), chaps. 4 and 5.

to "study" the presidency is discussed. Second, the two central features of the modern office—imagery and institution—are outlined. Third, several generalizations about the presidency that are related to its imagery and institution are addressed. These statements describe what usually happens in the office and outline regular patterns that are difficult for presidents to avoid and equally difficult for them to modify. Fourth, there is a consideration of several episodes of presidential mistakes that might have been avoided had presidents studied the office more carefully. Finally, the issue of what presidents can learn from how political scientists study the presidency is reexamined.

Studying the Presidency

There are three elements involved in studying the presidency or any subject: perspectives, methods, and content. The first two involve how to study a subject; the last pertains to what is studied. *Perspectives* define different ways of looking at the same subject. They give researchers a set of guidelines to follow in doing their work. In effect, perspectives act as researchers' blinders. Depending on their perspective, they will ask some questions and not others. In addition, from a particular perspective, they will get some answers and not others. Five main perspectives have dominated the study of the presidency: (1) historical—the evolution of the office, (2) constitutional—the expansion of constitutional powers and precedents set by presidents, (3) psychological—the effect of individual presidents' personalities and leadership styles on their decisions, (4) political power—individual presidents' influence on others through political give-and-take, and (5) institutional—the constraints placed on presidents' behavior by the White House organization that surrounds them.

Methods are the techniques scholars adopt to gain answers to the questions they derive from these several perspectives. The techniques involve gathering data or materials, analyzing them, and drawing conclusions. Two principal methods are used in political science: qualitative and quantitative. Although scholars may ask the same questions using either method, they obtain the answers differently.

Qualitative research involves in-depth descriptive analyses of an occurrence or a set of occurrences. Researchers cull diaries, documents, memoirs, newspapers, and other published accounts and interview presidents and presidential staffers. Their analyses may involve a case study of a presidential decision, a profile of a particular aspect of the office or a particular occupant, or a chronology of events that spans several presidencies. Scholars who conduct qualitative studies are most interested in a contextual understanding of what happens—that is, the sweep of events, people, and circumstances that define the subject of study.

Quantitative methods are used to test hypotheses about relationships between independent and dependent variables. The dependent variable is the phenomenon that researchers wish to explain. In order to measure the dependent variable, researchers count the number of times the phenomenon occurs during a given interval—a month, a quarter of a year, a year, or a presidential term. The independent variables are those factors that researchers hypothesize will help explain the dependent variable. They then determine how the frequency of the dependent variable is affected by the frequency of these other factors that happen during the same interval. The variables are defined and measured, after which various statistical techniques are applied to determine what effects the independent variables have on the dependent variable.

Quantitative studies of the presidency examine presidential activities as dependent variables. These activities include legislative victories, vetoes, public speeches, and the use of military force. Researchers then examine how factors such as presidents' approval ratings, press coverage, economic conditions, election results, the make-up of congressional parties, and certain highly visible events influence the occurrence of these types of activities. Scholars conducting quantitative analyses are especially interested in obtaining precise estimates of the effect of various factors on the activities of as many presidents over as long a period of time as possible.

Research perspectives and methods yield *content*. Content, of course, involves the various topics researchers investigate. But more than this, it includes the patterns and relationships found in these investigations. Content thus entails empirical generalizations about the presidency drawn from the various perspectives and methods.

Political scientists who study the presidency debate which perspective mixed with what method is best.[1] Table 2.1 depicts how the perspectives and methods combine. Both qualitative and quantitative methods are used to study the power and institutional perspectives, whereas qualitative techniques are most often used to study the historical, constitutional, and psychological perspectives. Currently, the power and institutional perspectives are dominant, and quantitative research is viewed as more scientifically rigorous than qualitative research. Yet if students of the presidency concentrate too heavily on the debate, they risk missing the larger picture offered by competent work that uses the several perspectives and methods. Qualitative and quantitative work that is done shoddily

Table 2.1. Perspectives and Methods in Studying the Presidency

	Perspective				
Method	Historical	Constitutional	Psychological	Power	Institutional
Qualitative	x	x	x	x	x
Quantitative	—	—	—	x	x

Note: x denotes a combination of perspectives and method that typically occurs. — denotes a combination of perspective and method that does not typically occur. This does not imply, however, that such a combination could not occur.

reveals nothing, no matter the perspective used. Qualitative and quantitative work that is done thoroughly can provide insights about the office, no matter the perspective used. These insights are what political scientists know about the presidency and what presidents can study. To be sure, perspectives and methods color content. But content that is acquired and synthesized from various perspectives and methods offers researchers a fair degree of confidence in its empirical validity. Presidents, it seems, are in need of a lesson in content, more than one in either perspectives or methods. Thus the rest of this chapter addresses the content of the field.

Imagery and Institution

The first thing presidents need to know about the presidency is that it has two major dimensions: imagery and institution.[2] The main *image* of the presidency is of the president, speaking with a clear lone voice, governing the country. The *institution* is the complex organization of people that surrounds the president, helps to make presidential decisions, and structures relations with other institutions, such as Congress, the media, the bureaucracy, and the courts.

These two features of the presidency appeared about the turn of the century.[3] Image and institution emerged through a philosophical shift from presidential restraint to presidential activism. As proponents of activism, Theodore Roosevelt (1901–1909) and Woodrow Wilson (1913–1921) argued that presidents have the ability to do anything on behalf of the people that does not directly violate the Constitution. Activism thus relies on two concepts, both of which forge the presidential image. First, presidents can do "anything"—they are to be active policy makers and problem solvers. Second, presidents do so on behalf of the people—they are, in Roosevelt's words, "stewards of the people." The institution is needed to carry out the responsibilities assumed by presidents in the new imagery. The one demands the other.

Neither of these features of the presidency existed in the nineteenth century, when presidents operated under notions of restraint—they exercised only those powers specified in the Constitution and existing laws. As a rule, presidents were neither seen nor heard. George Washington, Thomas Jefferson, Andrew Jackson, James K. Polk, and Abraham Lincoln aside, presidents before the twentieth century either did not take active roles in policy making and public leadership or were unsuccessful when they did so; both arenas were thus left to Congress.

The modern importance of image and institution indicates both that some of the five perspectives are more useful than others and that no one of them is enough. Obviously, scholars who use the institutional perspective place most of their emphasis on the institution and forgo the systematic study of imagery. Researchers who consider only personality and leadership may learn a great deal about the images of individual presidents but not about presidential imagery from a broader perspective of all presidents. Those who use the historical and constitutional perspectives seldom examine the development of image and institution historically and through the expansion of some constitutional powers. Those who study power are the most likely to recognize the significance of both image and institution. But these scholars are often captivated by the exercise of personal power by presidents to persuade others. They do not fully consider that image and institution are the sources of this power; therefore, the power is not personal but a feature of the office. Thus, image and institution are not adequately defined from any one perspective on the presidency. Yet, extracting content from all five perspectives clarifies the two dimensions. For presidents the key is to understand more specifically what the image and the institution are like.

On Imagery

The image of the presidency is the *single executive image*: the president is the most powerful, most important person in the government and in the nation. As the only official elected by the entire country, the president is the representative of the people. He professes compassion for the average American and passion for the American dream. He is the nation's principal problem solver, the one who identifies its most daunting challenges and offers solutions. He presses his leadership to ensure that the proposed solutions become law. In times of crisis, he single-handedly protects the nation. The image of the president is thus of a person who is omnicompetent (able to do all things) and omnipresent (working everywhere).

An image is a simplification. It is one's mental picture of an object, a product, a situation, or, in this case, a political office. The image usually magnifies certain features while glossing over other relevant details. Reality is typically checked against the image more than the other way around. For example, if you have an image of the perfect cat—big, white, and fluffy—then you are unlikely to enjoy cats who do not match this image. It is much less likely that if a scrawny, black, matted feline wanders by, you will adopt a new image of the perfect cat to accommodate it.

The single executive image is a simplification of both the presidency and American politics. It personalizes the office by embodying all its units, staff, and decisions in one person—the president. In the mind's eye of the nation, the president is the person who matters most. American politics is presidential politics. Many people's recollections of American politics are dominated by the day John F. Kennedy was shot, the day Richard M. Nixon resigned, the day George Bush declared war against Iraq, the day after day that Jimmy Carter could not free the hostages in Iran. People often simplify their views of both the presidency and American politics by focusing on the exploits of one man.

To be sure, people are aware that the government is immensely more complex than this—Congress is a powerful and, at times, dominant branch; the bureaucracy seems to do whatever it wants; the Supreme Court announces decisions that tell the rest of the government what to do. Yet, citizens look at this assemblage as if it were the scrawny cat. It does not fit their presidential image of the government. Similarly, when they find that a president appears to be in over his head with national economic difficulties, dissension within his own party in Congress, or civil wars abroad, they do not modify the single executive image to fit the harsh (and very typical) presidential circumstance. Instead, they revise their opinions of the incumbent chief executive, who comes out the loser in public opinion polls.

Sources of the Single Executive Image. The single executive image arises from three sources: the public, the press, and presidents themselves. Citizens are keenly interested in political figures as individuals, and presidents are the political figures they know best. The political scientist Fred Greenstein observes that people draw on the president as an important cognitive aid to simplify and ultimately understand politics.[4] Many Americans pay little attention to politics, but the one person they do know something about is the president. They can recall the most trivial details about a president, from his taste in food—whether it is President Bush's aversion to broccoli or President Clinton's affinity for McDonald's—to the names of the family pets: Fala (Roosevelt), King Timahoe (Nixon), Millie (Bush), and Socks (Clinton). Thus, people simplify the complex operations of government by concentrating on the actions of a single player—the president.

The media help produce the ubiquity of president-watching among the public. The most important national story that the press reports day in and day out is about the president. The press covers the presidency as if the person were the office—what he says, where he goes, whom he meets. They too are fascinated with the president as a person. It is not clear which fascination came first—that of the public or that of the press. Much press coverage has become known as the "body watch."[5] Reporters watch the president's every move just in case, as Ronald Reagan put it, the "awful awful" happens. As one television news executive producer observed, "We cover the president expecting he will die."[6] The body watch carries with it a vivid irony. Especially since the Kennedy assassination, the press assumes, probably correctly, that people want to know if a president becomes ill, is injured, or is killed. Yet on most days, nothing catastrophic happens. So the body watch captures the ordinary aspects of the president's life. Otherwise mundane activities, such as taking a morning walk, jogging, playing golf, eating at a restaurant, and boating, become news as part of the body watch. In addition, only when problems arise among members of the White House staff do viewers and readers learn about some of the well over one thousand people who work within the presidency. Most often the president stands alone in daily press coverage. This reinforces the image of the president as omnipresent and omnicompetent.

Presidents work to portray particular images of themselves. Many of these images first emerge during the election campaign as the candidates attempt to distinguish themselves from each other and often from the current occupant of the White House. A candidate portrays himself as smart when his predecessor or opponent is depicted as dumb. He portrays himself as energetic, hardworking, and eager for change when his predecessor is shown as lethargic. The personal image of a president also develops while he is in office. Some aspects of this image are built quite intentionally by the White House, such as the kind, gentle, family-oriented George Bush. Other aspects are shaped more unwittingly through selective media coverage of the president's daily activities, such as Gerald Ford being typecast as a bumbler after he slipped on ice and hit several errant golf balls. Whether crafted intentionally or occurring accidentally, a president's personal image is continually measured against the single executive image.

How to Study Presidential Imagery. How then should presidents study the single executive image so they can use it most effectively? Presidents may think

Early press coverage also reinforces the single executive image by depicting the president as a man of the people (complete with family, furniture, and daily routines) with bold new plans to lead the nation forward. The political scientists Michael Grossman and Martha Kumar found in a study of newspaper, television, and magazine coverage of presidents from 1953 to 1978 that during the early part of the term reporters are most attentive to human interest stories about the president. Indeed, a Ford White House official predicted that the first stories about the incoming Carter administration would be personality stories about the president: "First, who is Jimmy Carter? What is his personality? Does he get mad? Does he golf? Does he fish in a pond? How do you find out who somebody is? You look at his friends, his habits, his manner, his character, his personality."[15]

Taking the generalizations together, political scientists reveal two features of the presidential imagery. First, the single executive image rests on symbolism—the president symbolizes the nation, its people, and its government. There is a symbolic equivalence between the president and the public, with the two blurring together as one in presidents' speeches and in media coverage of the office. Presidents frequently use the pronoun *we* to refer to themselves and the American people.[16] As noted above, human interest news reports depict the president as one of the people. The symbolism is emotionally, not rationally, based. Ordinary citizens, who are often inattentive to government and politically unorganized, find it difficult to obtain tangible benefits from a president, unlike a major industry requesting relief from a regulation or an interest group seeking legislation. Instead, people seek "quiescence" in politics—reassurance that everything is all right or at least that someone is in charge.

People, then, may well be less concerned about what a president does than how he makes them feel. These emotions help to explain the otherwise ironic situations in which presidential failure garners public support. As one example, Kennedy's popularity rose ten points after the ill-fated Bay of Pigs invasion of Cuba in 1961. Had people judged the decision rationally, based on costs and benefits, their response would have been to disapprove of the president's performance. Instead the president benefited in the short term, because people sought quiescence that the "bad guys" were being challenged, no matter what the outcome of the challenge was.

Without studying the presidency, presidents may neglect this emotionally based symbolic connection and expect the American public to evaluate their proposals and achievements on their policy merits. Bill Clinton was frustrated, for example, that his legislative successes in 1993 were not accompanied by high public approval ratings. Following the single executive image, presidents must shape a visceral political experience through telling folksy stories, witnessing human tragedies and triumphs, and offering examples of old-fashioned American values. Presidents who try to do otherwise will find the public otherwise engaged.

Second, the single executive image is false. Although the image is a very real part of the American body politic, it is an exaggeration and distortion of grand proportions. The president does not single-handedly lead the people and govern the country. The president may be the single most powerful individual in the country, but Congress as a body is arguably more powerful. The president surely holds a unique position in the government, but he is not alone, either in the presidential institution or in the larger government.

In two ways, the falsehood of the single executive image may perplex presidents who have not adequately studied the presidency. Some presidents fail to see the falsehood. Instead, they act as though they are singularly powerful, flouting regular consultation with Congress and defying laws that prevent unilateral presidential action. In an interview with David Frost after resigning the presidency, Richard Nixon was asked about a president's breaking the law in the best interests of the nation. Nixon responded, "Well, when the President does it, that means that it is not illegal."[17] This was a contorted extension of the single executive image into a claim that the president can do no wrong.

Other presidents who know the image to be false risk pointing out the falsehood at their own peril. Jimmy Carter tried on several occasions to downplay people's expectations by suggesting that he was only one man who could not do it all. Although he was right, the public did not recognize that their expectations were unrealistic. Instead they judged Carter a failure for not living up to them. Presidents must both recognize the falsehood and live with it just as they must recognize the symbolic connection between the president and the public and do what they can to capitalize on both.

Closing the Image Gap

What can presidents do to capitalize on the single executive image? Political scientists offer four generalizations.

5. Short successful wars, sudden international crises, and significant diplomatic efforts temporarily improve the president's public approval rating.[18]

6. Major nationally televised addresses also temporarily improve public approval.[19]

7. Protracted wars, domestic riots, public protests and demonstrations, and declining economic conditions diminish public approval.[20]

8. During the course of the term, presidents face a decline in public approval. During the first and second terms, the decline begins in the first year and continues through the third. Public approval improves somewhat in the fourth year but does not return to its first year high.[21]

The size of the image gap that presidents endure between their personal images and the single executive image bears directly on presidents' public support—the wider the gap, the lower the public approval rating. Political scientists have recognized two aspects of the image gap: (1) the short-term events, activities, and circumstances that narrow or widen it and (2) the long-term pattern of public approval during a president's term as it relates to the gap.

In the Short Term. Presidents have a fair degree of control over some ventures that work to their advantage in closing the image gap, such as emergency military interventions, dramatic diplomatic efforts, and well-timed major television addresses. Presidents also face some circumstances beyond their control, such as international crises like the fall of the Berlin Wall and the collapse of the Soviet Union, which may work to their advantage. Whether presidents have control or not, a rally of national support typically takes place. Consistent with the emotional basis of public approval, presidents receive all but unconditional support for actions that place the United States in a clear-cut good-versus-evil, us-against-them position or that envelop the actions or positions of the administration in patriotic trappings.

But other sudden and unforeseen events or conditions at home—such as urban riots, skyrocketing consumer prices, and plummeting job prospects—may leave the public wondering what the president will do. Many of these exigencies will tarnish the president's reputation in relation to the single executive image. The single executive image suggests that presidents are responsible even for things that they cannot predict and over which they have no immediate control. Yet for the very reason that presidents can neither predict nor control what will happen, they are unable to capitalize on these events and conditions. The us-against-them focus changes; it is no longer the United States as a whole against foreign foes. Instead, it is more likely the president portraying his side as "us" and the opposition as "them," thereby ensuring domestic controversy rather than a popular mandate about how the issues should be handled.

Generalizations 5, 6, and 7 taken together—the mix of the controlled and the uncontrollable, the presidential rallying of public support, and the public questioning of presidential action—imply that presidents must engage in domestic, foreign, and economic policy making. The single executive image demands attention to all three policy spheres. Although presidents are likely to get less credit in domestic than in foreign affairs because the public rally feature is absent, they may come up short politically if they emphasize foreign over domestic initiatives. For example, because President Bush had so little in the way of a domestic agenda, he left himself open to charges of not caring sufficiently about the causes and consequences of the 1992 Los Angeles riots. The opposite is also true: it is unwise for presidents to develop high-profile domestic agendas and make short shrift of foreign policy. By doing so, they defy the symbolic importance of acting as the leader of the nation to the world and do not show skills of crisis management, both of which are expected parts of the single executive image. President Clinton initially appeared hesitant when discussing foreign affairs, leading many to speculate that he ordered the bombing of Baghdad in June 1993 specifically to gain public credit for a foreign initiative. (The official explanation was that the bombing was in retaliation for a government-sponsored assassination attempt against former President Bush.) Finally, although economic bad news widens the image gap, economic good news closes it. Even though presidents have limited control over what happens in the economy, they are credited with being economic wizards if the economy is robust. As President Carter observed, "When things go bad you get entirely too much blame. And I have to admit that when things go good, you get entirely too much credit."[22]

In the Long Run. If there is one pattern of the presidency that presidents understand, it is that public approval starts high, then diminishes. Only two presidents have escaped this canon since public opinion polls began when Franklin Roosevelt was president: Dwight Eisenhower, whose first-term popularity started high and stayed high, and George Bush, whose popularity started moderately high, soared, and then plummeted. Commentators noted that Bush's mid-term popularity was like a Texas river: a mile wide and an inch deep.

Political scientists have discovered two aspects of the rise and fall of popularity that go beyond this simple pattern. First, there are three phases to presidents' popularity. A honeymoon of high public approval characterizes the first phase, lasting six months to one year. Approval drops, often sharply, during the second and third years. In their fourth year, presidents begin to receive better ratings. People look to the election and discover that the president's opponent is mortal, too, or, if the president is leaving office, people conclude that he was not so bad after all.

Second, the three phases vary considerably in intensity and duration by president. Although approval generally starts high and finishes lower, the highs and lows differ widely from one president to the next. These variations depend on circumstances in the political and economic environment as much as on presidents' own efforts. Because of political and economic circumstances, some presidents enter office—having not yet done anything—suffering a wide image gap between the single executive image and their personal images, whereas others begin their terms—again having not yet done anything—enjoying a much narrower gap. For example, compare Truman in his own full term beginning in 1949 and Nixon in his first term in 1969. Both followed the general pattern. Their approval started high, hit bottom sometime in their third year in office, and began to recover at term's end. But Truman's inaugural high was 69 percent and Nixon's was ten points less at 59 percent. Scholars have speculated that Nixon's low start-up numbers reflected public disillusionment with the presidency because of the Vietnam War.[23]

Presidents cannot expect the American public to acknowledge the circumstances beyond the chief executive's control. Instead, many people believe that each new president writes on a tabula rasa. With these blank slates in hand, each president has a chance equal to all recent predecessors to do well in office. Yet, as the Truman-Nixon comparison makes clear, the slates presidents are given are far from blank. They are cluttered with different economic circumstances, different expectations from the campaign, and different impressions in the media about how well the administration is doing.

So what are presidents to do other than be lucky enough to preside over good times? In the long run, presidents undoubtedly find it a nasty realization that there is little they can do in office or little that can happen to them that will be better for their public support than doing nothing. Presidents may be equally disheartened to learn that no matter what they do in their second and third years, it will not halt the all but inevitable erosion of public support as the image gap widens. Even George Bush, whose popularity soared during his third year in office with the triumph of U.S. forces in the Persian Gulf War, saw his poll results tumble in the war's aftermath. But in the short term, there are things presidents can do to boost their approval ratings—deliver a nationally televised address, announce a diplomatic breakthrough, respond forthrightly to an international crisis—that may be sufficient to get a bill passed, cajole world leaders, or receive favorable press coverage. Thus, presidents must study the particular hands they are dealt upon entering office, realize that the public does not recognize this, and seize opportunities to close the image gap whenever they arise.

Generalizations about the Presidential Institution

In addition to image, political scientists have examined the presidential institution. They have done so by looking inward to the makeup of the organization and outward to the relations that the presidency has with other institutions, especially Congress, the media, and departments and agencies in the federal bureaucracy.

Inside the Institution

Political scientists offer three generalizations about the internal workings of the presidential institution.

9. Hierarchical staff systems with a single chief of staff are generally more successful than more collegial systems in which every top adviser reports directly to the president.[24]

10. Presidents' own rhetoric to the contrary, cabinet government does not work.[25]

11. Presidents are *not* in charge of the 1,600 people who are employed in the Executive Office of the President.[26]

In the early weeks after the election, many presidents-elect attempt to wrap their fledgling administrations in democratic expectations. They promise that, unlike past administrations, theirs will be run with great openness. As a symbol of such openness, presidents often promise to take great personal care in the daily running of the White House by granting access to divergent staff voices. As another symbol, presidents announce that the cabinet will meet frequently as a source of information, inspiration, and advice. Neither promise is kept for long.

Why are the promises so quickly abandoned? Political scientists observe that the presidential institution is too large for any of them to be kept. Several recent presidents have learned the hard way that collegial staff configurations lead to presidential overload. To give numerous staff members direct access to the president places a considerable burden on the president to keep abreast of the many major and minor issues being monitored by staff members, not to mention the task of resolving numerous major and minor personality and turf clashes within the staff.

For example, President Ford began his administration with a collegial staff system of nine people reporting directly to him, a spokes-of-the-wheel arrangement, with advisers at the rim of the wheel and the president at its hub. Ford soon bogged down in the collegiality and turned to a hierarchical arrangement, they operate under different timetables, and they do not know or serve as advocates for clients of the bureaucracy, whether farmers, welfare mothers, or some other group.

In that realization, presidents have attempted three strategies to win the hearts and minds of three million bureaucrats. Presidents Johnson and Nixon adopted one strategy—namely, to bring as many decisions about policy implementation as possible into the White House. The Johnson administration created the Office of Economic Opportunity (OEO) in the White House to fight the War on Poverty. The result was a disaster. OEO failed to coordinate community-based poverty programs adequately, leaving many without supervision and leaving the War on Poverty as a whole to flounder. The Nixon administration brought a variety of implementation functions into the White House. Yet, the resulting increase in the White House staff was not sufficient to alter bureaucratic patterns of thinking and procedures, especially in the areas of health, welfare, and poverty, over which Nixon sought the greatest control.

President Reagan promoted a second strategy: to groom people for positions in the bureaucracy who espoused the president's philosophy. This strategy met with early success, but as Reagan's term waned so did the strategy. After a year or two, many Reagan recruits returned to the private sector to make more money. In addition, when President Bush arrived at the White House with a less firmly defined ideological outlook than Reagan's, it was difficult to continue hiring people who fit the presidential outlook.

A third strategy, known as administrative clearance, began during the Nixon administration, greatly expanded under Carter, and was heavily relied on by the Reagan White House. It involved the Office of Management and Budget's approval of the rules and regulations proposed by departments and agencies. During the Reagan years, the clearance process had a significant effect on the proposed regulations of several agencies, notably the Environmental Protection Agency and the Departments of Housing and Urban Development, Education, and Energy, all of which Reagan disliked. Some agencies refused even to submit certain regulations to the OMB for fear they would be shot down. Similarly, many regulations that OMB rejected were never resubmitted.[35]

Administrative clearance shows the greatest promise for putting the presidency into the executive branch loop. It is the first *institutionalized* effort presidents have made to rein in the bureaucracy. By comparison, the other two strategies were decidedly ad hoc. The Office of Management and Budget has established procedures to investigate administrative regulations and acts as a watchdog for the rest of the government. As might be expected, because of the institutional nature of the clearance process, the president has very little personal involvement and essentially trusts the OMB to do what he wants.

Congressional Relations. Political scientists have uncovered important lessons for presidents working with Congress. First, presidents must not clutter the legislative agenda with lots of big issues or even lots of small ones. Nor must presidents meet Congress on its own terms, because its agenda is always cluttered with large and small issues. Instead, presidents benefit by presenting Congress with a small list of big-ticket items that spell out what the president wants.

Second, presidents must adjust to two kinds of presidential time that dictate many of their most important legislative strategies: electoral time and organizational time. Electoral time is a highly compressed four-year cycle that is geared toward the upcoming election. The electoral clock ticks fast and loud. As one White House aide put it, "You should subtract one year for the reelection campaign, another six months for the midterms, six months for the start-up, six months for the closing, and another month or two for an occasional vacation. That leaves you with a two-year presidential term."[36] In contrast, many Washington politicians—those elected, those appointed, and those hired—have long time frames for action. Their clocks tick slowly. They have careers—at least a decade but most likely two—in which to finish what they start. Many members of Congress, although they must look toward the next election, enjoy safe seats that ensure their political longevity. Most people in Washington are there to stay. Presidents come and go.

Organizational time is the slower pace at which the White House apparatus gathers information, follows existing procedures, and makes decisions. It reflects the start-up-and-slow-down rhythm of the presidency. Organizational time is at its slowest early in the term when staff members are just beginning to understand their jobs. It may speed up later in the term as people, including the president, learn the ropes.

Although electoral and organizational time run at opposite speeds, they are closely linked in two ways. In one way, electoral time helps to create the slower organizational time. Because electoral time forces presidents to act in a hurry and to keep acting, it creates a need for a large presidential institution to carry on the action. In such a compressed time frame, it is impossible for presidents and just a few close advisers to develop agendas, see them through Congress, and have the executive branch implement them. They must draw upon a presidential institution that operates on its own slow time schedule, made even slower by the coming and going of presidents every four or eight years.

In another way, the joining of electoral and organizational time poses a dilemma for presidents. What is the best time for presidents to put forward their legislative agenda during their terms? Electoral time says the best time to act is early in the term. Organizational time urges presidents to act later, when people are more settled into their jobs. Most presidents and their staffs acknowledge that electoral time takes precedence over organizational time. The organization must try to catch up with demands in the political arena. Electoral time allows presidents to use the single executive image most dramatically if they "hit the ground running" by presenting major policy initiatives to Congress with great public fanfare in the first months of the first year of their terms. "It's definitely a race," stated a Carter aide. "The first months are the starting line. If you don't get off the blocks fast, you'll lose the race."[37]

Yet hitting the ground running is neither easy nor fun. Presidents often stumble in their first months in office and delay their legislative goals. The presidential institution may not be ready to go. Like any large organization, it needs time to work properly. It may actually need more organizational time than many institutions because its flow of operation is interrupted every four to eight years by the arrival of a new president and new staff members. For example, the Nixon administration spent a great deal of organizational time developing a thorough welfare reform proposal; meanwhile political time was ticking away. Delaying the announcement gave opponents a better opportunity to organize their attack, and the plan stalled in Congress. A Nixon aide lamented, "We gave our opponents a great deal of time to fight the Family Assistance Plan. They had at least six months to prepare before the initial announcement. Then, because we were late, the program bogged down in congressional committee. We gave them too many chances to hit us."[38]

Finally, the presidential image and the presidential institution intertwine in the legislative process. Presidential addresses and public approval increase presidents' success in Congress. In turn, presidential success in Congress increases public approval. These relationships take place within a larger political-economic context. Presidential success in Congress is shaped by the size of the president's party, the year in his term (the later in the term, the less likely the president's position will prevail), economic circumstances, and international conflicts.[39]

Presidential Mistakes

The fifteen generalizations about imagery and institution embody much of what political scientists know about the presidency. Presidents, like everyone else, make mistakes. But many of them could be avoided if presidents carefully observed these generalizations and the broader discussions of imagery and institution from which they derive.

Presidents' mistakes can be defined as situations in which presidents adopt courses of action that bring about the opposite of what they want or significantly less than what they want. To be sure, mistakes are not always clear-cut. For example, when President Truman fired General Douglas MacArthur for insubordination at the height of an offensive against the Chinese during the Korean War, Truman incurred tremendous political opposition, especially when MacArthur returned to the United States to a hero's welcome. But the decision was not necessarily a military mistake, because MacArthur was pushing for a much wider war with China. Truman replaced MacArthur with General Matthew Ridgway, who was able to correct some of MacArthur's tactical excesses. There are, however, numerous instances in which mistakes are not subject to multiple interpretations. Presidents make mistakes on imagery, on institutional relations, and on the combination of the two.

Mistaken Images

Image mistakes involve the president's failure to live up to some central aspect of the single executive image. Many of these mistakes relate to the president as a person. They often involve small things, such as haircuts, walks on the beach, pets, and trips to the grocery store, because the single executive image depends on the symbolic connection between the president and the American public. People understand the connection best when it is based on activities in daily life that they share with the president. Everyone gets a haircut; everyone goes to the grocery store. As planes reportedly waited on nearby runways at Los Angeles International Airport, President Clinton paid $200 for a haircut by a Beverly Hills stylist aboard *Air Force One*. In a grocery store, President Bush was revealed as being unaware of how price scanners worked. President Nixon walked on the beach near his home in San Clemente, California, in a tie and dress shoes, looking stiff and uncomfortable. President Johnson played with his pet beagles, Him and Her, by pulling them up by their long floppy ears, outraging dog lovers. Because such image mistakes typically leave the president looking out of touch with average citizens, the gap between his personal image and the single executive image grows.

Image mistakes may also involve the president as a policy maker—breaking a promise, not doing what the single executive image demands under certain policy circumstances, or attempting to revise the image itself. President Bush made image mistakes not only when he went back on his "no new taxes" pledge, but also when he decided to ride the crest of public support after the Persian Gulf War without doing anything on the domestic scene. Bush's popularity peaked at a record 89 percent, the highest ever recorded for any president. During the war, he had effectively moved his personal image toward the single executive image, getting high marks for exercising good judgment in a crisis and engaging in a short, successful military encounter. After the war, there was an expectation on Capitol Hill (even among Republicans), in the media, and among many Americans that the president would convert this wave of public support into public deeds, notably on the sluggish economy. Instead, the long-time Bush strategist and secretary of state James Baker snapped to reporters, "When you're at 90 percent, you can do what you damn well please." Bush left the impression that the president was not willing to get the job done or try to understand the average American's plight in the midst of a very weak economy. As the economy continued to sour, Bush's image gap widened, his approval dropped to near 40 percent, and he lost the opportunity to take his case to the American people.

As may be imagined, the second type of image mistake is more likely to harm presidents than the first. Although the personal mistakes cause momentary embarrassment and for a time draw considerable press attention, the press and the public soon tire of the topic and move on to something else. The policy mistakes tend to have longer-range consequences and thus are more apt to characterize the failures of an administration.

Institutional Mistakes

Presidents are also prone to mistakes when they fail to address various institutional constraints adequately. Such mistakes involve relations in the White House and relations between the White House and other institutions, such as Congress, the Supreme Court, or a department or agency in the executive bureaucracy. Within the institution, presidents frequently fail to acknowledge tensions between units that share similar jurisdictions. Several presidents have let animosity fester between the national security adviser and the secretary of state on matters of diplomacy.[40] Information leaks also are common occurrences as units within the White House compete with each other to make decisions to their own advantage. In-house scandals or embarrassments also erupt because too many people are going in too many directions to be adequately monitored by the chief of staff or other staff members, let alone the president. Indeed, many of these instances have involved the chiefs of staff themselves, ranging from charges against Eisenhower's chief of staff, Sherman Adams, that he improperly accepted gifts to those leveled against Bush's chief of staff, John Sununu, for using government planes and cars for personal use. Many internal institutional mistakes prompt the question, "Who is minding the store?" And the answer often is, "No one." The mistakes are reflections of the complexity of the presidential institution and the limits to presidents' own control over it.

Presidents also make mistakes in relations between the presidency and other institutions. At the base of many of them is the recent presidential tendency to run against Congress. Presidents charge that Congress is unwieldy, irresponsible, and unable to do what the country needs. Although this tactic may play well with the folks back home, it does not play well with the people on Capitol Hill, who will support or oppose presidential legislative priorities.

President Reagan's ill-fated nomination of Robert Bork to the Supreme Court in 1987 revealed several dimensions of interinstitutional mistakes. Although the Reagan administration had been in office for six years, it violated several basic principles of the presidential institution during the nomination battle that lasted for three and one-half months and ended with the Senate's defeat of Bork by the largest margin in history—forty-two to fifty-eight. The Reagan people disregarded fundamental institutional constraints surrounding the nomination of Bork, an activist conservative: the Senate was solidly Democratic; it was late in Reagan's term; his popularity had slipped; Congress had been angered by the disclosures of the Iran-contra scandal; and several senators, notably Senate judiciary committee chair Joseph Biden, were running for president. Institutional miscalculations continued when the Reagan strategists pinned their hopes for victory on southern Democratic senators but did not conduct an aggressive lobbying campaign—either publicly or privately—for Bork until well after the swing senators had been pressured by their constituents not to back Bork. They also gave up a critical timing advantage when Reagan announced the nomination in July. The Senate adjourned for its summer recess in July and Biden did not call for hearings on the nomination until September. Had the Reagan people anticipated Biden's move, they could have delayed the president's own announcement of the nomination until after the Senate reconvened. This would have prevented Bork's opponents from mobilizing during July and August. Interinstitutional mistakes occur with Congress when presidents fail to take into account its composition, the link between presidential success and public approval, and the idea of timing issues in such a way as to gain the upper hand.

Image-Institutional Mistakes

Presidents also make mistakes that join lapses in imagery with those in institutional relations. The president chooses a course of action that widens his image gap. The gap then leaves space for other institutions to gain strategic advantages. President Clinton's attempt to end the forty-eight-year-old ban on gay men and lesbians in the military in 1993 is an example of this kind of image-institution mistake.

Clinton made a campaign promise to end the ban and reiterated the pledge as president-elect. At first glance, one might argue that Clinton did exactly what the single executive image demands. At the earliest possible opportunity—even before being sworn in—he announced that he would issue an executive order lifting the ban. Surely, this is the kind of swift, bold action the single executive image requires.

But the single executive image also dictates boundaries within which such swift actions must be taken. They must be done with average Americans in mind and in such a way that citizens will either not be aroused or will be unified. Instead, Clinton chose a highly controversial issue that tapped, among other things, homophobic prejudice both in and out of the military. In doing so he pushed away his own main agenda item, summarized in his campaign headquarters as "the economy, stupid." Nor did the Clinton team lay any rhetorical or public opinion groundwork for the decision. The apt comparison between lifting the gay ban and Truman's executive order desegregating the military was left to several members of Congress and gay-rights leaders to make. Furthermore, Clinton announced the decision at a time when few other administration decisions were being made. Indeed, this was the Clinton strategy. The president would look strong lifting the ban early with one stroke of the pen while more intricate plans were being developed for the economic programs at the core of Clinton's agenda. Yet the absence of other presidential news allowed the press to focus intense coverage on the matter of gays in the military rather than on the more typical stories of the new first family moving into the White House and the president's plans for the future. As a result, a public uproar ensued and Clinton lost much of his honeymoon support.

In an attempt to ameliorate the issue, Secretary of Defense Les Aspin announced that he would review the ban and make recommendations to the president in six months. The Clinton people hoped this would be a cooling-off period during which the controversy would diminish. Yet their timing decision set off a series of institutional machinations. Members of the armed forces and members of Congress, especially the Joint Chiefs of Staff and the Senate Armed Services Committee chair Sam Nunn, now had a full opportunity to organize against Clinton's proposal. The Joint Chiefs had threatened in November to resign en masse if an executive order not to their liking was forthcoming. Nunn held hearings and visited a submarine to dramatize the close quarters in which sailors, in particular, lived. The Joint Chiefs and Nunn were able to define the issue around their own alternatives. A compromise policy—"Don't ask; don't tell"—was ultimately worked out that permitted gay men and lesbians to serve in the military but not openly to acknowledge their sexual preference. The ban had been modified but not lifted. Thus, Clinton began his term with a wide image gap but also allowed two competing institutions—the military and Congress—to define an issue in such a way that the president had to acquiesce to them rather than the other way around.

Conclusion: Presidents and Political Scientists

Is it possible that, if President Clinton had a political scientist on his staff advising him on the nature of the presidency, the issue of gays in the military would have been resolved in a manner more in keeping with what the White House wanted? Could the Reagan administration have saved the Bork nomination? Could President Bush have translated public support into domestic policies after the Persian Gulf War? Political scientists are no more omniscient than presidents or their primary advisers. They would not get it right all of the time. But they have knowledge quite different from that offered by presidents' other advisers, knowledge that is pertinent to every decision that presidents make—namely, how the presidency operates.

Presidents have three main types of advisers. Policy advisers lay out various domestic and international policy problems that presidents may wish to address or may have to address. They also develop positions and programs for presidents to offer as solutions. Economic advisers spell out various options on how to keep the economy robust, how to make the good times return, and how to cut or add to the federal budget. Political advisers consider the politics of a decision—how it will play with the public, how the press will cast the issue, and how other politicians will respond. Political advisers then devise strategies to sell the president's decision with these political considerations in mind.

Missing are advisers skilled in telling presidents about the office they hold. Although each type of adviser teaches presidents a good deal about what they need to know in order to work in the White House, none of them is an expert on the presidency. The generalizations from political science research are not lessons that the other advisers would fully know. Even political advisers, who may be aware of some of the generalizations, such as those on public opinion, are not schooled in the presidency per se. Since many political advisers began their stint with the president during the campaign, they often have an electoral framework in mind that is much narrower than that offered by political scientists.

What presidents need is a fourth set of advisers—presidency advisers. Nor will it do to hire only those political scientists who view the presidency from a single perspective or advocate but one method. The generalizations about imagery and institution are a mix of qualitative and quantitative findings. Conclusions about different types of White House staff systems, cabinet government, and the limits to presidents' control of the Executive Office of the President and the bureaucracy are largely drawn from qualitative accounts. Conclusions about presidential success in Congress, presidential approval, and presidential speeches are drawn primarily from quantitative studies.

The generalizations also reveal the perspectives that political scientists adopt. Studies of presidential dealings with Congress and the public typically adopt the perspective of presidential power. Presidents must persuade members of Congress and the public to give them what they want. Accounts of the relations between presidents and their advisers, cabinet members, and the bureaucracy incorporate historical descriptions, interpretations of the power of presidents, and institutional analyses.

Thus, political scientists' understanding of the presidency rests on an accumulation of knowledge that cuts across methods and perspectives. Effective presidency advisers must have studied the office from several perspectives and must be knowledgeable about work using qualitative and quantitative methods. This permits them to understand the full scope of the office and its two central dimensions of imagery and institution. How presidents can succeed at using imagery and the institution is one of the main lessons political scientists offer in studying the presidency.

Notes

1. George C. Edwards III and Stephen J. Wayne, eds., *Studying the Presidency* (Knoxville: University of Tennessee Press, 1983); George C. Edwards III, John Kessel, and Bert Rockman, eds., *Researching the Presidency* (Pittsburgh: University of Pittsburgh Press, 1992).

2. For more details on these two concepts, see Lyn Ragsdale, *Presidential Politics* (Boston: Houghton Mifflin, 1993).

3. Jeffrey Tulis, *The Rhetorical Presidency* (New Haven: Yale University Press, 1987).

4. Fred Greenstein, "What the President Means to Americans," in *Choosing the President*, ed. D. Barber (Englewood Cliffs, N.J.: Prentice Hall, 1974), 144.

5. Michael Grossman and Martha Kumar, *Portraying the President* (Baltimore: Johns Hopkins University Press, 1981).

6. Herbert Gans, *Deciding What's News* (New York: Pantheon, 1979), 145.

7. Alfred de Grazia, "The Myth of the President," in *The Presidency*, ed. A. Wildavsky (Boston: Little, Brown, 1969), 50.

8. Hugh Heclo, "Introduction: The Presidential Illusion," in *The Illusion of Presidential Government*, ed. H. Heclo and L. Salamon (Boulder, Colo.: Westview Press, 1981), 3.

9. Barbara Hinckley, *The Symbolic Presidency* (New York: Routledge, 1990); Roderick Hart, *The Sound of Leadership* (Chicago: University of Chicago Press, 1987); Tulis, *The Rhetorical Presidency*.

10. George C. Edwards III, *The Public Presidency* (New York: St. Martin's Press, 1983), 196; Stephen Wayne, "Expectations of the President," in *The President and the Public*, ed. D. Graber (Philadelphia: Institute for the Study of Human Issues, 1982), 17–39.

11. Lyn Ragsdale, "Strong Feelings: Emotional Responses to Presidents," *Political Behavior* 13 (1991): 33–65; Greenstein, "What the President Means to Americans," 144–145.

12. Grossman and Kumar, *Portraying the President.*

13. "Remarks upon Taking the Oath of Office," *Public Papers of the Presidents, Gerald R. Ford, 1974* (Washington, D.C.: U.S. Government Printing Office, 1975), 1.

14. Quoted in Michael Novak, *Choosing Our King* (New York: Macmillan, 1974), 44.

15. Grossman and Kumar, *Portraying the President,* 275–276.

16. Hinckley, *The Symbolic Presidency,* 1990.

17. *New York Times,* May 21, 1977, A1.

18. Paul Brace and Barbara Hinckley, *Follow the Leader: Opinion Polls and Modern Presidents* (New York: Basic Books, 1992).

19. Lyn Ragsdale, "The Politics of Presidential Speechmaking," *American Political Science Review* 78 (December 1984): 971–984.

20. Ibid.; Samuel Kernell, "Explaining Presidential Popularity," *American Political Science Review* 72 (June 1978): 506–522; Charles Ostrom and Dennis Simon, "Promise and Performance: A Dynamic Model of Presidential Popularity," *American Political Science Review* 79 (June 1985): 334–358.

21. John Mueller, "Presidential Popularity from Truman to Johnson," *American Political Science Review* 64 (March 1970): 18–34; James Stimson, "Public Support for American Presidents: A Cyclical Model," *Public Opinion Quarterly* 40 (Spring 1976): 1–21; Brace and Hinckley, *Follow the Leader.*

22. Quoted in Godfrey Hodgson, *All Things to All Men: The False Promise of the Modern American Presidency* (New York: Simon and Schuster, 1980), 25.

23. Jack Dennis, "Dimensions of Public Support for the Presidency," *Society*, July/August 1976.

24. Samuel Kernell and Samuel Popkin, eds., *Chief of Staff* (Berkeley: University of California Press, 1986).

25. Richard Fenno, *The President's Cabinet* (New York: Vintage Books, 1959).

26. John Burke, *The Institutional Presidency* (Baltimore: Johns Hopkins University Press, 1992); Bradley Patterson, Jr., *The Ring of Power* (New York: Basic Books, 1988); Karen Hult, "Advising the President," in *Researching the Presidency*.

27. Quoted in James Pfiffner, *The Strategic Presidency* (Chicago: Dorsey Press, 1988), 29.

28. Ibid.

29. See Ragsdale, *Presidential Politics*, 191–196.

30. George Shultz, *Turmoil and Triumph: My Years as Secretary of State* (New York: Scribner, 1993).

31. Richard Nathan, *The Administrative Presidency* (New York: Wiley, 1983); Elizabeth Sanders, "The Presidency and the Bureaucratic State," in *The Presidency and the Political System*, 3d ed., ed. M. Nelson (Washington, D.C.: CQ Press, 1990), 409–442; Terry Moe, "The Political Presidency," in *The New Directions in American Politics*, ed. J. Chubb and P. Peterson (Washington, D.C.: Brookings Institution, 1985), 235–272.

32. Paul Light, *The President's Agenda* (Baltimore: Johns Hopkins University Press, 1982).

33. Ostrom and Simon, "Promise and Performance."

34. Brace and Hinckley, *Follow the Leader*; Lyn Ragsdale, "The Perpetual Campaign: Presidents' Public Appearances from Truman to Reagan" (University of Arizona, Tucson, mimeographed).

35. Ragsdale, *Presidential Politics*, 239.

36. Quoted in Light, *The President's Agenda*, 17.

37. Ibid., 43.

38. Ibid.

39. Ostrom and Simon, "Promise and Performance."

40. For example, a feud that developed in the Carter administration between Secretary of State Cyrus Vance and National Security Adviser Zbigniew Brzezinski affected the ill-fated helicopter rescue attempt of the American hostages held in Iran.

3 The American Presidency in Comparative Perspective: Systems, Situations, and Leaders

Bert A. Rockman

Whatever research methods or perspectives political scientists may bring to the study of the presidency, Bert A. Rockman argues in the concluding chapter of Part I that much can be learned by comparing the office to similar offices in other countries. "What does the American presidency look like from the vantage point of other political systems?" Rockman asks. He answers by reviewing the effects on national leadership of "the characteristics of political systems, such as their governmental arrangements and political cultures," the kinds of situations that affect leaders, and "leadership roles . . . as they differ across systems." One of Rockman's most provocative conclusions is that the obvious differences between the presidency and other national leadership roles, such as that of the prime minister of Great Britain, often mask more important similarities.

What does the American presidency look like when viewed from the vantage point of other political systems? How does it differ from other leadership posts? What differences derive from the characteristics of political systems, such as their governmental arrangements and political cultures? Such questions demand a comparative systems perspective on political leadership, which is central to an understanding of the American presidency. In this chapter, then, we assess the office of the presidency by looking at some of the conditions that act to enlarge or diminish its capacities. In so doing, we shall also be able to compare conditions that are relevant to the exercise of leadership across political systems. What kinds of situations make presidents more powerful? Which ones make them less so?

Another way to compare leadership roles is to analyze the style of the leaders themselves as they differ across systems. Definitions of the job and leadership styles vary from president to president and from prime minister to prime minister. Their styles of leadership will shape the contours of their roles. Style cannot be divorced, however, from situations and political systems; rather, it is shaped by and interacts with them. In short, our three elements for comparison—systems, situations, and leaders—are intertwined.

Although intertwined, these three elements shall be analyzed separately in this chapter in an effort to provide distinct bases for a comparative perspective. This perspective should lead us to ask how systems structure leadership roles, what situations influence leadership possibilities, the extent to which situations are structured by systems, and how leaders themselves vary. How are leaders selected and their roles defined? By undertaking such an exercise, inexact as it may be, we should be able to develop a more sophisticated perspective on the leadership role of the American presidency.

Systems

While American political rhetoric tends to lionize its system of government, scholars are inclined to be critical of it. These critical perspectives are especially prominent during times in which complacency toward the structure of American government is challenged either because of stark presidential aggrandizement or, more frequently, because of sustained policy stalemate. These occasions tend to produce a rash of reform proposals, some, indeed many, of which are meant to emulate what are perceived to be more effective forms of governance in other democracies. For a long time the British system of party government provided the model. Political turmoil and the waning economic fortunes of the United Kingdom, however, have suggested some limits to this model, although reformers are still drawn to it as if by magnetic force. The Scandinavian model (Sweden and Norway more than Denmark) of social corporatism and rationalized politics has also seemed attractive, yet is admittedly far more difficult to emulate because it would require not just institutional alteration but also a vast and probably impossible restructuring of American society and social and political norms. Japan's evident economic success has also attracted attention recently. The appeal here, however, has been based on Japan's business and industrial management techniques rather than its politics and government, which feature a heavy reliance on money, subsidies to inefficient but politically important sectors of production, and personal, if institutionalized, factions.

A comparative approach entails not a proclamation of the virtues of one institutional form over the other but an exploration of nuances. Thus, we begin with several broadly organized features of systems to guide our analysis, beginning with the attributes of national power and concluding with the role of political culture and its impact on public expectation.

Power Attributes

The great military and economic power of the United States translates into immense political power. How these political resources are actually used is another matter, but there is no doubt that on the world scene and at international gatherings, the United States is still the principal actor—not unchallenged as it was in the generation after World War II, but still more powerful than any other actor in international military, economic, and political spheres.

Under these circumstances it is nearly impossible for an American president to be anything less than important. In this regard, the president's stature reflects America's stature in the world rather than his more anemic capabilities to influence matters at home.[1] The president, of course, is not a free agent in world politics, which in any event is increasingly perceived as deeply interconnected with domestic matters. But a president more or less defines what a crisis is and in these matters has a freer hand than in domestic ones. Because an international crisis involving the United States inevitably includes far more than the United States, the American president is an inherently powerful figure and the presidency an exceedingly important vantage point.

The president's powerful presence also makes for mighty expectations at home and abroad. The leader's power naturally must be measured against his objectives and against the expectations built around his role, which are larger and greater for American presidents than for virtually any other national leader—greater, no doubt, than the prospects that they can be met. The simple point here is that we need to distinguish between importance and power. The president of the United States is important because his country has great power and corresponding influence on world politics, although such prominence does not necessarily make the president a powerful actor vis-à-vis his goals or the expectations of various domestic and international audiences.

Government Size

The size of the enterprise over which a leader presides says something about his power, or at least about the tools and instruments at his disposal. Presumably, the greater the government share of societal resources, the more leverage government has in negotiations between public policy makers and private interests. Two points need to be stressed. One is that the public sphere in the United States historically has been small in relation to those in western European democracies. The other is that the premises underlying the notion that big government makes for easier direction are not necessarily correct.

One of the elements of governmental size is the resource extraction, or taxing, arm of government, a function that can indicate the relative size of the public sphere, although not the distribution of activities within it. (A far higher proportion of government expenditures goes to the defense sector in the United States even in the post–cold war era than in comparable European countries.) In 1990, compared with the other twenty-three wealthy democracies located primarily in western Europe, the United States ranked next to last in extracting public resources, with only Turkey taxing less.[2] Although the federal government is large in absolute terms, it is comparatively small in relation to the private sector. By itself, however, big government does not necessarily make for a dominating government.

A large state also can be less than responsive to political direction from the top, especially if many of its expenditures are in the form of past program commitments. Ideally, leaders wish to set agendas free of past commitments. The accumulation of such commitments over time obviously sets stark limits on directional adaptations. Indeed, the meteoric growth in entitlements spending (health care, pensions, and various forms of income assistance) has set profound limits on funding new programs. In the present climate, therefore, the major imperative has been deficit reduction. A large state, consequently, may be merely a vastly overcommitted state and thus likely to be viewed by top political leaders more as an impediment in the path of leadership than a resource.

A big state, in sum, is neither inherently powerful nor inherently tractable. The extent to which resources are available for leadership is far more crucial than the size of the state, per se. Previous commitments place a lien on those resources, thus diminishing the space for maneuver. Regardless of the size of government, this is the predicament with which the heads of the affluent democracies, certainly including the president of the United States, are faced.

Centralization

Centralization of resources and authority is believed to provide assets to top national political leaders. Yet different forms of centralization need to be considered. One is the level of financial and political resources available to the central government in relation to other units of government. A reasonable presumption is that the higher the ratio of central government resources to those of regional and local governments, the greater the leverage of central political leaders. A second form of centralization is in the party apparatus providing the political power the leadership needs to govern. (The extreme example is the Leninist dogma of "democratic centrism," which means that once a decision is made at the top, discussion ceases and it is carried out.) A third form of centralization has to do with the relationship between the leader at the top and his cabinet.

Beginning with the relative centralization of government, we note that by almost any criterion, the resources commanded by the central government in the United States are considerably less than those found in European states. The American system is a federal one that grants considerable autonomy to the state governments, an arrangement that stems from the original unification of the American government and its embodiment in the constitutional doctrine of residual powers for states. Of the three European federal states—Austria, Germany, and Switzerland, respectively—two claim a somewhat higher (78 and 70 percent) and one a somewhat lower (62 percent) share of total governmental revenues for their central governments than does the United States (68 percent). But many more European states—those with unitary governments—keep a substantially greater share of revenues at the center, averaging 86 percent.[3]

These data have consequences for national political leaders. In 1981, for example, when Ronald Reagan launched his successful campaign to cut federal taxes, supply-siders believed the dollars saved in the private sector would be used to stimulate investment and therefore growth in the national economy. State governments commonly reacted to federal spending cuts, however, by increasing their own taxes.[4] Although the net effect of these countervailing activities is unclear, certainly the intended macroeconomic effects of presidential fiscal and tax policies were blunted.

Of course, as we have said, such outcomes are part of a federal system. Yet the American federal system is exceptionally decentralized and, unlike Germany's, for instance, has little ability to coordinate and homogenize public policies and budgets among the states. Virtually every American president has found his administration embroiled in conflicts between federal policy and one or more states or regions. The most notable of these conflicts in the post-World War II era was with southern states and communities over civil rights issues, especially school desegregation. More recently, conflicts have mainly centered on land use in the West; energy production in several states, notably in the oil-producing Southwest; and, in the Reagan era, the tax policies and rates of the higher-tax states of the Northeast and Upper Midwest. The states often prevail in such conflicts because of their ability to marshal political resources in Congress, a recent example of which was the relentless lobbying at the grass roots to compel key Democratic senators from high-energy-producing states to oppose President Clinton's proposed energy tax.

Unitary governments, to be sure, are no panacea for central policies that meet with deep regional unpopularity. Moreover, from Japan to Italy, the essence of grass-roots politics has been securing pork from the central government pork barrel. Still, an American president intent on pursuing "national" policies will find that goal more elusive than will his counterparts in western Europe. This, no doubt, is at least as much a function of the great size and territorial diversity of the United States as it is a consequence of its institutions. The institutions, however, give direct expression to this diversity.

Another, more finely grained form of centralizing resources for political leadership is the ability to enforce political discipline from the top. The model for such discipline, according to Richard Rose, is the "party government" model, which he defines as the "unique . . . claim to have the right to choose what solutions shall be binding upon the whole of society."[5]

The effective (and, in one view, proper) role of political parties, however, may be to prevent the leader either from straying from the party fold or from creating a personal political machine.[6] To the extent that a party is highly institutionalized, it may be able to exert as much pressure on the leader to adhere to party interests and values as the leader is able to command disciplined support from the party. Harold Wilson, for example, was a vintage conciliator of intraparty conflict in Great Britain, whereas Margaret Thatcher, with some success, sought to recast the Conservative party in her own image. When the party plays a dominating role, it sets boundaries for leadership behavior. A scholar of leadership in the former Soviet Union pointed out that support from the Communist party required ritualized incantations about the party role, which by implication meant the role of the massive party apparatus.[7]

Party support, in other words, comes at a high price and limits a leader's pursuit of innovations that may depart from accepted party policies and constituencies. No matter how centralized the political machinery may be, leaders have to build and sustain coalitions. In this regard, American presidents are not alone. In fact, because of the limited institutionalization of the parties in the United States, American presidents are often able to penetrate their official party organizations pretty thoroughly and thus ensure the responsiveness of the national party machinery to them. Party members in Congress, of course, have much more independence, but they are influenced by strong currents of presidential popularity.

Yet another, even more refined, form of centralization is the relative concentration of resources around the office of the leader. It is no straightforward matter, however, to describe precisely what a resource is. That the British prime minister inhabits an office staffed with very few people who are personally subordinate to him does not mean that he is an inherently less powerful person than an American president. Although many people work for the president and are thus accountable to him, staff size and leadership capacity are not equivalent. They may even be inversely related.[8]

Despite the buildup of staff around central leaders in other countries, most notably Germany and Canada, the modern American presidency is both more munificently staffed than any other leadership post and, perhaps, less institutionalized.[9] This reflects yet another irony. In relation to the other institutions of American government, the president is an important but, constitutionally, not a preeminent actor. With respect to the rest of the executive branch, though, the president is preeminent. Cabinet secretaries are a president's subordinates, not his colleagues.

In addition, the growth of the modern White House staff has reflected the need, as seen by most presidents, for presidential integration and direction of an otherwise fragmented government. The staff and other coordinating, budgetary, and monitoring organs of the Executive Office of the President (EOP) enhance the president's ability to counter the centrifugal tendencies of the departments and their political constituencies as expressed through Congress. It may be that this is a form of centralization that arises for the sole reason that, without it, presidents would be completely at the mercy of these centrifugal forces and subgovernmental arrangements. Yet presidents are given a kind of proprietary right (which they increasingly have come to exercise) over the executive branch. The White House staff thus embodies the assumption of executive preeminence in a government where the division of turf among many significant institutional actors is never very clear.

Presidential and Parliamentary Systems

What difference, per se, does governing structure make? In comparing the presidential and parliamentary systems, most attention has probably been given to the supposedly contrasting roles of the president and of the cabinet-government as initiators of legislative proposals. Presumably, in a parliamentary system once the cabinet decides, the deal is mostly done, but in the

American system presidential proposals merely begin a long and uncertain process in the Congress. It is reasonable, therefore, to suppose that presidents are more inhibited than prime ministers because of the legislature's independence from the executive. This supposition, however, is in need of review.

Advocates of parliamentary government, such as presidential adviser Lloyd N. Cutler,[10] assume that either the parliamentary system or some well-disguised form of it will produce the cohesion and authority that presidents need to govern according to their agendas. They assume that unified party government, rather than government by coalition (the far more frequent case), would prevail. Such advocates further assume that in a majority party government, few divisions would be intraparty. Finally, they neglect the relevance of other actors—interest groups, for example, who in a party government system would ply their influence within the parties and in the bureaucracy rather than in the legislature.

Although political machinery has some effect on how matters are handled, deeply divisive issues are not resolved simply through majoritarian rituals. Probably the most significant difference between the presidential and parliamentary systems is the manner in which the various interests and political factions struggle to shape the national agenda. The president tends to maximize and expand the agenda in public to accord both with his goals and with those of relevant party constituencies. Because of the separation between the executive and the legislature, his efforts to construct legislative majorities are necessarily open and visible. Such efforts generate confrontation, which makes presidents look more vulnerable when they lose and more potent when they win. In contrast, a potential prime minister is more typically engaged in striking inter- or intraparty bargains that the government can carry forward.[11] Once an agenda is formed, it is almost certain (assuming bargains are kept) that its most important elements will gain parliamentary approval. But such victories can be misleading because most of the cutting, shaping, and limitation of the agenda has occurred before the legislative stage. What is preshaped and thus basically certain of passage in a parliamentary system is shaped later in the presidential system and with more uncertainty about its ultimate disposition. This is, in the end, the real difference between the two systems.

Accountability

What forms of accountability undergird the systems that presidents and prime ministers lead? A broad summary of these accountability relationships is portrayed in Table 3.1. The pattern suggests that more of an insider's politi-

Table 3.1. Sources of Prime Ministerial and Presidential Accountability

Source of accountability	Extent of accountability	
	Prime ministers	Presidents
Party	Strong	Moderate to weak
Cabinet	Strong	Nonexistent
Legislature	Weak	Strong
Mass public	Strong	Very strong

cal game exists under a parliamentary-cabinet arrangement than under the American presidential arrangement.

Mass political accountability is strong, of course, for both kinds of leaders. In the parliamentary system the electoral verdict is, to a greater extent than in the presidential, about the parties, but it is also influenced by leading personalities. It is up to the party to decide on its leadership based on mass political signals. Such signals usually are followed if political disaster looms. Although the president does not start from scratch to build a coalition, his party's support cannot be taken for granted. This consequently makes him more susceptible than prime ministers to the effects of fluctuations in public opinion.

Presidents depend very little on cabinet or party approval, but they are greatly dependent on Congress, assuming, of course, that their activities require legislative approval. For prime ministers, however, party and cabinet are intimately connected—a connection that is much fainter in the United States, where the structures are less clearly demarcated. The president's cabinet is not a collegial body of peers or fellow party leaders. Its members are decidedly his underlings, and presidents often rely more deeply for counsel on friends (Bebe Rebozo to Richard M. Nixon, Charles Kirbo to Jimmy Carter), White House staff (Henry Kissinger to Nixon, Zbigniew Brzezinski and Hamilton Jordan to Carter), Washington icons (Averell Harriman and Clark Clifford to various Democratic presidents), or spouses (especially, but not exclusively, Hillary Rodham Clinton).

Party structures also differ. A president can control the formal party machinery at the national level, but (even though the national party organizations have become more prominent) most of the action in political parties remains at the state and local level: prime ministers, in contrast, are much more dependent on, and therefore more accountable to, their cabinets and their parties.

In sum, presidents are usually less, not more, inhibited than prime ministers. But they also tend to be more vulnerable because the process is more visible and open and thus not easily controlled through prearranged agreements.

Again, the systems tend to create different behavioral incentives. Naturally, leaders will differ as to how they interpret these incentives.

A Unitary or Collective Executive

The idea that presidents should not be inhibited in carrying out their executive powers is firmly asserted in *The Federalist*, no. 70. Hamilton argued:

> Those politicians and statesmen who have been the most celebrated for the soundness of their principles and for the justness of their views have declared in favor of a single executive and a numerous legislature. . . . Decision, activity, secrecy, and dispatch will generally characterize the proceedings of one man in a much more eminent degree than the proceedings of any greater number.[12]

The concept of a cabinet with collective decision-making responsibilities was not to be fully comprehended until many years later in the evolution of parliamentary government. Collective cabinet responsibility required the development of mass-based political parties to fuel modern parliamentary democracy.

The executive power produced by the modern mass-based political parties and collective cabinet responsibilities, ironically, seems to have been greater than that realized through the Hamiltonian conception of a unitary executive. The cabinets of modern parliamentary governments, which comprise the leading members of a political party or coalition, stand or fall together. The cabinet must be brought along by the prime minister and different positions reconciled. This accomplished, parliamentary support can then typically be assumed.

Almost the exact opposite holds true in the presidential system. Here, the cabinet members, being the president's subordinates, almost never make collective decisions; decisions are the president's responsibility, even if he feels compelled to use interdepartmental committees to make them. In this sense, the presidency is indeed the focus of governing energy that Hamilton had hoped to generate. But although the president need not put together agreements in the cabinet (still worrying, of course, about leaks from the disgruntled), his difficulties begin when he must persuade Congress to act on his behalf. Unity in the executive branch, without the use of other tools, merely displaces the locus of coalition building, making it more open and thus more likely to dissipate presidential energies in embarrassing political defeats.

The collective executive, in short, works through the modern political party. The unitary executive, however, cannot so easily channel energies in such a fashion. Even a deeply partisan president cannot always count on support from the leaders of his party in Congress; they, in turn, may or may not be in a position to help him work out agreements. In a Constitution written before the advent of mass political parties, it was natural to assume, as Hamilton did, that one person could produce sufficient executive energy. This assumption now appears to be largely untenable.

Selection Processes and "Selectorates"

The process of selecting a presidential candidate in the United States is a virtual three-ring circus, but the rings are concentric. They move from smaller audiences to bigger ones in an extraordinarily protracted process.

In modern politics, ambitious politicians have to draw attention to themselves or to their roles as political advocates. With the modest exception of France on the center-right, European and Japanese politics are organized exclusively around party organization as the stream in which political ambition is spawned—a condition that once held in the United States, especially in the nineteenth and early twentieth centuries. Party is now, however, merely one of the channels in the widened band through which politicians can beam their messages and direct their ambitions. As the candidacies of Carter in 1976 and of Ross Perot in 1992, and the more distant ones of Dwight D. Eisenhower and Wendell Willkie make clear, party is not always the dominant channel.

Two pertinent questions arise from this difference in the organization of leadership selection. First, who are the selectors? Next, what difference does the nature of the "selectorate" make for candidates and their behavior?

There is a relatively simple answer to the first question, but the simplicity is mostly superficial. The simple response is that selection is far more party-controlled in other democratic polities than in the United States. The direct primary, a distinctly American phenomenon, tends to remove an especially important lever from party organization—the ability to select candidates. But although the selectorate is broader for American presidential aspirants than for those who vie for equivalent posts in Europe, it is not precisely clear what the consequences are. Organization and money are important in American primary elections, and candidates who appeal to party activists are often able to generate more of both. In this sense, the primary election process actually can strengthen ideological consonance between candidates and party activists, especially when the traditional party apparatus is more dedicated to the patronage and particularistic elements of politics.

Thus, it is much easier to assert that American processes of candidate selection differ from those in other political democracies than it is to say what those differences mean. The American process of candidate selection is both visible and lengthy. It requires a lot of money and sustained public interest. The process produces a larger number and possibly greater variety of candidates; and it is inevitably less controlled and predictable. When an incumbent seeks reelection, the attention of the president (and therefore of the government) is riveted on creating effective political defenses (or attacks) for the numerous political judgment days ahead. When a sitting president is ineligible to run again or chooses not to, attention drifts from his administration to the succession.

Yet functional similarities between American and other democratic polities also exist, however differently they are manifested. All ambitious politicians must build bases for support so that when the opportunity strikes they are in a position to take advantage of it. Politicking, in this sense, does not occur all of a sudden. Rather, it is a continuous process. But the inside game does not always produce inside leaders, as the case of Thatcher indicates. In the view of Anthony King, her major claim to fame was that she was not Ted Heath, her predecessor as Conservative party leader.[13] Had she been an insider's politician, it is unlikely that she would have been so injudicious as to have taken Heath on. After James Callaghan's retirement, the Labour party made an unusual choice, too, when Michael Foote, an eccentric leftist, was selected as a compromise candidate between the party's vote-maximizing wing and its doctrinaire wing.

When reformers look for a fix, selection processes seem to be the natural target. One assumption that various reformers make is that altering the selectorates presumably will make the selected more moderate, more responsive, more likely to be victorious, more experienced, and more predictable. But this is less than obvious, even if one could define all of those virtues more sharply. The greater likelihood is that those who are selected will vary widely within any selection process.

Political Culture and Expectations

Expectations about leadership are said to run high in the United States.[14] These expectations arise partly because of the high level of trust that Americans invest in their political and governing institutions.[15] Even during the late 1960s and the 1970s, when the political alienation of Americans was a much discussed area of social research, confidence in government, although diminished, remained higher among U.S. citizens than among citizens of other democratic polities.

It may be that Americans are incurable optimists or simply naive innocents in regard to what political authority plausibly can achieve. Whatever the case, the irony is considerable. For the higher the expectations, the greater the fall when they are not met. George Bush's rapid descent from record-setting approval ratings after the Persian Gulf War to defeated incumbent burdened by a sluggish economy illustrates the point.

Before emphasizing, and possibly overemphasizing, the peculiarities of the American environment and system, we need to mention first some important similarities about modern mass politics. One is that the role of public expectation appears to be a generalized phenomenon of modern political life in all industrially advanced democratic systems. Mass expectations and governing realities are rarely compatible, particularly when times are bad. Maintaining political support thus appears to be a difficult undertaking in any system when bad news outraces the good. Dennis Kavanagh, for example, reports that only two postwar British prime ministers maintained the support of more than half of the British public for two years or more.[16] Treating several European countries, Michael Lewis-Beck has shown that the fortunes of political leaders rest greatly on public perceptions of the state of the economy.[17]

To be certain, the styles, structures, and norms of politics are not the same everywhere. Shared norms tend to moderate expectations and provide avenues for molding agreements, as in Norway and Sweden. (In Japan, the meliorating effect of shared norms was reinforced by the dominance of the Liberal Democratic party.) But the flow of events still tends to dictate the margin of political safety for the incumbent leadership. Thus, in Sweden, for example, in spite of an ameliorist style of politics, the rise of social turmoil and inflation did affect the stability of political coalitions in the 1970s and 1980s.

The great problem of modern democratic accountability is that mass publics typically are results oriented and are unrealistic about what governments can achieve at what cost. Although political leaders normally seek to satisfy such high performance expectations at low cost, they are less likely to be held responsible (except by other elites) for those behaviors for which they can realistically be held to account. Regardless of what goes into the decision, it is the outcome that counts. But this is not a peculiarly American malady.

The great-power status of the United States, however, does generate some unique expectations. So does its relative physical isolation. Great-power status in an era of mass political consciousness leads to an episodic, albeit fleeting, jingoism. The combination makes for the worst of all possible worlds—paroxysms of fervor without commitment. The American mass public is not of a single mind by any means, but its dominant tendency appears to be isolationist when engagement is likely to entail serious costs. Like other modern mass publics, Americans seem reluctant to be disturbed. Nowhere, including the United States, has public opinion been deeply roused toward action to halt the slaughter in the Balkans. Yet, although interventionism is more typically an elite-induced phenomenon, mass opinion, when it perceives that America has been provoked, will often support strong words and decisive (and, above all, immediately successful) actions, such as the invasions of Grenada in 1983 and Panama in 1989. Keep the peace, talk tough when necessary, but get it over with fast. Notably, the brief and successful war against Iraq in 1991 was more popular once it was over than it was in the protracted period leading to it.

Beyond the unusual considerations attendant to great-power status, two additional and related aspects of the American system generally enhance unrealistic expectations about presidents. One is, as Hugh Heclo has suggested, the illusion of national unity that is created by presidential candidates who are trying to build electoral coalitions independent of their party base. The other is the false but widespread belief that the president is the whole of government.

In regard to the illusion of unity, Heclo's argument amounts to the following: presidential nominees are not apprenticed through their party organization. Although they must play to partisans to gain support in primary elections and state caucuses, in a system in which party has a lesser, and, indeed, lessening, hold on voters, the general election evokes a broad public to which a candidate is apt to make only faintly partisan appeals.[18] Thus, according to Heclo:

By fleetingly raising expectations concerning the leader's unifying and governing powers, the selection process in the United States may actually make credible government all the more difficult. In popular conception the president is selected to reign in supreme command; in reality he will often be pulling strings and hoping that something somewhere will jump.[19]

Heclo's discussion of the consequences of the American presidential selection process—its lack of political apprenticeship, and consequently its emphasis on individualistic political entrepreneurship—resonates with some critiques of the American presidency.[20] These critiques portray a presidential office not only divorced from collective responsibility but also bereft of the sustaining power of collective institutions. Thus, public aspirations, centered in a single individual, can only rarely be fulfilled. Because of the mismatch of aspirations and actual assets, presidents (or those who speak for them and act on their behalf) will seek to expand their resources and gain control over other institutions, notably the bureaucracy.[21] The costs of this inflation of the presidency are probably twofold: an erosion of presidential judgment and, hence, of authority in the presidency.

In sum, expectations about leadership are founded essentially in the modern democratic ethos. Whether or not Americans hold excessively high expectations about what leadership and government can accomplish, they do not hold their institutions in lesser esteem than other publics. In spite of this, a view has developed that the American presidency is beset by unusually high expectations. This is partly because of the American projection of power in the world and the accompanying expectation that the president will keep intact both peace and national pride. But much of the diagnosis is grounded in the institutional nature of the American political system in general and the presidency in particular. The presidency, so individualized and plebiscitary, is linked neither to party organizations in politics nor to senior civil servants in government. Attention is drawn more to the person occupying the presidency than to the institution's governing capacities, whereby governing is taken to mean something more than the mere exertion of presidential will.

The American system creates incentives for a raw form of bottom-line accountability. Such incentives also can readily stimulate irresponsible behavior. Reformers' concerns over the president's abilities to exercise power often have neglected the issue of how such power would and should be exercised. Cut off from the sources of counsel of which most prime ministers can avail themselves, presidents more likely would be granted power unrestrained by prudence. The direction of reform too often unbalances the equation: more powers for political mobilization and fewer incentives for prudent behavior.

Situations

The foregoing analysis of systemic variations helps to illuminate differences in the situations or contexts in which leaders find themselves. Our quick tour of some of these varying situations includes: (1) short-run political coalitions; (2) long-run political coalitions; and (3) the role of crisis and foreign policy initiation.

Short-run Coalitions

As noted earlier, the aficionados of party government in the United States typically have in mind the clear majority-rule situation—the Westminster model. But majority party government is relatively rare in parliamentary systems. At a minimum, it rests on a winner-take-all, single-seat-district system that gives a seat to the candidate with either a plurality or a majority. Most parliamentary systems, however, have some form of mixed proportional representation and district voting.

Thus, various kinds of coalition arrangements prevail in most countries with parliamentary systems. The tendency of such coalitions (since most coalition patterns are generally stable) is to provide a certain stability to government. The tiny liberal Free Democratic party in Germany, for instance, has largely controlled or otherwise deeply influenced economic and foreign policy under both Christian Democratic and Social Democratic governments. Similarly, the small bloc of religious parties in Israel has consistently controlled policy and ministerial posts that deal with religious affairs. Such stability, of course, can turn into deadlock when new forces outside the coalition arise to challenge the status quo. It also gives a small political minority unusually great power.

Under normal circumstances, American presidents are in a complex coalition arrangement in spite of their presumptive control of the executive and the existence of only two parties in Congress.[22] But a president's coalitions (unlike those of a prime minister) are fluid rather than wholly structured by party. What remains unclear is whether the president's position is any more disadvantageous than that of the head of a coalition government, who is certainly constrained by arrangements made by the parties forming a government. A president can ask for more, but with greater risk of failure. Continued failure, or, more importantly, the perception of failure, corrodes his political standing.

In any event, rarely in American politics do elections create even a moment of party government. But such moments can occur, and when they do there are usually momentous legislative and policy consequences. One of the most critical conditions for producing party government has to do with the generation, dissipation, and regeneration of long-run political coalitions.

Long-Run Coalitions

The United States has both the oldest and the most volatile competitive party system in the world. Democrats and Republicans and their party ancestors have held different positions and taken on different constituencies during different eras of American history.[23] The process by which the partisan plates beneath the political surface shift over a period of time is referred to in the vocabulary of American politics as the cycle of realignment. The traditional pattern of realignment requires the slow exhaustion of prior party alignments, the emergence of new political appeals and constituencies and, ultimately, new patterns of voting. Typically, realigning moments are associated with unusual clarity in mass political cleavages and in partisan divisions among elites.[24] Considerable policy innovation usually occurs because of the relative ease of mobilizing political support in contrast to more normal times. These rare moments of realignment, in classic form, produce a kind of party government for a time in which substantial majorities in both houses of Congress are assembled in support of a party program. In modern times, this has meant support of the president's program.

These classic symptoms of realignment are uniquely American, although the more general phenomenon of coalition shift is not. The symptoms are unique because of the independence of the governing branches in the United States and the absence of the party discipline that is found in parliamentary systems. Long-term and substantial coalition shifts do occur in other systems, however, and effectively alter the political equation. For instance, the erosion of the French Communist party (which lost more than half its electoral support in a thirty-year period) enhanced the long-term prospects of the democratic Left in French politics, despite its present political deflation. The rise of green political movements in Europe also places pressure on more traditional political parties, especially on the Left.

During briefer periods of time, too, there can be an exhaustion of political initiative that results from the decay of a prevailing coalition or party. The ability to cope with larger problems declines. Such symptoms arose in the final years of the various Conservative governments in Britain from 1951 to 1964 and, again, during the sunset of the tattered Labour government in the late 1970s— a government sustained only by the forbearance of smaller parties in not bringing the Callaghan government to an end. Similarly, the victory of the Likud coalition in Israel in 1977 reflected the development of new political forces at a time when the Israeli Labor coalition had also lost its energy and direction.

The life cycle of political coalitions cannot have exactly the same symptoms in parliamentary systems as it does in the United States because parliamentary party discipline is the accepted norm under all conditions. The processes of energizing, of enervating, and of revitalizing go on everywhere, however. As the political forces that generate a government wind down, initiative declines, caution replaces risk taking, survivability displaces direction. Intraparty and intragovernmental rifts become more noticeable. In short, the prospects for governing on behalf of clear goals diminish.

In an absolute pinch, of course, an exhausted government can usually be saved in parliament, if not with the electorate. That, of course, is an advantage that presidents rarely have. Regime exhaustion and political travail are more directly and overtly connected in the American system. But even though party discipline can buffet some of the most severe challenges to a government, its ultimate effects on political vitality are far more limited than a purely legislative comparison between systems would suggest. Harold MacMillan in 1957–1959 was not in the same situation as Alec Douglas-Home in 1964; nor was Helmut Schmidt in 1981–1982 able to embark on the initiatives that Willy Brandt had in 1969–1971, and George Bush in 1989–1993 was in no position to energize policy change as Ronald Reagan had in 1981. "Political time"—the life cycle of regime creation and dissolution—needs different indicators across political systems, but the basic concept has universal properties (see Stephen Skowronek's chapter in this volume).

Crisis

Can the American president act quickly and decisively in a crisis? Is there any inherent difference between the president's ability to do so and that of a cabinet-parliamentary government? The word *inherent* in this formulation is important; but first we need to determine what a crisis is. A crisis generally is what someone in a leadership position declares it to be, but only if widespread agreement follows.

Usually, crisis entails the existence of a new and unanticipated situation that carries with it strong decisional costs and risks. The Argentine invasion of the Falklands/Malvinas in 1982 produced a crisis in London because the costs of any reaction would be strong and risk bearing. Either the fleet would go to war and risk defeat thousands of miles away or it would stay home and the Thatcher government, along with the British nation, would risk political humiliation.

Foreign policy crises are apt to generate greater support for leadership responses because they engage the entire nation. The American reaction to the Soviet invasion of Afghanistan demonstrates, though, how closely foreign and domestic interests are linked. Recall the protests of grain farmers and their representatives in Washington when the embargo of American wheat to the Soviet Union was imposed by the Carter administration. Domestic crises are less likely to elicit agreement on leadership response because they engage the attention of diverse interests, which see their concerns linked positively or, more often, adversely to proposed solutions.

Two aspects of crisis management are especially illustrative of the differences between presidential and parliamentary systems. In the American system, the ability to initiate action decisively is a presidential advantage, and, if the crisis is exceptionally brief, decision and action can usually be implemented to some resolution. If, however, the president's action requires congressional approval or if there is litigation, the system of separation of powers can be limiting. On the one hand, we have the Supreme Court's rejection of Truman's seizure of the steel mills in the midst of a steelworkers' strike during the Korean War as an obvious case of the blunting of leadership initiative. Prime ministers, on the other hand, tend to feel the limits of response early because they have to carry their cabinets with them, especially if the government is a multiparty coalition. Granted, presidents have an advantage when decisive and brief action is possible before others have much of an opportunity to act. But the more protracted the action, the more the complexity of the American system tends to take effect and the greater the inclination of normal politics to prevail. In parliamentary systems, the advantages and disadvantages appear to be the mirror image of the presidential system: initial action involves a fair amount of consultation, but fewer impediments arise thereafter.

Although system does structure the management of crises, more is likely to depend both on the individual leader's definition of a crisis and on the leader's temperament when making decisions under stress. In this regard, because of the status of the president as decision maker in chief, presidents vary more than prime ministers. Some presidents, such as Nixon, will have an obsession with secrecy; others, like Eisenhower, will make greater use of consultative processes. The political system itself, however, is unlikely to influence the probabilities for successful outcomes. In Suez in 1956, Anthony Eden acted decisively and failed; in the Falklands/Malvinas crisis, Thatcher acted decisively and succeeded. In the *Mayaguez* incident of 1975, Gerald Ford acted decisively and, reputedly at least, won, even though more Americans were killed than were rescued from the revolutionary Cambodian forces. Five years later a similar, although much more complicated, rescue effort failed in Iran, probably sealing Carter's political fate.

In sum, the American president can act quickly and decisively in a crisis. That does not mean that he will. Kennedy took his time during the Cuban missile crisis, both to size up alternatives and to reach a consensus among his advisors. Nor does it mean that, after he acts, the president's initiatives will be accepted by the other branches of government. Above all, decisiveness does not necessarily mean success. Luck may be at least as good a guide here as design. That consideration leads us naturally enough to leaders and to leadership roles.

Leaders

Leadership Roles

The American president, Clinton Rossiter points out in his classic book on the presidency, wears many hats.[25] He plays more roles than top leaders in other systems. Despite the familiar separation-of-powers system, American institutions do not have sharply differentiated functions. Rather, they share power. Modern European political institutions, to the contrary and to differing degrees, tend to differentiate functions while concentrating power.[26]

Among the many hats worn by the American president, according to Rossiter, are those of chief of state, chief executive, chief diplomat, commander in chief, and chief legislator. Yet these are only the constitutional roles. Rossiter adds several others that have been grafted onto the modern presidency through practice: party chief, opinion leader and representative, manager of prosperity, leader of the Western alliance (a now diminished role), and chief administrator. Of the five formal roles, the one that is most emphasized in contrasting the American system with others (usually, as rendered, to the detriment of the American system) is that of chief legislator.

We have noted that presidents as party leaders normally embody their party and penetrate the apparatus of its national organization. Even the exceptions to this rule—Truman and Ford, who as vice-presidential successors had difficulties controlling their parties, and Carter—ultimately were able to secure the apparatus and to win over the minds if not the hearts of their party elites. In general, the personalized control of a party is more difficult to attain for parliamentary political leaders, whose parties are far better organized and institutionalized than their American equivalents. On the whole, within their parties European prime ministers are at least as much a representative or internal mediator as the dominant leader. In countries as different as Italy and Japan, for example, the larger parties have distinctive factions. In Japan, these are formalized. The factions encourage deal cutting, logrolling, and rotation.

Some of the American president's many roles—notably, commander in chief, chief diplomat, alliance leader, and prosperity manager (in an increasingly internationalized economy)—result from, or have become more important because of, the United States' central role in world affairs. The president's functions as chief executive and administrator have also been altered. Since 1956, when Rossiter published *The American Presidency*, the role of the White House staff and the EOP have grown markedly in importance. The growth of the White House and the EOP gives the president a corporate presence. The frequent invocation of a president's reported preferences by those who are at a distance from his physical presence creates new problems of presidential management. The Reagan presidency in the halcyon days before the Iran-contra scandal seemed to suggest that it was far more important that a president be a chief than a chief executive.[27] In the aftermath of that scandal, however, we are reminded that a president also cannot avoid being a chief executive. The management difficulties that have so beset the first half of the Clinton presidency, in fact, suggest the importance of both functions. If the role of chief is ineffectively performed, no president can expect to be an effective chief executive. But without a head for the details and the seemingly small matters, a president's hopes for effective leadership may be derailed.

Presidents come wrapped in the cloak of the state and are not, as are prime ministers, merely the heads of governments. That could be one reason why presidents' elections are so often greeted as a process of national legitimation and unity instead of just the outcome of a partisan struggle. Efforts to diminish the pomp of the chief-of-state role also strip away the notion that the occupant of the office is someone special. Playing on populist sentiments and, perhaps, his own instincts, Carter managed, to his detriment, to strip away all illusions of state majesty from the presidency. Ford and Truman also thought better of humility than majesty (having followed particularly "royal" presidencies). But as Rossiter put it, the American presidency is both the most and the least political of offices.[28] In its guise as chief of state, it is the least directly political— although, of course, astute presidents know how to extract maximum political mileage from this aspect of the presidential role.

All political leaders have been placed in the position of "managing prosperity." Their fortunes are tied to their success or sheer luck with the economy. Yet economic interdependence and the emergence of a global economy have made the economic forces to be managed less obviously manipulable.

It is in the roles of chief legislator and opinion leader and representative that—aside from the party leadership role—institutional differences between prime minister and president are at their purest. As we have seen, one of the main differences between a president and a prime minister is that the former builds political coalitions after legislation is introduced and the latter, who serves in a parliamentary-cabinet government where political party discipline is paramount and assumed, is involved in building coalitions beforehand. A president is constantly engaged in calculating and recalculating legislative prospects and strategies. This requires a form of continuous political mobilization in a highly unpredictable environment.

Blending the roles of opinion leader (spokesman for the people), chief of state, and keeper of the peace and the economy with more overt political roles such as chief legislator and party leader means that the president must bring highly diverse skills to the office. A good compass and the ability to articulate direction clearly are crucial requirements of the job; the test, however, as Rossiter himself observed, is how well all of these diverse elements are integrated—if indeed they are. Surely, in this regard, the president's job is the most complex of all leadership positions. It contains elements that provide it with both unusual power and unusual vulnerability.

Leadership Definitions

In view of the complexity of any leadership position, especially the American presidency, how can one define the job, and to what extent can definitions make a difference?

Any leader in any organization of both reasonable complexity and competing goals and strategies is hostage to the priorities of others. However self-starting a leader may be, a president or prime minister is running a kind of variety show with different acts commanding attention. Some acts are staples; others vary according to the momentary rise of certain issues or perceived needs. As every variety show host needs a stand-up comedian and a singer, so every governmental leader needs a finance or budget minister and a foreign minister. But a health or education minister, like a juggler or dancing bear, does not have to be a constant booking for the leader.[29] A top leader must have the former and may desire to have the latter.

There are, of course, differences between variety show hosts and, thus, between shows. During television's first two decades in the United States, there were two enormously successful variety shows, one hosted by Ed Sullivan, a show business columnist for one of the New York tabloids, the other by Bob Hope, one of the most popular comedians of the era. Ed Sullivan had no discernible skills as an entertainer. His acts dominated the show; he merely introduced them. Bob Hope, in contrast, was a big part of his show. People tuned in to watch him. The acts kept him from being exhausted by filling up an hour's space.

Consider the analogy to leadership styles: Harold Wilson, Jimmy Carter, George Bush, or Helmut Kohl as Ed Sullivan, mostly serving as host to the agendas of others. Margaret Thatcher, Ronald Reagan, or Willy Brandt, fulfilling the Bob Hope role, provided unmistakable direction and flavor to the operation of government. Thatcher and Reagan were both endowed with a strong sense of what they wanted done and the ability to articulate their purposes with stunning clarity. It was difficult to misperceive their signals. For various reasons, neither Wilson nor Carter was clearly directive. Nor was George Bush or, arguably so far, Clinton. In the cases of Wilson and Carter, their parties were, of course, divided. Wilson sought to smooth over deep intraparty differences whereas Thatcher dumped dissidents overboard. Unlike Reagan, who made decisions out of deep inner conviction, Carter was open to facts or arguments that could move a decision this way or that, thus creating uncertainty as well as providing an invitation for more acts to gain a spot on his "show." Much like Carter, Clinton is affected by an attraction to facts and details but suffers also, as did Carter, from putting forth an agenda more extensive than his level of political support allows. In Clinton's case, the combination of policy ambition and the weakness of his political resources leads him toward compromise and, thus, the charge of inconstancy. Bush, too, suffered from a weak political hand but had few policy ambitions. At least in the first half of his term, Bush's desire for accommodation rather than confrontation (a desire that diminished after Bush's fellow Republicans virtually impaled him for violating his "no new taxes" pledge in late 1990) reflected both the limits of his political circumstances—a Democratic Congress and no mandate—and a political personality that had a large "comfort zone" for accommodating seemingly dissonant policy choices.

Holding individual differences constant, however, there is also something different about the presidential and prime ministerial roles that makes the president more of an emcee for others' agendas (an Ed Sullivan) than the prime minister is. This is partly because the prime minister is a party leader first and government leader second; for the president it is the reverse. Much of the agenda pressing for the prime minister is done inside the party; a great deal is also done inside the cabinet or in forming it. Presidents may encounter some pressures at their party conventions, but only in rare instances (Ford in 1976, Carter to a much lesser degree in 1980, and, if indifference counts, Bush in 1992) do nominees fail to control the party platform. But a president, once installed, is theoretically at the head of an executive hierarchy. Whatever the reality, the expectation is that the buck will stop with the president, not with the secretary of some department. For administrations, such as those of Carter or Bush, that are bent on booking many acts and pleasing a wide array of their party's varying constituencies, the Ed Sullivan model becomes evident.[30] Little direction is seen to be forthcoming, whether or not the president is really possessed of any. Unlike Ed Sullivan, such presidents receive few plaudits.

What difference, finally, does leadership make? The question tantalizes because we have no clear way of connecting leadership behavior to outcomes. We can begin at either end of this problem—the behavioral side or the results side. The behavioral side, we quickly see, depends greatly on which aspects of leadership we deem situationally appropriate. In energizing government, simplicity is of the essence. One need not be a philosopher-king, but one needs to be a king (or queen). That, at least, appears to be the lesson we derive from those who have succeeded at giving direction to government, regardless of its ultimate wisdom. In this context, the extent to which constraints fail to paralyze choice is partly a consequence of the willingness to take risks. The more risk-averse leaders are, the greater the constraints will seem to be.

On the results side, we can infer the effects of leadership if we look carefully. Robert Putnam and his colleagues, for instance, illustrate both the limitations and the possibilities of leadership.[31] By studying various Italian regional governments, they conclude that performance is predicted almost perfectly by broad indicators of regional, social, economic, and historical characteristics. When they look at regions with similar characteristics, however, they note departures from the expected outcome. The greater the difference, the more it appears that entrepreneurial leadership (or, alternatively, its absence) has made a difference in the region's performance.

Clearly, citizens of modern democracies tend to expect too much from leaders. The study of Putnam and his colleagues is sobering in that regard. Yet, we can err excessively in the opposite direction too. And the Putnam saga equally well suggests that possibility. What remains clouded, unfortunately, is the connection between outcomes and institutional factors, situations, and leadership styles.

A Final Word

Comparison is the basis of judgment. False comparisons idealize at least one of the alternatives or generalize from momentary discomforts. The perspective provided by sound comparative analysis makes complex what seemed so simple. Stark contrasts recede on closer inspection. Sometimes, institutions give us differences in form rather than in result.

The American political system generates a good deal of overt but often un-crystallized conflict. Because so much agenda generating and coalition building is done openly in the United States, conflict is more visible and presidents often appear to be stymied. But governing is nowhere an easy matter. Political leaders in all democracies are subject to public disapproval and diminished political resources. Among the G-7 leaders at the Tokyo economic summit in July of 1993, President Clinton, whose level of popular approval at home reached record-breaking lows for this point in his term, nevertheless had, except for Kim Campbell, the then newly installed but now notably ex–Canadian prime minister, the highest approval rating among the leaders there. In the absence of a Stalinist-like concentration of power, politics makes governing hard. Democratic politics makes it harder still. That understanding is necessary if we are to refine our questions about the capacity for political leadership in the United States and avoid drifting off into idealized alternatives.

Notes

1. Anthony King, "Foundations of Power," in *Researching the Presidency*, ed. George C. Edwards III, John H. Kessel, and Bert A. Rockman (Pittsburgh: University of Pittsburgh Press, 1993), 415–451.

2. *Revenue Statistics of OECD Member Countries, 1965–1991* (Paris: OECD Publications, 1992), 14.

3. Ibid., 198–199. The cited figures include social security taxes.

4. Richard P. Nathan and Fred C. Doolittle, "The Untold Story of Reagan's 'New Federalism,'" *Public Interest* 77 (Fall 1984): 96–105.

5. Richard Rose, "The Variability of Party Government: A Theoretical and Empirical Critique," *Political Studies* 17 (December 1969): 414.

6. James W. Ceaser, "Political Parties and Presidential Ambition," *Journal of Politics* 40 (August 1978): 708–741.

7. George W. Breslauer, *Khrushchev and Brezhnev as Leaders: Building Authority in Soviet Politics* (London: George Allen and Unwin, 1982).

8. See King, "Foundations of Power."

9. See, for example, Colin Campbell, *Governments under Stress: Political Executives and Key Bureaucrats in Washington, London, and Ottawa* (Toronto: University of Toronto Press, 1983); and Margaret J. Wyszomirski, "The De-Institutionalization of Presidential Staff Agencies," *Public Administration Review* 42 (1982): 448–457.

10. Lloyd N. Cutler, "To Form a Government," *Foreign Affairs* 59 (Fall 1980): 126–143.

11. Rose, "Variability of Party Government"; see also Anthony King, "Political Parties in Western Democracies: Some Skeptical Reflections," *Polity* 2 (Fall 1969): 111–141.

12. Alexander Hamilton, in *The Federalist Papers*, ed. Clinton Rossiter (New York: New American Library, 1961), no. 70, 424.

13. Anthony King, "Margaret Thatcher: The Style of a Prime Minister," in *The British Prime Minister*, 2d ed., ed. Anthony King (Durham, N.C.: Duke University Press, 1985), 96–140.

14. See, for example, Theodore J. Lowi, *The Personal President: Power Invested, Promise Unfulfilled* (Ithaca, N.Y.: Cornell University Press, 1985); and Bert A. Rockman, *The Leadership Question: The Presidency and the American System* (New York: Praeger, 1984).

15. See, for instance, Rose, *The Capacity of the President: A Comparative Analysis* (Strathclyde, Scotland: Centre for the Study of Public Policy, 1984), 62–78.

16. Dennis Kavanagh, "From Gentlemen to Players: Changes in Political Leadership," in *Britain: Progress and Decline*, ed. William L. Gwyn and Richard Rose, Tulane Studies in Political Science, vol. 17 (New Orleans: Tulane University Press, 1980), 90–91; see also Rose, *Capacity of the President*, 72–73.

17. Michael Lewis-Beck, "Comparative Economic Voting: Britain, France, Germany, Italy," *American Journal of Political Science* 30 (May 1986): 315–346.

18. On the declining grip of parties, see, for instance, Martin P. Wattenberg, *The Decline of American Political Parties, 1952-1980* (Cambridge: Harvard University Press, 1984). On the "unifying" aspects of American presidential elections, see John H. Kessel, "The Seasons of Presidential Politics," *Social Science Quarterly* 58 (December 1977): 419–435; and Hugh Heclo, "Presidential and Prime Ministerial Selection," in *Perspectives on Presidential Selection*, ed. Donald R. Matthews (Washington, D.C.: Brookings Institution, 1973): 19–48.

19. Heclo, "Presidential and Prime Ministerial Selection," 48.

20. Rose, *Capacity of the President*; Lowi, *Personal President*; and Rockman, *Leadership Question*.

21. See, for example, Joel D. Aberbach and Bert A. Rockman, "Clashing Beliefs within the Executive Branch: The Nixon Administration Bureaucracy," *American Political Science Review* 70 (June 1976): 456–468. A lengthy discussion of Reagan administration efforts to gain control of the bureaucracy is in Bert A. Rockman, "USA: Government under President Reagan," in *Jahrbuch zur Staats- und Verwaltungswissenschaft*, ed. Thomas Ellwein et al. (Baden-Baden: Nomos Verlag, 1987): 286–308. For a straightforward articulation of the president's need to gain control over the bureaucracy, see Terry M. Moe, "The Politicized Presidency," in *The New Direction in American Politics*, ed. John E. Chubb and Paul E. Peterson (Washington, D.C.: Brookings Institution, 1985), 235–272.

22. In assessing a number of studies that compare governmental policy-making capabilities across a variety of advanced democracies, Weaver and Rockman conclude, "The U.S. separation of powers system tends to cluster closely with the coalitional parliamentary regime types in terms of its associated risks and opportunities." R. Kent Weaver and Bert A. Rockman, eds., *Do Institutions Matter? Government Capabilities in the United States and Abroad* (Washington, D.C.: Brookings Institution, 1993), 450.

23. See, for instance, Benjamin Ginsberg, *The Consequences of Consent: Elections, Citizen Control and Popular Acquiescence* (Reading, Mass.: Addison-Wesley, 1982).

24. For example, see Paul Allen Beck, "The Electoral Cycle and Patterns of American Politics," *British Journal of Political Science* 9 (April 1979): 129–156; and David W. Brady, "Critical Elections, Congressional Parties and Clusters of Policy Changes," *British Journal of Political Science* 8 (January 1978): 79–99.

25. Clinton Rossiter, *The American Presidency* (New York: Mentor Books, 1956).

26. Samuel P. Huntington, "Political Modernization: America vs. Europe," in *Political Order in Changing Societies*, ed. Samuel P. Huntington (New Haven: Yale University Press, 1968), 93–139.

27. Richard Rose, "The President: A Chief but Not an Executive," *Presidential Studies Quarterly* 7 (Winter 1977): 5–20.

28. Rossiter, *American Presidency.*

29. See, in this regard, Richard Rose, "British Government: The Job at the Top," in *Presidents and Prime Ministers*, ed. Richard Rose and Ezra N. Suleiman (Washington, D.C.: American Enterprise Institute, 1980), 1–49.

30. According to Heclo, the White House Office of Public Liaison virtually became another interest group making claims on the presidential agenda. See Hugh Heclo, "The Changing Presidential Office," in *Politics and the Oval Office: Towards Presidential Governance*, ed. Arnold J. Meltsner (San Francisco: Institute for Contemporary Studies, 1981), 161–184.

31. Robert D. Putnam et al., "Explaining Institutional Success: The Case of Italian Regional Government," *American Political Science Review* 77 (March 1983): 55–74.

Part II   Elements of Presidential Power

4 The Two Constitutional Presidencies

Jeffrey K. Tulis

The design of the presidency may be found in Article II of the Constitution. Yet, according to Jeffrey K. Tulis, two constitutional presidencies exist—not just the enduring, large-C version that the framers invented at the Constitutional Convention of 1787, whose formal provisions remain substantially unaltered, but also the adapted, small-c constitution that Woodrow Wilson devised and that most twentieth-century presidents, including Bill Clinton, have practiced. Regrettably, Tulis argues, the fit between the formal and the informal constitutional presidencies is not always close. Both constitutions value "energy" in the presidency, but the exercise of popular rhetorical leadership that is proscribed by the framers' Constitution is prescribed by Wilson's constitution. As a result, Tulis concludes, "Many of the dilemmas and frustrations of the modern presidency may be traced to the president's ambiguous constitutional station, a vantage place composed of conflicting elements."

The modern presidency is buffeted by two "constitutions." Presidential action continues to be constrained, and presidential behavior shaped, by the institutions created by the original Constitution. The core structures established in 1789 and debated during the founding era remain essentially unchanged. For the most part, later amendments to the Constitution have left intact the basic features of the executive, legislative, and judicial branches of government. Great questions, such as the merits of unity or plurality in the executive, have not been seriously reopened. Because most of the structure persists, it seems plausible that the theory upon which the presidency was constructed remains relevant to its current functioning.[1]

Presidential and public understanding of the constitutional system and of the president's place in it have changed, however. This new understanding is the "second constitution" under whose auspices presidents attempt to govern. Central to this second constitution is a view of statecraft that is in tension with the original Constitution—indeed it is opposed to the founders' understanding of the presidency's place in the political system. The second constitution, which puts a premium on active and continuous presidential leadership of popular opinion, is buttressed by several institutional, albeit extraconstitutional, developments. These include the proliferation of presidential primaries as a mode of selection and the emergence of the mass media as a pervasive force.[2]

Many of the dilemmas and frustrations of the modern presidency may be traced to the president's ambiguous constitutional station, a vantage place composed of conflicting elements. The purpose of this chapter is to lay bare the theoretical core of each of the two constitutions in order to highlight those elements that are in tension between them.

To uncover the principles that underlie the original Constitution, this chapter relies heavily on *The Federalist*. A set of papers justifying the Constitution, the text was written by three of the Constitution's most articulate proponents, Alexander Hamilton, James Madison, and John Jay. The purpose of this journey back to the founders is not to point to their authority or to lament change. Neither is it meant to imply that all the supporters of the Constitution agreed with each of their arguments. *The Federalist* does represent, however, the most coherent articulation of the implications of, and interconnections among, the principles and practices that were generally agreed upon when the Constitution was ratified.[3]

The political thought of Woodrow Wilson is explored to outline the principles of the second constitution. Wilson self-consciously attacked *The Federalist* in his writings; as president he tried to act according to the dictates of his reinterpretation of the American political system. Presidents have continued to follow his example, and presidential scholars tend to repeat his arguments. Of course, most presidents have not thought through the issues Wilson discussed—they are too busy for that. But if pushed and questioned, modern presidents would probably (and occasionally do) justify their behavior with arguments that echo Wilson's. Just as *The Federalist* represents the deepest and most coherent articulation of generally held nineteenth-century understandings of the presidency, Wilson offers the most comprehensive theory in support of contemporary impulses and practices.

The Founding Perspective

Perhaps the most striking feature of the founding perspective, particularly in comparison with contemporary political analyses, is its synoptic character. The founders' task was to create a whole government, one in which the executive would play an important part, but only a part. By contrast, contemporary scholars of American politics often study institutions individually and thus tend to be partisans of "their institution" in its contests with other actors in American politics.[4] Presidency scholars often restrict their inquiries to the strategic concerns of presidents as they quest for power. Recovering the founding perspective gives one a way to think about the systemic legitimacy and utility of presidential power as well. To uncover such a synoptic vision, one must range widely in search of the principles that guided or justified the founders' view of the executive. Some of these principles are discussed most thoroughly in *The Federalist* in the context of other institutions, such as Congress or the judiciary.

The founders' general and far-reaching institutional analysis was preceded by a more fundamental decision of enormous import. Federalists and anti-Federalists alike sought a government devoted to limited ends. In contrast to polities that attempt to shape the souls of their citizenry and foster certain excellences or moral qualities by penetrating deeply into the "private" sphere, the founders wanted their government to be limited to establishing and securing such a sphere. Politics would extend only to the tasks of protecting individual rights and fostering liberty for the exercise of those rights. Civic virtue would still be necessary, but it would be elicited from the people rather than imposed on them.

Proponents and critics of the Constitution agreed about the proper ends of government, but they disagreed over the best institutional means to secure them.[5] Some critics of the Constitution worried that its institutions would actually undermine its limited liberal ends. Although these kinds of arguments were settled politically by the federalist victory, *The Federalist* concedes that they were not resolved fundamentally because they continued as problems built into the structure of American politics.

Is a vigorous executive consistent with the genius of republican government? Hasty readers of *The Federalist* think yes, unequivocally. Closer reading of *The Federalist* reveals a deeper ambivalence regarding the compatibility of executive power and republican freedom.[6]

Demagoguery

The founders worried especially about the danger that a powerful executive might pose to the system if his power were derived from the role of popular leader.[7] For most Federalists, *demagogue* and *popular leader* were synonyms, and nearly all references to popular leaders in their writings are pejorative.

Demagoguery, combined with majority tyranny, was regarded as the peculiar vice to which democracies were susceptible. Although much historical evidence supported this insight, the founders were made more acutely aware of the problem by the presence in their own midst of popular leaders such as Daniel Shays, who led an insurrection in Massachusetts. The founders' preoccupation with demagoguery may appear today as quaint, yet it may be that we do not fear it today because the founders were so successful in institutionally proscribing some forms of it.

The original Greek meaning of *demagogue* was simply "leader of the people," and the term was applied in premodern times to champions of the people's claim to rule as against that of aristocrats and monarchs. As James Ceaser points out, the term has been more characteristically applied to a certain *quality* of leadership—that which attempts to sway popular passions. Because most speech contains a mix of rational and passionate appeals, it is difficult to specify demagoguery with precision. But as Ceaser argues, one cannot ignore the phenomenon because it is difficult to define, suggesting that it possesses at least enough intuitive clarity that few would label Dwight Eisenhower, for example, a demagogue, while most would not hesitate to so label Joseph McCarthy. The key characteristic of demagoguery seems to be an *excess* of passionate appeals. Ceaser categorizes demagogues according to the kinds of passions that are summoned, dividing these into "soft" and "hard" types.

The soft demagogue tends to flatter his constituents, "by claiming that they know what is best, and makes a point of claiming his closeness (to them) by manner or gesture."[8] The hard demagogue attempts to create or encourage divisions among the people in order to build and maintain his constituency. Typically, this sort of appeal employs extremist rhetoric that panders to fear. James Madison worried about the possibility of class appeals that would pit the poor against the wealthy. But the hard demagogue might appeal to a very different passion. "Excessive encouragement of morality and hope" might be employed to create a division between those alleged to be compassionate, moral, or progressive, and those thought insensitive, selfish, or backward. Hard demagogues are not restricted to the right or to the left.[9]

Demagogues can also be classified by their object. Here the issue becomes more complicated. Demagoguery might be good if it were a means to a good end, such as preservation of a decent nation or successful prosecution of a just war. The difficulty is to ensure by institutional means that demagoguery would be employed only for good ends and not simply to satisfy the overweening ambition of an immoral leader or potential tyrant. How are political structures created that permit demagoguery when appeals to passion are needed but proscribe it for normal politics?

The founders did not have a straightforward answer to this problem, perhaps because there is no unproblematic institutional solution. Yet they did address it indirectly in two ways: they attempted both to narrow the range of acceptable demagogic appeals through the architectonic act of founding itself and to mitigate the effects of such appeals in the day-to-day conduct of governance through the particular institutions they created. Certainly they did not choose to make provision for the institutional encouragement of demagoguery in time of crisis, refusing to adopt, for example, the Roman model of constitutional dictatorship for emergencies.[10] Behind their indirect approach may have been the thought that excessive ambition needs no institutional support and the faith that in extraordinary circumstances popular rhetoric, even forceful demagoguery, would gain legitimacy through the pressure of necessity.

Many references in *The Federalist* and in the ratification debates over the Constitution warn of demagogues of the hard variety who through divisive appeals would aim at tyranny. *The Federalist* literally begins and ends with this issue. In the final paper Hamilton offers "a lesson of moderation to all sincere lovers of the Union [that] ought to put them on their guard against hazarding anarchy, civil war, a perpetual alienation of the states from each other, and perhaps the military despotism of a victorious demagogue."[11] The founders' concern with hard demagoguery was not merely a rhetorical device designed to facilitate passage of the Constitution. It also reveals a concern to address the kinds of divisions and issues exploited by hard demagoguery. From this perspective, the founding can be understood as an attempt to settle the large issue of whether the one, few, or many ruled (in favor of the many "through" a constitution), to reconfirm the limited purposes of government (security, prosperity, and the protection of rights), and thereby to give effect to the distinction between public and private life. At the founding, these large questions were still matters of political dispute. Hamilton argued that adoption of the Constitution would settle these perennially divisive questions for Americans, replacing those questions with smaller, less contentious issues. Hamilton called this new American politics a politics of "administration," distinguishing it from the traditional politics of disputed ends. If politics were transformed and narrowed in this way, thought Hamilton, demagogues would be deprived of part of their once powerful arsenal of rhetorical weapons because certain topics would be rendered illegitimate for public discussion. By constituting an American understanding of politics, the founding would also reconstitute the problem of demagoguery.[12]

If the overriding concern about demagoguery in the extraordinary period before the ratification of the Constitution was to prevent social disruption, division, and possibly tyranny, the concerns expressed through the Constitution for normal times were broader: to create institutions that would be most likely to generate and execute good policy or to resist bad policy. Underlying the institutional structures and powers created by the Constitution are three principles designed to address this broad concern: representation, independence of the executive, and separation of powers.

Representation

As the founders realized, the problem with any simple distinction between good and bad law is that it is difficult to provide clear criteria to distinguish the two in any particular instance. It will not do to suggest that in a democracy good legislation reflects the majority will. A majority may tyrannize a minority, violating its rights; even a nontyrannical majority may be a foolish one, preferring policies that do not further its interests. These considerations lay behind the founders' distrust of "direct" or "pure" democracy.[13]

Yet an alternative understanding—that legislation is good if it objectively furthers the limited ends of the polity—is also problematic. It is perhaps impossible to assess the "interests" of a nation without giving considerable attention to what the citizenry considers its interests to be. This consideration lies behind the founders' animus toward monarchy and aristocracy.[14] Identifying and embodying the proper weight to be given popular opinion and its appropriate institutional reflections is one of the characteristic problems of democratic constitutionalism. The founders' understanding of republicanism as representative government reveals this problem and the Constitution's attempted solution.

Practically, the founders attempted to accommodate these two requisites of good government by four devices. First, they established popular election as the fundamental basis of the Constitution and of the government's legitimacy. They modified that requirement by allowing "indirect" selection for some institutions (for example, the Senate, Court, and presidency), that is, selection by others who were themselves chosen by the people. With respect to the president, the founders wanted to elicit the "sense of the people," but they feared an inability to do so if the people acted in a "collective capacity." They worried that the dynamics of mass politics would at best produce poorly qualified presidents and at worst open the door to demagoguery and regime instability. At the same time, the founders wanted to give popular opinion a greater role in presidential selection than it would have if Congress chose the executive. The institutional solution to these concerns was the electoral college, originally designed as a semiautonomous locus of decision for presidential selection and chosen by state legislatures at each election.[15]

Second, the founders established differing lengths of tenure for officeholders in the major national institutions, which corresponded to the institutions' varying "proximity" to the people. House members were to face reelection every two years, thus making them more responsive to constituent pressure than members of the other national institutions. The president was given a four-year term, sufficient time, it was thought, to "contribute to the firmness of the executive" without justifying "any alarm for the public liberty."[16]

Third, the founders derived the authority and formal power of the institutions and their officers ultimately from the people but immediately from the Constitution, thus insulating officials from day-to-day currents of public opinion, while allowing assertion of deeply felt and widely shared public opinion through constitutional amendment.

Finally, the founders envisioned that the extent of the nation itself would insulate governing officials from sudden shifts of public opinion. In his well-known arguments for an extended republic, Madison reasoned that large size would improve democracy by making the formation of majority factions difficult. But again, argued Madison, extent of the territory and diversity of factions would not prevent the formation of a majority if the issue were an important one.[17]

The brakes on public opinion, not the provision for its influence, are what cause skepticism today.[18] Because popular leadership is so central to modern theories of the presidency, the rationale behind the founders' distrust of "direct democracy" should be noted specifically. This issue is raised dramatically in *The Federalist* no. 49, in which Madison addresses Jefferson's suggestion that "whenever two of the three branches of government shall concur in [the] opinion . . . that a convention is necessary for altering the Constitution, *or correcting breaches of it*, a convention shall be called for the purpose." Madison recounts Jefferson's reasoning: because the Constitution was formed by the people, it rightfully ought to be modified by them. Madison admits "that a constitutional road to the decision of the people ought to be marked out and kept open for great and extraordinary occasions." But he objects to bringing directly to the people disputes among the branches about the extent of their authority. In the normal course of governance, such disputes could be expected to arise fairly often. In our day they would include, for example, the war powers controversy, the impoundment controversy, and the issue of executive privilege.

Madison objects to recourse to "the people" on three basic grounds. First, popular appeals would imply "some defect" in the government: "Frequent appeals would, in great measure, deprive the government of that veneration which time bestows on everything, and without which perhaps the wisest and freest governments would not possess the requisite stability." *The Federalist* points to the institutional benefits of popular veneration—stability of government and the enhanced authority of its constitutional officers. Second, the tranquility of the society as a whole might be disturbed. Madison expresses the fear that an enterprising demagogue might reopen disputes over "great national questions" in a political context less favorable to their resolution than the Constitutional Convention.

Finally, Madison voices "the greatest objection of all" to frequent appeals to the people: "The decisions which would probably result from such appeals would not answer the purpose of maintaining the constitutional equilibrium of government." The executive might face political difficulties if frequent appeals to the people were permitted because other features of his office (his singularity, independence, and executive powers) would leave him at a rhetorical disadvantage in contests with the legislature. Presidents will be "generally the objects of jealousy and their administrations . . . liable to be discolored and rendered unpopular," Madison argued. "The Members of the legislatures on the other hand are numerous. . . . Their connections of blood, of friendship, and of acquaintance embrace a great proportion of the most influential part of society. The nature of their public trust implies a personal influence among the people."[19]

Madison realizes that there may be circumstances "less adverse to the executive and judiciary departments." If the executive power were "in the hands of a peculiar favorite of the people . . . the public decision might be less swayed in favor of the [legislature]. But still it could never be expected to turn on the true merits of the question." The ultimate reason for the rejection of "frequent popular appeals" is that they would undermine *deliberation,* and result in bad public policy:

The *passions,* not the *reason,* of the public would sit in judgment. But it is the reason alone, of the public, that ought to control and regulate the government. The passions ought to be controlled and regulated by the government.[20]

There are two frequent misunderstandings of the founders' opinion on the deliberative function of representation. The first is that they naively believed that deliberation constituted the whole of legislative politics—that there would be no bargaining, logrolling, or nondeliberative rhetorical appeals. The discussion of Congress in *The Federalist* nos. 52 to 68 and in the Constitutional Convention debates reveals quite clearly that the founders understood that the legislative process would involve a mixture of these elements. The founding task was to create an institutional context that made deliberation most likely, not to assume that it would occur "naturally" or, even in the best of legislatures, predominantly.[21]

The second common error, prevalent in leading historical accounts of the period, is to interpret the deliberative elements of the founders' design as an attempt to rid the legislative councils of "common men" and replace them with "better sorts"—more educated and, above all, more propertied individuals.[22] Deliberation, in this view, is the byproduct of the kind of person elected to office. The public's opinions are "refined and enlarged" because refined individuals do the governing. Although this view finds some support in *The Federalist* and was a worry of several anti-Federalists, the founders' Constitution places much greater emphasis on the formal structures of the national institutions than on the background of officeholders.[23] Indeed, good character and high intelligence, they reasoned, would be of little help to the government if it resembled a direct democracy: "In all very numerous assemblies, of whatever characters composed, passion never fails to wrest the sceptre from reason. Had every Athenian citizen been a Socrates, every Athenian assembly would still have been a mob."[24]

The presidency was thus intended to be representative of the people, but not merely responsive to popular will. Drawn from the people through an election (albeit an indirect one), the president was to be free enough from the daily shifts in public opinion so that he could refine it and, paradoxically, better serve popular interests. Hamilton expresses well this element of the theory in a passage in which he links the problem of representation to that of demagoguery:

There are those who would be inclined to regard the servile pliancy of the executive to a prevailing current in the community of the legislature as its best recommendation. But such men entertain very crude notions, as well of the purposes for which government was instituted, as of the true means by which public happiness may be promoted. The republican principle demands that the deliberative sense of the community should govern the conduct of those to whom they intrust the management of the affairs; but it does not require an unqualified complaisance to every transient impulse which the people may receive from the arts of men, who flatter their prejudices to betray their interests. . . . When occasions present themselves in which the interests of the people are at variance with their inclinations, it is the duty of the persons whom they have appointed to be the guardians of those interests to withstand the temporary delusion in order to give them time and opportunity for more cool and sedate reflection.[25]

Independence of the Executive

To "withstand the temporary delusion" of popular opinion, the executive was made independent. The office would draw its authority from the Constitution rather than from another governmental branch. The framers were led to this decision from their knowledge of the states, where, according to John Marshall, the governments (with the exception of New York) lacked any structure "which could resist the wild projects of the moment, give the people an opportunity to reflect and allow the good sense of the nation time for exertion." As Madison stated at the convention, "Experience had proved a tendency in our governments to throw all power into the legislative vortex. The executives of the states are in general little more than Cyphers; the legislatures omnipotent."[26]

Independence from Congress was the immediate practical need, yet the need was based on the close connection between legislatures and popular opinion. Because independence from public opinion was the source of the concern about the legislatures, the founders rejected James Wilson's arguments on behalf of popular election as a means of making the president independent of Congress.

Independence of the executive created the conditions under which presidents would be most likely to adopt a different perspective from Congress on matters of public policy. Congress would be dominated by local factions that, according to plan, would give great weight to constituent opinion. The president, as Thomas Jefferson was to argue, was the only national officer "who commanded a view of the whole ground." Metaphorically, independence gave the president his own space within, and his own angle of vision on, the polity. According to the founding theory, these constituent features of discretion are entailed by the twin activities of executing the will of the legislature *and* leading a legislature to construct good laws to be executed, laws that would be responsive to long-term needs of the nation.[27]

Separation of Powers

The constitutional role of the president in lawmaking raises the question of the meaning and purpose of separation of powers. What is the sense of separation of power if power is shared among the branches of government? Clearly, legalists are wrong who have assumed that the founders wished to distinguish so carefully among executive, legislative, and judicial power as to make each the exclusive preserve of a particular branch. However, their error has given rise to another.

Political scientists, following Richard Neustadt, have assumed that because powers were not divided according to the principle of "one branch, one function," the founders made no principled distinction among kinds of power. Instead, according to Neustadt, they created "separate institutions sharing power."[28] The premise of that claim is that power is an entity that can be divided up to prevent any one branch from having enough to rule another. In this view, the sole purpose of separation of powers is to preserve liberty by preventing the arbitrary rule of any one center of power.

The Neustadt perspective finds some support both in the founders' deliberations and in the Constitution. Much attention was given to making each branch "weighty" enough to resist encroachment by the others. Yet this "checks and balances" view of separation of powers can be understood better in tandem with an alternative understanding of the concept: powers were separated and structures of each branch differentiated in order to equip each branch to perform different tasks. Each branch would be superior (although not the sole power) in its own sphere and in its own way. The purpose of separation of powers was to make effective governance more likely.[29]

Ensuring the protection of liberty and individual rights was one element of effective governance as conceived by the founders, but not the only one. Government also needed to ensure the security of the nation and to craft policies that reflected popular will.[30] These three governmental objectives may conflict; for example, popular opinion may favor policies that violate rights. Separation of powers was thought to be an institutional way of accommodating the tensions between governmental objectives.

Table 4.1 presents a simplified view of the purposes behind the separation of powers. Note that the three objectives of government—popular will, popular rights, and self-preservation—are mixed twice in the Constitution; they are mixed among the branches and within each branch so that each objective is given priority in one branch. Congress and the president were to concern themselves with all three, but the priority of their concern differs, with "self-preservation" or national security of utmost concern to the president.

The term *separation of powers* has perhaps obstructed understanding of the extent to which different structures were designed to give each branch the special quality needed to secure its governmental objectives. Thus, although the

Table 4.1. Separation of Powers

Objectives (in order of priority)	Special qualities and functions (to be aimed at)	Structures and means
CONGRESS		
1. Popular will	Deliberation	a. Plurality
2. Popular rights		b. Proximity (frequent
3. Self-preservation		House elections)
		c. Bicameralism
		d. Competent powers
PRESIDENT		
1. Self-preservation	Energy and "steady	a. Unity
2. Popular rights	administration of law"	b. Four-year term
3. Popular will		and reeligibility
		c. Competent powers
COURTS		
1. Popular rights	"Judgment, not will"	a. Small collegial body
		b. Life tenure
		c. Power linked to argument

founders were not so naive as to expect that Congress would be simply "deliberative," they hoped its plural membership and bicameral structure would provide necessary, if not sufficient, conditions for deliberation to emerge. Similarly, the president's "energy," it was hoped, would be enhanced by unity, the prospect of reelection, and substantial discretion. As we all know, the Court does not simply "judge" dispassionately; it also makes policies and exercises will. But the founders believed it made no sense to have a Court if it were intended to be just like a Congress. The judiciary was structured to make the dispassionate protection of rights more likely, if by no means certain.

The founders differentiated powers as well as structures in the original design. These powers ("the executive power" vested in the president in Article II and "all legislative power herein granted," given to Congress in Article I) overlap and sometimes conflict. Yet both the legalists' view of power as "parchment distinction" and the political scientists' view of "separate institutions sharing power" provide inadequate guides to what happens and what was thought ought to happen when powers collided. The founders urged that "line drawing" among spheres of authority be the product of political conflict among the branches, not the result of dispassionate legal analysis. Contrary to more contemporary views, they did not believe that such conflict would lead to deadlock or stalemate.[31]

Consider the disputes that sometimes arise from claims of "executive privilege."[32] Presidents occasionally refuse to provide information to Congress that its members deem necessary to carry out their special functions. They usually justify assertions of executive privilege on the grounds of either national security or the need to maintain the conditions necessary to sound execution, including the unfettered canvassing of opinions.

Both Congress and the president have legitimate constitutional prerogatives at stake: Congress has a right to know and the president a need for secrecy. How does one discover whether in any particular instance the president's claim is more or less weighty than Congress's? The answer will depend on the circumstances—for example, the importance of the particular piece of legislation in the congressional agenda versus the importance of the particular secret to the executive. There is no formula independent of political circumstance with which to weigh such competing institutional claims. The most knowledgeable observers of those political conflicts are the parties themselves: Congress and the president.

Each branch has weapons at its disposal to use against the other. Congress can threaten to hold up legislation or appointments important to the president. Ultimately, it could impeach and convict him. For his part, a president may continue to "stonewall"; he may veto bills or fail to support legislation of interest to his legislative opponents; he may delay political appointments; and he may put the issue to public test, even submitting to an impeachment inquiry for his own advantage. The lengths to which presidents and Congresses are willing to go was thought to be a rough measure of the importance of their respective constitutional claims. Nearly always, executive-legislative disputes are resolved at a relatively low stage of potential conflict. In 1981, for example, President Ronald Reagan ordered Interior Secretary James Watt to release information to a Senate committee after the committee had agreed to maintain confidentiality. The compromise was reached after public debate and "contempt of Congress" hearings were held.

It is important to note that this political process is dynamic. Viewed at particular moments, the system may appear deadlocked; considered over time, considerable movement becomes apparent. Similar scenarios could be constructed for the other issues over which congressional and presidential claims to authority conflict, such as the use of executive agreements in place of treaties, the deployment of military force, or the executive impoundment of appropriated monies.[33]

Although conflict may continue to be institutionally fostered or constrained in ways that were intended by the founders, one still may wonder whether their broad objectives have been secured and whether their priorities should be ours.

At the outset of the present century, Woodrow Wilson mounted an attack on the founders' design, convinced that it had not achieved its objectives. More important, his attack resulted in a reordering of these objectives in the understandings that presidents have of their roles. His theory underlies the second constitution that buffets the presidency.

The Modern Perspective

Woodrow Wilson's influential critique of *The Federalist* contains another synoptic vision. Yet his comprehensive reinterpretation of the constitutional order appears, at first glance, to be internally inconsistent. Between writing his classic dissertation, *Congressional Government,* in 1884, and publishing his well-known series of lectures, *Constitutional Government in the United States,* in 1908, Wilson shifted his position on important structural features of the constitutional system.

Early in his career Wilson depicted the House of Representatives as the potential motive force in American politics and urged reforms to make it more unified and energetic. He paid little attention to the presidency or judiciary. In later years he focused his attention on the presidency. In his early writings Wilson urged a plethora of constitutional amendments that were designed to emulate the British parliamentary system, including proposals to synchronize the terms of representatives and senators with that of the president and to require presidents to choose leaders of the majority party as cabinet secretaries. Later Wilson abandoned formal amendment as a strategy, urging instead that the existing Constitution be reinterpreted to encompass his parliamentary views.

Wilson also altered his views at a deeper theoretical level. Christopher Wolfe has shown that while the "early" Wilson held a "traditional" view of the Constitution as a document whose meaning persists over time, the "later" Wilson adopted a historicist understanding, claiming that the meaning of the Constitution changed as a reflection of the prevailing thought of successive generations.[34]

As interesting as these shifts in Wilson's thought are, they all rest on an underlying critique of the American polity that Wilson maintained consistently throughout his career. Wilson's altered constitutional proposals—indeed, his altered understanding of constitutionalism itself—ought to be viewed as a series of strategic moves designed to remedy the same alleged systemic defects. Our task here is to review Wilson's understanding of those defects and to outline the doctrine he developed to contend with them—a doctrine whose centerpiece would ultimately be the rhetorical presidency.

Wilson's doctrine counterpoises the founders' understanding of demagoguery, representation, independence of the executive, and separation of powers. For clarity, these principles will be examined here in a slightly different order from before: separation of powers, representation, independence of the executive, and demagoguery.

Separation of Powers

For Wilson, separation of powers was the central defect of American politics. He was the first and most sophisticated proponent of the now conventional argument that separation of powers is a synonym for "checks and balances," that is, the negation of power by one branch over another. Yet Wilson's view was more sophisticated than its progeny because his ultimate indictment of the founders' conception was a functionalist one. Wilson claimed that under the auspices of the founders' view, formal and informal political institutions failed to promote true deliberation in the legislature and impeded energy in the executive.

Wilson characterized the founders' understanding as "Newtonian," a yearning for equipoise and balance in a machinelike system:

The admirable positions of the *Federalist* read like thoughtful applications of Montesquieu to the political needs and circumstances of America. They are full of the theory of checks and balances. The President is balanced off against Congress, Congress against the President, and each against the Court. . . . Politics is turned into mechanics under [Montesquieu's] touch. The theory of gravitation is supreme.[35]

The accuracy of Wilson's portrayal of the founders may be questioned. He reasoned backward from the malfunctioning system as he found it to how they must have intended it. Wilson's depiction of the system rather than his interpretation of the founders' intentions is of present concern.

Rather than equipoise and balance, Wilson found a system dominated by Congress, with several attendant functional infirmities: major legislation frustrated by narrow-minded committees, lack of coordination and direction of policies, a general breakdown of deliberation, and an absence of leadership. Extraconstitutional institutions—boss-led political parties chief among them—had sprung up to assume the functions not performed by Congress or the president, but they had not performed them well. Wilson also acknowledged that the formal institutions had not always performed badly, that some prior

Congresses (those of Webster and Clay) and some presidencies (those of Washington, Adams, Jefferson, Jackson, Lincoln, Roosevelt, and, surprisingly, Madison) had been examples of forceful leadership.[36]

These two strands of thought—the growth of extraconstitutional institutions and the periodic excellence of the constitutional structures—led Wilson to conclude that the founders had mischaracterized their own system. The founders' rhetoric was "Newtonian," but their constitutional structure, like all government, was actually "Darwinian." Wilson explains:

The trouble with the Newtonian theory is that government is not a machine but a living thing. It falls, not under the theory of the universe, but under the theory of organic life. It is accountable to Darwin, not to Newton. It is modified by its environment, necessitated by its tasks, shaped to its functions by the sheer pressure of life.[37]

The founders' doctrine had affected the working of the structure to the extent that the power of the political branches was interpreted mechanically and that many of the structural features reflected the Newtonian yearning. A tension arose between the "organic" core of the system and the "mechanical" understanding of it by politicians and citizens. Thus, "the constitutional structure of the government has hampered and limited [the president's] actions but it has not prevented [them.]" Wilson tried to resolve the tension between the understanding of American politics as Newtonian and its actual Darwinian character to make the evolution self-conscious and thereby more rational and effective.[38]

Wilson attacked the founders for relying on mere "parchment barriers" to effectuate a separation of powers. This claim is an obvious distortion of founding views. In *Federalist* nos. 47 and 48, the argument is precisely that the federal Constitution, unlike earlier state constitutions, would *not* rely primarily on parchment distinctions of power but on differentiation of institutional structures.[39] Through Wilson's discussion of parchment barriers, however, an important difference between his and the founders' view of the same problem becomes visible. Both worried over the tendency of legislatures to dominate in republican systems.

To mitigate the danger posed by legislatures, the founders had relied primarily on an independent president with an office structured to give its occupant the personal incentive and means to stand up to Congress when it exceeded its authority. These structural features included a nonlegislative mode of election, constitutionally fixed salary, qualified veto, four-year term, and indefinite reeligibility. Although the parchment powers of Congress and the president overlapped (contrary to Wilson's depiction of them), the demarcation of powers proper to each branch would result primarily from political interplay and conflict between the political branches rather than from a theoretical drawing of lines by the judiciary.[40]

Wilson offered a quite different view. First, he claimed that because of the inadequacy of mere parchment barriers, Congress, in the latter half of the nineteenth century, had encroached uncontested on the executive sphere. Second, he contended that when the president's institutional check was employed, it took the form of a "negative"—prevention of a bad outcome rather than provision for a good one. In this view, separation of powers hindered efficient, coordinated, well-led policy.[41]

Wilson did not wish to bolster structures to thwart the legislature. He preferred that the president and Congress be fully integrated into, and implicated in, each other's activities. Rather than merely assail Congress, Wilson would tame or, as it were, domesticate it. Separation would be replaced by institutionally structured cooperation. Cooperation was especially necessary because the president lacked the energy he needed, energy that could be provided only by policy backed by Congress and its majority. Although Congress had failed as a deliberative body, it could now be restored to its true function by presidential leadership that raised and defended key policies.

These latter two claims actually represent the major purposes of the Wilsonian theory: leadership and deliberation. Unlike the founders, who saw these two functions in conflict, Wilson regarded them as dependent on each other. In "Leaderless Government" he stated:

I take it for granted that when one is speaking of a representative legislature he means by an "efficient organization" an organization which provides for deliberate, and deliberative, action and which enables the nation to affix responsibility for what is done and what is not done. The Senate is deliberate enough; but it is hardly deliberative after its ancient and better manner. . . . The House of Representatives is neither deliberate nor deliberative. We have not forgotten that one of the most energetic of its recent Speakers thanked God, in his frankness, that the House was not a deliberative body. It has not the time for the leadership of argument. . . . For debate and leadership of that sort the House must have a party organization and discipline such as it has never had.[42]

At this point, it appears that the founders and Wilson differed on the means to common ends. Both wanted "deliberation" and an "energetic" executive, but each proposed different constitutional arrangements to achieve those objectives. In fact, their differences went much deeper, for each theory defined deliberation and energy differently. These differences, hinted at in the above quotation, will become clearer as we examine Wilson's reinterpretation of representation and independence of the executive.

Representation

In the discussion of the founding perspective, the competing requirements of popular consent and insulation from public opinion as a requisite of impartial judgment were canvassed. Woodrow Wilson gave much greater weight to the role of public opinion in the ordinary conduct of representative government than did the founders. Some scholars have suggested that Wilson's rhetoric and the institutional practices he established (especially regarding the nomination of presidential candidates) are the major sources of contemporary efforts to create a more "participatory" democracy. However, Wilson's understanding of representation, like his views on separation of powers, was more sophisticated than that of his followers.[43]

Wilson categorically rejected the Burkean view of the legislator who is elected for his quality of judgment and position on a few issues and then left free to exercise that judgment:

It used to be thought that legislation was an affair to be conducted by the few who were instructed for the benefit of the many who were uninstructed: that statesmanship was a function of origination for which only trained and instructed men were fit. Those who actually conducted legislation and conducted affairs were rather whimsically chosen by Fortune to illustrate this theory, but such was the ruling thought in politics. The Sovereignty of the People, however . . . has created a very different practice. . . . It is a dignified proposition with us—is it not?—that as is the majority, so ought the government to be.[44]

Wilson did not think his view was equivalent to "direct democracy" or to subservience to public opinion (understood, as it often is today, as response to public opinion polls). He favored an interplay between representative and constituent that would, in fact, educate the constituent. This process differed, at least in theory, from the older attempts to "form" public opinion: it did not begin in the minds of the elite but in the hearts of the masses. Wilson called the process of fathoming the people's desires (often only vaguely known to the people until instructed) "interpretation." Interpretation was the core of leadership for him.[45] Before we explore its meaning further, it will be useful to dwell on Wilson's notion of the desired interplay between the "leader-interpreter" and the people so that we may see how his understanding of deliberation differed from the founders'.

For the founders, deliberation meant reasoning on the merits of policy. The character and content of deliberation would thus vary with the character of the policy at issue. In "normal" times, there would be squabbles by competing interests. Deliberation would occur to the extent that such interests were compelled to offer and respond to arguments made by the others. The arguments might be relatively crude, specialized, and technical or they might involve matters of legal or constitutional propriety. But in none of these instances would they resemble the great debates over fundamental principles—for example, over the question whether to promote interests in the first place. Great questions were the stuff of crisis politics and the founders placed much hope in securing the distinction between crisis and normal political life.

Wilson effaced the distinction between "crisis" and "normal" political argument.

Crises give birth and a new growth to statesmanship because they are peculiarly periods of action . . . [and] also of unusual opportunity for gaining leadership and a controlling and guiding influence. . . . And we thus come upon the principle . . . that governmental forms will call to the work of the administration able minds and strong hearts constantly or infrequently, according as they do or do not afford *at all times* an opportunity of gaining and retaining a commanding authority and an undisputed leadership in the nation's councils.[46]

Woodrow Wilson's lament that little deliberation took place in Congress was not that the merits of policies were left unexplored but rather that, because the discussions were not elevated to the level of major contests of principle, the public generally did not interest itself. True deliberation, he urged, would rivet the attention of press and public, while what substituted for it in his day were virtually secret contests of interest-based factions. Wilson rested this view on three observations. First, the congressional workload was parceled out to specialized standing committees, whose decisions usually were ratified by the respective houses without any general debate. Second, the arguments that did take place in committee were technical and structured by the "special pleadings" of interest groups, whose advocates adopted the model of legal litigation as their mode of discussion. As Wilson characterized committee debates:

They have about them none of the searching, critical, illuminating character of the higher order of parliamentary debate, in which men are pitted against each other as equals, and urged to sharp contest and masterful strife by the inspiration of political principle and personal ambition, through the rivalry of parties and the competition of policies. They represent a joust between antagonistic interests, not a contest of principles.[47]

Finally, because debates were hidden away in committee, technical, and interest-based, the public cared little about them. "The ordinary citizen cannot be induced to pay much heed to the details, or even the main principles of lawmaking," Wilson wrote, "unless something more interesting than the law itself be involved in the pending decision of the lawmaker." For the founders this would not have been disturbing, but for Wilson the very heart of representative government was the principle of publicity: "The informing function of Congress should be preferred even to its legislative function." The informing function was to be preferred both as an end in itself and because the accountability of public officials required policies that were connected with one another and explained to the people. Argument from "principle" would connect policy and present constellations of policies as coherent wholes to be approved or disapproved by the people. "Principles, as statesmen conceive them, are threads to the labyrinth of circumstances."[48]

Wilson attacked separation of powers in an effort to improve leadership for the purpose of fostering deliberation. "Congress cannot, under our present system . . . be effective for the instruction of public opinion, or the cleansing of political action." As mentioned at the outset of this chapter, Wilson first looked to Congress itself, specifically to its Speaker, for such leadership. Several years after the publication of *Congressional Government*, Wilson turned his attention to the president. "There is no trouble now about getting the president's speeches printed and read, every word," he wrote at the turn of the century.[49]

Independence of the Executive

The attempt to bring the president into more intimate contact with Congress and the people raises the question of the president's "independence." Wilson altered the meaning of this notion, which had originally been that the president's special authority came independently from the Constitution, not from Congress or the people. The president's station thus afforded him the possibility and responsibility of taking a perspective on policy different from either Congress or the people. Wilson urged us to consider the president as receiving his authority independently through a mandate from the people. For Wilson, the president remained "special," but now because he was the only governmental officer with a national mandate.[50]

Political scientists today have difficulty in finding mandates in election years, let alone between them, because of the great number of issues and the lack of public consensus on them. Wilson understood this problem and urged the leader to sift through the multifarious currents of opinion to find a core of issues that he believed reflected majority will even if the majority was not yet fully aware of it.

The leader's rhetoric could translate the people's felt desires into public policy. Wilson cited Daniel Webster as an example of such an interpreter of the public will:

The nation lay as it were unconscious of its unity and purpose, and he called it into full consciousness. It could never again be anything less than what he said it was. It is at such moments and in the mouths of such interpreters that nations spring from age to age in their development.[51]

"Interpretation" involves two skills. First, the leader must understand the true majority sentiment underneath the contradictory positions of factions and the discordant views of the masses. Second, the leader must explain the people's true desires to them in a way that is easily comprehended and convincing.

Wilson's desire to raise politics to the level of rational disputation and his professed aim to have leaders educate the masses are contradictory. Candidly, he acknowledges that the power to command would require simplification of the arguments to accommodate the masses: "The arguments which induce popular action must always be broad and obvious arguments; only a very gross substance of concrete conception can make any impression on the minds of the masses."[52] Not only is argument simplified, but disseminating "information"—a common concern of contemporary democratic theory—is not the function of a deliberative leader in Wilson's view:

Men are not led by being told what they don't know. Persuasion is a force, but not information; and persuasion is accomplished by creeping into the confidence of those you would lead.... Mark the simplicity and directness of the arguments and ideas of true leaders. The motives which they urge are elemental; the morality which they seek to enforce is large and obvious; the policy they emphasize, purged of all subtlety.[53]

Demagoguery

Wilson's understanding of leadership raises again the problem of demagoguery. What distinguishes a leader-interpreter from a demagogue? Who is to make this distinction? The founders feared there was no institutionally effective way to exclude the demagogue if popular oratory during "normal" times was encouraged. Indeed, the term *leader,* which appears a dozen times in *The Federalist,* is used disparagingly in all but one instance, and that one is a reference to leaders of the Revolution.[54]

Wilson was sensitive to this problem. "The most despotic of governments under the control of wise statesmen is preferable to the freest ruled by demagogues," he wrote. Wilson relied on two criteria to distinguish the demagogue from the leader, one based on the nature of the appeal, the other on the character of the leader. The demagogue appeals to "the momentary and whimsical popular mood, the transitory or popular passion," while the leader appeals to "true" and durable majority sentiment. The demagogue is motivated by the desire to augment personal power, while the leader is more interested in fostering the permanent interests of the community. "The one [trims] to the inclinations of the moment, the other [is] obedient to the permanent purposes of the public mind."[55]

Theoretically, there are a number of difficulties with these distinctions. If popular opinion is the source of the leader's rhetoric, what basis apart from popular opinion itself is there to distinguish the "permanent" from the "transient"? If popular opinion is constantly evolving, what sense is there to the notion of "the permanent purposes of the public mind"? Yet the most serious difficulties are practical ones. Assuming it is theoretically possible to distinguish the leader from the demagogue, how is that distinction to be incorporated into the daily operation of political institutions? Wilson offered a threefold response to this query.

First, he claimed his doctrine contained an ethic that could be passed on to future leaders. Wilson hoped that politicians' altered understanding of what constituted success and fame could provide some security. He constantly pointed to British parliamentary practice, urging that long training in debate had produced generations of leaders and few demagogues. Indeed, Wilson had taught at Johns Hopkins, Bryn Mawr, Wesleyan, and Princeton, and at each of those institutions he established debating societies modeled on the Oxford Union.[56]

Second, Wilson placed some reliance on the public's ability to judge character:

Men can scarcely be orators without that force of character, that readiness of resource, that cleverness of vision, that grasp of intellect, that courage of conviction, that correctness of purpose, and that instinct and capacity for leadership which are the eight horses that draw the triumphal chariot of every leader and ruler of free-men. We could not object to being ruled by such men.[57]

According to Wilson, the public need not appeal to a complex standard or theory to distinguish demagoguery from leadership, but could easily recognize "courage," "intelligence," and "correctness of purpose"—signs that the leader was not a demagogue. Wilson does not tell us why prior publics *have* fallen prey to enterprising demagogues, but the major difficulty with this second source of restraint is that public understanding of the leader's character would come from his oratory rather than from a history of his political activity or from direct contact with him. The public's understanding of character might be based solely on words.

Finally, Wilson suggests that the natural conservatism of public opinion, its resistance to innovation that is not consonant with the speed and direction of its own movement, will afford still more safety:

Practical leadership may not beckon to the slow masses of men from beyond some dim, unexplored space or some intervening chasm: it must daily feel the road to the goal proposed, knowing that it is a slow, very slow, evolution to the wings, and that for the present, and for a very long future also, Society must walk, dependent upon practicable paths, incapable of scaling sudden heights.[58]

Woodrow Wilson's assurances of security against demagogues may seem unsatisfactory because they do not adequately distinguish the polity in which he worked from others in which demagogues have prevailed, including some southern states in this country. However, his arguments should be considered as much for the theoretical direction and emphases that they imply as for the particular weaknesses they reveal. Wilson's doctrine stands on the premise that the need for more energy in the political system is greater than the risk incurred through the possibility of demagoguery.[59] This represents a major shift, indeed a reversal, of the founding perspective. If Wilson's argument regarding demagoguery is strained or inadequate, it was a price he was willing to pay to remedy what he regarded as the founders' inadequate provision for an energetic executive.

Conclusion

Both constitutions were designed to encourage and support an energetic president, but they differ over the legitimate sources and alleged virtues of popular leadership. For the founders, the president draws his energy from his authority. His authority rests on his independent constitutional position. For Woodrow Wilson and for presidents ever since, power and authority are conferred directly by the people. *The Federalist* and the Constitution proscribe popular leadership. Woodrow Wilson prescribes it. Indeed, Wilson urges the president to minister continually to the moods of the people as a preparation for action. The founders' president was to look to the people, but less frequently, and to be judged by them, but usually after acting.

The second constitution gained legitimacy because presidents were thought to lack the resources necessary for the energy promised but not delivered by the first. The second constitution did not replace the first, however. Because many of the founding structures persist while our understanding of the president's legitimate role has changed, the new view should be thought of as superimposed on the old, altering without obliterating the original structure.

Many commentators have noted the tendency of recent presidents to raise public expectations about what they can achieve. Indeed, public disenchantment with government altogether may stem largely from disappointment in presidential performance, inasmuch as the presidency is the most visible and important American political institution. Yet, rather than being the result of the peculiar personality traits of particular presidents, raised expectations are grounded in an institutional dilemma common to all modern presidents. Under the auspices of the second constitution, presidents must continually craft rhetoric that pleases their popular audience. But although presidents are always in a position to promise more, the only additional resource they have to make good on their promises is public opinion itself. Because Congress retains the independent status conferred on it by the first Constitution, it can resist the president.

Of course, presidents who are exceptionally popular or gifted as orators can overcome the resistance of the legislature. For the political system as a whole, this possibility is both good and bad. To the extent that the system requires periodic renewal through synoptic policies that reconstitute the political agenda, it is good. But the very qualities that are necessary to achieve such large-scale change tend to subvert the deliberative process, which makes unwise legislation or incoherent policy more likely.

Ronald Reagan's major political victories as president illustrate both sides of this systemic dilemma.[60] On the one hand, without the second constitution, it would be difficult to imagine Reagan's success at winning tax reform legislation. His skillful coordination of a rhetorical and a legislative strategy overcame the resistance of thousands of lobbies that sought to preserve advantageous provisions of the existing tax code. Similarly, Social Security and other large policies that were initiated by Franklin D. Roosevelt during the New Deal may not have been possible without the second constitution.

On the other hand, Reagan's first budget victory in 1981 and the Strategic Defense Initiative (known as "Star Wars") illustrate how popular leadership can subvert the deliberative process or produce incoherent policy. The budget cuts of 1981 were secured with virtually no congressional debate. Among their effects was the gutting of virtually all of the Great Society programs passed by Lyndon B. Johnson, which themselves were the product of a popular campaign that circumvented the deliberative process.

When Congress does deliberate, as it has on Star Wars, the debate is often structured by contradictory forms of rhetoric, the product of the two constitutions. The arguments presidents make to the people are different from those they make to Congress. To the people, President Reagan promised to strive for a new defense technology that would make nuclear deterrence obsolete. But to Congress, his administration argued that Star Wars was needed to supplement, not supplant, deterrence.[61] Each kind of argument can be used to impeach the other. Jimmy Carter found himself in the same bind on energy policy. When he urged the American people to support his energy plan, Carter contended that it was necessary to remedy an existing crisis. But to Congress he argued that the same policy was necessary to forestall a crisis.[62]

The second constitution promises energy, which is said to be inadequately provided by the first. This suggests that the two constitutions fit together to form a more complete whole. Unfortunately, over the long run, the tendency of the second constitution to make extraordinary power routine undermines, rather than completes, the logic of the original Constitution. Garry Wills has described how presidents since John F. Kennedy have attempted to pit public opinion against their own executive establishment. Successors to a charismatic leader then inherit "a delegitimated set of procedures" and are themselves compelled "to go outside of procedures—further delegitimating the very office they [hold]."[63] In President Reagan's case, this cycle was reinforced by an ideology opposed to big government. "In the present crisis," Reagan said at his first inaugural, "government is not the solution to our problem; government *is* the problem." Although fiascoes like the Iran-contra affair are not inevitable, they are made more likely by the logic and legitimacy of the second constitution.

Perhaps because the dilemmas of the hybrid presidency were so manifest in the Reagan era, or because critiques of popular leadership found their way into the political culture, Reagan's successors have attempted to alter presidential practice. Yet Presidents George Bush and Bill Clinton each have responded to the problem of popular leadership quite differently. One can clearly see these differences through brief comparisons both of their attitudes toward rhetoric and of a major speech delivered by each one during the first year of his administration.

At the outset of his presidency George Bush tried to abandon the leadership style of Reagan. As one astute commentator noted:

Reagan made the rhetorical presidency the rage in Washington. How else could a President operate effectively, except by going over the head of Congress to the American people? Stirring the nation to action was supposed to be the President's first priority. It's not Bush's. "This is as unrhetorical a Presidency as you'll get," says a White House official.[64]

Bush delivered considerably fewer major speeches than Reagan did in his first year. In addition, by leaving much of the task of popular rhetoric to surrogates such as William Bennett and by placing his principal political strategist, Lee Atwater, in charge of the Republican National Committee instead of in the White House, Bush reestablished the important distinction between governing and campaigning.

Thus, in a number of respects Bush resembled the constitutional officer of the first Constitution more than the rhetorical president of the second. One must not strain this comparison, however. Like the president of the first Constitution, Bush seemed to realize that popular rhetoric was a problem, not a panacea. Unlike the president that is idealized in that Constitution, however, Bush apparently did not know what to say in place of popular rhetoric or how to say it. The president as constitutional officer needs a principled rhetoric, a form of speech that makes sense of the polity, its constitutive principles, and its political tendencies. Bush did not seem to understand this.

Consider Bush's first State of the Union address. The president began the speech like a "constitutional officer":

Tonight, I come not to speak about the "state of the Government"—not to detail every new initiative we plan for the coming year, nor to describe every line item in the budget. I'm here to speak to you and to the American people about the State of the Union—about our world—the changes we've seen, the challenges we face. And what that means for America.[65]

After this promising beginning, Bush proceeded like an inarticulate "rhetorical president," reciting a brief catalog of the extraordinary events taking place in Eastern Europe and around the world with almost no effort to instruct as to their meaning. The bulk of the speech was the sort of laundry list of new legislative and budgetary proposals the president had just promised to avoid.

President Clinton has responded to the dilemma of the hybrid constitution quite differently. Instead of seeking to abandon modern practices only to be coopted by the continued public demand for them, Clinton has embraced the rhetorical presidency while seeking to modify or reform it and the public's understanding of leadership.

Like Reagan and unlike Bush, Clinton imported the skills and talents of his campaign into the core leadership of his White House. During his first months in office Clinton experienced firsthand the difficulties of translating the strategies and techniques of campaigning into the processes of governance. Yet his response to these political difficulties was not to abandon the modern conception of leadership but, rather, to invite Ronald Reagan's former communications director, David Gergen, to be his chief strategist. Gergen had worked for Nixon and Bush as well as for Reagan but never before for a Democrat. It is safe to surmise that no political operative is as familiar with the promise and pitfalls of the rhetorical presidency as is David Gergen. Educated in the practices of popular leadership, Clinton's Gergen seems wiser than Reagan's Gergen.

Gergen and Clinton learned that some of the power of the rhetorical presidency may be appropriately harnessed to the tasks of modern governance without many of the common costs of popular leadership. This harnessing can be effected if the president can find a way to avoid utopian visionary speech that overpromises, on the one hand, and detailed policy speeches that seem to preempt and preclude legislative deliberation, on the other. In this spirit, Clinton has developed a leadership style that has four key attributes:

1. The president personally sets direction and establishes priorities through major speeches. These speeches emphasize the principles upon which the president wants policy constructed rather than the concrete rules, regulations, or appropriations that would be the means to realize those principles.

2. The executive branch as a whole is given the task of preparing concrete policies that illustrate and exemplify the president's principles and provide a focus for congressional deliberation.

3. The president and his surrogates reserve for smaller, appropriately chosen audiences arguments regarding the details and technical aspects of specific proposals.

4. Members of Congress are invited to deliberate—to refine, to develop, or even to replace the president's concrete proposals as long as their efforts are consonant with the president's publicly articulated principles.

Clinton's leadership style was strikingly evident in the kickoff of his campaign for health care reform. Clinton structured his nationally televised address to a joint session of Congress around an articulation, illustration, and defense of six principles that he believed "must embody our efforts to reform America's health care system: security, simplicity, savings, choice, quality, and responsibility."[66] The president explained the meaning of each of these principles, but he did not review the details of his proposal. The speech was neither visionary nor specific. Some news commentators, schooled by the rhetorical presidency, faulted the president on just those grounds. They failed to see that his speech may come to be regarded as the finest domestic policy speech since World War II because it reset the *terms of debate* on health care, while at the same time leaving considerable room for legislative deliberation. President Clinton invited Congress to offer specific proposals that measured up to standards articulated in his speech.

In the days following the speech, the president, the First Lady, and advisers such as Ira Magaziner displayed their considerable command of detail as the administration's elaborate proposal was unfolded before congressional committees and other audiences. In each of these settings the particular proposals were offered as *exemplary* of the principles articulated in the major address, not as proposals that need be accepted as is. Thus, the president invited deliberation while attempting to structure and lead it.

President Clinton has discovered that it is impossible to return to the first Constitution even if one wished to. Instead of, like Bush, attempting such a return, only to be carried along willy-nilly by demands born of the second constitution, Clinton is seeking to advance the second constitution by infusing it with principles borrowed from the first.

Although President Clinton's speeches and actions reveal this new conception of leadership, he has not made it an explicit topic for public instruction. To successfully navigate the dilemmas of the two constitutions he will have to do so. Left uninstructed, political pundits and popular opinion may mark President Clinton as unsuccessful by the lights of the second constitution. With his guidance, however, Americans could come to reinterpret, and thereby reform, the rhetorical presidency.

Notes

1. Notable structural changes in the Constitution are the Twelfth, Seventeenth, Twentieth, and Twenty-second Amendments, which deal, respectively, with change in the electoral college system, the election of senators, presidential succession, and presidential reeligibility. Although all are interesting, only the last seems manifestly inconsistent with the founders' plan. For a defense of the relevance of the constitutional theory of the presidency to contemporary practice, see Joseph M. Bessette and Jeffrey Tulis, eds., *The Presidency in the Constitutional Order* (Baton Rouge: Louisiana State University Press, 1981).

2. James W. Ceaser, *Presidential Selection: Theory and Development* (Princeton, N.J.: Princeton University Press, 1979); Nelson Polsby, *Consequences of Party Reform* (New York: Oxford University Press, 1983); Doris A. Graber, *Mass Media and American Politics,* 2d ed. (Washington, D.C.: CQ Press, 1984); David L. Paletz and Robert M. Entman, *Media, Power, Politics* (New York: Free Press, 1981); and Harvey C. Mansfield, Jr., "The Media World and Democratic Representation," *Government and Opposition* 14 (Summer 1979): 35–45.

3. This essay does not reveal the founders' personal and political motives except as they were self-consciously incorporated into the reasons offered for their Constitution. The founders' views are treated on their own terms, as a constitutional theory; Hamilton's statement in the first number of *The Federalist* is taken seriously: "My motives must remain in the depository of my own breast. My arguments will be open to all and may be judged by all." James Madison, Alexander Hamilton, and John Jay, *The Federalist Papers,* ed. Clinton Rossiter (New York: New American Library, 1961), no. 1, 36. For a good discussion of the literature on the political motives of the founding fathers, see Erwin C. Hargrove and Michael Nelson, *Presidents, Politics, and Policy* (New York: Knopf, 1984), chap. 2.

4. The most influential study of the presidency is by Richard Neustadt. See *Presidential Power: The Politics of Leadership from FDR to Carter* (New York: Wiley, 1979), vi: "One must try to view the Presidency from over the President's shoulder, looking out and down with the perspective of *his* place."

5. Herbert J. Storing, *What the Anti-Federalists Were For* (Chicago: University of Chicago Press, 1981), 83n.

6. *The Federalist,* no. 70, 423.

7. In the first number "Publius" warns "that of those men who have overturned the liberties of republics, the greatest number have begun their career by paying obsequious court to the people, commencing demagogues and ending tyrants." And in the last essay, "These judicious reflections contain a lesson of moderation to all the sincere lovers of the Union, and ought to put them upon their guard against hazarding anarchy, civil war, and perhaps the military despotism of a victorious demagogue, in the pursuit of what they are not likely to obtain, but from TIME and EXPERIENCE."

8. Ceaser, *Presidential Selection,* 12, 54–60, 166–167, 318–327. See also V. O. Key, *The Responsible Electorate* (New York: Random House, 1966), chap. 2; Stanley Kelley, Jr., *Political Campaigning: Problems in Creating an Informed Electorate* (Washington, D.C.: Brookings Institution, 1960), 93; Pendleton E. Herring, *Presidential Leadership* (New York: Holt, Rinehart and Winston, 1940), 70; and *The Federalist,* no. 71, 432.

9. *The Federalist,* no. 10, 82; and Ceaser, *Presidential Selection,* 324.

10. Clinton Rossiter, *Constitutional Dictatorship: Crisis Government in the Modern Democracies* (Princeton, N.J.: Princeton University Press, 1948), chap. 3.

11. *The Federalist,* no. 85, 527.

12. Harvey Flaumenhaft, "Hamilton's Administrative Republic and the American Presidency," in *The Presidency in the Constitutional Order,* 65–114. Of course, the Civil War and turn-of-the-century progressive politics show that Hamilton's "administrative republic" has been punctuated with the sorts of crises and politics Hamilton sought to avoid.

13. *The Federalist,* no. 10, 77; no. 43, 276; no. 51, 323–325; no. 63, 384; and no. 73, 443. Moreover, the factual quest to find a "majority" may be no less contestable than dispute over the merits of proposals. Contemporary political scientists who provide ample support for the latter worry when they suggest that it is often both theoretically and practically impossible to discover a majority will—that is, to count it up—owing to the manifold differences of intensity of preferences and the plethora of possible hierarchies of preferences. Kenneth Arrow, *Social Choice and Individual Values* (New York: Wiley, 1963); and Benjamin I. Page, *Choices and Echoes in Presidential Elections* (Chicago: University of Chicago Press, 1978), chap. 2.

14. *The Federalist,* no. 39, 241; see also Martin Diamond, "Democracy and the Federalist: A Reconsideration of the Framers' Intent," *American Political Science Review* 53 (March 1959): 52–68.

15. *The Federalist,* no. 39, 241; no. 68, 412–423. See also James Ceaser, "Presidential Selection," in *The Presidency in the Constitutional Order,* 234–282. Ironically, the founders were proudest of this institutional creation; the electoral college was their most original contrivance. Moreover, it escaped the censure of and even won a good deal of praise from antifederal opponents of the Constitution. Because electors were chosen by state legislatures for the sole purpose of selecting a president, the process was thought *more* democratic than potential alternatives, such as selection by Congress.

16. *The Federalist,* no. 72, 435. The empirical judgment that four years would serve the purpose of insulating the president is not as important for this discussion as the *principle* reflected in that choice, a principle that has fueled recent calls for a six-year term.

17. *The Federalist,* nos. 9 and 10.

18. Gordon Wood, *The Creation of the American Republic: 1776–1787* (New York: Norton, 1969); Michael Parenti, "The Constitution as an Elitist Document," in *How Democratic Is the Constitution?* ed. Robert Goldwin (Washington, D.C.: American Enterprise Institute, 1980), 39–58; and Charles Lindblom, *Politics and Markets* (New York: Basic Books, 1979), conclusion.

19. *The Federalist,* no. 49, 313–317.

20. Ibid., 317.

21. See *The Federalist,* no. 57; Joseph M. Bessette, "Deliberative Democracy," in *How Democratic Is the Constitution?* 102–116; and Michael Malbin, "What Did the Founders Want Congress to Be—and Who Cares?" (Paper presented at the annual meeting of the American Political Science Association, Denver, September 2, 1982). On the status of legislative deliberation today, see Joseph M. Bessette, *The Mild Voice of Reason: Deliberative Democracy and American National Government* (Chicago: University of Chicago Press, 1994); William Muir, *Legislature* (Chicago: University of Chicago Press, 1982); and Arthur Maass, *Congress and the Common Good* (New York: Basic Books, 1983).

22. Wood, *Creation of the American Republic,* chap. 5; and Ceaser, *Presidential Selection,* 48.

23. *The Federalist*, no. 62; no. 63, 376–390; and Storing, *What the Anti-Federalists Were For*, chap. 7.

24. *The Federalist*, no. 55, 342; Max Farrand, ed., *The Records of the Federal Convention of 1787*, 4 vols. (New Haven: Yale University Press, 1966), 1:53.

25. *The Federalist*, no. 71, 432; Madison expresses almost the identical position in no. 63, where he states,

As the cool and deliberate sense of the community, ought in all governments, and actually will in all free governments, ultimately prevail over the views of its rulers; so there are particular moments in public affairs when the people, stimulated by some irregular passion, or some illicit advantage, or misled by the artful misrepresentations of interested men, may call for measures which they themselves will afterwards be most ready to lament and condemn. In these critical moments how salutary will be [a Senate].

26. John Marshall, *Life of George Washington*, quoted in Charles Thatch, *The Creation of the Presidency* (1923; reprint, Baltimore: Johns Hopkins University Press, 1969), 51; and Farrand, *Records*, 2:35, 22, 32.

27. *The Federalist*, no. 68, 413; no. 71, 433; and no. 73, 442; see also Storing, "Introduction," *Creation of the Presidency*, vi–viii. Thomas Jefferson, "Inaugural Address," March 4, 1801, in *The Life and Writings of Thomas Jefferson*, ed. Adrienne Koch and William Peden (New York: Modern Library, 1944), 325.

28. Neustadt, *Presidential Power*, 26, 28–30, 170, 176, 204. See also James Sterling Young, *The Washington Community* (New York: Columbia University Press, 1964), 53. This insight has been the basis of numerous critiques of the American "pluralist" system which, it is alleged, frustrates leadership as it forces politicians through a complicated political obstacle course.

29. Farrand, *Records*, vol. 1, 66–67; *The Federalist*, no. 47, 360–380; see also U.S. Congress, *Annals of Congress*, vol. 1, 384–412, 476–608. See generally Louis Fisher, *Constitutional Conflict between Congress and the President* (Princeton, N.J.: Princeton University Press, 1985).

30. In many discussions of separation of powers today, the meaning of *effectiveness* is restricted to only one of these objectives—the implementation of policy that reflects popular will. See, for example, Donald Robinson, ed., *Reforming American Government* (Boulder: Westview Press, 1985).

31. See, for example, Lloyd N. Cutler, "To Form a Government," *Foreign Affairs* 59 (Fall 1980): 126–143.

32. Gary J. Schmitt, "Executive Privilege: Presidential Power to Withhold Information from Congress," in *Presidency in the Constitutional Order*, 154–194.

33. Richard Pious, *The American Presidency* (New York: Basic Books, 1979), 372–415; Gary J. Schmitt, "Separation of Powers: Introduction to the Study of Executive Agreements," *American Journal of Jurisprudence* 27 (1982): 114–138; and Louis Fisher, *Presidential Spending Power* (Princeton, N.J.: Princeton University Press, 1975), 147–201.

34. Woodrow Wilson, *Congressional Government: A Study in American Politics* (1884; reprint, Gloucester, Mass.: Peter Smith, 1973), preface to 15th printing, introduction; Wilson, *Constitutional Government in the United States* (New York: Columbia University Press, 1908); and Christopher Wolfe, "Woodrow Wilson: Interpreting the Constitution," *Review of Politics* 41 (January 1979): 131. See also Woodrow Wilson, "Cabinet Government in the United States," in *College and State*, ed. Ray Stannard Baker and William E. Dodd, 2 vols. (New York: Harper and Brothers, 1925), 1:19–42; Paul Eidelberg,

A Discourse on Statesmanship (Urbana: University of Illinois Press, 1974), chaps. 8 and 9; Harry Clor, "Woodrow Wilson," in *American Political Thought,* ed. Morton J. Frisch and Richard G. Stevens (New York: Scribner, 1971); and Robert Eden, *Political Leadership and Nihilism* (Gainesville: University of Florida Press, 1984), chap. 1.

35. Wilson, *Constitutional Government,* 22, 56; and Wilson, "Leaderless Government," in *College and State,* 337.

36. Wilson, *Congressional Government,* 141, 149, 164, 195.

37. Wilson, *Constitutional Government,* 56.

38. Ibid., 60; see also Wilson, *Congressional Government,* 28, 30, 31, 187.

39. *The Federalist,* nos. 47 and 48, 300–313. Consider Madison's statement in *Federalist* no. 48, 308–309:

Will it be sufficient to mark with precision, the boundaries of these departments in the Constitution of the government, and to trust to these parchment barriers against the encroaching spirit of power? This is the security which appears to have been principally relied upon by the compilers of most of the American Constitutions. But experience assures us that the efficacy of the provision has been greatly overrated; and that some more adequate defense is indispensably necessary for the more feeble against the more powerful members of the government. The legislative department is everywhere extending the sphere of its activity and drawing all power into its impetuous vortex.

40. Schmitt, "Executive Privilege."

41. Woodrow Wilson, "Leaderless Government," 340, 357; Wilson, *Congressional Government,* 158, 201; and Wilson, "Cabinet Government," 24–25.

42. Wilson, "Leaderless Government," 346; at the time he wrote this, Wilson was thinking of leadership internal to the House, but he later came to see the president performing this same role. Wilson, *Constitutional Government,* 69–77; see also Wilson, *Congressional Government,* 76, 97–98.

43. Eidelberg, *Discourse on Statesmanship,* chaps. 8 and 9; and Ceaser, *Presidential Selection,* chap. 4, conclusion.

44. Woodrow Wilson, *Leaders of Men,* ed. T. H. Vail Motter (Princeton, N.J.: Princeton University Press, 1952), 39. This is the manuscript of an oft-repeated lecture that Wilson delivered in the 1890s. See also Wilson, *Congressional Government,* 195, 214.

45. Wilson, *Leaders of Men,* 39; and Wilson, *Constitutional Government,* 49. See also Wilson, *Congressional Government,* 78, 136–137.

46. Wilson, "Cabinet Government," 34–35. See also Wilson, "Leaderless Government," 354; and Wilson, *Congressional Government,* 72, 136–137.

47. Wilson, *Congressional Government,* 69, 72.

48. Ibid., 72, 82, 197–198; Wilson, "Cabinet Government," 20, 28–32; and Wilson, *Leaders of Men,* 46.

49. Wilson, *Congressional Government,* 76; ibid., preface to 15th printing, 22–23.

50. Ibid., 187.

51. Wilson, *Constitutional Government,* 49. Today, the idea of a mandate as objective assessment of the will of the people has been fused with the idea of leader as interpreter. Presidents regularly appeal to the results of elections as legitimizing those policies that they believe ought to reflect majority opinion. On the "false" claims to represent popular will, see Stanley Kelley, Jr., *Interpreting Elections* (Princeton, N.J.: Princeton University Press, 1984).

52. Wilson, *Leaders of Men,* 20, 26.

53. Ibid., 29.

54. I am indebted to Robert Eden for the point about *The Federalist*. See also Ceaser, *Presidential Selection*, 192–197.

55. Wilson, "Cabinet Government," 37; and Wilson, *Leaders of Men*, 45–46.

56. See, for example, Wilson, *Congressional Government*, 143–147.

57. Ibid., 144.

58. Wilson, *Leaders of Men*, 45.

59. Wilson, *Congressional Government*, 144.

60. I discuss this and other dilemmas more fully in *The Rhetorical Presidency* (Princeton, N.J.: Princeton University Press, 1987).

61. Steven E. Miller and Stephen Van Evera, eds., *The Star Wars Controversy* (Princeton, N.J.: Princeton University Press, 1986), preface.

62. Sanford Weiner and Aaron Wildavsky, "The Prophylactic Presidency," *Public Interest* 52 (Summer 1978): 1–18.

63. Garry Wills, "The Kennedy Imprisonment: The Prisoner of Charisma," *Atlantic*, January 1982, 34; and H. H. Gerth and C. Wright Mills, eds., *From Max Weber* (New York: Oxford University Press, 1958), 247–248.

64. Fred Barnes, "Mr. Popularity," *New Republic*, January 8 and 15, 1990, 13.

65. "Text of the President's State of the Union Message to Nation," *New York Times*, February 1, 1990, C18.

66. "Address to a Joint Session of Congress on Health Care Reform, September 22, 1993," *Weekly Compilation of Presidential Documents* (Washington, D.C.: U.S. Government Printing Office), vol. 29, no. 38, p. 1837.

5 Presidential Leadership in Political Time

Stephen Skowronek

Much recent scholarship on the presidency has emphasized the cyclical aspects of the office. Stephen Skowronek explains one recurring sequence in presidential history—namely, the rise and fall of regimes, or governing coalitions—in terms of the passage of what he calls "political time." Each sequence begins when an established regime is defeated soundly in a presidential election, bringing to power a new coalition led by a new president, such as Andrew Jackson in 1828 and Franklin D. Roosevelt in 1932. The challenges to the president who would create a regime are to undermine the "institutional support for opposition interests," to restructure "institutional relations between state and society," and to secure "the dominant position of the new political coalition." As Skowronek argues, not all presidents succeed in this endeavor, and the efforts of even those presidents who do succeed eventually will crumble as the new regime becomes old and vulnerable. Skowronek concludes by offering some thoughts about the place of Ronald Reagan, George Bush, and Bill Clinton in the cyclical history of national regimes.

Three general dynamics are evident in presidential history. The locus of the first is the constitutional separation of powers. It links presidents past and present in a timeless and constant struggle over the definition of their institutional prerogatives, and suggests that, although much has changed in two hundred years, the basic structure of presidential action has remained essentially the same. A second dynamic can be traced through the modernization of the nation. It links presidents past and present in an evolutionary sequence culminating in the expanded powers and governing responsibilities of the "modern presidency," and it suggests that the post-World War II incumbents stand apart—their shared leadership situation distinguished from that of earlier presidents by the scope of governmental concerns, the complexity of national and international issues, and the sheer size of the institutional apparatus. The third dynamic is less well attended by students of the American presidency. Its locus is the changing shape of the political regimes that have organized state-society relations for broad periods of American history, and it links presidents past and present at parallel junctures in "political time."[1] This third dynamic is the point of departure for our investigation.

To read American history with an eye toward the dynamics of political change is to see that within the sequence of national development there have been many beginnings and many endings. Periods are marked by the rise to power of new political coalitions, one of which comes to exert a dominant influence over the federal government. The dominant coalition operates the federal government and perpetuates its position through the development of a distinctive set of institutional arrangements and approaches to public policy questions. Once established, however, coalition interests have an enervating effect on the governing capacities of these political-institutional regimes. From the outset conflicts among interests within the dominant coalition threaten to cause political disaffection and may weaken regime support. Then—beyond the problems posed by conflicts among these established interests—more basic questions arise concerning the interests themselves. As the nation changes, the regime's traditional approach to problems appears increasingly outmoded, and the government it dominates appears increasingly hostaged to sectarian interests with myopic concerns, insufferable demands, and momentary loyalties. In all, the longer a regime survives, the more its approach to national affairs becomes encumbered and distorted. Its political energies dissipate, and it becomes less competent in addressing the manifest governing demands of the day.

Thinking in terms of regime sequences rather than linear national development, one can distinguish many different political contexts for presidential leadership *within* a given historical period. Leadership situations might be characterized by the president's posture vis-à-vis the dominant political coalition. In the modern Democratic period, for example, regime outsiders like Republicans Dwight D. Eisenhower and Richard M. Nixon faced different political problems from those confronted by regime insiders like John F. Kennedy and Lyndon B. Johnson.

Leadership situations might also be differentiated according to political time; that is, when in a regime sequence the president engages the political-institutional order. Thus, presidents Franklin D. Roosevelt, John F. Kennedy, and Jimmy Carter—all Democrats who enjoyed Democratic majorities in Congress—may be said to have faced different problems in leading the nation as they were arrayed along a sequence of political change that encompassed the generation and degeneration of the New Deal order.

This view of the changing relationship between the presidency and the political system can easily be related to certain outstanding patterns in presidential leadership across American history. First, the presidents who traditionally make the historians' roster of America's greatest—George Washington, Thomas Jefferson, Andrew Jackson, Abraham Lincoln, Woodrow Wilson, and Franklin D. Roosevelt—all came to power in an abrupt break from a long-established political-institutional regime; and each led a movement of new political forces into control of the federal government.[2] Second, after the initial break with the past and the consolidation of a new system of government control, a general decline in the political effectiveness of regime insiders is notable. Take, for example, the sequence of Jeffersonians. After the galvanizing performance of Jefferson's first term, we observe increasing political divisions and a managerial-style presidency under James Madison. Asserting the sanctity of an indivisible Republican majority, James Monroe opened his administration to unbridled sectarianism and oversaw a debilitating fragmentation of the federal establishment. A complete political and institutional breakdown marked the abbreviated tenure of John Quincy Adams.

But is it possible to go beyond these general observations and elaborate a historical-structural analysis of political leadership in the presidency? What characteristic political challenges face a leader at any given stage in a regime sequence? How is the quality of presidential performance related to the changing shape of the political-institutional order? These questions call for an investigation that breaks presidential history into regime segments and then compares leadership problems and presidential performances at similar stages in regime development across historical periods. Taking different regimes into account simultaneously, this essay will group presidents together on the basis of the parallel positions they hold in political time.

The analysis focuses on three pairs of presidents drawn from the New Deal and Jacksonian regimes: Franklin D. Roosevelt and Andrew Jackson; John F. Kennedy and James K. Polk; and Jimmy Carter and Franklin Pierce. All were Democrats and thus affiliated with the dominant coalition of their respective periods. None took a passive, caretaker view of his office. Indeed, each aspired to great national leadership. Paired comparisons have been formed by slicing into these two regime sequences at corresponding junctures and exposing a shared relationship between the presidency and the political system.

We begin with two beginnings—the presidency of Franklin D. Roosevelt and its counterpart in political time, the presidency of Andrew Jackson. Coming to power upon the displacement of an old ruling coalition, these presidents became mired in remarkably similar political struggles. Although separated by more than a century of history, they both faced the distinctive challenge of constructing a new regime. Leadership became a matter of securing the political and institutional infrastructure of a new governmental order.

Beyond the challenges of regime construction lie the ever more perplexing problems of managing an established regime in changing times. The regime manager is constrained on one side by the political imperatives of coalition maintenance and on the other by deepening divisions within the ranks. Leadership does not penetrate to the basics of political and institutional reconstruction. It is caught up in the difficulties of satisfying regime commitments while stemming the tide of internal disaffection. Consequently, the president is challenged at the level of interest control and conflict manipulation. Our examination of the manager's dilemma focuses on John F. Kennedy and his counterpart in political time, James K. Polk.

Finally, we come to the paradoxes of establishing a credible leadership posture in an enervated regime. Jimmy Carter and Franklin Pierce both came to power at a time when the dominant coalition had degenerated into myopic sects that appeared impervious to the most basic problems facing the nation. Neither of these presidents penetrated to the level of managing coalition interests. Each found himself caught in the widening disjunction between established power and political legitimacy. Their affiliation with the old order in a new age turned their respective bids for leadership into awkward and superficial struggles to avoid the stigma of their own irrelevance.

All six of these presidents had to grapple with the erosion of political support that inevitably comes with executive action. But, if this problem plagued them all, the initial relationship between the leader and his supporters was not the same, and the terms of presidential interaction with the political system changed sequentially from stage to stage. Looking within these pairs, we can identify performance challenges that are shared by leaders who addressed the political system at a similar juncture. Looking across the pairs, we observe an ever more tenuous leadership situation, an ever more constricted universe of political action, and an ever more superficial penetration of the political system.

Jackson and Roosevelt:
Upheaval and the Challenge of Regime Construction

The presidencies of Andrew Jackson and Franklin D. Roosevelt were both launched on the heels of a major political upheaval. Preceding the election of each, a party long established as the dominant and controlling power within the federal government had begun to flounder and fragment in an atmosphere of national crisis. Finally, the old ruling party suffered a stunning defeat at the polls, losing its dominant position in Congress as well as its control of the presidency. Jackson and Roosevelt assumed the office of chief executive with the old ruling coalition thoroughly discredited by the electorate and, at least temporarily, displaced from political power. They each led into control of the federal establishment a movement based on general discontent with the previously established order of things.

Of the two, Jackson's election in 1828 presents this crisis of the old order in a more purely political form. New economic and social conflicts had been festering in the United States since the financial panic of 1819, but Jackson's campaign gained its special meaning from the confusion and outrage unleashed by the election of 1824. In that election, the Congressional Caucus collapsed as the engine of national political unity, and the once monolithic Republican party disintegrated into warring factions. After an extended period of political maneuvering, an alliance between John Quincy Adams and Henry Clay secured Adams a presidential victory in the House of Representatives, despite Jackson's pluralities in both popular and electoral votes. The Adams administration was immediately and permanently engulfed in charges of conspiracy, intrigue, and profligacy in high places. Jackson, the hero of 1815, became a hero wronged in 1824. The Jackson campaign of 1828 launched a broadside assault on the degrading "corruption of manners" that had consumed Washington and on the conspiracy of interests that had captured the federal government from the people.[3]

In the election of 1932 the collapse of the old ruling party dovetailed with and was overshadowed by the Great Depression. The Democratic party of 1932 offered nothing if not hope for economic recovery, and in this Roosevelt's candidacy found special meaning almost in spite of the candidate's rather conservative campaign rhetoric. The depression had made a mockery of President Herbert Hoover's early identification of his party with prosperity, and the challenge of formulating a response to the crisis broke the Republican ranks and threw the party into disarray. Roosevelt's appeal was grounded, not in substantive proposals or even partisan ideology, but in a widespread perception of Republican incompetence, if not intransigence, in the face of national economic calamity. As future secretary of state Cordell Hull outlined Roosevelt's leadership situation in January 1933: "No political party at Washington [is] in control of Congress or even itself . . . there [is] no cohesive nationwide sentiment behind any fundamental policy or idea today. The election was an overwhelmingly negative affair."[4]

Thus, Jackson and Roosevelt each engaged a political system cut from its moorings by a wave of popular discontent. Old commitments of ideology and interest suddenly had been thrown into question. New commitments were as yet only vague appeals to some essential American value (republican virtue, economic opportunity) that had been lost in the indulgences of the old order. With old political alliances in disarray and new political energies infused into Congress, these presidents had an extraordinary opportunity to set a new course in public policy and to redefine the terms of national political debate. They recaptured the experience of being first.

But this situation is not without its characteristic leadership challenge. The leader who is propelled into office by a political upheaval in governmental control ultimately confronts the imperatives of establishing a new order in government and politics. This challenge is presented directly by the favored interests and residual institutional supports of the old order; once the challenge has been posed, the unencumbered leadership environment that was created by the initial break with the past quickly fades. The president is faced with the choice of either abandoning his new departure or consolidating it with structural reforms. Situated just beyond the old order, presidential leadership crystallizes as a problem of regime construction.

The president as regime builder grapples with the fundamentals of political regeneration—institutional reconstruction and party building. At these moments, when national political power has been shaken to its foundational elements, we see the president join at center stage a set of activities that other leaders, less favorably situated, engage only indirectly or piecemeal—destroying residual institutional support for opposition interests, restructuring institutional relations between state and society and securing the dominant position of a new political coalition. Success in these tasks is hardly guaranteed. Wilson had to abandon this course when the Republicans reunited and preempted his efforts to broaden the Democratic base. Lincoln was assassinated just as the most critical questions of party building and institutional reconstruction were to be addressed, a disaster that ushered in a devastating confrontation between president and Congress and left the emergent Republican regime hanging precariously for the next three decades. Even Jackson and Roosevelt—America's quintessential regime builders—were not uniformly successful. Neither could keep the dual offensives of party building and institutional reconstruction moving in tandem long enough to complete them both.

Andrew Jackson

Republican renewal was the keynote of Jackson's first term. The president was determined to ferret out the political and institutional corruption that he believed had befallen the Jeffersonian regime. This meant purging incompetence and profligacy from the civil service, initiating fiscal retrenchment in national projects, and reviving federalism as a system of vigorous state-based government.[5] Jackson's appeal for a return to Jefferson's original ideas about government certainly posed a potent indictment of the recent state of national affairs and a clear challenge to long-established interests. But there was a studied political restraint in his repudiation of the recent past that defied the attempts of his opponents to characterize it as revolutionary.[6] Indeed, while holding out an attractive standard with which to rally supporters, Jackson was careful to yield his opposition precious little ground upon which to mount an effective counterattack. He used the initial upheaval in governmental control to cultivate an irreproachable political position as the nation's crusader in reform.

Significantly, the transformation of Jackson's presidency from a moral crusade into a radical program of political reconstruction was instigated, not by the president himself, but by the premier institution of the old regime, the Bank of the United States.[7] At the time of Jackson's election, the bank was long established as both the most powerful institution in America and the most important link between state and society. It dominated the nation's credit system, maintained extensive ties of material interest with political elites, and actively involved itself in electoral campaigns to sustain its own political support. It embodied all the problems of institutional corruption and political degradation toward which Jackson addressed his administration. The bank was a concentration of political and economic power able to tyrannize over people's lives and to control the will of their elected representatives.

During his first years in office Jackson spoke vaguely of the need for some modification of the bank's charter. But since the charter did not expire until 1836, there appeared to be plenty of time to consider appropriate changes. Indeed, although Jackson was personally inclined toward radical hard-money views, he recognized the dangers of impromptu tinkering with an institution so firmly entrenched in the nation's economic life and hesitated to embrace untested alternatives. Moreover, he foresaw an overwhelming reelection endorsement for his early achievements and knew that to press the bank issue before the election of 1832 could only hurt him politically. After a rout of Henry Clay, the architect of the bank and the obvious challenger in the forthcoming campaign, Jackson anticipated a free hand to deal with the institution as he saw fit.

But Jackson's apparent commitment to some kind of bank reform and the obvious political calculations surrounding the issue led the bank president, Nicholas Biddle, to join forces with Clay. They orchestrated a preelection push to recharter the institution without any reforms a full four years before its charter expired. Biddle feared for the bank's future in a Jackson second term, and Clay needed to break Jackson's irreproachable image as a national leader and to expose his political weaknesses. An early recharter bill promised to splinter Jackson's support in Congress. If the president signed the bill, his integrity as a reformer would be destroyed; if he vetoed it, he would provide a sorely needed coherence to anti-Jackson sentiment.

As expected, the recharter bill threw Jackson enthusiasts into a quandary and passed through Congress. The bill pushed Jackson beyond the possibility of controlling the modification of extant institutions without significant opposition, and forced him to choose between retreat and an irrevocable break with established governmental arrangements. He saw the bill not only as a blatant attempt by those attached to the old order to destroy him politically but also as proof certain that the bank's political power threatened the very survival of republican government. Accepting the challenge, he set out to destroy the bank. The 1828 crusade for republican renewal became in 1832 an all-fronts offensive to establish an entirely new political and institutional order.

The president's veto of the recharter bill clearly marked this transition. The political themes of 1828 were turned against the bank with a vengeance. Jackson said his stand would extricate the federal government from the interests of the privileged and protect the states from encroaching federal domination. He appealed directly to the interests of the nation's farmers, mechanics, and laborers, claiming that this great political majority stood to lose control over the government to the influential few. This call to the "common man" for a defense of the republic had long been a Jacksonian theme, but now it carried the portent of sweeping governmental changes. Jackson not only was declaring open war on the premier institution of the old order but was also challenging long-settled questions of governance. The Supreme Court, for example, had upheld the constitutionality of the bank decades before. Jackson's veto challenged the assumption of executive deference to the Court and asserted presidential authority to make an independent and contrary judgment about judicial decisions. Jackson also challenged executive deference to Congress, perhaps the central operating principle of the Jeffersonian regime. His veto message went beyond constitutional objections to the recharter bill and asserted the president's authority to make an independent evaluation of the social, economic, and political implications of congressional action. In all, the message was a regime builder's manifesto for mobilizing a broad-based political coalition, shattering established institutional relationships between state and society, and transforming power arrangements within the government itself.

Of course, new political regimes are not built by presidential proclamation. Jackson had his work cut out for him at the beginning of his second term. His victory over Clay in 1832 was certainly sweeping enough to reaffirm his leadership. In addition, having used the veto as a campaign document, Jackson could now claim a mandate to complete the work it outlined. But the veto had also been used as an issue by Clay, and the threat to the bank was fueling organized political opposition in all sectors of the country.[8] More important still, the Senate, which had been shaky enough in Jackson's first term, moved completely beyond his control in 1833, and his party's majority in the House returned in a highly volatile condition. Finally, the bank's charter had three more years, and bank president Biddle had every intention of exploiting Jackson's political vulnerabilities in the hope of securing his own future.

Thus, the election victory drew Jackson deeper into the politics of reconstruction. To maintain his leadership, he needed to neutralize the bank's significance for the remainder of its charter and to prevent any new recharter movement from emerging in Congress. His plan was to remove the federal government's deposits from the bank on his own authority and to transfer them to a select group of politically friendly state banks. The president would thus simultaneously circumvent his opponents and offer the nation an alternative banking system. The new banking structure had several potential advantages. It promised to work under the direct supervision of the executive branch, to forge direct institutional connections between the presidency and local centers of political power, and to secure broad political support against a revival of the national bank.

This plan faced formidable opposition from the Treasury Department, the Senate, and, most of all, from the Bank of the United States. Biddle responded to the removal of federal deposits with an abrupt and severe curtailment of loans. By squeezing the nation into a financial panic, Biddle hoped to turn public opinion against Jackson. The Senate followed suit with a formal censure of the president, denouncing his pretensions to independent action on the presumption of a direct mandate from the people.

The so-called Panic Session of Congress (1833–1834) posed the ultimate test of Jackson's resolve to forge a new regime. Success now hinged on consolidating the Democratic party in Congress and reaffirming its control over the national government. The president moved quickly to assign blame for the panic to the bank. Having destroyed Biddle's credibility, he was able by the spring of 1834 to solidify Democratic support in the House and to gain an endorsement of his actions (and implicitly, his authority to act) from that chamber. Then, undertaking a major grass-roots party-building effort in the midterm elections of 1834, Jackson and his political lieutenants were able to secure a loyal Democratic majority in the Senate. The struggle was over, and in a final acknowledgment of the legitimacy of the new order, the Democratic Senate expunged its censure of the president from the record.

But even as Congress was falling into line, the limitations of the president's achievement were manifesting themselves throughout the nation. Jackson had successfully repudiated the old governmental order, consolidated a new political party behind his policies, secured that party's control over the entire federal establishment, and redefined the position of the presidency in its relations with Congress, the courts, the states, and the electorate. The problem lay with his institutional alternative for reconstructing financial relations between state and society. From the outset, the state deposit system proved a dismal failure.

In truth, Jackson had latched onto the deposit banking scheme as much out of political necessity as principle. The president had been caught between his opponents' determination to save the bank and his supporters' need for a clear and attractive alternative to it. Opposition to Biddle and Clay merged with opposition to any national banking structure, and what might otherwise have been an interim experiment with state banking quickly became a political commitment. Unfortunately, the infusion of federal deposits into the pet state banks fueled a speculative boom and threatened a major financial collapse.

Hoping to stem this disaster, the Treasury Department began to choose banks of deposit less for their political soundness than for their financial health. Jackson threw his support behind a gradual conversion to hard money. In the end, however, the president was forced to accept the grim irony of his success as a regime builder. As Congress moved more solidly behind him, its members began to see for themselves the special political attractions of the state deposit system. With the passage of the Deposit Act of 1836, Congress expanded the number of state depositories and explicitly limited executive discretion in controlling them.[9]

Thus, although Jackson had reconstructed American government and politics, he merely substituted one irresponsible and uncontrollable financial system for another. Institutional ties between state and society emerged as the weak link in the new order. Jackson's chosen successor, Martin Van Buren, understood this all too well as he struggled to extricate the federal government from the state banks in the midst of the nation's first great depression.

Franklin D. Roosevelt

As a political personality, the moralistic, vindictive, and tortured Jackson stands in marked contrast to the pragmatic, engaging, and buoyant Franklin D. Roosevelt. Yet their initial triumphs over long-established ruling parties and the sustained popular enthusiasm that accompanied their victories propelled each into grappling with a similar set of leadership challenges. By late 1934 Roosevelt himself seemed to sense the parallels, writing to Vice President John Nance Garner, "The more I learn about Andy Jackson, the more I love him."[10]

The timing of this remark is noteworthy. In 1934 and 1935 Roosevelt's emergency program caused mounting discontent among the favored interests of the old order. Moreover, the president saw that the residual institutional bulwark of that order was capable of simply sweeping his programs aside. Like Jackson in 1832, Roosevelt was being challenged either to reconstruct the political and institutional foundations of the national government or to abandon the initiative he had sustained virtually without opposition in his early years of power.

The revival of the economy had been the keynote of Roosevelt's early program.[11] Although collectivist in approach and boldly assertive of a positive role for the federal government, the early policies of the New Deal did not present a broadside challenge to long-established political and economic interests. Roosevelt had adopted the role of a bipartisan national leader reaching out to all interests in a time of crisis. He carefully courted the southern Bourbons, who controlled the old Democratic party, and directly incorporated big business into the government's recovery program. But if Roosevelt's program did not ignore the interests attached to and supported by the governmental arrangements of the past, it did implicate those interests in a broader coalition. The New Deal had also bestowed legitimacy on the interests of organized labor, the poor, and the unemployed, leaving southern Bourbons and northern industrialists feeling threatened and increasingly insecure.

This sense of unease manifested itself politically in the summer of 1934 with the organization of the American Liberty League. Though the league mounted an aggressive assault on Roosevelt and the New Deal, Roosevelt's party received a resounding endorsement in the midterm elections, actually broadening the base of enthusiastic New Dealers in Congress. The congressional elections vividly demonstrated the futility of political opposition, but in the spring of 1935 a more potent adversary arose within the government itself. The

Supreme Court, keeper of the rules of governance for the old regime, handed down a series of anti-New Deal decisions. The most important of these nullified the centerpiece of Roosevelt's recovery program, the National Industrial Recovery Act.

With the American Liberty League clarifying the stakes of the New Deal departure and the Court pulling the rug out from under the cooperative approach to economic recovery, Roosevelt turned his administration toward structural reform. If he could no longer lead all interests toward economic recovery, he could still secure the interests of a great political majority within the new governmental order.

Roosevelt began the transition from national leader to regime builder with a considerable advantage over Jackson. He could restructure institutional relations between state and society simply by reaching out to the radical and irrepressibly zealous Seventy-fourth Congress (1935–1937) and offering it sorely needed coherence and direction. The result was a second round of New Deal legislation. The federal government extended new services and permanent institutional supports to organized labor, small business, the aged, the unemployed, and later, the rural poor. At the same time, the president revealed a new approach to big business and the affluent by pressing for tighter regulation and graduated taxation.[12]

The scope and vision of these achievements far surpassed the makeshift and flawed arrangements that Jackson had improvised to restructure institutional relations between state and society in the bank war. But Roosevelt's comparatively early and more thoroughgoing success on this score proved a dubious advantage in subsequent efforts to consolidate the new order. After his overwhelming reelection victory in 1936, Roosevelt pressed a series of consolidation initiatives. Like Jackson in his second term, he began with an effort to neutralize the remaining threat within the government.

Roosevelt's target, of course, was the Supreme Court. He was wise not to follow Jackson's example in the bank war by launching a direct ideological attack on the Court. After all, Roosevelt was challenging a constitutional branch of government and could hardly succeed in labeling that branch a threat to the survival of the republic. The president decided instead to kill his institutional opposition with kindness. He called for an increase in the size of the Court, ostensibly to ease the burden on the elder justices and to increase overall efficiency. Unfortunately, the real stakes of the contest never were made explicit, and the Chief Justice deflected the attack by simply denying the need for help. More importantly, the Court, unlike the bank, did not further exacerbate the situation. Instead, it reversed course in the middle of the battle and displayed a willingness to accept the policies of the second New Deal.

The Court's turnabout was a great victory for the new regime. It relegated to the irretrievable past the old strictures surrounding legitimate governmental activity that Roosevelt had been repudiating from the outset of his presidency. But in so doing, the justices eliminated even the implicit justification for Roosevelt's proposed judicial reforms. With the constituent services of the New Deal secure, Congress had little reason to challenge the integrity of the Court. Bound by his own inefficiency arguments, Roosevelt did not withdraw his proposal.

Although stalwart liberals stood by the president to the end, traditional Democratic conservatives deserted him. A bipartisan opposition took open ground against Roosevelt, defeated the "Court-packing" scheme, and divided the ranks of the New Deal coalition. It was a rebuke every bit as portentous as the formal censure of Jackson by the Senate.

With Roosevelt, as with Jackson, the third congressional election of his tenure called forth a major party-building initiative. Stung by his defeat, the president sought to reaffirm his hold over the Democratic party and to strengthen its liberal commitments. Ironically, this effort was handicapped by Roosevelt's early and sweeping successes. Unlike Jackson in 1834, Roosevelt in 1938 could not point to any immediate threat to his governing coalition. The liberal program was already in place. The Court had capitulated, and despite deep fissures manifested during the Court battle, the overwhelming Democratic majorities in Congress gave no indication of abandoning the New Deal. Even the southern delegations in Congress maintained majority support for Roosevelt's domestic reform initiatives.[13] Under these conditions, party building took on an aura of presidential self-indulgence. Although enormously important from the standpoint of future regime coherence, at the time it looked like heavy-handed, selective punishment of personal enemies. In this guise, it evoked little popular support, let alone enthusiasm.

The party-building initiative failed. Virtually all of the conservative Democrats targeted for defeat were reelected, and the Republicans showed a resurgence of strength. As two-party politics returned to the national scene, the awkward division within the majority party between the old southern conservatism and the new liberal orthodoxy became a permanent feature of the new regime.

Despite these setbacks, Roosevelt pressed forward with the business of consolidating a new order, and a final effort met with considerable success. In 1939 the president received congressional approval of a package of administrative reforms that promised to bolster the president's position vis-à-vis the other branches of government. Following the precepts of his Committee on Administrative Management, the president had asked for new executive offices to provide planning and direction for governmental operations. The Congress endorsed a modest version of the scheme, but while deflating Roosevelt's grand design, it clearly acknowledged the new governing demands presented by the large federal programs and permanent bureaucratic apparatus he had forged. The establishment of the Executive Office of the President closed the New Deal with a fitting symbol of the new state of affairs.[14]

Polk and Kennedy:
Reaffirmation and the Dilemmas of Interest Management

The administrations of Jackson and Roosevelt shared much in both the political conditions of leadership and the challenges undertaken. An initial upheaval, the ensuing political confusion, and the widespread support for a decisive break from the institutional strictures of the past framed America's quintessential regime-building presidencies. Opposition from the favored interests of the old order and their residual institutional supports eventually pushed these presidents from an original program to meet the immediate crisis at hand into structural reforms that promised to place institutional relations between state and society on an entirely new footing. After a second landslide election, Jackson and Roosevelt each moved to consolidate their new order by eliminating the institutional opposition and forging a more coherent base of party support. As the nation redivided politically, they secured a new ruling coalition, reset the political agenda, and institutionalized a new position of power for the presidency itself.

It is evident from a comparison of these performances that where Rooseveltian regime building was triumphant, that of Jackson faltered and vice versa: Roosevelt thoroughly reconstructed institutional relations between state and society, but his performance as a party builder was weak and his achievement flawed. Jackson left institutional relations between state and society in a dangerous disarray, but his performance and achievement as a party builder remain unparalleled. The more important point lies, however, beyond these comparisons. It is that few presidents can engage in a wholesale political repudiation of the past and address the political system at the level of institutional reconstruction and party building. Most presidents must use their skills and resources—however extensive these may be—to work within the already established governmental order.

The successful regime builder leaves in his wake a more constricted universe for political leadership. To his partisan successors, in particular, he leaves the difficult task of keeping faith with a ruling coalition. In an established regime, the majority party president comes to power as a representative of the dominant political alliance and is expected to offer a representative's service in delegate style. Commitments of ideology and interest are all too clear, and the fusion of national political legitimacy with established power relationships argues against any attempt to tinker with the basics of government and politics. The leader is challenged, not to break down the old order and forge a new one, but to complete the unfinished business, adapt the agenda to changing times, and defuse the potentially explosive choices among competing obligations. He is partner to a highly structured regime politics, and, to keep the partnership working, he must sustain a preemptive control over impending disruptions. The political problem is to get innovation without repudiation and to present creativity as a vindication of orthodoxy.

The presidencies of James K. Polk and John F. Kennedy clearly illustrate the problems and prospects of leadership that is circumscribed by the challenge of managing an established coalition. Both men came to the presidency after an interval of opposition party control and divided government. The intervening years had seen some significant changes in the tenor of public policy, but there had been no systemic transformations of government and politics. Ushering in a second era of majority party government, Polk and Kennedy promised at once to reaffirm the commitments and revitalize the program of the dominant regime.

Neither Polk nor Kennedy could claim the leadership of any major party faction. Indeed, their credibility as regime managers rested largely on their second-rank status in regular party circles. Each schooled himself in the task of allaying mutual suspicions among the great centers of party strength. Their nominations to the presidency were the result of skillful dancing around the conflicts that divided the party. What they lacked in deep political loyalties, they made up for with their freedom to cultivate widespread support.

Once the office was attained, the challenge of interest management was magnified. Each of these presidents had accepted one especially virulent bit of orthodoxy that claimed majority support within the party as a necessary part of the new regime agenda. Their ability to endorse their party's most divisive enthusiasm (Texas annexation, civil rights) without losing a broad base of credibility within it was fitting testimony to their early education in the art of aggressive maintenance of the regime party. But their mediating skills did not alter the fact that each came into office with a clear commitment to act on an issue which had long threatened to split the party apart. In addition, Polk and Kennedy each won astonishingly close elections. There was no clear mandate for action, no discernible tide of national discontent, no mass rejection of what had gone before. The hairbreadth Democratic victories of 1844 and 1960 suggested that the opposition could continue to make a serious claim to the presidency and reinforced an already highly developed sense of executive dependence on all parts of the party coalition. With maintenance at a premium and an ideological rupture within the ranks at hand, Polk and Kennedy carried the full weight of the leadership dilemma that confronts the majority party president of an established regime.

James K. Polk

For the Democratic party of 1844, the long-festering issue was the annexation of Texas, with its attendant implication of a war of aggression for the expansion of slave territory.[15] Andrew Jackson, an ardent nationalist with a passion for annexation, had steered clear of any definitive action on Texas during the last years of his presidency. He had just consolidated the Democratic party, and the threat of dividing it anew along sectional lines argued for a passive posture of merely anticipating the inevitable.[16]

Democratic loyalists followed Jackson's lead until 1843, when the partyless "mongrel president," John Tyler, desperate to build an independent political base of support for himself, latched onto the annexation issue and presented a formal proposal on the subject to Congress. With Texas finally pushed to the forefront, expansionist fever heated up in the South and the West and antislavery agitation accelerated in the North.

Jackson's political nightmare became a reality on the eve of his party's nominating convention in 1844. Martin Van Buren, Jackson's successor to the presidency in 1837 and still the nominal head of the Democracy, risked an all but certain nomination by coming out against the *immediate* annexation of Texas. Despite its carefully orthodox wording, the New Yorker's pronouncement roused a formidable opposition in the southern and western wings of the party and left the convention deadlocked through eight ballots. With Van Buren holding a large bloc of delegates but unable to get the leaders of the South and West to relinquish the necessary two-thirds majority, it became clear that only a "new man" could save the party from disaster. That man had to be firm on immediate annexation without being openly opposed to Van Buren. On the ninth ballot, James Knox Polk became the Democratic nominee.

Polk was well aware of the circumstances of his nomination. As leader of the Democratic party in Tennessee and stalwart friend of Andrew Jackson, he had unimpeachable credentials as an orthodox party regular. He had served loyally as floor leader of the House during the critical days of the bank war and had gone on to win his state's governorship. But after Polk tried and failed to gain his party's vice-presidential nomination in 1840, his political career fell on hard times.

Calculating his strategy for a political comeback in 1844, Polk made full use of his second-rank standing in high party circles. Again he posed as the perfect vice-presidential candidate and cultivated his ties to Van Buren. Knowing that this time Van Buren's nomination would be difficult, Polk also understood the special advantages of being a Texas enthusiast with Van Buren connections. As soon as that calculation paid off, Polk ventured another. In accepting the presidential nomination, he pledged that, if elected, he would not seek a second term. Although he thus declared himself a lame duck even before he was elected, Polk reckoned he would not serve any time in office at all unless the frustrated party giants in all sections of the nation expended every last ounce of energy for the campaign—an effort they might not make if it meant foreclosing their own prospects for eight years.[17]

The one-term declaration was a bid for party unity and a pledge of party maintenance. But the divisions that were exposed at the convention of 1844 and their uncertain resolution in a Texas platform and a dark-horse nomination suggested that the party was likely to chew itself up under a passive caretaker presidency. If Polk were to avoid a disastrous schism in the party of Jackson, he would have to order, balance, and service the major contending interests in turn. He would have to enlist each contingent within the party in support of the policy interests of all the others. Polk submerged himself in a high-risk strategy of aggressive maintenance in which the goal was to satisfy each faction of his party enough to keep the whole from falling apart. The scheme was at once pragmatic and holistic, hardheaded and fantastic. The most startling thing of all is how well it worked.

The president opened his administration (appropriately enough) with a declaration that he would "know no divisions of the Democratic party." He promised "equal and exact justice to every portion."[18] His first action indicated, however, that the going would be rough. Scrutinizing the cabinet selection process, Van Buren (whose electoral efforts had put Polk over the top) judged that his interests in New York had not been sufficiently recognized. The frustrated ex-president presumed a determination on the new president's part to turn the party toward the slave South. Polk tried to appease Van Buren with other patronage offers, but relations between them did not improve. From the outset Van Buren's loyalty was laden with suspicion.

The outcry over patronage suggests that any action the president took would cloud Polk's orthodoxy in charges of betrayal. Van Buren's accusations were but the first in an incessant barrage of such charges.[19] But Polk was not powerless in the face of disaffection. He had an irresistible agenda for party government to bolster his precarious political position.

Polk's program elaborated the theme of equal justice for all coalition interests. On the domestic side, he reached out to the South with support for a lower tariff, to the Northwest with support for land price reform, to the Northeast by endorsing a warehouse storage system advantageous to import merchants, and to the old Jackson radicals with a commitment to a return to hard money and a reinstatement of the independent treasury. (Van Buren had dedicated his entire administration to establishing the independent treasury as a solution to Jackson's banking dilemma, but his work had been undermined in the intervening four years.) It was in foreign affairs, however, that the president placed the highest hopes for his administration. Superimposed on his carefully balanced program of party service in the domestic arena was a missionary embrace of the United States' "Manifest Destiny." Reaching out to the South, Polk promised to annex Texas; to the Northwest, he promised Oregon; and to bind the whole nation together, he made a secret promise to himself to acquire California. In all, the president would complete the orthodox Jacksonian program of party services and fuse popular passions in an irresistible jingoistic campaign to extend the Jacksonian Republic across the continent.

Driven by the dual imperatives of maintenance and leadership, Polk sought to transform the nation without changing its politics. Party loyalty was the key to success, but it would take more than just a series of favorable party votes to make Polk's strategy of aggressive maintenance work. The sequence, pace, and symbolism of Polk's initiatives had to be assiduously controlled and coordinated with difficult foreign negotiations so that the explosive moral issues inherent in the program would not enter the debate. Sectional paranoia and ideological heresies had to be held in constant check. Mutual self-interest had to remain at the forefront so that reciprocal party obligations could be reinforced. Polk's program was much more than a laundry list of party commitments. If he did not get everything he promised in the order he promised it, he risked a major political rupture that would threaten whatever he did achieve. Here, at the level of executive management and interest control, the president faltered.

After the patronage tiff with Van Buren demonstrated Polk's problems with the eastern radicals, disaffection over the Oregon boundary settlement exposed his difficulties in striking an agreeable balance between western and southern expansionists. The president moved forward immediately and simultaneously on his promises to acquire Oregon and Texas. In each case he pressed an aggressive, indeed belligerent, border claim. He demanded "all of Oregon" (extending north to the 54∞ 40' parallel) from Great Britain and "Greater Texas" (extending south of the Nueces River to the Rio Grande) from Mexico.

The pledge to get "all of Oregon" unleashed a tidal wave of popular enthusiasm in the Northwest. But Great Britain refused to play according to the presidential plan, and a potent peace movement spread across the South and the East out of fear of impending war over the Oregon boundary. Polk used the belligerence of the "54∞ 40' or fight" faction to counter the peace movement and to prod the British into coming to terms, but he knew the risks of war on that front. An impending war with Mexico over the Texas boundary promised to yield California in short order, but a war with both Mexico and Great Britain promised disaster.

When the British finally agreed to settle the Oregon boundary at the forty-ninth parallel, Polk accepted the compromise. Then, after an appropriate display of Mexican aggression on the Texas border, he asked Congress for a declaration of war on Mexico. Abandoned, the 54∞ 40' men turned on the president, mercilessly accusing him of selling out to the South and picking on defenseless Mexico instead of standing honorably against the British. A huge part of the Oregon territory had been added to the Union, but a vociferous bloc of westerners now joined the Van Burenites in judging the president deceptive and dangerously prosouthern. Polk had miscalculated both British determination and western pride. His accomplishment deviated from the pace and scope of his grand design and in so doing undermined the delicate party balance.

Polk's designs were further complicated by the effects of wartime sensibilities on his carefully balanced legislative program. The independent treasury and warehouse storage bills were enacted easily, but old matters of principle and simple matters of interest were not enough to calm agitated eastern Democrats. They demanded the president's assurance that he was not involved in a war of conquest in the Southwest. Polk responded with an evasive definition of war aims. There was little else he could do to ease suspicions.

More portentous still was the influence of the tariff initiative on wartime politics. Polk had to court northwestern Democrats to make up for expected eastern defections on a vote for a major downward revision of rates. To do so, he not only used land price reform as an incentive to end debate but also withheld his objections to a legislative initiative brewing among representatives of the South and West to develop the Mississippi River system. The northwesterners swallowed their pride over Oregon in hopeful expectation and threw their support behind the tariff bill.

After the bill was enacted, Polk vetoed the internal improvement bill. It had never been a part of his program and was an offense to Jacksonian orthodoxy. But the president's maneuverings were an offense to the West and all but eclipsed the veto's stalwart affirmation of Jacksonian principles. To make matters worse, the land bill failed. The president made good his pledge to press the measure, but he could not secure enactment. Burned three times after offering loyal support to southern interests, the northwesterners were no longer willing to heed the counsels of mutual restraint. The president's effort to bring the war to a quick and triumphant conclusion provided them with their opportunity to strike back.

The war with Mexico was in fact only a few months old, but that was already too long for the president and his party. To speed the advent of peace, Polk decided to ask Congress for a $2 million appropriation to settle the Texas boundary dispute and to pay "for any concessions which may be made by Mexico." This open offer of money for land was the first clear indication that the United States was engaged in—perhaps had consciously provoked—a war of conquest in the Southwest. With it, the latent issue of 1844 manifested itself with a vengeance. Northern Democrats, faced with growing antislavery agitation at home, saw unequal treatment in the administration's handling of matters of interest, intolerable duplicity in presidential action, and an insufferable southern bias in national policy. They were ready to take their stand on matters of principle.

It is ironic that Polk's implicit acknowledgment of the drive for California, with its promise of fulfilling the nationalistic continental vision, would fan the fires of sectional conflict. Surely he had intended just the opposite. The president was, in fact, correct in calculating that no section of the party would oppose the great national passion for expansion to the Pacific. But he simply could not curb party disaffection in the East, and unfulfilled expectations fueled dissatisfaction in the West. He was thus left to watch in dismay as the malcontents joined forces to take their revenge on the South.

Northern Democrats loyally offered to support the president's effort to buy peace and land, but added a demand that slavery be prohibited from entering any of the territory that might thus be acquired. This condition was known as the "Wilmot Proviso" after Democrat David Wilmot, a Van Buren enthusiast from western Pennsylvania. Once introduced, it splintered the party along the dreaded sectional cleavage. An appropriations bill with the proviso was passed in the House, but it failed in the Senate when an effort to remove the proviso was successfully filibustered. Now it was Polk's turn to be bitter. In a grim confession of the failure of his grand design, he claimed he could not comprehend "what connection slavery had with making peace with Mexico."[20]

Ultimately, Polk got his peace, and with it he added California and the greater Southwest to the Union. He also delivered on tariff revision, the independent treasury, the warehouse storage system, Oregon, and Texas. Interest management by Polk had extorted a monumental program of party service from established sources of power in remarkably short order. Indeed, except for the conclusion of peace with Mexico, everything had been put in place between the spring of 1845 and the summer of 1846. But the Jacksonian party had ruptured under the pressures of enacting this most orthodox of party programs. Polk's monument to Jacksonian nationalism proved a breeding ground for sectional heresy, and his golden age of policy achievement was undermined at its political foundations.

The failure of interest management to serve the dual goals of political maintenance and policy achievement manifested itself in political disaster for the Democratic party. By the fall of 1846 the New York party was divided into two irreconcilable camps, with Van Buren leading the radicals, who were in favor of the Wilmot Proviso and opposed to the administration. Although Polk maintained an official stance of neutrality toward the schism, party regulars rallied behind Lewis Cass, a westerner opposed to the proviso. Cass's alternative—"popular" or "squatter" sovereignty in the territories—promised to hold together the larger portion of the majority party by absolving the federal government of any role in resolving the questions of slavery extension and regional balance that were raised by Polk's transformation of the nation. When the Democrats nominated Cass in 1848, the Van Buren delegation bolted the convention. Joining "Conscience Whigs" and "Liberty party" men, they formed the Free Soil party, dedicated it to the principles of the Wilmot Proviso, and nominated Van Buren as their presidential candidate.[21]

Polk abandoned his studied neutrality after the convention. In the waning months of his administration he withdrew administration favors from Free Soil sympathizers and threw his support behind the party regulars.[22] But it was Van Buren who had the last word. Four years after putting personal defeat aside, loyally supporting the party, and electing Polk, he emerged as the leader of the "heretics" and defeated Cass.

John F. Kennedy

John F. Kennedy had every intention of spending eight years in the White House, but this ambition only compounded the leadership dilemma inherent in his initial political situation. Kennedy's presidential campaign harkened back to Rooseveltian images of direction and energy in government. It stigmatized Republican rule as a lethargic, aimless muddle, and roused the people with a promise to "get the country moving again."

At the same time, however, the party of Roosevelt maintained its awkward division between northern liberals and southern conservatives. The candidate assiduously courted both wings, and the narrowness of his victory reinforced his debts to each. The president's prospects for eight years in the White House seemed to hinge on his ability to vindicate, in his first four, the promise of vigorous national leadership without undermining the established foundations of national political power.

Kennedy's "New Frontier" was eminently suited to these demands for aggressive maintenance. It looked outward toward placing a man on the moon and protecting the free world from Communist aggression. It looked inward toward pragmatic adaptations and selected adjustments of the New Deal consensus. Leadership in the international arena would bring the nation together behind bold demonstrations of American power and determination. In the domestic arena it would contain party conflict through presidential management and executive-controlled initiatives.

Kennedy's leadership design had more in common with Polk's pursuits than frontier imagery. Both presidents gave primacy to foreign enthusiasms and hoped the nation would do the same. Facing a politically divided people and a fractionated party, they both set out to tap the unifying potential of America's missionary stance in the world and to rivet national attention on aggressive (even provocative) international adventures. By so doing, they claimed the high ground as men of truly national vision. At the same time, each countered deepening conflicts of principle in the ruling coalition with an attempt to balance interests. They were engaged in a constant struggle to mute the passions that divided their supporters and to stem coalition disaffection. Resisting the notion of irreconcilable differences within the ranks, Polk and Kennedy held out their support to all interests and demanded in return the acquiescence of each in executive determination of the range, substance, and timing of policy initiatives.

Of course, there are some notable differences in the way these presidents approached regime management. Kennedy, not unaware of Polk's failings, avoided Polk's tactics.[23] Polk had gone after as much as possible as quickly as possible for as many as possible in the hope that conflicts among interests could be submerged through the ordered satisfaction of each. Kennedy seemed to feel that conflicts could be avoided best by refraining from unnecessarily divisive action. He was more circumspect in his choice of initiatives and more cautious in their pursuit. Interest balance translated into legislative restraint, and aggressive maintenance became contained advocacy. Kennedy's "politics of expectation" kept fulfillment of the liberal agenda at the level of anticipation.[24]

At the heart of Kennedy's political dilemma was the long-festering issue of civil rights for black Americans. Roosevelt had seen the fight for civil rights coming, but he refused to make it his own, fearing the devastating effect it would have on the precarious sectional balance in his newly established party coalition.[25] Harry S. Truman had seen the fight break out and temporarily rupture the party in 1948.[26] His response was a balance of executive amelioration and legislative caution. When the Republicans made gains in southern cities during the 1950s, the prudent course Truman had outlined appeared more persuasive than ever. But by 1961 black migration into northern cities, Supreme Court support for civil rights demands, and an ever more aggressive civil rights movement in the South had made it increasingly difficult for a Democratic president to resist a more definitive commitment.

In his early campaign for the presidential nomination, Kennedy developed a posture of inoffensive support on civil rights.[27] While keeping himself abreast of the liberal position, he held back from leadership and avoided pressing the cause on southern conservatives. Such maneuvering became considerably more difficult at the party convention of 1960. The liberal-controlled platform committee presented a civil rights plank that all but committed the nominee to take the offensive. It pledged presidential leadership on behalf of new legislation, vigorous enforcement of existing laws, and reforms in congressional procedures to remove impediments to such action. Adding insult to injury, the plank lent party sanction to the civil rights demonstrations that had been accelerating throughout the South.

Although the Democratic platform tied Kennedy to the cause that had ruptured the party in 1948, it did not dampen his determination to hold on to the

South. Once nominated, he reached out to the offended region and identified himself with more traditional Democratic strategies. Indeed, by offering the vice-presidential nomination to Lyndon B. Johnson, he risked a serious offense to the left. Johnson was not only the South's first choice and Kennedy's chief rival for the presidential nomination, but his national reputation was punctuated by conspicuous efforts on behalf of ameliorative civil rights action in the Senate. Kennedy himself seems to have been a bit surprised by Johnson's acceptance of second place. The liberals were disheartened.[28] Together, however, Kennedy and Johnson made a formidable team of regime managers. Riding the horns of their party's dilemma, they balanced the boldest Democratic commitment ever on the side of civil rights with a determination not to lose the support of its most passionate opponents. Their narrow victory owed as much to those who were promised a new level of action as to those who were promised continued moderation.

The president's inaugural and State of the Union addresses directed national attention to imminent international dangers and America's world responsibilities. Civil rights received only passing mention. Stressing the need for containment in the international arena, these speeches also reflected the president's commitment to containment in the domestic sphere. In the months before the inauguration Kennedy had decided to keep civil rights off his legislative agenda. Instead, he would prod Congress along on other liberal issues, such as minimum wage, housing, area redevelopment, aid to education, mass transit, and health care. The plan was not difficult to rationalize. If on the one hand the president pressed for civil rights legislation and failed, his entire legislative program would be placed in jeopardy, and executive efforts on behalf of blacks would be subject to even closer scrutiny. If on the other he withheld the civil rights issue from Congress, southerners might show their appreciation for the president's circumspection. His other measures might have a better chance for enactment, and blacks would reap the benefits of this selected expansion of the liberal legislation as well as the benefits of Kennedy's executive-controlled civil rights initiatives.

Accordingly, Kennedy avoided personal involvement in a preinaugural fight in the Senate over the liberalization of the rules of debate. The effort failed. He did lend his support to a liberal attempt to expand the House Rules Committee, but this was a prerequisite to House action on Kennedy's chosen legislative program. The rules effort succeeded, but the new committee members gave no indication of an impending civil rights offensive.[29]

Feelings of resentment and betrayal among civil rights leaders inevitably followed the decision to forgo the bold legislative actions suggested in the party platform. But by giving substance to the promise of aggressive executive action, the president sought to allay this resentment and to persuasively demonstrate a new level of federal commitment. The administration moved forward on several fronts.

The centerpiece of the administration's strategy was to use the Justice Department to promote and protect voter registration drives among southern blacks. This promised to give blacks the power to secure their rights and also to minimize the electoral costs of any further Democratic defections among southern whites. On other fronts, the president liberalized the old Civil Rights Commission and created the Committee on Equal Employment Opportunity to investigate job discrimination. When Congress moved to eliminate the poll tax, the president lent his support. When demonstrations threatened to disrupt southern transportation terminals, Attorney General Robert F. Kennedy enlisted the cooperation of the Interstate Commerce Commission in desegregating the facilities. When black applicant James Meredith asserted his right to enroll at the University of Mississippi, the administration responded with protection and crisis mediation. Even more visibly, the president appointed a record number of blacks to high civil service positions.

Kennedy pressed executive action on behalf of civil rights with more vigor and greater effect than any of his predecessors. Still, civil rights enthusiasts were left with unfulfilled hopes and mounting suspicions. Ever mindful of the political imperatives of containing advocacy, the president was trying not only to serve the interests of blacks but also to manage those interests and serve the interests of civil rights opponents. Indeed, there seemed to be a deceptive qualification in each display of principle. For example, the president's patronage policies brought blacks into positions of influence in government, but they also brought new segregationist federal judges to the South. The Federal Bureau of Investigation (FBI) that provided support for the voter registration drive also tapped the phone of civil rights activist Martin Luther King, Jr. The poll tax was eliminated with administration support, but the administration backed away from a contest over literacy tests. Kennedy liberalized the Civil Rights Commission, but he refused to endorse its controversial report, which recommended withholding federal funds from states that violated the Constitution. While he encouraged the desegregation of interstate transportation terminals, the president put off action on a key campaign pledge to promote the desegregation of housing by executive order. (When the housing order was finally issued, it adopted the narrowest possible application and was not made retroactive.) And although the administration ultimately saw to the integration of the University of Mississippi, the U.S. attorney general first tried to find some way to allow the racist governor of the state to save face.

Executive management allowed Kennedy to juggle mutually contradictory expectations for two years. But as an exercise in forestalling a schism within the ranks, the administration's efforts to control advocacy and to balance interests ultimately satisfied no one and offered no real hope of resolving the issue at hand. The weaknesses in the president's position became more and more apparent early in 1963 as civil rights leaders pressed ahead with their own timetable for action.

Although civil rights leaders clearly needed the president's support, they steadfastly refused to compromise their demands or to relinquish de facto control over their movement to presidential management. The president and his brother became agitated when movement leaders contended that the administration was not doing all that it could for blacks. Civil rights groups, in turn, were outraged by the administration's implication that the movement comprised an interest like any other and that its claims could be pragmatically "balanced" against those of racism and bigotry in a purely political calculus. Independent action had already blurred the line between contained advocacy and reactive accommodation in the administration's response to the movement. Continued independence and intensified action promised to limit the president's latitude still further and to force him to shift his course from interest balancing to moral choice.

The first sign of a shift came on February 28, 1963. After a season of rising criticism of presidential tokenism, embarrassing civil rights advocacy by liberal Republicans in Congress, and portentous planning for spring demonstrations in the most racially sensitive parts of the South, the president recommended some mild civil rights measures to Congress. His message acknowledged that civil rights was indeed a moral issue and indicated that it no longer could be treated simply as another interest. But this shift was one of words more than action. Kennedy did not follow up his legislative request in any significant way.

Although civil rights agitation clearly was spilling over the banks of presidential containment, the prospect for passing civil rights legislation in Congress had improved little since Kennedy had taken office. His circumspect attitude toward civil rights matters during the first two years of his administration had succeeded in winning only modest support from southern Democrats for his other social and economic measures. On the one hand, several of the administration's most important victories—minimum wage, housing, and area rede-velopment legislation—clearly demonstrated the significance of southern sup-port. On the other, the president had already seen southern Democrats defect in droves to defeat his proposed Department of Urban Affairs, presumably be-cause the first department head was to be black.[30] If Kennedy could no longer hope to contain the civil rights issue, he still faced the problem of containing the political damage that would inevitably come from spearheading legislative action.

Kennedy's approach to this problem was to press legislation as an irresistible counsel of moderation. This meant holding back still longer, waiting for the ex-treme positions to manifest themselves fully, then offering real change as the only prudent course available. He did not have to wait long. In 1963 a wave of spring civil rights demonstrations that began in Birmingham, Alabama, and extended throughout the South brought mass arrests and ugly displays of police brutality to the center of public attention. Capitalizing on the specter of social disintegration, the administration argued that a new legislative initiative was essential to the restoration of order and sought bipartisan support for it on this basis. Congressional Republicans were enlisted with the argument that the only way to get the protesters off the streets was to provide them with new legal remedies in the courts. Kennedy then seized an opportunity to isolate the radical right. On the evening of the day Gov. George Wallace made his sym-bolic gesture in defiance of federal authority at the University of Alabama (physically barring the entrance of a prospective black student), the president gave a hastily prepared but impassioned television address on the need for new civil rights legislation.

In late June the administration sent its new legislative proposal to Congress. The bill went far beyond the mild measures offered in February. It contained significantly expanded voting rights protections and for the first time called for federal protection to enforce school desegregation and to guarantee equal access to public facilities. But even with this full bow to liberal commitments, the struggle for containment continued. The administration tried to counter the zeal of urban Democrats by searching for compromises that would hold a bipartisan coalition of civil rights support. When civil rights leaders planned a march on Washington in the midst of the legislative battle, the president tried without success to dissuade them.

Containing the zeal of the left was the least of the president's problems. Kennedy had struggled continually to moderate his party's liberal commitments and thus avoid a rupture on the right. With a landmark piece of civil rights legislation inching its way through Congress, the president now turned to face the dreaded party schism. His popularity had plummeted in the South. George Wallace was contemplating a national campaign to challenge liberal control of the Democratic party, and an ugly white backlash in the North made the prospects for such a campaign brighter than ever. Conservative reaction, party schism, and the need to hold a base in the South were foremost in the president's thinking as he embarked on his fateful trip to Texas in November 1963.

Pierce and Carter: Disjunction and the Struggle for Credibility

For Polk and Kennedy, leadership was circumscribed by a political test of aggressive maintenance and the corresponding dilemmas of interest management. With a preemptive assertion of executive control, each attempted to orchestrate a course and pace for regime development that would change the nation without changing its politics. Their governing strategies involved them in convoluted conflict manipulations that were calculated to reconcile divergent coalition interests, stave off a political rupture, and move forward on outstanding regime commitments. Grounded in established power, leadership cast a dark cloud of duplicity over its greatest achievements.

Indeed, it would be difficult to choose the greater of these two presidential performances. Polk was able to deliver on an impressive array of policy promises, but his success was premised on excluding from the political arena the basic moral issue raised by these policies. Kennedy delivered little in the way of outstanding policy, but he ultimately acknowledged the great moral choice he confronted and he made a moral decision of enormous national significance. These differences notwithstanding, Polk and Kennedy dealt with the unraveling of interest management in a similar way. Executive control and a promise of delivering significant policy support to all the interests of the majority party gave way within two years to an effort to limit the effects of an open rupture. When interest management could no longer stave off disaffection and hold the old coalition together, these presidents took their stand with the larger part and tried to isolate the heretics.

The irony in these performances is that, although upholding their respective regime commitments and affirming their party orthodoxies, Polk and Kennedy raised serious questions about the future terms of regime survival and thus left orthodoxy itself politically insecure. Because Polk's nationalism and Kennedy's liberalism ultimately came at the expense of the old majority coalition, a new appeal to the political interests of the nation seemed imperative. In vindicating orthodoxy, Polk and Kennedy set in motion a pivotal turn toward sectarianism in regime development.

For the Jacksonian Democrats, the turn toward sectarianism grew out of a political defeat. The election of 1848 exposed the weaknesses of stalwart Jacksonian nationalism and spurred party managers to overcome the political damage wrought by sectional divisiveness. In 1850 Democratic votes secured passage of a bipartisan legislative package designed to smooth the disruptions wrought by the Polk administration.[31] This incongruous series of measures, collectively labeled the "Compromise of 1850," repackaged moderation in a way that many hoped would isolate the extremists and lead to the creation of a new Union party. But the dream of a Union party failed to spark widespread interest, and Democratic managers grasped the sectarian alternative. Using the compromise as a point of departure, they set out to reassemble their broken coalition. While supporting governmental policies that were designed to silence ideological conflict, they renewed a partnership in power with interests at the ideological extremes.[32]

For the New Deal regime, the turn came on the heels of a great electoral victory. Running against a Republican extremist, Lyndon B. Johnson swept the nation. But the disaffection stemming from the Kennedy administration was clearly visible: southern Democrat Johnson lost five states in his own region to the Republican outlier. In 1965 and 1966 Johnson tried to fuse a new consensus with policies that ranged across the extremes of ideology and interest. He dreamed of superseding the New Deal with a Great Society, but his vast expansion of services to interests added more to governmental fragmentation than to regime coherence. He also hoped to supplant the old Democratic party with a "party for all Americans," but his extension of regime commitments did more to scatter political loyalties than to unify them.[33]

By the time of the next incarnation of majority party government (1852 and 1976, respectively), the challenge of presidential leadership had shifted categorically once again. By 1852 the nationalism of Jackson had degenerated into a patchwork of suspect compromises sitting atop a seething sectional division. By 1976 the liberalism of Roosevelt had become a grab bag of special interest services all too vulnerable to political charges of burdening a troubled economy with bureaucratic overhead. Expedience eclipsed enthusiasm in the bond between the regime and the nation. Supporters of orthodoxy were placed on the defensive. The energies that once came from advancing great national purposes had dissipated. A rule of myopic sects defied the very notion of governmental authority.

Expedience also eclipsed enthusiasm in the bond between the majority party and its president. Franklin Pierce and Jimmy Carter each took the term *dark horse* to new depths of obscurity. Each was a minor local figure, far removed from the centers of party strength and interest. Indeed, each hailed from the region of greatest erosion in majority party support. Pierce, a New Hampshire attorney who had retired from the Senate almost a decade before, was called to head the Democratic ticket in 1852 after forty-eight convention ballots failed to yield a consensus on anyone who might have been expected to actually lead the party. His appeal (if it may be so called) within regular party circles lay first in his uniquely inoffensive availability and, second, in his potential to bring northeastern Free Soil Democrats back to the standard they had so recently branded as proslavery. Carter, a former governor of Georgia, was chosen to head the Democratic ticket in 1976 after mounting a broadside assault on the national political establishment. To say he appealed to regular party circles would be to mistake the nature of his campaign and to exaggerate the coherence of the Democratic organization at that time. Still, Carter offered the Democrats a candidate untainted by two decades of divisive national politics, and one capable of bringing the South back to the party of liberalism.

The successful reassembling of broken coalitions left Pierce and Carter to ponder the peculiar challenge of leading an enervated regime. These presidents engaged the political system at a step removed from a claim to managing coalition interests and orchestrating agenda fulfillment. Tenuously attached to a governmental establishment that itself appeared dangerously out of step with the most pressing problems of the day, their leadership turned on a question so narrow that it is really prerequisite to leadership—that of their own credibility. Despite determined efforts to establish trustworthiness, neither Pierce nor Carter could reconcile his own awkward position in the old order with the awkward position of the old order in the nation at large. Caught between the incessant demands of regime interests and the bankruptcy of the assumptions about the government and the nation that had supported those interests in the past, neither could find secure ground on which to make a stand and limit the political unraveling that comes with executive action. What began in expedience simply dissolved into irrelevance.

Franklin Pierce

In 1852 Franklin Pierce carried twenty-seven of the thirty-one states for a hefty 250 out of 296 electoral votes.[34] In the process, the Democratic party strengthened its hold over both houses of Congress. Still, the Pierce landslide was more apparent than real, and the election was anything but a mandate for action. As a presidential candidate, Pierce had merely endorsed the work of a bipartisan group of Senate moderates. His campaign had been confined to a simple declaration of support for the Compromise of 1850 and a pledge to resist any further agitation on slavery, the issue that underlay all other national concerns. The Pierce campaign was nothing if not a dutiful bow to senatorial authority and moderate political opinion.

It is possible that the new president might have enhanced his position at the start of his term by taking a second bow to the center and placing the largesse of his office at the disposal of the Senate moderates. But other aspects of the election argued against this strategy. Pierce actually had received less than 51 percent of the popular vote. He had won the presidency, not because the moderate center of national opinion had rallied to his standard but because the party managers working in the field had reassembled support at the extremes of Democratic party opinion. To the extremists, the Compromise of 1850 was a cause for suspicion rather than satisfaction; it was a matter of reluctant acquiescence rather than loyal support.

Pierce was sensitive to the precariousness of his victory but thought the logic of his situation was fairly clear. He believed the election of 1848 had shown it was not enough for the Democratic party to stand with the moderates and let the extremes go their own way and that the narrow victory of 1852 amply demonstrated the electoral imperative of consolidating party loyalties across the spectrum of party opinion. He was gratified by the election's renewed display of party loyalty—however reluctantly given—and he found farfetched and unimpressive the possibility that the centrists of both parties might join him on independent ground in a kind of national coalition government. He therefore decided to reach out to the old party coalition in an effort to heal the wounds of 1848 once and for all.

In a bold bid for leadership, Pierce held himself aloof from the moderate senators and set out to rebuild the political machinery of Jacksonian government under presidential auspices. As the mastermind of a party restoration, he hoped to gain respectability in his dealings with Congress, to take charge of national affairs, and ultimately—in 1856—to lay claim to the mantle of Andrew Jackson. The basic problem with this plan for establishing a credible leadership posture was that no interest of any significance depended on the president's success. Pierce had exhausted his party's national strength and legitimacy simply by letting the various party leaders elect him. These leaders had no stake in following their own creation and no intention of suspending their mutual suspicions in order to enhance the president's position. Pierce quickly discovered that his claim to the office of Andrew Jackson had no political foundation and that by asserting his independence at the outset, he had robbed the alternative strategy—a bow to senatorial power—of any possible advantage.

As for political vision, Pierce's goal of resuscitating the old party machinery was ideologically and programmatically vacuous. It was conceived as a purely mechanical exercise in repairing and perfecting the regime's core institutional apparatus and thereby restoring its operational vitality. There was no reference to any of the substantive concerns that had caused the vitality of the party apparatus to dissipate in the first place. Those concerns were simply to be forgotten. Pierce recalled Polk's dictum of "equal and exact justice" for every portion of the party but neglected the wide-ranging appeal to unfinished party business that had driven Polk's administration. He held up to the nation the vision of a political machine restored and purged of all political content.[35]

The rapid unraveling of the Pierce administration began with the president's initial offer to forget the Free Soil heresy of 1848 and provide all party factions in the North their due measure of presidential favor for support given in 1852. Much to the president's dismay, many of the New York Democrats who had remained loyal in 1848 refused to forgive the heretics and share the bounty. The New York party disintegrated at a touch, and in 1853 the Whigs swept the state elections.

Within months of Pierce's inauguration, then, the president's strategy for establishing his credibility as a leader was in a shambles. His key appointment to the collectorship of the Port of New York had yet to be confirmed by the Senate, and if the party leaders withheld their endorsement (a prospect that Pierce's early standoffishness and the New York electoral debacle made all too real), the rebuke to the fledgling administration would be devastating. Pierce was at the mercy of the Senate. Worse, he had placed the Senate at the mercy of the radical states' rights advocates of the South. This small but potent faction of southern senators felt shortchanged by the distribution of patronage in their own region and resolved to use the president's appeal for the restoration of Free Soilers as a basis for their revenge. The administration's distribution of rewards in the North, they said, represented a heightened level of commitment to the Free Soil element, and they challenged their more moderate southern cohorts to extract an equal commitment to their region as well.

The radical southerners found their opportunity in Illinois senator Stephen Douglas's bill to organize the Nebraska Territory. Douglas pushed the Nebraska bill because it would open a transcontinental railroad route through the center of his own political base. His bill followed the orthodox party posture, a stance confirmed in the Compromise of 1850, stipulating that the new territory would be organized without reference to slavery and that the people of the territory would decide the issue. Southerners who had ostensibly accepted this formula for settling new lands by electing Pierce in 1852 were offended by the president's northern political strategy in 1853 and felt compelled to raise the price of their support in 1854. They demanded that the Douglas bill include a repeal of the Missouri Compromise of 1820 and thus explicitly acknowledge that slavery could become permanently established anywhere in the national domain. Douglas evidently convinced himself that the expected benefits of his Nebraska bill were worth the price extracted by the South. After all, it could be argued that the repeal would only articulate something already implicit in the doctrine of squatter sovereignty. The change in the formal terms of sectional peace would be more symbolic than real. In any case, Douglas accepted the repeal, and by dividing the Nebraska Territory in two (Nebraska and Kansas) hinted that both sections might peacefully lay claim to part of the new land.

In January 1854, less than a year into Pierce's administration, Douglas led his southern collaborators to the White House to secure a presidential endorsement for the Kansas-Nebraska bill. With Douglas's railroad and the confirmation of Pierce's New York collector nominee hanging in the balance, the cornerstone of the Pierce presidency gave way. In his very first legislative decision, the president was being told to disregard his electoral pledge not to reopen the issue of slavery and to tie his leadership to the repudiation of the Missouri Compromise. To endorse the handiwork of the party leaders was to risk his credibility in the nation at large. But if he chose to stand by his pledge, he was certain to lose all credibility within the party. Pierce chose to stand with the party leaders. Like Douglas, he apparently convinced himself that the Kansas-Nebraska bill was consistent enough with the spirit of the Compromise of 1850 to not raise any new issues concerning slavery. He then offered to help Douglas convince the northern wing of the party. The administration's candidate for collector of the Port of New York was confirmed.

Between March 1853 and January 1854 Pierce tried and failed to prove himself to his party on his own terms; between January and May of 1854 he struggled to prove himself to his party on the Senate's terms. The president threw all the resources of the administration behind passage of the Kansas-Nebraska bill in the House. Despite a Democratic majority of 159–76, he fought a no-win battle to discipline a party vote. Midway into the proceedings, sixty-six of the ninety northern Democrats stood in open revolt against this northern Democratic president. A no-holds-barred use of presidential patronage ultimately persuaded forty-four representatives to give a final assent. Instead of perfecting the political machine, Pierce found himself defying a political revolution. Passage of the bill was secured through the support of southern Whigs. Forty-two northern Democrats openly voted no. Not one northern Whig voted yes.[36]

Pierce lost his gamble with national credibility in the winter of 1854. Exhausted after the passage of Douglas's bill, the administration turned to reap northern revenge for the broken pledge of 1852. The Democrats lost every northern state except New Hampshire and California in the elections of 1854. The once huge Democratic majority in the House disappeared, and a curious new amalgam of political forces prepared to take over. Adding to the rebuke was the threat of civil war in the territories. Free Soil and proslavery factions rushed into Kansas and squared off in a contest for control. The president called for order, but his plea was ignored.

Pierce never gave up hope that his party would turn to him. But once the North had rejected his administration, the South had no more use for him, and the party Pierce had so desperately wanted to lead became increasingly eager to get rid of him. Ironically, when faced with the unmitigated failure of his leadership and his political impotence at midterm, Pierce seemed to gain his first sense of a higher purpose. He threw his hat into the ring for a second term with a spirited defense of the Kansas-Nebraska Act and a biting indictment of the critics of the Missouri Compromise repeal. He appealed to the nation to reject treason in Kansas, wrapped his party in the Constitution, and cast its enemies in the role of uncompromising disunionists bent on civil war.[37]

This was the president's shining hour. Rejecting the specter of party illegitimacy and the stigma of his own irrelevance, standing firm with the establishment against the forces that would destroy it, Pierce pressed the case for his party in the nation and with it, his own case for party leadership. Still, no one rallied to his side. The party took up the "friends of the Constitution" sentiment, but it hastened to bury the memory of the man who had articulated it. Pierce's unceasing effort to prove his significance to those who had called him to power never bore fruit. The Democratic convention was an "anybody but Pierce" affair.

Jimmy Carter

There is no better rationale for Jimmy Carter's mugwumpish approach to political leadership than Franklin Pierce's unmitigated failure. No sooner had Pierce identified his prospects for gaining credibility with revitalizing the old party machinery under presidential auspices than he fell victim to party interests so factious that the desperate state of national affairs was all but ignored. The sect-ridden party of Jackson proved itself bankrupt as a governing instrument. Its operators could not even recognize that they were toying with explosive moral issues of national significance. Pierce's plan to claim party leadership first and then to take charge of the nation dissolved with its initial action, pushing the president down a path as demoralizing for the nation as it was degrading to the office. The quest for credibility degenerated into saving face with the Senate over patronage appointments, toeing the line on volatile territorial legislation for the sake of Douglas's railroad, and forswearing a solemn pledge to the nation.

It was Jimmy Carter's peculiar genius to treat his remoteness from his party and its institutional power centers as a distinctive asset rather than his chief liability in his quest for a credible leadership posture. He called attention to moral degeneration in government and politics, made it his issue, and then compelled the political coalition that had built that government to indulge his crusade against it. In a style reminiscent of Andrew Jackson, Carter identified himself with popular disillusionment with political insiders, entrenched special interests, and the corruption of manners in Washington. He let the liberals of the Democratic party flounder in their own disarray until it became clear that liberalism could no longer take the political offensive on its own terms. Then, in the 1976 Florida primary, Carter pressed his southern advantage. The party either had to fall in line behind his campaign against the establishment or risk another confrontation with the still greater heresies of George Wallace.

The obvious problem in Carter's approach to the presidency was that while it claimed a high moral stance of detachment from the establishment, it also positioned itself within an established governing coalition. This curiosity afforded him neither the regime outsider's freedom to oppose established interests nor the insider's license to support them. The tension in Carter's campaign between the effort to reassemble the core constituencies of the traditional Democratic regime and the promise to reform the governmental order that served it suggested the difficulties he would face establishing a credible leadership posture in office. Carter's narrow victory magnified those difficulties by showing the regime's supporters in Congress to be a good deal more secure politically than their strange new affiliate in the executive mansion.

On what terms, then, did Carter propose to reconcile his outsider's appeal with his position within the old order? The answer of the campaign lay in Carter's preoccupation with problems of form, procedure, and discipline rather than in the substance of the old order. It was not bureaucratic *programs*, Carter argued, but bureaucratic *inefficiency* that left the people estranged from their government. It was not the system *per se* that was at fault but the way it was being run. In the eyes of this late regime Democrat, the stifling weight and moral decay of the federal government presented problems of technique and personnel, not substance.

Like Jackson's early efforts, Carter's reform program called for governmental reorganization, civil service reform, and fiscal retrenchment. But coming from an outsider affiliated with the old order, the political force and ideological energy of this revitalization program were largely nullified. What Jackson presented as an ideological indictment of the old order and a buttress for supporters newly arrived in power, Carter presented as institutional engineering plain and simple. Carter's Jackson-like appeal to the nation translated into an ideologically passionless vision of reorganizing the old order without challenging any of its core concerns.[38]

It is in this respect that the shaky ground on which Carter staked his credibility as a leader begins to appear a good deal more like that claimed by Franklin Pierce than their different party postures would at first lead us to suppose. Both pinned their hopes on the perfectibility of machinery. Carter would do for the bureaucratic apparatus of the liberal regime what Pierce had intended to do for the party apparatus of the Jacksonian regime—repair the mechanical defects and realize a new level of operational efficiency. By perfecting the apparatus, they hoped to save the old regime from its own self-destructive impulses and, at the same time, eliminate the need to make any substantive choices among interests. Political vitality was to be restored simply by making the engines of power run more efficiently.

Sharing this vision, Pierce and Carter also shared a problem of action. Neither could point to any interest of political significance that depended on his success in reorganization. Carter's plan for instilling a new level of bureaucratic discipline was not the stuff to stir the enthusiasm of established Democrats, and once the plan became concrete action, there was plenty for party interests to vehemently oppose. Carter's vision of institutional efficiency dissolved in a matter of weeks into institutional confrontation.

The Carter administration immediately engaged the nation in an elaborate display of symbolism that was designed to build a reservoir of popular faith in the president's intentions and confidence in his ability to change the tenor of government.[39] The economic difficulties the old regime faced in simply maintaining its programmatic commitments at current levels dampened whatever enthusiasm there was for reaching out to the interests with expansive new programs in orthodox Democratic style. The impulse to lead thus focused on an early redemption of the pledge to be different. With his "strategy of symbols," the president bypassed Congress and claimed authority in government as an extension of his personal credibility in the nation at large.

The first material test of this strategy came in February 1977, when Carter decided to cut nineteen local water projects from the 1978 budget. As mundane as this bid for leadership was, it placed the disjunction between the president's appeal to the people and his political support in government in the starkest possible light. For the president, the water projects were a prime example of the wasteful expenditures inherent in the old ways government did business. The cuts offered Carter a well-founded and much needed opportunity to demonstrate to the nation how an outsider with no attachments to established routines could bring a thrifty discipline to government without really threatening any of its programmatic concerns. Congress—and, in particular, the Democratic leadership in the Senate—saw the matter quite differently. The president's gesture was received as an irresponsible and politically pretentious assault on the bread and butter of congressional careers. Its only real purpose was to enhance the president's public standing, yet its victims were those upon whom presidential success in government must ultimately depend. The Democratic leaders of the Senate pressed the confrontation. They reinstated the threatened water projects on a presidentially sponsored public works jobs bill. Carter threatened to stand his ground, and majority party government floundered at the impasse.

As relations with Congress grew tense, the president's bid for national leadership became even more dependent on public faith and confidence in his administration's integrity. By standing aloof from "politics as usual," the administration saddled itself with a moral standard that any would find difficult to sustain. A hint of shady dealing surfaced in the summer of 1977, and by the fall, the symbolic supports of Carter's leadership were a shambles.

Like the water projects debacle, the Bert Lance affair is remarkable for its substantive insignificance. The administration's "scandal" amounted to an investigation of financial indiscretions by one official before he took office. But the Carter administration was nothing if not the embodiment of a higher morality, and the budget director was the president's most important and trusted political appointee. The exposé of Lance, whose hand was on the tiller of the bureaucratic ship, not only indicted the administration's claim to ethical superiority but also made a sham of the Democratic Senate's nomination review process. Shorn of its pretensions to a higher standard, the administration's outsider status became a dubious asset. Attention was now directed to the apparent inability of the outsiders to make the government work and address the nation's manifest problems.

Despite these first-year difficulties in establishing a credible leadership posture on his own terms, Carter still refused to abdicate to the party leaders. Indeed, as time went on the intransigence of the nation's economic difficulties seemed to stiffen the president's resistance to social policy enthusiasms he felt the nation could no longer afford to support. There was to be no recapitulation of the Pierce-Douglas disaster in an alliance between Carter and Sen. Edward M. Kennedy, D-Mass. But what of the prospects for continued presidential resistance? The core constituencies of the Democratic party—blacks and organized labor in particular—found the president's program of governmental reorganization and fiscal retrenchment tangential at best to their concerns. They had little use for a Democratic president who seemed to govern like a Republican, and their disillusionment added to the dismay of the congressional leadership. Stalwart liberals admonished the president not to forsake the traditional interests but to rally them and, in Kennedy's words, "sail against the wind."[40] If the nation's shaky economy made this message perilous for the president to embrace, his awkward political position made it equally perilous to ignore.

Following the Lance affair, Carter did attempt to dispel disillusionment with an appeal to the neoliberal theme of consumerism. He had identified himself with consumer issues during his campaign and opened the second year of his administration with a drive to establish a consumer protection agency. The proposal could hardly be said to address the demands of the old Democratic constituencies, but it had enthusiastic backing from consumer groups, a general popular appeal, support from the Democratic leadership in Congress, and the rare promise of serving all these at little direct cost to the government. In consumer protection, Carter found the makings of a great victory, one that would not only wash away the memory of the first year but also define his own brand of political leadership. But the legislation failed, and with the failure his prospects for leadership all but collapsed.

Indeed, this defeat underscored the paradox that plagued Carter's never-ending struggle for credibility. Opposition fueled by business interests turned the consumer protection issue against the administration with devastating effect. Identifying governmental regulation of industry with the grim state of the national economy, business made Carter's neoliberalism appear symptomatic of the problem and counterproductive to any real solution.[41] Carter's own critique of undisciplined government expansion actually became the property of his critics, and the distinctions he had drawn between himself and the old liberal establishment became hopelessly blurred. While this most distant of Democratic presidents was alienating the liberal establishment by his neglect of its priorities, he was being inextricably linked to it in a conservative assault on the manifest failings of the New Deal liberal regime. Carter's liberalism-with-a-difference simply could not stand its ground in the sectarian controversies that racked the liberal order in the 1970s. It was as vulnerable to the conservatives for being more of the same as it was vulnerable to the liberals for being different.

As tensions between the old regime politics and new economic realities intensified, all sense of political definition was eclipsed. Notable administration victories—the Senate's ratification of a bitterly contested treaty with Panama, the endorsement of a version of the much heralded administrative reorganization, the negotiation of an accord between Israel and Egypt—offered precious little vindication of the promise of revitalization. Moreover, the president's mugwumpish resolve to find his own way through deepening crises increasingly came to be perceived as rootless floundering. His attempt to assert forceful leadership through a major cabinet shake-up in the summer of 1979 only added credence to the image of an administration out of control. His determination to support a policy of inducing recession to fight inflation shattered the political symbolism of decades past by saddling a Democratic administration with a counsel of austerity and sacrifice and passing to the Republicans the traditional Democratic promise of economic recovery and sustained prosperity.

The administration was aware of its failure to engage the political system in a meaningful way well before these momentous decisions. By early 1979 the president had turned introspective. It was readily apparent that his credibility had to be established anew and imperative that the administration be identified with some clear and compelling purpose. Carter's response to the eclipse of political definition was not, of course, a Pierce-like defense of the old order and its principles. It was, if anything, a sharpened attack on the old order and a renewed declaration of presidential political independence.

In what was to be his most dramatic public moment, Carter appeared in a nationally televised appeal to the people in July 1979 with a revised assessment of the crisis facing the nation.[42] Carter began his new bid for leadership credibility by acknowledging widespread disillusionment with the administration and its "mixed success" with Congress. But the president detached himself from the "paralysis, stagnation, and drift" that had marked his tenure. He issued a strong denunciation of the legislative process and reasserted his campaign image as an outsider continuing the people's fight against degenerate politics.

Attempting to restore the people's faith in themselves and to rally them to his cause, Carter all but declared the bankruptcy of the federal government as he found it. Thirty months in office only seemed to reveal to him how deeply rooted the government's incapacities were. It was the system itself, not simply its inefficiencies, that the president now placed in question.

Trying once again to identify his leadership with the people's alienation from the government, Carter again exposed himself as the one with the most paralyzing case of estrangement. The awkward truth in this presidential homily lent credence to the regime's most vehement opponents by indicting the establishment controlled by the president's ostensible allies. On the face of it, Carter had come to embrace a leadership challenge of the greatest moment— the repudiation of an entire political-institutional order—but beneath the challenge lay the hopeless paradox of his political position. The Democratic party tore itself apart in a revolt against him and the sentiments he articulated. It rejected his message, discredited his efforts, and then, in its most pathetic display of impotence, revealed to the nation that it had nothing more to offer. Carter finally may have seen the gravity of the problems he confronted, but as the people saw it, he was not part of the solution.

Rethinking the Politics of Leadership

The politics of leadership is often pictured as a contest between the man and the system. Political fragmentation and institutional intransigence threaten to frustrate the would-be leader at every turn. Success, if it is possible at all, is reserved for the exceptional individual. It takes a person of rare political skill to manipulate the system in politically effective ways. It takes a person of rare character to give those manipulations national meaning and constructive purpose.

Although the significance of the particular person in office cannot be doubted, this individual-centered perspective on leadership presents a rather one-sided view of the interplay between the presidency and the larger political system. It is highly sensitive to differences among incumbents, but it tends to obscure differences in the political situations in which they act. If presidential leadership is indeed something of a struggle between the individual and the system, it must be recognized that the system changes as well as the incumbent. Indeed, the political conditions for presidential action can shift radically from one administration to the next, and with each change the challenge of exercising political leadership will be correspondingly altered.

Within any one historical period the shifting political contexts encountered by leaders are likely to appear idiosyncratic and the political changes effected by each incumbent, erratic. To catch the patterns and sequences in the politics of leadership, we need to adopt a much broader view of the relevant historical experience than is customary. On this larger canvas, similar kinds of situations elicit from leaders similar premises and projects for political action. Moreover, the situations, premises, and projects that tend to recur over long stretches of time have correspondingly similar political effects. Presidential history in this perspective is episodic rather than evolutionary, with leadership opportunities gradually dissipating after an initial upheaval in political control of the government. Presidents intervene in—and their leadership is mediated by—the generation and degeneration of political orders, or partisan regimes. The clock at work in presidential leadership keeps *political* rather than historical time.

The leaders who stand out at a glance—Washington, Jefferson, Jackson, Lincoln, and Franklin Roosevelt—are closer to each other in the political conditions of leadership than they are to any of their respective neighbors in historical time. In political time each is a first, a regime builder. The regime builders ride into power on an upheaval in governmental control and test their leadership in efforts to secure the political and institutional infrastructure for a new governing coalition. Their success creates a new establishment, thrusts their partisan successors into the position of regime managers, and poses the test of aggressive maintenance.

As the analysis of the Jacksonian and New Deal regimes has shown, successive incarnations of majority party government produce progressively more tenuous challenges for regime managers. Politically affiliated with already established commitments of ideology and interest, these presidents approach the ever more perplexing problems of managing the regime's commitments with ever more superficial governing solutions. Regime supporters, in turn, approach ever more perplexing leadership choices with ever less forbearance. Ultimately, visions of regime management dissolve into politically vacuous mechanical contrivances, and leadership is foreclosed by the political dilemmas of simply establishing the president's credibility. In this way, the exercise of presidential power drives each regime further into a crisis of legitimacy, gradually preparing the ground for another reconstructive breakthrough.

It is worth noting that the critical issue in each of the six cases reviewed has not been success or failure in enacting some momentous new program for national action. Franklin Pierce, in pitched battle, succeeded in enacting the Kansas-Nebraska Act but failed miserably as a political leader; in contrast,

Franklin Roosevelt, the most formidable political leader of the twentieth century, was thwarted time and again on matters of program, from the voiding of the "first" New Deal by the Supreme Court to the failure of his party purge. Nor has the critical issue in these cases been the success of the policies enacted in solving national problems. After all, the New Deal failed to pull the nation out of the Great Depression, and Andrew Jackson's alternative banking scheme exacerbated an economic depression. The incumbents in these two historical sequences are distinguishable from one another—and paired individually with counterparts in very different historical periods—by their ability to set the terms and conditions of legitimate political action. In this view, the critical issue on which leadership turns is the president's political authority, his control over the meaning of his initiatives and accomplishments in the face of the contending interpretations of friends and foes alike. A president's authority over political definitions changes with the passage of political time and hinges in large measure on the relationship between the incumbent and received governing commitments.[43]

Thus, the paradigmatic expressions of political leadership in the presidency come from incumbents, such as Jackson and Roosevelt, who stand free of the commitments of the recent past and are able to define their leadership projects against the backdrop of the manifest failures of a recently displaced governing coalition. Able to hammer relentlessly against a failed and discredited course of national action, they are best situated to reset the terms and conditions of legitimate national government.

For Polk and Kennedy, whose ascension to power revived and reaffirmed commitments drawn from the recent past, leadership was quite different. It was their job to make good on long-heralded promises, to continue the work of the established regime and implement a robust policy agenda. Leadership was a matter of managing interests and implementing policies in the manner best calculated to stave off warfare within the ranks. In exercising power on these terms, however, Polk and Kennedy were constrained by the authority of faithful followers to challenge their particular rendition of the true meaning and implications of received commitments. Their leadership sent sectarian schisms deep into the ranks of regime supporters.

The difficulties of exercising political leadership mounted apace under Pierce and Carter. They came to power affiliated with an old orthodoxy that was on the defensive. Each offered to repair the political machinery of a faltering regime, one whose basic commitments of ideology and interest were increasingly seen as the very source of the nation's problems. Caught between the demands of their nominal supporters for further action along the old course and frontal assaults on the old course from a resurgent opposition, these leaders were unable to establish clear warrants for any course of action, and their exercises of power accelerated the crises of legitimacy they were intended to abate.

Comparisons that move across broad stretches of history help us make sense of the shifting parameters of the politics of leadership that are notable within a historical period. Still, they leave a major question outstanding: what has been the effect of the secular changes that, over time, have transformed the organization of governmental power itself? Roosevelt did not simply repeat Jackson's performance. He directed his leadership against interests and institutions that were more firmly entrenched in government and more fully integrated into the social and economic life of the nation. For this reason he was more constrained as a reconstructive leader than Jackson. Although Roosevelt was able to set the general terms for a reordering of political commitments, his initiatives repeatedly went down to defeat. The new order was not imposed from the top down as in Jackson's case but was fashioned more systemically by interests and institutions beyond Roosevelt's direct control.

In the Pierce-Carter comparison, secular changes in the organization of American government seem to have had the opposite effect. Jimmy Carter had at his disposal institutional resources for independent action that Franklin Pierce could scarcely have imagined. When Stephen Douglas marched to the White House demanding that Pierce take on the party's latest enthusiasm as his own, the senator had the balance of governmental power on his side. As president, Pierce had no resources of comparable institutional weight with which to counter his party's leadership in Congress. But when Edward Kennedy demanded that Carter buck the conservative tide and take on new liberal commitments, Carter was able to resist by employing the political resources of the modern presidency to distance his administration from the liberal agenda and defeat the Kennedy challenge. It would seem then that secular changes in the organization of American government have cut in two directions at once. They serve both to delimit the possibilities for a presidentially imposed reconstruction of American government and politics and to bolster the independence of those who are nominally affiliated with previously established commitments of ideology and interest.

If the recurrent patterns of presidential leadership in political time are in fact being reshaped by this subtle undercurrent of secular change, we might expect that the differences among presidents' political capacities will begin to flatten out. The most recent examples of leadership in the familiar modes are suggestive of the current state of affairs in this regard. On the one hand, Ronald Reagan's rendition of reconstructive leadership and George Bush's rendition of the faithful son indicate the still pervasive influence of political time on the politics of leadership. Reagan came to power as another great repudiator, and like the reconstructive leaders of the past, he transformed the national political landscape, resetting the terms and conditions of legitimate national government more thoroughly and effectively than any president since Franklin Roosevelt. George Bush came to power promising to affirm and continue Reagan's course: indeed, he professed his faith belligerently with an iron-clad pledge—"no new taxes."

Yet even as we have been treated in recent years to especially strident renditions of these classic leadership postures, the disparity between the old premises being offered for political leadership and the ability of contemporary presidents to follow through has been magnified. Reagan's reconstruction tracked Roosevelt's as a further narrowing of the political range of their common leadership stance. Reagan met with even more formidable resistance than FDR in trying to dislodge old political commitments from the government, and the shortfall left Bush to manage a new ordering that was more rhetorical than institutional. Indeed, the limitations on Reagan's efforts to impose a new order from on high quickly weighed in against Bush's efforts to stay the course. Before mid-term, the governing responsibilities of the modern presidency got the better of political consistency, and Bush abruptly broke his foremost pledge of continuity by agreeing to raise taxes. That the standards of appropriate political action still change radically from one administration to the next was indicated in the stark contrast between Bush's futile efforts to reestablish his political authority after his reversal on taxation and Reagan's seeming immunity from his own reversals and shortfalls. But in his initial response to the charges of betrayal that arose within the Republican ranks—"I'm doing like Lincoln did, 'think anew'"—Bush went far toward acknowledging the absurdity of even trying to play the faithful son in the modern presidency.[44]

The growing disparity between premise and practice in presidential leadership is a prime source of frustration and cynicism in modern American politics. To bring premises into line with a more candid assessment of presidential prospects today, our leaders will have to discard the old leadership postures and fashion new claims to political authority. Opposition leaders will have to recognize that designs for change can no longer be imposed holistically from above and that proposals to alter course will have to withstand the test of exhaustive deliberation. Affiliated leaders will have to recognize the vast responsibilities for independent action that are now built into the office they occupy and take care not to hostage the presidency to hollow pledges of consistency and continuity with received governing formulas. A constructive escape from political time hinges on our leaders' embracing a politics that is at once more pragmatic and more deliberative. But as the Clinton presidency is now demonstrating, that will be easier said than done.

Notes

1. Other works investigating distinctly political patterns in presidential history include Erwin C. Hargrove and Michael Nelson, *Presidents, Politics, and Policy* (New York: Knopf, 1984); and James David Barber, *The Pulse of Politics: Electing Presidents in the Media Age* (New York: W. W. Norton, 1980).

2. Thomas A. Bailey, *Presidential Greatness: The Image and the Man from George Washington to the Present* (New York: Appleton-Century-Croft, 1966), 23–24. Bailey critically discusses the ratings by professional historians. The important point here, however, is that the presidents who rated highest in the Schlesinger surveys of 1948 and 1962 all shared this peculiarly structured leadership situation at the outset of their terms.

3. Robert Remini, *Andrew Jackson and the Course of American Freedom, 1822–1832*, vol. 2 (New York: Harper and Row, 1981), 12–38, 74–142.

4. Quoted in Frank Freidel, *FDR and the South* (Baton Rouge: Louisiana State University Press, 1965), 42.

5. Remini, *Andrew Jackson*, 152–202, 248–256.

6. The famous veto of the Maysfield Road, for example, was notable for its limited implications. It challenged federal support for *intrastate* projects and was specifically selected as an example for its location in Henry Clay's Kentucky. On Jackson's objectives in civil service reform, see Albert Somit, "Andrew Jackson as an Administrative Reformer," *Tennessee Historical Quarterly* 13 (September 1954): 204–223; and Eric McKinley Erickson, "The Federal Civil Service under President Jackson," *Mississippi Valley Historical Review* 13 (March 1927): 517–540. Also significant in this regard is Richard G. Miller, "The Tariff of 1832: The Issue That Failed," *The Filson Club History Quarterly* 49 (July 1975): 221–230.

7. The analysis in this and the following paragraphs draws on the following works: Remini, *Andrew Jackson;* Robert Remini, *Andrew Jackson and the Bank War: A Study in the Growth of Presidential Power* (New York: W. W. Norton, 1967); Marquis James, *Andrew Jackson: Portrait of a President* (New York: Grosset and Dunlap, 1937), 283–303, 350–385; and Arthur M. Schlesinger, Jr., *The Age of Jackson* (Boston: Little, Brown, 1945), 74–131.

8. Charles Sellers, Jr., "Who Were the Southern Whigs?" *American Historical Review* 49 (January 1954): 335–346.

9. Harry Scheiber, "The Pet Banks in Jacksonian Politics and Finance, 1833–1841," *Journal of Economic History* 23 (June 1963): 196–214; Frank Otto Gatell, "Spoils of the Bank War: Political Bias in the Selection of Pet Banks," *American Historical Review* 70 (October 1964): 35–58; and Frank Otto Gatell, "Secretary Taney and the Baltimore Pets: A Study in Banking and Politics," *Business History Review* 39 (Summer 1965): 205–227.

10. Quoted in James MacGregor Burns, *Roosevelt: The Lion and the Fox* (New York: Harcourt, Brace and World, 1956), 208.

11. The analysis in this and the following paragraphs draws on Burns, *Roosevelt*, and Freidel, *FDR and the South*.

12. Burns, *Roosevelt*, 223–241.

13. Freidel, *FDR and the South*.

14. Richard Polenberg, *Reorganizing Roosevelt's Government: The Controversy over Executive Reorganization, 1936–1939* (Cambridge: Harvard University Press, 1966).

15. The analysis in this and the following paragraphs draws on the following works: Charles Sellers, *James K. Polk: Continentalist, 1843–1846* (Princeton: Princeton University Press, 1966); John Schroeder, *Mr. Polk's War: American Opposition and Dissent, 1846–1848* (Madison: University of Wisconsin Press, 1973); Norman A. Graebner, "James Polk," in *America's Ten Greatest Presidents*, ed. Morton Borden (Chicago: Rand McNally, 1961), 113-138; and Charles McCoy, *Polk and the Presidency* (Austin: University of Texas Press, 1960).

16. Sellers, *James K. Polk*, 50.

17. Ibid., 113–114, 123.

18. Ibid., 282–283.

19. Ibid., 162–164; Joseph G. Raybeck, "Martin Van Buren's Break with James K. Polk: The Record," *New York History* 36 (January 1955): 51–62; and Norman A. Graebner, "James K. Polk: A Study in Federal Patronage," *Mississippi Valley Historical Review* 38 (March 1952): 613–632.

20. Sellers, *James K. Polk*, 483.

21. Frederick J. Blue, *The Free Soilers: Third Party Politics, 1848–54* (Urbana: University of Illinois Press, 1973), 16–80; and John Mayfield, *Rehearsal for Republicanism: Free Soil and the Politics of Antislavery* (Port Washington, N.Y.: Kennikat Press, 1980), 80–125.

22. McCoy, *Polk and the Presidency*, 197–198, 203–204.

23. Arthur M. Schlesinger, Jr., *A Thousand Days: John F. Kennedy in the White House* (Boston: Houghton Mifflin, 1965), 675–676.

24. Carroll Kilpatrick, "The Kennedy Style and Congress," *The Virginia Quarterly Review* 39 (Winter 1963): 1–11; and Henry Fairlie, *The Kennedy Promise: The Politics of Expectation* (New York: Doubleday, 1973), esp. 235–263.

25. Freidel, *FDR and the South*, 71–102.

26. Herbert S. Parmet, *The Democrats: The Years after FDR* (New York: Oxford University Press, 1976), 80–82.

27. The analysis in this and the following paragraphs draws on material presented in the following works: Carl M. Bauer, *John F. Kennedy and the Second Reconstruction* (New York: Columbia University Press, 1977); Schlesinger, *Thousand Days*; Parmet, *Democrats*, 193–247; Bruce Miroff, *Pragmatic Illusions: The Presidential Politics of John F. Kennedy* (New York: David McKay, 1976), 223–270; and Fairlie, *Kennedy Promise*, 235–263.

28. Bauer, *John F. Kennedy*, 30-38; and Schlesinger, *Thousand Days*, 47–52.

29. Bauer, *John F. Kennedy*, 61–88; and Schlesinger, *Thousand Days*, 30–31.

30. Parmet, *Democrats*, 211; and Bauer, *John F. Kennedy*, 128–130.

31. Holman Hamilton, *Prologue to Conflict: The Crisis and Compromise of 1850* (Lexington: University of Kentucky Press, 1964), esp. 156–164.

32. Roy F. Nichols, *The Democratic Machine, 1850–54* (New York: AMS Press, 1967).

33. Parmet, *Democrats*, 220–228.

34. The analysis in this and the following paragraphs draws on Roy F. Nichols,

Franklin Pierce: Young Hickory of Granite Hills (Philadelphia: University of Pennsylvania Press, 1969); and Nichols, *Democratic Machine,* 147–226.

35. Nichols, *Franklin Pierce,* 292–293, 308–310; and Nichols, *Democratic Machine,* 224.

36. Roy F. Nichols, "The Kansas-Nebraska Act: A Century of Historiography," *Mississippi Valley Historical Review* 43 (September 1956): 187-212; and Nichols, *Franklin Pierce,* 292–324, 333–338.

37. Nichols, *Franklin Pierce,* 360–365, 425–434.

38. Jack Knott and Aaron Wildavsky, "Skepticism and Dogma in the White House: Jimmy Carter's Theory of Governing," *Wilson Quarterly* 1 (Winter 1977): 49–68; and James Fallows, "The Passionless Presidency: The Trouble with Jimmy Carter's Administration," *Atlantic Monthly,* May 1979, 33–58, and June 1979, 75–81.

39. The analysis in this and the following paragraphs draws on the following works: Robert Shogun, *Promises to Keep: Carter's First Hundred Days* (New York: Thomas Y. Crowell, 1977); Haynes Johnson, *In the Absence of Power: Governing America* (New York: Viking, 1980); Robert Shogun, *None of the Above: Why Presidents Fail and What Can Be Done about It* (New York: New American Library, 1982), 177–250; Thomas Ferguson and Joel Rogers, eds., *The Hidden Election: Politics and Economics in the 1980 Presidential Campaign* (New York: Pantheon, 1981), 200–230; and Alan Wolfe, *America's Impasse: The Rise and Fall of the Politics of Growth* (New York: Pantheon, 1981), 200–230.

40. Shogun, *None of the Above,* 220.

41. Johnson, *Absence of Power,* 233–245.

42. *New York Times,* July 16, 1979, 1, 10.

43. See Stephen Skowronek, *The Politics Presidents Make: Leadership from John Adams to George Bush* (Cambridge: Harvard University Press, Belknap Press, 1993).

44. "The President's News Conference, June 29, 1990," *Public Papers of the President: George Bush* (Washington, D.C.: U.S. Government Printing Office, 1991), 885.

6 Presidential Competence

Paul J. Quirk

The skills of political leadership that a president requires are a recurring theme of modern presidential scholarship. Most students of political skill have dwelled on leadership technique: bargaining, persuasion, rhetoric, management, and the like. Paul J. Quirk approaches the subject differently, asking "What must presidents know?" Quirk rejects as impossibly demanding the widely advocated "self-reliant" model that is patterned after Franklin D. Roosevelt. He is even less approving of the "minimalist" or "chairman of the board" model that Ronald Reagan adopted, which Quirk regards as not demanding enough. Quirk's own model calls for "strategic competence" of the kind occasionally practiced during the Bush administration and the early Clinton administration: presidents need not know everything, but they must know how to find what they need to know.

The presidency of Ronald Reagan drew attention to a simple, yet rarely examined question about American government: What must the president know? To have a good chance to succeed politically and serve the country well, must presidents be highly knowledgeable on the issues and processes of government? Must they have long experience in national government, or spend hours daily immersed in briefing papers? Or can they rely on other officials—especially the cabinet and White House staff—to provide the necessary expertise and information?

Although Reagan had passionate convictions and a remarkable talent for conveying them to the public, he was notoriously lacking in specific information about the affairs of government. Critics ridiculed his frequent misinformed comments and his inability to speak to issues without a script. Most of the public did not mind: Reagan served two terms and left office a popular president. But his reputation has weathered considerably in succeeding years.[1] Was Reagan's knowledge adequate? Considering the enormous complexity of modern government, is adequate presidential knowledge even feasible?

Although the requirements for a competent presidency cannot be reduced to a formula, they should be possible to define in general terms. Drawing primarily from the experiences of presidents from Franklin D. Roosevelt to Reagan, I present three distinct and competing conceptions of the president's personal tasks and expertise—that is, of presidential competence. I criticize two of them—one an orthodox approach of long standing, the other mainly associated with Reagan. I then offer a third model, based on a notion of "strategic competence," and discuss the requirements of that model in three major areas of presidential activity. In the last section I test the relevance of the analysis by assessing the performance of the two presidents who followed Reagan: George Bush and Bill Clinton.

The Self-Reliant Presidency

Most commentary on the presidency assumes a concept of the president's personal tasks that borders on the heroic. Stated simply, the president must strive to be self-reliant and personally bear a large share of the burden of governing. And he must therefore meet intellectual requirements that are correspondingly rigorous.

The classic argument for the self-reliant presidency is presented in Richard Neustadt's *Presidential Power.*[2] In arguing for an enlarged conception of the presidential role, Neustadt stressed that the president's political interests, and therefore his perspective on decisions, are unique. Only the president has political stakes that arguably correspond with the national interest. For no other government official is individual achievement so closely identified with the well-being of the entire nation. Thus a president's chances for success depend on what he can do for himself: his direct involvement in decisions, his personal reputation and skill, his control over subordinates.[3]

It is in this spirit that students of the presidency often hold up Franklin D. Roosevelt as the exemplary modern president—if not for his specific policies or administrative practices, at least for his personal orientation to the job. A perfect "active-positive" in James David Barber's typology of presidential personalities, Roosevelt made strenuous efforts to increase his control and to improve his grasp of issues and situations.[4] For example, he would set up duplicate channels within the government to provide him information and advice. When this did not seem enough, he looked outside the government for persons who could offer additional perspectives.[5] The ideal president, in short, is one with a consuming passion for control, and thus for information.

This image of the president—as one who makes the major decisions himself, depends on others only in lesser matters, and firmly controls his subordinates—appeals to the general public, which seems to evaluate presidents partly by how well they live up to this image. But is the self-reliant presidency sensible, even as an ideal? Both experience and the elementary facts of contemporary government indicate strongly that it is not.

Even for Roosevelt, self-reliance carried certain costs. In an admiring description of Roosevelt's administrative practices, Arthur Schlesinger, Jr., concedes that his methods hampered performance in some respects. Roosevelt's creation of unstructured, competitive relations among subordinates, a method he used for control, caused "confusion and exasperation on the operating level"; it was "nerve-wracking and often positively demoralizing." Because Roosevelt reserved so many decisions for himself, he could not make all of them promptly, and aides often had to contend with troublesome delays.[6] The overall effect of Roosevelt's self-reliant decision making on the design, operation, and success of New Deal programs is open to question. Indeed, the New Deal is revered mainly for its broad assertion of governmental responsibility for the nation's well-being, not for the effectiveness of its specific programs. Roosevelt took pride in an observer's estimate that for each decision made by Calvin Coolidge, he was making at least thirty-five. Perhaps some smaller ratio would have been better.

In later administrations the weaknesses of the self-reliant presidency have emerged more clearly. Presidents who have aspired to self-reliance have ended up leaving serious responsibilities badly neglected. Lyndon B. Johnson, another president with prodigious energy and a need for control, gravitated naturally to the self-reliant approach.[7] Eventually, however, he directed his efforts narrowly and obsessively to the Vietnam War. Meeting daily with the officers in charge, Johnson directed the military strategy from the Oval Office, going into such detail, at times, as to select specific targets for bombing. Every other area of presidential concern he virtually set aside. Although such detailed involvement would have been unobjectionable had there been any cause to believe it would help to resolve the conflict, the reverse seems more likely. Guided by the president's civilian subordinates, the military officers themselves should have been able to decide matters of strategy at least as well as the president, probably better. Moreover, Johnson's direct operational control of military strategy may have impaired his ability to take a broader, "presidential" perspective. After all, doing a general's job, to some inevitable degree, means thinking like a general. Johnson illustrated a dangerous tendency for self-reliance to become an end in itself.

Jimmy Carter, although less driven than Johnson, preferred self-reliance as a matter of conviction. It led him toward a narrowness of a different kind. From the first month in office, Carter signaled his intention to be thoroughly involved, completely informed, and prompt. "Unless there's a holocaust," he told the staff, "I'll take care of everything the same day it comes in." Thus he spent long hours daily poring over stacks of memoranda and took thick briefing books with him for weekends at Camp David. Initially, he even checked arithmetic in budget documents. Later he complained mildly about the number of memoranda and their length, but he still made no genuine effort to curb the flow.[8] Carter's extreme attention to detail cannot have contributed more than very marginally to the quality of his administration's decisions. Yet it took his attention from other, more essential tasks. Carter was criticized as having failed to articulate the broad themes or ideals that would give his presidency a sense of purpose—a natural oversight, if true, for a president who was wallowing in detail. He certainly neglected the crucial task of nurturing constructive relationships with other leaders in Washington.[9]

The main defect of the self-reliant presidency, however, is none of these particular risks, but rather the blunt, physical impossibility of carrying it out. Perhaps Roosevelt, an extraordinary man who served when government was still relatively manageable, could achieve some sort of approximation of the ideal. But the larger and more complex government has become, the more presidents have been forced to depend on the judgments of others. Today, any single important policy question produces enough pertinent studies, positions, and proposals to keep a conscientious policy maker fully occupied. In any remotely literal sense, therefore, presidential self-reliance is not so much inadvisable as inconceivable.

Even as an inspirational ideal (like perfect virtue), the self-reliant presidency is more misleading than helpful. It can lead to an obsessive narrowness, and it is too far removed from reality to offer any concrete guidance. Rather than such an ideal, presidents need a conception of what a competent, successful performance would really consist of—one that takes the nature of government and the limits of human ability as they exist.

The Minimalist Presidency

A second approach to presidential competence rejects the heroic demands of self-reliance altogether. In this approach, the president requires little or no understanding of specific issues and problems and instead can rely almost entirely on subordinates to resolve them. Although rarely if ever advocated by commentators, the "minimalist" approach commands close attention if only because of the Reagan administration's attempt to use it.

Minimalism does not imply a passive conception of the presidency as an institution, the view of some nineteenth-century American presidents. Accepting the Whig theory of government, they believed that Congress, as the most representative branch, should lead the country, and thus they left it to Congress to shape and pass legislation without much presidential advice.[10] The Whig theory has been abandoned in the twentieth century, and minimalism, as here defined, is not an attempt to restore it. With the help of a large personal staff, the Office of Management and Budget (OMB), and other presidential agencies in the Executive Office of the President, a minimalist president can exercise his powers as expansively as any.

Nor does minimalism describe the "hidden-hand" leadership ascribed to Dwight D. Eisenhower in the notable reinterpretation of his presidency by Fred Greenstein.[11] Long viewed as a passive president, who reigned rather than ruled, Eisenhower has been thoroughly misinterpreted, according to Greenstein's provocative thesis. In truth, Eisenhower, seeing a political advantage, merely cultivated this image. He worked longer hours, gave closer attention to issues, and exercised more influence than the public was allowed to notice.

Eisenhower's methods of influence were indirect. In the long dispute between the administration and Joseph McCarthy over the senator's charges of Communist infiltration of the government, Eisenhower resolutely withheld any public criticism of McCarthy by name. Privately, however, the president and his aides arranged the format of the Senate's Army-McCarthy hearings and plotted strategy for the executive branch, which ultimately led to the senator's downfall.[12]

The hidden-hand style, Greenstein argues, generally permitted Eisenhower to get what he wanted, yet insulated him from politically harmful controversy. By remaining "above politics," Eisenhower could achieve a political feat as yet unmatched by any of his successors—serving two complete four-year terms, popular to the end. Eisenhower was no minimalist; he was merely a closet activist.

The only recent minimalist president was Ronald Reagan, whose administration often flatly rejected the self-reliant approach. President Reagan's role in decision making, his spokesmen said during the first year, would be that of a chairman of the board. He would personally establish the general policies and goals of his administration, select cabinet and other key personnel who shared his commitments, then delegate broad authority to them so that they could work out the particulars.[13]

In part, the very limited role for the president was clearly designed to accommodate Reagan's particular limitations—especially his disinclination to do much reading or sit through lengthy briefings—and to answer critics who questioned his fitness for office. By expounding a minimalist theory, the Reagan administration was able to defend the president's frequent lapses and inaccuracies in news conferences as harmless and irrelevant. It is a "fantasy of the press," said communications director David Gergen, that an occasional "blooper" in a news conference has any real importance.[14]

Nevertheless, the administration presented this minimalist model not merely as an ad hoc accommodation but as a sensible way in general for a president to operate. The model has at least one claim to be taken seriously: unlike self-reliance, it has the merit of being attainable. For several reasons, however, it can neither be defended in general nor even judged satisfactory in Reagan's case.

First, chairman-of-the-board notions notwithstanding, a minimalist president and his administration will have serious difficulties reaching intelligent decisions. This is so if only because a minimalist president—or rather, the sort of president to whom minimalism might be suited—will not fully appreciate his own limitations. By consistently neglecting the complexities of careful policy arguments, one never comes to understand the importance of thorough analysis. In politics and government, at least, people generally do not place a high value on discourse that is much more sophisticated than their own habitual mode of thought.

That President Reagan showed no particular humility about his ability to make policy judgments was most apparent in his decisions about budgets, taxes, and the federal deficit. In late 1981 Reagan's key economic policy makers—the OMB director, David A. Stockman; the treasury secretary, Donald Regan; and the White House chief of staff, James Baker—recommended unanimously that the president propose a modest tax increase to keep the budget deficit to an acceptable level.

After the last holdout, Regan, came on board, the press began to treat the president's concurrence as a foregone conclusion. To the humiliation of his advisers, however, Reagan instead followed his own instinct not to retreat and rejected their recommendation. The resulting 1983 presidential budget was so far in deficit that it was dismissed out of hand even by the Republican Senate, and the president ended up accepting a package of "revenue enhancements" that

Congress virtually forced on him. In 1983 and 1984 Reagan repeatedly rejected pleas for a deficit-reducing tax increase that were made by Stockman and Martin Feldstein, the administration's second chairman of the Council of Economic Advisers (CEA) and its most distinguished economist.

Second, even if a minimalist president is willing to delegate authority and accept advice, his aides and cabinet members cannot make up for his limitations. Rather, as they compete for the president's favor, they will tend to assume his likeness. That is, they will take cues from his rhetoric and descend to his level of argumentation; advocates will emerge for almost any policy he is inclined to support. Such imitation apparently produced the scandals in the Environmental Protection Agency (EPA) that embarrassed the Reagan administration during the first term and led to the removal of numerous high-level officials. These officials, including Administrator Anne Gorsuch Burford, interpreted Reagan's sweeping antiregulatory rhetoric to mean that, requirements of the law notwithstanding, they should hardly regulate at all.

The effect of Reagan's relaxed approach to policy decisions on the quality of debate in his administration is illustrated by a White House meeting on the defense budget in September 1981, recounted in Stockman's revealing memoir.[15] The OMB was proposing a moderate reduction in the planned growth of defense spending—still giving the Pentagon an inflation-adjusted increase of 52 percent over five years and 92 percent of its original request. In a presentation that Stockman calls "a masterpiece of obfuscation," Secretary of Defense Caspar W. Weinberger compared American and Soviet capabilities as if the OMB were refusing to endorse any increase. Almost all of his comparisons, displayed in elaborate charts, concerned weapons categories that Stockman wasn't trying to cut. Weinberger stressed that the B-52 bomber was outdated, even though the OMB supported full funding for the B-1 and Stealth bombers that were planned to replace it; and he detailed the superiority of Warsaw Pact forces in numbers of divisions, even though the OMB had agreed to buy the full complement of sixteen active divisions the Pentagon wanted. (The secretary concluded all of this by showing a blown-up cartoon depicting the OMB budget as "a four-eyed wimp who looked like Woody Allen, carrying a tiny rifle.") In the end, Weinberger got his way. Whatever the merits of the decision, a well-prepared, attentive president would have dismissed such a presentation as largely irrelevant to what was actually in dispute. A defense secretary who anticipated such a response would have felt compelled to address the real issues.

Finally, if a president openly delegates significant decisions or almost always accepts subordinates' advice, the press is likely to comment adversely and make this a source of embarrassment for him. Because the public likes presidents who seem in command, it makes good copy for a reporter to suggest that aides are assuming the president's job—even though relying heavily on them may be a sensible adaptation to the president's personal limitations. The press sometimes challenged Reagan to demonstrate his involvement in decisions, and this may have led him to make more decisions in certain areas than he would have otherwise. During Reagan's summit meetings with the Soviet president Mikhail Gorbachev, for example, the president negotiated with the Soviet leader one-to-one on arms control, a subject of daunting complexity for any president.

Neither self-reliance nor minimalism offers a reliable, or even a plausible, route to presidential competence. The question is whether there is another possible model that corrects the defects of both—making feasible demands on the president yet allowing for competent performance.

Strategic Competence

The third conception of presidential competence, set forth in the rest of this chapter, lies between the two extremes of minimalism and self-reliance. But it does not represent merely a vague compromise between them. It is based on a notion of *strategic competence,* from which it derives definition.

Strategic competence does not refer to the correct but not very helpful observation that presidents need to be competent in the choice of strategies. It refers primarily to the idea that, in order to achieve competence, presidents must have a well-designed (even if mostly implicit) strategy *for* competence. This strategy, it seems, must take into account three basic elements of the president's situation.

1. The president's time, energy, and talent, and thus his capacity for direct, personal competence, must be regarded as a scarce resource. *Choices must be made concerning what things a president will attempt to know.*

2. Depending on the task (for example, deciding issues, promoting policies), the president's ability to substitute the judgment and expertise of others for his own and still get satisfactory results varies considerably. *Delegation works better for some tasks than for others.*

3. The success of such substitutions will depend on a relatively small number of presidential actions and decisions concerning the selection of subordinates, the general instructions they are given, and the president's limited interactions with them. *How well delegation works depends on how it is done.*

Achieving competent performance, then, can be viewed as a problem of allocating resources. The president's personal abilities and time to use them are the scarce resources. For each task, the possibilities and requirements for effective delegation determine how much of these resources should be used, and how they should be employed.

In the rest of this chapter, I will work out the implications of strategic competence in three major areas of presidential activity: policy decisions, policy processes, and policy promotion.[16] The test of the model is twofold. For each area of presidential activity, does it provide adequately for competent performance? Taken as a whole, does it call for a level of expertise and attentiveness that an average president can be expected to meet?

Policy Decisions

When it comes to substantive issues, vast presidential ignorance is simply inevitable. No one understands more than a few significant issues very well. Fortunately, presidents can get by—controlling subordinates reasonably well and minimizing the risk of policy disasters—on far less than a thorough mastery. Some prior preparation, however, is required.

As a matter of course, each president has a general outlook or philosophy of government. The principal requirement beyond this is for the president to be familiar enough with the substantive policy debates in each major area to recognize the signs of responsible argument. This especially includes having enough exposure to the work of policy analysts and experts in each area to know, if only in general terms, how they reach conclusions and the contribution they make. The point is not that the president will then be able to work through all the pertinent materials on an issue, evaluate them properly, and reach a sound, independent conclusion—that is ruled out if only for lack of time. As he evaluates policy advice, however, the president will at least be able to tell which of his subordinates are making sense. Whatever the subject at hand, the president will be able to judge whether an advocate is bringing to bear the right kinds of evidence, considerations, and arguments, and citing appropriate authorities.

One can observe the importance of this ability by comparing two, in some respects similar, episodes. Both John F. Kennedy in 1963 and Ronald Reagan in 1981 proposed large, controversial reductions of the individual income tax, each in some sense unorthodox. But in the role played by respectable economic opinion, the two cases could not be more different.

Kennedy brought to bear the prescriptions of Keynesian economics, which by then had been the dominant school of professional economic thought for nearly three decades. The Kennedy administration took office when the economy was in a deep recession. From the beginning, therefore, Walter Heller, a leading academic economist and Kennedy's CEA chairman, sought tax reductions to promote economic growth—the appropriate Keynesian response even though it might increase the federal deficit. Already aware of the rationale for stimulation, Kennedy did not require persuasion on the economic merits, but he did have political reservations. "I understand the case for a tax cut," he told Heller, "but it doesn't fit my call for sacrifice." Nor did it fit the economic views of Congress or the general public—both of which remained faithful on the whole to the traditional belief in an annually balanced budget. But the CEA continued lobbying, and Kennedy—first partially, later completely—went along. Finally, in 1963 Kennedy proposed to reduce income taxes substantially.

The novelty of this proposal, with the economy already recovering and the budget in deficit, alarmed traditionalists. "What can those people in Washington be thinking about?" asked former president Eisenhower in a magazine article. "Why would they deliberately do this to our country?" Congress, which also had doubts, moved slowly but eventually passed the tax cut in 1964. The Keynesian deficits proved right for the time: the tax cut stimulated enough economic activity that revenues, instead of declining, actually increased.[17]

Aside from being a tax cut and being radical, Reagan's proposal bore little resemblance to Kennedy's. Pushed through Congress in the summer of 1981, the Kemp-Roth tax bill (named for its congressional sponsors Congressman Jack F. Kemp and Sen. William V. Roth, Jr.) represented an explicit break with mainstream economic thinking, both liberal and conservative. The bill embodied the ideas of a small fringe group of economists whose views the conservative Republican economist Herbert Stein dismissed in the *Wall Street Journal* as "punk supply-side economics." In selling the bill to Congress, which was submissive in the aftermath of the Reagan election landslide, the administration made bold, unsupported claims. Despite tax rate reductions of 25 percent in a three-year period, it promised that the bill would so stimulate investment that revenues would increase and deficits decline. This resembled the claims for the Kennedy bill except that, under the prevailing conditions, nothing in conventional economic models or empirical estimates remotely justified the optimistic predictions. The Senate Republican leader Howard Baker, a reluctant supporter, termed the bill "a riverboat gamble." The gamble did not pay off. Within a year, policy makers were contemplating deficits in the $200 billion range—twice what they had considered intolerable a short time earlier and enough, nearly all agreed, to damage the economy severely.[18]

A president with some measure of sophistication about economic policy would have dismissed as economic demagoguery the extraordinary claims made for the Kemp-Roth bill.[19] He would have become aware of several things: that mainstream economists have worked out methods for estimating the effects of tax policies; that these estimates are imprecise and subject to a certain range of disagreement; but that, nevertheless, they are the best estimates anybody has. President Reagan undoubtedly knew (it would have been impossible not to) that most economists did not endorse Kemp-Roth. But it seems he had never paid enough attention to economic debate to recognize an important distinction between ideological faith and empirical measurement.

None of this is to suggest that presidents should set aside their ideologies and simply defer to experts, conceived somehow as ideologically neutral. Gerald Ford, the most conservative recent president next to Reagan, had an abiding commitment to the free market and assembled a cabinet and staff largely from individuals who shared his perspective. Yet the Ford administration also insisted that sound professional analysis underlie its decisions and took pains to consider a variety of views. Ford's CEA chairman, Alan Greenspan, was a devout conservative, but he encouraged the president to meet with diverse groups of outside economists (including former advisers in liberal Democratic administrations). He relied on conventional economic models and forecasting methods to fashion his own advice to the president. None of this prevented Ford's conservatism from shaping the policies of his administration, which held down government spending, stressed controlling inflation more than reducing unemployment, and started the process of deregulation.[20]

In much the same way, Reagan achieved conservative goals (cutting tax rates and reducing governmental distortion of economic decisions)—along with some liberal ones (tax relief for low-income people)—in the historic Tax Reform Act of 1986. The president's proposal was based on a massive study of the tax system by economists and tax specialists in the Treasury Department, which had advocated such reforms since the 1960s, and it embodied a consensual judgment among experts both inside and outside of government that the proliferation of credits, exemptions, and deductions in the federal tax code was harmful to the economy.[21]

Adequate policy expertise cannot be acquired in a hurry. A president needs to have been over the years the kind of politician who participates responsibly in decision making and debate and who does his homework. This means occasionally taking the time to read some of the advocacy documents (such as hearing testimony and committee reports) that are prepared especially for politicians and their staff. Such documents tend to be pitched toward the politician's sophistication and tolerance for detail and yet can provide a fairly rigorous education.

If properly prepared, a president need not spend long hours immersed in memoranda, the way Jimmy Carter did. If, after a thorough briefing on a decision of ordinary importance, the president still does not see which course he prefers, he is probably just as well off delegating the decision or taking a vote of his advisers. Other tasks will make more of a contribution to his success than further reading or discussion on a decision that is a close call anyway.

Policy Processes

In addition to policy issues, presidents must be competent in the processes of policy making.[22] Most presidential policy decisions are based on advice from several agencies or advisory groups in the executive branch, each with different responsibilities and points of view. To be useful to the president, all the advice must be brought together in a timely, intelligible way, with proper attention to all the significant viewpoints and considerations. Unfortunately, complex organizational and group decision processes like these have a notorious capacity to produce self-defeating and morally unacceptable results. The specific ways in which they go awry are numerous, but in general terms there are three major threats: intelligence failures, in which critical information is filtered out at lower organizational levels (sometimes because subordinates think the president would be upset by or disagree with it);[23] groupthink, in which a decision-making group commits itself to a course of action prematurely and adheres to it because of social pressures to conform;[24] and noncoordination, which may occur in formulating advice, in handling interdependent issues, or in carrying out decisions.[25]

Many of the frustrations of the Carter administration resulted from its failure to organize decision processes with sufficient care and skill. Carter's original energy proposals, which affected numerous federal programs, were nonetheless formulated by a single drafting group under the direction of Energy Secretary James Schlesinger. The group worked in secrecy and isolation, as well as under severe time pressure, which the president had imposed. The resulting proposals had serious flaws that, combined with resentment of the secrecy, led to a fiasco in Congress. Such problems were typical. The Carter administration's system of interagency task forces for domestic policy making generally was chaotic and not well controlled by the White House.[26] Moreover, the

White House itself was weakly coordinated. Not only did Carter's White House have fewer high-level coordinators than Reagan's, but, as John Kessel's comparative study has shown, those it did have were less active in communicating with the rest of the staff.[27]

In foreign policy, the major criticisms of the Carter administration concerned its propensity for vacillation and incoherence. Those tendencies resulted largely from its failure to manage the conflict between National Security Adviser Zbigniew Brzezinski and Secretary of State Cyrus R. Vance. Despite their different approaches to foreign policy, neither their respective roles nor the administration's operative doctrines were ever adequately clear. One crucial issue was whether the American stance toward negotiating with the Soviets on strategic arms would be linked with Soviet activities in the Horn of Africa (as Brzezinski wanted) or decided solely for its direct effects on American strategic interests (the preference of Vance). Instead of being reconciled, both policies were stated in public, each by the official who favored it, which cast doubt on America's ability to act consistently on either of them.[28] In part this problem resulted from Carter's personal unwillingness to discipline subordinates—to insist, for example, that Brzezinski abide by the more modest role that in theory had been assigned to him.

In short, serious presidential failures will often result not from individual ignorance—his own or that of his advisers—but from an administration's collective failure to maintain reliable processes for decision. But what must a president know to avoid this danger, and how can he learn it?

The effort to design the best possible organization for presidential coordination of the executive branch is exceedingly complex and uncertain—fundamentally a matter of hard trade-offs and guesses, not elegant solutions. Rather than adopt any one organizational plan or carefully study the debates about them, a president needs to have a high degree of generalized *process sensibility.* He should be generally conversant with the risks and impediments to effective decision making and strongly committed to avoiding them; he should recognize the potentially decisive effects of structure, procedures, and leadership methods; and he should be prepared to assign these matters a high priority. In short, the president should see organization and procedure as matters both difficult and vital.

The main operational requirements are straightforward. One or more of the president's top-level staff should be a process specialist—someone with experience managing large organizations, ideally the White House, and whose role is defined primarily as a manager and guardian of the decision process, not as an adviser on politics and policy.[29] Certainly one such person is needed in the position of White House chief of staff; others, perhaps much lower in rank, are needed to manage each major area of policy. A suitable person is one who is sophisticated about the problems of organizational design and the subtleties of human relationships—in addition to just being orderly. The president should invest such a person with the support and authority needed to impose a decision-making structure and help him or her insist on adherence to it. Since any organizational arrangement will have weaknesses, some of them unexpected, the president and other senior officials must give the decision-making process continual attention—monitoring its performance, and making adjustments.

Finally, if any of this is to work, the president also must be willing to discipline his own manner of participation. A well-managed, reliable decision-making process sometimes requires the president to perform, so to speak, unnatural acts. For example, in the heat of debate about a major decision, the inclination to enforce general plans about structures and roles does not come naturally. A "point of order" about procedures appears to distract from urgent decisions. In any case, the president's temptation is to react according to the substantive outcome he thinks he prefers: if an official who is supposed to be a neutral coordinator has a viewpoint the president likes, let him be heard; if an agency will make trouble over a decision that seems inevitable, let it stay out of it. Whatever the established procedures, senior officials sometimes will try to bypass them—asking for more control of a certain issue or ignoring channels to give the president direct advice.

On important decisions that require intensive discussion—decisions in major foreign policy crises, for example—the requirements are even more unnatural. In order to avoid serious mistakes, it is crucial not to suppress disagreement or close off debate prematurely. Thus, it is important for the president to assume a neutral stance until the time comes to decide. According to the psychologist Irving Janis's study of the Kennedy administration's disastrous decision to invade the Bay of Pigs, the president unwittingly inhibited debate just by his tone and manner of asking questions, which made it obvious that he believed, or wanted to believe, the invasion would work.[30] The president must restrain tendencies that are perfectly normal: to form opinions, perhaps optimistic ones, before all the evidence is in, and then want others to relieve his anxiety by agreeing. He must have a strong process sensibility if only because, without it, he would lack the motivation to do his own part.

The performance of Reagan and his aides in organization and policy management was mixed. In establishing effective advisory systems, especially at the outset of the administration, they did well. The administration's principal device for making policy decisions, a system of "cabinet councils," was planned and run largely by Chief of Staff James Baker, who had a knack for organization and previous experience in the Ford administration.[31] Each cabinet council was a subcommittee of the full cabinet, staffed by the White House and chaired by a cabinet member or sometimes the president. The system generally worked well in blending departmental and White House perspectives and reaching decisions in a timely manner, and it kept cabinet members attuned to the president's goals. Inevitably, adjustments were made with the passage of time. A White House Legislative Strategy Group (LSG) ended up making many of the decisions. Among the cabinet councils, the one assigned to coordinate economic policy, chaired by Treasury Secretary Regan, assumed a broad jurisdiction. To a degree, Reagan played his part in making these arrangements work. He enforced roles—removing a secretary of state, Alexander Haig, who was prone to exceed the limits of his charter—and invested the chief of staff with the authority to run an orderly process.

Nevertheless, the Reagan administration often failed to make decisions through a reasonably sound, deliberate process. One difficulty was that some of the officials Reagan selected to manage decision making lacked the appropriate skills or disposition for the task. In 1985 he allowed an exhausted Baker and an ambitious Regan to switch jobs. Although Regan by then had plenty of experience, he was less suited than Baker to the coordinating role of a chief of staff, and he soon came under attack for surrounding himself with weak subordinates and seeking to dominate the decision process. Until the appointment of Frank D. Carlucci in December 1986, the administration went through a series of four undistinguished national security advisers—one of them, William P. Clark, a long-time associate of Reagan's with minimal experience in foreign policy.

On a number of occasions an even more important source of difficulty was the conduct of the president himself. Instead of exercising self-restraint and fostering discussion, Reagan gave his own impulses free rein. He ignored bad news and responded with anger to unwelcome advice.[32] His role in decisions was unpredictable. Reagan's announcement in March 1983 of the effort to develop a "Star Wars" missile defense system was made, as John Steinbrunner says, "without prior staff work or technical definition . . . [and] rather astonished professional security bureaucracies throughout the world."[33] During the 1986 summit meeting in Reykjavík, Iceland, Reagan again acted without prior staff work as he tentatively accepted a surprise Soviet proposal to do away with long-range nuclear weapons—a Utopian notion that ignored the vast superiority of Soviet conventional forces and was soon disavowed by the administration.

Finally, a lack of concern for the integrity of the decision process figured prominently in the Iran-contra scandal that emerged in late 1986, a disaster for U.S. foreign policy and the worst political crisis of the Reagan presidency. The secret arms sales to Iran were vehemently opposed by Secretary of State George P. Shultz and Defense Secretary Weinberger, who wrote on his copy of the White House memorandum proposing the plan that it was "almost too absurd for comment." To get around their resistance, the White House largely excluded the two officials from further discussions and carried out the sales, in some degree, without their knowledge. Moreover, to escape the normal congressional oversight of covert activities, the transfers were handled directly by the staff of the National Security Council (NSC), theoretically an advisory unit, instead of the Defense Department (DOD) or the Central Intelligence Agency (CIA). In short, the White House deprived itself of the advice of the two principal cabinet members in foreign policy, the congressional leadership on intelligence matters, and the operational staff of DOD and the CIA—any of whom would have been likely to point out, aside from other serious objections, that the weapons transfers almost inevitably would become public.

Policy Promotion

Good policy decisions, carefully made, are not enough. Presidents also need competence in policy promotion—the ability to get things done in Washington and especially in Congress.[34] For no other major presidential task, it seems, is the necessary knowledge any more complicated or esoteric. Nevertheless, it is also a task in which delegation can largely substitute for the president's own judgment and thus one in which strategic competence places a modest burden on the president.

To promote his policies effectively, a president must make good decisions on complex, highly uncertain problems of strategy and tactics. Which presidential policy goals are politically feasible and which must be deferred? With which groups or congressional leaders should coalitions be formed? When resistance is met, should the president stand firm, perhaps taking the issue to the public, or should he compromise? In all these matters what is the proper timing? Such decisions call for a form of political expertise that has several related elements (all of them different from those involved in winning elections): a solid knowledge of the main coalitions, influence relations, and rivalries among groups and individuals in Washington; personal acquaintance with a considerable number of important or well-informed individuals; and a fine-grained, practical understanding of how the political institutions work. This expertise can be acquired, clearly enough, only through substantial and recent experience in Washington. For a president who happens to lack this experience, however, this need not pose much difficulty. Like any technical skill, which in a sense it is, the necessary expertise can easily be hired; the president needs merely to see his need for it.

Because the government has many jobs that require political skill, people with the requisite experience abound. Many of them (to state the matter politely) would be willing to serve in the White House, and by asking around, it is not hard to get good readings on their effectiveness. Most important, having hired experienced Washington operatives, a president can delegate to them the critical judgments about feasibility, strategy, and political technique. It is not that such judgments are clear-cut, of course. But unlike questions of policy, in these matters the boundary between the realm of expertise and that of values and ideology is not difficult to discern. Political strategy, in the narrow sense of how to realize given policy objectives to the greatest possible extent, is ideologically neutral. It is even nonpartisan: Republican and Democratic presidents attempt to influence Congress in much the same way.[35] In any case, a political expert's performance in the White House can be measured primarily by short-term results, that is, by how much the administration's policy goals are actually being achieved.

Both the value and the necessity of delegating policy promotion emerge from a comparison of Carter and Reagan—two recent presidents who had no prior Washington experience. If there was a single, root cause of the Carter administration's failure (underlying even its mismanagement of decision making), it was its refusal to recruit people with successful experience in Washington politics for top advisory and political jobs in the White House.

One of the more unfortunate choices was that of Frank Moore to direct legislative liaison. Although he had held the same job in Georgia when Carter was governor, Moore had no experience in Washington and came to be regarded in Congress as out of his depth. Among Moore's initial staff, which consisted mostly of Georgians, two of the five professionals had worked neither in Congress nor as lobbyists. In organizing them, Moore chose a plan that had been opposed by the former Democratic liaison officials who had been asked for advice. Instead of using the conventional division by chambers and major congressional groups, Moore assigned each lobbyist to specialize in an area of policy. This kept them from developing the stable relationships with individual members of Congress that would enhance trust, and it ignored the straight-forward consideration that not all the issues in which the lobbyists specialized would be actively considered at the same time.[36] The Carter administration's reputed incompetence in dealing with Congress might have been predicted: the best of the many Georgians on the Carter staff were able and effective, but others were not, and collectively they lacked the orientation to operate well in Washington.[37]

After this widely condemned failure of his immediate predecessor, it is not surprising that President Reagan did not make the same mistake. But it is still impressive how thoroughly he applied the lesson, even setting aside sectarian considerations for some of the top White House positions. James Baker, who was mainly responsible for political operations during the first term, had not only been a Ford administration appointee and campaign manager for George Bush but was also considered too moderate for a high-level position by many of Reagan's conservative supporters. The congressional liaison director, Max Friedersdorf, was a mainstream Republican who had worked on congressional relations for Nixon and Ford.[38] In short, the political strategy by which the "Reagan revolution" was pushed through Congress in 1981 was devised and exe-cuted by hired hands who were latecomers, at most, to Reaganism. Although there was some change in personnel in subsequent years, including the job switch by Baker and Regan, the organization and management of this function was essentially stable.[39]

Although the task of formulating strategy for policy promotion can be dele-gated, much of the hard work cannot. Nothing can draw attention to a pro-posal and build public support like a well-presented speech by the president. Furthermore, there are always certain votes available in Congress if the presi-dent makes the necessary phone calls or meets with the right members. The latter task is often tedious, however, if not somewhat degrading—pleading for support, repeating the same pitch over and over, and promising favors to some while evading requests from others. Presidents therefore often neglect this duty, a source of frustration for their staffs. Carter "went all over the country for two years asking everybody he saw to vote for him," his press secretary complained, "but he doesn't like to call up a Congressman and ask for his support on a bill."[40] Reagan, in contrast, spared no personal effort to pass his program. During the debate on funding for the MX missile in 1985, he had face-to-face meetings with more than two hundred members of Congress and followed up with dozens of phone calls. When House Republicans felt they were being ig-nored in negotiations on tax reform, he went to Capitol Hill to make amends.

Of course, a president's effectiveness in lobbying and making speeches depends very much on his basic skills in persuasive communication. A lack of such skills cannot be made up by presidential aides, nor can it be overcome to any great extent by additional learning.

The Possibility of Competence

The presidency is not an impossible job. The requirements for personal knowledge, attention, and expertise on the president's part seem wholly manageable—but only if the president has a *strategy* for competence that puts his own, inherently limited capacities to use where and how they are most needed.

With regard to the substance of *policy decisions,* it is enough if the president over the years has given reasonably serious attention to the major national issues and thus is able to recognize the elements of responsible debate. Waking before sunrise to read stacks of policy memoranda is neither necessary nor especially productive.

To maintain an effective *policy process,* the president mainly needs to have a strong process sensibility, that is, a clear sense of the need for careful and self-conscious management of decision making and a willingness to discipline himself as he participates in it. He need not claim any facility in drawing the boxes and arrows of organization charts himself. Although this substantive and procedural competence will not ensure that the president will always make the "right" decision—the one he would make with perfect understanding of the issues—it will minimize the likelihood of decisions that are intolerably far off the mark. Finally, and easiest of all, the president must know enough to avail himself of the assistance of persons experienced in *policy promotion* in the political environment of Washington, and especially in dealing with Congress—whether they have been long-time supporters or not. Then he must respect their advice and do the work they ask of him.

Bush, Clinton, and Strategic Competence

The requirements of strategic competence help account for some of the successes and failures of the two most recent presidents, George Bush and Bill Clinton. Both presidents had significant achievements but also serious troubles. Some of their difficulties were caused by forces beyond their control—in other words, bad luck. But in differing degrees, each also had deficiencies of competence for which he paid a price.

The Bush presidency is generally regarded as a failure, mostly because Bush ended his term with low popularity ratings and was defeated in his bid for re-election.[41] For the most part, however, these developments were not under his control and did not reflect on his competence. In spring 1991, even as Bush was basking in the glory of America's victories over Soviet communism in the cold war and over Saddam Hussein in the Persian Gulf War and was enjoying such high approval ratings that the leading potential Democratic challengers were declining to enter the presidential race, the economy slipped into a recession. The weak economy hung on through most of 1992. It gradually but dramatically eroded Bush's standing with the public and, more than anything else, caused his defeat in the election.[42]

In the midst of the recession, Bush refused to support a tax cut or spending increase to prime the economy, arguing that either course would only make the situation worse. His refusal to act was later portrayed by the Democrats as indifference to the nation's economic distress. In truth, Bush was following the advice not only of his staff but also of most economists, who warned that increasing an already oversized budget deficit would harm the economy in the long run and predicted that the economy would recover quickly even without stimulation.[43] That these predictions proved wrong virtually killed Bush's chances for reelection.

However, Bush's decision was reasonable in light of the information he had at the time. Even in hindsight, it is not clear that a stimulative fiscal policy in 1991 would have produced a better economic result. Fundamentally, Bush was a victim not of misguided decisions or ineffectual leadership but rather of economic forces that he could neither predict nor control.

Yet the course of Bush's presidency also turned on his own competence. He was in several respects naturally skilled and strategically competent. By all accounts, Bush was well versed on public policy. He used reasonably orderly and informative decision processes.[44] He was an eager self-starter in using his extensive personal contacts to push his policies in Congress.

Nevertheless, Bush made some of his own difficulties in ways that reflected deficiencies in his decision making. His major strategic failing was that he imposed very little discipline on his own participation in the decision process. Specifically, Bush had some unusual and potentially harmful personal dispositions toward decision making and political action that he allowed to shape the advisory process and determine decisions. He had a hard time maintaining balanced and stable attitudes toward risk and conflict. Although such attitudes are difficult to pin down without detailed analyses of particular decisions, Bush seems to have vacillated between the extremes of caution and risk taking, and also between the extremes of conciliation and hostility. For example, in 1989 Bush surprised observers by caving in to Congress on aid to the Nicaragua contras; but then he invaded Panama under dubious authority of international law. He attacked Iraq with massive force in 1991, then pulled back without securing a complete victory. According to a scathing critique by former President Richard M. Nixon, Bush shrank from the critical task of leading the country to support democratization and economic reform in Russia.[45] One of Bush's riskiest moves was his unconditional "read-my-lips" promise during the 1988 campaign that he would not raise taxes. His eventual abandonment of the promise as part of a 1990 deficit reduction agreement was a political disaster for Bush that placed a major burden on his reelection effort.

Moreover, Bush had little patience for thinking broadly about plans and purposes. Critics dismissed him as shallow and complained that he had no vision of the country's future. Bush rejected the criticism as irrelevant, belittling what he called "the vision thing." But in fact, his overly concrete style of thinking constrained deliberation in the White House. Even in the early stages of Bush's term, the staff focused on reacting to events, thereby neglecting broad goals and long-range plans.[46]

Finally, Bush had limited patience for thinking, whether broadly or narrowly, about domestic policy. Bush had some good reasons for preferring to spend his time on foreign affairs: his extensive experience in that area (as former envoy to China and director of the Central Intelligence Agency), a lack of popular support for conservative reforms in domestic policy, fiscal barriers to new or expanded social programs, and the likelihood of conflict over domestic issues with a solidly Democratic Congress. But instead of exercising self-discipline, Bush indulged his preference for foreign policy freely. He allowed his lack of interest in domestic issues to be generally known and widely commented upon.[47]

Bush's attitude skewed the advisory process and his administration's decisions. Remarkably, the Bush administration offered no legislative agenda in its first year.[48] His staff undertook a lengthy study of the welfare system only to conclude that nothing useful could be done about it. A few Bush staffers, notably Secretary of Housing and Urban Development Jack Kemp and White House aide James Pinkerton, tried to advance an innovative, conservative domestic agenda, but they were consistently defeated within the administration. In 1991, Bush's political advisers recommended that he rely on his high popularity and the political "war dividend" from the victory in the Persian Gulf to carry him to reelection in 1992.[49]

In the end, Bush learned that the public will not allow presidents to write off domestic policy. His lack of a domestic agenda was itself an effective issue for the Democrats in the 1992 campaign; and Bush was reduced to promising, pathetically, that he would replace his White House staff and work mainly on domestic problems in his second term. It is not clear that Bush would either have had significant additional policy accomplishments or would have won re-election if he had managed risk and conflict better, paid more attention to goals and plans, and tried harder to develop a respectable record of domestic achievement. But he certainly would have improved his chances.

An assessment of President Clinton's competence, necessarily tentative after only fourteen months in office, also reveals areas of strength and weakness.[50] Indeed, the contrasts are stark. On the one hand, Clinton has shown an extraordinary grasp of policy issues. In a lengthy televised economic summit conference shortly before his inauguration, Clinton traded ideas and insights, seemingly on equal terms, with an assemblage of leading economists, business leaders, and other experts. His ability to discourse cogently and in detail on a broad range of policy matters was widely admired. Moreover, he performed with energy, skill, and strategic intelligence in promoting his major policies—fighting successful uphill battles in Congress to pass his 1993 deficit reduction plan and the North American Free Trade Agreement. With his combination of policy knowledge, rhetorical ability, interpersonal skills, and energy, Clinton had prodigious raw talent for presidential leadership.

On the other hand, Clinton failed profoundly and in multiple ways to meet the requirements of strategic competence in the management of decision processes. His chief of staff, Thomas F. "Mack" McLarty, was a lifelong Arkansas friend and successful businessman who had no Washington or government experience. McLarty had a suitable concept of the chief of staff's role, seeking to broker the decision process without interjecting his own views, but he was out of his element in White House politics. The president's chief counsel, Bernard Nussbaum, was a distinguished Wall Street lawyer who also had minimal experience in Washington.[51] In fact, many Clinton staff members had little experience of any kind: they were in their twenties or early thirties, just beginning their professional careers.

The decision-making process in the early Clinton White House was haphazard, without much explicit management or planned structure. Although "war rooms" were organized to deal with a handful of major issues, decisions were arrived at informally.[52] The roles and influence of the staff depended mainly on personal relationships; several overlapping networks centered, respectively, on the president (the so-called "Friends of Bill"); his wife, Hillary Rodham Clinton; Vice President Al Gore; the 1992 campaign staff; and a circle of Arkansas friends.[53] In some ways Clinton seemed to adopt the impractical ideal of self-reliant presidential leadership, making up for the lack of structured advisory processes by investing enormous personal energy in decision making. Strangely, the early Clinton White House failed to reflect the president's apparent ideological commitments. It lacked a significant number of the relatively conservative Democrats for whom Clinton had long been a leading spokesman and instead was dominated by liberal Democrats. The staff's liberalism raised questions about whether Clinton had abandoned his 1992 campaign stance as a "new Democrat" and planned to govern in the interests of traditional Democratic constituencies.[54]

Finally, Clinton used questionable judgment in setting up the advisory process that formulated his health care reform plan—an extraordinarily complex undertaking with direct bearing on almost one-sixth of the national economy. The health care reform task force was headed by Hillary Rodham Clinton, with the help of Ira Magaziner, an academic policy analyst. Although it was probably sensible to assign this task to someone the president could trust implicitly to protect his political interests, and Mrs. Clinton and Magaziner were both knowledgeable about social policy, both were associated with the liberal wing of the Democratic party.

More important, neither Mrs. Clinton nor Magaziner had ever managed or even been part of a complex executive-branch policy-making process. The two created an unwieldy structure with numerous working groups and more than 500 participants from government and the private sector.[55] In an ill-advised effort at secrecy reminiscent of the formation of the Carter administration's energy plan, they not only shielded the task force's deliberations from public view but even tried to keep its membership confidential.

The inexperienced, disorganized, and ideologically unbalanced White House staff was responsible in varying degrees for a legion of political difficulties that beset Clinton in his first fourteen months as president. These included a costly clash with Congress about the rights of gays and lesbians in the military; the inability to win confirmation of several major cabinet and subcabinet appointments; a scandal concerning the unwarranted dismissal of civil servants in the White House travel office; an embarrassing gaffe in which Clinton held up air traffic at Los Angeles International Airport for two hours while he got a $200 haircut on Air Force One; the need to drop energy taxes and infrastructure investments from his economic program; and criticism of administration policies on Somalia, Haiti, Bosnia, and China as incoherent. Clinton's health care proposal, inevitably controversial, was too costly and bureaucratic for many Democrats and faced, at best, major surgery in Congress. In March 1994, Clinton suffered revelations that his chief counsel had held meetings of dubious propriety with Treasury Department officials who were looking into some of the Clintons' past financial dealings with the Whitewater Development Corporation.

In contrast to Bush, Clinton learned from his early mistakes. Responding to the White House foul-ups of the first year, he brought in a respected Republican political analyst and former White House aide, David R. Gergen, as counselor in order to give the staff more political depth and provide a conservative counterweight to its liberal tendency. Later, when the chief counsel was forced to resign in the Whitewater scandal, Clinton picked a renowned Washington lawyer and former counsel to President Carter, Lloyd N. Cutler, as his replacement. With an improving economy, respectable showings in opinion polls, and significant policy achievements under his belt, Clinton began his second spring in office with every chance for a successful presidency—provided of course that he was not derailed by past indiscretions and that he continued to grow in the ways of strategic competence.

Notes

This chapter is an extensively revised and elaborated version of "What Must a President Know?" by Paul J. Quirk in *Transaction/SOCIETY*, no. 23 (January/February 1983) © 1983 by Transaction Publishers. The author would like to acknowledge the following people for their very helpful advice: Stella Herriges Quirk, Irving Louis Horowitz, A. James Reichley, Robert A. Katzmann, Martha Derthick, and Michael Nelson. Susan Green and James Sopp helped to update the chapter.

1. As one Republican political analyst has observed in an article for a conservative magazine, "The years . . . [since 1989] have not so far been kind to Reagan's standing, either with the general public or with scholars of the presidency." See A. James Reichley, "Reagan in Retrospect," *The World and I*, May 1994. Most of the diminution of Reagan's standing is the result of the budget deficits and other economic troubles of the 1990s.

2. Richard E. Neustadt, *Presidential Power: The Politics of Leadership* (New York: Wiley, 1960). Later editions, most recently in 1980, have updated the analysis and in some ways modified the argument.

3. Ibid., chap. 7.

4. James David Barber, *The Presidential Character: Predicting Performance in the White House*, 2d ed. (Englewood Cliffs, N.J.: Prentice-Hall, 1977).

5. Arthur M. Schlesinger, Jr., "Roosevelt as Administrator," in *Bureaucratic Power in National Politics*, 2d ed., ed. Francis E. Rourke (Boston: Little, Brown, 1972), 126–138.

6. Ibid., 132–133, 137.

7. On Johnson's personality and his presidency, see Doris Kearns, *Lyndon Johnson and the American Dream* (New York: Harper and Row, 1976).

8. James Fallows, "The Passionless Presidency," *Atlantic*, May 1979, 33–48.

9. See Nelson W. Polsby, *The Consequences of Party Reform* (New York: Oxford University Press, 1983), 108–109.

10. On the Whig theory and the changing conceptions of the presidency as an institution, see James L. Sundquist, *The Decline and Resurgence of Congress* (Washington, D.C.: Brookings Institution, 1981), chap. 2.

11. Fred I. Greenstein, *The Hidden-Hand Presidency: Eisenhower as Leader* (New York: Basic Books, 1982).

12. Ibid., 61, 155–227.

13. Dick Kirschten, "White House Strategy," *National Journal*, February 21, 1981, 300–303.

14. Quoted in John Herbers, "The Presidency and the Press Corps," *New York Times Magazine*, May 9, 1982, 45ff.

15. David A. Stockman, *The Triumph of Politics: How the Reagan Revolution Failed* (New York: Harper and Row, 1986), 276–295.

16. For the sake of brevity, I omit the president's problems and potential strategies for managing policy implementation by the bureaucracy. See Richard P. Nathan, *The Administrative Presidency* (New York: Wiley, 1983). This function depends heavily on the appropriate selection of political executives. See G. Calvin Mackenzie, *The Politics of Presidential Appointments* (New York: Free Press, 1980).

17. Arthur M. Schlesinger, Jr., *A Thousand Days: John F. Kennedy in the White House* (Boston: Houghton Mifflin, 1965), 628–630, 1002–1008.

18. At least one Reagan administration leader has been candid about the role of faith in its 1981 economic proposals. See William Greider, "The Education of David Stockman," *Atlantic*, December 1981, 27ff.

19. The same cannot be said of members of Congress, whom one expects to be more prone to demagoguery, and who came under intense political pressure, stimulated in large part by the president.

20. See A. James Reichley, *Conservatives in an Age of Change: The Nixon and Ford Administrations* (Washington, D.C.: Brookings Institution, 1981), chap. 18; Roger Porter, *Presidential Decision Making: The Economic Policy Board* (New York: Cambridge University Press, 1980), chap. 3; and Martha Derthick and Paul J. Quirk, *The Politics of Deregulation* (Washington, D.C.: Brookings Institution, 1985), chap. 2.

21. Timothy B. Clark, "Strange Bedfellows," *National Journal*, February 2, 1985. For a penetrating study of the politics of taxation, see John F. Witte, *The Politics and Development of the Federal Income Tax* (Madison: University of Wisconsin Press, 1985).

22. The president's task in managing decision making is more difficult than that of chief executives in some of the parliamentary democracies because they have more elaborate and better institutionalized coordinating machinery. See Colin Campbell and George J. Szablowski, *The Super-Bureaucrats: Structure and Behavior in Central Agencies* (New York: New York University Press, 1979). For insightful analyses of the influences on presidential ability to use information effectively, see John P. Burke and Fred I. Greenstein, *How Presidents Test Reality: Decisions on Vietnam, 1954 and 1965* (New York: Russell Sage Foundation, 1989); and Bert A. Rockman, "Organizing the White House: On a West Wing and a Prayer," *Journal of Managerial Issues* 5 (Winter 1993): 453–464.

23. Harold Wilensky, *Organizational Intelligence: Knowledge and Policy in Government and Industry* (New York: Basic Books, 1967).

24. Irving Janis, *Victims of GroupThink: A Psychological Study of Foreign-Policy Decisions and Fiascoes* (Boston: Houghton Mifflin, 1972).

25. Fundamentally, all organization theory concerns the problem of coordination. See Anthony Downs, *Inside Bureaucracy* (Boston: Little, Brown, 1967), chap. 11; and Jay R. Galbraith, *Organization Design* (Reading, Mass.: Addison-Wesley, 1977). Problems of coordination in the executive branch are emphasized in I. M. Destler, *Making Foreign Economic Policy* (Washington, D.C.: Brookings Institution, 1980).

26. Lester M. Salamon, "The Presidency and Domestic Policy Formulation," in *The Illusion of Presidential Government*, ed. Hugh Heclo and Lester Salamon (Boulder, Colo.: Westview Press, 1982), 177–212.

27. For this and other Reagan-Carter comparisons, see John H. Kessel, "The Structures of the Reagan White House" (Paper presented at the annual meeting of the American Political Science Association, Chicago, September 1–4, 1983). More generally on Carter, however, see Kessel, "The Structures of the Carter White House," *American Journal of Political Science* 22 (August 1983).

28. The resulting mutual recriminations constitute leading themes in the recently published memoirs of the two officials. See Cyrus Vance, *Hard Choices: Critical Years in America's Foreign Policy* (New York: Simon and Schuster, 1983); and Zbigniew Brzezinski, *Power and Principle: Memoirs of the National Security Advisor, 1977–1981* (New York: Farrar, Straus and Giroux, 1983).

29. An influential argument for separating the roles of process manager and policy adviser is in Alexander George, "The Case for Multiple Advocacy in Making Foreign Policy," *American Political Science Review* 66 (September 1972): 751–785; see also George, *Presidential Decision Making: The Effective Use of Information and Advice* (Boulder, Colo.: Westview Press, 1980).

30. Janis, *Victims of GroupThink*, chap. 2.

31. For an account of the Reagan administration's organizational strategy, see James P. Pfiffner, "White House Staff versus the Cabinet: Centripetal and Centrifugal Roles," *Presidential Studies Quarterly* 16 (Fall 1986): 666–690.

32. Reagan's capacity for ignoring bad news is documented in Stockman, *The Triumph of Politics*; and Laurence I. Barrett, *Gambling with History: Reagan in the White House* (New York: Penguin Books, 1984), esp. 174.

33. John D. Steinbrunner, "Security Policy," in *The New Direction in American Politics*, ed. John E. Chubb and Paul E. Peterson (Washington, D.C.: Brookings Institution, 1985), 351.

34. On the president's relations with Congress, see Anthony King, ed., *Both Ends of the Avenue: The Presidency, the Executive Branch, and Congress in the 1980s* (Washington, D.C.: American Enterprise Institute, 1983); Barbara Kellerman, *The Political Presidency* (New York: Oxford University Press, 1984); and Mark A. Peterson, *Legislating Together: The White House and Capitol Hill from Eisenhower to Reagan* (Cambridge: Harvard University Press, 1990).

35. For a historical treatment and analysis of organization for White House liaison, see Stephen J. Wayne, *The Legislative Presidency* (New York: Harper and Row, 1978).

36. Eric L. Davis, "Legislative Liaison in the Carter Administration," *Political Science Quarterly* 95 (Summer 1979): 287–302. Eventually, organization of the staff by issues was dropped.

37. In *Consequences of Party Reform*, 105–114, Polsby details the Carter administration's major mistakes in dealing with Congress and argues persuasively that its difficulties were not importantly the result of internal changes in Congress.

38. Dick Kirschten, "Second Term Legislative Strategy Shifts to Foreign Policy and Defense Issues," *National Journal*, March 30, 1985, 696–699.

39. Samuel Kernell, *Going Public: New Strategies of Presidential Leadership* (Washington, D.C.: CQ Press, 1986); and Theodore J. Lowi, *The Personal President: Power Invested, Promise Unfulfilled* (Ithaca, N.Y.: Cornell University Press, 1985).

40. Quoted in Polsby, *Consequences of Party Reform*, 109.

41. For early assessments of the Bush presidency, see Colin Campbell and Bert A. Rockman, eds., *The Bush Presidency: First Appraisals* (Chatham, N.J.: Chatham House, 1991); and Ryan J. Barilleaux and Mary E. Stuckey, eds., *Leadership and the Bush Presidency: Prudence or Drift in an Era of Change?* (Westport, Conn.: Greenwood Press, 1992).

42. See Paul J. Quirk and Jon K. Dalager, "The Election: A 'New Democrat' and a New Kind of Presidential Campaign," in *The Elections of 1992*, ed. Michael Nelson (Washington, D.C.: CQ Press, 1993), 57–88.

43. See Paul J. Quirk and Bruce Nesmith, "Explaining Deadlock: Domestic Policy-making in the Bush Presidency," in *New Perspectives on American Politics*, ed. Lawrence C. Dodd and Calvin Jillson (Washington, D.C.: CQ Press, 1994), 200–201.

44. Richard Cohen, "The Gloves Are Off," *National Journal*, October 14, 1989, 2508–2512; and "Mr. Consensus," *Time*, August 21, 1989, 17–22.

45. Richard M. Nixon, "The Challenge We Face in Russia," *Wall Street Journal*, March 11, 1992, 14.

46. Paul J. Quirk, "Domestic Policy: Divided Government and Cooperative Presidential Leadership," in *The Bush Presidency: First Appraisals*, ed. Colin Campbell and Bert A. Rockman (Chatham, N.J.: Chatham House, 1991), 69–92.

47. Robert Shogun, *The Riddle of Power: Presidential Leadership from Truman to Bush* (New York: Penguin, 1982), chap. 10.

48. Quirk, "Domestic Policy: Divided Government and Cooperative Presidential leadership," 69–92.

49. Fred Barnes, "White House Watch: Logjam," *New Republic*, May 11, 1992, 10–11; James Pinkerton, "Life in Bush Hell," *New Republic*, December 14, 1992, 22–27; Mickey Kaus, "Paradigm's Loss," *New Republic*, July 27, 1992, 16–22; Fred Barnes, "White House Watch: War Dividend," *New Republic*, March 25, 1991, 12–13; and Burt Solomon, "White House Notebook: Bush Plays Down Domestic Policy in Coasting Towards Reelection," *National Journal*, February 30, 1991, 752–753.

50. For a thoughtful, although very early view, see Fred I. Greenstein, "The Presidential Leadership Style of Bill Clinton: An Early Appraisal," *Political Science Quarterly* 108 (Winter 1993–1994): 589–602.

51. W. John Moore, "West Wing Novice," *National Journal*, June 5, 1993, 1339–1343. Two decades earlier, Nussbaum had worked on the Watergate prosecution team.

52. Burt Solomon, "White House Notebook: A Modish Management Style Means Slip-Sliding around the West Wing," *National Journal*, October 30, 1993, 2606–2607.

53. Burt Solomon, "Crisscrossed with Connections . . . West Wing Is a Networker's Dream," *National Journal*, January 15, 1994, 256–257.

54. Fred Barnes, "Neoconned," *New Republic*, January 25, 1993, 14–16.

55. Julie Kosterlitz, "Changing of the Guard," *National Journal*, March 6, 1993, 575; Burt Solomon, "Boomers in Charge," *National Journal*, June 19, 1993, 1472.

7 The Psychological Presidency

Michael Nelson

Several delegates to the Constitutional Convention of 1787 noted during the first week of debate that to invest enormous power in a one-person office was to invest enormous power in one person. Not until James David Barber wrote The Presidential Character, *however, was a systematic effort made to explore the psychological consequences of that important truism. Michael Nelson examines this influential book, along with another that Barber wrote about the voters' supposed contributions to the "psychological presidency," called* The Pulse of Politics. *Although Nelson finds Barber's theories wanting (the healthiest of Barber's character types, for example, are not always successful presidents), he praises Barber for drawing attention to the psychological aspects of the presidency and for encouraging political journalists to do the same in their coverage of presidential campaigns.*

The United States elects its president every four years, which makes it unique among democratic nations. During several recent election campaigns, *Time* magazine has run a story about James David Barber, which makes him equally singular among political scientists. The two quadrennial oddities are not unrelated.

The first *Time* article was about Barber's just published book, *The Presidential Character: Predicting Performance in the White House,* in which he argued that presidents could be divided into four psychological types: "active-positive," "active-negative," "passive-positive," and "passive-negative." What's more, according to Barber via *Time,* by taking "a hard look at men before they reach the White House," voters could tell in advance what candidates would be like if elected: healthily "ambitious out of exuberance," like the active-positives; or pathologically "ambitious out of anxiety," "compliant and other-directed," or "dutiful and self-denying," like the three other, lesser types, respectively. In the 1972 election, Barber told *Time,* the choice was between an active-positive,

George McGovern, and a psychologically defective active-negative, Richard M. Nixon.[1]

Nixon won the election, but Barber's early insights into Nixon's personality won notoriety for both him and his theory, especially in the wake of Watergate. So prominent had Barber become by 1976 that Hugh Sidey used his entire "Presidency" column in the October 4 issue of *Time* to tell readers that Barber was refusing to type candidates Gerald R. Ford and Jimmy Carter this time around. "Barber is deep into an academic study of this election and its participants, and he is pledged to restraint until it is over," Sidey reported solemnly.[2] (Actually, more than a year before, Barber had told interviewers from *U.S. News & World Report* that he considered Ford an active-positive.)[3] Carter, who read Barber's book twice when it came out, was left to tell the *Washington Post* that active-positive is "what I would like to be. That's what I hope I prove to be."[4] And so Carter would be, wrote Barber in a special postelection column for *Time.*[5]

The 1980 election campaign witnessed the appearance of another Barber book, *The Pulse of Politics: Electing Presidents in the Media Age,* and in honor of the occasion, two *Time* articles. This was all to the good, because the first, a Sidey column in March, offered more gush than information: "The first words encountered in the new book by Duke's Professor James David Barber are stunning: 'A revolution in presidential politics is under way.' . . . Barber has made political history before."[6] A more substantive piece in the magazine's May 19 "Nation" section described the new book's cycle theory of twentieth-century presidential elections: since 1900, steady four-year beats in the public's psychological mood, or "pulse," have caused a recurring alternation among elections of "conflict," "conscience," and "conciliation." *Time* went on to stress, although not explain, Barber's view of the importance of the mass media, both as a reinforcer of this cycle and as a potential mechanism for helping the nation to break out of it.[7]

In 1984, 1988, and 1992, Barber wrote for and was written about in numerous other national publications. But it was *Time*'s infatuation with Barber that brought him a level of fame that comes rarely to scholars, more rarely still to political scientists. For Barber, fame has come at some cost. Although widely known, his ideas are little understood. The media's cursory treatment of them has made them appear superficial or even foolish—instantly appealing to the naive, instantly odious to the thoughtful. Partly as a result, Barber's reputation in the intellectual community as an *homme sérieux* has suffered. In the backrooms and corridors of scholarly gatherings, one hears "journalistic" and "popularizer," the worst academic epithets, muttered along with his name. Indeed, in a 1991 assessment of recent scholarly research on the presidency, Paul Quirk observed of the whole field of presidential psychology that "researchers seem to have kept their distance from the subject as if to avoid guilt by association" with Barber.[8]

This situation is in need of remedy. Barber's theories may be seriously flawed, but they are serious theories. For all their limitations—some of them self-confessed—they offer one of the more significant contributions a scholar can make: an unfamiliar but useful way of looking at a familiar thing that we no longer see very clearly. In Barber's case, the familiar thing is the American presidency, and the unfamiliar way of looking at it is through the lenses of psychology.

Psychological Perspectives on the Presidency

Constitutional Perspectives

To look at politics in general, or the American presidency in particular, from a psychological perspective is not new. Although deprived of the insights (and spared the nonsense) of twentieth-century psychology, the framers of the Constitution constructed their plan of government on a foundation of Hobbesian assumptions about what motivates *homo politicus*. (They called what they were doing moral philosophy, not psychology.) James Madison and most of his colleagues at the Constitutional Convention assumed that "men are instruments of their desires"; that "one such desire is the desire for power"; and that "if unrestrained by external checks, any individual or group of individuals will tyrannize over others."[9] Because the framers believed these things, a basic tenet of their political philosophy was that the government they were designing should be a "government of laws and not of men." Not just psychology but history had taught them to associate liberty with law and tyranny with rulers who depart from law, as had George III and his colonial governors.

In the end the convention yielded to those who urged, on grounds of "energy in the executive," that the Constitution lodge the powers of the executive branch in a single person, the president.[10] There are several explanations for why the framers were willing to put aside their doubts and inject such a powerful dose of individual "character" (in both the moral and the psychological senses of the word) into their new plan of government. One is the framers' certain knowledge that George Washington would be the first president. They knew that Washington aroused powerful and, from the standpoint of winning the nation's support for the new government, vital psychological reponses from the people. As Seymour Martin Lipset has shown, Washington was a classic example of Max Weber's charismatic leader, a man "treated [by the people] as endowed with supernatural, superhuman, or at least specifically exceptional powers or qualities."[11] Marcus Cunliffe notes:

[B]abies were being christened after him as early as 1775, and while he was still President, his countrymen paid to see him in waxwork effigy. To his admirers he was "godlike Washington," and his detractors complained to one another that he was looked upon as a "demigod" whom it was treasonous to criticize. "Oh Washington!" declared Ezra Stiles of Yale (in a sermon of 1783). "How I do love thy name! How have I often adored and blessed thy God, for creating and forming thee the great ornament of human kind!"[12]

Just as Washington's "gift of grace" would legitimize the new government, the framers believed, so would his personal character ensure its republican nature. The powers of the president in the Constitution "are full great," wrote Pierce Butler, a convention delegate from South Carolina, to a British kinsman,

and greater than I was disposed to make them. Nor, entre nous, do I believe they would have been so great had not many of the delegates cast their eyes towards General Washington as President; and shaped their Ideas of the Powers to be given to a President, by their opinions of his Virtue.[13]

The framers were not so naive or shortsighted as to invest everything in Washington. To protect the nation from power-mad tyrants after he left office, they provided that the election of presidents, whether by electors or members of the House of Representatives, would involve selection by peers—personal acquaintances of the candidates who could screen out those of defective character. And even if someone of low character slipped through the net and became president, the framers believed that they had structured the office to protect the nation from harm. "The founders' deliberation over the provision for indefinite reeligibility," writes Jeffrey Tulis, "illustrates how they believed self-interest could sometimes be elevated."[14] Whether motivated by "avarice," "ambition," or "the love of fame," argued Alexander Hamilton in the *Federalist,* a president will behave responsibly in order to secure reelection to the office that allows that desire to be fulfilled.[15] Underlying this confidence was the assurance that in a relatively slow-paced world, a mad or wicked president could do only so much damage before corrective action could remove him. As John Jay explained, "So far as the fear of punishment and disgrace can operate, that motive to good behavior is amply afforded by the article on the subject of impeachment."[16]

Scholarly Perspectives

The framers' decision to inject personality into the presidency was a conscious one. But it was made for reasons that eventually ceased to pertain, the last of them crumbling on August 6, 1945, when on orders of an American president, an atomic bomb was dropped on Hiroshima. The destructive powers at a modern president's disposal are ultimate and swift; the impeachment process now seems uncertain and slow. Peer review never took hold in the Electoral College. The rise of the national broadcast media makes the president's personality all the more pervasive. In sum, the framers' carefully conceived defenses against a president of defective character are gone.

Clearly, then, a sophisticated psychological perspective on the presidency was overdue in the late 1960s, when Barber began offering one in a series of articles and papers that culminated in *The Presidential Character*.[17] Presidential scholars had long taken it as axiomatic that the American presidency is an institution shaped in some measure by the personalities of individual presidents. But rarely had the literature of personality *theory* been brought to bear, in large part because scholars of the post–Franklin D. Roosevelt period no longer seemed to share the framers' assumptions about human nature, at least as far as the presidency was concerned. As we saw in Chapter 1, historians and political scientists exalted not only presidential power but also presidents who were ambitious for power. Richard Neustadt's influential book, *Presidential Power*, published in 1960, was typical in this regard:

The contributions that a president can make to government are indispensable. Assuming that he knows what power is and wants it, those contributions cannot help but be forthcoming in some measure as by-products of his search for personal influence.[18]

As Erwin Hargrove reflected in post-Vietnam, post-Watergate 1974, this line of reasoning was the source of startling deficiencies in scholarly understandings of the office: "We had assumed that ideological purpose was sufficient to purify the drive for power, but we forgot the importance of character."[19]

Scholars also had recognized for some time that Americans' attitudes about the presidency, like presidents' actions, are psychologically as well as politically rooted. Studies of schoolchildren indicated that they first come into political awareness by learning of, and feeling fondly toward, the president. As adults, they "rally" to the president's support, both when they inaugurate a new one and in times of crisis.[20] Popular nationalistic emotions, which in constitutional monarchies are directed toward the king or queen, are deflected in American society onto the presidency. Again, however, scholars' awareness of these psychological forces manifested itself more in casual observations (Dwight D. Eisenhower was a "father figure"; the "public mood" is fickle) than in systematic thought.

The presidencies of John F. Kennedy, Lyndon B. Johnson, and Nixon altered this scholarly quiescence. Surveys taken shortly after the Kennedy assassination recorded the startling depth of the feelings that citizens have about the presidency. A large share of the population experienced symptoms classically associated with grief over the death of a loved one. Historical evidence suggests that the public has responded similarly to the deaths of all sitting presidents, popular or not, by murder or natural causes.[21]

If Kennedy's death illustrated the deep psychological ties of the public to the presidency, the experiences of his successors showed even more clearly the importance of psychology in understanding the connection between president and presidency. Johnson, the peace candidate who rigidly pursued a self-defeating policy of war, and Nixon, who promised "lower voices" only to angrily turn political disagreements into personal crises, projected their personalities onto policy in ways that were both obvious and destructive. The events of this period brought students of the presidency up short. As they paused to consider the "psychological presidency," they found Barber standing at the ready with the foundation and first floor of a full-blown theory.

James David Barber and the Psychological Presidency

Barber's theory offers a model of the presidency as an institution shaped largely by the psychological mix between the personalities of individual presidents and the public's deep feelings about the office. It also proposes methods of predicting what those personalities and feelings are likely to be in particular circumstances. These considerations govern *The Presidential Character* and *The Pulse of Politics*, books that we shall examine in turn. The question of how we can become masters of our own and of the presidency's psychological fate is also treated in these books, but it receives fuller exposition in other works by Barber.

Presidential Psychology

The primary danger of the Nixon administration will be that the President will grasp some line of policy or method of operation and pursue it in spite of its failure. . . . How will Nixon respond to challenges to the morality of his regime, to charges of scandal and/or corruption? First such charges strike a raw nerve, not only from the Checkers business, but also from deep within the personality in which the demands of the superego are so harsh and hard. . . . The first impulse will be to hush it up, to conceal it, bring down the blinds. If it breaks open and Nixon cannot avoid commenting on it, there is a real setup here for another crisis.

James David Barber is more than a little proud of that prediction, mainly because he made it in a talk he gave at Stanford University on January 19, 1969, the eve of Nixon's first inauguration. It was among the first in a series of speeches, papers, and articles whose purpose was to explain his theory of presidential personality and how to predict it, always with his forecast for Nixon's future prominently, and thus riskily, displayed. The theory received its fullest statement in *The Presidential Character.*

"Character," in Barber's usage, is not quite a synonym for personality.[22] A politician's psychological constitution also includes two other components: an adolescence-born "worldview," which Barber defines as "primary, politically relevant beliefs, particularly his conceptions of social causality, human nature, and the central moral conflicts of the time"; and a "style," or "habitual way of performing three political roles: rhetoric, personal relations, and homework," which develops in early adulthood. But clearly Barber considers character, which forms in childhood and shapes the later development of style and worldview, to be "the most important thing to know about a president or candidate." As he defines the term, "character is the way the President orients himself toward life—not for the moment, but enduringly." It "grows out of the child's experiments in relating to parents, brothers and sisters, and peers at play and in school, as well as to his own body and the objects around it." Through these experiences, the child—and thus the adult to be—arrives subconsciously at a deep and private understanding of fundamental self-worth.

For some, this process results in high self-esteem, the vital ingredient for psychological health and political productiveness. Others must search outside themselves for evidence of worth that at best will be a partial substitute. Depending on the source and nature of their limited self-esteem, Barber suggests, they will concentrate their search in one of three areas: the affection from others that compliant and agreeable behavior brings, the sense of usefulness that comes from performing a widely respected duty, or the deference attendant with dominance and control over other people. Because politics is a vocation rich in opportunities to find all three of these things—affection from cheering crowds and backslapping colleagues, usefulness from public service in a civic cause, dominance through official power—it is not surprising that some insecure people are attracted to a political career.

This makes for a problem, Barber argues: if public officials, especially presidents, use their office to compensate for private doubts and demons, it follows that they will not always use it for public purposes. Affection-seekers will be so concerned with preserving the goodwill of those around them that they seldom will challenge the status quo or otherwise rock the boat. The duty-doers will be similarly inert, although in their case inertia will result from their feeling that to be useful they must be diligent guardians of time-honored practices and procedures. Passive presidents of both kinds may provide the nation with "breathing spells, times of recovery in our frantic political life," or even "a refreshing hopefulness and at least some sense of sharing and caring." Still, in Barber's view, their main effect is to "divert popular attention from the hard realities of politics," thus leaving the country to "drift." And "what passive presidents ignore, active presidents inherit."[23]

Power-driven presidents pose the greatest danger. They will seek their psychological compensation not in inaction but in intense efforts to maintain or extend their personal sense of domination and control through public channels. When things are going well for power-driven presidents and they feel they have the upper hand on their political opponents, there may be no problem. But when things cease to go their way, as eventually things will in a democratic system, such a president's response almost certainly will take destructive forms, such as rigid defensiveness or aggression against opponents. Only those with high self-esteem will be secure enough to lead as democratic political leaders must lead, with persuasion and flexibility as well as action and initiative.

Perhaps more important than the theoretical underpinnings of Barber's character analysis is the practical purpose that animates *The Presidential Character:* to help citizens choose their presidents wisely. The book's first words herald this purpose:

When a citizen votes for a presidential candidate he makes, in effect, a prediction. He chooses from among the contenders the one he thinks (or feels, or guesses) would be the best president. . . . This book is meant to help citizens and those who advise them cut through the confusion and get at some clear criteria for choosing presidents.

How, though, in the heat and haste of a presidential election, with candidates notably unwilling to bare their souls for psychological inspection, are we to find out what they are really like? Easy enough, argues Barber. To answer the difficult question of what motivates a political leader, just answer two simpler questions in its stead: Active or Passive? ("How much energy does the man invest in his presidency?"); and Positive or Negative? ("Relatively speaking, does he seem to experience his political life as happy or sad, enjoyable or discouraging, positive or negative in its main effect?") According to Barber, the four possible combinations of answers to these questions turn out to be almost synonymous with the four psychological strategies that people use to enhance self-esteem. The active-positives are the healthy ones in the group. Their high sense of self-worth enables them to work hard at politics, have fun at what they do, and thus be fairly good at it. Of the four eighteenth- and nineteenth-century presidents and the sixteen twentieth-century presidents whom Barber has typed, he places Thomas Jefferson, Franklin D. Roosevelt, Harry S. Truman, Kennedy, Ford, Carter, George Bush, and Bill Clinton in this category. The passive-positives (James Madison, William H. Taft, Warren G. Harding, Ronald Reagan) are the affection-seekers; although not especially hard-working, they enjoy the office. The passive-negatives (Washington, Calvin Coolidge, Eisenhower) neither work nor play; it is duty, not pleasure or zest, that gets them into politics. Finally, there are the power-seeking active-negatives, who compulsively and with little satisfaction throw themselves into their presidential chores.

In Barber's view, active-negative presidents John Adams, Woodrow Wilson, Herbert Hoover, Johnson, and Nixon all shared one important personality-rooted quality: they persisted in disastrous courses of action (Adams's repressive Alien and Sedition acts, Wilson's League of Nations battle, Hoover's depression policy, Johnson's Vietnam, Nixon's Watergate) because to have conceded error would have been to cede their sense of con- trol, something their psychological constitutions would not allow them to do. Table 7.1 summarizes Barber's four types and his categorizations of individual presidents.

Not surprisingly, *The Presidential Character* was extremely controversial when it came out in 1972. Many argued that Barber's theory was too simple, that his four types did not begin to cover the range of human complexity. At one level, this criticism is as trivial as it is true. In spelling out his theory, Barber states clearly that "we are talking about tendencies, broad directions; no individual man exactly fits a category." His typology is offered as a method for sizing up potential presidents, not for diagnosing and treating them. Given the nature of election campaigning, a reasonably accurate shorthand device is about all we can hope for. The real question, then, is whether Barber's shorthand device is reasonably accurate.

Barber's intellectual defense of his typology's soundness, quoted here in full, is not altogether comforting:

Table 7.1. Barber's Character Typology, with Presidents Categorized According to Type

Energy directed toward the Presidency	Affect toward the Presidency	
	Positive	*Negative*
Active	Thomas Jefferson Franklin Roosevelt Harry Truman John Kennedy Gerald Ford Jimmy Carter George Bush Bill Clinton	John Adams Woodrow Wilson Herbert Hoover Lyndon Johnson Richard Nixon
	"consistency between much activity and the enjoyment of it, indicating relatively high self-esteem and relative success in relating to the environment. . . . shows an orientation to productiveness as a value and an ability to use his styles flexibly, adaptively"	"activity has a compulsive quality, as if the man were trying to make up for something or escape from anxiety into hard work. . . . seems ambitious, striving upward, power-seeking. . . . stance toward the environment is aggressive and has a problem in managing his aggressive feelings."
Passive	James Madison William Taft Warren Harding Ronald Reagan	George Washington Calvin Coolidge Dwight Eisenhower
	"receptive, compliant, other-directed character whose life is a search for affection as a reward for being agreeable and cooperative. . . . low self-esteem (on grounds of being unlovable)."	"low self-esteem based on a sense of uselessness . . . in politics because they think they ought to be. . . . tendency is to withdraw, to escape from the conflict and uncertainty of politics by emphasizing vague principles (especially prohibitions) and procedural arrangements."

Sources: Barber's discussions of all presidents but Clinton are in *The Presidential Character: Predicting Performance in the White House,* 4th ed. (Englewood Cliffs, N.J.: Prentice-Hall, 1992). Clinton is characterized by Barber in Doyle McManus, "Key Challenges Await Clinton," *Los Angeles Times,* January 20, 1993, A6.

Why might we expect these two simple dimensions [active-passive, positive-negative] to outline the main character types? Because they stand for two central features of anyone's orientation toward life. In nearly every study of personality, some form of the active-passive contrast is critical; the general tendency to act or be acted upon is evident in such concepts as dominance-submission, extraversion-introversion, aggression-timidity, attack-defense, fight-flight, engagement-withdrawal, approach-avoidance. In every life we sense quickly the general energy output of the people we deal with. Similarly we catch on fairly quickly to the affect dimension—whether the person seems to be optimistic or pessimistic, hopeful or skeptical, happy or sad. The two baselines are clear and they are also independent of one another: all of us know people who are very active but seem discouraged, others who are quite passive but seem happy, and so forth. The activity baseline refers to what one does, the affect baseline to how one feels about what he does.

Both are crude clues to character. They are leads into four basic character patterns long familiar in psychological research.[24]

In the library copy of *The Presidential Character* from which I copied this passage, there is a handwritten note in the margin: "Footnote, man!" But there was no footnote to the psychological literature, here or anywhere else in the book. Casual readers might take this to mean that none was necessary, and they would be right if Barber's types really were "long familiar in psychological research" and "appeared in nearly every study of personality."[25] But they aren't and they don't; as Alexander George has pointed out, personality theory itself is a "quagmire" in which "the term 'character' in practice is applied loosely and means many different things."[26] Barber's real defense of his theory—that it works; witness Nixon—is not to be dismissed, but one wishes he had explained better why he thinks it works.[27]

Interestingly, Barber's typology also has been criticized for not being simple enough, at least not for purposes of accurate preelection application. Where, exactly, is one to look to decide if deep down, candidate Jones is the energetic, buoyant person her image makers say she is? Barber is quite right to warn analysts away from their usual hunting ground—the candidate's recent performances in other high offices. These offices "are all much more restrictive than the Presidency is, much more set by institutional requirements,"[28] and thus much less fertile cultures for psychopathologies to grow in. (This is Barber's only real mention of what might be considered a third, equally important component of the psychological presidency: the rarefied, court-like atmosphere—so well described in George Reedy's *The Twilight of the Presidency*[29]—that surrounds presidents and allows those whose psychological constitutions so move them to seal themselves off from harsh political realities.)

Barber's alternative to performance-based analysis—namely, a study of the candidate's "first independent political success," or "fips," in which a personal formula for success in politics was discovered—is not very helpful either. How, for example, is one to tell which "ips" was first? According to Barber's appropriately broad definition of *political*, Johnson's first success was not his election to Congress but his work as a student assistant to his college president. Hoover's was his incumbency as student body treasurer at Stanford. Sorting through a candidate's life with the thoroughness necessary to determine the "fips" may or may not be an essential task. But it is clearly not a straightforward one.

Some scholars question not only the technical basis or practical applicability of Barber's psychological theory of presidential behavior but also the importance of psychological explanation itself. Psychology appears to be almost everything to Barber, as this statement from his research design for *The Presidential Character* reveals:

What is de-emphasized in this scheme? Everything which does not lend itself to the production of potentially testable generalizations about presidential behavior. Thus we shall be less concerned with the substance or content of particular issues . . . less concern[ed] for distant phenomena, such as relationships among other political actors affecting events without much reference to the president, public opinion, broad economic or historical trends, etc.—except insofar as these enter into the president's own approach to decision-making.[30]

But is personality all that matters? Provocative though it may be, Barber's theory seems to unravel even as he applies it. A "healthy" political personality turns out not to be a guarantor of presidential success: Barber classed Ford, Carter, and Bush early in their presidencies as active-positives, for example. Carter, in fact, seemed to take flexibility—a virtue characteristic of active-positives—to such an extreme that it approached vacillation and inconsistency, almost as if in reading *The Presidential Character* he had learned its lessons too well.

Nor, as Table 7.2 shows, does Barber's notion of psychological unsuitability seem to correspond to failure in office. The ranks of the most successful presidents in three recent surveys by historians include some whom Barber classified as active-positives (Jefferson, Truman, and Franklin Roosevelt), but an equal number of active-negatives (Wilson, Lyndon Johnson, and John Adams), and others whom Barber labeled passive-negatives (Washington and Eisenhower).[31] The most perverse result of classifying presidents by this standard involves Abraham Lincoln, whom Jeffrey Tulis, correctly applying Barber's theory, found to be an active-negative.[32]

Hargrove finds the active-positive category equally unhelpful because

active-positive presidents vary so as individuals that the category lacks the capacity to analyze and explain actions of presidential leadership. A schema that puts Franklin Roosevelt and Jimmy Carter in the same cell tells us that they shared high self-esteem and the capacity to learn and adapt to circumstances, but it says noth-

Table 7.2. "Great" Presidents and Barber's Character Typology

	Positive	Negative
Active	Thomas Jefferson Franklin Roosevelt Harry Truman	John Adams Woodrow Wilson Lyndon Johnson [Abrahm Lincoln]
Passive		George Washington Dwight Eisenhower

Note: For purposes of this table, a "great" president is defined as one who ranked among the first ten in at least one of these three polls of historians: Steve Neal, "Our Best and Worst Presidents," *Chicago Tribune Magazine*, January 10, 1982, 9-18; Robert K. Murray and Tim H. Blessing, *Greatness in the White House: Rating the Presidents, Washington through Carter* (University Park: Pennsylvania State University Press, 1988); and David L. Porter, letter to author, January 15, 1982. Four others who achieved this ranking (Jackson, Polk, T. Roosevelt, and McKinley) are not included because Barber did not classify them according to his typology. Lincoln's name is bracketed because Jeffrey Tulis classified him using Barber's typology.

ing about the great differences in political skill between them or the psychological bases for such differences.[33]

One could raise similar doubts about categories that lump together Harding and Reagan (passive-positive) or Coolidge and Eisenhower (passive-negative).

Clearly, personality is not all that matters in the presidency. As Tulis notes, Lincoln's behavior as president can be explained much better by his political philosophy and skills than by his personality. Similarly, one need not resort to psychology to explain the failures of active-negatives Hoover and, in the latter years of his presidency, Lyndon Johnson. Hoover's unbending opposition to instituting federal relief in the face of the depression may have stemmed more from ideological beliefs than psychological rigidity. Johnson's refusal to change the administration's policy in Vietnam could be interpreted as the action of a self-styled consensus leader trying to steer a moderate course between hawks who wanted full-scale military involvement and doves who wanted unilateral withdrawal.[34] These presidents' actions were ineffective, but not necessarily irrational.

The theoretical and practical criticisms mentioned here are important, and they do not exhaust the list. (Observer bias is one. Since Barber's published writings provide no clear checklist of criteria by which to type candidates, subjectivity is absolutely inherent.) But they should not blind us to his major contributions in *The Presidential Character*: a concentration (albeit excessive) on the importance of presidential personality in explaining presidential behavior, a sensitivity to personality's role as a variable (power does not always corrupt; nor does the office always make the man), and a boldness in approaching the problems voters face in predicting what candidates will be like if elected.

Public Psychology

The second side of the psychological presidency—the public's side—is Barber's concern in *The Pulse of Politics: Electing Presidents in the Media Age*. The book is about elections, those occasions when, because citizens are deciding who will fill the presidential office, they presumably feel (presidential deaths aside) their emotional attachment to it most deeply. Again Barber presents us with a typology. The public's election moods come in three varieties: *conflict* ("we itch for adventure, . . . [a] blood-and-guts political contest"), *conscience* ("the call goes out for a revival of social conscience, the restoration of the constitutional covenant"), and *conciliation* ("the public yearns for solace, for domestic tranquility").[35] This time the types appear in recurring order as well, over a twelve-year cycle.

Barber's question in *The Pulse of Politics*—what is "the swirl of emotions" with which Americans surround the presidency?—is as important and original as the questions he posed in *The Presidential Character*. But again, his answer is as puzzling as it is provocative. Although Barber's theory applies only to American presidential elections in this century, he seems to feel that the psychological "pulse" has beaten deeply, if softly, in all humankind for all time. Barber finds conflict, conscience, and conciliation in the "old sagas" of ancient peoples and in "the psychological paradigm that dominates the modern age: the *ego*, instrument for coping with the struggles of the external world [conflict]; the *superego*, warning against harmful violations [conscience]; the *id*, longing after the thrill and ease of sexual satisfaction [conciliation]." He finds it firmly reinforced in American history. Conflict is reflected in our emphasis on the war story ("In isolated America, the warmakers repeatedly confronted the special problem of arousing the martial spirit against distant enemies. . . . Thus our history vibrates with *talk* about war"). Conscience is displayed in America's sense of itself as an instrument of divine providence ("our conscience has never been satisfied by government as a mere practical arrangement"). Conciliation shows up in our efforts to live with each other in a heterogeneous "nation of nationalities." In the twentieth century, Barber argues, these three themes became the controlling force in the political psychology of the American electorate, so controlling, in fact, that every presidential election since the conflict of 1900 has fit its place within the cycle (conscience in 1904, conciliation in 1908, conflict again in 1912, and so on). What caused the pulse to start beating so strongly, he feels, was the rise of national mass media.

The modern newspaper came first, just before the turn of the century. "In a remarkable historical conjunction," writes Barber, "the sudden surge into mass popularity of the American daily newspaper coincided with the Spanish-American War." Since war stories sold papers, daily journalists also wrote about "politics as war"—that is, conflict. In the early 1900s national mass circulation magazines arrived on the scene, taking their cues from the Progressive reformers who dominated the politics of that period. "The 'muckrakers'—actually positive thinkers out to build America, not destroy reputations"—wrote of "politics as a moral enterprise," an enterprise of conscience. Then came the broadcast media, radio in the 1920s and television in the 1950s. What set them apart was their commercial need to reach not just a wide audience but the widest possible audience. "Broadcasting aimed to please, wrapping politics in fun and games . . . conveying with unmatched reach and power its core message of conciliation."

As for the cyclic pulse, the recurring appearance of the three public moods in the same order, Barber suggests that the dynamic is internal: each type of public mood generates the next. After a conflict election ("a battle for power . . . a rousing call to arms"), a reaction sets in. Conscience calls for "the cleansing of the temple of democracy." But "the troubles do not go away," and four years later "the public yearns for solace," or conciliation. After another four years, Barber claims, "the time for a fight will come around again," and so on.

In *The Pulse of Politics*, difficulties arise not in applying the theory (a calendar will do: if it's 1996, this must be a conflict election), but in the theory itself. Barber needs an even more secure intellectual foundation here than in his character theory, for this time he not only classifies all presidential elections into three types but also asserts that they will recur in a fixed order. Once again, however, one finds no footnotes; if Barber is grounding his theory in external sources, then it is impossible to tell—and hard to imagine—what they are. Nor does the theory stand up sturdily under its own weight. If, for example, radio and television are agents of conciliation, why did we not have fewer conciliating elections before they became our dominant political media and more since? Perhaps that is why some of the postdictions to which Barber's theory leads are as questionable as they are easy to make: Did conflict really typify the (by most accounts) placid Reagan-Mondale election in 1984, conscience the mean-spirited 1988 contest between Bush and Dukakis, or conciliation the bitterly fought election between Clinton, Bush, and Perot in 1992?

The most interesting criticism pertinent to Barber's pulse theory, however, was made in 1972 by a political scientist concerned with the public's presidential psychology, which he described as a "climate of expectations" that "shifts and changes." This scholar wrote:

Wars, depressions, and other national events contribute to that change, but there is also a rough cycle, from an emphasis on action (which begins to look too 'political') to an emphasis on legitimacy (the moral uplift of which creates its own strains) to an emphasis on reassurance and rest (which comes to seem like drift) and back to action again. One need not be astrological about it.

A year earlier this same scholar had written that although "the mystic could see the series . . . marching in fateful repetition beginning in 1900 . . . the pattern is too astrological to be convincing." Careful readers will recognize the identity between the cycles of action-legitimacy-reassurance and conflict-conscience-conciliation. Clever ones will realize that the passages above were written by James David Barber.[36]

Person, Mood, and the Psychological Presidency

There is, in fact, a good deal about the public's political psychology sprinkled through *The Presidential Character*, and the more of it one discovers, the more curious things get. Most significant is the brief concluding chapter, "Presidential Character and the Moods of the Eighth Decade" (reprinted in the three subsequent editions of the book, most recently in 1992), which contains Barber's bold suggestion of a close fit between the two sides of his model. For each type of public psychological climate, Barber posits a "resonant" type of presidential personality. This seems to be a central point in his theory of the presidency: "Much of what [a president] is remembered for," he argues, "will depend on the fit between the dominant forces in his character and the dominant feelings in his constituency." Further, "the dangers of discord in that resonance are severe."[37]

What is the precise nature of this fit? When the public cry is for action (conflict), Barber argues, "it comes through loudest to the active-negative type, whose inner struggle between aggression and control resonates with the popular plea for toughness. . . . [The active-negative's] temptation to stand and fight receives wide support from the culture." In the public's reassurance (conciliation) mood, he writes, "they want a friend," a passive-positive. As for the "appeal for a moral cleansing of the Presidency," or legitimacy (conscience), Barber suggests that it "resonates with the passive-negative character in its emphasis on *not doing* certain things." This leaves the active-positive, Barber's president for all seasons.[38] Blessed with a "character firmly rooted in self-recognition and self-love," Barber's "active-positive can not only *perform* lovingly or aggressively or with detachment, he can *feel* those ways."[39]

What Barber first offered in *The Presidential Character,* then, was the foundation for a model of the psychological presidency that was not only two-sided but integrated as well, one in which the "tuning, the resonance—or lack of it"—between the public's "climate of expectations" and the president's personality "sets in motion the dynamic of his Presidency." He concentrated on the personality half of his model in *The Presidential Character,* then firmed it up and filled in the other half—the public's—in *The Pulse of Politics.* And here is where things become especially curious. Most authors, when they complete a multivolume opus, trumpet their accomplishment. Barber does not. In fact, one finds in *The Pulse of Politics* no mention at all of presidential character, of public climates of expectations, or of "the resonance—or lack of it"—between them.[40]

At first blush, this seems doubly strange, because there is a strong surface fit between the halves of Barber's model. As Table 7.3 indicates, in the twenty-two elections since Taft's in 1908 (Barber did not type twentieth-century presidents before Taft), presidential character and public mood resonated fifteen times. The exceptions—active-negative Wilson's election in the conscience year of 1916, passive-negative Coolidge's in conflictual 1924, active-negative Hoover's in the conscience election of 1928, passive-negative Eisenhower's in the conciliating election of 1956, active-negative Johnson's in conscience-oriented 1964, active-negative Nixon's in conciliating 1968, and passive-positive Reagan's in conflict-dominated 1984—perhaps could be explained by successful campaign image management, an argument that would also support Barber's view of the media's power in presidential politics. In that case, a test of Barber's model would be: Did these "inappropriate" presidents lose the public's support when it found out what they were really like after the election? In every presidency but those of Coolidge, Eisenhower, and Reagan, the answer would have been yes.

On closer inspection, however, it also turns out that in every case but these, the presidents whose administrations were unsuccessful were active-negatives, who, Barber tells us, will fail for reasons that have nothing to do with the public mood. As for the model's overall success rate of fifteen out of twenty-two, it includes nine elections that were won by active-positives, who, he says, resonate with every public mood. A good hand in a wild-card game is not necessarily a good hand in straight poker; Barber's success rate in the elections not won by

Table 7.3. Resonance of Character Type and Public Mood in Presidential Elections, 1908–1992

	Election		Winning Presidential Candidate	
Year	Public mood	"Resonant" character types	Name	Character type
1908	Conciliation	Passive-positive (Active-positive)	Taft	Passive-positive
1912	Conflict	Active-negative (Active-positive)	Wilson	Active-negative
1916	Conscience	Passive-negative (Active-positive)	Wilson	Active-negative
1920	Conciliation	Passive-positive (Active-positive)	Harding	Passive-positive
1924	Conflict	Active-negative (Active-positive)	Coolidge	Passive-negative
1928	Conscience	Passive-negative (Active-positive)	Hoover	Active-negative
1932	Conciliation	Passive-positive (Active-positive)	Roosevelt	Active-positive
1936	Conflict	Active-negative (Active-positive)	Roosevelt	Active-positive
1940	Conscience	Passive-negative (Active-positive)	Roosevelt	Active-positive
1944	Conciliation	Passive-positive (Active-positive)	Roosevelt	Active-positive
1948	Conflict	Active-negative (Active-positive)	Truman	Active-positive
1952	Conscience	Passive-negative (Active-positive)	Eisenhower	Passive-negative
1956	Conciliation	Passive-positive (Active-positive)	Eisenhower	Passive-negative
1960	Conflict	Active-negative (Active-positive)	Kennedy	Active-positive
1964	Conscience	Passive-negative (Active-positive)	Johnson	Active-negative
1968	Conciliation	Passive-positive (Active-positive)	Nixon	Active-negative
1972	Conflict	Active-negative (Active-positive)	Nixon	Active-negative
1976	Conscience	Passive-negative (Active-positive)	Carter	Active-positive
1980	Conciliation	Passive-positive (Active-positive)	Reagan	Passive-positive
1984	Conflict	Active-negative (Active-positive)	Reagan	Passive-positive
1988	Conscience	Passive-negative (Active-positive)	Bush	Active-positive
1992	Conciliation	Passive-positive (Active-positive)	Clinton	Active-positive

active-positives is only six of thirteen. In the case of conscience elections, only once did a representative of the resonant type (passive-negative) win, whereas purportedly less suitable active-negatives won three times.

Barber's Prescriptions

In *The Presidential Character* and *The Pulse of Politics* Barber developed a suggestive and relatively complete model of the psychological presidency. Why he has failed even to acknowledge the connection between the theories in each book, much less present them as a unified whole, remains unclear. Perhaps he feared that the lack of fit between his mood and personality types—the public and presidential components—would have distracted critics from his larger points.

In any event, the theoretical and predictive elements of Barber's theory of the presidency are sufficiently provocative to warrant him a hearing for his prescriptions for change. Barber's primary goal for the psychological presidency is that it be "de-psychopathologized." He wants to keep active-negatives out of the White House and put healthy active-positives in. He wants the public to become the master of its own political fate, breaking out of its electoral mood cycle, which is essentially a cycle of psychological dependency. Freed of their inner chains, the president and the public, Barber claims, will be able to forge a "creative politics" or "politics of persuasion," as he has variously dubbed it. Just what this kind of politics would be like is not clear, but apparently it would involve greater sensitivity on the part of both presidents and citizens to the ideas of the other.[41]

It will not surprise readers to learn that Barber, by and large, dismisses constitutional reform as a method for achieving his goals: if the presidency is as shaped by psychological forces as he says it is, then institutional tinkering will be, almost by definition, beside the point.[42] Change, to be effective, will have to come in the hearts and minds of people: in the information they get about politics, the way they think about it, and the way they feel about what they think. Because of this, Barber believes, the central agent of change will have to be the most pervasive—media journalism—and its central channel, the coverage of presidential elections.[43]

It is here, in his prescriptive writings, that Barber is on most solid ground, here that his answers are as good as his questions. Unlike many media critics, he does not assume imperiously that the sole purpose of newspapers, magazines, and television is to elevate the masses. Barber recognizes that the media is made up of commercial enterprises that must sell papers and attract viewers. He recognizes, too, that the basic format of news coverage is the story, not the scholarly treatise. His singular contribution is his argument that the media can improve the way it does all of these things at the same time, that better election stories will attract bigger audiences in more enlightening ways.

The first key to better stories, Barber argues, is greater attention to the candidates. Election coverage that ignores the motivations, developmental histories, and basic beliefs of its protagonists is as lifeless as dramas or novels would be if they neglected these crucial human attributes. Such coverage is also uninformative; elections, after all, present choices among people, and as Barber has shown, the kinds of people candidates are influences the kinds of presidents they would be. Good journalism, according to Barber, would "focus on the person as embodying his historical development, playing out a character born and bred in another place, connecting an old identity with a new persona—the stuff of intriguing drama from Joseph in Egypt on down. That can be done explicitly in biographical stories."[44]

Barber is commendably diffident here; he does not expect reporters to master and apply his own character typology. But he does want them to search the candidates' lives for patterns of behavior, particularly the rigidity that is characteristic of active-negatives. (Of all behavior patterns, rigidity, he feels, "is probably the easiest one to spot and the most dangerous one to elect.")[45] With public interest ever high in "people" stories and psychology, Barber probably is right in thinking that this kind of reporting would not only inform readers but engage their interest as well.

Press coverage of the 1988 election bears out Barber's expectation. During the nomination stage of the campaign, the "character" issue drove two Democratic candidates from the field, much to the relief of most political leaders and (eventually) most voters. Former senator Gary Hart's extramarital escapades, which were revealed by the *Miami Herald,* were politically harmful less because of his moral weakness than because of the recklessness the incidents typified in his character.

Similarly, serious doubts were raised about Sen. Joseph Biden's intellectual and personal depth when the press discovered that he had lied to voters about his success in school and then had tried to pass off stories from an autobiographical speech by a British politician as if they were drawn from his own life. On the Republican side, Sen. Robert Dole's candidacy self-destructed when, in snarling "Tell him to stop lying about my record" to George Bush on live network television, he opened up for public display the volatile temper and resentments that Washington insiders had long seen in his character. As for Bush, he triumphed in part because he was able to lay to rest the so-called wimp factor—that is, the suspicion that he was too weak to be a successful president.

In a curious way, the 1992 election bore out Barber as well. To be sure, the concerns about character that were expressed during that campaign centered on one candidate, Clinton, and were moral rather than psychological—the opposite of what Barber had intended. Clinton's truthfulness and fidelity were first called into question when an Arkansas acquaintance, Gennifer Flowers, publicly charged that she and Clinton had enjoyed a long-standing extramarital affair while he was governor. (Clinton denied the charge but conceded that he and his wife had endured some marital problems in the past.) Soon after, letters in Clinton's own hand were published suggesting that he had dodged the draft during the Vietnam War. In contrast to their severe response to the candidates whose psychological character was questioned in 1988, however, reporters and voters overcame their doubts about Clinton's moral character and elected him—an active-positive, in Barber's reckoning—as president.

Engaging readers' interest is Barber's second key to better journalism. He finds reporters and editors notably, sometimes belligerently, ignorant of their audiences, quoting Richard Salant of CBS News: "I really don't know and I'm not interested. Our job is to give people not what they want, but what we decide they ought to have." Barber suggests that what is often lost in such a stance is an awareness of what voters need to make voting decisions, namely, information about who the candidates are and what they believe. According to a study of network evening news coverage of the 1972 election campaign, which he cites, almost as much time was devoted to the polls, strategies, rallies, and other "horse-race" elements of the election as to the candidates' personal qualifications and issue stands combined. As Barber notes, "The viewer tuning in for facts to guide his choice would, therefore, have to pick his political nuggets from a great gravel pile of political irrelevancy."[46] Critics who doubt the public's interest in long, fleshed-out stories about what candidates think, what they are like, and what great problems they would face as president would do well to check the quarter-century of ratings for CBS's *60 Minutes.*

An electorate whose latent but powerful interest in politics is engaged by the media will become an informed electorate because it wants to, not because it is supposed to. This is Barber's strong belief. So sensible a statement of the problem is this, and so attractive a vision of its solution, that one can forgive him for cluttering it up with types and terminologies.

Notes

1. "Candidate on the Couch," *Time*, June 19, 1972, 15–17; James David Barber, *The Presidential Character: Predicting Performance in the White House* (Englewood Cliffs, N.J.: Prentice-Hall, 1972); a second edition was published in 1977, a third edition in 1985, and a fourth edition in 1992. Unless otherwise indicated, the quotations cited in this essay appear in all four editions, with page numbers drawn from the first edition.

2. Hugh Sidey, "The Active-Positive Searching," *Time*, October 4, 1976, 23.

3. "After Eight Months in Office—How Ford Rates Now," *U.S. News & World Report*, April 28, 1975, 28.

4. David S. Broder, "Carter Would Like to Be an 'Active Positive,'" *Washington Post*, July 16, 1976, A12.

5. James David Barber, "An Active-Positive Character," *Time*, January 3, 1977, 17.

6. Hugh Sidey, "'A Revolution Is Under Way,'" *Time*, March 31, 1980, 20.

7. "Cycle Races," *Time*, May 19, 1980, 29.

8. Paul J. Quirk, "What Do We Know and How Do We Know It? Research on the Presidency," in *Political Science: Looking to the Future*, ed. William J. Crotty and Alan D. Monroe, vol. 4 (Evanston, Ill.: Northwestern University Press, 1991), 52. Psychologists, on the other hand, recently have been paying more attention to the presidency. See, for example, Dean Keith Simonton, *Why Presidents Succeed: A Political Psychology of Leadership* (New Haven: Yale University Press, 1987), and Harold M. Zullow, Gabriele Oettingen, Christopher Peterson, and Martin E. P. Seligman, "Pessimistic Explanatory Style in the Historical Record," *American Psychologist* 43 (September 1988): 673–681.

9. Robert A. Dahl, *A Preface to Democratic Theory* (Chicago: University of Chicago Press, 1956), 6–8.

10. The phrase is Alexander Hamilton's. See Alexander Hamilton, James Madison, and John Jay, *The Federalist Papers*, with an introduction by Clinton Rossiter (New York: New American Library, 1961), nos. 70, 423.

11. Seymour Martin Lipset, *The First New Nation* (New York: Basic Books, 1963), chap. 1; and Max Weber, *The Theory of Social and Economic Organization* (New York: Oxford University Press, 1947), 358.

12. Marcus Cunliffe, *George Washington: Man and Monument* (New York: New American Library, 1958), 15.

13. Max Farrand, *The Records of the Federal Conventions of 1787*, 4 vols. (New Haven: Yale University Press, 1966), 1:65.

14. Jeffrey Tulis, "On Presidential Character," in *The Presidency in the Constitutional Order*, ed. Jeffrey Tulis and Joseph M. Bessette (Baton Rouge: Louisiana State University Press, 1981), 287.

15. *Federalist*, nos. 71 and 72, 431–440.

16. *Federalist*, no. 64, 396.

17. See, for example, James David Barber, "Adult Identity and Presidential Style: The Rhetorical Emphasis," *Daedalus* 97 (Summer 1968): 938–968; Barber, "Classifying and Predicting Presidential Styles: Two 'Weak' Presidents," *Journal of Social Issues* 24 (July 1968): 51–80; Barber, "The President and His Friends" (Paper presented at the annual meeting of the American Political Science Association, New York, September 1969); and Barber, "The Interplay of Presidential Character and Style: A Paradigm and Five Illustrations," in *A Source Book for the Study of Personality and Politics*, ed. Fred I. Greenstein and Michael Lerner (Chicago: Markham, 1971), 383–408.

18. Richard E. Neustadt, *Presidential Power: The Politics of Leadership* (New York: Wiley, 1960), 185.

19. Erwin C. Hargrove, *The Power of the Modern Presidency* (New York: Knopf, 1974), 33.

20. See, for example, Fred I. Greenstein, *Children and Politics* (New Haven: Yale University Press, 1965); and John E. Mueller, *War, Presidents, and Public Opinion* (New York: Wiley, 1973).

21. Paul B. Sheatsley and Jacob J. Feldman, "The Assassination of President Kennedy: Public Reactions," *Public Opinion Quarterly* 28 (Summer 1964): 189–215.

22. Unless otherwise indicated, all quotes from Barber in this section are from *The Presidential Character,* chap. 1.

23. Ibid., 145, 206. In more recent writings, Barber's assessment of presidential passivity has grown more harsh. A passive-positive, for example, "may . . . preside over the cruelest of regimes." *Presidential Character,* 3d ed., 529–530.

24. Barber, *Presidential Character,* 12.

25. Thirteen years after *The Presidential Character* was first published, in an appendix to the third edition, Barber described a variety of works to show that his character types "are not a product of one author's fevered imagination," but rather keep "popping up in study after study." In truth, most of the cited works are not scholarly studies of psychological character at all, nor are they claimed to be by their authors.

26. Alexander George, "Assessing Presidential Character," *World Politics* 26 (January 1974): 234–282.

27. Ibid. George argues that Nixon's behavior was not of a kind that Barber's theory would lead one to predict.

28. Barber, *Presidential Character,* 99.

29. George Reedy, *The Twilight of the Presidency* (New York: New American Library, 1970). See also Bruce Buchanan, *The Presidential Experience: What the Office Does to the Man* (Englewood Cliffs, N.J.: Prentice-Hall, 1978).

30. James David Barber, "Coding Scheme for Presidential Biographies," January 1968, mimeographed, 3.

31. The surveys are reported in Steve Neal, "Our Best and Worst Presidents," *Chicago Tribune Magazine,* January 10, 1982, 9–18; Robert K. Murray and Tim H. Blessing, *Greatness in the White House: Rating the Presidents, Washington through Carter* (University Park: Pennsylvania State University Press, 1988); and David L. Porter, letter to author, January 15, 1982.

32. Tulis, "On Presidential Character."

33. Erwin C. Hargrove, "Presidential Personality and Leadership Style," in *Researching the Presidency: Vital Questions, New Approaches,* ed. George C. Edwards III, John H. Kessel, and Bert Rockman (Pittsburgh: University of Pittsburgh Press, 1993), 96.

34. Erwin C. Hargrove, "Presidential Personality and Revisionist Views of the Presidency," *Midwest Journal of Political Science* 17 (November 1973): 819–836.

35. James David Barber, *The Pulse of Politics: Electing Presidents in the Media Age* (New York: Norton, 1980). Unless otherwise indicated, all quotes from Barber in this section are from chapters 1 and 2.

36. The first quote appears in *The Presidential Character,* 9; the second in "Interplay of Presidential Character and Style," n. 2.

37. Barber, *Presidential Character,* 446.

38. Ibid., 446, 448, 451.

39. Ibid., 243.

40. Barber did draw a connection between the public's desire for conciliation and its choice of a passive-positive in the 1980 election: "Sometimes people want a fighter in the White House and sometimes a saint. But the time comes when all we want is a friend, a pal, a guy to reassure us that the story is going to come out all right. In 1980, that need found just the right promise in Ronald Reagan, the smiling American." James David Barber, "Reagan's Sheer Personal Likability Faces Its Sternest Test," *Washington Post*, January 20, 1981, 8.

41. James David Barber, "Tone-Deaf in the Oval Office," *Saturday Review/World*, January 12, 1974, 10–14.

42. James David Barber, "The Presidency after Watergate," *World*, July 31, 1973, 16–19.

43. Barber, *Pulse of Politics*, chap. 15. For other statements of his views on how the press should cover politics and the presidency, see James David Barber, ed., *Race for the Presidency: The Media and the Nominating Process* (Englewood Cliffs, N.J.: Prentice-Hall, 1978), chaps. 5–7; Barber, "Not Quite the *New York Times*: What Network News Should Be," *Washington Monthly*, September 1979, 14–21; and Barber, *Politics by Humans: Research on American Political Leadership* (Durham, N.C.: Duke University Press, 1988), chaps. 17–18.

44. Barber, *Race for the Presidency*, 145.

45. Ibid., 171, 162–164.

46. Ibid., 174, 182–183.

Part III   Presidential Selection

8 The Presidency and the Nominating Process

Bruce Buchanan

The process by which political parties in the United States select their nominees for president, which emerged from the McGovern-Fraser Commission and other reform efforts of the 1970s and 1980s, is bafflingly complex both to foreign observers and to many Americans. In this chapter, Bruce Buchanan explains that process. He also assesses how well the presidential nominating process performs the five important tasks that must be accomplished if government is to be both democratic and effective: to empower and inform the voters, to prepare the voters to make well-grounded choices, to produce two or more well-qualified nominees for president, to set the stage for a consensus-building general election campaign, and to contribute to effective presidential leadership. Drawing extensively on evidence from the 1992 election and other recent campaigns, Buchanan concludes that the nominating process, on the whole, is working. To the extent that the process contains flaws, "the burden of future improvement [rests] more on voters than on would-be reformers."

The founders made no constitutional provision for the nomination of presidential candidates. The vacuum they left was filled initially by party caucuses in Congress, then by national party nominating conventions, and since 1968 by party-organized presidential primaries.

Six nomination seasons have now passed in the quarter-century since the move to binding primaries. During that time, three independent candidates—George C. Wallace (1968), John B. Anderson (1980), and H. Ross Perot (1992)—have challenged the major parties' dominance of the road to the White House. This, added to declining voter participation in the primaries and a growing list of critics, convince some observers of the need for another overhaul of the nominating process.

On the whole, however, although it needs certain improvements, the nominating process is working. Untidiness and some disenchantment are to be expected from a process that attempts to do two potentially incompatible things: operate democratically and produce candidates who are able and willing to provide effective presidential leadership. Nevertheless, the nominating process is not self-executing. It requires constant effort and close appraisal if adequate service to both *democracy* and *effectiveness* is to be maintained. After a brief sketch of its basic structure, we will look closely at how well the process is managing each of the several tasks we ask it to perform.

How the Nominating Process Works

Through state primaries and caucuses, candidates for major party nominations for president acquire delegates who are pledged to vote for them at the national nominating conventions that take place in the summer before the general election. The Democratic and Republican parties organize and manage these primaries and caucuses in which the voters select the delegates.

Delegates are apportioned to candidates after each state primary according to a mix of national party rules and varying state rules and laws. In most Republican primaries, for example, the governing principle is still "winner take all"; Democrats now allocate delegates in rough proportion to each candidate's share of the popular vote. Delegate selection and allocation rules vary widely and can get complicated. But the important fact is that primary and caucus voters, and not party insiders, select the delegates and thus the presidential nominees.

The nomination campaign season formally begins in February of the presidential election year with the Iowa caucuses and extends through June, with late primaries in, for example, New Jersey and North Dakota. States are generally free to schedule their primaries when they wish. One result is that like-minded regional blocs such as the southern states schedule their primaries early to try to maximize their collective influence on the nominations. In 1992, for example, about one-third of the Democratic party delegates had been selected by the time the polls closed on "Super Tuesday" (the second Tuesday in March). This is usually enough to identify a clear front-runner with sufficient momentum to draw media attention and money away from the other candidates. That is why most candidates start campaigning so early; often a year or more before the Iowa caucuses. It is also why the last three months of a nomination season sometimes seem anticlimactic and unsatisfying to voters and journalists alike.

Five Tasks for the Nominating Process

With the basic structure of the nominating process in mind, we can probe more deeply into how well it works.[1] The completion of five tasks is needed to keep the nominating process both democratic and able to produce effective presidential leadership.

- Provide three important forms of nomination democracy
- Prepare voters to make well-grounded choices
- Produce two or more well-qualified nominees
- Set the stage for a consensus-building general election campaign
- Contribute to effective presidential leadership

How closely has recent political practice come to completing each of these tasks? What barriers stand in the way? These questions concern us next.

Nomination Democracy

To nominate is simply to propose candidates for election to the presidency. To do so democratically can mean many things. Here we focus on the three standards—two familiar, one less so—that are most revealing of the current democratic status of the nominating process.

Voters Choose the Nominees

The first democratic standard is that ordinary voters, not party professionals, should choose presidential nominees. Ever since the congressional party caucus system of the Jefferson era gave way to party nominations by convention in the Jackson administration, the unhappiness of outsiders with dominance by party professionals has put pressure on those professionals to allow the voters to choose the convention delegates in state primaries and caucuses. Reforms initiated by the Democrats and partially adopted by the Republicans since 1968 have defined "democratization" as "the spread of direct primaries, the inclusion of more women and minorities as delegates, the elimination of winner-take-all selection systems, and a requirement that delegates carry out their pledges to vote for certain candidates at the conventions."[2]

Because it dominates most of the state legislatures that write the election laws, the Democratic party has driven the nomination reform process since 1968. The conventional wisdom about the results of these reforms has emerged largely from the thinking of Democratic leaders about the fortunes of Democratic candidates. Many of these leaders believe that democratization has yielded too many unelectable candidates, like George McGovern, and ill-suited candidates, like Jimmy Carter, because the new rules permit liberal activists or little-known outsiders to capture the nominating process.

"The solution," wrote the 1984 Democratic nominee, Walter F. Mondale, during the 1992 primary season, "is to reduce the influence of the primaries and boost the influence of party leaders, who can be held accountable for the personal and political character of a nominee."[3] Indeed, that had been the spirit behind the Democrats' decision in 1984 to reserve 14 percent of the convention seats for unpledged "superdelegates" drawn from the ranks of established party leaders.

But neither superdelegates nor other 1984 concessions to party leaders (all of which had the result of partly reversing the move toward nomination democracy) have had much discernible effect on the electability or the presidential qualifications of Democratic nominees.[4] The qualified party centrists, Walter Mondale and Michael Dukakis, although nominated under the modified rules, still went on to lose in 1984 and 1988. And Bill Clinton's nomination and victory in 1992, although aided by his strategy of distancing himself from the liberal Jesse Jackson wing of the Democratic party, owed little or nothing to the changes in the rules favoring establishment candidates.

Instead, it was a different kind of reform, also aimed at nominating more electable candidates, that seemed to help the Democrats in 1992. The simultaneous and relatively early scheduling of mostly southern state primaries on Super Tuesday was invented in 1988 to give well-financed southern party moderates a competitive advantage against liberal candidates. Super Tuesday backfired in 1988, when Jesse Jackson tied with Sen. Albert Gore of Tennessee for the lead, with each getting 29 percent of the region's vote. But it appeared to work in 1992, when an electable southern moderate—Gov. Bill Clinton of Arkansas—emerged from Super Tuesday as nearly unstoppable.

Super Tuesday alone did not propel Clinton to victory. He probably would not have been nominated at all had not much better known candidates like Gov. Mario Cuomo of New York, Congressman Richard Gephardt of Missouri, and Sen. Al Gore decided not to run in the mistaken belief that George Bush was unbeatable. And it is just as unlikely that, once nominated, Clinton could have won the general election had the economic news been better, or even had the race not included Ross Perot as well as George Bush. Bush's precipitous drop in the polls as the economic climate worsened, along with Ross Perot's ability to siphon off Republican votes, were at least as important as the early southern state primaries in determining Clinton's "electability" in 1992.

Still, Super Tuesday can at least be said to have put the Democrats in a good position to take advantage of unexpectedly favorable political circumstances. It did so by identifying a probable nominee early, which gave the party ample time to unite behind him. It also allowed time for Clinton's moderate "New Democrat" image to influence voters' perceptions of a party previously stereotyped by its liberal wing. And although underfinanced candidates like the former Massachusetts senator Paul Tsongas and the Nebraska senator Bob Kerrey were hurt by the financial requirements of waging simultaneous campaigns in multistate primaries, the reform had no other obvious antidemocratic features.

Conclusions about the effects of democratizing reforms on the Democratic party's ability to nominate electable, qualified candidates must be tempered by the realization that many other influential factors compete with reforms as explanations for nomination and election outcomes. But this much is clear: after 1992, the democratization of the delegate selection rules seemed less of a threat to either electability or candidate qualifications than it had as recently as 1980.

Voter turnout, never impressive during primary elections, sank to a record low in 1992: only 19.6 percent of the voting age population in all states that had primaries for one or both parties.[5] This figure falls far short of the comfort zone of even bare majority participation.

Polls from 1968 to 1992 have shown that more people are unhappy than content with the choice of nominees they have in each presidential election.[6] Yet the electorate has not moved en masse to improve those dissatisfying choices by taking part in the primary elections and caucuses that produce them. That leaves the party faithful and activists—groups likely to be unrepresentative of the broad membership of either major political party or of voters in general—in control by default.[7]

Voters above Monied Interests

Primary season presidential candidates, like the eventual major party nominees and anyone else who is taken seriously as a candidate at any point on the road to the White House, should be more beholden to ordinary voters than to monied interests. This, however, is plainly not the case. Despite reform laws like the Federal Election Campaign Act of 1975, which was intended to reduce the influence of private money on presidential campaigns, enough loopholes have been opened in the law to make it possible for candidates' campaign organizations to accept and spend virtually every dollar that their fund-raising operations can produce.[8] Because many of these funds are contributed by wealthy organizations and individuals who implicitly or explicitly expect—and often enjoy—privileged access in return for their money, a chronic problem of diminished influence for ordinary citizens arises.[9]

The victorious Clinton nominating campaign, although initially undercapitalized and forced to borrow funds, was nevertheless the best financed Democratic campaign in 1992. Candidates like Paul Tsongas, who won the New Hampshire primary, were forced from the race for lack of money. Tsongas lacked the funds to stay competitive when the campaign moved from the single small state "retail" level to the "wholesale" level required by multiple simultaneous large-state primaries. A study conducted by the nonpartisan National Library on Money and Politics of contributions of more than $200 to the Clinton campaign during the 1992 primary season found that most were from law firms, investment houses, and real estate companies.[10]

Clinton refused to accept money from political action committees and made campaign finance reform a major issue during his campaign. But he also made indirect use of the special interest "soft" money that became available during the general election campaign because of loopholes in the campaign finance laws.[11] Thus, like most successful American politicians, Clinton entered office with apparent and troubling obligations to various special interest campaign contributors.[12]

Ironically, public disgust with well-heeled special interests helped increase the appeal of the billionaire Ross Perot in 1992. Many voters considered an independently wealthy candidate as more trustworthy than those who had to scrounge for campaign funds from special interests. But unless future presidential candidates are to come exclusively from the ranks of the superrich, a prospect with major democratic problems of its own, the money cloud will continue to hang over the nominating process. Its effect is to reduce the relative influence of ordinary citizens in elections and governance and thus to fuel their cynicism about politics.

Nomination by Ballot Petition

Finally, nomination democracy means that nominations for president are open—that is, persons outside the two-party system can secure a place on state ballots simply by accumulating enough signatures on petitions to meet the various state ballot access requirements. The Perot candidacy—ensured by his registration on all fifty state ballots—shows the potential significance of this openness for candidates who have the financial resources and personal qualities needed to attract public notice and support. "Ross Perot has already triumphantly demonstrated something recently unimaginable," opined the *New York Times* at the close of the 1992 primary season. "It is now possible to mount a plausible campaign for President without backing from any political party at all."[13]

The emergence of Perot is a vivid reminder of where the power to effect change really resides. A public disgusted with traditional partisan politics, when presented with a credible alternative, is powerful enough and potentially quite willing to overturn a party-dominated nominating structure when its candidates do not inspire. The *New York Times* editorial expressed some trepidation but was ultimately supportive of this development:

[Perot's plausibility] may portend a scary future, leading away from the certitudes of two-party politics to a system open to manipulation by the super-rich. But to judge by the present campaign, this evolution also could produce highly welcome results—involving more citizens in politics, bringing politics closer to questions that affect their lives and giving them more say in how those questions are answered."

Perot, however, sparks fear in those who, like James Madison, instinctively distrust mass public power and want it filtered and channeled through the institutions—in this case the parties—that Perot sidestepped.[14] Such observers argue that historically the party-dominated presidential selection system has played a structuring and moderating role in American politics. As James Ceaser and Andrew Busch argue, "The party system has served to screen candidates in the nominating phase and to channel national political conflict inside two known and 'safe' institutions."[15] By operating outside this moderating machinery in 1992, Perot evaded the revealing test of mettle that is imposed by the traditional rigors of primary campaigning.

Ceaser and Busch also point out that another restraining institution, the electoral college, kept Perot's 19 percent share of the popular vote from preventing a first-round winner, as a direct election plan might have done. Instead, Bill Clinton won the election with a comfortable electoral college majority, despite receiving only 43 percent of the popular vote.

Whether this outcome seems reassuring or not ultimately depends on the extent of one's faith in the voters. It is worth remembering that it was the judgment of the American people, not some institutional mechanism, that caused

Perot's drop from first in the polls in May 1992 to just 19 percent of the vote in the general election.

Informed Voters

The second major task of the presidential nominating process is to prepare the voters to make well-grounded candidate choices in the primary elections. Ensuring that the nominees chosen by ordinary voters are as carefully screened as those chosen by party leaders is the best way to make effectiveness and democracy more compatible. This requirement also is rooted in the logic of representative government, which is designed to protect citizens' interests from abuse by elites.[16] But citizens can't vote their interests unless they first learn how the candidates' plans and capacities might affect them.

Primary and other campaigns thus should involve a substantial educational component, including a review of the national policy agenda, the candidates' proposals for addressing it, and attention to the qualifications—that is, the experience-based competence and relevant personal qualities—of the candidates so that the voters can become informed enough to make reasonable choices.

Such exposure is particularly important for primary voters because they function as de facto surrogates for the mass electorate during that crucial period when a large pool of candidates is reduced to two or possibly three serious finalists in the general election. It is often said that the nomination race is too long, sometimes beginning years before the first primaries and caucuses.[17] But two considerations argue that such length has its uses. The first is that virtual unknowns, which Bill Clinton and Ross Perot were in 1991, can arise from obscurity to finalist status, and time is needed to take their measure. The second is that American voters, famously indifferent to politics, are more likely to absorb useful information if they are given ample time to do so before voting.

How Much Do They Know?

How well informed are primary voters? Larry Bartels's analysis of the survey data from the 1984 National Election Studies led him to conclude that "information is especially plentiful in the local political context generated by a primary election," and that "actual prospective voters tend to be substantially better informed than the national audience at the same time."[18] Alexander Heard cites claims that voters in recent years have shown an increased ability to identify candidates' stands on the issues.[19] But national surveys of voters' knowledge in 1988 and 1992 are less reassuring.

In early September of 1988 and 1992, twenty-item tests of presidential candidates' positions on issues were administered by telephone to random national samples of eligible voters. The results for both election years provide a measure of what the voters had learned about the candidates' stands by the time the primaries, caucuses, and national party conventions were over. In 1988, half or more of the respondents matched the issue position with the correct candidate only five of twenty times. In 1992, half or more correctly attributed positions to candidates nine times out of twenty.[20]

Although the electorate of 1992 had learned more during the nominating season than that of 1988 about the candidate issue positions, the performance in neither year is especially impressive. Indeed, only 10 percent of the 1992 sample identified "keeping informed" as an obligation of citizenship. Such findings are not unusual. Most political scientists consider it unrealistic to expect voters to be any more motivated or better informed about politics than surveys have shown they are.[21]

If the screening of candidates is entirely in the hands of primary and caucus voters, however, voter preparedness is a real concern. It may be that primary electorates are better informed than the mass electorate, but the evidence for this proposition is scanty, and the assumption on which it rests is debatable. It requires an information-seeking citizenry to evaluate previously unknown candidates like Ross Perot and Bill Clinton. Some minimal preparation is needed to know what the issue agenda is and when candidates are evading, misrepresenting, or overpromising. To be sure, vague awareness of candidate positions and qualifications has not prevented primary and caucus voters from choosing capable nominees in the past.[22] But ignorance can only decrease the odds of success. It also reduces the quality and usefulness of campaign discourse, as candidates substitute emotion for information and the media emphasize the sensational in order to attract support and attention. All this makes it harder to ensure that popular nomination is also competent nomination.

Sources of Information

Information is plentiful in presidential elections, especially during a nomination season like that of 1992, which was dominated by economic anxiety. Candidates and the media both supply information in abundance. But both are driven by their own interests to present it selectively, in ways that complicate the voters' task.

Candidates, for example, are not expected to be objective. It is understood that they will bend information to serve their electoral prospects. When the public demand is for substance, as in 1992, they will provide substance. The Democratic candidate Paul Tsongas set the tone for the 1992 nomination season with an eighty-six-page booklet describing his economic plans in great detail. His emphasis on substance helped propel him to a New Hampshire primary victory over the front-runner and eventual nominee Bill Clinton. Soon Clinton, the Democratic primary contender and Iowa senator Tom Harkin, President George Bush, and Ross Perot followed suit with issue pamphlets of their own, making 1992 the year of the booklet.[23]

Primary candidates also are sometimes helpfully revealing about themselves and their plans in televised debates. The third nationally televised debate among the 1992 Democratic primary candidates, for example, took place on February 1 and for the first time featured an open, informal discussion without a fixed rotation of questions, time limits, or closing statements. Wrote one reviewer: "The discussion sometimes got bogged down in bureaucratese, but the candidates' personalities and philosophies emerged as they bickered about infrastructure, capital gains taxes and health care plans. Unlike so many debates, this one left a television viewer with a sense of what distinguished each candidate."[24]

But candidates often dissemble, whether in their advertising, speechmaking, or publications. Reviewers of the booklets published by primary candidates in 1992 noted, for example, that they were usually long on attractive proposals but short on discussion of costs. All three presidential finalists were accused of evading tough questions about the costs and effectiveness of their economic plans. And after his election, President Clinton was charged with pretending as a candidate that he had not been informed that the deficit would be much bigger than was officially estimated in the summer of 1992.

The news media called attention to each of these evasions, thereby illustrating one of the most important services they perform for voters: testing the truth of the candidate's claims.[25] But it is not the only service that is required of the media. Television and print coverage of the candidates, campaigns, and issues are the only nonpartisan sources of information about such matters that are available to the voters. That makes their coverage practices especially important.

A content analysis of all 1,559 stories about the presidential nominating campaign that were broadcast on the ABC, CBS, and NBC evening news programs from January 1, 1992, until the end of the Republican National Convention on August 21, 1992, showed that only 544 stories dealt with policy issues. As for the rest, 520 stories were on campaign strategies, 473 were on campaign controversies, and 373 were on "horse race standings." Thus, although policy issues was the top story category in 1992 (horse race standings were first in 1988), most of the 1992 coverage still featured campaign-related topics.[26]

News organizations now routinely substitute for the political parties as the screening agency for presidential candidates seeking party nominations. Several screening tendencies, rooted in the news values, customs, and organizational constraints of news-gathering organizations, have emerged. These include overcoverage of the earliest caucuses and primaries and neglect of the later ones, premature labeling of front-runners, and letting "expectations" (that is, whether particular candidates do better or worse than expected in a primary) rather than actual primary results determine which candidates get positive attention and which get the sort of negative coverage, or neglect, that can drive candidates out of the race.[27] Some scholars regard the irrational effects of such practices on candidates' fortunes as evidence that the press is ill-equipped to fulfill the screening function.[28] Needless to say, many winnowed candidates have felt unfairly victimized.

During the 1992 primary and general election campaign, the candidates fought back. Ross Perot, Jerry Brown, Bill Clinton, and eventually George Bush managed to wrest some control of their message from the traditional news media by turning to unconventional practices and new media outlets. Perot's candidacy emerged from an offhand pledge on CNN's *Larry King Live* that he would run for president if people got him on the ballot in all fifty states. He and other candidates made frequent appearances on *Larry King* and other entertainment shows that previously had been considered beneath the dignity of presidential aspirants. The formats were less confrontational than those of traditional press conferences and panel shows. The questioners were mostly ordinary voters. One poll found that viewers felt they learned more when candidates answered the questions of ordinary citizens instead of journalists.[29]

Jerry Brown irritated primary season debate moderators by repeating his 800 number at every opportunity. Bill Clinton distributed videocassettes to undecided voters in New Hampshire, played the saxophone on the *Arsenio Hall Show*, discussed marital infidelity and marijuana use with Phil Donahue, and took questions from young people eighteen to twenty-four years old on MTV. Ross Perot used direct-access video to reach voters with satellite dishes and paid for network time to broadcast his thirty-minute "infomercials" to large, appreciative audiences.

The effects of the new media are not yet fully understood, and their durability remains to be tested. But they were much watched and listened to in 1992. In a poll taken in September 1992, 40 percent of respondents said they had obtained news or information about the campaign from talk shows or call-in programs on radio or television. That figure increased to 50 percent by early November.[30]

Do voters learn more from the new media? One study of North Carolina voters found that exposure to nonconventional media, primarily talk shows, accounted for a far greater increase in public knowledge about the candidates' positions on policy issues than did either print media or conventional television news.[31] Should this finding recur, the new formats may be recognized as a boon to voter learning.

Still, voters in 1992 were less motivated to participate in the primaries, and thus probably less motivated to learn about the issues and candidates, than in the general election. As we have seen, primary season turnout reached a record low of 19.6 percent, even as the general election turnout reached a twenty-four-year high of 55 percent.[32] A Gallup poll showed that in June 1992, at the end of the primary season, only 38 percent of all voters—compared with 48 percent at a similar point in 1988—said the primaries had been an effective way to select the best-qualified nominees for president.[33]

Primary voters in 1992 were especially disenchanted with the major party front-runners, as Ross Perot's dominance of the media and the polls between late February and early June suggests. But feelings of disappointment—in candidates and in the primary process itself—are standard for voters in every nomination season. One reason is that most of them are forced to accept the defeat of their favorite candidate and reconcile themselves to second and third choices. Such disillusionment seems to reduce the voters' investment in learning about and screening the early field of presidential candidates.

Qualified Nominees

The third major task of the nominating process is to produce two or more qualified nominees. To be "qualified" is to be electable and to be both professionally and personally capable of fulfilling the demands of the presidency. Such a capability is minimally indicated by a record of successful experience in positions of high public trust—governor, senator, congressman, general. It is reinforced by credible performance of the public and organizational tasks required during the long campaign for the presidency.

Understood this way, competence does not guarantee success in office, only the presumptive fitness to seek it. Anyone who has held high state or national public office and performed adequately can, by this standard, plausibly claim a reasonable chance to do the same as president. Among the contenders in 1992, both George Bush and Bill Clinton met this test, as did Bob Kerrey, Tom Harkin, L. Douglas Wilder, and Jerry Brown. Pat Buchanan and Ross Perot did not. Interestingly, lack of political experience seems to have figured importantly in Perot's third-place finish in the 1992 general election.[34]

The personal qualities that are most helpful in navigating the presidency may be separated into those demanded by the electorate and those demanded by the office. Among the first is a leaderly gift for reaching and inspiring audiences. Reaganesque likeability is a related quality that is bankable as political capital because it helps to sustain public support and deflect criticism. Another is old-fashioned morality, of the kind implied by the media's preoccupation with the "character question" while covering candidates like Gary Hart in 1988 and Bill Clinton in 1992. Although Clinton's election suggests that public standards are relaxing, a president's moral standing—his reputation for integrity, honesty, fidelity, and trustworthiness—can still affect his political support and thus his effectiveness.

Among the personal qualities demanded by the office are a president's habits of coping in the face of frustrating roadblocks, the lure of expedient deceit, a taxing workload, and head-turning flattery and glory. Candidates and presidents who tend to respond angrily to frustration (Nixon), to overload or underload on work (Carter and Reagan, respectively), to rely on deception (Hart), or to surround themselves with yes men (Woodrow Wilson) invite trouble of one sort or another.[35]

Ideally, the nominating process is a mechanism for winnowing the pack. In theory, those of questionable electability, competence, and personal qualities will be eliminated and the nominees who are politically viable leaders with acceptable personal and professional qualifications and who differ primarily in terms of policy will survive to enter the fall campaign.

In reality, some apparently well-qualified candidates are eliminated for lack of money or supportive media coverage. But those who clear these less legitimate hurdles still face many others more directly revealing of presidency-relevant competence. The nominating process is a multistep endurance test for candidates that includes the scrutiny accompanying exposure to some thirty-nine primary elections, including both face-to-face contacts with voters in "retail" primary states like New Hampshire and the media-driven, simultaneous, big-state contests of Super Tuesday.[36]

The vetting begins during the "invisible primary" period, often a year or more before the first electoral test, and extends through early June of the election year, when the last primaries are held. During this one- to two-year period, candidates try to demonstrate their ability to do the following:

- Withstand the results of journalistic background checks into their character and their record of political experience and performance
- Staff and maintain an effective, political organization
- Mobilize the support of party factions and unify them
- Generate financial support
- Attract the votes of millions of ordinary citizens
- Appear credible and persuasive as speechmakers and television performers
- Test their wits and knowledge against critical opponents in numerous freewheeling debates
- Answer the attacks of political opponents
- Devise and constantly refine a political strategy
- Articulate a resonant policy vision
- Recover and learn from inevitable, potentially fatal, mistakes

The lengthy, arduous nominating process wears down candidates and wears out voters. After long, tedious months of often anticlimactic primaries and un-edifying media coverage, both find it draining, punishing, and distinctly unsatisfying. The process does not feel redemptive, ennobling, or even particularly useful while it is being experienced. Instead, it seems only to diminish candidates and intensify public distaste for politics. All this was particularly true in 1992, when the primary season was dominated by Gennifer Flowers, "but I didn't inhale," and caustic criticism by the Texas entrepreneur who seemed to many at the time to offer the hope of something different and better.[37]

But away from the moment, the view is different. Unlike other democracies, which allow only familiar party stalwarts to reach the top, we ask our nominating process to convert virtual unknowns into presidents in a few months. (In a poll conducted in January 1992, 78 percent of the respondents said that they hadn't heard enough about Bill Clinton to have an opinion!)[38] In such a system the present marathon, or something very much like it, is essential. The sequential primary process not only winnows the pack while disclosing and testing the candidates' qualifications; it also helps to school the next president for much (although not all) of what he will encounter during the fall campaign and in office. And it forces on a reluctant public the concentrated exposure it needs to get to know him, to watch him deal with and recover from adversity, and eventually to adjust to him and his leadership. Both candidates and the citizen-audience, although sobered and often depressed by the experience, are undeniably readier for what comes next.

Thus, a major concern about Perot-style independent candidates is their sidestepping of the rigors of the primary process. Perot's drop from first in the polls (before announcing his withdrawal from the race in July 1992) to last in the final election tally (after his October 1 reentry) had many causes. But surely one was his reluctance to hang in when the going got tough and to prove he could bear up under the kind of trial by fire that Clinton endured in riding out the Gennifer Flowers, marijuana, and draft evasion crises. Clinton's resilience when most expected him to fold did much to convince observers that he could handle the pressures of the presidency. The primaries also revealed Clinton's ability to learn and recover from his mistakes.

The critics of the primary process do make worthwhile points. It might be possible, for example, to achieve what is needed with fewer primaries. Some primaries in 1992, such as New Hampshire's with its focus on issue booklets, produced more useful information than did others, like New York's, with its circuslike atmosphere. Saner primary spacing might increase the chances for voter reflection. And it might be useful to introduce additional forums to the process, like issues conventions, where representative voters can engage the candidates.[39]

But as it is, the nomination gauntlet provides ample opportunity for media and public scrutiny. And it brings to the surface abundant, highly relevant evidence of candidate character and ability, as well as of policy plans. Improving the quality of the scrutiny—better, more relevant media issue probing, background checks, and candidate questioning, and greater public attention to available information—would do as much or more to generate thorough, effective reviews of the candidates' suitability for office than a revised primary format.

A Consensus-Building National Campaign

If the primaries, caucuses, and nominating conventions have succeeded, then two qualified nominees will emerge whose parties have each embraced a distinguishable set of policies and who have introduced themselves to a mass electorate that is beginning to tune in to the election as Labor Day approaches. Voters will have had the opportunity to learn the important differences between the candidates and their platforms, and the stage will have been set for a useful presidential campaign—that is, one that positively engages the electorate and further clarifies the choices to be made between broad policy directions and specific individuals.

In both 1988 and 1992 the nominating process, for the most part, delivered these goods. Both preconvention seasons produced vigorous, reasonably substantive debates on the issues. The 1992 primaries featured issues booklets and a focus on the economy. In 1988 the primaries "stimulated a wider and deeper discussion of issues than did the subsequent general election campaign."[40]

Both sets of primaries also produced competent nominees of acceptable character—the Republican George Bush and the Democrats Michael Dukakis and Bill Clinton—whose most important differences with their opponents concerned policy and governing philosophy. Although the nominating conventions of the Democrats in 1988 and the Republicans in 1992 were less effective than their opponents' at uniting the party and projecting enthusiasm and confidence to the television audience, neither side lost the general election for that reason alone.

Aided by a nominating process that worked, the 1992 presidential campaign went on to produce something like a national consensus on the need for budgetary discipline and economic change. It was widely regarded as a generally positive, issue-oriented, and thus useful presidential campaign.[41] The 1988 nominating process was just as effective, but it had less of a beneficial effect on the general election campaign, in which a serious discussion of issues was avoided. Indeed, because of its evasiveness and mean-spirited tone, many considered the presidential campaign of 1988 to be the worst in memory.[42]

Apparently a successful nominating process can facilitate a useful national campaign, but it cannot guarantee one. In 1988 the process delivered qualified candidates, reasonably unified parties, and policy distinctions. But the policy debate did not continue into the fall campaign. Why was the 1992 issues debate sustained, while that of 1988 was not?

Three reasons stand out. The first two involve factors at work in 1992 (but not in 1988) that kept the issue momentum alive through the fall: widespread economic anxiety and Ross Perot. Anxious voters forced the candidates to stay focused on the economy from January through November. "From the New Hampshire primary on, the voters provided a merciless reality check on the candidates; those who strayed from the economy for very long were quickly punished."[43]

Perot's role was to use his ability to attract attention in ways that intensified the voters' interest in the campaign in general and on the economic and budget deficit positions of Bush and Clinton in particular. He reduced their ability to change the subject. Perot also reduced the incidence of negative advertising by increasing uncertainty about its effects.[44]

The third reason that the 1992 campaign was better is something that happened in 1988 and that could happen in any election in which there is no countervailing pressure from voters or other candidates. George Bush decided to make the central focus of the fall campaign an attack on Dukakis's "liberalism" instead of the major policy debates of the 1988 primaries. Dukakis's inability to generate enough public pressure to force Bush off this message meant that Bush's decision canceled out the positive influence that the 1988 nominating process might otherwise have had on the discussion of national priorities. Bush had found a way to win. But he hijacked the policy debate in the process.

In sum, a nominating process that sets the stage with qualified candidates, the developed outline of an issues debate, a unified campaign organization, and an introduction to the voting audience is a helpful, even necessary, condition for a positive, consensus-building fall campaign. But it is not a sufficient condition. An insistent public demand that disciplines the candidates is also needed.

Effective Presidential Leadership

The final task of the nominating process is to contribute to effective presidential leadership. The process will inevitably affect such leadership, for good or ill, in at least four ways.

The most obvious way that the nominating process will affect presidential leadership is by the kind of president it produces. The process "selects for" certain kinds of human traits (and thus presidents) and keeps others out. Specifically, it anoints intensely ambitious people who have great energy, stamina, and resilience, as well as the chutzpah to imagine that they deserve to be elected and can succeed in office. Such people must also prove themselves willing and able to endure setbacks and other trials, to sacrifice private life, and to take big risks. The process does not attract those who are uncomfortable with self-promotion, who are risk-averse, who are reluctant to commit extraordinary energy and resources to the task, or who are unwilling to sacrifice other, surer opportunities to fight for such an uncertain prize.

People of great talent and leadership can be found in both the "self-selected" and the "not interested" groups. That many competent and qualified people do not run for president is sometimes mentioned as a drawback of our system.[45] But in view of the turbulent intensity of presidential work, the unrealistic public expectations that presidents face, and the uncertain prospects for success, it is clear that the human traits now encouraged by the nominating process are a good fit to the demands of the job.

Second, the staff and operational strategies that are road-tested in the primaries are sure to affect at least early presidential functioning. Many of President Clinton's top advisers began in primary campaign roles, including the senior presidential adviser George Stephanopoulos (who was campaign communications director, deputy manager, and alter ego); the White House personnel director, Bruce Lindsey (campaign director, chief adviser, and flak catcher); and the health care coordinator, Hillary Rodham Clinton, who played a central role at every stage of the campaign.

Because of its ambitious legislative agenda, the Clinton administration believed that a permanent campaign for public pressure on Congress was necessary. Thus it continued to rely heavily on the political advisory team that it had assembled before, during, and after the primaries. "One of our main roles," said the pollster Stanley Greenberg, "is to help build popular support for major Administration initiatives." Other important figures from the campaign included the strategists James Carville and Paul Begala and the advertising director, Mandy Grunwald.[46]

Relationships forged in the heat of the campaign clearly affected presidential decision making during the early part of the administration. It was, in James Carville's words, "like a family thing." The bonds of trust that Clinton's political consultants developed with the president, his wife, and the senior White House staff gave them significant influence on questions "ranging from whether to limit cost-of-living increases for social security recipients to how to label the administration's health care proposals."[47]

Unsurprisingly, the Clinton team repeated in office many of the techniques that had worked in the campaign. For example, its damage control system, which was effective during the primary season when problems like Gennifer Flowers arose, was revived to cope with the early political fallout from the controversy over gays and lesbians in the military.[48] Then the political team went to work selling the president's economic and health care packages. The informal, ad hoc system of task forces and study groups that was used at every stage of the Clinton campaign also came to characterize White House operations.[49]

The administration came under fire for trying to carry the agenda-controlling techniques of the campaign too far. Reporters' complaints about their treatment at the hands of the communications director, George Stephanopoulos, led to his reassignment and to the hiring of the former Reagan strategist David R. Gergen as counselor with communications responsibilities. As Bush press secretary Marlin Fitzwater said:

I think George was the victim of the Administration's initial mistake of thinking they could govern as they campaigned. . . . If you make a decision that your campaign strategy is to be used in a governing mode, you tend to think you can go over the heads of everybody. You go over the heads of the press. You ignore the Republicans, as they did in their budget submission. You ignore doctors and others, as they did in the health task force. And when you ignore all those components, you're going to get into trouble.[50]

Clinton apparently agreed, as shown by the Gergen appointment and by his expressed intent, reflecting on the highly partisan budget struggle, not to "go through another six months where we have to get all of our votes within one party."[51]

Third, presidential leadership will be affected by what becomes of the political coalition that was put together to secure the nomination. Almost by definition, anyone who wins a presidential election has managed to avoid a too-narrow identification with a party faction and has reached beyond the party to capture a substantial share of the political center.

But the most valuable postelection legacies of a party nomination are the base of hard-core party and personal support at the center of the nomination drive, the most loyal partisan voters in the electorate, and the presumptive claim to party support in Congress. Although not enough by themselves, these are valuable starting points and potential safety nets in the struggle for success and survival in office. An independent candidate like Ross Perot may develop a personal following. But he would be at a severe disadvantage in the White House without hard-core support from loyal party voters and the established legislative party traditions that benefit a major party nominee.

The benefits of the nominating base, although real, are neither automatic nor sufficient unto themselves. Much depends on what the president does with that initial seed grant of party-based support. In an age of party decline, legislative independence, and public skepticism, any president must struggle, issue-by-issue, to hold the coalition together and add to it at the margins. If it is strengthened and enlarged by leadership that sparks wider affection and respect and reinforces partisan loyalty, the president is in a better position to pass legislation, weather political hard times, and get reelected.

Ronald Reagan is the best recent example of a president who sustained and enlarged his support. After seizing the momentum from George Bush in a New

Hampshire primary debate in 1980, he went on as president to convert nomination and election support into a sustained and unusually loyal personal following among political conservatives. His supporters, who included both Republicans and southern Democrats, were instrumental in the 1981 legislative successes—budget and tax cuts—that launched and defined his presidency. He forged a relationship with a broad segment of the American electorate, including the "Reagan Democrats," that helped to ensure his reelection. Good feeling toward Reagan also helped him to weather the Iran-contra affair, a presidential mistake that might have forced a less trusted president from office.[52] He sustained and enlarged his support through two terms by appearing to stick resolutely to his conservative principles while also projecting a modest likeability.

In contrast, Reagan's successor built no loyal personal following in his party or the electorate, alienated conservatives by straying from the Reagan agenda, and lost his reelection bid because Reagan Democrats, independents, southerners, white Protestants, and Catholics who were displeased with his economic policies abandoned him at the polls.[53] George Bush might not have survived an election dominated by a sluggish economy even with an intensely loyal partisan following. But without it, victory was impossible.

For his part, Bill Clinton led in the formation and development of the moderate, centrist Democratic Leadership Council and captured the nomination as a "New Democrat" who had succeeded in moving his party away from its leftist leanings back toward the center.[54] His election reassembled the core Democratic constituency of African-Americans, Latinos, the unemployed, blue-collar workers, the young, the poor, and the less well educated. To this he added significant numbers of wealthy Americans, male college graduates, middle-aged people, and suburban residents.[55] Even so, he was a minority president, elected with just 43 percent of the vote.

Clinton's task of forging a durable political coalition thus remained incomplete, and the early prospects for success were mixed. Despite a creditable record of accomplishment in his first six months as president, Clinton's standing in the polls stayed below 50 percent.[56] Some people complained that his early emphasis on such liberal issues as gays and lesbians in the military weakened his claim to be a new kind of Democrat. Others believed that his highly partisan approach to selling his initial budget and economic plan, which narrowly survived congressional review without a single Republican vote, risked limiting his ability to expand his constituency. Still other observers worried that Clinton had not communicated a set of principles around which a core following might coalesce.[57] His ability to do so, and to survive the political consequences of pressing an ambitious and expensive policy agenda, would ultimately decide how durable and expandable his nomination and electoral coalitions turned out to be.

Fourth, presidential fortunes are affected by the expectations the candidate created on the campaign trail, beginning with the primaries. At issue is the implicit contract between leaders and followers in a democracy. Postelection mandates for policy action, which are useful for bridging the constitutional chasm between the president and Congress, can be fashioned by clearly signaling a policy direction or governing philosophy during the campaign. The election of the signaler implies voter approval of the signal. That carries weight with Congress if the claim of voter endorsement is credible. Election also creates expectations among voters that the president will try to do what the candidate promised.

Ronald Reagan made the most successful claim to a policy mandate in recent history. He had a simple message, which he made plain from the earliest 1980 primaries: government is the country's major problem. That clear stance later allowed him to sell the argument that specific legislative proposals had actually been endorsed by the voters. Despite evidence to the contrary from exit polls, Congress was persuaded that the voters had given Reagan a mandate for his 1981 proposals for cuts in taxes and spending.[58]

The Bush and Clinton presidencies offer less positive examples of the relation between campaigns and governance. Both Clinton and Bush made campaign promises that they broke in office: Bush's famous "read my lips, no new taxes" pledge, and Clinton's endorsement of a middle-class tax cut.[59] Many observers believe that Bush's political decline began when he broke his tax promise in 1990.[60] And some analysts see Clinton's abandonment of a tax cut as part of a pattern of irresolution that harms his credibility.[61]

Conclusion

A nominating process that helps to equip voters to choose well-qualified candidates who go on to seek policy mandates that facilitate governance can claim to be both democratic and effective. This review of the five tasks that must be accomplished to keep these values compatible, however, shows that such a process is difficult to achieve. On the one hand, the nominating process has produced acceptably qualified nominees. The 1992 experience shows it can bring to the surface the qualifications of political unknowns in remarkably short order. On the other hand, dismal primary election turnout, the money cloud, and spotty attention by candidates and the media to assisting voter learning are threats to both democracy and effectiveness.

Experience with structural nomination reforms, particularly their inconclusive and sometimes unintended results, suggests the limits of that approach to improvement. Nominees are not always willing to act in ways that convert nomination momentum into substantive, consensus-building fall campaigns.

That leaves the burden of future improvement more on voters than on would-be reformers. And in the 1992 nomination season as well as during the fall campaign, voters did manage to force some improvement over the evasive general election campaign of 1988 by signaling their expectations for an economic debate. But they were aroused by economic anxiety and assisted by candidates like Paul Tsongas and Ross Perot, who helped to put pressure on the major party nominees to focus on substance. The less voters are aroused and focused, the more likely is campaign politics to veer into self-interested gamesmanship of the 1988 variety.

Currently the nominating process does a better job of preparing candidates than it does voters. Yet it takes engaged and informed voters to assess newcomers and outsiders like Perot and Clinton and to keep the candidates focused on the public's issue agenda. Are the voters up to the task? The historical record is discouraging. But widespread alienation from traditional politics, coupled with the unprecedented response to the political maverick Ross Perot in 1992, suggest that the political habits of the American voter may not be as immutable as we often think.

Notes

1. For different conceptions of the basic aims of the nomination system, see James W. Ceaser, *Presidential Selection: Theory and Development* (Princeton, N.J.: Princeton University Press, 1979), 3–40; and Nelson W. Polsby and Aaron Wildavsky, *Presidential Elections*, 8th ed. (New York: Free Press, 1991), 288. For a compatible view, see Michael Nelson, "The Case for the Current Presidential Nominating Process," in *Before Nomination*, ed. George Grassmuck (Washington, D.C.: American Enterprise Institute, 1985), 24–34.

2. Mark A. Peterson and Jack L. Walker, "The Presidency and the Nominating System," in *The Presidency and the Political System*, 3d ed., ed. Michael Nelson (Washington, D.C.: CQ Press, 1990), 237. Also see Earl Black and Merle Black, *The Vital South: How Presidents Are Elected* (Cambridge: Harvard University Press, 1992), 241.

3. Walter F. Mondale, "Primaries Are No Test of Character," *New York Times*, February 26, 1992, A15.

4. Ross K. Baker, "Sorting Out and Suiting Up: The Presidential Nominations," in *The Election of 1992*, ed. Gerald M. Pomper et al. (Chatham, N.J.: Chatham House, 1993), 45.

5. Associated Press, *Austin American-Statesman*, July 2, 1992, A4. In 1972, the first year the majority of states chose convention delegates through primaries, turnout was 29.5 percent. Before 1992 the low point came in 1984, with a turnout of 22.42 percent.

6. Maxwell E. McCombs, "Explorers and Surveyors: Expanding Strategies for Agenda-Setting Research," *Journalism Quarterly* 69 (1993): 819.

7. For an analysis of the characteristics of primary voters, see Larry M. Bartels, *Presidential Primaries and the Dynamics of Public Choice* (Princeton, N.J.: Princeton University Press, 1988), 140–148.

8. F. Christopher Arterton, "Campaign '92: Strategies and Tactics," in *The Election of 1992*, 83.

9. See Ellen S. Miller, "Money, Politics, and Democracy," *Boston Review*, March/April 1993, 5; Jill Abramson, "Special Interests Give $205 Million to Campaigns," *Wall Street Journal*, October 23, 1992, A4. See also Neil A. Lewis, "Limits on Donating to Candidates Aren't Deterring the Big Spenders," *New York Times*, May 16, 1992, 1; and Stephen Labaton, "Where the 'Soft Money' Comes From," *New York Times*, July 10, 1992, A10.

10. Stephen Labaton, "Democrats Have Money Machine Up and Running," *New York Times*, July 27, 1992, A8.

11. According to a *New York Times* editorial, the Clinton campaign and the Democratic National Committee collected some $29 million from special interests during the last election cycle. See "Please Hold for the President," March 14, 1993, IV 16.

12. For details on Clinton's ties and potential obligations to campaign contributors, see Peter H. Stone, "Lying in Wait," *National Journal*, November 21, 1992, 2656; and W. John Moore, "The Gravy Train," *National Journal*, October 10, 1992, 2294. Stephen Labaton, "With Gifts from All Sides, Who Gets Clinton's Ear?" *New York Times*, November 15, 1992, I 16.

13. "The No-Party System," *New York Times*, June 3, 1992, A14.

14. Drew McCoy, *The Last of the Fathers: James Madison and the Republican Legacy* (Cambridge: Cambridge University Press, 1989), 50.

15. James Ceaser and Andrew Busch, *Upside Down and Inside Out: The 1992 Elections and American Politics* (Lanham, Md.: Rowman and Littlefield, 1993), 120.

16. For a discussion of the idea of "protective democracy," and representative government's role in affording such protection, see David Held, *Models of Democracy* (Stanford, Calif.: Stanford University Press, 1987), 36–71.

17. See David Yepsen, "Looking to '96, GOP Hopefuls Begin Pilgrimages to Iowa," *Des Moines Sunday Register*, June 20, 1993, 6B.

18. Bartels, *Presidential Primaries*, 289.

19. Alexander Heard, *Made in America: Improving the Nomination and Election of Presidents* (New York: HarperCollins, 1991), 34.

20. The 1988 results are in Bruce Buchanan, *Electing a President: The Markle Commission Research on Campaign '88* (Austin: University of Texas Press, 1991), 93. The 1992 results are in Bruce Buchanan, "A Tale of Two Campaigns" (Paper presented at the annual meeting of the American Political Science Association, Washington, D.C., September 1–4, 1993), 16.

21. See Robert C. Luskin, "Measuring Political Sophistication," *American Journal of Political Science* 31 (1987): 856–899, and "Explaining Political Sophistication," *Political Behavior* 12 (1990): 353.

22. See Samuel L. Popkin, "Campaigns That Matter," in *Under the Watchful Eye: Managing Presidential Campaigns in the Television Era*, ed. Mathew D. McCubbins (Washington, D.C.: CQ Press, 1992), 153–170.

23. Elizabeth Kolbert, "Campaign's New Prop: A Prescription in Print," *New York Times*, January 25, 1992, 8. See also Mike Feinsilber, "Battling Booklets by Bush, Clinton," *Austin American-Statesman*, September 13, 1992, A14.

24. John Tierney, "Longer Debate Shows Issues and Personalities," *New York Times*, February 2, 1992, 15.

25. On evasive booklets, see Kolbert, "Campaign's New Prop." Gaps in the three finalists' economic plans are discussed in David E. Rosenbaum, "Bush's, Clinton's Economic Plans Just Don't Figure," *Austin American-Statesman*, September 25, 1992, A1, and in Rosenbaum's "Where They Stand on the Deficit," *New York Times*, October 5, 1992, A15. On Clinton's primary season evasiveness, see Dan Balz, "Clinton Is Long on Vision, Short on Ways and Means," *Washington Post National Weekly Edition*, April 13–19, 1992, 13. And on Clinton's deficit memory, see "Reading Mr. Clinton's Lips," *New York Times*, January 28, 1993, A12.

26. S. Robert Lichter and Linda S. Richter, eds., "Battle of the Sound Bites: TV News Coverage of the 1992 Presidential Election Campaign," *Media Monitor* (Washington, D.C.: Center for Media and Public Affairs, August/September, 1992), 2. The authors note that stories may have more than one topic.

27. Cf. Bartels, *Presidential Primaries*, 33–41. See also A. M. Rosenthal, "Skewing the Primaries," *New York Times*, January 17, 1992, A13.

28. Gary R. Orren and William G. Mayer, "The Press, Political Parties, and the Public-Private Balance in Elections," in *The Parties Respond: Changes in the American Party System* (Boulder, Colo.: Westview Press, 1990); Thomas Patterson, "The Press and Its Missed Assignment," in *The Elections of 1988*, ed. Michael Nelson (Washington, D.C.: CQ Press, 1989).

29. Press release, *Columbia Journalism Review*, November–December 1992, 35.

30. Buchanan, "A Tale of Two Campaigns."

31. Philip Meyer, "The Media Reformation: Giving the Agenda Back to the People," in Nelson, *The Elections of 1992*, 91.

32. Adam Clymer, "Turnout on Election Day '92 Was the Largest in 24 Years," *New York Times*, December 17, 1992, A13.

33. Princeton Survey Research Associates, "Report to the Markle Foundation," Princeton, N.J., July 1993.

34. See Buchanan, "A Tale of Two Campaigns," 6–8.

35. For elaboration of the discussion of qualifications in the text, see Bruce Buchanan, *The Citizens' Presidency: Standards of Choice and Judgment* (Washington, D.C.: CQ Press, 1987).

36. See "Almanac: Presidential Primaries," *New York Times*, January 21, 1992, A9. There were only 13 primaries in 1968; 21 in 1972; 27 in 1976; 36 in 1980; 30 in 1984, and 36 in 1988.

37. The dispirited primary end-season atmosphere is nicely captured in Robin Toner, "Here Comes the Finale: No Need to Applaud," *New York Times*, May 31, 1992, IV 1.

38. See "Early Impressions of the Candidates," *New York Times*, January 10, 1992, A10.

39. See, for example, Polsby and Wildavsky, *Presidential Elections*, 290, on fewer primaries; Bartels, *Presidential Primaries*, 291, on spacing and momentum; David Broder, "No Way to Pick a President," *Washington Post National Weekly Edition*, April 27–May 3,

1992, 4, on what qualifications are and are not tested in primaries; and James Fishkin, *Democracy and Deliberation* (New Haven: Yale University Press, 1991), on issues conventions.

40. Heard, *Made in America*, 29.

41. Tom Price, "Voters Happier about Politics at End of Angry Year, Poll Says," *Austin American-Statesman*, November 15, 1992, A7.

42. See Paul J. Quirk and Jon K. Dalager, "The Election: A 'New Democrat' and a New Kind of Presidential Campaign," in Nelson, *The Elections of 1992*, 57.

43. Robin Toner, "Political Metamorphoses: Voters Impose Discipline on the Candidates As Perot Finds a New Way of Campaigning," *New York Times*, November 3, 1992, A1.

44. For a more thorough discussion of the effects of economic anxiety and Ross Perot on the 1992 campaign, see Buchanan, "A Tale of Two Campaigns." For a discussion of how Perot's presence made negative advertising riskier, see David Shribman, "In a Three-Way Presidential Race, the Old Rules of Campaigning Suddenly Have Become Obsolete," *Wall Street Journal*, May 27, 1992, A1. Also see Robin Toner, "In 3-Way Races the Old Rules Can Trip You," *New York Times*, July 5, 1992, IV 1.

45. A thoughtful recent example is Vernon Smith, "Best, Brightest in Private Sector Largely Shun Politics," *Dallas Morning News*, November 1, 1992, 35A.

46. James A. Barnes, "They Can Sell, But Can They Close?" *National Journal*, March 20, 1993, 712.

47. Ibid.

48. I do not mean to imply that the Clinton campaign was a continuously flawless operation. See Dan Balz, "The Campaign Wasn't All That Smooth, Either," *Washington Post National Weekly Edition*, May 24–30, 1993, 12.

49. See Michael K. Brisby, "At the White House, Titles Offer Few Clues about Real Influence," *New York Times*, March 26, 1993, A1. See also Burt Solomon, "A One-Man Band," *National Journal*, April 24, 1993, 970. The effort to educate the public on the administration's health care plan used all the campaign devices first deployed in the campaign for the nomination, including polls, focus groups, political strategy, and spin control. See Robin Toner, "Clinton's Health Care Plan: A Push to Sell Peace of Mind, *New York Times*, April 7, 1993, A1.

50. Quoted in Robin Toner, "After Fall, Stephanopoulos Remains at Center, but Out of the Public Eye," *New York Times*, July 26, 1993, A6.

51. See "Excerpts from President's Speech to Governors on Health Care," *New York Times*, August 17, 1993, A8.

52. See Lou Cannon, *President Reagan: The Role of a Lifetime* (New York: Simon and Schuster, 1991), 738.

53. See David Shribman, "Factions of Bush '88 Coalition Break Away," *Wall Street Journal*, October 23, 1992, A4.

54. See Harold F. Bass, Jr., "Bill Clinton's Presidential Party Leadership: A Preliminary Assessment" (Paper presented at the annual meeting of the American Political Science Association, Washington, D.C., September 2–5, 1993).

55. See Gerald M. Pomper, "The Presidential Election," in *The Election of 1992*, 132.

56. In the *Wall Street Journal*/NBC News poll, Clinton fell below 50 percent in April 1993 and did not reach 50 percent again until September 1993. See "Poll Shows Half Approve of Clinton's Performance," *Wall Street Journal*, September 15, 1993, A24.

57. See, for example, Thomas L. Friedman, "Clinton's Gay Policy: Cave-In or Milestone?" *New York Times*, July 25, 1993, IV 1.

58. On the clarity of Reagan's primary message, see Theodore H. White, *America in Search of Itself: The Making of the President 1956–1980* (New York: Harper and Row, 1982), 304–306. On how Reagan sold Congress on his mandate, see Fred Greenstein, *The Reagan Presidency: An Early Assessment* (Baltimore: Johns Hopkins University Press, 1983), 174.

59. Bush's vow to oppose all tax increases dates from the early 1988 primary season. See Amy Brooke Baker, "Campaign '88: Issues Scorecard," *Christian Science Monitor*, February 4, 1988, 16. Clinton's middle-class tax cut dates from the 1992 primary season. See Dan Balz, "Clinton Is Long on Vision, Short on Ways and Means," *Washington Post*, April 13–19, 1992, 13.

60. See R. W. Apple, Jr., "Bush Trips, Capital Reels: Dizzying Tax Course Endangers His Image," *New York Times*, October 11, 1990, A1.

61. See "Promises, Promises," *Wall Street Journal*, April 30, 1993, A10, and Thomas B. Edsall, "Time Is Not on Clinton's Side," *Washington Post National Weekly Edition*, May 10–16, 1993, 23.

9 The Presidency and the Election Campaign: Framing the Choice in 1992

John H. Aldrich and Thomas Weko

The outcome of the presidential election of 1992 between the Republican nominee, President George Bush; the Democratic nominee, Arkansas governor Bill Clinton; and independent candidate H. Ross Perot, a wealthy businessman, resembled the outcome of all recent presidential elections: it was determined by the interaction of the voters' goals and the candidates' strategies, all within the context of the political realities of the day. The voters, argue John H. Aldrich and Thomas Weko, have a meaningful vision of what the nation should be and what is wrong with it. To win, candidates must convince the voters that they share this vision and, if elected, are capable of acting on it. Presidential efforts thus become complex efforts to "frame" the choice for voters in a way that is likely to win their support. Yet, Aldrich and Weko conclude, even though the more successful framer will probably be elected president, it will be hard to govern successfully if the winning frame is devoid of policy content.

In March 1991, just weeks after the victory of U.S. and allied forces in the Persian Gulf War, George Bush's approval rating soared to levels unprecedented in the history of modern opinion polling: nearly nine out of ten Americans approved of Bush's handling of the presidency.[1] Not surprisingly, he and his advisers foresaw an easy path to renomination and reelection in 1992: they simply would claim credit for the twin victories of the Persian Gulf War and the cold war, then reap the harvest of votes on election day. To be sure, the economy was not doing particularly well, but the downturn presumably would be short-lived and the president would be able to ride the peace issue and his high approval ratings to easy reelection. Bush's expectations seemed to hold true through much of 1991; his popularity remained uncommonly high, and the Democrats were in disarray. As the fall began, it appeared as if no major Democrats would be brave—or foolhardy—enough even to contend for their party's nomination.

By the end of 1991, however, Bush's prospects of reelection had begun to dim. Prominent Democrats did enter the race; seven in all pursued the Democratic nomination in 1992. Moreover, Bush faced two contenders within his own party, one of whom, Pat Buchanan, mounted a credible challenge. Bush's approval ratings slid, and the nation's economic downturn turned out to be neither slight nor short-lived. Perhaps most ominously, in November 1991 his former attorney general, Richard Thornburgh, lost a special Senate election in Pennsylvania to Harris Wofford, a little-known Democrat who rode the issue of health care to an upset victory.

Bush did win his party's nomination in 1992, but only after being challenged more strongly by Buchanan than he had anticipated. His poll standings continued to slip badly as his renomination drew near. By early summer, the certain Democratic nominee, Gov. Bill Clinton of Arkansas, had become a serious competitor. And the independent (if undeclared) candidacy of H. Ross Perot, billionaire and electoral ingenue, had captured the public's imagination and the television networks' attention, permitting him to surge to the top of the polls in June. Dogged by questions about his background and eroding poll standings, Perot withdrew from the race on July 16, the same day that Clinton accepted his party's nomination. Clinton's strong showing at the Democratic National Convention and Perot's exit combined to produce a significant "bounce" in the polls, putting Clinton well ahead of Bush. Many expected a similar bounce for Bush after the Republican National Convention, but the president appeared to lose control of the agenda to conservatives, especially those, such as Buchanan and Pat Robertson, who were pushing an extreme social agenda. As a result, the campaign opened with Bush decidedly behind Clinton in the polls.

George Bush was not able to overtake his Democratic adversary in the fall campaign of 1992, as he had in 1988. Moreover, many voters who had supported Ross Perot before his withdrawal returned to his camp after he reentered the race in October. In the final analysis, Perot's 19 percent of the popular vote was about evenly divided between those who would have supported Bush if Perot were not a candidate and those who would have favored Clinton. Clinton won a popular vote plurality of 43 percent and an electoral college majority of 370 votes.

Clinton won the election by following a strategy that was best summed up in a sign that hung on the wall of his campaign headquarters: "Change vs. more of the same. The economy, stupid. Don't forget health care." As we will show, "the economy, stupid" mattered to the electorate. Also, in contrast to Bush, Clinton remembered the importance of health care. Most of all, Clinton and his aides were right in thinking that the voters' first priority was change: more than 60 percent of the electorate voted for change in 1992, a third of them opting for the changes promised by Ross Perot.

The argument of this chapter is that campaign strategies matter. The campaign strategies of the presidential candidates shaped both the voters' choices in the 1992 election and Bill Clinton's prospects for leadership while in office.[2]

The campaign strategies of presidential candidates are designed to frame the context of choice for voters. As decades of research have shown, voters' are relatively ill informed about presidential elections. Nonetheless, they do have goals they would like to see the society achieve and problems they hope the political system will solve. Voters choose, therefore, the candidate they believe is most likely to achieve their goals and solve those problems.

Presidential campaign strategies are attempts by candidates to convince a majority of voters that they would make the best president. Such strategies are constrained by current political realities; by the natures and political histories of the candidates and their opponents; by the electorate's image of the parties; and by the competitive environment of the election, notably by each candidate's attempts to lead voters to conclude that he or she would be the best president. Yet the complexity of politics leaves the candidates with room to maneuver strategically. Campaign strategists try to simplify that complexity by framing the criteria of choice for voters in terms that are favorable to each nominee's candidacy. In 1980, for example, Ronald Reagan proposed that voters ask whether they were better off in 1980 than they had been in 1976. Reagan was confident that if voters saw the choice in those terms, a majority would decide not to return a "failed" incumbent to office. Jimmy Carter tried to persuade voters to consider not only his successes and failures but also the alternative. He hoped that a majority would then conclude that Reagan would be worse than he. Thus, campaign strategies are not just attempts to change people's minds. They are attempts to get voters to see the choice in the candidate's terms, which should, if the candidate reasons wisely, lead more of them to decide that he or she would indeed make the best president.

Campaign strategy not only frames the choices of the electorate; it also shapes the victor's postelection political agenda. Reagan was successful in Congress in 1981 because his legislative proposals had been central both to his electoral victory and to the victories of many members of the House of Representatives and the Senate. He was especially successful among relatively junior southern Democrats in Congress, who reasonably feared electoral retribution if they opposed Reagan's proposals—not the least because Reagan had run strongly in most of their districts.[3] Reagan was far less successful in dealing with Congress in his second term, even though his margin of victory in 1984 was considerably larger than in 1980, because his reelection strategy was based on virtually no policy proposals at all. Bush's strategy in 1988, like Reagan's in 1984, was not centered on policy proposals, and he held no more sway with Congress than Reagan had in his second term. Because Clinton's proposals for change, although real, were less focused than Reagan's had been in 1980, in regard to any claim for a "mandate" from the people for congressional action his victory falls someplace between the election of 1980 and those of 1984 and 1988. The rest of this chapter expands on these arguments, beginning with the nature of the public's choice in presidential elections.

The Public's Choice

Any analysis of candidates and their strategies must be predicated on a basic understanding of the public and its decision making. Four characteristics of voting are especially important. First, the goal of voters is quite straightforward: choose the candidate who would make the best president. Since 1964, the National Election Studies (NES) surveys have included "feeling thermometer" questions, in response to which individuals score each candidate according to their overall feelings about that candidate. In every election, more than nine out of ten voters select the major party nominee they rank higher. Stanley Kelley and Thad Mirer proved this point another way, demonstrating that there is a direct and strong translation of voters' likes and dislikes of the candidates to their vote. So clear and obvious is this relationship that they entitled their article "The Simple Act of Voting."[4]

Second, voters have goals and values concerning politics and governance, a meaningful vision of what the nation should be and what is wrong with it. Simply put, the public desires peace, prosperity, and tranquility; it holds presidents accountable for achieving these ends; and it evaluates presidential candidates accordingly. These concerns, and especially how they are used to decide for whom to vote, are rooted in actual conditions, as shaped mostly by the flow of information from the mass media. Thus, the particular manifestations of the public's concerns shift as the conditions it experiences and the information it receives change.

Third, the voters bring their goals and concerns to bear in deciding which candidate would make the best president. For example, in the 1988 NES survey, 94 percent of those who thought one party was better able to solve what they considered to be the most important national problem voted for the nominee of that party, whereas those who thought neither party was better able to do so voted nearly evenly for the two candidates.[5] This evidence suggests that voters prefer one candidate to the others because they believe that candidate is best able to handle the concerns that are most important to them.

Fourth, candidates can shape the voters' perceptions and hence their votes. The act of voting may be simple, but the political world is complex. Voters deal with this complexity and uncertainty much as other decision makers—even experts—do: they simplify. They choose on the basis of a limited set of criteria that diminishes the complexity of the choice—a few major concerns, issues, and characteristics of the candidates.[6] In the language of social psychologists, voters "frame" their decision. In doing so they receive assistance. Indeed, the candidates' campaign strategies can be seen as attempts to frame the voters' decision, to manipulate the criteria of choice in terms favorable to each candidate.

The NES data support the first three characteristics about voting at least as strongly in 1992 as in other recent elections. (The fourth characteristic is the subject of later sections.) On the first characteristic, 97 percent of those who ranked Clinton highest on the NES's 100-point "feeling thermometer" voted for him, and 93 percent of those who rated Bush highest voted for him. "Only" 77 percent of those who scored Perot highest on the thermometer voted for him, apparent testimony to the concern about casting a "wasted" vote for an independent candidate.[7]

As to the second characteristic, the concerns of the electorate were relatively focused in 1992. Nearly two out of three voters (64 percent) cited some aspect of the economy as the most important problem facing the country, second only to the three out of four who did so in 1976. Most of the rest (28 percent) cited some other domestic concern, led specifically (although by only 6 percent of all respondents) by health care. Barely three out of one hundred voters cited any aspect of foreign affairs or defense policy as their central concern; this was a lower number than in any election since the Vietnam War. Thus, it was "the economy, stupid" and, a distant second, health care that mattered to the public. Unfortunately for Bush, voters no longer were worried about foreign and defense problems, nor did they evince much concern about "family values" and other issues on the agenda of social conservatives.

Although it was the economy that concerned most of the public, their specific economic concerns were diffuse. Indeed, the single most common economic "problem" that voters cited was "economy (unspecified)," followed by unemployment-recession and the federal budget deficit or government spending. Their unspecified concern about the economy may have reflected reality (inflation was low, the recession was technically over, and unemployment was worrisome but not very high by historical standards), but it was quite unlike the voters' more specific economic concerns in previous elections. By being general, the economic issue did not respond directly either to Clinton's proposals, which gave priority to economic stimulus and job creation, or to Perot's, which emphasized deficit reduction. But it did harm Bush. Four of five respondents disapproved of the way Bush had handled the economy. Only 2 percent felt that the government was doing a good job handling their most important concern, with 28 percent saying it was doing "only fair," and 69 percent saying "poor." These were the lowest ratings received on these two measures by an incumbent president and by the government he led in recent elections.[8]

Concerning the third characteristic—that voters bring their goals and concerns to bear in deciding which candidate would make the best president—although all of the measures discussed above are strongly related to the vote, they do not ask directly for comparisons between the parties or candidates. Respondents were, however, asked by NES which political party would better handle the problem they believed to be most important (unfortunately, therefore, not including Perot). Although 48 percent thought neither party would do better than the other, the other half chose the Democrats by a three to one margin, slightly better for the Democrats even than in 1976, their best showing in elections from 1972 through 1988. Further, among major party voters, 93 percent voted for the candidate of the party they thought would handle their chief concern better, whereas those who thought that neither party was better split their votes fairly evenly. In other words, when they saw a choice involving their major concern, voters overwhelmingly acted on it; when not, they divided their vote. Thus, in 1992 as in the past, voters chose the person they thought would make the best president; had goals and concerns related to peace, tranquility, and especially prosperity; and brought those concerns to bear in deciding who would make the best president.

The Candidate's Choice of Strategies

Seldom, if ever, are the constraints on a candidate's strategic options so imposing as to allow only a single choice. Thus, the candidate faces a decision problem: "Which strategy should I choose?" The answer comes in two parts.

First, candidates choose strategies to attempt to achieve their goals. As with the voters, candidates' goals are straightforward. They want to win the election. Even those who face massive electoral defeat, such as Barry Goldwater, George S. McGovern, and Walter Mondale, persist in the hope of victory—and act accordingly. Candidates also have beliefs about the problems facing the nation and the policies appropriate for solving these problems. Thus, candidates have both electoral and policy goals.

Second, candidates fashion their strategies from the raw material of the setting in which the campaign is conducted. This setting provides them with both constraints and opportunities. It includes the conditions of the nation (is unemployment high? are international tensions diminishing?), the concerns of the public (based in large part on the conditions of the nation as revealed to them through the mass media), and the political history of the candidates and their parties. The Democrats are popularly seen as the party of liberals, often beholden to special interests such as those of African-Americans and pro-choice feminists. It is only with difficulty that Democratic candidates can convince the public that they are different. Michael Dukakis in 1988 was never able to shake the "L-word" strategy that Bush used—namely, that Dukakis was just another *liberal* Democrat from Massachusetts. Clinton, with effort, was able to convince enough voters in 1992 that he was a new kind of Democrat, but he did not convince all.[9] Bush was even more tightly constrained by the Republican image as a conservative party, especially after twelve years in the White House and the party's inability (or unwillingness) to disprove that it was beholden to the religious right for its social agenda. Bush also was constrained by the perception that he was part of "inside-the-beltway" Washington politics.[10] Although Clinton was less bound by the Washington establishment image, he was, of course, a part of the two-party system that had brought years of alleged "gridlock" under divided partisan control of government. Perot was about as free as any candidate ever was to fashion an image.

The candidates' choices, like those of the voters, are made under conditions of uncertainty. They cannot be sure about the concerns of the public or how to shape them, much less about how to frame the voters' choice to fashion majority support. They also face opponents who are seeking to lead the voters to different choices and news media that may challenge—or ignore—central elements of their campaign strategy.

Consider how goals and constraints shaped Dukakis's strategic choices in 1988. He could not run on a platform that promised higher taxes; such a claim would lose him the election. He would not promise massive reductions in domestic programs; such a claim was personally unpalatable. And he could not argue that he had the greater experience in foreign affairs and so would better reduce international tensions than Bush; such a claim was not believable. Nonetheless, Dukakis did have room to maneuver. The public had concerns, such as the deterioration of American manufacturing and the loss of economic world leadership, that were not auspicious to Bush's candidacy. The problem was to persuade voters to see the choice on these and other grounds that were favorable to Dukakis, not on the grounds on which Bush wanted them to choose. "If the issues on voters' minds are America's place in the world and the family squeeze, we win," observed his senior strategist, John Sasso. "If it is peace and prosperity, we lose."[11]

In 1992, as we noted earlier, Bush hoped to frame the choice as whether to return to office or to abandon the incumbent who had presided over the collapse of the Soviet Union, ending the cold war, and crushed an aggressive dictator in Iraq. He hoped to be seen, that is, as a successful world leader who vanquished the foes of democracy and brought peace to the world. His very successes, however, constrained him. Having seen international problems solved but not domestic ones, the public, almost inevitably, turned from concerns about the new world order to concerns at home.

Framing the choice of voters requires more than a desire to do so; it also requires a means of shaping the concerns that voters bring to their choice. Television has become the instrument of framing. Television news powerfully shapes the importance that voters attach to national problems: it shapes, that is, the political agenda. Television news also influences the criteria voters use in assessing the character and performance of presidents.[12] Candidates can only partially control the "free advertising" of television news, although they go to great lengths to influence how their campaigns are covered. But the "paid media"—that is, the candidates' advertising campaigns—also help to shape the agenda and criteria of evaluation, and this, of course, is fully under the control of the campaign and its strategists.[13] In 1992, Clinton and especially Perot were innovative in their media strategies, using both new technologies and old ones in new ways.

No candidate frames the choices of voters unilaterally. Reality and believability—that is, actual political conditions and the candidate's political background—constrain candidates, because people will not accept an unrealistic frame, and the media will point out its lack of realism and believability. More important, because elections are contested, voters will be confronted with, and can choose among, the contending frames of the candidates. They can even develop frames of their own.

Not all campaigns are the same. In 1984, for example, Reagan held a distinct advantage as a popular incumbent.[14] This afforded him not only greater room to maneuver, but also the ability to set the agenda and tone of the campaign. Reagan, in effect, got to move first, whereas Mondale was forced to react to the president's campaign strategy. For his part, Reagan could—and did—all but ignore Mondale's strategy. The 1984 election, then, was *asymmetric*.[15] In general, the incumbent has the advantage of being the leader to whom the follower must react, as in the elections of 1956, 1964, 1972, and 1984. But those of 1976, 1980, and 1992 were different, because the incumbents were unusually weak. In 1980, for example, Carter was plagued by Iran's continued holding of American hostages and by soaring inflation and interest rates. By the time the general election campaign began, many of the advantages of incumbency were lost to Carter, among them the ability to be the campaign leader. So, too, did Bush lose the advantages of incumbency in 1992 by his inability to resolve the nation's economic woes. (He also suffered from his apparently high expectations of victory, which led him to ignore the task of developing a campaign strategy, or even to campaign, until far later than usual.)[16] These elections were unusually *symmetric*: the incumbents and challengers began on an equal competitive footing. Elections without an incumbent are also usually symmetric.

George Bush

Clearly, Bush entered his reelection campaign with one overriding liability: the economy. Bush could not credibly say that the economy was doing well; it wasn't. Having failed in his effort to frame the election in terms of picking either a proven and successful or an untested world leader, Bush had two means by which he could convince a majority of voters that he was the best candidate to handle the economy. Both were long shots.

First, Bush could put domestic, especially economic, policy at the center of his campaign frame. He could claim that he had been compelled to deal with foreign policy during his first term, guiding the nation through the collapse of communism and into a new world order. During the next four years, Bush could promise, he would focus on affairs at home, bringing the same resolve to them that he had brought to world affairs. He could proclaim, as he did during his 1991 State of the Union message, "If we can change the world, we can change America."

Alternatively, Bush could eschew discussion of what policies he would adopt during a second term and instead try to exploit the liabilities of Clinton and the Democratic party. If successfully executed, this strategy would shift public evaluations away from the economy and toward social issues, such as crime and family values, which had been used to great effect by the Republicans in past presidential elections, while reinforcing deep public doubts about Clinton's personal integrity. In short, Bush could tell voters, "Things may be bad, but if you elect an untrustworthy liberal like 'Slick Willie,' they will be much worse." This frame would be reminiscent of Carter's attempted frame of the 1980 campaign.

The policy-based frame had two problems. First, Bush had campaigned in 1988 as an agent of continuity, not change, and throughout his tenure as president Bush's watchword had been "prudence." In addition, Bush had been indifferent to domestic policy, preferring instead to devote himself to international affairs.[17] He had broken the most important policy commitment of his 1988 campaign, "no new taxes." Any Bush promises about sweeping changes in domestic policy were likely to be heavily discounted by skeptical news organizations and voters.

Second, it was not clear that Bush *could* devise a policy-based frame. Bush had shown no capacity to explain why he wanted to govern during the first three and one-half years of his presidency. Asked in April 1992 about the single most important domestic policy goal of a second term, Bush replied:

Single goal? There are several goals, and I've been spelling them all out. But if you had to single out one, education covers so many of these fields and our goals to achieve those goals cover more, because I'm talking about—one of them is being ready to learn. That's Head Start. And another one is a place where you can learn. That is drug-free schools. So when I talk about education, I'm talking about all of these things.

Unable to articulate a frame with which to orient his own thinking, how could Bush frame the choice of millions of voters?

The second alternative, a negative frame, had its problems, too. Roundly criticized by scholars and journalists for the negative character of his 1988 campaign, Bush could anticipate harsh criticism if he mounted a similar effort in 1992. A campaign that focused on the Republican icons of God, family, and country had successfully shaped the concerns of voters in 1988 because there were no substantive problems dominating their attention.[18] In 1992, voters did have a clearly focused concern, the economy, and a negative frame risked being scorned as humbuggery by pundits and dismissed by voters as irrelevant to their concerns.

Ultimately, the Bush campaign began the election season with the second, negative, frame. It was chosen by default. Try as they might, Bush and his senior advisers could not develop and sustain a policy frame.[19] Thus, as the campaign got under way during the summer of 1992, the vice president and others in the right wing of the Republican party tried to cast the choice as one based on "family values." Bush, too, weighed in, portraying himself as a defender of those values, and his Democratic opponent as a man whose political and personal life showed contempt for them, including marital fidelity and religious faith.[20]

Quickly, however, the shortcomings of a "family values" frame became apparent. First, its harsh, negative, ultraconservative character repelled moderate Republicans.[21] More important, it was regarded by voters as irrelevant to their concerns. Two weeks after the Republican National Convention, voters were asked, "What one issue do you wish the candidates would talk about most?" Forty-six percent cited the economy, another 8 percent cited health care, and only 1 percent volunteered family values.[22] By late August Bush's campaign advisers acknowledged the obvious: "You don't have to be a rocket scientist to figure out that . . . family values took on a connotation that was a giant negative."[23]

During September and early October the Bush campaign struggled once more to fashion a serviceable, positive policy frame. On September 10 the president gave a speech entitled "An Agenda for America's Economic Renewal"; the next day he delivered a brief version of the speech in a five-minute commercial on national television. In October the president continued to search for ways to "dramatize that his second term would be different from his first": he publicly rebuked his economic aides and pledged to appoint James Baker as his economic czar after the election.[24]

But the "agenda for renewal" quickly vanished, and the pledge to fire his advisers did not evoke much of a response. The central problem was clear. Bush had been in office for four years, during which time the economy went into recession and emerged only slowly and weakly. Having proposed no new economic agenda for the 1988 campaign (except his broken promise on taxes), having introduced no new economic programs as president, and having served in all twelve years of the Reagan and Bush administrations, why, voters wondered, would Bush change? There were, after all, two other candidates who could claim more plausibly that they would change the Reagan-Bush approach.

Eventually, lacking effective alternatives, Bush returned to a negative frame, albeit with a new focus, "trust and taxes."[25] In doing so, he remained who and what he was: a politician unable to articulate what he once described as "the vision thing." "At the end of the day," one campaign official acknowledged, "Bush was always more comfortable attacking Clinton and tearing him down than he was articulating his own vision."[26] In contrast to 1988, however, in 1992 the public had substantive concerns on which they were focused. Unlike 1988, too, in 1992 Bush faced two serious opponents—and his attack ads could focus on only one.

Bill Clinton

As Clinton and his campaign advisers began to devise a campaign frame, two conditions dominated their thinking. First, Bush, not Clinton, would be saddled with the problems of the nation's economy. Second, Clinton was a known quantity to the American public, unlike most challengers who lack long careers in national politics.[27] Unfortunately for Clinton, he had entered the voters' consciousness during February and March of 1992, as allegations about his marital infidelity and draft avoidance dominated the news. As the Clinton pollster Stanley Greenberg warned in April in a memo to the candidate: "Bill Clinton is viewed unfavorably by a sizable minority of Democratic primary voters (about 30 percent) and a plurality of general election voters (about 40 percent)."[28] In the waning days of April 1992, public polling revealed the same: negative evaluations of Clinton (40 percent) were much more common than positive evaluations (26 percent).[29] No candidate had ever successfully campaigned for the presidency with such high "negatives."[30]

At a minimum the Clinton campaign would need to adopt a frame that both reinforced a *preexisting* frame among the public—namely, widespread discontent with Bush's handling of the economy—and convinced voters that they would not be abandoning the frying pan for the fire by choosing Clinton. Specifically, the campaign had to convince the public that Clinton's character was adequate to the task of leading the country, and that Clinton was a "new kind of Democrat," not an incompetent and too-extreme liberal.[31]

Alternatively, the Clinton campaign could work to spell out what Clinton would do if elected president—it could offer a policy-based frame, as the Reagan campaign did in 1980 under similar circumstances. Following the example of Reagan in 1980 (and Perot in 1992), Clinton could say, "If elected, I will raise taxes, reduce defense and entitlement spending, and balance the budget."

The first frame had its risks, but they were not electoral risks. Rather, the problem with the first frame would come later: if Clinton won by promising to be "not Bush," how could he plausibly claim a mandate to govern? The risks of the second frame were far more immediate. What would happen if Clinton adopted a policy frame that proved to be an electoral liability, as Mondale did in 1984 by pledging to raise voters' taxes?

Not surprisingly, Clinton adopted the first frame, coupled with enough policy proposals to make credible his claim to be the candidate of "change." In an effort to reduce the balance of Clinton's negatives to positives, the campaign worked to "construct a new image for Mr. and Mrs. Clinton: an honest, plain-folks idealist and his warm and loving wife."[32] His staff discovered in focus groups in the spring that voters were aware of the allegations about marital infidelity and avoidance of the draft, but they knew nothing of his rise from a difficult early life. When informed of this background, focus group members changed their opinion of Clinton. These findings led to the development of the highly personal, biographical film that introduced Clinton at the national convention.[33] Moreover, the frame assiduously presented Clinton as "a different kind of Democrat": a Democrat who was willing to use military force abroad in pursuit of American interests and values, and who was willing to stand up to "special interests," such as African-Americans, at home.[34] This frame characterized Clinton as the progeny of a small town, southern Baptist upbringing and as the leader of the moderate Democratic Leadership Council, rather than as a relentlessly ambitious career politician whose pedigree included elite academic institutions like Yale and Oxford.

H. Ross Perot

Neither a career politician nor a partisan, Ross Perot was unconstrained by either an established political reputation or a party image. Thus, he was free to do what no "regular" candidate—that is, no major party nominee with a public record—could do in 1992: campaign against "gridlock, entrenched interests, and the whole mess of politics." Perot's rise to the top in the early summer trial-heat polls was the product of his harnessing public discontent and credibly claiming to be a successful manager and "do-er." During this phase of the campaign, he could be free of specifics about how to clean up the mess; he also received the positive media coverage ordinarily given to rising candidates early in the nomination season.[35]

Predictably, after Perot became a serious contender in the polls, he was subjected to serious and critical scrutiny from the media. Problems quickly surfaced, including his reference to African-Americans as "you people" and behavior that gave credence to claims that he was a deeply suspicious, perhaps even paranoid, leader. In addition, pressure mounted for him to indicate just what he would do when he "got under the hood" to fix the nation's problems. Perot responded by releasing a budget plan that proposed tax increases and spending reductions to trim the deficit—just after he withdrew his undeclared candidacy in July.[36]

When Perot returned to the campaign in October he seized on a twofold campaign frame much like his first frame. He continued his attack on Washington politics, arguing that it was not the bad intentions of politicians but the structure of "politics as usual" that led to gridlock, budget deficits, and other maladies. One of his campaign slogans addressed this concern, simultaneously attacking the "wasted vote" theory that often discouraged voters from supporting independent candidates: "Don't waste your vote on politics as usual." Institutional reform, Perot argued, could most easily be accomplished by a leader who was an outsider to partisan, and especially to Washington, politics. This part of his frame, although directed at both opponents, was more tellingly applied against Bush than Clinton. Indeed, Perot's attacks were, during most of the fall, far more anti-Bush than anti-Clinton.

In the second part of his frame, Perot argued that the most important substantive cost of politics as usual was the massive federal budget deficit. His emphasis on the deficit addressed the public's most important concern, the economy. He argued that only if the nation reduced its deficit could the economy grow in the long term. Failure to reduce it would rob the country, and especially its younger generations, of the American dream. Emphasizing the budget also neatly distinguished Perot from his opponents. Bush was the candidate of the status quo that had wrought the deficits, in Perot's frame. Clinton, although a candidate of change who emphasized the economy, argued that short-term stimulus was needed before deficit reduction. Implicit in Perot's view (and perhaps his failure was not to make it more explicit) was that Clinton's approach was the typical Democratic formula of "tax and spend."

In sum, Perot offered a cohesive, two-part frame that took context (the public's concern about the economy and dissatisfaction with politics) into account and that argued for change, reform, and a new nonpartisan kind of candidate. In many respects, Perot's frame aligned with Clinton's. Together they reinforced the call for change. Together they kept the focus on the economy. Together they reduced Bush's options—and thus his chances for victory—severely.

With Bush's choices for framing and chances for success narrowed, two questions remained for the Perot campaign. First, would jobs and growth or deficits be considered the most important problem? About this, the public was unsure. As noted above, the most common response to the "most important problems" question was "economy (unspecified)," followed by jobs and the deficit. Second, was Clinton, a partisan politician but a non-Washingtonian of a new generation, a sufficient change from politics as usual, or would voters think it was worth the risk to go to a complete outsider? In the end, of course, Perot faced in Clinton a candidate who was just enough outside of Washington politics as usual to be a plausible agent for change in the opinion of a plurality of the voting public.

The Voters' Choice

Bush's campaign frame proved to be much less successful than Clinton's. To be sure, the Bush frame was partially successful: voters' evaluations of Clinton's trustworthiness declined noticeably after it became the focus of Bush's campaign.[37] Moreover, large numbers of voters concluded that Clinton would likely raise their taxes, as Bush claimed he would. More critical, however, the public's assessment of Bush on both of these matters—trust and taxes—was not significantly better than their assessment of his opponents.[38]

Ultimately, the Bush frame failed because few voters based their choice on "trust and taxes." Rather, the efforts of Clinton and Perot to keep the electorate's attention focused on Bush's economic stewardship succeeded. Asked what issues were most important to them when casting their vote, voters overwhelmingly replied that it was the economy and jobs (43 percent), the deficit (21 percent), and health care (19 percent)—rather than family values (15 percent), taxes (14 percent), or foreign policy (8 percent). Not surprisingly, voters who were most concerned about the economy and jobs voted for Clinton rather than Bush by a margin of two to one (52 percent to 24 percent), and those most concerned about health care voted for Clinton by more than three to one (67 percent to 19 percent). Asked to identify which personal qualities were most important in a president, voters most often mentioned their candidate's ability to "bring change" (37 percent) and to offer the "best plan" for solving the nation's ills (25 percent). Honesty and crisis judgment, two aspects of choice that stood at the center of Bush's frame, were far less frequently cited as a basis for choice (14 percent and 16 percent, respectively).[39] In the end, Perot convinced large numbers of voters that he was a choice to be taken seriously— and likely raised public concern about the deficit higher than it otherwise would have been. Most of all, he reinforced the frame of "change," thereby hurting Bush. By three to two, voters said they preferred change to continuity, and by two to one, those who preferred change believed that Clinton was a good enough risk to support for change.

Framing and Governance

The election of 1992 was unmistakably a mandate for change—together, Clinton and Perot won 62 percent of the vote. But what sort of change did voters want? Deficit reduction? Job creation? Institutional reforms? The election failed to resolve these questions—or to provide Clinton with a policy mandate—for two reasons.

First, although Clinton *and* Perot received a majority of the popular vote, Clinton alone won only 43.2 percent. As R. W. Apple observed, "a large majority rejected Mr. Bush and thus backed change, but it was divided on who was a better agent of change. Perot clouded the results of the election."[40]

Moreover, even if Perot had chosen not to rejoin the race, Clinton would have been unable to claim a policy mandate, as Reagan had done in 1980. Having chosen to be unclear about where he wanted to take the country once elected, Clinton could not lay claim to a mandate for a specific set of proposals.[41] As David Rosenbaum of the *New York Times* presciently observed on November 1, "Mr. Clinton, if he wins, will have a harder time rallying Congress and the public than would be the case if he had been more specific in the campaign about what he wanted to do as president."[42]

In the days after the election, Clinton did claim that he had received a mandate from the voters—but a mandate that was devoid of policy content. At his first news conference Clinton volunteered, "I think that the clear mandate of this election . . . was an end to politics as usual, an end to the gridlock in Washington, [and] an end to finger-pointing and blame."[43]

Democrats in Congress, most of whom had served only under Republican presidents, expressed their desire to cooperate with Clinton and claimed that their fortunes were tied to the success of his presidency. However, no members of Congress felt themselves beholden to or threatened by President-elect Clinton. Having won only 43 percent of the vote, Clinton ran well behind the typical member, outpolling House members in only 5 of 435 congressional districts.[44] And, since Clinton's party lost ten seats in the House and gained none in the Senate, politicians and political commentators concluded, as Thomas Edsall of the *Washington Post* did, "Coattails? There Were None."[45]

Republicans, dismissive of Clinton's claims to a mandate, were little disposed to embrace his proposals, particularly those that ran directly against their goals and public image, such as increased taxes and expanded domestic programs. Senate Minority Leader Robert Dole set the tone for Capitol Hill Republicans, arguing, "He didn't get a majority. The country obviously didn't want Bush, but they weren't ready for Perot and they had plenty of doubts about Clinton. They want change. Well, we want to be responsible and deliver change, whatever that means, but we're skeptical."[46]

As the Clinton administration got under way it quickly encountered serious problems in winning adoption of the president's legislative program. Clinton's proposal to stimulate the nation's economy ran aground in the Senate, filibustered to death by Republican members. His taxing and spending legislation, particularly his proposal to raise taxes, met with stiff opposition on Capitol Hill, from both Republicans and conservative Democrats, and barely was enacted. Republicans and conservative democrats also fiercely attacked Clinton's health care legislation.

Conclusion

We have put forth four basic arguments. First, campaign strategies matter in presidential elections because they frame the nature of the voters' choices, thereby simplifying the complexity of politics by offering two, or in 1992 three, basic ways to think about the alternatives. Second, candidates' choices of frames are constrained by the real-world context in which the election takes place (as filtered through the media to the public) and by the backgrounds and preexisting images of the candidates and their parties. Third, the choices—and the effectiveness—of the candidates' frames are shaped competitively, as the other candidates offer frames of their own. Finally, the successful campaign frame shapes the possibilities facing the victor in office. A campaign frame that features relatively specific policy proposals will give the victor considerable leverage with Congress, at least on those proposals. A frame that does not have relatively specific content yields the victor little leverage.

Could Bush have adopted a winning frame in 1992? Perhaps—depending on the frames his opponents adopted. By concentrating on Bush's major liability, the economy, and by leading voters to conclude that change was needed, Clinton and Perot defeated him. If one or both opponents chose different frames, they may well have given Bush the space he needed to win reelection.

The winning frame of change, with its emphasis on the economy, presented Clinton with both an opportunity and a risk for the future. The opportunity was to claim a mandate for new economic policies, and the risk was that the victor's administration—and chances for reelection in 1996—would be judged primarily on his ability to enact new economic programs *and* on the apparent success of those programs as measured by improvements of the economy.

Notes

1. A *Los Angeles Times* poll recorded his approval rating at 86 percent between March 9 and 11, as reported in *The Election of 1992: Reports and Interpretations*, ed. Gerald M. Pomper et al. (Chatham, N.J.: Chatham House, 1993), 40.

2. For more on the topic of campaign strategies, see John H. Aldrich and Thomas Weko, "The Presidency and the Election Process: Campaign Strategy, Voting, and Governance," in *The Presidency and the Political System*, 2d ed., ed. Michael Nelson (Washington, D.C.: CQ Press, 1988); and Thomas Weko and John H. Aldrich, "The Presidency and the Election Campaign: Framing the Choice in 1988," in *The Presidency and the Political System*, 3d ed., ed. Michael Nelson (Washington, D.C.: CQ Press, 1990).

3. See David W. Rohde, *Parties and Leaders in the Postreform House* (Chicago: University of Chicago Press, 1991).

4. Stanley Kelley, Jr., and Thad W. Mirer, "The Simple Act of Voting," *American Political Science Review* 68 (June 1974): 572–591.

5. See Paul R. Abramson, John H. Aldrich, and David W. Rohde, *Change and Continuity in the 1988 Elections*, rev. ed. (Washington, D.C.: CQ Press, 1991).

6. See, for example, Daniel Kahneman, Paul Slovic, and Amos Tversky, eds., *Judgment under Uncertainty: Heuristics and Biases* (New York: Cambridge University Press, 1982). For an application of the "social cognitive" perspective in political psychology to presidential voting, see Wendy M. Rahn, John H. Aldrich, Eugene Borgida, and John L. Sullivan, "A Social-Cognitive Model of Candidate Appraisal," in *Information and Democratic Processes*, ed. John A. Ferejohn and James H. Kuklinski (Urbana: University of Illinois Press, 1990): 136–159.

7. This argument is made in Paul R. Abramson, John H. Aldrich, and David W. Rohde, *Change and Continuity in the 1992 Elections* (Washington, D.C.: CQ Press, 1994). Note that, of those who rated Perot highest, 13 percent voted for Clinton and 10 percent voted for Bush.

8. See Abramson, Aldrich, and Rohde, *Change and Continuity in the 1992 Elections*, for comparative data back to the 1980 election concerning the incumbent's handling of the economy and back to 1972 for the government's performance on the problem respondents mentioned as most important.

9. For instance, respondents to the 1992 NES survey were asked to place themselves, Bush, and Clinton on three seven-point issue scales, the same three scales that had been used in prior surveys. On average, the respondents placed Clinton at positions very close to where Mondale and Dukakis had been placed in 1984 and 1988, respectively. See Abramson, Aldrich, and Rohde, *Change and Continuity in the 1992 Elections*.

10. See James Ceaser and Andrew Busch, *Upside Down and Inside Out: The 1992 Elections and American Politics* (Lanham, Md.: Rowman and Littlefield, 1993).

11. Peter Goldman and Tom Mathews, *The Quest for the Presidency: The 1988 Campaign* (New York: Simon and Schuster, 1989), 346.

12. Shanto Iyengar and Donald Kinder, *News That Matters: Television and American Opinion* (Chicago: University of Chicago Press, 1987).

13. By the closing weeks of the 1988 campaign, 25 percent of all likely voters reported that candidate advertisements had helped them make their choice between the candidates, as reported in the *New York Times*, October 30, 1988.

14. This argument about asymmetry is developed more fully in Aldrich and Weko, "The Presidency and the Election Process."

15. An important basis of this asymmetry is media coverage of incumbents. Incumbents continue to be president, and all their actions as president are as newsworthy as ever. Moreover, the challengers' reactions to presidential actions are tainted by the appearance of self-interest. Carter used these advantages by following the "Rose Garden" strategy in his 1980 nomination contest against Ted Kennedy. For much of this contest, Carter refused to campaign, staying in the White House to try to resolve the hostage crisis. Kennedy could not challenge that stance without appearing unpatriotic. By the fall, the hostage crisis had dragged on for too long for this strategy to continue to be effective.

16. See "How He Won: The Untold Story of Bill Clinton's Triumph," *Newsweek*, Special Election Issue, November/December 1992, esp. 58–61.

17. Bush's chief of staff, John Sununu, told a conservative gathering in November 1990: "There's not a single piece of legislation that needs to be passed in the next two years for this president. In fact, if Congress wants to come together, adjourn, and leave, it's all right with us." (Quoted in Michael Duffy and Dan Goodgame, *Marching in Place: The Status Quo Presidency of George Bush* [New York: Simon and Schuster, 1992], 29.)

18. Weko and Aldrich, "The Presidency and the Election Campaign: Framing the Choice in 1988."

19. The Bush campaign first began its struggle to establish a policy frame in April 1992 (see "Despite Grip on Nomination, Bush Still Gropes for Agenda," *New York Times*, April 30, 1992, A1). In mid-October the president's aides were *still* groping for a workable policy frame. Michael Wines, "How the President Lost: A Campaign of Disorganization and Disappointment," *New York Times*, November 29, 1992, I 26.

20. As Bush remarked in his nomination acceptance speech, "the other party took words to put together their platform, but left out G-O-D."

21. Michael Kelly, "Republicans Rethink 'Family Values' Focus," *New York Times*, August 27, 1992, A20.

22. Robin Toner, "Clinton Retains a Wide Lead in Latest Poll," *New York Times*, September 16, 1992, A1.

23. Andrew Rosenthal, "Bush Tries to Recoup from Harsh Tone on Values," *New York Times*, August 27, 1992, A1.

24. Thomas Friedman, "Off-Again, On-Again Speech Is Off, Again," *New York Times*, October 14, 1992, A20.

25. By early October journalists were commenting on the similarity between Bush's 1988 and 1992 frames. See, for example, Andrew Rosenthal, "Bush Escalates Attack on Clinton for His Anti-Vietnam War Protests," *New York Times*, October 6, 1992, A20.

26. Andrew Rosenthal, "As Bush's Loss Sinks In, Finger Pointing Begins," *New York Times*, November 5, 1992, A1.

27. Pomper et al., *The Election of 1992*, 114–116.

28. Quoted in Michael Kelly, "The Making of a First Family: A Blueprint," *New York Times*, November 14, 1992, I 1.

29. Robin Toner, "Polls Show Perot Gaining Strength to Rival Clinton's," *New York Times*, April 26, 1992, A1.

30. Pomper et al., *The Election of 1992*, 116.

31. Mandy Grunwald, Clinton's advertising chief, described the aims of the campaign succinctly: "This campaign must be focused on George Bush and the country's problems, not on Bill Clinton" and "We must not allow the Bush campaign to discredit Clinton to the point where he is disqualified as an alternative to Bush." *Newsweek*, Special Election Issue, November/December, 1992, 78.

32. Michael Kelly, "The Making of a First Family: A Blueprint," *New York Times*, November 14, 1992, I 1.

33. See *Newsweek*, Special Election Issue, November/December 1992, 40–57.

34. Clinton's carefully staged confrontation with "Sistah Souljah" and his arm's-length relationship with Jesse Jackson played an important role in convincing white voters that Clinton was a "different kind of Democrat." Thomas Edsall, "The Disguised Debate for White America's Vote," *Washington Post National Weekly Edition*, August 10–16, 1992.

35. On the evolution of news coverage during the nomination season, see Larry Bartels, *Presidential Primaries and the Dynamics of Public Choice* (Princeton, N.J.: Princeton University Press, 1988).

36. "Advisers Describe Perot Disillusion," *New York Times*, July 18, 1992, I 1. See also "Bold Perot Plan to Attack Deficit Thrusts Issue at Bush and Clinton," *New York Times*, September 28, 1992, A1.

37. The percentage of respondents saying that Clinton had the honesty and integrity to serve as president declined from 70 percent in August 1992 to 56 percent in late October 1992. Pomper et al., *The Election of 1992*, 124.

38. Ibid., 124.

39. Data from the Voter Research and Surveys Exit Poll, November 2, 1992.

40. R. W. Apple, "Clinton, Savoring Victory, Starts Sizing Up Job Ahead," *New York Times*, November 5, 1992, A1.

41. Of course, if Perot had not been a candidate, Clinton might have adopted a different campaign frame, possibly one with a sharper and more specific policy focus.

42. David E. Rosenbaum, "Clinton Could Claim a Mandate, But It Might Be Hard to Define," *New York Times*, November 1, 1992, I 30.

43. "Excerpts from President-Elect's News Conference in Arkansas," *New York Times*, November 13, 1992, A18.

44. Richard E. Cohen, "What Coattails?" *National Journal*, May 29, 1993, 1285–1291.

45. Thomas Edsall, "Coattails? There Were None," *Washington Post National Weekly Edition*, January 4–10, 1993, 15.

46. Apple, "Clinton, Savoring the Victory, Starts Sizing Up Job," 1. Elsewhere Dole suggested that Senate Republicans held 43 percent of Senate seats, just as Clinton had received 43 percent of the presidential vote. Both were equally entitled to claim a "mandate," Dole concluded. Michael Nelson, "Clinton and the Cycle of Politics and Policy," in *The Elections of 1992*, ed. Michael Nelson (Washington, D.C.: CQ Press, 1993), 146.

Part IV Presidents and Politics

10 The Presidency and the Public: Leadership as Spectacle

Bruce Miroff

To govern successfully, presidents have always needed political support from the public. What is new in the modern presidency is the extent to which they work hard to achieve such support. As Bruce Miroff argues, the modern president "not only responds to popular demands and passions but also actively reaches out to shape them." The president does so in speeches and in symbol-ridden events, which Miroff, borrowing from the language of cultural anthropology, calls "spectacles." Understood properly, for example, the highly popular war against Iraq that George Bush launched in February 1991 resembled nothing so much as a professional wrestling match, in which the audience (the American people) was gratified by the sight of the good guy (President Bush) overpowering the bad guy (the Iraqi leader Saddam Hussein). For Bill Clinton, the challenge has been to plant the appealing spectacle of populism more prominently in the public consciousness than the negative spectacle of presidential weakness.

One of the most distinctive features of the modern presidency is its constant cultivation of popular support. The framers of the United States Constitution envisioned a president substantially insulated from the demands and passions of the people by the long duration of his term and the dignity of his office. The modern president, in contrast, not only responds to popular demands and passions but also actively reaches out to shape them. Both the possibilities opened up by modern technology and the problems presented by the increased fragility of parties and institutional coalitions lead presidents to turn to the public for support and strength. If popular backing is to be maintained, the public must believe in the president's leadership qualities.

Observers of presidential politics are increasingly recognizing the centrality of the president's relationship with the American public. George Edwards speaks of "the public presidency" and argues that the "greatest source of influence for the president is public approval."[1] Samuel Kernell suggests that presidential appeals for popular favor now overshadow more traditional methods of seeking influence, especially bargaining. Presidents today, Kernell argues, are "going public"; he demonstrates their propensity to cultivate popular support by recording the mounting frequency of their public addresses, public appearances, and political travel. These constitute, he claims, "the repertoire of modern leadership."[2]

This new understanding of presidential leadership can be carried further. A president's approach to, and impact on, public perceptions is not limited to overt appeals in speeches and appearances. Much of what the modern presidency does, in fact, involves the projection of images whose purpose is to shape public understanding and gain popular support. A significant—and growing—part of the presidency revolves around the enactment of leadership as a *spectacle*.

To examine the presidency as a spectacle is to ask not only how a president seeks to appear but also what it is that the public sees. We are accustomed to gauging the public's responses to a president with polls that measure approval and disapproval of the president's overall performance in office and his effectiveness in managing the economy and foreign policy. Yet these evaluative categories may say more about the information desired by politicians or academic researchers than about the terms in which most members of a president's audience actually view him. A public that responds mainly to presidential spectacles will not ignore the president's performance, but its understanding of that performance, as well as its sense of the more overarching and intangible strengths and weaknesses of the administration, will be colored by the terms of the spectacle.

The Presidency as Spectacle

A spectacle is a kind of symbolic event, one in which particular details stand for broader and deeper meanings. What differentiates a spectacle from other kinds of symbolic events is the centrality of character and action. A spectacle presents intriguing and often dominating characters not in static poses but through actions that establish their public identities.

Spectacle implies a clear division between actors and spectators. As Daniel Dayan and Elihu Katz have noted, a spectacle possesses "a narrowness of focus, a limited set of appropriate responses, and . . . a minimal level of interaction. What there is to see is very clearly exhibited; spectacle implies a distinction between the roles of performers and audience."[3] A spectacle does not permit the audience to interrupt the action and redirect its meaning. Spectators can become absorbed in a spectacle or can find it unconvincing, but they cannot become performers. A spectacle is not designed for mass participation; it is not a democratic event.

Perhaps the most distinctive characteristic of a spectacle is that the actions that constitute it are meaningful not for what they achieve but for what they signify. Actions in a spectacle are gestures rather than means to an end. What is important is that they be understandable and impressive to the spectators. This distinction between gestures and means is illustrated by Roland Barthes in his classic discussion of professional wrestling as a spectacle. Barthes shows that professional wrestling is completely unlike professional boxing. Boxing is a form of competition, a contest of skill in a situation of uncertainty. What matters is the outcome; because this is in doubt, we can wager on it. But in professional wrestling, the outcome is preordained; it would be senseless to bet on who is going to win. What matters in professional wrestling are the gestures made during the match, gestures by performers portraying distinctive characters, gestures that carry moral significance. In a typical match, an evil character threatens a good character, knocks him down on the canvas, abuses him with dirty tricks, but ultimately loses when the good character rises up to exact a just revenge.[4]

It may seem odd to approach the presidency through an analogy with boxing and wrestling—but let us pursue it for a moment. Much of what presidents do is analogous to what boxers do—they engage in contests of power and policy with other political actors, contests in which the outcomes are uncertain. But a growing amount of presidential activity is akin to wrestling. The contemporary presidency is presented by the White House (with the collaboration of the media) as a series of spectacles in which a larger-than-life main character, along with his supporting team, engage in emblematic bouts with immoral or dangerous adversaries.

A number of contemporary developments have converged to foster the rise of spectacle in the modern presidency. The mass media have become the principal vehicle for presidential spectacle. Focusing more of their coverage on the president than on any other person or institution in American life, the media keep him constantly before the public and give him unmatched opportunities to display his leadership qualities. Television provides the view most amenable to spectacle; by favoring the visual and the dramatic, it promotes stories with simple plot lines over complex analyses of causes and consequences. But other kinds of media are not fundamentally different. As David Paletz and Robert Entman have shown, American journalists "define events from a short-term, anti-historical perspective; see individual or group action, not structural or other impersonal long run forces, at the root of most occurrences; and simplify and reduce stories to conventional symbols for easy assimilation by audiences."[5]

The mass media are not, to be sure, always reliable vehicles for presidential spectacles. Reporters may frame their stories in terms that undermine the meanings the White House intends to convey. Their desire for controversy can feed off presidential spectacles, but it also can destroy them. The media can contribute to spectacular failures in the presidency as well as to successful spectacles.

Spectacle has also been fostered by the president's rise to primacy in the American political system. A political order originally centered on institutions has given way, especially in the public mind, to a political order that centers on the person of the president. Theodore Lowi writes, "Since the president has become the embodiment of government, it seems perfectly normal for millions upon millions of Americans to concentrate their hopes and fears directly and personally upon him."[6] The "personal president" that Lowi describes is the object of popular expectations; these expectations, Stephen Wayne and Thomas Cronin have shown, are both excessive and contradictory.[7] The president must attempt to satisfy the public by delivering tangible benefits, such as economic growth, but these will almost never be enough. Not surprisingly, then, presidents turn to the gestures of the spectacle to satisfy their audience.

To understand the modern presidency as a form of spectacle, we must consider the presentation of the president as a spectacular character, his team's role as supporting performers, and the arrangement of gestures that convey to the audience the meaning of his actions.

A contemporary president is, to borrow a phrase from Guy Debord, "the spectacular representation of a living human being."[8] An enormous amount of attention is paid to the president as a public character; every deed, quality, and even foible is regarded as fascinating and important. The American public may not learn the details of policy formulation, but they know that Gerald Ford bumps his head on helicopter doorframes, that Ronald Reagan likes jellybeans, and that Bill Clinton enjoys hanging out with Hollywood celebrities. In a spectacle, a president's character possesses intrinsic as well as symbolic value; it is to be appreciated for its own sake. The spectators do not press the president to specify what economic or social benefits he is providing or denying them; nor do they closely inquire into the truthfulness of the claims he makes. (To the extent that they do evaluate the president in such terms, they step outside the terms of the spectacle.) His featured qualities are presented as benefits in themselves. Thus, John F. Kennedy's glamour casts his whole era in a romanticized glow, while Reagan's amiability relieves the grim national mood that had developed under his predecessor.

The president's character must not only be appealing but must also be magnified by the spectacle. The spectacle makes the president appear exceptionally decisive, tough, courageous, prescient, or prudent. Whether he is in fact all or any of these things is obscured. What matters is that he is presented as having these qualities, in magnitudes far beyond what ordinary citizens can imagine themselves to possess. The president must appear confident and masterful before spectators whose very position, as onlookers, denies the possibility of mastery.[9]

The most likely presidential qualities to be magnified will be ones that contrast dramatically with those attributes that drew criticism to the previous president. Thus, Jimmy Carter, coming after a Nixon administration disgraced for its power-hungry immorality, was featured in spectacles of modesty and honesty. Ronald Reagan, following a president perceived as weak, was featured in spectacles that highlighted his potency. George Bush, succeeding a president notorious for his disengagement from the workings of his own administration, was featured in spectacles of "hands-on" management.

The president is the principal figure in presidential spectacles, but he has the help of aides and advisers. The star performer is surrounded by a *team*. Members of the president's team can, through the supporting parts they play, enhance or detract from the spectacle's effect on the audience. For a president's team to enhance his spectacles, its members should project attractive qualities that either resemble the featured attributes of the president or make up for the president's perceived deficiencies. A team will diminish presidential spectacles if its members project qualities that underscore the president's weaknesses.

A performance team, Erving Goffman has shown, contains "a set of individuals whose intimate cooperation is required if a given projected definition of the situation is to be maintained."[10] There are a number of ways the team can disrupt presidential spectacles. A member of the team can call too much attention to himself, partially upstaging the president. This was one of the disruptive practices that made the Reagan White House eager to be rid of Secretary of State Alexander Haig. He can give away important secrets to the audience; Budget Director David Stockman's famous confessions about supply-side economics to a reporter for the *Atlantic* jeopardized the mystique of economic innovation that the Reagan administration had created in 1981. Worst of all, a member of the team can, perhaps inadvertently, discredit the central meanings that a presidential spectacle has been designed to establish. Thus, revelations of

Budget Director Bert Lance's questionable banking practices deflated the lofty moral tone established at the outset of the Carter presidency.

The audience watching a presidential spectacle is, the White House hopes, as impressed by gestures as by results. Indeed, the gestures are sometimes preferable to the results. Thus, a "show" of force by the president is preferable to the death and destruction that are the results of force. The ways in which the invasion of Grenada in 1983, the bombing of Libya in 1986, and the seizing of Panamanian dictator Manuel Noriega in 1989 were portrayed to the American public suggest an eagerness in the White House to present the image of military toughness but not the casualties from military conflict—even when they are the enemy's casualties.

Gestures overshadow results. They also overshadow facts. But facts are not obliterated in a presidential spectacle. They remain present; they are needed, in a sense, to nurture the gestures. Without real events, presidential spectacles would not be impressive; they would seem contrived, mere pseudoevents. However, some of the facts that emerge in the course of an event might discredit its presentation as spectacle. Therefore, a successful spectacle, such as Reagan's "liberation" of Grenada, must be more powerful than any of the facts upon which it draws. Rising above contradictory or disconfirming details, the spectacle must transfigure the more pliant facts and make them carriers of its most spectacular gestures.

Presidential spectacles are seldom pure spectacles in the sense that a wrestling match can be a pure spectacle. Although they may involve a good deal of advance planning and careful calculation of gestures, they cannot be completely scripted in advance. Unexpected and unpredictable events will emerge during a presidential spectacle. If the White House is fortunate and skillful, it can capitalize upon some of these events by using them to enhance the spectacle. If the White House is not so lucky or talented, such events can detract from, or even undermine, the spectacle.

Also unlike wrestling or other pure spectacles, the presidential variety often has more than one audience. Its primary purpose is to construct meanings for the American public. But it also can direct messages to those whom the White House has identified as its foes or the sources of its problems. In 1981, when Reagan fired the air traffic controllers of the Professional Air Traffic Controllers' Organization (PATCO) because they engaged in an illegal strike, he presented to the public the spectacle of a tough, determined president who would uphold the law and, unlike his predecessor, would not be pushed around by grasping interest groups. The spectacle also conveyed to organized labor that the White

House knew how to feed popular suspicions of unions and could make things difficult for a labor movement that became too assertive.

As the PATCO firing shows, some presidential spectacles retain important policy dimensions. One could construct a continuum in which one end represented pure policy and the other pure spectacle. Toward the policy end one would find behind-the-scenes presidential actions, including quiet bargaining over domestic policies (such as Lyndon Johnson's lining up of Republican support for civil rights legislation) and covert actions in foreign affairs (the Nixon administration's use of the CIA to "destabilize" a Socialist regime in Chile). Toward the spectacle end would be presidential posturing at home (law-and-order and drugs have been handy topics) and dramatic foreign travel (from 1972 until the 1989 massacre in Tiananmen Square, China was a particular presidential favorite). Most of the president's actions are a mix of policy and spectacle.

The Possibilities of Spectacle: John F. Kennedy

It was the administration of John F. Kennedy that first disclosed the possibilities in presidential spectacle. Certainly there were precursors—especially the two Roosevelts—but the coming together of vast media coverage, inflated popular expectations, and talent at producing spectacle is first evident in the New Frontier era. To be sure, the possibilities of spectacle were too new, and the pull of important policy issues too great, for spectacle to be at the center of the most important events of the Kennedy presidency. But spectacle was present even in those events—and more evident still in secondary undertakings.

Kennedy became, in the course of his brief presidency, a remarkable spectacle character. His candidacy had evoked doubts about his age, experience, and qualifications. But these seeming handicaps were turned into virtues. His would be a presidency that projected youth, vigor, and novelty, that recast the institution itself as a headquarters for intelligence and masterful will. Qualities of the president that signified power were supplemented by other qualities—wealth, physical attractiveness, and wit—that signified glamour. Kennedy's character was portrayed by the media as pleasurable in its own right. Yet it also carried symbolic value, representing, on the surface, the national will to excellence, and, at a deeper level, the nation's excitement with its status as a great imperial power.

Although some of the glitter of Kennedy's character has been rubbed off by later revelations, his winning attributes have remained a model for many of his successors. Even if other presidents could not hope to emulate all of his appealing features, they could strive for that grace in being president that was

Kennedy's ultimate charm. Nixon had some talent at producing spectacles—witness the handling of his 1972 trip to China—but the grace of Kennedy continued to elude him. Nixon and his advisers recognized, for example, the value in all those photographs of Kennedy walking along the beach or sailing at Hyannis Port. But their attempt to project the same relaxed grace produced comedy rather than spectacle. When photographers were taken out to snap pictures of the president walking at San Clemente, they found Nixon "traipsing along the beach in an ill-fitting windbreaker, a pair of dress trousers, and *street* shoes."[11]

The Kennedy team also received exceptional media coverage— and revealed thereby that the people surrounding the president could contribute their own spectacle value. Members of Kennedy's staff and cabinet were portrayed as a "ministry of talent," a constellation of exceptionally intelligent and able men revolving around a brilliant star. Even more engaging was the image, favored by Kennedy himself, of his team as a "band of brothers." In reality, Patrick Anderson has observed, Kennedy's staff "hummed with an undercurrent of jealousy, rivalry, and friction."[12] But what the public saw was a team of youthful, impressive men bound together by their dedication to an equally young and impressive leader. Kennedy's team thus served as an extension of their leader, magnifying his qualities to add to his luster.

Intelligence and toughness were particularly featured in the area of foreign policy. With McGeorge Bundy as the president's special assistant for national security affairs and Robert McNamara as his secretary of defense, Kennedy had team members who underscored his own claim to foreign policy mastery. McNamara became a legend for his analytical and statistical sharpness, while Bundy, the former Harvard dean, came across, in the words of David Halberstam, as "the sharpest intellect of a generation, a repository of national intelligence."[13] Each projected unflagging drive and steely determination; as Halberstam wrote of McNamara: "He was a man of force, moving, pushing, getting things done, . . . the can-do man in the can-do society, in the can-do era."[14] McNamara and Bundy seemed to be running the national security apparatus as extensions of Kennedy.

An even more direct extension of John Kennedy was his brother, the attorney general. Robert Kennedy's intelligence and drive recalled those of the president, and his special closeness to JFK made their strengths seem intertwined. Yet Robert also projected intensity and what his detractors dubbed "ruthlessness," qualities that could undercut his brother's charm. John Kennedy was not tarnished by his brother or by any aides on staff, both because of his own self-deprecating wit and because his team included an especially good-humored member. Press Secretary Pierre Salinger became one of the best known of the New Frontiersmen not because he shared their vaunted strengths but because he supplied comic leavening. As Patrick Anderson has written, Salinger "was Kennedy's Falstaff and he made the most of the role."[15]

The most dramatic actions of the Kennedy presidency were designed to produce results rather than to feature gestures; spectacle was not yet a very deliberate motive. Yet even in such actions as the steel crisis of 1962, the civil rights struggle of 1963, the Berlin and Cuban crises, the Kennedy administration provided moments of spectacle that would impress its successors and help shape future media expectations. Sometimes it was the image of the president at the center of a White House command post, personally making cool and effective decisions in the heat of crises. There also was the image of the president denouncing the greed of steel company executives and invoking a higher public interest before a national television audience.

Where spectacle predominated on the New Frontier was in more peripheral areas. The space race was one such area: Kennedy's public pledge to send a man to the moon had little to do with scientific advancement, but a great deal to do with demonstrating the superiority of America's (and the president's) spirit in the face of the Communist challenge. Physical fitness was a minor spectacle; much-publicized fifty-mile hikes by New Frontiersmen highlighted the theme of restoring vigor to American life. The presidential press conference was adapted to the purposes of spectacle and became one of Kennedy's greatest successes. As the first president to permit live television coverage of his press conferences, Kennedy used this forum to demonstrate to the public his mastery of facts, quick intelligence, and sense of humor. What was said during Kennedy's press conferences was less important than his appealing ways of saying it; the press was a less important audience than the wider public.

The Triumph of Spectacle: Ronald Reagan

The Reagan presidency was a triumph of spectacle. In the realm of substantive policy, it was marked by striking failures as well as significant successes. But even the most egregious of these failures—public exposure of the disastrous covert policy of selling arms to Iran and diverting some of the profits from the sales to the Nicaraguan contras—proved to be only a temporary blow to the political fortunes of the most spectacular president in decades. With the help of two heartwarming summits with Soviet leader Mikhail Gorbachev, Reagan recovered from the Iran-contra debacle and left office near the peak of his popularity. His presidency had, for the most part, floated above its flawed processes and failed policies, secure in the brilliant glow of its successful spectacles.

The basis of this success was the character of Ronald Reagan. His previous career in movies and television made Reagan comfortable with and adept at spectacles; he moved easily from one kind to another.[16] Reagan presented to his audience a multifaceted character, funny yet powerful, ordinary yet heroic, individual yet representative. He was a character richer even than Kennedy in mythic resonance.

Coming into office after a president who was widely perceived as weak, Reagan as a spectacle character projected potency. His administration featured a number of spectacles in which Reagan displayed his decisiveness, forcefulness, and will to prevail. The image of masculine toughness was played up repeatedly. The American people saw a president who, even though in his seventies, rode horses and exercised vigorously, a president who liked to cite (and thereby identify himself with) movie tough guys such as Clint Eastwood and Sylvester Stallone. Yet Reagan's strength was nicely balanced by his amiability; his aggressiveness was rendered benign by his characteristic one-line quips. The warm grin took the edge off, removed any intimations of callousness or violence.

Quickly dubbed the Great Communicator, Reagan presented his character not through eloquent rhetoric but through storytelling. As Paul Erickson has demonstrated, Reagan liked to tell tales of "stock symbolic characters," figures whose values and behavior were "heavily colored with Reagan's ideological and emotional principles."[17] Although the villains in these tales ranged from Washington bureaucrats to Marxist dictators, the heroes, whether ordinary people or inspirational figures like Knute Rockne, shared a belief in America. Examined more closely, these heroes turned out to resemble Reagan himself. Praising the heroism of Americans, Reagan, as representative American, praised himself.

The power of Reagan's character rested not only on its intrinsic attractiveness but also on its symbolic appeal. The spectacle specialists who worked for Reagan seized upon the idea of making him an emblem for the American identity. In a June 1984 memo, White House aide Richard Darman sketched a campaign strategy that revolved around the president's mythic role: "Paint RR as the personification of all that is right with or heroized by America. Leave Mondale in a position where an attack on Reagan is tantamount to an attack on America's idealized image of itself."[18] Having come into office at a time of considerable anxiety, with many Americans uncertain (according to polls and interviews) about the economy, their future, and America itself, Reagan was an immensely reassuring character. He had not been marked by the shocks of recent American history—and he denied that those shocks had meaning. He told Americans that the Vietnam War was noble rather than appalling, that Watergate was forgotten, that racial conflict was a thing of the distant past, and that the American economy still offered the American dream to any aspiring individual. Reagan (the character) and America (the country) were presented in the spectacles of the Reagan presidency as timeless, above the decay of aging and the difficulties of history.

The Reagan team assumed special importance because Reagan ran what Lou Cannon has called "the delegated presidency."[19] His team members carried on, as was well known to the public, most of the business of the executive branch; Reagan's own work habits were decidedly relaxed. Reagan's team did not contain many performers who reinforced the president's character, as did Kennedy's New Frontiersmen. But it featured several figures whose spectacle role was to compensate for Reagan's deficiencies or to carry on his mission with a greater air of vigor than the amiable president usually conveyed. The Reagan presidency was not free of disruptive characters—Alexander Haig's and James Watt's unattractive features and gestures called the president's spectacle into question. Unlike the Carter presidency, however, the Reagan administration removed these characters before too much damage had been done.

David Stockman was the most publicized supporting player in the first months of 1981. His image in the media was formidable. *Newsweek*, for example, marveled at how "his buzz-saw intellect has helped him stage a series of bravura performances before Congress," and acclaimed him "the Reagan Administration's boy wonder."[20] There was spectacle appeal in the sight of the nation's youngest-ever budget director serving as the right arm of the nation's oldest-ever chief executive. More important, Stockman's appearance as the master of budget numbers compensated for a president who was notoriously uninterested in data. Stockman faded in spectacle value after his disastrous *Atlantic* confessions in the fall of 1981. His admission that budget numbers had been doctored to show the results the administration wanted, and that the across-the-board tax cut was a "Trojan horse" to make politically palatable a large reduction in the rates paid by the wealthiest taxpayers, left his credibility wounded. But Stockman's contribution had been substantial when it was most needed, in the crucial budget and tax battles of Reagan's early months as president.

As Reagan's longtime aide, Edwin Meese III was one of the most prominent members of the president's team. Meese's principal spectacle role was not as a White House manager but as a cop. Even before he moved from the White

House to the Justice Department, Meese became the voice and the symbol of the administration's tough stance on law-and-order issues. Although the president sometimes spoke about law-and-order, Meese took on the issue with a vigor that his more benign boss could not convey.

In foreign affairs, the Reagan administration developed an effective balance of images in the persons of Caspar Weinberger and George Shultz. Weinberger quickly became the administration's most visible cold war hard-liner. As the tireless spokesman and unbudging champion of a soaring defense budget, he was a handy symbol for the Reagan military buildup. Nicholas Lemann notes that while "Weinberger's predecessor, Harold Brown, devoted himself almost completely to management, Weinberger . . . operated more and more on the theatrical side."[21] His grim, hawklike visage was as much a reminder of the Soviet threat as the alarming paperback reports on the Russian behemoth that his Defense Department issued every year. Yet Weinberger could seem too alarming, feeding the fears of those who worried about Reagan's warmaking proclivities.

Once Haig was pushed out as secretary of state, however, the Reagan administration found the ideal counterpoint to Weinberger in George Shultz. In contrast to both Haig and Weinberger, Shultz was a reassuring figure. He was portrayed in the media in soothing terms: low-key, quiet, conciliatory. In form and demeanor, he came across, in the words of *Time*, "as a good gray diplomat."[22] Shultz was taken to be a voice of foreign policy moderation in an administration otherwise dominated by hard-liners. Actually, Shultz had better cold war credentials than Weinberger, having been a founding member of the hard-line Committee on the Present Danger in 1976. And he was more inclined to support the use of military force than was the secretary of defense, who reflected the caution of a Pentagon burned by the Vietnam experience. But Shultz's real views were less evident than his spectacle role as the gentle diplomat.

The Reagan presidency benefited not only from a spectacular main character and a useful team but also from talent and good fortune at enacting spectacle gestures. It is not difficult to find events during the Reagan years—the PATCO strike, the Geneva summit, the Libyan bombing, and others—whose significance primarily lay in their spectacle value. The most striking Reagan spectacle of all was the invasion of Grenada. Grenada deserves a close look; it can serve as the archetypal presidential spectacle.

American forces invaded the island of Grenada in October 1983. Relations between the Reagan administration and the Marxist regime of Grenada's Maurice Bishop had been increasingly tense. When Bishop was overthrown and murdered by a clique of more militant Marxists, the Reagan administration began to consider military action. It was urged to invade by the Organization of Eastern Caribbean States, composed of Grenada's island neighbors. And it had a pretext for action in the safety of the Americans—most of them medical students—on the island. Once the decision to invade was made, American troops landed in force, evacuated most of the students, and seized the island after encountering unexpectedly stiff resistance. Reagan administration officials announced that in the course of securing the island U.S. forces had discovered large caches of military supplies and documents, indicating that Cuba planned to turn Grenada into a base for the export of revolution and terror.

Examination of the details that eventually came to light cast doubt on the Reagan administration's claims of a threat to the American students and a buildup of "sophisticated" Cuban weaponry on the island. Beyond such details, there was a sheer incongruity between the importance bestowed on Grenada by the Reagan administration and the insignificance that the facts seemed to suggest. Grenada is a tiny island, with a population of 100,000, a land area of 133 square miles, and an economy whose exports totaled $19 million in 1981.[23] That American troops could secure it was never in question; as Richard Gabriel has noted, "in terms of actual combat forces, the U.S. outnumbered the island's defenders approximately ten to one."[24] Grenada's importance did not derive from the facts of the event, or from the military, political, and economic implications of America's actions, but from its value as a spectacle.

What was the spectacle of Grenada about? Its meaning was articulated by a triumphant President Reagan: "Our days of weakness are over. Our military forces are back on their feet and standing tall."[25] Reagan, even more than the American military, came across in the media as "standing tall" in Grenada.

The spectacle actually began with the president on a weekend golfing vacation in Augusta, Georgia. His vacation was interrupted first by planning for an invasion of Grenada and then by news that the U.S. Marine barracks in Beirut had been bombed. Once the news of the Grenada landings replaced the tragedy in Beirut on the front page and television screen, the golfing angle proved to be an apt beginning for a spectacle. It was used to dramatize the ability of a relaxed and laid-back president to rise to a grave challenge. And it supplied the White House with an unusual backdrop to present the president in charge, with members of his team by his side. As Francis X. Clines reported in the *New York Times*,

The White House offered the public some graphic tableaux, snapped by the White House photographer over the weekend, depicting the President at the center of various conferences. He is seen in bathrobe and slippers being briefed by Mr. Shultz and Mr. McFarlane, then out on the Augusta fairway, pausing at the wheel of his golf cart as he receives another dispatch. Mr. Shultz is getting the latest word in another, holding the special security phone with a golf glove on.[26]

Pictures of the president as decision maker were particularly effective because pictures from Grenada itself were lacking; the American press had been barred by the Reagan administration from covering the invasion. This outraged the press but was extremely useful to the spectacle, which would not have been furthered by pictures of dead bodies or civilian casualties, or by independent sources of information with which congressional critics could raise unpleasant questions.

The initial meaning of the Grenada spectacle was established by Reagan in his announcement of the invasion. The enemy was suitably evil: "a brutal group of leftist thugs." American objectives were purely moral—to protect the lives of innocent people, namely American medical students, on the island, and to restore democracy to the people of Grenada. And the actions taken were unmistakably forceful: "The United States had no choice but to act strongly and decisively."[27]

But the spectacle of Grenada soon expanded beyond this initial definition. The evacuation of the medical students provided one of those unanticipated occurrences that heighten the power of spectacle: when several of the students kissed the airport tarmac to express their relief and joy at returning to American soil, the resulting pictures on television and in the newspapers were better than anything the administration could have orchestrated. They provided the spectacle with historical as well as emotional resonance. Here was a second hostage crisis—but where Carter had been helpless to release captive Americans, Reagan had swiftly come to the rescue.

Rescue of the students quickly took second place, however, to a new theme: the claim that U.S. forces had uncovered and uprooted a hidden Soviet-Cuban base for adventurism and terrorism. In his nationally televised address, Reagan did not ignore the Iran analogy: "The nightmare of our hostages in Iran must never be repeated." But he stressed the greater drama of defeating a sinister Communist plot. "Grenada, we were told, was a friendly island paradise for tourism. Well, it wasn't. It was a Soviet-Cuban colony being readied as a major military bastion to export terror and undermine democracy. We got there just in time."[28] Grenada was turning out to be an even better spectacle for Reagan: he had rescued not only the students but the people of all the Americas as well. (Later there would be another bonus: the happiness of the Grenadian people at the overthrow of the military clique that had murdered Maurice Bishop. Reagan thus became not just rescuer but liberator.)

As the spectacle expanded and grew more heroic, public approval increased. The president's standing in the polls went up. *Time* reported that "a post-invasion poll taken by the *Washington Post* and ABC News showed that 63% of Americans approve the way Reagan is handling the presidency, the highest level in two years, and attributed his gain largely to the Grenada intervention."[29] Congressional critics, although skeptical of many of the claims made by the administration, began to stifle their doubts and chime in with endorsements in accordance with the polls. An unnamed White House aide, quoted in *Newsweek*, drew the obvious lesson: "You can scream and shout and gnash your teeth all you want, but the folks out there like it. It was done right and done with dispatch."[30]

In its final gestures, the Grenada spectacle commemorated itself. Reagan invited the medical students to the White House, and, predictably, basked in their praise and cheering. The Pentagon contributed its symbolic share, awarding some eight thousand medals for the Grenada operation—more than the number of American troops that set foot on the island. In actuality, Gabriel has shown, "the operation was marred by a number of military failures."[31] Yet these were obscured by the triumphant appearances of the spectacle.

That the spectacle of Grenada was more potent, and would prove more lasting in its effects, than any disconfirming facts was observed at the time by Anthony Lewis. Reagan "knew the facts would come out eventually," wrote Lewis. "But if that day could be postponed, it might make a great political difference. People would be left with their first impression that this was a decisive President fighting communism."[32] Grenada became for most Americans a highlight of Reagan's first term. Insignificant in military or diplomatic terms, as spectacle it was one of the most successful acts of the Reagan presidency.

A Schizoid Spectacle: George Bush

Time accorded George Bush a unique honor: it named him its "Men of the Year" for 1990. There were really two President Bushes, the magazine explained, a strong and visionary leader in international affairs and a fumbling and directionless executive at home.[33] The split in Bush's presidency that *Time* highlighted was as evident in the realm of spectacle as in the realm of policy. The foreign affairs spectacle of the Bush presidency featured a masterful leader, a powerhouse team, and thrilling gestures. The domestic spectacle featured a confused leader, a colorless team, and gestures of remarkable ineptitude. Together, they created a schizoid spectacle.

Critics could find much to fault in Bush's foreign policy. He had, for example, been slow to respond to the momentous changes that led to the demise of the Soviet Union, and he had helped to build up the power of Iraq's Saddam Hussein almost to the eve of the invasion of Kuwait. Bush's foreign policy was considered more reactive than proactive, and his vision of "a new world order" was vague.[34] Still, Bush did possess genuine talents in foreign affairs. Equally important, he was lucky enough to be in office when Communism collapsed. Everything went his way abroad (at least until an ill-starred trip to Japan early in 1992), and as spectacle, his foreign policy leadership was a great triumph.

The main character in the Bush administration's foreign policy spectacle was experienced, confident, decisively in charge. Bush seemed bred to foreign policy stewardship in a patrician tradition dating back to Theodore Roosevelt and Henry Stimson. He came across to the public as the master diplomat, successfully cajoling and persuading other world leaders through well-publicized phone calls; in truth, he moved easily among international elites, obviously in his element. He was an even more triumphant spectacle character when featured in winning tableaux as commander in chief of Operation Desert Storm.

The foreign policy team made a superb contribution to the global side of the Bush spectacle. Not since the administration of Richard Nixon had a president's skill at diplomacy been so effectively magnified by his top civilian advisers; not since World War II had a commander in chief been blessed with such popular military subordinates. James Baker, Bush's one-time Houston neighbor and long-time political manager, was both courtly and canny as secretary of state. Richard Cheney was a cool, cerebral secretary of defense, with an air of mastery reminiscent of Robert McNamara. Colin Powell, chairman of the Joint Chiefs of Staff, radiated dignity and authority as the highest-ranking African American in the history of the military and was almost universally admired. Gen. Norman Schwarzkopf was a feisty commander for Desert Storm—an appealing emblem for a military finally restored to glorious health after two decades of licking its Vietnam wounds.

More than anything else, military gestures produced exciting drama in the Bush foreign affairs spectacle. Panama was the prelude to the Persian Gulf War. It featured, in Manuel Noriega, a doubly immoral adversary—a drug smuggler as well as a dictator. The U.S. military operation to depose Noriega was swift and efficient, and a victorious outcome was assured once the Panamanian strongman was seized and transported to the United States to face drug-trafficking charges.

The Gulf War victory dwarfed Panama, not only as significant policy accomplishment but also as spectacle. Bush depicted Saddam Hussein, the Iraqi dictator, as a second Hitler, a figure whose immense record of evil made Noriega look like a small-time thug. To be sure, Operation Desert Storm lacked the satisfying climax of destroying the evil adversary. But as a military display, it provided Americans with numerous scenes to cheer. The indisputable favorites were Defense Department videos of laser-guided bombs homing in on Iraqi targets with pinpoint accuracy. In the cinematic terms that President Reagan had made popular, Desert Storm was not the cavalry rescue of Grenada or the capture of the pirate captain in Panama; it was high-tech epic, the return of the American Jedi.

Bush's foreign policy spectacle was successful—perhaps too successful. Once the Soviet Union crumbled and Iraq was militarily humiliated, foreign policy seemed much less relevant to most Americans. According to Walter Dean Burnham, "In 1992 foreign policy issues and public concerns about them played the smallest role in any American presidential election since 1936."[35] As Americans began to focus almost exclusively on the home front, they witnessed a domestic Bush spectacle utterly unlike the foreign affairs version.

The domestic Bush was an uncertain, awkward character, especially in the electorally decisive field of economic policy. Inheriting what he had once derided as Reagan's "voodoo economics," Bush presided over an economic crisis when the policy's magic failed. In the face of this crisis, which was evident by the second year of his administration, Bush drifted, seemingly without a clue as to how to restore the economy to health. The only economic prescription he ever put forward with any conviction was a cut in the capital gains tax rate that would have most directly benefited wealthy investors. Comfortable dealing with the problems that beset international elites, Bush seemed ill at ease with the economic problems bothering ordinary Americans.

Bush's economic team only magnified his weaknesses. His secretary of the treasury, Nicholas Brady, and chairman of the Council of Economic Advisers, Michael Boskin, were pale, dim figures who barely registered in the public's consciousness. To the extent that anyone did notice them, they seemed to epitomize inaction, holding the fond but false hope that the economy would right itself without major government action. A more visible economic team member was the budget director, Richard Darman. But he was portrayed in the media as arrogant and abrasive. A trial to many Republican members of Congress, Darman's more important spectacle role was as an irritant to the Democratic members; he represented the warfare between the Bush White House and Capitol Hill that resulted in domestic policy gridlock.

It was through a series of small gestures, some intended and others inadvertent, that Bush's disengagement from the economic difficulties of ordinary people was most dramatically demonstrated. Touring a grocery store, the president expressed amazement at the electronic scanners that read prices. To those who stood by every week as these scanners recorded their food purchases, here was a president unfamiliar with how families struggled to pay their grocery bills. Visiting a suburban mall on the day after Thanksgiving (the busiest shopping day of the year) in 1991, Bush brought along reporters who publicized his purchases: athletic socks for himself, Christmas presents for his family. Bush's shopping expedition seemed designed to convey the message that Americans could lift themselves out of recession just by taking a few more trips to the local mall. The most telling gesture of disengagement came early in 1992 at a campaign stop in New Hampshire, when Bush blurted out a stage cue from one of his speechwriters: "Message: I care." The message that came through, of course, was that the president had to be prompted to commiserate with the economic woes of the American people.

Real economic fears and pains denied Bush reelection in 1992. But the fears and pains were made worse by the ineptitude of his domestic spectacle. A president who lacked not only a credible economic plan but also credible gestures that would communicate concern and effort to restore economic health went down to a landslide defeat, with 63 percent of the electorate voting against him. The schizoid spectacle of George Bush, triumphant in its foreign policy performance, disastrous in his domestic policy performance, was over.

A Populist Spectacle: Bill Clinton

If George Bush sounded insincere while blurting out, "Message: I care," Bill Clinton's campaign was designed to communicate exactly the same message with authenticity and depth. Following the pattern described earlier, Clinton displayed qualities that Bush had been criticized for lacking. Where Bush was tongue-tied, Clinton was articulate; where Bush drifted, Clinton was awash in plans and programs; where Bush dreamed distractedly of foreign policy triumphs, Clinton concentrated with apparent intelligence on the economy. The most striking contrast, however, was between Bush's disengagement from the problems of ordinary Americans and Clinton's desire for intimate engagement with their lives. Clinton's campaign spectacle promised to redirect the presidency from foreign policy elitism to domestic populism. Its main character was neither a war hero nor a powerful authority figure but rather an actively helpful friend of ordinary citizens in their time of trouble.

Clinton's populist intimacy, his proclivity for touching ordinary people physically as well as symbolically, was successfully transferred from his campaign into his transition to the presidency. The public saw the president-elect in the guise of policy expert at an "economic summit" in Little Rock. But they also watched him connect directly with ordinary people in scenes that evoked the diversity of American life. Pictures on television and in the newspapers depicted Clinton, on his first postelection visit to Washington, D.C., strolling down a gritty street in a black neighborhood. Other pictures captured him playing saxophone with a high-school band in Georgia and joining in a volleyball game on a California beach. Equally at ease in the ghetto, the small-town South, and the California good life, Clinton as president-elect previewed a spectacle in which Americans of every kind would be heard and helped.[36]

The first weeks of the Clinton presidency proved rocky, with the new chief executive buffeted by a failed nomination for attorney general and a costly controversy over gays and lesbians in the military. So, as he prepared to launch his deficit-reduction package, Clinton resurrected the town hall meeting—described by the *New York Times* as "a festival of populist imagery"—from his campaign.[37] Leaving Washington for the first time since the inauguration, getting back among ordinary folks in Detroit, Clinton appeared exuberant; once the forum began, he promptly stepped down from the stage to get closer to the audience. Along with a nationally televised, partly extemporaneous presidential speech before Congress, the town hall meeting was an effective kick-off for Clinton's budget drive.

Viewing Clinton's town hall meeting on television, Walter Goodman, the media critic of the *New York Times*, was reminded of Frank Capra, the director of such classic films as *Mr. Smith Goes to Washington* and *It's a Wonderful Life.* "On Monday night," Goodman wrote,

you could practically hear the big us-against-them speeches of James Stewart and Gary Cooper as the youthful-looking President pleaded, 'We're all in this together' and perorated with an evocation of patriotism and the Almighty. All that was missing was a small boy looking on, aglow with admiration.[38]

Jaded by the train of spectacles that presidents had offered the public for decades, Goodman, like most journalists, was cynical about Clinton's populist version. Yet watching Clinton mingle with the masses, it was hard to gainsay the emotional intensity that he displayed in these moments. It seemed just possible that Clinton's was a spectacle that might transcend itself, breaking down the barrier between performer and audience and producing an authentic connection between president and people.

In the months that followed, however, Clinton did not transcend spectacle; indeed, he did not even carry off his populist spectacle in an engaging manner. Preoccupied with passing his budget, he became enmeshed in the inside politics of Washington and neglected to take his case to the people in further town hall meetings and similar events. Literally losing touch with the public, he appeared a typical rather than a novel politician, a deal maker more than an intimate of the people.

Deeper damage to Clinton's spectacle of populism came from politically clumsy gestures that called its central premises into question. When his chief of staff, Thomas "Mack" McLarty, abruptly sacked every employee in the White House travel office for alleged corruption, White House reporters revealed that several of Clinton's closest cronies stood to benefit from the firings. Favoring friends by harshly treating low-level subordinates undercut the image of a caring Clinton. Even worse was the almost simultaneous episode of the two hundred dollar haircut. When reporters revealed that Clinton had delayed the departure of Air Force One from the Los Angeles airport so that he could have his hair cut by a pricey Beverly Hills stylist, Christophe, the contradiction between the populist from Hope, Arkansas, and the president gone Hollywood became an instant topic of national gossip and derision. (Initial press reports also suggested that Clinton's delay held up other flights, adding to the image of elitist arrogance, but later news stories disputed this.) Typical of the caustic commentary from the media was a *Newsweek* barb: "Hopes for the Clinton presidency seemed to be waning on supermarket lines and in barbershops across America (at least, those that charged less than three figures a trim)."[39]

Whatever other qualities a president projects through spectacle, an indispensable quality that every chief executive must appear to possess is strength. As Clinton's populist spectacle wobbled, his image as a strong leader also began to fall apart. Washington insiders filled the press with complaints about the president: he was uncertain of purpose, he vacillated in his decision making, he compromised too readily, he was too easily "rolled" by tough, determined opponents. The issue that became an emblem of these criticisms was Clinton's stand on admitting homosexuals into the military. After initially staking out a strong position against discriminatory treatment of gays and lesbians, the president was forced into a succession of retreats, backed down not only by the popular Gen. Colin Powell but also by a rival southern politician, Sen. Sam Nunn of Georgia.

Clinton's team could not help him much as he plummeted in the polls. His most visible White House aide, George Stephanopoulos, had made a cardinal blunder at the outset of the administration: he alienated the White House press corps with his cold and contemptuous air. In retaliation, the press made the baby-faced Stephanopoulos the symbol of an immature and inexperienced White House staff. Greater age and gravity marked Clinton's foreign policy team, which was headed by such experienced Washington hands as Secretary of State Warren Christopher and Secretary of Defense Les Aspin. But both had floundered indecisively over the agonizing dilemmas of the war in Bosnia, magnifying Clinton's own flip-flops on the biggest foreign policy issue of his first months in office. In a novel development for presidential spectacle, the only members of the president's team who conveyed strength were women: the president's wife, Hillary Rodham Clinton, and his attorney general, Janet Reno. Hillary was a superb asset to her husband, taking charge of the health care reform issue with mastery and determination. As for Janet Reno, her take-charge manner and readiness to concede error were pointedly compared by the press with the president's alleged deficiency in these qualities.

Two-thirds of the way through Clinton's first year in office, with David Gergen, an experienced specialist from the Reagan administration, now in charge of spectacle, the president's performance improved. It was not easy to restore the populist spectacle's original appeal to the public. But the show was far from over for a self-styled "comeback kid." Perhaps Clinton was fortunate to have made so many of his mistakes so early in his term. For by the fall of 1993, there were signs, particularly in the skillfully orchestrated unveiling of his health care reform plan, that he had learned from his initial blunders. In September the president dazzled Washington and the country alike with a passionate nationally televised speech before Congress on the health issue. He kept up the momentum by reconnecting to his public in a Tampa town hall meeting and in emotional visits with tragic victims of the existing health care system. If Clinton pulled off health care reform, and if the American economy at last gathered steam, this intimate friend of the American people, who helped them to overcome their domestic woes, might turn out to have a heartwarming populist spectacle after all.

Conclusion

It is tempting to blame the growth of spectacle on individual presidents, their calculating advisers, and compliant journalists. It is more accurate, however, to attribute the growth of spectacle to larger structural forces: the extreme personalization of the modern presidency, the excessive expectations of the president that most Americans possess, and the voluminous media coverage that fixes on presidents and treats American politics largely as a report of their adventures. Indeed, presidential spectacles can be linked to a culture of consumption in which spectacle is the predominant form that relates the few to the many.

Spectacle, then, is more a structural feature of the contemporary presidency than a strategy of deception adopted by particular presidents. In running for the presidency, then carrying out its tasks, any contemporary chief executive is likely to turn to spectacle. Spectacle has become institutionalized, as specialists in the White House routinely devise performances for a vast press corps that is eager to report every colorful detail. Spectacle is expected by the public as the most visible manifestation of presidential leadership. A president who deliberately eschewed its possibilities would probably encounter the same kind of difficulties as a president who tried to lead by spectacle and failed.

Still, the rise of spectacle in the presidency remains a disturbing development. It is harmful to presidents, promoting gesture over accomplishment and appearance over fact. It is even more harmful to the public, since it obfuscates presidential activity, undermines executive accountability, and encourages passivity on the part of citizens. The presentation of leadership as spectacle has little in common with the kind of leadership that American democratic values imply.

Notes

1. George C. Edwards III, *The Public Presidency: The Pursuit of Popular Support* (New York: St. Martin's Press, 1983), 1.

2. Samuel Kernell, *Going Public: New Strategies of Presidential Leadership*, 2d ed. (Washington, D.C.: CQ Press, 1993), 91. For a valuable historical perspective on the president's relationship with the public, see Jeffrey K. Tulis, *The Rhetorical Presidency* (Princeton, N.J.: Princeton University Press, 1987).

3. Daniel Dayan and Elihu Katz, "Electronic Ceremonies: Television Performs a Royal Wedding," in *On Signs*, ed. Marshall Blonsky (Baltimore: Johns Hopkins University Press, 1985), 16. For a view of spectacle as encompassing all political reality, see Murray Edelman, *Constructing the Political Spectacle* (Chicago: University of Chicago Press, 1988).

4. Roland Barthes, *Mythologies* (New York: Hill and Wang, 1972), 15–25.

5. David L. Paletz and Robert M. Entman, *Media Power Politics* (New York: Free Press, 1981), 21.

6. Theodore J. Lowi, *The Personal President* (Ithaca, N.Y.: Cornell University Press, 1985), 96.

7. See Stephen J. Wayne, "Great Expectations: What People Want from Presidents," in *Rethinking the Presidency*, ed. Thomas E. Cronin (Boston: Little, Brown, 1982), 185–199, and Thomas E. Cronin, *The State of the Presidency*, 2d ed. (Boston: Little, Brown, 1980), 2–25. Cronin was one of the first to recognize the relation between inflated public expectations and the emergence of public relations strategies at the center of presidential politics. See his "The Presidency Public Relations Script," in *The Presidency Reappraised*, ed. Rexford G. Tugwell and Thomas E. Cronin (New York: Praeger, 1974), 168–183.

8. Guy Debord, *Society of the Spectacle* (Detroit: Black and Red, 1983), para. 60.

9. On the confidence of the public personality and the anxiety of his audience, see Richard Sennett, *The Fall of Public Man* (New York: Knopf, 1977).

10. Erving Goffman, *The Presentation of Self in Everyday Life* (Garden City, N.Y.: Anchor Books, 1959), 104.

11. Dan Rather and Gary Paul Gates, *The Palace Guard* (New York: Warner Books, 1975), 285.

12. Patrick Anderson, *The President's Men* (Garden City, N.Y.: Anchor Books, 1969), 239.

13. David Halberstam, *The Best and the Brightest* (Greenwich, Conn.: Fawcett Crest Books, 1973), 57.

14. Ibid., 265.

15. Anderson, *The President's Men*, 279.

16. For a discussion of how his movie roles helped transform Reagan's character, see Michael Rogin, *Ronald Reagan, the Movie, and Other Episodes in Political Demonology* (Berkeley: University of California Press, 1987), 1–43.

17. Paul D. Erickson, *Reagan Speaks: The Making of an American Myth* (New York: New York University Press, 1985), 49, 51, 52.

18. Quoted in ibid., 100.

19. Lou Cannon, *Reagan* (New York: Putnam, 1982), 371–401.

20. "Meet David Stockman," *Newsweek*, February 16, 1981.

21. Nicholas Lemann, "The Peacetime War," *Atlantic*, October 1984, 88.

22. "Coolly Taking Charge," *Time*, September 6, 1982.

23. "From Bad to Worse for U.S. in Grenada," *U. S. News and World Report*, October 31, 1983.

24. Richard A. Gabriel, *Military Incompetence: Why the American Military Doesn't Win* (New York: Hill and Wang, 1985), 154.

25. Quoted in "Fare Well, Grenada," *Time*, December 26, 1983.

26. *New York Times*, October 26, 1983.

27. Ibid.

28. Ibid., October 28, 1983.

29. "Getting Back to Normal," *Time*, November 21, 1983.

30. "'We Will Not Be Intimidated,'" *Newsweek*, November 14, 1983.

31. Gabriel, *Military Incompetence*, 186.

32. Anthony Lewis, "What Was He Hiding?" *New York Times*, October 31, 1983.

33. "A Tale of Two Bushes: One Finds a Vision on the Global Stage; The Other Still Displays None at Home," *Time*, January 7, 1991.

34. See, for example, Larry Berman and Bruce W. Jentleson, "Bush and the Post-Cold-War World: New Challenges for American Leadership," in *The Bush Presidency: First Appraisals*, ed. Colin Campbell and Bert A. Rockman (Chatham, N.J.: Chatham House, 1991), 93–128.

35. Walter Dean Burnham, "The Legacy of George Bush: Travails of an Understudy," in *The Election of 1992: Reports and Interpretations*, ed. Gerald M. Pomper et al. (Chatham, N.J.: Chatham House, 1993), 21.

36. *New York Times*, November 30, 1992.

37. Ibid., February 10, 1993.

38. Ibid., February 17, 1993.

39. "What's Wrong?" *Newsweek*, June 7, 1993.

11 The President and the Press: Negotiating Newsworthiness at the White House

Timothy E. Cook and Lyn Ragsdale

Presidents and the press need each other to do their jobs. In order to govern effectively, the president must communicate with the American people. The press, in turn, relies on the president for information to provide to its readers, listeners, and viewers. Yet each party in this relationship has its own goals: the president wants to be portrayed favorably in order to win public support, and the press wants to be independent and interesting in order to keep and attract an audience. To fulfill their respective needs, argue Timothy E. Cook and Lyn Ragsdale, presidents and journalists engage in an ongoing "negotiation of newsworthiness." The subjects of these negotiations include the process of press-president interactions (how presidents and reporters will come together to make news), the content of news stories (what each story will be about), valence (are the stories positive or negative?), and results ("Stories about the president have strong consequences for presidential governance and presidential power").

I think the watchdog function is fine. But it's often carried to extremes in a search for headlines. For instance, the missing pages from my State Department file—here was a deal where Newsweek *bit on a rumor. So you had these serious reporters who just wanted to grill me about that—when the economy is in the tubes, when 100,000 people a month are losing their health insurance. And I'm supposed to take these people seriously as our sole intermediaries to the voters of this country? Sure, they should do their watchdog function, but anyone who lets himself be interpreted to the American people through these intermediaries alone is nuts.*

President-elect Bill Clinton, TV Guide, *November 21, 1992*

They feel we are expendable, and if they make an end run, they will get a better press, if you will, with the people. Eventually, they should realize the president has to be interrogated, and has to be accountable, and we're the ones to do it.

Helen Thomas, of United Press International, on
National Public Radio, *January 24, 1993*

Whatever happened to the honeymoon? Political folklore tells us that presidents can count on an early partnership with the media. The personalities of presidents and their families are new material for the public; presidents initially are judged on proposing policy rather than on performance; and open disagreement with the president within the administration and Congress is generally presumed not to arise until later in the presidential term.[1]

But Bill Clinton never had a honeymoon with the press. From the start, tension and conflict underlay the relationship. His first several months, for example, were marked by coverage that leaned toward the negative. According to a content analysis by the Center for Media and Public Affairs of the nightly news broadcasts of ABC, CBS, and NBC from January 20 to May 12, 1993, statements about Clinton that could be coded positively or negatively were negative 64 percent of the time. Although the degree of negativity varied from issue to issue (least negative on Bosnia, most negative on taxes and social security), on no issue during this period did Clinton receive more good marks than bad.[2] To be sure, from week to week, these "news ratings" bounced around quite a bit. Clinton's bad first weeks, with the storm over his proposal to lift the ban on gay men and lesbians in the military, were followed by a relatively good fourth week, with his State of the Union message. The coverage then reached a new low with the miniscandals in May 1993 about the White House travel office and a $200 presidential haircut. Highly positive coverage returned with Clinton's trip to the G-7 summit and his tour of the flood-ravaged Midwest. Thus, little evidence exists of either a honeymoon or consistently increasing antagonism. Instead, the relations between the president and the press seem to be variable, even volatile, perhaps so unpredictable as to be inexplicable.

In this chapter we ask the questions: Is there a way to explain the relationship between American presidents and the American news media? What defines and influences the relationship? And why does it matter?

Dependence and Independence

Presidents and the news media rely heavily on one another to do their jobs.[3] Presidents need the news media to get their messages out, to set the political agenda, to create favorable public moods, and to pressure otherwise recalcitrant political actors. Similarly, the news media use presidents as central protagonists around whom they can organize their daily production of news. The top news story is typically a presidential story; the top domestic newsbeat is at the White House.

Amid this mutual reliance, however, presidents and journalists are also independent of one another. The interests of presidents and the press, although intertwined, are fundamentally different. Presidents, like all politicians, want to get their information to the public (and to other politicians) in a form that is as favorable as possible to their own interests. But reporters, partly because of their commitment to serving their audiences, partly because of their commitment to balance and neutrality, and partly because of their professional aspirations, are not willing to be "unwitting adjuncts" to the White House. The result is what we call an ongoing *negotiation of newsworthiness* within the White House, within the news media, and between the two regarding which of the thousands of things that presidents, their families, and their advisers do in a given day will become news.[4]

This negotiation of newsworthiness involves what gets covered, who gets asked about a story, and how and for how long the story is covered. It is a negotiation that evolves between the White House and the press, as stories rise, develop, and fall; as alternative sources speak out or clam up; and as presidential and journalistic strategies change during the course of a president's term and from one president's term to another's. What is newsworthy one day may be old news the next. What is good news coverage for one president may be critical news coverage for another.

The negotiation of newsworthiness has four aspects. In somewhat chronological order, these aspects are process, content, valence, and result.

The White House press corps and the White House press office negotiate first over the *process* of their interactions—that is, how the president and reporters will come together to make news. The most important and perhaps the most mysterious part of the negotiation of newsworthiness is how an event is elevated to the status of a news item. An equally intriguing part of the process is how some events receive days of coverage whereas other, similar events are barely noticed at all. For example, the Bush administration's first, failed, attempt to capture the Panamanian leader Manuel Noriega on drug charges received exhaustive coverage. Yet the Clinton administration's failed attempt to detain a Somali warlord (which ended instead with the mistaken capture of United Nations workers) received less attention—until Americans were killed. The rules by which the process takes place are not at all straightforward. What would seem to be obviously newsworthy one day is not the next.

Once the press corps and press office begin to interact, negotiations occur about the *content* of presidential news. News, whether initiated by reporters or by the White House, can range from big stories about a president's policy decisions concerning the economy, diplomacy, legislative initiatives, and military involvements to seemingly trivial tales of presidential pets, haircuts, golf shots, and vacation plans. Presidents may wish to stress one story, whereas journalists may be preoccupied with another. Even when the president and the press converge on the same event, reporters can seize on a particular tidbit and elevate it into a story.

Even when the content is agreed upon, negotiations take place about the *valence* of the story—whether it will be handled positively, negatively, or neutrally. Although the White House wants positive press coverage, it is not always lucky enough to get it. Much of the negotiation involves the White House putting a particular spin on a story (that is, casting an event in an especially favorable light), which the press in turn may attempt to expose. In other instances, a president may make a mistake—miscalculate a key vote in Congress, err in a military decision, or break a campaign promise—which is likely to receive negative coverage.

Finally, negotiations influence the *results* or consequences of the selection of stories for both presidents and the press. These results, by weakening or strengthening each side, set the stage for the next round of negotiations about process, content, and valence. The selection of newsworthy stories can affect the president's relations with other political actors, including members of Congress, foreign leaders, and the public. Many people felt that Ronald Reagan's "teflon presidency," in which bad news stories seldom reflected directly on the president, benefited him with Congress and the public. The press may also be judged as being too tough or too soft on a president by its selection of stories. Even before the Watergate scandal, President Nixon said the media were "out to get him" in their coverage, and other presidents have felt free to criticize the media as having an ax to grind. Such criticism puts the press on guard in its dealings with the White House.

The Negotiation of Process

Before considering these four specific aspects of the negotiation of newsworthiness, we describe the general characteristics of the negotiation and how the negotiation has become a cornerstone of modern American politics.

Negotiations in Earlier Times

The negotiation of newsworthiness at the White House began in earnest at the start of the twentieth century, when presidents first turned to the news media to convey their messages about policy and public leadership. In the nineteenth century, as Jeffrey Tulis has documented, presidents generally were not visible in the press—partly because the White House had no place to accommodate journalists, but also because most presidents saw their primary role as executing the will of Congress rather than stepping out front with policies and proposals.[5] Washington reporters focused their attention on congressional debates and reported the activities of senators and representatives far more extensively than those of presidents.[6] In addition, few presidents did much either to assert themselves as leaders of the people or to woo reporters. All that began to change toward the end of the nineteenth century, when the Progressive Era saw three changes occur that influenced news coverage in the new century.

First, news became big business. Newspapers, in pursuit of mass circulation, began to abandon their emphasis on congressional debate in favor of color and spectacle organized around familiar protagonists. Even before the end of the century, events such as the assassination of President James Garfield and the marriage of President Grover Cleveland fit the new emphasis well. By the end of Cleveland's second term, reporters had begun to gather at the White House gates. President William McKinley held White House receptions for journalists. Theodore Roosevelt welcomed them into the White House, thereby creating the White House press corps.[7] Reporters had first obtained bylines identifying them as the writers of their stories during the Civil War so that their dispatches could be monitored; they soon became more central players, displacing the nineteenth-century ascendancy of the editor and the editorial page as they began to specialize, professionalize, and find a niche for themselves as nonpartisan "muckrakers."[8]

Second, the Progressive reforms for clean government—most notably, the ascent of direct primaries and the secret ballot—undermined the practice of party-line voting that had dominated the nineteenth century. As members of Congress, preoccupied by reelection and increasingly parochial concerns, figured out new ways to stay in office and build a career, partisanship in Congress began to wane.[9] Congress had been the focus of news attention throughout the nineteenth century, but members were quickly becoming inclined to avoid reporters in order to cut deals behind closed doors.

Third, the power vacuum left by Congress was filled by enterprising presidents, starting with Theodore Roosevelt, who viewed the president as a "steward of the people" who was "bound actively and affirmatively to do all he could for the people," and Woodrow Wilson.[10] Roosevelt and Wilson saw the presidency not only as an energetic office, closely involved in the legislative process, but as a visible office that would use press attention in governing. Although later presidents, such as Warren Harding and Calvin Coolidge, were not activists in the Rooseveltian vein, even they continued to play a prominent role with the press. After Wilson, no presidents would wonder why they should bother to meet with reporters—as his predecessor, President William Howard Taft, did ("Must I see those men again!" Taft once complained. "Didn't I see them just the other day?")[11] The negotiation of newsworthiness thus became a permanent feature of relations between the White House and the press.

Why the News Matters to Presidents

Dealing with the news media has been especially attractive to activist presidents, who face the traditional problem of persuasion. Although Richard Neustadt's classic *Presidential Power*, published in 1960, is often remembered as an encomium to a strong, activist president, its greatest insight is that formal presidential powers do not add up to genuine presidential influence.[12] As Neustadt argues, because no one has the range of tasks that presidents are expected to pursue, presidents cannot expect anyone else to work for them on their own terms. Indeed, other political actors often regard the president's powers as ways of getting their own goals accomplished. The challenge for activist presidents, therefore, is to leverage their powers to persuade others to do what the president wants done. (Hence Neustadt's maxim that presidential power is "the power to persuade.")

When Neustadt talked about persuasion, he meant one-on-one bargaining. But bargaining between presidents and other political actors, such as members of Congress, world leaders, top-ranking military officers, and governors, although still important, has become more problematic as the political system has become more complex and dispersed.[13] Since the 1960s, the executive branch has grown significantly because of the burgeoning role of government that was launched by Lyndon Johnson's Great Society programs. Congress has gone from being an insulated institution dominated by a few party and committee leaders to a considerably more open and permeable body whose powers are dispersed among a much larger set of individuals. The number of interest groups has skyrocketed, with a surge in single-issue citizen groups and business and labor groups that have been able to exert power through their political action committees' contributions to congressional campaigns. Finally, national television news has been transformed from a cursory fifteen-minute show with occasional film footage to a system of large-scale nightly news programs on the three broadcast networks and round-the-clock coverage on the Cable News Network and the two channels of C-SPAN.

Direct Public Appeals. The increasingly complex policy environment places limits on presidential bargaining for the simple reason that there are more actors with whom to bargain. As one solution, presidents have adopted a strategy to persuade others en masse. By giving speeches, making public appearances, and generating news, presidents can hope to set the policy agenda, to put their spin on particular issues, to raise the stakes of opposition to the presidential program, and to create the perception of a public mood that is beneficial to their causes. Theodore Roosevelt and Woodrow Wilson began this practice well before the complexity of the modern presidential policy environment developed. Roosevelt attempted to rally public support for the Hepburn Act to regulate railroad rates in advance of the congressional debate. Wilson expanded Roosevelt's practice by making direct appeals to the public even as the Senate was debating ratification of the Versailles Treaty, which ended World War I. With the ascendancy of radio in the 1920s and television in the 1950s, presidents devoted increasing time, energy, and resources to giving major national speeches, holding press conferences, and making ceremonial public appearances as visible efforts at persuasion.[14] Their use of major speeches, especially, shows presidents to be strategic communicators. Presidents since Truman have tended to deliver major nationally televised addresses when their popularity and legislative success are low, but have avoided making such speeches when economic conditions and military involvements worsen.[15] Most fundamentally, presidents also are strategic in their recognition that they cannot go to the public well too often.[16]

Although presidents may hope that these efforts provide them with a public avenue around the media, speeches and other appearances remain intrinsically part of the negotiation of newsworthiness. The news media have their own ways of ensuring that presidents do not take to the airwaves too often. Presidents can ask the major television networks for prime air time, but the networks can and do turn them down, as President Bush discovered in mid-1992 when his request to televise an evening press conference was rejected by ABC, CBS, and NBC. With the increased availability of cable television, UHF channels, and VCRs, a presidential prime-time address, even when it is carried by all the networks, reaches a smaller potential audience than in the past.[17] The president's ability to go directly to a national audience also is limited by the current readiness of the networks to give the opposition party equal time and to allow journalists to offer "instant analyses"—that is, interpretations that help to shape the public response to the president—immediately after the speech.[18] Finally, the president must rely on the media to cover various other public appearances in addition to the national speeches. Since much of the importance of these appearances rests on visual images rather than on the words uttered, television coverage is essential. In short, presidents can use public activities as avenues of persuasion, but journalists have their own views about how and how much those avenues should be pursued.

White House Press Strategies. In addition to presidential speeches and other public appearances, presidents have devoted increasing staff to press operations, as the estimates from Hoover to Reagan in Table 11.1 show. These press operations accord the White House considerable clout in the negotiation of newsworthiness. Starting with the Nixon presidency, the press operations have included the White House Press Office, which is headed by the president's press secretary and handles day-to-day press relations, and the Office of Communications, which handles the president's long-range communication strategies.[19] Presidents' press secretaries hold daily news briefings, which numbered well over ten thousand from the Kennedy through the Reagan administrations.[20] During the briefings, press secretaries provide the official White House response to an event or announce the president's position on a policy or political matter. The sheer volume of briefings gives the White House tremendous influence on what is deemed to be newsworthy. Mere presidential involvement can give new life to a languishing issue. One White House correspondent went so far as to say

Table 11.1. Growth of White House Press Operations

President	Total Staff	Professional Staff
Hoover	1	1
FDR	2	2
Truman	4-6	2-3
Eisenhower	3	2
Kennedy	7	3
Johnson	10	5
Nixon	58	13
Ford	45	10
Carter	46	24
Reagan	50	17

Source: Karen M. Hult and Charles Walcott, "To Meet the Press: Tracing the Evolution of White House Press Operations." (Paper presented at the annual meeting of the Midwest Political Science Association, Chicago, April 13–15, 1989). Reprinted by permission of the authors.

that "every day when the [press secretary] gets out there he determines, with his opening statement, what the news is going to be for that day." [21]

Presidents also develop long-range communication strategies to identify a White House priority or story line, coordinate who says what, plan the public schedules of the president and other top administration officials to highlight the White House position, and attempt to prevent any contrary messages from emerging within the administration. To be sure, the term "long-range" is a bit misleading. Long-range media planning involves a day rather than an hour, or a few weeks rather than a day. But it is clearly planning because the strategies are geared toward tomorrow's reactions to today's stories, rather than just to responding to today's questions. Such planning originated with President Nixon, who established the Office of Communications. Nixon wanted to develop long-range publicity efforts to avoid embarrassing coverage; in response the Office of Communications created a "line-of-the-day operation," in which single topics and angles were disseminated throughout the administration as *the* matter for all discussion on that day.[22] William Safire, a Nixon speechwriter, explained: "The purpose of the [office] was to plan the public activities of the president and to see that Administration figures were lined up to make news in an orderly fashion—that is, no two major stories purposely broken on the same day, or if a bad story was due, to try and smother it with other news."[23]

Press Opportunities. Thus, public appearances and speeches, daily press briefings, and long-range communication strategies provide the White House with opportunities to gain an upper hand in the negotiation of newsworthiness. The White House not only can help to define the day's news; it also can try to control other ongoing stories and limit the ability of reporters to seek other interpretations to a particular event. Nonetheless, presidents cannot always use these opportunities as effectively as they might wish. The press has its own ways of approaching White House news—and its own advantages in the ongoing negotiation.

Why Presidents Matter to the News

The eternal problem for journalists is how to generate a news product day in and day out, when "news," by definition, is supposed to be new and unexpected. To solve this problem, reporters gravitate to the places where they expect news to occur and where they can latch on to a continuing story that serves as both an ongoing focus for the reporter and a multi-episode serial for the audience. Thus, news operations are broken down into "newsbeats," the territorial or topical domains that individual reporters are assigned to cover.[24] Taken together, these newsbeats make up a system through which the media can routinely generate stories on a variety of topics. Designating an institution or a subject as a newsbeat both reflects and confers newsworthiness, because a newsbeat embodies a continuing organizational commitment to stories from that site or on that subject. At each newsbeat, certain individuals are seen to be in key positions and thus become "authoritative sources" worth citing; in addition, stereotypical story lines tend to emerge to guide reporters' search for news.[25]

In recent decades, the White House has become more and more the central newsbeat in Washington, making the president the central protagonist not only of that beat, but perhaps of the entire national news—especially of television news, in which the White House story commonly leads the broadcast. To a greater extent than any other political actors in the United States, presidents have reporters come to them rather than having to seek the reporters out. The media presume that, because of the president's centrality as head of state and head of government, virtually anything that presidents do could well be newsworthy. Indeed, the president is probably the only political figure in the United States whose activities are followed twenty-four hours a day. As one Washington bureau chief morbidly (but candidly) told the sociologist Herbert Gans, "We cover the president expecting he will die."[26]

Because of their near-automatic news value, presidents, more than other sources, can dictate the terms of access. Consequently, reporters can easily end up as virtual prisoners in the all but hermetically sealed White House pressroom, reluctant to roam far from their connection to fame and fortune in the news business. Instead of encouraging innovation and enterprise, the White House breeds anxiety among reporters about missing the story that everyone else is chasing.

Thus, presidents rarely have to use the ultimate sanction of "freezing out" individual reporters. Instead, presidents work to manage the news by serving reporters in ways that will prove beneficial: anticipating reporters' questions in news conferences and preparing accordingly; designing prescheduled events that meet news values of drama, color, and terseness; and providing frequent access, albeit in constrained and directed ways. The president's monopoly of good information and the ability to regulate access to key newsmakers means that news opportunities can be meted out on a basis decided by the newsmakers themselves—as long as those newsmakers are aware of the habits and routines of the news media. But "as long as" is an important caveat, because it suggests that the president has to take news reporters and their standards of the news into account when deciding what to do and how and when to do it.

Just because presidents matter to the news does not mean that they can consistently get into the news on their own terms. In other words, the constant attention to what presidents do and say is not always to their benefit, because they cannot hide from the spotlight when things are going badly. Neustadt, in one of his afterthoughts regarding *Presidential Power*, worried as much in looking back at the Carter presidency: the president's "duties now include providing White House visuals for the TV network news most days each week. No law requires it but woe betide the President who seeks to be selective about that!"[27]

The president may be a wonderful source for routine news, but, to use Herbert Gans's terms, although presidential news may be regularly *available*, journalists may not always find it *suitable*.[28] For news to "fit," it must meet standards of vividness, clarity, and terseness. So, for example, to dramatize an issue, White House press operations stage media events and scatter sound bites throughout presidential speeches. As Tom Griscom, President Reagan's director of communications, noted, "We wrote trying to give the lead to the media of what we hoped they would cover, rather than find it out. . . . [T]hose speeches were written with four or five points in them that were short enough and that the president would say in short enough time so they could probably fit into a newscast."[29]

But the White House cannot control so neatly what other sources are saying, let alone what other stories are being reported from other newsbeats in Washington, across the country, and around the globe. Big stories may emerge that deflect attention away from carefully crafted presidential events—which necessitates skill at riding the wave created by the intervening event. Thus, in the fall of 1993, during the buildup to President Clinton's long-awaited unveiling of the administration's health care reforms, the news media, which had prepared a multitude of stories on the subject, were distracted by the dissolution of parliament by the Russian president, Boris Yeltsin. Clinton responded with a quick declaration of support for Yeltsin so that he could get back to his main message. Then, just as health care seemed to be coming back to the top of the agenda, an Amtrak train derailment in Alabama killed scores of people on the morning of Clinton's speech to a joint session of Congress. The president, in a Reaganesque move, began his speech by asking a moment of silence for those who had lost their lives in the accident—acknowledging the importance of the story and then moving on.

Even on stories instigated by presidents, White House beat reporters at times may be stranded, but while waiting for the president to do something newsworthy, they can weave comments and quotes gathered by their colleagues into their report. In particular, the open access that Washington reporters have to a wide range of members of Congress means that, although Congress itself is less frequently in the news than the president, journalists are often informed by congressional opinion about presidential actions.[30] Moreover, since journalists must find conflict to report—in the case of television, to produce tension that will be resolved by the end of the story—reliance on Congress can fit into two familiar Washington scripts: Democrat-versus-Republican and Congress-versus-president. Add the plethora of interest groups cranking out press releases, think-tank experts whose job includes providing pithy (even glib) analysis, and the ever-present possibility of taking a poll or going out to the hinterlands to see what the person-in-the-street thinks, and one understands how the president's power over the news may be quite limited.

Even reporters with little access to critical commentary are uncomfortable thinking of themselves as mere disseminators of presidential words and actions. Adhering to norms of professional autonomy and service to the audience, they aspire to be savvy interpreters and find ways to distance themselves from complicity in presidential news.[31]

In short, news from the White House newsbeat is not always news from the White House's chosen perspective. According to a study of how seven different media events were covered in nightly network news programs during the first six months of the Bush presidency, presidential quotes take up considerably less than half the time of White House reporters' accounts of presidential speeches, statements, and actions, and visuals of the president rarely fill more than half the time. In other words, a typical White House story is mostly made up of audio and video segments from other sources—members of Congress, Washington experts, file footage, or the journalists themselves. And journalists can be highly selective, not only of whom to quote, but of what to show from the presidential appearances. In the Bush examples, the nightly news never included more than 10 percent of the total number of seconds of presidential statements or presidential visuals that were contained in the original media event.[32]

Thus, although each side relies on the other in the negotiation of newsworthiness, neither dominates. The presidency and the news media are independent institutions that command important and unique resources. Journalists worry about maintaining access to powerful sources such as the president, but only if such access leads to a product that their superiors—who, after all, pay their salaries—will assess favorably. They need to provide stories that maximize both the production values of vividness and clarity and the journalistic norms of balance and neutrality. Reporters, moreover, derive satisfaction and self-esteem from their professional autonomy. Any indication that they are mere press agents, or "flacks," for the president would lead to a loss of prestige within a profession that lacks traditional markers for membership and accomplishment. Finally, as we shall see, even if presidents can restrict reporters' access and focus them on some topics, the news media still have the final say about the ultimate product—by raising certain issues, interjecting doubts, questioning motives, and seeking out critical sources for balance.

Balanced Negotiations

Basic differences exist between presidential and journalistic notions of "good news." But to depict the newsbeat as filled with constant conflict would overlook the daily trade-offs that both sides make and the ways in which they learn to live with each other in order to put out a routine product. Interactions between the White House and the news media partake of both cooperation and opposition. In short, the negotiation of newsworthiness, whether explicit or implicit, is constant.

The Negotiation of Content

Within the general negotiation of newsworthiness, presidents and journalists engage in more specific negotiations about the content of the actual stories that will appear on the news—that is, what each story will be about—before determining the valence (positive, negative, or neutral) of the story and the results that it will have for the future negotiation of newsworthiness.

Importance and Interest

News, it is often said, is supposed to be both important and interesting. The president has the greatest control in ascertaining importance, but the news media are more influential in designating interest. This division of labor was best captured by a plaque that appeared on the desk of Reagan's chief White House spokesperson, Larry Speakes: "You don't tell us how to stage the news, and we won't tell you how to cover it." Although jocular, Speakes's plaque reveals the area that each side is presumed to dominate—and suggests that the news from the White House is a *co-production.*

Presidential Definitions of Importance. Presidents designate importance in three ways. First, they select issues (or ignore them) for presidential involvement. Thus, by choosing to speak on a certain issue, the president defines it as inherently important. A good recent example of this tendency is the reporting of the civil war in Bosnia and Herzegovina. When President Clinton publicly mulled over the possibility of American military involvement in Bosnia in the spring of 1993, the Serbian threats to various Bosnian towns suddenly became important news; when Clinton backed away from that option, the news from the civil war waned, even though the death toll continued unabated.

Second, presidents can stage events that will draw attention to particular issues and concerns. Consider, for example, President Bush's response to the 1989 Supreme Court decision that struck down a Texas law banning the burning of the American flag as an unconstitutional restriction on free speech. Bush, who had won the presidency in part because of a flag-waving campaign, decided to support a constitutional amendment to overturn the Court decision. To do so, he spoke as part of a spectacular rally in front of the Iwo Jima memorial, surrounded by soldiers and red, white, and blue bunting on a cloudless June day. The visual impact of the rally and its easily described objective were apparently strong enough to make the event the lead story on all three networks' nightly news shows. The event thereby symbolized Bush's resolve, conferred importance on the issue, and put pressure on the Democrats in Congress in a way that a mere statement or response to a question in a press conference presumably would not have done.

Finally, and relatedly, presidents can choose the venues for involvement with the media. When they do not want to be sidetracked with questions from the press that could easily become the focus for a story, presidents can give public speeches. At other times, press conferences may be preferable, especially when the president would like to deflect criticism on an issue without at the same time elevating the importance of the issue. Carolyn Smith calls this strategy the "hidden-agenda press conference," although sometimes reporters have to be goaded into posing the right questions.[33] Photo opportunities can provide attractive visuals for a story, sometimes accompanied by a pithy sound bite that may represent the only presidential communication of the day, and thus become a good candidate for the nightly news.

Media Definitions of Interesting Stories. Although the president can designate importance, the media have an advantage in indicating what is interesting. Reporters must "sell" their stories to superiors, who decide both how much to "budget" for a story (paragraphs in print, minutes and seconds in broadcast), and what will go into the news and where.[34] Lacking specific indicators of what the audience wants to read or see, and doubtful, in any case, of the audience's ability to know what is of most value, reporters rely on seat-of-the-pants journalistic standards of interest.

In particular, journalists rely on two sets of considerations. First, news must correspond to what Gans calls "product considerations" or what others term "production values."[35] Journalists for all media presume that the more timely, clear-cut, easily described, vivid, colorful, and visualizable something is, the more newsworthy it is. The less the president pays attention to these concerns of the news media, the more journalists will have to find ways to boost the news quotient in their reports. Stated differently, the more difficult the president makes it for journalists to accomplish their routine tasks of reporting quality news that is timely, colorful, visualizable and important, the greater will be journalistic dissatisfaction with the material that the president provides and the greater will be the incentive to look elsewhere for news.

Second, reporters pay attention to cultural standards of what makes a "good story." These standards evolve in two ways. In one way, reporters return to what Gans has called the "enduring values" of the news, most overtly displayed in feature stories that celebrate rugged individualism, mourn the passage of rural, small-town traditions, and discover altruistic leaders in American life.[36] But hard news, especially crises, evokes these strains of the dominant American culture, too. For example, the massive midwestern floods during the summer of 1993 almost invariably were treated by television news as opportunities to show communities pulling together in the face of an ongoing disaster, using individual ingenuity and determination selflessly to help each other out. In the process, the policy implications of the floods—including the attitude that the government should take toward individuals who settle in high-risk locales and fail to take out flood insurance—were shortchanged.

In another way, today's "good stories" are rooted in yesterday's news. Since nobody knows just what news is, reporters often have to rely on what big news items were in the past. Even extraordinarily unexpected stories, such as President Johnson's televised announcement in 1968 that he would not run for reelection, hark back to previous stories. The sociologist Gaye Tuchman called this a "what-a-story," based on her observation of a newsroom that night: "Lifting their heads to answer telephones, bark orders, and then clarify them, the editors periodically announced, 'What a story! . . . The story of a century . . . What a night, what a night! . . . Who would have believed it? . . . There's been nothing like it since Coolidge said, "I do not choose to run."'"[37] As Tuchman's example suggests, reporters have a large stock of past news narratives upon which to rely. These constitute a collective memory that journalists use to judge what is news and to decide how to make sense of current happenings.

This collective memory is especially strong about presidents. Past presidential exemplars (and the legends associated with each one) provide an accumulated knowledge of past presidential successes and failures. One of the longest-lasting ways in which yesterday's news serves as the basis for today's stories is the media's focus on each president's first hundred days in office. This time frame was initially marked out during Franklin Roosevelt's first months in office, when he put various emergency measures into effect and introduced other social welfare proposals to combat the Great Depression. Since FDR, the media have concentrated on the hundred-day time frame as the make-or-break period for the president. Some presidents have fallen into the trap by suggesting that they will accomplish long lists of projects during this artificially designated time period. Ironically, no president since Roosevelt has had a similar hundred-day period of success; nor are there any intrinsic political or institutional reasons to concentrate on this number of days, the first 200 days, the first 365 days, or the first 730 days. But the time frame continues to bracket the early part of presidents' terms and saddle them with expectations of program initiation and legislative success that may be wildly unrealistic. In short, the media have defined the first hundred days as a period of interest, and stories of success and failure are judged accordingly within the time frame.

Presidential Narratives

Importance and interest dovetail in presidential narratives.[38] These are stories about what presidents can do, should do, and should not do. The stories are familiar, with well-known beginnings and endings. The narratives repeat themselves over and over; they may vary in details from one president to the next, but not in their basic progress. Some are stories the president is supposed to live up to. Others are stories the president must live down. In either case, journalists expect to be able to retell the stories at various times during each president's term.

In all of the stories, journalists and presidents alike depict a particular kind of protagonist. The narratives stem from an image of the president as the one person in charge of the government, speaking with a clear, lone voice. In this view, the president is the nation's principal problem solver, the one who identifies the nation's most pressing issues and offers solutions. In times of crisis, presidents single-handedly protect the nation. They symbolize the nation and embody its moral and patriotic values. Thus, when journalists express concern about a president's "drift," "lack of focus," "indecision," "muddle," and "inconsistency," they are implicitly endorsing the single executive image about how presidents should act—decisively, clearly, and with determination. This sounds harmless enough until one realizes that presidents thereby are pressured *not* to take their time in making careful decisions, *not* to consult with others in Washington, *not* to consider the complexity of a situation, and *not* to reassess past campaign promises in light of new developments.

From the single executive image, several presidential narratives arise. The four most familiar narratives are: (1) the president at work presenting solutions to major national problems; (2) the president as international leader directing military involvements or diplomatic solutions to world crises; (3) the president acting as the moral, religious, and patriotic representative of the people; and (4) the president making major mistakes—whether by exercising bad political judgment or engaging in seemingly illegal actions.

The Story of the President as Problem Solver. The story of the president as domestic problem solver has become a familiar one. Since Theodore Roosevelt first introduced the Square Deal to the country and Woodrow Wilson followed suit with the New Freedom, presidents have offered packages of legislative proposals designed to cure the most pressing ills of the nation. Some presidents have obligingly made the story more interesting by giving these proposals names—the New Deal (Franklin Roosevelt), the Fair Deal (Truman), the New Frontier (Kennedy), and the Great Society (Johnson). The story typically begins at the time of the first State of the Union message, during which the president lays out the problems of the country and promises to fix them. The story is then revisited off and on during the next weeks, months, and years, as the president succeeds or fails in Congress, in the executive branch, and in the public eye. The story almost always ends the same way—with some degree of disappointment that the president did not accomplish all that he set out to achieve.

The Story of the President as International Leader. This story is as familiar as that of the president as problem solver. It depicts the president as the world leader whose decisions keep the free world free or make the oppressed world free. In the story, the president acts boldly, dramatically, with a sense of crisis, and alone. Even when the secretaries of defense and state, the national security adviser, members of the Joint Chiefs of Staff, and the director of the Central Intelligence Agency are intimately involved in the decisions, the single executive image casts the president as the solitary decision maker, leading the forces of good against the forces of evil. During the cold war, the story was of presidents fighting the red menace of Communism. Since the collapse of the Soviet Union, presidents now fight other tyrants and dictators. For example, the story pictured George Bush as representing the forces of democracy against the "butcher of Baghdad," the Iraqi leader Saddam Hussein. The story ends on an upbeat note with the president successfully protecting the nation's and world's best interests.

The Story of the President as Representative of the People. Presidents also are part of a story about the American people in which the president articulates the American dream, American reinvigoration, and American success. In the story, the president acts as national cheerleader, boosting the collective morale of the country. The story is about presidents who match the values, aspirations, even the very lives of their fellow citizens. Thus, the story captures presidents in their ceremonial roles: lighting Christmas trees, laying wreaths at the tombs of war dead, visiting devastated disaster areas, and congratulating victorious athletes and returning astronauts. It also reveals presidents as ordinary people who enjoy vacations, develop illnesses, and have wayward siblings. This narrative, which resembles the timeless human interest stories that fill out a newspaper or close a television broadcast, is not a continuing story and has no real ending beyond "another day in the life of. . . ." The ceremonial and ordinary-person aspects of the story capture press attention throughout presidents' terms, even when their popularity is low and news coverage is negative.

The Story of the President's Mistakes. This story depicts the president as having committed a major public, political, or policy gaffe. At worst, presidents are presented as villains or, more ambiguously, as naive fools. The story takes two twists. In the first, the president does something that backfires in the world, in Congress, or in public opinion. So, for example, there is the story of Jimmy Carter's ill-fated helicopter rescue attempt of the American hostages in Iran. There is the story of George Bush's broken promise of "no new taxes," which Bush himself acknowledged was the worst mistake of his presidency. There is the story of Gerald Ford's pardon of Richard Nixon, which prompted the largest drop in public approval ever for a president. Perhaps the most significant story about presidents' mistakes is one that shows the president unable to live up to the other narratives and, therefore, unable to live up to the single executive image. Particularly telling stories of presidential mistakes arise when a president does little or nothing to address major national problems, when a president is unable to win diplomatic or military victories against the unrelenting foe, and when a president fails to reinforce people's expectations about the American dream.

In another story line, the president acts illegally, appears to lie, says things publicly that contradict other reports about an event, or denies being aware of the apparently questionable actions of aides. In each instance, the president acts in a way that is contrary to the single executive image. One of the dominant stories during the Vietnam War was about President Johnson's "credibility gap." Johnson was routinely criticized for claiming ignorance about various efforts that intensified the American involvement in the war, many of which he had expressly ordered and each of which the press exposed in extensive daily war coverage. President Nixon faced a credibility gap of another sort when tapes of private conversations that directly contradicted his public statements about Watergate were released. Still, the story does not necessarily end with the disgrace of the president. Presidents can assert "plausible deniability," as Ronald Reagan did during the Iran-contra scandal by saying he was not aware that two aides, Oliver North and John Poindexter, had funneled money from Iranian arms sales to the Nicaraguan contra rebels. Presidents can also attempt to shift attention away from the mistake by providing the media with other narratives—not always successfully. Thus, in the waning days of his presidency, Richard Nixon tried (but failed) to distract attention from the Watergate story by reviving briefly the "international leader" narrative through high-profile foreign trips to the Middle East and the Soviet Union.

In sum, the four narratives tell the public, the press, and the president what to expect and when to expect it during the course of a presidential term. The narratives effectively establish boundaries to the negotiation of newsworthiness. They provide a set number of story lines that journalists are likely to pursue. What is newsworthy depends on whether the event fits within one or more of the narratives. If the president does something outside the narratives or acts in ways that the narratives do not acknowledge, journalists are less likely to be cooperative in getting the president's message out. In particular, if the president cannot convincingly present himself as problem solver, international leader, or representative of the people, the media can simply turn to the fourth available narrative: presidential mistakes and failure.

The Negotiation of Valence

To hear presidents tell it, they rarely receive favorable press coverage. Since Thomas Jefferson protested that "nothing in a newspaper is to be believed [because it] presents only a caricature of disaffected minds," presidents have invariably held an all-but-paranoid perspective on press treatment of their activities.[39] Perhaps George Shultz, Reagan's secretary of state, best described the view from the White House when he tersely complained, "Reporters are always against us."[40] Yet the evidence presented by political scientists paints a very different picture of news valence. In a study of press coverage from 1953 through 1978, Michael Grossman and Martha Kumar found that stories about presidents in newspapers, news magazines, and on network news broadcasts were more often positive or neutral than negative.[41] Negative stories exceeded positive stories only during the Watergate scandal. What remains a mystery is how and when presidents receive their most favorable coverage. Based on the foregoing discussion of the content of presidential news, we can now explain when presidents receive favorable coverage that helps them to pursue their interests and when they receive unfavorable coverage that hampers them.

When presidents' activities conform to the story lines of the three narratives of problem solver, international leader, and representative of the people, they are likely to receive favorable or at least neutral coverage. But how do reporters know if the presidential master script is being followed? Simply put, they rely upon the president and other authoritative sources in Washington to tell them. The sociologist Mark Fishman has elegantly outlined how journalists try to figure out what are the "facts of the case" and "the two sides of the story." He noted that in working on a story reporters would go to sources whom they expected to disagree because of their institutional positions. The comments that accorded with one another became "the facts of the case"; the disagreements were "the two sides of the story."[42] Thus, when alternative authoritative sources in Washington—especially members of the opposition party and members of Congress—raise no objections, the president must be presumed to be doing something right and receives not only favorable news coverage but a boost in the polls.[43]

To be sure, reporters must always include some opposition and conflict in news stories, whether for dramatic tension or for balance. When authoritative sources in Washington are silent—or, because of attacks from the White House, silenced—the coverage can shift to less legitimate presidential antagonists (such as social movements), foreign leaders, or abstract enemies like crime, inflation, or government waste. This dynamic is especially strong in foreign affairs, an area in which the news media's willingness to criticize presidential initiatives is directly linked to the degree of dissent among Washington elites. Thus, contrary to the legend that the news media (usually personified as Walter Cronkite of CBS) single-handedly turned the country against the Vietnam War after the 1968 Tet offensive, the media actually took their cue from the dissent that was building in Congress and within the Johnson administration.[44] Likewise, in the first two months after the Iraqi invasion of Kuwait, the reluctance of members of Congress to criticize President Bush's military buildup made the "two sides of the story" a personalized battle between the White House and Baghdad.[45]

News, then, can go in cycles—either an elite variant of "the spiral of silence," in which positive presidential stories discourage potentially critical perspectives from being expressed, or the inverse, in which dissent encourages more dissent. Moreover, because journalists, sensitive to their inability to define news precisely, are attentive to other journalists' reporting, consensus can swiftly emerge about the presidential performance. Although this style of "pack journalism" has been long recognized, the way it contributes to waves of presidential media coverage has not. Daniel Hallin and Paolo Mancini, in an inventive comparison of American and Italian television news during a trip to Italy by President Reagan, noted that whereas Italian newscasters maintained a consistently cool neutrality about their sources, American reporters, in pursuit of simple drama, tended to swerve toward highly positive or highly negative stories.[46]

In other words, presidential news is subject to what the reporter Jonathan Alter, reflecting upon Clinton's first week in office, nicely termed "the manic-depressive media."[47] Increasingly overheated and dramatic reporting, seeking to make every roll-call vote into a make-or-break moment for the president, exaggerates these trends. As a presidential term goes on, the news increasingly settles down. Certain issues provoke continuing stories that are not easily displaced unless and until they are resolved, and since new issues constantly appear, a presidential term sees an ever greater repertoire of possible topics—some positive, some not—for White House reporters to cover. But as the political scientist Mark Rozell suggests in his analysis of editorial commentary during the Ford and Carter presidencies, presidents' later actions tend to be interpreted in the context of the earliest understandings of how they act and decide—understandings that solidify during the first year of their presidencies.[48]

Presidents are thus constrained in their ability to control the valence of the news, which puts pressure on them to act in particular ways. If a continuing story has not been resolved, they may wish to resolve it, even if the results are not palatable, simply so that reporters will stop asking about it. Clinton's so-called compromise (closer to a capitulation) on the issue of gays in the military is a prime example. Or they may try to change the subject, because a shift in focus can result in dramatically different kinds of coverage. The contrast between how George Bush was covered during the negotiations over the budget in late 1990 and the coverage he received during the Persian Gulf crisis could scarcely be starker. But this contrast also foreshadowed the disastrous slump in Bush's news coverage and ultimately his popularity once the Gulf War was over and Americans' attention returned to the stagnant economy.

The Negotiation in Action

Ultimately, which White House stories appear in the news and the valence of those stories rest on the daily process of how stories are initiated, selected, and negotiated. This most central aspect of the negotiation of newsworthiness at the White House unfolds in three ways. The first is the explicit battle over the forums in which president-press relations will occur, as presidents and journalists seek to specify the conditions and circumstances under which they will meet. The second is the explicit interaction within those forums, best exemplified by the give-and-take of press conferences. The third is the indirect and implicit negotiation that goes on when each party is out of sight of the other—that is, as the president anticipates what will make news, and as reporters go back to their home organizations with the raw material that the president provides them and reshape it into a coherent news account.

Since these negotiations proceed on a day-to-day basis among a relatively stable set of actors, open warfare is discouraged. Instead, conflict has been largely institutionalized and, even then, cushioned by the interconnections between the White House press office and the White House press corps. For one thing, press officers and reporters usually have similar backgrounds; indeed, presidential press secretaries are often former (and occasionally, future) journalists themselves.[49]

More important, the White House newsbeat is a social system encompassing both press officers and beat reporters, who together bridge the gap between news organizations and the government.[50] Recall that reporters must find ways to take the material that their sources provide them and persuade their editors to use it. Journalists wish to get their stories in the news on a regular basis and, reinforced by other reporters at the White House, they end up defending the presidential perspective within their home news organization. In the words of Gaye Tuchman, newsbeat journalists "ask the questions appropriate to their sources' world."[51] Similarly, press secretaries who deal with journalists' queries day in and day out become sensitized to the media's concerns and difficulties in covering the beat. In short, White House beat reporters and White House press secretaries are ambassadors from their home institutions to each other— with consequent divided loyalties.

There are additional limits on open warfare. Presidents rarely freeze out reporters or challenge their credentials. Attacks on individual journalists are deemed unpresidential. And if reporters feel overtly pressured, they can always reveal the attempts to shut them up—as a CNN reporter did in early 1993 when Clinton's then-director of communications, George Stephanopoulos, was discovered behind a camera instructing CNN's White House correspondent, Wolf Blitzer, that the president had never said what Blitzer was alleging.

Journalists are vulnerable, too—especially to the question, Who elected *you*? In general, they find ways, in the words of Don Hewitt (the executive producer of *60 Minutes*), to be "critical without being partisan," because their legitimacy rests on not being seen as autonomous political actors. Thus, reporters have to find ways to criticize the president that do not seem like politically based vendettas—whether by relying on already extant dissent in Washington, by judging the president according to the president's own standards (especially campaign promises), or by critiquing presidential style more than substance and methods more than goals.

Despite these limits on open warfare, the process does not and cannot work smoothly because of continuing differences about what constitutes news and the perception by both the press and the presidency that it alone bears primary responsibility for communicating with the American public. This perception is perfectly captured in the quotations by Bill Clinton and Helen Thomas that began this chapter. Thus, the negotiation of newsworthiness is constant but often subtle, indirect, and implicit.

Although presidents may vary during their terms in how much they rely on press conferences, photo opportunities, press secretaries' briefings, and speeches, the conditions of access are seldom drastically rethought. In contrast, at the beginning of presidential terms, newly elected presidents, fresh from the campaign, anticipate the biases of the news media and seek ways to get the best coverage possible. Thus, John Kennedy was convinced when he took office in 1961 that the editorial pages of the nation's newspapers were hopelessly favorable to Republicans, and so, to reach the people directly, he began to hold live televised press conferences. Richard Nixon, even more convinced of the antipathy of the national news media at the beginning of his first term, in 1969, established the Office of Communications to find ways to woo what he deemed the more favorable local reporters. Ronald Reagan, in 1981, uncomfortable with the give-and-take of press conferences, preferred "photo opportunities," which provided little chance for questions but lots of possibilities for winning visuals of the former actor. And when Bill Clinton entered the White House, in 1993, as we have seen, he was highly suspicious of "intermediaries," refusing to hold a press conference for weeks and turning instead to electronic town meetings in which ordinary citizens, rather than professional reporters, could question him.

The news media do not always defer to the president's choice of issues and events. Photo opportunities may be interrupted by reporters yelling out questions on unrelated issues. Journalists' questions routinely diverge from the president's opening statements at press conferences, even during the initial months of a presidency.[52] And reporters can and do complain publicly when presidents de-emphasize direct contact with the media in favor of highly stage-managed media events. But for all the journalistic loyalty to the give-and-take of presidential press conferences, these occasions are often as easily controlled by the president as by the press. Opportunities for sustained follow-up are few. Since presidents choose the questioners, they can recover from a tough question by searching for someone who will toss them a softball. Because of the usually sacrosanct time limit of a half hour, presidents can also run out the clock by blathering on in evasive or convoluted language. Finally, if all else fails, they can refuse to take any further questions on a particular subject.

Consider this telling example from a Rose Garden press briefing in 1989. President Bush met with a small number of reporters who, with Oliver North's Iran-contra trial approaching, had been speculating about Bush's possible involvement in the scandal. Bush declined to comment. With the trial in progress, he said he would have more to say at a later date, but added, "Let me say this; my conscience is clear." At this point, the following exchange ensued between President Bush and Lesley Stahl, then the CBS White House correspondent.

STAHL: Mr. President, when you say your conscience is clear, do you mean that the interpretation that has been made of the documents in this trial, which I gather were made by Mr. North himself, are not entirely accurate?

BUSH: I'm not discussing anything about my role in this except to say that everything I've said I'll stand behind.

STAHL: You won't even—since they're sequestered—just give us a—

BUSH: I've just told the gentleman that I'm not going to go into that. So, please don't ask me to do that which I've just said I'm not going to do, because you're burning up time.

STAHL: Right. Assault weapons.

BUSH: The meter is running through the sand on you. (general hubbub among reporters)

STAHL: Assault weapons.

BUSH: And I am now filibustering, so—

STAHL: Sir, can I ask you about assault weapons?
BUSH: Oh, no, you've already used up your ticket.
STAHL: No, no, no.
BUSH: Go ahead.
STAHL: Assault weapons. [PROCEEDS TO QUESTION][53]

The most intriguing part of the negotiation of content may well occur not between the White House and the news media but within the White House and within the news organizations themselves. It is routine by now for presidents to anticipate what the media will cover and how. By deciding what issue to emphasize in which forum, presidents seek advantages with the press. And by conducting practice sessions before press conferences or anticipating what questions are likely to be asked and the best responses, by crafting glossy media events, or by sending out first ladies, vice-presidents, and Cabinet members as surrogates on issues, presidents can attempt to gain the edge—most often by trying to give the media a news item that they simply cannot resist.

Ironically, however, presidents, in seeking to gain dominance over the news, end up incorporating journalistic definitions of newsworthiness into their decision-making process. Mark Hertsgaard has vividly described the early-morning meetings in the Reagan administration in which the participants devised the line-of-the-day and then sent it out through other meetings and press briefings to the world at large.[54] Although Hertsgaard intended to demonstrate the Reagan administration's brilliance at manipulating the media, it is worth noting how much the line-of-the-day both anticipated journalistic production values and reacted to the news itself—the stories that had been in the previous evening's network news or on the front page of that morning's *Washington Post* or the *New York Times*.

Reporters can take the initiative as well, especially when what the White House has provided them is lacking in apparent newsworthiness. An excellent example occurred in the second week of Bush's presidency, when Japan's Prime Minister Takeshita was the first foreign leader to visit the White House. This event, both its visuals and its speeches, was formulaic and provided little movement in the continuing story of the relationship between Japan and the United States. On C-SPAN, the event unrolled as follows: Takeshita's limousine arrived at the front of the White House; he entered; he emerged with Bush for a photo opportunity, at which Bush, looking for something to do, took one question about his health, saying only, "Totally new man. All well. Totally recovered." Later, Bush and Takeshita reappeared and stiffly read statements of goodwill and friendship.

If journalists were to cover any of this event, they would have to find creative ways to rework it into a more newsworthy item. The three broadcast networks chose different strategies. ABC ignored the visit. NBC chose to make it the peg for a story that otherwise would not have been considered timely: an excerpt from Bush's talk was used as the lead-in to a commentary by John Chancellor on what the United States could learn from Japan's investment in research and development. CBS zeroed in on Bush's off-the-cuff statement about his health and made it into an example of a "failed event" that could be fit into a separate, larger story on the difficulties the Bush administration was having with some of its appointees:

DAN RATHER: President Bush planned to showcase his foreign policy credentials and experience today as he met with Japan's Prime Minister Takeshita. Instead, as CBS White House correspondent Lesley Stahl reports, Mr. Bush was dogged by questions about the ethics of some of his nominees for high office and by questions about his own health.

LESLEY STAHL: President Bush is having trouble getting his message across. Today's well-laid plans—highlight the importance of U.S.-Japanese relations with his first foreign visitor, Prime Minister Takeshita. But what was the president asked? How's your health.

BUSH: Totally new man. All well. Totally recovered.

STAHL: More questions. What about John Tower's personal conduct? The White House spokesman said that the President had confidence in Tower and urges prompt consideration of his nomination. And more questions about other nominees—ethical questions that muddle the central message of President Bush's first thirteen days in office, the importance of ethics in government.[55]

This may be an unusually strong example of reportorial initiative in the face of unpromising material, but it reveals the potential power of reporters to take presidential actions and statements out of context and to alter the story line with the reporter's voiceover, not to mention juxtaposition of the president with other sources and with file footage.

The Negotiation of Results

Stories about the president have strong consequences for presidential governance and presidential power. Put simply, presidents cannot use the news media to magnify their power on all issues all of the time. The pursuit of favorable news coverage directs them toward some policies and issues and away from others.

As we have seen, presidential activities, to be covered favorably, need to fit the three presidential narratives of action and empathy—problem solver, international leader, and representative of the people. Failing that, the residual narrative of presidential failure is most accessible to the news media. In addition, these activities must fit journalistic production values; for example, they will be covered in their own terms more effectively if they are timely, clear-cut, vivid, easily described, colorful, and visualizable.

Production values become political values in this process of mutual anticipation and negotiation. Presidents in search of advantages through the media have two choices—stress simple, perhaps symbolically charged issues and clear-cut commitments *or* make complex issues seem simpler than they actually are. For presidents and their co-workers it is important to package actions in such a way as to strike balances between the complexity of policies and the simplicity of news and between the news media's desire for clarity and closure and the president's need to keep options open as long as possible.

Ronald Reagan was considered a "great communicator" as president because he favored simple issues stated clearly, consistently, and without nuance. But Reagan's media style fit well with his approach to legislation—stake out a clear, immovable position on a larger principle (such as lowering the highest tax rates) toward which others will have to move, once they are in the spotlight. The close linkage of production values and political values also explains the contrast between what was perceived as George Bush's success in the Gulf War and his failure on the budget for fiscal year 1991. From the start, Bush laid out a simple, straightforward line in the Gulf—pushing Saddam Hussein out of Kuwait—with remarkable intransigence and in a decisive way that fit the presidential narratives of action. In contrast, the complex negotiations on the budget in the fall of 1990 made Bush seem drifting, confused, and contradictory. Whether, in retrospect, the war was a policy success and the budget a policy failure is debatable. The war solved few of the problems that occasioned Iraq's invasion of Kuwait and opened up new problems by sparking rebellions by Iraqi Shiites and Kurds. The budget agreement actually staunched the growth of the budget deficit by establishing the principle that new spending would have to be matched by new taxes. But it is precisely because of Bush's abilities and inabilities to manage his media image effectively that we may remember the war and the budget negotiations quite differently.

In short, the more presidents rely on the press to help them out in policy making, the more journalists establish the criteria for presidential decisions. These criteria become especially widespread when the negotiation of newsworthiness extends not only to the interactions of White House staffers with the White House press corps but to the staffers' anticipation of how the media are likely to react to different presidential initiatives and activities.

Correspondingly, the increasing reliance by journalists on the president as the key protagonist of the news reinforces a "presidentialist" understanding of government. In this, there is both good news and bad news for presidents. The media's concentration on the presidency, and on the person of the president in particular, gives the incumbent numerous opportunities to set the agenda, to turn public attention toward some issues instead of others, to influence public moods, and to pressure recalcitrant political actors.

Still, as we have seen, the momentum can change quickly, even during the best of times. The news media can shift stories or events out of the president's control, raising new problems for political and news management. And far from gaining mastery over the news, presidents may be less able to manage it to their benefit as their terms progress. The first year seems to be crucial in setting the news media's understanding of what a presidency is all about, what issues are at its core, how the president goes about making decisions and setting priorities, and how effective these efforts are. Other dynamics that are connected to the unfolding of the four-year term—how unresolved issues and promises pile up, how dissent builds within the executive branch as cabinet secretaries become restive, how presidential popularity declines, and how presidents themselves shift their rhetorical emphasis away from new policies and toward accomplishing what has already been proposed—are not likely to help the president receive favorable news coverage either.[56] Thus, as the president's term wears on, presidential control of the agenda wanes.

Moreover, the presidentialist understanding of governance means that problems land squarely in the president's lap. Journalists demand presidential reaction and action concerning virtually any breaking news—from blizzards to bomb blasts. If the president ends up being portrayed as overwhelmed by events and unsure of how to act, media attention can serve to diminish presidential power, as Neustadt suggested. Yet because the narratives of presidential action and empathy are constantly evoked, the mythic vision dies hard. The news media may end up elevating the centrality of the presidency as an institution with uneven results for the incumbents of that office.

For public policy and American democracy, as for presidents, there is both good and bad news in the relationship between the presidency and the media. By "going public," presidents can push political debate to a new level stated in terms of the public interest. It may well be that for the public to enter into the debate, the terms must be clarified and simplified—as the news media can do—so that people can connect their own personal concerns with larger political issues and ideas.[57]

If we need the news to start a public debate and discussion, then we must concern ourselves about the terms of that discourse. As noted earlier, quality journalism may be clear-cut, decisive, vivid, terse, and visualizable without making its stories more understandable or more relevant to the public. Moreover, policy making is frequently and necessarily complex, gradual, technical, protracted, and abstract. Since the news media often establish benchmarks for presidents that reward them for making news on journalists' own terms, presidents cannot ignore their demands. But policy making can suffer if journalistic values become the primary political values.

A fascinating case study seems to be emerging, as of this writing, with President Clinton's proposed health care policy reforms. The legislation that he has sent to Capitol Hill is one of the most complex and lengthy presidential proposals in history. Yet Clinton began the health care campaign with a speech to a joint session of Congress that emphasized several basic "principles"—"security, simplicity, savings, choice, quality, and responsibility"—that in their terseness are closer to buzzwords than overarching theoretical guides. As Elizabeth Kolbert noted in the *New York Times* two days after Clinton's speech:

It may be that over the next few months, the battle over President Clinton's health care proposal will turn on the fractious details of providing medical coverage to all Americans. Yesterday, however, the struggle was rather more elemental. As Clinton Administration officials and their Republican critics fanned out across the networks, it was channel-to-channel combat for the best catchwords of the health care debate. By the end of the day, the Administration had established a firm hold on "security" and had mounted a strong offensive for "simplicity" and "responsibility." Republicans had laid siege to "job loss" and "cost" and had staged a tough counteroffensive for "quality."[58]

Whether Clinton will be able to keep "on message" is certainly an open question. But a more central one is whether Clinton will be able to respond to journalists in their own terms with news that meets their needs and that helps the president to keep the issue on the front burner and convince Congress of the impossibility of inaction. At the same time he will have to deal with the many affected groups, handle the extraordinary diversity of claims and issues, and come up with a proposal that neither raises taxes too severely nor raises the budget deficit.

Presidents in the late twentieth century may no longer have the choice, as did some of their distant predecessors, of whether or not to use the news media in governing. As Todd Gitlin has noted in a rather different context, the New Left social movement he studied had an unpalatable choice:

Even reformist movements must work industriously to broadcast their messages without having them discounted, trivialized, fragmented, rendered incoherent. Awareness of the media's routines and frames is no guarantee that a movement will be able to achieve publicity for its analysis and program on its own terms. . . . But surely ignorance of the media's codes condemns a movement to marginality.[59]

Although presidents clearly have more access and thus more power than social movements do to get their issues, concerns, and perspectives into the news on a regular basis, they are faced with the same dilemma as other political actors. Above all, presidents cannot count on journalists to be either consistent allies or consistent enemies. Instead, the negotiation of newsworthiness at the White House is uncertain, constant, and increasingly central to the course of American presidencies.

Notes

1. Michael Baruch Grossman and Martha Joynt Kumar, "The White House and the News Media: The Phases of Their Relationship," *Political Science Quarterly* 94 (1979): 37–53; and Grossman and Kumar, *Portraying the President: The White House and the News Media* (Baltimore: Johns Hopkins University Press, 1981), chap. 11.

2. S. Robert Lichter, in a presentation on the panel "Clinton and the Press: The First Hundred Days" at the annual meeting of the International Communication Association, Washington, D.C., May 29, 1993. Lichter did not count statements that could not be coded as either positive or negative, so his figures may overestimate the negativity of the press.

3. For an early statement of this point, see Michael Baruch Grossman and Francis E. Rourke, "The Media and the Presidency: An Exchange Analysis," *Political Science Quarterly* 91 (Fall 1976): 455–470.

4. The term comes from Timothy E. Cook, *Making Laws and Making News: Media Strategies in the U.S. House of Representatives* (Washington, D.C.: Brookings Institution, 1989), 169. For similar interpretations, see Jay G. Blumler and Michael Gurevitch, "Politicians and the Press: An Essay on Role Relationships," in *Handbook of Political Communication*, ed. Dan D. Nimmo and Keith R. Sanders (Beverly Hills, Calif.: Sage Publications, 1981), 467–493; and F. Christopher Arterton, *Media Politics: The News Strategies of Presidential Campaigns* (Lexington, Mass.: Lexington Books, 1984).

5. Jeffrey Tulis, *The Rhetorical Presidency* (Princeton, N.J.: Princeton University Press, 1987).

6. Samuel Kernell and Gary C. Jacobson, "Congress and the Presidency as News in the Nineteenth Century," *Journal of Politics* 49 (November 1987): 1016–1035.

7. George Juergens, *News from the White House: The Presidential-Press Relationship in the Progressive Era* (Chicago: University of Chicago Press, 1981), chap. 2.

8. See, for example, Michael Schudson, *Discovering the News: A Social History of American Newspapers* (New York: Basic Books, 1978), chap. 3.

9. See, for example, Joseph Cooper and David W. Brady, "Institutional Context and Leadership Style: The House from Cannon to Rayburn," *American Political Science Review* 75 (June 1981): 411–425.

10. Theodore Roosevelt, *Theodore Roosevelt: An Autobiography* (New York: Macmillan, 1913), 389.

11. Quoted in Elmer E. Cornwell, *Presidential Leadership of Public Opinion* (Bloomington: Indiana University Press, 1965), 28.

12. Richard Neustadt, *Presidential Power* (New York: Wiley, 1960).

13. Samuel Kernell, *Going Public: New Strategies of Presidential Leadership* (Washington, D.C.: CQ Press, 1986).

14. Presidents since Truman have made an increasing number of appearances, including major speeches, news conferences, minor speeches on specific policy proposals, and ceremonial public appearances both in and out of Washington. See Gary King and Lyn Ragsdale, *The Elusive Executive: Discovering Statistical Patterns in the Presidency* (Washington, D.C.: CQ Press, 1988).

15. Roderick Hart, *The Sound of Leadership* (Chicago: University of Chicago Press, 1987); Lyn Ragsdale, "Presidents' Perpetual Campaigns: Public Appearances from Truman to Bush" (University of Arizona, Tucson, mimeographed).

16. Lyn Ragsdale, "The Politics of Presidential Speechmaking, 1949–1980," *American Political Science Review* 78 (December 1984): 971–984.

17. Joe S. Foote, *Television Access and Political Power: The Networks, the Presidency, and the "Loyal Opposition"* (New York: Praeger, 1990), table 7.2.

18. On the latter point, see especially the experimental study that compared viewers' responses to a Nixon speech with and without the journalists' interpretations: David L. Paletz and Richard J. Vinegar, "Presidents on Television: The Effects of Instant Analysis," *Public Opinion Quarterly* 41 (1977/1978): 488–497. A recent study of the effects of presidential election debates makes much the same point; see James B. Lemert, William R. Elliott, James M. Bernstein, William L. Rosenberg, and Karl J. Nestvold, *News Verdicts, the Debates, and Presidential Campaigns* (New York: Praeger, 1991). On the increase of equal time for the opposition, see Foote, *Television Access and Political Power*, esp. chap. 5.

19. For the development of this structure, see John Anthony Maltese, *Spin Control: The White House Office of Communications and the Management of Presidential News* (Chapel Hill: University of North Carolina Press, 1992).

20. Bradley Patterson, Jr., *The Ring of Power: The White House Staff and Its Expanding Role in Government* (New York: Basic Books, 1988), 170.

21. Quoted in Grossman and Kumar, *Portraying the President*, 33.

22. The historical development of the line-of-the-day is nicely delineated in Maltese, *Spin Control*; see also Mark Hertsgaard, *On Bended Knee: The Press and the Reagan Presidency* (New York: Farrar, Straus and Giroux, 1988), esp. chap. 3.

23. William Safire, *Before the Fall: An Inside View of the Pre-Watergate White House* (Garden City, N.J.: Doubleday, 1975), 361.

24. The best book on newsbeats is Mark Fishman, *Manufacturing the News* (Austin: University of Texas Press, 1980).

25. The best and most thought-provoking of the internal studies of news organizations are Robert Darnton, "Writing News and Telling Stories," *Daedalus* 104 (Spring 1975): 175–194; Gaye Tuchman, *Making News: A Study in the Construction of Reality* (New York: Free Press, 1978); and Herbert J. Gans, *Deciding What's News: A Study of CBS Evening News, NBC Nightly News, Newsweek, and Time* (New York: Pantheon, 1979).

26. Quoted in Gans, *Deciding What's News*, 145.

27. Richard E. Neustadt, "Presidential Leadership: The Clerk against the Preacher," in *Problems and Prospects for Presidential Leadership in the 1980s*, vol. 1, ed. J. S. Young (Lanham, Md.: University Press of America, 1983), 2.

28. Gans, *Deciding What's News*, 81.

29. Quoted in Daniel C. Hallin, ed., *The Presidency, the Press, and the People* (La Jolla: University of California, San Diego, 1992), 158–159.

30. As the political scientist Stephen Hess stated in *The Washington Reporters* (Washington, D.C.: Brookings Institution, 1981), "Capitol Hill is the dominant location of news gathering" (48).

31. For example, a representative sample of 1,001 journalists conducted in 1981–1982 showed that 62 percent favored an interpretive and investigative role, but that 50 percent also favored an information dissemination role. Importantly, about half of each group opted for both roles. Only 17 percent wished to play an adversary role. See David H. Weaver and G. Cleveland Wilhoit, *The American Journalist: A Portrait of U.S. News People and Their Work* (Bloomington: Indiana University Press, 1986), figure 5.1.

32. Timothy E. Cook, "Staging the News and Covering the News: Media Events, Broadcast Network News, and the First Six Months of the Bush Presidency" (Paper presented at the research conference "Off the Video Record," held at Purdue University, West Lafayette, Indiana, November 1992).

33. Carolyn Smith makes this point about what she calls "the hidden-agenda press conferences" in *Presidential Press Conferences: A Critical Approach* (New York: Praeger, 1990), esp. 84–88, and describes one of President Reagan's press conferences in December 1983, shortly after White House counselor Edwin Meese had suggested that people were showing up at soup kitchens in order to avoid paying for food. Six days later, Reagan appeared in the White House pressroom and claimed no agenda: "I don't have an opening statement. But I just figured that it might be a good idea to come in here and get your questions now. And then, I won't have to tonight at the press party at the White House." After ten questions and after White House spokesperson Larry Speakes indicated that the press conference was over—with nothing about the Meese gaffe—Reagan went on:

> Could I just volunteer some information, though I'm sorry that none of you—maybe one of you that I didn't call on would have asked about Mr. Meese and hunger.
> Press: Yes, we were going to.
> President: You were? [Laughter] Well, let me just say—I'll volunteer, instead of an opening statement, a closing statement on that. (88)

34. Gans, *Deciding What's News*, 90–93.

35. Ibid., 157–176.

36. Ibid., 41.

37. Tuchman, *Making News*, 61 (ellipses in original).

38. We have been influenced in our discussion of presidential narratives by works such as Alfred de Grazia, "The Myth of the President," in *The Presidency*, ed. Aaron Wildavsky (Boston: Little, Brown, 1969), 49–73; Fred I. Greenstein, "What the President

Means to Americans," in *Choosing the President*, ed. James David Barber (Englewood Cliffs, N.J.: Prentice-Hall, 1974), 121–148; and James Oliver Robertson, *American Myth, American Reality* (New York: Hill and Wang, 1980), esp. 308–321.

39. Quoted in George C. Edwards III, *The Public Presidency: The Pursuit of Popular Support* (New York: St. Martin's Press, 1983), 106.

40. Quoted in Hedrick Smith, *The Power Game: How Washington Works* (New York: Random House, 1988), 435.

41. Grossman and Kumar, *Portraying the President*, chap. 10.

42. Fishman, *Manufacturing the News*, chap. 5, esp. 125.

43. See, for example, Richard Brody, *Assessing the President: The Media, Elite Opinion, and Public Support* (Stanford, Calif.: Stanford University Press, 1991).

44. Daniel C. Hallin, *The "Uncensored War": The Media and Vietnam* (New York: Oxford University Press, 1986), chap. 5.

45. Timothy E. Cook, "Domesticating a Crisis: Washington Newsbeats and Network News after the Iraqi Invasion of Kuwait," in *Taken by Storm: The News Media, U.S. Foreign Policy, and the Gulf War*, ed. W. Lance Bennett and David L. Paletz (Chicago: University of Chicago Press, forthcoming).

46. Daniel C. Hallin and Paolo Mancini, "Speaking of the President: Political Structure and Representational Form in U.S. and Italian Television News," *Theory and Society* 13 (1984): 829–846.

47. Jonathan Alter, "The Manic-Depressive Media," *Newsweek*, February 8, 1993, 29.

48. Mark Rozell, *The Press and the Ford Presidency* (Ann Arbor: University of Michigan Press, 1992); Rozell, *The Press and the Carter Presidency* (Boulder, Colo.: Westview Press, 1988).

49. Thus, for example, of the twelve press secretaries from Kennedy through Bush, Pierre Salinger (Kennedy) had reported for the *San Francisco Chronicle* and *Collier's*; George Reedy (Johnson) had been a congressional reporter for UPI for eight years; George Christian (Johnson) had been an International News Service correspondent for seven years; both of Ford's press secretaries (Jerald ter Horst and Ron Nessen) went directly from long journalistic careers to the White House; and even Larry Speakes (Reagan) had been editor of several small Mississippi papers for seven years. The same is true of White House directors of communication, such as Herbert Klein (Nixon), Patrick Buchanan (Reagan), Tom Griscom (Reagan), and Mark Gearan (Clinton). In a bit of a reversal, three of those who had worked only in politics beforehand—Bill Moyers, Jody Powell, and David Gergen—became journalists after their White House stint.

50. See the concept of "boundary roles" in Blumler and Gurevitch, "Politicians and the Press," 485.

51. Tuchman, *Making News*, 152.

52. Jarol B. Manheim, "The Honeymoon's Over," *Journal of Politics* 41 (1979): 55–74.

53. This excerpt is taken directly from the C-SPAN compilation tape from the Public Affairs Video Archive, which differs slightly from the version in the *Public Papers of the President: George Bush, 1989* (Washington, D.C.: U.S. Government Printing Office, 1990), 1:450.

54. Hertsgaard, *On Bended Knee*, chap. 3, esp. 33–36.

55. *CBS Evening News*, February 2, 1989.

56. This point is inspired by Grossman and Kumar, "The White House and the News Media," but we see more variability in this process than their smooth alliance-competition-détente model implies.

57. See, in particular, W. Russell Neuman, Marion R. Just, and Ann N. Crigler, *Common Knowledge: News and the Construction of Political Meaning* (Chicago: University of Chicago Press, 1992).

58. Elizabeth Kolbert, "Across the Networks, a Partisan Battle for Best Catchwords on Health Care," *New York Times*, September 24, 1993, A19.

59. Todd Gitlin, *The Whole World Is Watching: The Mass Media in the Making and Unmaking of the New Left* (Berkeley: University of California Press, 1980), 286–287.

12 The Presidency and Interest Groups: Why Presidents Cannot Govern

Benjamin Ginsberg, Walter R. Mebane, Jr., and Martin Shefter

Why have so many recent presidents failed politically? According to Benjamin Ginsberg, Walter R. Mebane, and Martin Shefter, the source of presidential failure has not been personal but systemic. The American political system, in their view, has degenerated from one in which the primary arena of political conflict between political parties and interest groups was elections to one in which political conflict takes place between institutions. The Democrats and their interest group supporters have entrenched themselves primarily in the social service and regulatory agencies of the domestic state; the Republicans and their allies have sought to create a similar base in the military and national security apparatus. From these and other bastions, "present-day political forces are as likely to employ judicial and investigatory proceedings as presidential elections" in their pursuit of power. One victim of new-style political conflict, the authors conclude, is the presidency; another may be democracy itself.

For the past thirty years the history of the American presidency has been one of disappointment and failure. Of America's last six presidents, five were compelled to leave office sooner than they wished. Gerald R. Ford, Jimmy Carter, and George Bush were defeated in their efforts to win a second term. Richard M. Nixon was forced to resign by the Watergate scandal. Lyndon B. Johnson declined to seek another term after his administration was wrecked by the Vietnam War. Only Ronald Reagan, among recent chief executives, was able to complete two full terms in office. And even Reagan saw his second term disrupted by the Iran-contra scandal.

In November 1992, Americans elected a new president who promised to address the nation's economic and social problems and to bring "change" to Washington. During Bill Clinton's first weeks in office, his popular standing was high; his relations with Congress excellent; and the media described him as the most skillful politician in America. Indeed, some journalists compared him favorably to Franklin D. Roosevelt and Abraham Lincoln.

After only six months, however, Clinton's standing in the public opinion polls had plummeted to the lowest level of any president in history at a comparable point in his term; one of his major policy initiatives, the North American Free Trade Agreement (NAFTA), was openly and vehemently opposed by two of the three top leaders of his party in the House of Representatives; and the national media were characterizing him as without leadership ability, inept, and lacking a moral compass.[1] Instead of comparing him *favorably* to Roosevelt and Lincoln, the media were now comparing Clinton *unfavorably* to George Bush— a president whom they previously had likened to the unfortunate Herbert Hoover and the hapless James Buchanan.

Commentators are often inclined to explain the difficulties encountered by public officials in terms of personal failings. The collapse of so many presidencies, however, cannot be attributed entirely to the shortcomings of the individual incumbents. Instead, Clinton's problems and those of his predecessors can, in large measure, be seen as consequences of the American political process. During the past several decades a new political pattern has emerged in the United States, characterized by low rates of voter turnout, weak political parties, a central role for interest groups and the media, and the use of new political weapons that have, in some respects, supplanted elections as instruments of political warfare.[2] It is this new political process, which might be termed "postelectoral politics," that accounts for many of the difficulties encountered by President Clinton and his predecessors.

In this chapter we examine the central features of America's current political process and how they developed. We then consider their institutional and policy implications. Students of American politics may well ask whether, under present conditions, any president can govern. As the Clintonites might say, "It's the process—stupid!"

Elite Conflict and Popular Mobilization

For much of America's history, elections were the central arenas of popular choice and political conflict. Full white manhood suffrage was achieved in the United States in the early 1800s; by the end of the nineteenth century this electorate was highly mobilized. During the 1880s and 1890s, turnout generally exceeded 80 percent of eligible voters in presidential elections and approached 70 percent in midterm congressional races. Outside the South, presidential election turnout stood at nearly 90 percent.[3]

These high levels of voting participation were achieved because, in nineteenth-century America, contending political forces waged their struggles largely through competitive popular mobilization. Debates about policies and battles for power among rival elites were seldom confined to the conference rooms and corridors of the Capitol. Instead, political struggles typically extended into the electoral arena. In a pattern that E. E. Schattschneider characterized as "expanding the scope of the conflict," opposing parties and interest groups mobilized their supporters throughout the country, "lining up the unwashed," as V. O. Key put it, in an effort to defeat their political opponents by outvoting them.[4]

The resulting style of nineteenth-century political campaigns has been characterized by Richard Jensen as "militarist."[5] Contending political forces were organized and active in every constituency. Voters in each precinct were "drilled" by party "captains," who, in turn, were organized and provided with supplies, equipment, and intelligence by an elaborate, well-staffed, and well-financed organization. Party propaganda was disseminated by a rabidly partisan press. Throughout the country, hundreds of thousands of party workers marched from house to house on election day, handing out leaflets, helping voters to the polls, and, on occasion, offering voters financial inducements to support the candidate of *their* choice.

When the stakes were high, as during the critical election of 1896, party machines were capable of extraordinary feats of popular mobilization. According to Jensen, during William McKinley's "front porch" campaign of 1896, 750,000 persons—about 13 percent of GOP voters that year—were brought from all over the United States to the candidate's Ohio home by Republican party workers. These same party workers and their Democratic counterparts then led nearly 90 percent of all eligible voters outside the South to the polls on election day. This prodigious feat, in a semiagrarian nation in which the horse and buggy was still a major mode of transportation, illustrates the close relationship between elite struggle and electoral mobilization in nineteenth-century America. Each side devoted its energies to mobilizing and winning the maximum possible number of votes. To be sure, policy contention during the late nineteenth century was not solely a matter of electoral mobilization. The period from the Civil War through World War I saw numerous indictments, impeachments, and assassinations of political leaders.[6] The question of who would be permitted to participate in elections was settled during Reconstruction by violence and other extralegal means.[7] Allegations of conspiracy and corruption were the normal currency of party politics.[8] Fraudulent voting was commonplace in elections.[9] (Thus the efforts of the Populists and Progressives to reform the electoral and administrative processes by establishing primaries and formal civil service systems were not unrelated to the practices of the day.) Nevertheless, the attempt to mobilize maximum support in elections was a central strategy for anyone seeking to control the government and to influence public policy.

The nineteenth-century pattern of active public involvement is a far cry from how politics is conducted in present-day America. Recent voter turnout has been extremely low. Less than 56 percent of those eligible to vote actually voted in the 1992 presidential election—and this represented a four-point increase in turnout from the 1988 election! In midterm congressional elections, barely one-third of eligible voters go to the polls.

Interestingly, however, these low levels of voter turnout are not associated with a decline in political conflict. For example, conflict within Congress, as measured by the closeness of roll-call votes, has *increased* significantly in recent years.[10]

It is indicative of the intensity of conflict in contemporary American politics that many political forces have castigated President Clinton for his willingness to compromise with their opponents. The liberal *New York Times* vehemently denounced Clinton's appointment of a moderate Republican, David Gergen, to the White House staff; the *Times* asserted that as a spokesman for the Reagan administration, Gergen had presented in a favorable light policies that had "coarsened" American life.[11] Similarly, Clinton's withdrawal of Lani Guinier's nomination to be assistant attorney general for civil rights was bitterly denounced by the Congressional Black Caucus, the NAACP, and NOW. Clinton abandoned the Guinier nomination as part of his effort to move to the political center, and because reservations about Guinier's appointment had been expressed by numerous mainstream Democratic senators and by several major publications—including the *Washington Post*, the *New York Times*, and the *New Republic*—that had endorsed Clinton's presidential candidacy. Nonetheless Guinier's supporters denounced the president's withdrawal of her nomination as "caving in to the Radical Right."

During the 1950s and 1960s, most observers of American politics had considered the tendency of American politicians to compromise with their opponents to be a virtue—reflecting the "genius of American politics."[12] By contrast, many contemporary political commentators have asserted that President Clinton's compromises are a sign of his complete lack of moral convictions.[13]

Also indicative of the intensity of conflict among elites in contemporary American politics are the number of President Clinton's legislative proposals that have been filibustered by Republicans in the Senate and the unanimous opposition among both Senate and House Republicans that several of his bills have encountered. It is noteworthy, however, that such struggles among contending political forces no longer lead to major efforts to mobilize voters in elections.

In view of the intensity of contemporary political struggles concerning such questions as how to cope with the federal budget deficit and whether abortions should be publicly financed or totally outlawed, the limited involvement of the mass electorate in recent years is striking. During the nineteenth century, voter mobilization (as manifested in electoral turnout) and elite conflict (as manifested in close congressional roll calls) were directly associated. In recent years, however, the relationship between levels of conflict at the elite and mass levels has collapsed. In sharp contrast to the militarist elections of the nineteenth century, contemporary political forces no longer are willing to engage in all-out struggle in the electoral arena.

American politicians purport to deplore the nation's low levels of voter turnout. It is interesting to note, however, that even modest efforts to boost voter turnout inspire only lukewarm support in Washington. For example, the so-called motor voter act, signed into law by President Clinton in 1993, was bitterly opposed by most Republicans.[14] For their part, congressional Democrats were willing to delete those portions of the bill that were most likely to maximize registration among the poor, such as providing automatic voter registration to all clients at welfare offices. Indeed, many Democrats had been happy to see the bill vetoed by President Bush in 1992, even though "motor voter" is expected to have only a modest effect on the size and composition of the electorate.[15] Why are political forces that are locked in bitter struggles less than eager to engage in full-scale popular mobilization in an effort to overwhelm their foes at the polls?

State-Building versus Party-Building

The collapse of electoral turnout in the twentieth century is usually attributed to the decline of political parties. Strong party organizations, or so the argument goes, are necessary for securing high levels of voting participation, especially among poor and uneducated voters.

The decline-of-party thesis is certainly true as far as it goes. However, it is more a description than an explanation of what happened. To observe that parties have declined is simply to note that political elites have not maintained organizations through which they mobilize mass publics to defeat their rivals. It is not to say why they have failed to do so. We will propose an explanation for their failure.

Contemporary elites could not eschew a strategy of mass mobilization if they lacked alternative means to gain or retain power. Such alternatives, however, do exist. Elites have been able to secure power without building a strong popular base by fashioning institutional bastions for themselves in governmental agencies. In lieu of full-scale popular mobilization, contemporary political forces have entrenched themselves in the structure of the American state.

Democrats, especially organized labor, public employees, and other elements of the party's liberal camp, began to entrench themselves in the apparatus of the American welfare state during Franklin Roosevelt's New Deal. Segments of the Republican party, especially in the Sunbelt, undertook to entrench themselves in America's national security state during the Reagan military build-up, sometimes in alliance with southern and conservative Democrats. Competitive entrenchment by the Republicans and Democrats has come to substitute for mass electoral mobilization as the means of securing power in the United States. This is a major reason that high levels of partisan conflict coexist with low rates of voting participation in contemporary American politics.

Democratic Entrenchment

Since the 1930s, Democratic presidents and Congresses have managed to enact a large number of social and regulatory programs. To administer these programs, they created or expanded numerous government agencies. These federal bureaucracies are in turn linked by grant-in-aid programs to public agencies and nonprofit organizations at the state and local levels, and through these to the Democratic party's political base.[16] This entire complex is tied back to Democrats in Congress, who affirm the worth of federal social and regulatory policies and defend the authority and budgets of the agencies responsible for their administration when they come under attack.

After Bill Clinton's victory in 1992 gave the Democrats control of the White House for the first time in twelve years, the new administration moved to entrench the liberal wing of the Democratic party further in the domestic state. The most important such programs of the Clinton administration were in the fields of economic policy, health care, and political reform.

In economic policy, President Clinton introduced a package of tax increases and spending cuts that, according to the White House, would reduce the nation's projected budget deficit by some $500 billion in five years without damaging the economy. The burden of the proposed tax increases was to be borne chiefly by wealthier taxpayers, although virtually all but the poorest Americans would see some increase in their taxes. A middle-class tax cut, which Clinton had proposed during the campaign, was dropped. A tax on energy was to provide substantial new revenues. A second element in the president's economic proposal was a $16 billion "stimulus package" containing new spending for a variety of domestic programs.

In the area of health policy, the president asserted that the escalating cost of medical care amounted to a national social and economic crisis. Clinton created a 500-person task force under the leadership of his wife, Hillary Rodham Clinton. This group developed a proposal for a complete overhaul of the nation's health care system. Although the deliberations, and even the membership, of the task force were secret, it soon became known that the administration favored some form of "managed competition." In such a system the federal government would oversee the creation of large groups of health care purchasers who would contract with health care providers for a complete package of medical services. All Americans would receive a basic package of health insurance. The annual costs of the program to the federal government, estimated between $50 billion and $100 billion, would be funded primarily by new payroll taxes.

As for political reform, Clinton proposed changes in both campaign spending rules (limiting private contributions and providing public funding for congressional campaigns) and the Hatch Act, permitting federal civil servants to play a larger role in the political process. Clinton also urged Congress to enact a new set of rules that would prohibit lobbyists from making campaign contributions to national legislative or executive officials if they had lobbied these officials within the previous twelve months. Finally, the president sought legislation to stipulate that companies employing lobbyists be prohibited from deducting lobbying costs from their federal taxes as a business expense, thereby making it more costly for firms to employ lobbyists.

Taken together, the three main elements of Clinton's program can be seen as a recipe for expanding the power of liberal Democrats in national politics. Clinton's economic package entailed substantial tax increases and cuts in military spending. Under the rubric of "investment," it channeled additional revenues into Democratic social programs and agencies that had faced restrictive funding during the preceding twelve years of Republican rule. Thus, in the name of deficit reduction, Clinton actually proposed to step up domestic spending.[17]

Clinton's health care reform proposals would create an extensive set of new government agencies and institutions that would permit liberal Democrats to expand their influence substantially over a sector that represents nearly 15 percent of the national economy. Politically, health care promises to achieve for the Clintonians what Social Security accomplished for the New Dealers in the 1930s—that is, provide millions of voters with an ongoing reason to support the Democratic party while giving the Democrats a new means to manage the national economy. Indeed, in his nationally televised speech before a joint session of Congress, Clinton explicitly argued that his "health security" program was styled after Social Security.

Finally, Clinton's proposed changes in campaign spending rules would generally work to the advantage of his political allies, including liberal public interest groups and Democratic incumbents. Reform of the Hatch Act promised to permit the heavily Democratic federal civil service to play a larger role in the political process.[18]

Thus, through his policy initiatives, the president was attempting to create programs and institutions that would help maintain Democratic control of the government. Adoption of these proposals would solidify the Democratic party's institutional base in the bureaucracies of the federal, state, and local governments while making it more difficult for the Republicans to dislodge the Democrats through the electoral process.

Republican Entrenchment

As the Democrats have entrenched themselves primarily in the social service and regulatory agencies of the domestic state, the Republicans, in alliances with some conservative and Southern Democrats, have sought to create a similar base of power in the government's military and national security apparatus. The Republicans are not as firmly rooted in their sector of the state as the Democrats are in theirs. Still, Republicans evidently have calculated that all-out electoral mobilization would not serve their interests and have preferred the known risks of limited electoral participation and competitive entrenchment to what Benjamin Disraeli termed the "leap in the dark" of expanding the electorate.

Beginning in the 1980s, the Republicans undertook to enhance the size and power of America's military and national security apparatus and to use it as an instrument for governing and perpetuating their party's power. Toward this end, the Reagan administration sponsored the largest peacetime military buildup in the nation's history.[19] Annual military expenditures in constant 1982 dollars were increased by more than 40 percent, from $171 billion at the end of the Carter administration to $242 billion by the middle of President Reagan's second term. Liberal opposition in Congress limited further increases to the annual rate of inflation. But the enormous military buildup of the first Reagan administration had enlarged the base upon which even these modest changes in spending were calculated.

When the Democrats returned to the White House in 1992, they attacked the military and national security sectors. President Clinton proposed substantial cuts in defense spending. Moreover, Clinton and some congressional Democrats were sharply critical of the military for closing its eyes to the sexual abuse of women in the ranks and for prohibiting the recruitment and retention of gay and lesbian personnel.

Indeed, the congressional investigation of the "Tailhook" affair and the entire conflict regarding homosexuals in the armed services can be seen as efforts by Democrats to stigmatize and delegitimate an institution, the military, that had become an important Republican bastion. In October 1993, Clinton's navy secretary, John Dalton, cited the sexual harassment that had occurred at the 1991 Tailhook Association convention both in demanding the resignation of Admiral Frank Kelso, the chief of naval operations, and in instituting disciplinary proceedings against a dozen admirals and marine generals.

The attempted decapitation of the navy's chain of command (the secretary of defense refused to fire Kelso) was announced just one day after the Pentagon indicated that it would delay implementing the compromise ("Don't ask; don't tell; don't pursue") that it had worked out with the Clinton administration concerning gays and lesbians in the military. The Pentagon attributed the delay to the technical difficulty of informing base commanders about the new regulations. But the actions on both sides can be seen as an escalation in the struggle between the Clinton administration and the military establishment. An earlier episode had been the scathing public criticism of the commander in chief by an air force major general, for which the general was only mildly rebuked by his superiors and advised to take early retirement.

Other incidents bespeak the hostility between the military and the Clinton administration. For example, when Gen. Colin Powell, the chairman of the Joint Chiefs of Staff, introduced the former Republican defense secretary Dick Cheney at a Pentagon function in 1993, he saluted and called Cheney "Boss." The entire room, filled with military officers, erupted into loud and sustained cheering at this suggestion that the wrong people were now in power. In truth, Republican officials tend to develop close relationships with military personnel as officers rise through the ranks. Republican defense secretaries typically recruit their assistants from the military rather than from civilian institutions (Colin Powell, for example, had served as assistant to Secretary of Defense Caspar Weinberger); they also rely heavily on the Pentagon's joint staff (the uniformed staff of the Joint Chiefs) for policy planning. In contrast, Democratic secretaries of defense, such as Les Aspin, recruit their assistants mainly from congressional staffs and university faculties. These civilian officials regard the joint staff with suspicion. The military brass, in turn, is disdainful of a group it calls the "Faculty Club."

It remains to be seen whether the Democrats will be able to undermine or capture a sector of the state that has come to be closely linked to their political rivals. Just as the officials of domestic agencies, such as the Environmental Protection Agency, appealed to Democrats and liberal Republicans in Congress for support when they came under attack during the Reagan and Bush years, the military has sought the support of congressional Republicans and conservative Democrats in its conflicts with the Clinton administration. For example, during Senate Armed Services Committee hearings in 1993, Republican senator John Warner arranged with the Joint Chiefs of Staff to subject Secretary Aspin's military readiness plan to a withering attack. Conservative Democrat Sam Nunn took up the Pentagon's fight against admitting and retaining openly homosexual individuals in the military.

Early Democratic efforts to control the military establishment produced bitter struggles between Secretary Aspin and the leaders of the uniformed services. Aspin charged that the military had not provided him with accurate information, whereas military leaders accused Aspin and his staff of failing to consult them and of taking actions that threatened the nation's military readiness.[20]

Indeed, within the first months of the Clinton presidency, the military launched a counterattack against the "Faculty Club." Acting on a complaint from career officers, the Pentagon's inspector general charged that Assistant Secretary of Defense-designate Graham Allison had twice broken government ethics rules during the period that he served as a special consultant to Aspin while awaiting Senate confirmation of his permanent appointment. The inspector general's report alleged that Allison, a former dean of Harvard's Kennedy School of Government, had arranged for his Harvard colleague, Robert Blackwill, to receive a Pentagon consulting contract. The report further charged that Allison had subsequently used a meeting with the Russian defense attaché in Washington to encourage the Russian government to make a donation to Harvard University that would guarantee the inclusion of its officials in a military exchange program organized by Blackwill. Career officers claimed, moreover, that Blackwill had used the position secured for him by Allison to lobby for federal funding of yet another Harvard program. All of these charges were reported to have infuriated some conservative members of the Senate Armed Services Committee and to have threatened Allison's confirmation.[21]

Within a year of Clinton's taking office, this bureaucratic warfare led him to fire Defense Secretary Aspin, just as leaks to their congressional allies by bureaucrats in the Environmental Protection Agency had compelled President Reagan to dismiss his initial EPA administrator, Anne Gorsuch Burford, whose conservative policies were vehemently opposed by her subordinates. Indeed, the military's triumph over the White House was so complete that at the televised announcement of Aspin's replacement by Admiral Bobby Inman, Clinton found it necessary to stand in silence as Inman told the press that his interview with the president left him with a "comfort level" concerning Clinton's service as commander in chief sufficient to accept the president's offer to appoint him as secretary of defense.

Electoral Mobilization versus Institutional Struggle

Entrenchment in governmental institutions provides modern political parties and interest groups with access to public resources and power without requiring them to engage in full-scale electoral mobilization. This explains how high levels of elite conflict can coexist with low levels of popular participation in contemporary politics. Rather than "expand the scope of conflict" to include voters, elites now compete by seeking to colonize existing governmental agencies, establish new ones, and undermine agencies controlled by their opponents. For example, Republican presidents in the 1980s drastically reduced federal tax revenues and amassed enormous budget deficits in an effort to make it impossible for liberal congressional Democrats to expand the domestic programs and agencies in which their wing of the Democratic party is entrenched. In the 1990s, a Democratic president seeks both to overcome the constraint of the deficit by raising taxes and to attack the military and national security agencies that are linked to the Republicans.

In their struggles for power, present-day political forces are as likely to employ judicial and investigatory proceedings as presidential elections. Courts and investigations by congressional committees and government commissions are used to assail administrative arrangements that favor the opposition and to drive administration appointees and even elected officials from office without the need for appeals to voters.

Indeed, the growing political use of the criminal justice system is an indication of how conflict has been displaced from the electoral arena into institutional combat. From the early 1970s to the early 1990s, nearly a twentyfold increase occurred (from roughly 50 to almost 1,000) in the number of indictments brought by federal prosecutors against national, state, and local officials.[22]

Administration opponents have also taken to launching attacks upon individuals whom the president seeks to appoint to office. In recent years, such attacks were most intense in the cases of President Reagan's Supreme Court nominee Robert Bork, President Bush's initial choice for secretary of defense, John Tower, and Bush's Supreme Court nominee Clarence Thomas.[23] Character assassination has become such a routine aspect of American politics that the end of "divided government" in the 1992 election has not halted partisan efforts to discredit presidential appointees. Such attacks compelled President Clinton to withdraw his initial nominees for attorney general, Zoë Baird and Kimba Wood, as well as his choice for assistant attorney general, Lani Guinier. To ensure that Clinton would not have to withdraw his first official nominee for the Supreme Court, the White House leaked the names of the president's choices. Two of the potential nominees who were "hung out to dry" in this way, Bruce Babbitt and Stephen Breyer, were dropped after encountering opposition.

As his first year in office was drawing to a close, President Clinton himself was subject to a comparable series of attacks. The conservative *American Spectator* published an article reporting that two Arkansas state troopers claimed that as members of Gov. Bill Clinton's security detail they had helped him arrange liaisons with women. The troopers said that they continued performing these services after Clinton won the presidential election in November 1992 but before he left Arkansas. In addition, other critics alleged that Clinton and his wife were guilty of various improprieties involving a real estate investment in the now defunct Whitewater Development Corporation of Arkansas. As governor, Clinton allegedly loosened regulatory supervision of a savings and loan institution that had lent money to Whitewater and that had helped pay off Clinton's gubernatorial campaign debts. The institution in question later went bankrupt, and protecting its depositors imposed great costs on the public. It was also alleged that President Clinton's aides removed material concerning Whitewater from the files of deputy White House counsel Vincent Foster, prior to turning the files over to the police investigating Foster's suicide. Republican members of Congress (subsequently joined by some Democrats) immediately called for the appointment of an independent counsel to investigate the president's conduct in this matter.

Thus, political forces that shrink from mobilizing voters are perfectly happy to destroy the reputations of or even to imprison their opponents. Indeed, investigations and criminal proceedings are used routinely today by those seeking to reverse electoral outcomes. For example, in 1993, Sen. Bob Packwood's political opponents asked the Senate Ethics Committee to refuse to seat Packwood despite his recent reelection victory. They claimed that his electoral success should be ignored because he had misled voters by denying to reporters the truth of the charges of sexual harassment that were made by some of his former employees, thereby discouraging the press from reporting these allegations until after the 1992 elections. In June 1993, just one day after the landslide election of Kay Bailey Hutchison, the Texas state treasurer, to the U.S. Senate, her opponents announced a grand jury probe into her conduct as state treasurer. (She was indicted a few months later.) In this way, those who were defeated decisively in the electoral arena hope to obtain a more favorable outcome. It may be only a matter of time before such techniques are used in presidential elections.

Politics and Governance

The emergence of a politics of diminished electoral mobilization undermines presidential power; it is problematic in other respects as well. First, the contemporary pattern of American politics is profoundly undemocratic. Obviously, the nineteenth-century voters who were mobilized so effectively by Boss Tweed and his brethren were not exactly the free agents of democratic theory. Nevertheless, when voter mobilization is the key to political success, ordinary citizens at least have an opportunity to play a role in making policy and resolving political disputes.

A political process in which only half of those who are potentially eligible actually take part, in which politicians secure power through entrenchment in government bureaucracies, and in which investigatory and judicial processes are routinely invoked to limit the effect of, or even to reverse, electoral outcomes can hardly be called democratic. Perhaps "quasi-democratic" would be a more appropriate label.

Second, and of particular importance to the presidency, contemporary political patterns promote weak and indecisive government. However much presidents may talk about "change," governments that do not actively mobilize voters and that lack a stable base of popular support have no reliable foundation from which to confront vested interests and take decisive action.

For example, after his election in 1992, President Clinton felt compelled to reassure powerful banking and financial interests that his administration would be responsive to their concerns. This was a major reason that Clinton—who had campaigned in 1992 as a staunch opponent of business-as-usual in Washington—named Ron Brown to be his secretary of commerce and Lloyd Bentsen as secretary of the treasury. Brown was a veteran Washington corporate lobbyist, well known to the business community. Bentsen, as chairman of the Senate Finance Committee, was noted for his close and cordial relationship with banking, financial, insurance, and real estate interests.[24] President Clinton was no more anxious than his Republican predecessors to confront these interests.

Later in his term, the opposition of the Southwestern energy industry forced Clinton to abandon his plan for a tax based on the energy content of fuels, or British thermal units (BTUs). Even before he formally abandoned the BTU tax, Clinton had been compelled to grant concessions and exemptions to so many industries and interests that the tax had all but disappeared.

Similarly, the health care plan that President Clinton unveiled in September 1993 made so many concessions to powerful interest groups that the fiscal viability of the entire program was jeopardized.[25] Because of the opposition of the senior citizens' lobby to a potential loss of benefits, Medicare recipients were exempted from the plan. (Indeed, they were promised expensive new benefits under the Medicare system.) Because the politically powerful postal workers' union was determined to continue administering its own health insurance program, it demanded and received an exemption from the Clinton plan. Other public employee unions vowed to seek similar treatment for their members. Physicians' groups demanded and won provisions that would allow them to continue to practice fee-for-service medicine. As a concession to veterans' groups, the Veterans Administration medical system was exempted from the plan. Large corporations were permitted to opt out of the plan even though their health care costs were expected to decline as the federal government began to pick up the tab for citizens who previously had no health insurance. Clinton's proposal to change the medical malpractice system was immediately dropped when trial lawyers, who are major beneficiaries of the current health care system, objected.

All of these concessions were made before the health care plan was even introduced. There was little doubt—as even the president admitted—that once the plan was actually submitted to Congress, other powerful interests would demand and receive costly special considerations for their members. The danger was that health care reform might, like the BTU tax, die the death of a thousand concessions from Clinton's need to purchase the support of powerful interests. Once again, Clinton was unable to stand up to any organized interest to bring about the change he claimed to seek.

Indeed, lacking a firm popular base, contemporary presidents are much more vulnerable than their predecessors to all manner of political attack, especially media criticism. Traditional party organizations had stable popular followings that could be counted on when their leaders came under fire. As Chicago's long-time mayor, the late Richard J. Daley, once said in response to media attacks, "When you've got the people behind you, you don't need the media. . . . The media can kiss my _____!" Contemporary presidents lack Mayor Daley's well-organized popular base. Lacking such an underpinning of support, they cannot afford his indifference to their media images.

Presidents and other contemporary elected officials who are subjected to attack often find that their standing in public opinion polls (today's superficial substitute for an organized popular base) can evaporate overnight and with it their capacity to govern. Thus, the Nixon administration was paralyzed for eighteen months by the Watergate affair and the Reagan White House for two years by the Iran-contra affair. Congress was nearly immobilized for a year by the imbroglios in regard to Jim Wright, Tony Coehlo, and Barney Frank and for another year by the House Post Office scandal. In 1993, the Clinton administration found its political leverage declining as the president's standing in the polls dipped. This is hardly a recipe for a strong government that might be able to solve America's long-term deficit and trade problems.

Finally, because they tend to produce what John Chubb and Paul Peterson have correctly called a "government that cannot govern," contemporary political patterns have contributed to the growth of extraordinary levels of popular cynicism and distrust of government.[26] It is worth observing that in Latin America, angry and frustrated publics have recently supported the modern-day embodiment of the political savior—the "businessman on horseback," such as Peru's Alberto Fujimoro—who promises to restore order and bring an end to the foolishness of the politicians. Those who feel confident that such things cannot happen in the United States would do well to ponder the meaning of the Ross Perot phenomenon.[27]

Notes

1. Clinton's fortunes were revived in September 1993 by his proposal for a national health care system. Whether the spurt in the president's approval could survive the effort to work out a health plan that could win majority support in Congress was very much an open question. It is clear, however, that the pummeling that Clinton experienced during his first six months in office indicates the extraordinary vulnerability of modern presidents.

2. Benjamin Ginsberg and Martin Shefter, *Politics by Other Means: The Declining Importance of Elections in America* (New York: Basic Books, 1990).

3. In the late nineteenth century, electoral turnout was lower in the states of the former Confederacy than in the rest of the country because blacks were excluded from voting and there was no party competition in the "Solid South."

4. E. E. Schattschneider, *The Semi-Sovereign People* (New York: Holt, Rinehart and Winston, 1960), 5; V. O. Key, Jr., *Politics, Parties and Pressure Groups*, 4th ed. (New York: Crowell, 1958), 201.

5. Richard Jensen, *The Winning of the Midwest* (Chicago: University of Chicago Press, 1971), chap. 6.

6. In 1868 President Andrew Johnson was impeached by the House of Representatives and avoided conviction and removal by only a single vote in the Senate. Presidents Abraham Lincoln, James Garfield, and William McKinley were assassinated in 1865, 1881, and 1901, respectively. Among the numerous public officials subject to criminal indictments and prosecutions were the agents of the Treasury Department involved in the Whiskey Ring scandals of the 1870s.

7. Southern politics was beset with extralegal violence by groups such as the Ku Klux Klan. See J. Morgan Kousser, *The Shaping of Southern Politics: Suffrage Restriction and the Establishment of the One-Party South, 1890–1910* (New Haven: Yale University Press, 1974).

8. Mark W. Summers, *The Era of Good Stealings* (New York: Oxford University Press, 1993).

9. Philip E. Converse, "Change in the American Electorate," in *The Human Meaning of Social Change*, ed. Angus Campbell and Philip Converse (New York: Russell Sage Foundation, 1972), 263–337; Walter Dean Burnham, "Theory and Voting Research," *American Political Science Review* 68: 1002–1023. The issue of magnitude and effect on reported voter turnout remains controversial.

10. Benjamin Ginsberg, Walter R. Mebane, Jr., and Martin Shefter, "The Disjunction between Political Conflict and Electoral Mobilization in the Contemporary United States" (Paper presented at the annual meeting of the American Political Science Association, Washington, D.C., September 1993).

11. *New York Times*, June 2, 1993.

12. Daniel Boorstin, *The Genius of American Politics* (Chicago: University of Chicago Press, 1953).

13. David von Drehle, "Feat of (Henry) Clay: A Defense of the Lost Art of Compromise," *Washington Post*, June 20, 1993, C1; Thomas L. Friedman, "Clinton's Gay Policy: Cave-In or Milestone," *New York Times*, July 25, 1993, IV 1.

14. The "motor voter" act authorizes government agencies, such as motor vehicle bureaus, to enroll as registered voters the members of the public with whom they deal.

15. Chuck Alston, "Democrats Flex New Muscle with Trio of Election Bills," *Congressional Quarterly Weekly Report*, March 20, 1993, 643–645.

16. Lester M. Salamon, "Rethinking Public Management: Third Party Government and the Changing Forms of Government Action," *Public Policy* 29 (Summer 1981): 255–275.

17. See E. J. Dionne, "Clinton's Clever Plan," *Washington Post*, February 22, 1993, A19.

18. Alston, "Democrats Flex New Muscle."

19. Daniel Wirls, *Buildup: The Politics of Defense in the Reagan Era* (Ithaca, N.Y.: Cornell University Press, 1992).

20. Barton Gellman, "Rumblings of Discord Heard in Pentagon," *Washington Post*, June 20, 1993, 1.

21. Barton Gellman, "Report Cites Breaches by Pentagon Nominee," *Washington Post*, July 8, 1993, A15.

22. Ginsberg and Shefter, *Politics by Other Means*, 6.

23. Martin Shefter, "Institutional Conflict over Presidential Appointments: The Case of Clarence Thomas," *PS: Political Science and Politics* 25 (December 1992): 676–679.

24. Jill Abramson and John Harwood, "Some Say Likely Choice of Bentsen, the Insider, for Treasury Post Could Send the Wrong Signals," *Wall Street Journal*, December 9, 1992, A26.

25. See Steven Pearlstein and Dana Priest, "Ensuring a Healthy Chance: Reform Plan Tailored to Attract Base of Allies," *Washington Post*, September 22, 1993, 1. See also Jeffrey Birnbaum, "Clinton Health Package Has a Little Something for Just Enough Factions to Splinter Opposition," *Wall Street Journal*, September 23, 1993, A18.

26. John Chubb and Paul Peterson, *Can the Government Govern?* (Washington, D.C.: Brookings Institution, 1985), chap. 1.

27. For a discussion of the recent political success of businessmen in formerly liberal constituencies, see "Return of Ears," *Economist*, May 22, 1993, 34.

13 The Presidency and Political Parties

Sidney M. Milkis

The modern presidency has been anything but supportive of the modern Republican and Democratic parties. According to Sidney M. Milkis, President Franklin D. Roosevelt and most of his successors have found the traditional party system to be too grounded in state and local organizations to be of much help in the effort to forge presidential policies and programs. Indeed, to the extent that the parties have exercised influence through Congress, presidents have sometimes perceived them to be an impediment to national leadership. Roosevelt, Lyndon B. Johnson, and Richard M. Nixon each took steps to replace party influence with centralized administration in the bureaucracy and the White House. Ronald Reagan, George Bush, and Bill Clinton have tried to restore some (but not all) of the traditional importance of the political parties, Milkis argues, by refashioning them into highly untraditional but politically potent national organizations. But their efforts have been uneven and have met with limited success.

The relationship between the presidency and the American party system has always been difficult. The architects of the Constitution established a nonpartisan president who, with the support of the judiciary, was intended to play the leading institutional role in checking and controlling the "violence of faction" that the framers feared would rend the fabric of representative democracy. Even after the presidency became a more partisan office during the early part of the nineteenth century, its authority continued to depend on an ability to transcend party politics. The president is nominated by a party but, unlike the British prime minister, is not elected by it.

The inherent tension between the presidency and the party system reached a critical point during the 1930s. The institutionalization of the modern presidency, arguably the most significant constitutional legacy of Franklin D. Roosevelt's New Deal, ruptured severely the limited, albeit significant, bond that linked presidents to their parties. In fact, the modern presidency was crafted with the intention of reducing the influence of the party system on American politics. In this sense Roosevelt's extraordinary party leadership contributed to the decline of the American party system. This decline continued—even accelerated—under the administrations of subsequent presidents, notably Lyndon B. Johnson and Richard M. Nixon. Under Ronald Reagan, however, the party system showed at least some signs of transformation and renewal. Reagan and his successor, George Bush, supported efforts by Republicans in the national committee and congressional campaign organizations to restore some of the importance of political parties by refashioning them into highly untraditional but politically potent national organizations. Yet the 1992 election and its aftermath raised serious doubts about the capacity of these emergent national parties to build popular support for political principles and programs.[1]

New Deal Party Politics, Presidential Reform, and the Decline of the American Party System

The New Deal seriously questioned the adequacy of the traditional natural rights liberalism of John Locke and the framers, which emphasized the need to limit constitutionally the scope of government's responsibilities. The modern liberalism that became the public philosophy of the New Deal entailed a fundamental reappraisal of the concept of rights. As Roosevelt first indicated in his 1932 campaign speech at the Commonwealth Club in San Francisco, effective political reform would require, at a minimum, the development of "an economic declaration of rights, an economic constitutional order," grounded in a commitment to guarantee a decent level of economic well-being for the American people. Although equality of opportunity had traditionally been promoted by limited government interference in society, recent economic and social changes, such as the closing of the frontiers and the growth of industrial combinations, demanded that America now recognize "the new terms of the old social contract."

The establishment of a new constitutional order would require a reordering of the political process. The traditional patterns of American politics, characterized by constitutional mechanisms that impeded collective action, would have to give way to a more centralized and administrative government. As Roosevelt put it, "The day of enlightened administration has come."[2]

The concerns Roosevelt expressed in the Commonwealth Club speech are an important guide to understanding the New Deal and its effects on the party system. The pursuit of an economic constitutional order presupposed a fundamental change in the relationship between the presidency and the party system.

In Roosevelt's view, the party system, which was essentially based on state and local organizations and interests and was thus suited to congressional primacy, would have to be transformed into a national, executive-oriented system organized on the basis of public issues.

In this understanding, Roosevelt was no doubt influenced by the thought of Woodrow Wilson. The reform of parties, Wilson believed, depended on extending the influence of the presidency. The limits on partisanship inherent in American constitutional government notwithstanding, the president represented his party's "vital link of connection" with the nation: "He can dominate his party by being spokesman for the real sentiment and purpose of the country, by giving the country at once the information and statements of policy which will enable it to form its judgments alike of parties and men."[3]

Wilson's words spoke louder than his actions; like all presidents after 1800, he reconciled himself to the strong fissures within his party.[4] Roosevelt, however, was less willing to work through existing partisan channels, and more important, the New Deal represented a more fundamental departure than did Wilsonian progressivism from traditional Democratic policies of individual autonomy, limited government, and states' rights.

As president-elect, Roosevelt began preparations to modify the partisan practices of previous administrations. For example, convinced that Wilson's adherence to traditional partisan politics in staffing the federal government was unfortunate, Roosevelt expressed to Attorney General Homer S. Cummings his desire to proceed along somewhat different lines, with a view, according to the latter's diary, "to building up a national organization rather than allowing patronage to be used merely to build Senatorial and Congressional machines."[5] Roosevelt followed traditional patronage practices during his first term, allowing the chair of the Democratic National Committee (DNC), James Farley, to coordinate appointments in response to local party organizations and Democratic senators. After his reelection in 1936, however, the recommendations of these organization people were not followed as closely. Beginning in 1938, especially, as Edward Flynn, who became the Democratic chair in 1940, indicated in his memoirs, "the President turned more and more frequently to the so-called New Dealers," so that "many of the appointments in Washington went to men who were supporters of the President and believed in what he was trying to do, but who were not Democrats in many instances, and in all instances were not organization Democrats."[6]

Moreover, although Wilson took care to consult with legislative party leaders in the development of his policy program, Roosevelt relegated his party in

Congress to a decidedly subordinate status. He offended legislators by his use of press conferences to announce important decisions and, again unlike Wilson, eschewed the use of the party caucus in Congress. Roosevelt rejected as impractical, for example, the suggestion of Congressman Alfred Phillips, Jr., "that those sharing the burden of responsibility of party government should regularly and often be called into caucus and that such caucuses should evolve party policies and choice of party leaders."[7]

The most dramatic aspect of Roosevelt's attempt to remake the Democratic party was his twelve-state effort, involving one gubernatorial and several congressional primary campaigns, to unseat conservative Democrats in 1938. Such intervention was not unprecedented; in particular, William H. Taft and Wilson had made limited efforts to remove recalcitrant leaders from their parties. Yet Roosevelt's campaign took place on an unprecedentedly large scale and, unlike previous efforts, made no attempt to work through the regular party organization. The degree to which his action was viewed as a shocking departure from the norm is indicated by the press's labeling of it as "the purge," a term associated with Adolf Hitler's attempt to weed out dissension from Germany's National Socialist party and Joseph Stalin's elimination of "disloyal" party members from the Soviet Communist party.

Finally, in 1936 the Roosevelt administration successfully pushed to abolish the Democratic National Convention rule that required support from two-thirds of the delegates for the nomination of president and vice president. This rule had been defended in the past because it guarded the most loyal Democratic region—the South—against the imposition of an unwanted ticket by the less habitually Democratic North, East, and West.[8] To eliminate the rule, therefore, both weakened the influence of southern Democrats (whom the journalist Thomas Stokes described as "the ball and chain which hobbled the Party's forward march") and facilitated the adoption of a national reform program.[9]

After the 1938 purge campaign, the columnist Raymond Clapper noted that "no President ever has gone as far as Mr. Roosevelt in striving to stamp his policies upon his party."[10] This massive partisan effort began the process of transforming the party system from local to national and programmatic party organizations. At the same time, the New Deal made partisanship less important. Roosevelt's partisan leadership, although it did effect important changes in the Democratic party organization, ultimately was based on a personal link with the public that would better enable him to make use of his position as leader of the nation, not just of the party that governed the nation.[11] For example, in all but one of the 1938 primary campaigns in which he participated personally,

Roosevelt chose to make a direct appeal to public opinion rather than attempt to work through or to reform the regular party apparatus. This strategy was encouraged by earlier reforms, especially the direct primary, which had begun to weaken the grip of party organizations on the voters. Radio broadcasting also had made direct presidential appeals an enticing strategy, especially for as popular a president with as fine a radio presence as Roosevelt. After his close associate Felix Frankfurter urged him to go to the country in August 1937 to explain the issues that gave rise to the bitter Court-packing controversy, Roosevelt, perhaps in anticipation of the purge campaign, responded: "You are absolutely right about the radio. I feel like saying to the country—'You will hear from me soon and often. This is not a threat but a promise.'"[12]

In the final analysis, the "benign dictatorship" that Roosevelt sought to impose on the Democratic party was more conducive to corroding the American party system than to reforming it. His prescription for party reform—extraordinary presidential leadership—posed a serious, if not intractable, dilemma: on the one hand, the decentralized character of politics in the United States can be modified only by strong presidential leadership; on the other, a president determined to alter fundamentally the connection between the executive and the party eventually will shatter party unity.[13]

Roosevelt, in fact, was always aware that the extent to which his purposes could be achieved by party leadership was limited. He felt that a full revamping of partisan politics was impractical, given the obstacles to party government that are so deeply ingrained in the American political experience. The immense failure of the purge campaign reinforced this view: in the dozen states where the president acted against entrenched incumbents, he was successful in only two—Oregon and New York.[14] Moreover, New Dealers did not view the welfare state as a partisan issue. The reform program of the 1930s was conceived as a "second bill of rights" that should be established as much as possible in permanent programs beyond the vagaries of public opinion and elections.[15]

Thus, the most significant institutional reforms of the New Deal did not promote party government but fostered instead a program that would help the president to govern in the absence of party government. This program, as embodied in the 1937 executive reorganization bill, would have greatly extended presidential authority over the executive branch, including the independent regulatory commissions. The president and the executive agencies would also be delegated extensive authority to govern, making unnecessary the constant cooperation of party members in Congress. As the *Report of the President's Committee on Administrative Management* put it, with administrative reform the "brief exultant commitment" to progressive government that was expressed in the elections of 1932 and, especially, 1936 would now be more firmly established in "persistent, determined, competent, day by day administration of what the Nation has decided to do."[16]

Interestingly, the administrative reform bill, which was directed to making politics less necessary, became, at Roosevelt's urging, a party government-style "vote of confidence" for the administration in Congress. Roosevelt initially lost this vote in 1938, when the reorganization bill was defeated in the House of Representatives, but he did manage, through the purge campaign and other partisan actions, to keep administrative reform sufficiently prominent in party councils that a compromise version passed in 1939. Although considerably weaker than Roosevelt's original proposal, the 1939 Executive Reorganization Act was a significant measure. It not only provided authority for the creation of the Executive Office of the President, which included the newly formed White House Office and a strengthened and refurbished Bureau of the Budget, but also enhanced the president's control of the expanding activities of the executive branch. As such, this legislation represents the genesis of the institutional presidency, which was equipped to govern independently of the constraints imposed by the regular political process.

The civil service reform carried out by the Roosevelt administration was another important part of the effort to replace partisan politics with executive administration. The original reorganization proposals of 1937 had contained provisions to make the administration of the civil service more effective and to expand the merit system. The reorganization bill passed in 1939 was shorn of this controversial feature; but Roosevelt found it possible to accomplish extensive civil service reform through executive action. He did so by extending merit protection to personnel appointed by the administration during its first term, four-fifths of whom had been brought into government outside of merit channels.[17] Patronage appointments had traditionally been used to nourish the party system; the New Deal celebrated an administrative politics that fed instead an executive department oriented to expanding liberal programs. As the administrative historian Paul Van Riper has noted, the new practices created a new kind of patronage, "a sort of intellectual and ideological patronage rather than the more traditional partisan type."[18]

Roosevelt's leadership transformed the Democratic party into a way station on the road to administrative government. As the presidency developed into an elaborate and ubiquitous institution, it preempted party leaders in many of their limited, but significant, duties: providing a link from government to interest groups, staffing the executive department, contributing to policy development, and organizing election campaigns. Moreover, New Deal administrative reform was directed not just to creating presidential government but to embedding progressive principles (considered tantamount to political rights) in a bureaucratic structure that would insulate reform and reformers from electoral change.

Lyndon Johnson's Great Society and the Transcendence of Partisan Politics

Presidential leadership during the New Deal prepared the executive branch to be a government unto itself and established the presidency rather than the party as the locus of political responsibility. But the modern presidency was created to chart the course for, and direct the voyage to, a more liberal America. Roosevelt's pronouncement of a "second bill of rights" proclaimed and began this task, but it fell to Johnson, as one journalist noted, to "codify the New Deal vision of a good society."[19]

Johnson's attempt to create the Great Society marked a significant extension of programmatic liberalism and accelerated the effort to transcend partisan politics. Roosevelt's ill-fated efforts to guide the affairs of his party were well remembered by Johnson, who came to Congress in 1937 in a special House election as an enthusiastic supporter of the New Deal. He took Roosevelt's experience to be the best example of the generally ephemeral nature of party government in the United States, and he fully expected the cohesive Democratic support he received from Congress after the 1964 election to be temporary.[20] Thus Johnson, like Roosevelt, looked beyond the party system toward the politics of "enlightened administration."

Although Johnson avoided any sort of purge campaign and worked closely with Democratic congressional leaders, he took strong action to de-emphasize the role of the traditional party organization. For example, the Johnson administration undertook a ruthless attack on the Democratic National Committee beginning in late 1965, slashing its budget to the bone and eliminating several of its important programs, such as the highly successful voter registration division. The president also ignored the pleas of several advisers to replace the amiable but ineffective John Bailey as DNC chair. Instead, he humiliated Bailey, keeping him on but turning over control of the scaled-back committee's activities to the White House political liaison, Marvin Watson.[21]

Journalists and scholars have generally explained Johnson's lack of support for the regular party organization by referring to his political background and personality. Some have suggested that Johnson was afraid the DNC might be built into a power center capable of challenging his authority in behalf of the Kennedy wing of the party.[22] Others have pointed to Johnson's roots in the one-party system in Texas, an experience that inclined him to emphasize a consensus style of politics, based on support from diverse elements of the electorate that spanned traditional party lines.[23]

These explanations are surely not without merit. Yet to view Johnson's failures as a party leader in purely personal terms is to ignore the imperative of policy reform that influenced his administration. Like Roosevelt, Johnson "had always regarded political parties, strongly rooted in states and localities, capable of holding him accountable, as intruders on the business of government."[24] Moreover, from the beginning of his presidency Johnson envisioned the creation of an ambitious program that would leave its (and his) mark on history in the areas of government organization, conservation, education, and urban affairs. Such efforts to advance not only the New Deal goal of economic security but also the "quality of American life" necessarily brought Johnson into sharp conflict with unreconstructed elements of the Democratic party.[25] As one Johnson aide put it, "Because of the ambitious reforms [LBJ] pushed, it was necessary to move well beyond, to suspend attention to, the party."[26]

Considerable evidence exists that the Johnson administration lacked confidence in the ability of the Democratic party to act as an intermediary between the White House and the American people. For example, an aide to Vice President Hubert Humphrey wrote Marvin Watson that "out in the country most Democrats at the State and local level are not intellectually equipped to help on such critical issues as Vietnam and the riots." After a meeting with district party leaders of Queens, New York, the White House domestic adviser Joseph Califano reported that "they were . . . totally unfamiliar with the dramatic increases in the poverty, health, education and manpower training areas."[27] The uneasy relationship between the Johnson presidency and the Democratic party was particularly aggravated by the administration's aggressive commitment to civil rights, which created considerable friction with local party organizations, especially, but not exclusively, in the South. It is little wonder, then, that when trouble erupted in the cities, the president had his special assistants spend time in ghettos around the country, instead of relying on the reports of local party leaders.[28]

Lack of trust in the Democratic party encouraged the Johnson administration to renew the New Deal pattern of institutional reform. In the area of policy development, one of the most significant innovations of the Johnson administration was to create several task forces under the supervision of the

White House Office and the Bureau of the Budget. These working groups were made up of leading academics throughout the country who prepared reports in virtually all areas of public policy. The specific proposals that came out of these groups, such as the Education Task Force's elementary-education proposal, formed the heart of the Great Society program. The administration took great care to protect the task forces from political pressures, even keeping them secret. Moreover, members were told to pay no attention to political considerations; they were not to worry about whether their recommendations would be acceptable to Congress and party leaders.[29]

The de-emphasis of partisan politics that marked the creation of the Great Society was also apparent in the personnel policy of the Johnson presidency. As his main talent scout, Johnson chose not a political adviser but John Macy, who was also chairman of the Civil Service Commission. Macy worked closely with the White House staff, but, especially during the earlier days of the administration, he was responsible for making recommendations directly to the president. As the White House staff rather grudgingly admitted, Macy's "wheel ground exceedingly slow but exceedingly fine."[30] Candidates with impressive credentials and experience were uncovered after careful national searches.

The strong commitment to merit in the Johnson administration greatly disturbed certain advisers who were responsible for maintaining the president's political support. James Rowe, who was Johnson's campaign director in both 1964 and 1968, constantly hounded Macy, without success, to consider political loyalists more carefully. Rowe believed Johnson's personnel policy was gratuitously inattentive to political exigencies. At one point he ended a memo to Macy by saying, "Perhaps you can train some of those career men to run the political campaign in 1968. (It ain't as easy as you government people appear to think it is.)" Macy never responded, but the president called the next day to defend the policies of his personnel director and to chastise Rowe for seeking to interfere in the appointment process.[31]

The rupture between the presidency and the party made it difficult to sustain political enthusiasm and organizational support for the Great Society. The Democrats' poor showing in the 1966 congressional elections precipitated a firestorm of criticism about the president's inattention to party politics, criticism that continued until Johnson withdrew from the presidential campaign in 1968. Yet Johnson and most of his advisers felt that this de-emphasis on partisanship was necessary if the administration was to achieve programmatic reform and coordinate the increasingly unwieldy activities of government. During the early days of the Johnson presidency, one of his more thoughtful aides, Horace Busby, wrote Johnson a long memo in which he stressed the importance of establishing an institutional basis for the Great Society. About a year later, that same aide expressed great satisfaction that the Johnson presidency had confounded its critics in achieving notable institutional changes. In fact, these changes seemed to mark the full triumph of the Democrats as the party to end party politics:

Most startling is that while all recognize Johnson as a great politician his appointments have been the most consistently free of politics of any President—in the Cabinet or at lower levels.

On record, history will remember this as the most important era of nonpartisanship since the "Era of Good Feeling" more than a century ago at the start of the nineteenth century. Absence of politics and partisanship is one reason the GOP is having a hard time mounting any respectable offense against either Johnson or his program.[32]

As in the case of the New Deal, however, the institutional innovations of the Great Society did not eliminate "politics" from the activities of the executive branch. Rather, the Great Society extended the merging of politics and administration that had characterized executive reform during the 1930s. For example, in order to improve his use of the appointment process as a tool of political administration, Johnson issued an executive order to create a new category of positions in the executive branch, called Noncareer Executive Assignments (NEAs). In recognition of their direct involvement in policy making, NEAs were exempted from the usual civil service requirements.

To be sure, NEAs gave Johnson a stronger foothold in the agencies.[33] But the criteria his administration used to fill these positions emphasized loyalty to Johnson's program rather than a more narrow, personal commitment to the president. Consequently, Johnson's active role as manager of the federal service, which John Macy considered unprecedented for a "modern-day Chief Executive," helped to revive the high morale and programmatic commitment that had characterized the bureaucracy during the 1930s.[34] As the White House aide Bill Moyers urged in a memo to the newly created Department of Housing and Urban Development, the goal of the Great Society was to renew "some of the zeal—coupled with sound, tough executive management of the New Deal days."[35]

The legacy of Johnson's assault on party politics was apparent in the 1968 election. By 1966, Democratic leaders no longer felt they were part of a national coalition. As 1968 approached, the Johnson administration was preparing a campaign task force that would work independently of the regular party apparatus.[36] These actions greatly accelerated the breakdown of the state and local Democratic machinery, placing party organizations in acute distress in nearly every large state.[37] By the time Johnson withdrew from the election in March 1968, the Democratic party was already in the midst of a lengthy period of decay that was accentuated, but not really caused, by the conflict over the Vietnam War.

Thus, the tumultuous 1968 Democratic convention and the party reforms, spawned by the McGovern-Fraser Commission, that followed in its wake should be viewed as the culmination of long-standing efforts to free the presidency from traditional partisan influences. In many respects, the expansion of presidential primaries and other changes in nomination politics initiated by the commission were a logical extension of the modern presidency. The very quietness of the revolution in party rules that took place during the 1970s is evidence in itself that the party system was forlorn by the end of the Johnson era. These changes could not have been accomplished over the opposition of alert and vigorous party leaders.[38]

Johnson was well aware that elements were in place for the collapse of the regular party apparatus by 1968. From 1966 on, his aides bombarded him with memos warning of the disarray in the Democratic party organization. Johnson also was informed that reform forces in the states were creating "a new ball game with new rules." These memos indicated that the exploitation of a weakened party apparatus by insurgents would allow someone with as little national prominence as the antiwar senator Eugene McCarthy to mount a head-on challenge against Johnson.[39] The president expressed his own recognition of the decline of party politics in a private meeting with Humphrey on April 3, 1968, a few days after he announced his decision not to run for reelection. Although indicating his intention to remain publicly neutral, Johnson wished the vice president well. But he expressed concern about Humphrey's ability to win the support of the party organization: "This the president cannot assure the Vice President because he could not assure it for himself."[40] Like Roosevelt, Johnson had greatly diminished his political capital in pursuit of programmatic innovation.

Richard Nixon, Nonpartisanship, and the Demise of the Modern Presidency

Considering that the New Deal and Great Society were established by replacing traditional party politics with administration, it is not surprising that when a conservative challenge to liberal reform emerged, it entailed the creation of a conservative "administrative presidency."[41] This development further contributed to the decline of partisan politics.

Until the 1960s, opponents of the welfare state were generally opposed to the modern presidency, which had served as the fulcrum of liberal reform. Nevertheless, by the end of the Johnson administration, it became clear that a strong conservative movement would require an activist program of retrenchment in order to counteract the enduring effects of the New Deal and Great Society. Once the opponents of liberal public policy, primarily housed in the Republican party, recognized this, they looked to the possibility that, ideologically, the modern presidency could be a two-edged sword.

The administrative actions of the Nixon presidency were a logical extension of the practices of Roosevelt and Johnson. The centralization of authority in the White House and the reduction of the regular Republican organization to perfunctory status during the Nixon years was hardly new.[42] The complete autonomy of the Committee for the Re-Election of the President (CREEP) from the regular Republican organization in the 1972 campaign was but the final stage of a long process of White House preemption of the national committee's political responsibilities. And the administrative reform program that was pursued after Nixon's reelection, in which executive authority was concentrated in the hands of White House operatives and four cabinet "supersecretaries," was the culmination of a long-standing tendency in the modern presidency to reconstitute the executive branch as a formidable and independent instrument of government.[43]

Thus, just as Roosevelt's presidency anticipated the Great Society, Johnson's presidency anticipated the administrative presidency of Richard Nixon. Indeed, the strategy of pursuing policy goals through administrative capacities that had been created for the most part by Democratic presidents was considered especially suitable by a minority Republican president who faced a hostile Congress and bureaucracy intent on preserving those presidents' programs. Nixon actually surpassed previous modern presidents in viewing the party system as an obstacle to effective governance.

Yet, mainly because of the Watergate scandal, Nixon's presidency had the effect of strengthening opposition to the unilateral use of presidential power, even as it further attenuated the bonds that linked presidents to the party system. The evolution of the modern presidency now left the office in complete institutional isolation. This isolation continued during the Ford and Carter years, so much so that by the end of the 1970s scholars were lamenting the demise of the presidency as well as of the party system.

The Reagan Presidency and the Revitalization of Party Politics

The development of the modern presidency fostered a serious decline in the traditional local and patronage-based parties. Yet some developments during the Reagan presidency suggested that a phoenix had emerged from the ashes. The erosion of old-style partisan politics had allowed a more national and issue-oriented party system to develop, forging new links between presidents and their parties.

The Republican party in particular developed a formidable organizational apparatus, which displayed unprecedented strength at the national level. The refurbishing of the GOP organization was largely due to the efforts of William Brock, who during his tenure as chair of the Republican National Committee (RNC) from 1976 to 1980 set out to rejuvenate and ultimately to revolutionize the national party. After 1976 the RNC and the two other national Republican campaign bodies, the National Republican Senatorial Committee and the National Republican Congressional (House) Committee, greatly expanded their efforts to raise funds and provide services at the national level for state and local GOP candidates. Moreover, these efforts carried the national party into activities, such as the publication of public policy journals and the distribution of comprehensive briefing books for candidates, that demonstrated its interest in generating programmatic proposals that might be politically useful. The Democrats lagged behind in party-building efforts, but the losses they suffered in the 1980 elections encouraged them to modernize the national political machinery, openly imitating some of the devices employed by the Republicans. As a result, the traditional party apparatus, based on patronage and state and local organizations, gave way to a more programmatic party politics, based on the national organization. Arguably, a party system had finally evolved that was compatible with the national polity forged on the anvil of the New Deal.[44]

The revival of the Republican party as a force against government by administration seemed to complete the development of a new American party system. The nomination and election of Ronald Reagan, a far more ideological conservative than Nixon, galvanized the Republican commitment to programs, such as "regulatory relief" and "new federalism," that severely challenged the institutional legacy of the New Deal. Had such a trend continued, the circumvention of the regular political process by administrative action may well have been displaced by the sort of full-scale debate about political questions usually associated with critical realignments.

Significantly, it was Reagan who broke with the tradition of the modern presidency and identified closely with his party. The president worked hard to strengthen the Republicans' organizational and popular base, surprising his own political director with his "total readiness" to shoulder such partisan responsibilities as making numerous fund-raising appearances for the party and its candidates.[45] Apparently, after having spent the first fifty years of his life as a Democrat, Reagan brought the enthusiasm of a convert to Republican activities.

The experience of the Reagan administration suggests how the relationship between the president and the party can be mutually beneficial. Republican party strength provided Reagan with the support of a formidable institution, solidifying his personal popularity and facilitating the support of his program in Congress. As a result, the Reagan presidency was able to suspend the paralysis that seemed to afflict American government in the 1970s, even though the Republicans never attained control of the House of Representatives. In turn, Reagan's popularity served the party by strengthening its fund-raising efforts and promoting a shift in voters' party loyalties, placing the Republicans by 1985 in a position of virtual parity with the Democrats for the first time since the 1940s.[46] It may be, then, that the 1980s marked the watershed both for a new political era and for a renewed link between presidents and the party system.

Nevertheless, the separation of political institutions in the United States provides a precarious setting for comprehensive party programs. It is unlikely that the emergence of strong national party organizations will fundamentally alter the limited possibilities for party government under the American Constitution, a fact that will continue to encourage modern presidents, particularly those intent on ambitious policy reform, to emphasize popular appeal and administrative action rather than "collective responsibility." It is not surprising, therefore, that the Reagan presidency frequently pursued its program with acts of administrative discretion that short-circuited the legislative process and weakened efforts to carry out broad-based party policies. The Iran-contra scandal, for example, was not simply a matter of the president's being asleep on his watch. Rather, it revealed the Reagan administration's determination to assume a more forceful anti-communist posture in Central America in the face of a recalcitrant Congress and bureaucracy.[47]

Sen. Richard Lugar, who as chair of the Foreign Relations Committee from 1985 to 1987 acted as Reagan's Senate floor leader in matters of foreign policy, considers the Iran-contra affair to have been a "glaring exception" to Reagan's general willingness to consult with Congress and to work closely with the Republican leadership. The irony, according to Lugar, is that this uncharacteristic inattention to partisan responsibility made possible the president's "most signal policy failure."[48]

Yet a close examination of policy making during the Reagan years provides other examples of the administration's resorting to unilateral executive action. From the start, in fact, the Reagan White House often pursued programmatic change by using the administrative tactics that characterized the Nixon years. Not only was policy centered in the White House Office and other support agencies in the Executive Office of the President, but much care was taken to plant White House loyalists in the departments and agencies—persons who could be relied on to ride herd on civil servants and carry forth the president's program. Most significant, a wide range of deregulation policies were pursued, not through legislative change, but by administrative inaction, delay, and repeal. President Reagan's Executive Orders 12,291 and 12,498 mandated a comprehensive review of proposed agency regulations and centralized the review process in the Office of Management and Budget (OMB).[49] Reagan also appointed a Task Force on Regulatory Relief, headed by Vice President Bush, to apply cost-benefit analyses to existing rules. In this light, the Iran-contra scandal may be seen not as an aberration but as an extreme example of how the Reagan administration reacted when it anticipated or was confronted with resistance to its proposals by Congress.

Indeed, the importance of presidential politics and executive administration in the Reagan presidency may actually have weakened the prospects for a Republican realignment. The journalist Sidney Blumenthal has argued that Reagan "did not reinvent the Republican party so much as transcend it. His primary political instrument was the conservative movement, which inhabited the party out of convenience."[50] Blumenthal's observation is only partly correct—Reagan's commitment to strengthening his party was sincere and, in many respects, effective. Nevertheless, his administration's devotion to certain tenets of conservative ideology led it to rely on unilateral executive action and on the mobilization of conservative citizen groups in a way that ultimately compromised the president's support for the Republican party. "Too many of those around [the president] seem to have a sense of party that begins and ends in the oval office," William Brock, then secretary of labor, lamented in 1987. "Too many really don't understand what it means to link the White House to a party in a way that creates an alliance between the presidency, the House, and the Senate, or between the national party and officials at the state and local level."[51] This criticism was echoed by many GOP officials during the final two years of the Reagan presidency.

As such, Reagan did not transform Washington completely. Rather, he strengthened the Republican beachhead in the nation's capital, solidifying his party's recent dominance of the presidency and providing better opportunities for conservatives in the Washington community. Reagan's landslide reelection in 1984 did not prevent the Democrats from maintaining control of the House of Representatives; nor did his plea to the voters during the 1986 congressional campaign to elect Republican majorities prevent the Democrats from recapturing control of the Senate.

Concomitantly, Reagan's two terms witnessed a revitalization of the struggle between the executive and legislative branches; indeed, his conservative program became the foundation for more fundamental philosophical and policy differences between them than in the past. The Iran-contra affair and the battles to control regulatory policy were marked not just by differences between the president and Congress about policy, but by each branch's efforts to weaken the other. The efforts of Republicans to compensate for their inability to control Congress by seeking to circumvent legislative restrictions on presidential conduct were matched by Democratic initiatives to burden the executive with smothering legislative oversight.[52] The opposition to liberal reform, then, did not end in a challenge to national administrative power but in a raw and disruptive battle to control its services.

Reagan's Legacy and the Accession of George Bush

The 1988 election seemed to indicate that divided government had become an enduring characteristic of American politics. The Bush campaign took its shape from the Reagan legacy: in the final analysis, Bush's nomination by the Republican party and his victory by a substantial margin against his Democratic opponent, Gov. Michael Dukakis of Massachusetts, were expressions of the voters' approval of the Reagan administration.[53] Yet the 1988 election also revealed the limits of the Reagan revolution, reflecting in its outcome the underlying pattern that had characterized American politics since 1968: Republican dominance in the White House, Democratic ascendancy almost everywhere else. In fact, the 1988 election represented an extreme manifestation of this pattern. Never before had a president been elected while the other party gained ground in the House, Senate, the state legislatures, and the state governorships. Never before had voters given a newly elected president fewer fellow partisans in Congress than they gave Bush.[54]

Bush's first year as president revealed both his skill as a political conciliator and the continuing obstacles to the restoration of partisanship to the presidency. Facing a Democratic Congress and lacking his predecessor's rhetorical ability, Bush had little choice but to reach across party lines to accomplish his goals. This "kinder, gentler" approach to Congress was often reciprocated during his first year. After intensive negotiations, Bush managed to reach agreements with Congress on two of the most troublesome issues he faced upon taking office—aid to the contra rebels in Nicaragua and the crisis of the savings and loan industry. The president won high marks from many legislators for his give-and-take approach to domestic and foreign policy, as well as for the personal attention he paid to the political needs of Democrats and Republicans alike. But several Republicans, especially the party's more conservative members, grew restless at Bush's disinclination to lead in a partisan style. Jeffrey A. Eisenach, who was the adviser for the 1988 presidential campaign of Gov. Pierre S. Dupont of Delaware, expressed the widespread fear of conservatives that the Republican party would not gain control of Congress in the 1990s should Bush "submerge the difference between the parties so it's impossible to create a set of issues to distinguish Republicans and Democrats."[55]

In many ways, however, Bush's conciliatory approach camouflaged an aggressive partisanship aimed at extending the political effects of the Reagan revolution beyond the presidency. Having served as a Republican county chair in Texas during the 1960s and as RNC chair during the Watergate scandal (the first president ever to have served as national party chair), Bush came to the White House with a zest for his partisan duties. He not only continued the Reagan practice of campaigning for fellow Republicans and of raising funds for the regular party apparatus, but he also gave his party's national organization a higher profile than any modern president. Significantly, Bush placed his principal political adviser, Lee Atwater, not in the White House (the usual practice of modern presidents), but in the national party chair.[56]

With the president's approval Atwater did not confine himself to the party chair's customary role of presiding over the party's institutions. Instead, he sought to transform the RNC into an aggressive political organization that would highlight the differences between Republicans and Democrats on economic, social, and foreign policy issues at every level of government. As such, Atwater's aggressive partisanship provided balance to a presidency that otherwise preferred consultation and compromise to confrontation.

Yet the Bush administration's efforts to consolidate and extend the Republican gains of the Reagan years were not successful. In the final analysis, the failure of this project can be explained by fundamental disagreements between liberals and conservatives that defied Bush's efforts to forge a more inclusive Republican party. In the fall of 1990, a serious intraparty struggle emerged over the 1991 budget. Seeking to work out a compromise with the Democratic congressional leadership, Bush accepted a fiscal package that included excise tax hikes on gasoline and home heating oil. In turn, the Democratic leadership agreed to cut Medicare spending. The deal left liberal Democrats and conservative Republicans furious. Especially strong resistance arose in the House, where the Democratic opposition abhorred the Medicare cuts and the regressive nature of the new taxes and many Republicans, led by Minority Whip Newt Gingrich, felt betrayed by Bush's willingness to abandon his celebrated campaign pledge to oppose new taxes.[57]

At the urging of Democratic and Republican supporters of the tax agreement, Bush went on television to try to sell the package to the American people. This was the president's first attempt to mobilize public opinion to pressure Congress; it ended in dismal failure. Despite Bush's rhetorical appeal and feverish administration lobbying efforts on Capitol Hill, a majority of House Republicans followed Gingrich in opposing the compromise, dooming it to defeat. The subsequent budget agreement that passed the House and the Senate included a hike in the tax rate on high-income taxpayers, a proposal that Bush had bitterly opposed. The agreement passed with the support of Democratic majorities, but most Republicans in Congress voted against it.

Bush's problems were compounded by the loss of Atwater, who had collapsed in early March while delivering a speech. Physicians soon diagnosed a brain tumor, and Atwater, although he continued to occupy the party chair, had to abandon his political responsibilities. This left the Republican headquarters without effective leadership for almost a year, before Bush, after receiving several rejections, finally tapped Secretary of Agriculture Clayton Yeutter, to replace Atwater.[58] Atwater's illness returned the center of political strategy to the White House, leaving Chief of Staff John Sununu as Bush's main political adviser. Lacking his predecessor's close personal relationship with the president, Yeutter was not in a position to challenge the preeminence of the White House staff in the conduct of political operations.[59] Reflecting on the low morale at party headquarters in the face of its declining importance, a former member of the Research Division wrote, "RNC is a sad place. . . . Few people there care about issues. The only 'policy'-oriented material coming out of the First Street [RNC] bureaucracy consists of brief pamphlets that are nothing more than rewrites of White House press releases. Working there was the most frustrating experience of my life."[60]

The bitter feud over the 1991 budget and the loss of Atwater left the Republican party in a state of disarray during the 1990 midterm election campaign. Bush's offers to help his fellow partisans were spurned by some, who could not forgive the president for reneging on his "no new taxes" pledge. Conservatives believed that Bush had deserted not only a sacred pledge but the party's best hope of becoming a majority in the House and Senate. In addition, the budget debacle obscured the differences between the parties, thus undercutting Republican congressional candidates' chances to campaign in 1990 on what they considered the party's most fundamental and effective issue. Finally, in late October, Bush became embroiled in a feud with the co-chair of the Republican Congressional Campaign Committee, Ed Rollins, who circulated a memo urging House GOP candidates not to hesitate to distance their campaigns from the president. This spectacle embarrassed the White House, which pressured Rollins to resign in early 1991. But the damage had been done— Republicans had lost their philosophical compass along with further ground in the House and Senate.[61]

In sum, the closer ties that Reagan and Bush tried to forge between the modern presidency and the Republican party did not alter the unprecedented partisan and electoral divisions that characterized the era of divided government. Indeed, the persistence of divided government itself retarded the restoration of partisanship to the presidency. During the early days of his presidency, Bush attempted to reach out to Democrats in Congress in order to restore the badly frayed consensus in American politics. But he gave no reasonable defense of his pragmatism. Thus, once he abandoned his antitax pledge and lost his top political strategist to illness, Bush's presidency floated adrift. His search for agreement with Congress in the absence of any clear principles threatened the modern presidency with the same sort of isolation and weakness that had characterized the Ford and Carter years.[62]

The 1992 Election and Beyond

The Bush presidency was a painful reminder of the modern executive's "extraordinary isolation."[63] Since FDR, the president had been freed from the constraints of party, only to be enslaved by a volatile political environment that often would rapidly undercut popular support. In 1991, Bush basked in the triumphs of the Gulf and cold wars, his popularity rating at a historic high of about 90 percent; in 1992, he was soundly defeated in his bid for reelection by the governor of Arkansas, William "Bill" Clinton. The Democrats not only captured the presidency but also preserved their majorities in the House and the Senate. For twelve years, the voters' striking ambiguity about the parties had left the government in a cross-fire between a Republican president and Democratic Congress. In 1992, however, an exit poll revealed that a plurality of voters now preferred to have the presidency and Congress controlled by the Democratic party, in the hope that ideological polarization and institutional conflict would be brought to an end.[64] This hope was urged on by Clinton's promise to govern as a "new Democrat," an "agent of change" who would restore political consensus in American politics.

In truth, the 1992 election contained both optimistic and pessimistic portents for the modern presidency. Although the Democrats ran an effective campaign and Clinton skillfully, if not always boldly, addressed his party's liabilities, the election results showed that fundamental conflicts continued to divide Americans, even as they seemed united in their dissatisfaction with the way government worked. Clinton won only 43 percent of the popular vote, roughly the same percentage that losing Democratic candidates had received in the previous three elections. The strong support for the independent candidate H. Ross Perot reflected the continuing erosion of partisan loyalties in the electorate.

Indeed, Perot's campaign, which garnered 19 percent of the popular vote (the most serious electoral challenge to the two-party system since Theodore Roosevelt's 1912 Progressive party campaign), suggested just how much presidential politics had been emancipated from the constraints of party. Perot had never held political office of any kind, and his campaign, dominated by thirty-minute commercials and hour-long appearances on talk shows, set a new standard for direct, plebiscitary appeals that threatened to sound the death knell of the party campaign. Disdaining importunities to form a third party from those interested in party renewal, Perot launched his campaign without the bother of a nominating convention. Instead, his supporters were called to arms on the popular Cable News Network talk show *Larry King Live*.[65]

Just as significant, Perot's call for better planning as a solution to government "gridlock" testified to the powerful appeal of simplified notions of "enlightened administration" in contemporary democratic politics. Perot proposed a novel forum in which to link the president to public opinion—the "electronic town hall." Somehow—in ways he never quite explained—public opinion would be used as a supplement to, or a substitute for, the deliberations and conflicts of constitutional government. With polls showing Perot leading both Bush and Clinton in the early part of the summer, his novel concept of presidential leadership seemed destined to play an important and disconcerting part in American politics. "Perot hints broadly at an even bolder new order," the historian Alan Brinkley wrote in July 1992, "in which the president, checked only by direct expressions of popular desire, will roll up his sleeves and solve the nation's problems."[66]

In the end, however, the American people invested their hope for constructive change more cautiously, in the possibility that Clinton embodied a new form of Democratic politics that could correct and renew the progressive tradition as shaped by the New Deal. During the 1980s, Clinton was a leader of the Democratic Leadership Council, a moderate group in the Democratic party that developed many of the ideas that became the central themes of his run for the presidency. As Clinton declared frequently during the campaign, these ideas represented a new philosophy of government that would "honor middle class values, restore public trust, create a new sense of community and make America work again." He heralded "a new social contract," a "new covenant"—one that in the name of responsibility and community would seek to constrain the demands for economic rights that had been unleashed by the Roosevelt revolution. The essence of Clinton's message was that the liberal commitment to guaranteeing economic welfare through entitlement programs such as Social Security, Medicare, Medicaid, and Aid to Families with Dependent Children had gone too far. The objective of the new covenant was to correct the tendency of Americans to celebrate individual rights and government entitlements without any sense of the mutual obligations they had to each other and their country.[67]

Clinton's commitment to educational opportunity best exemplified the objective of restoring a balance between rights and responsibility. Its central feature, a national service corps, was emblematic of the heart of the new covenant principle—national community. According to Clinton, a trust fund would be created, from which any American could draw money for a college education as long as they paid it back either as a small percentage of their life's income or with two years of service as teachers, as police officers, as child care workers, or in other activities that "our country desperately needs."[68]

Clinton pledged to dedicate his party to the new concept of justice he espoused. But his commitment to control government spending and recast the welfare state was obscured during the early days of his presidency by many traditional liberal actions. No sooner had he been inaugurated than Clinton announced his intention to issue executive orders to reverse the policy of Reagan and Bush of forbidding abortion counseling at federally funded clinics (the so-called "gag rule")—and to lift the long-standing ban on homosexuals in the military. These policies could be carried out "with a stroke of the pen," Clinton believed, leaving him free, as he promised during his quest for the presidency, to focus "like a laser" on the economy.[69]

There was no prospect, however, that such divisive social issues could be resolved through executive orders. To be sure, the development of the administrative presidency gave presidents more power to exercise domestic policy autonomously. Yet with the expansion of national administration to issues that shaped the direction and character of American public life, this power proved to be illusory. The proposal to lift the ban on gays and lesbians in the military plagued Clinton throughout the critical early months of his presidency. Intense opposition from the respected head of the Joint Chiefs of Staff, Colin Powell, and the influential chair of the Senate Armed Services Committee, Sam Nunn of Georgia, forced Clinton to defer his executive order for six months while he sought a compromise solution. But the delay and the compromise aroused the ire of gay and lesbian activists, who had given strong financial and organizational support to Clinton during the election. Most damaging for the new president was that the issue became a glaring benchmark of his inability to revitalize progressive politics as an instrument to redress the economic insecurity and political alienation of the middle class.

The bitter partisan fight in the summer of 1993 over the administration's budgetary program served only to reinforce doubts about Clinton's ability to lead the nation in a new, more harmonious direction. Even though Clinton's budget plan promised to reduce the deficit, it involved new taxes and an array of social programs that Republicans and conservative Democrats perceived as standard "tax and spend" liberalism. In August 1993 Congress enacted a modified version of the plan, albeit by a razor-thin margin and without any support from Republicans, who voted unanimously against it in the House and Senate. Clinton won this narrow, bruising victory only after promising moderate Democrats that he would put together another package of spending cuts in the fall. But this uneasy compromise failed to dispel the view that Clinton had failed to live up to his campaign promise to transcend the bitter philosophical and partisan battles of the Reagan and Bush years.[70]

In fact, Clinton said and did little about a new covenant during the first year of his presidency. He appointed Donna Shalala to head the Department of Health and Human Services, even though she had expressed little support for reshaping social welfare policy. In the February address to Congress, in which he laid out his administration's goals, Clinton, instead of trumpeting the reciprocal obligations between citizens and their government, proposed a new set of entitlements in the form of job training, a college education, and health care. Clinton's proposal to make college loans available to all Americans did include the much touted plan to form a national service corps. But the enactment of a scaled-down version of this program in August was lost amid Clinton's promises to expand the welfare state.[71]

The apologetic stance that Clinton displayed in the face of traditional liberal causes was, to a point, understandable; it was a logical response to the modern institutional separation between the presidency and the party. The moderate wing of the Democratic party that he represented—including the Democratic Leadership Council—was a minority wing. The majority of liberal interest group activists and Democratic members of Congress still preferred entitlements to obligations and regulations to responsibilities. The media-driven caucuses and primaries, a legacy of the McGovern-Fraser reforms, had given him the opportunity to seize the Democratic label as an outsider candidate but offered no means to effect a transformation of his party when he took office. To bring about the new mission of progressivism that he advocated during the election, Clinton would have to risk a brutal confrontation with the major powers in the Democratic party.[72]

Yet no president had risked such a confrontation with his party since Roosevelt's failed purge campaign. It is not surprising, therefore, that Clinton's allies in the Democratic Leadership Council urged him to renew his "credentials as an outsider" by going over the heads of the party leadership in Congress and taking his message directly to the people. The new president could "break gridlock," they argued, only by appealing to the large number of independents in the electorate who had voted for Perot—that is, by "forging new and sometimes bipartisan coalitions around an agenda that moves beyond the polarized left-right debate."[73]

In the fall of 1993, Clinton took a page from his former political associates in his successful campaign to secure congressional approval of the North American Free Trade Agreement (NAFTA) with Canada and Mexico. The fight for NAFTA caused Clinton to defend free enterprise ardently and to oppose the protectionism of labor unions, which still represented one of the most important constituencies in the national Democratic party. Clinton's victory was owed partly to the active support of the Republican congressional leadership; in fact, a majority of Republicans in the House and Senate supported the free trade agreement, whereas a majority of Democrats, including the House majority leader and majority whip, opposed it. No less important, however, was the Clinton administration's mobilization of popular support. The turning point in the struggle came when the administration challenged Perot, the leading opponent of NAFTA, to debate Vice President Albert Gore on *Larry*

King Live. Gore's optimistic defense of open markets was well received by the large television audience, rousing enough support for the treaty to persuade a majority of legislators in both houses of Congress to approve the trade agreement.[74]

With the successful fight over NAFTA, moderate Democrats began to hope that Clinton had finally begun the task of dedicating his party to the principles and policies he had espoused during the campaign. But the next major legislative battle would be for the administration's health care program, which promised to "guarantee all Americans a comprehensive package of benefits over the course of an entire lifetime." As such it would create a new government entitlement program and an administrative apparatus that would signal the revitalization rather than the reform of the traditional welfare state.[75] Although the administration made conciliatory overtures to the plan's opponents, hoping to forge bipartisan cooperation on Capitol Hill and a broad consensus among the general public, the possibilities for comprehensive reform hinged on settling differences about the appropriate role of government, which had divided the parties and the country for the past two decades. Thus, long after being elected to the presidency, Clinton still faced the profound challenge of establishing the boundaries in which his party and domestic policy could be reformed.

Yet it might be unreasonable, indeed, dangerous, to rely so heavily on presidents to determine the contours of political action. The modern presidency operates in a political arena that is seldom congenial to meaningful political debate and that all too often is guilty of deflecting attention from the painful struggles about the appropriate meaning of liberalism or the relative merits of contemporary liberalism and conservatism. With the liberation of the executive from many of the constraints of party leadership and the rise of the mass media, presidents have resorted to rhetoric and administration, tools with which they have sought to forge new, more personal ties with the public. But this form of politics has perhaps promised the people more security for economic welfare than a free society can tolerate, and it has exposed them to the kind of public figures who will exploit citizens' impatience with the difficult tasks involved in sustaining a healthy constitutional democracy.

Presidents who enjoy prominent places in history have taken the American people to school, educating them about new policy proposals and persuading them to make difficult choices. But they have done so as great party leaders, in the midst of critical partisan realignments. Public education of this sort is rarely encountered on talk shows or in electronic town meetings. Instead, in such forums candidates and presidents are tempted to seek the devotion of the American people in order to manipulate them.

Critical partisan elections have enabled each generation to claim its right to redefine the Constitution's principles and reorganize its institutions. The New Deal continued this unending task to ensure that each generation could affirm its attachment to constitutional government. The burden of this generation is to hold the modern presidency to account, to recapture the understanding of democracy that has made such momentous deliberation and choice so central to the pursuit of America's political destiny. In the nation's present hour of discontent, this effort requires above all the will to acknowledge the limits and appropriate tasks of national administrative power.

Notes

1. For a more detailed treatment of the issues discussed in this chapter, see Sidney M. Milkis, *The President and the Parties: The Transformation of the American Party System Since the New Deal* (New York: Oxford University Press, 1993).

2. Franklin D. Roosevelt, *Public Papers and Addresses*, 13 vols. (New York: Random House, 1938–1950), 1:751–752.

3. Woodrow Wilson, *Constitutional Government in the United States* (New York: Columbia University Press, 1908), 68–69.

4. Arthur S. Link, "Woodrow Wilson and the Democratic Party," *Review of Politics* 18 (April 1956): 146–156. Wilson effectively established himself as the principal spokesman for the Democratic party. But he accepted traditional partisan practices concerning legislative deliberations and appointments in order to gain support for his program in Congress, thus failing to strengthen either the Democratic party's national organization or its fundamental commitment to progressive principles.

5. Personal and Political Diary of Homer Cummings, January 5, 1933, box 234, no. 2, 90, Homer Cummings Papers (no. 9973), Manuscripts Department, University of Virginia Library, Charlottesville.

6. Edward J. Flynn, *You're the Boss* (New York: Viking, 1947), 153.

7. Alfred Phillips, Jr., to Franklin D. Roosevelt, June 9, 1937; and Roosevelt to Phillips, June 16, 1937, President's Personal File, 2666, Franklin D. Roosevelt Library, Hyde Park, New York.

8. Franklin Clarkin, "Two-Thirds Rule Facing Abolition," *New York Times*, January 5, 1936, IV 10.

9. Thomas Stokes, *Chip Off My Shoulder* (Princeton, N.J.: Princeton University Press, 1940), 503. For an assessment of Roosevelt's role in the abolition of the two-thirds rule that also addresses the significance of this party reform, see Harold F. Bass, Jr., "Presidential Party Leadership and Party Reform: Franklin D. Roosevelt and the Abrogation of the Two-Thirds Rule" (Paper presented at the annual meeting of the Southern Political Science Association, Nashville, Tennessee, November 7–9, 1985).

10. Raymond Clapper, "Roosevelt Tries the Primaries," *Current History*, October 1938, 16.

11. Morton Frisch, *Franklin D. Roosevelt: The Contribution of the New Deal to American Political Thought and Practice* (Boston: S. T. Wayne, 1975), 79.

12. Frankfurter to Roosevelt, August 9, 1937, box 210, Papers of Thomas G. Corcoran; Roosevelt to Frankfurter, August 12, 1937, reel 60, Felix Frankfurter Papers; both in Manuscript Division, Library of Congress, Washington, D.C.

13. Herbert Croly, a fellow Progressive, criticized Wilson's concept of presidential party leadership along these lines. Although he shared Wilson's view that executive power needed to be strengthened, Croly argued that the "necessity of such leadership [was] itself an evidence of the decrepitude of the two-party system." A strong executive would not reform parties but instead would establish the conditions in which partisan responsibility would decline and a more direct and palpable link between the president and public opinion would be created. The emergence of a modern executive and the destruction of the two-party system, Croly wrote, "was an indispensable condition of the success of progressive democracy." *Progressive Democracy* (New York: Macmillan, 1914), 345, 348.

14. The purge campaign galvanized opposition throughout the nation, apparently contributing to the heavy losses the Democrats sustained in the 1938 general elections.

15. The term "second bill of rights" comes from Roosevelt's 1944 State of the Union message, which reaffirmed the New Deal's commitment to an economic constitutional order. Roosevelt, *Public Papers and Addresses*, 13:40.

16. *Report of the President's Committee on Administrative Management* (Washington, D.C.: U.S. Government Printing Office, 1937), 53. The President's Committee on Administrative Management, headed by Louis Brownlow, played a central role in the planning and politics of executive reorganization from 1936 to 1940. For a full analysis of the commission, see Barry Karl, *Executive Reorganization and Reform in the New Deal* (Cambridge: Harvard University Press, 1963).

17. Memorandum, Herbert Emmerich to Louis Brownlow, June 29, 1938, on "Extending the Competitive Classified Civil Service"; and Civil Service Commission, statement regarding executive order of June 24, 1938, extending the merit system; both in Papers of the President's Committee on Administrative Management, Roosevelt Library; see also Richard Polenberg, *Reorganizing Roosevelt's Government* (Cambridge: Harvard University Press, 1966), 22–23, 184. With the passage of the Ramspeck Act in 1940, this convulsive movement to reshape the civil service was virtually completed. The Ramspeck Act authorized the president to extend the merit system to nearly 200,000 positions previously exempted by law, many of them occupied by supporters of the New Deal. Roosevelt took early advantage of this authorization in 1941. By executive order he extended the coverage of the civil service protection to include about 95 percent of the permanent service. Leonard White, "Franklin Roosevelt and the Public Service," *Public Personnel Review* 6 (July 1945): 142.

18. Paul Van Riper, *History of the United States Civil Service* (Evanston, Ill.: Row, Peterson, 1958), 327. The merging of politics and administration took an interesting course as a result of the Hatch Act, which was passed in 1939. Until the passage of this bill, which barred most federal employees from participating in campaigns, the Roosevelt administration was making use of the growing army of federal workers in state and local political activity, including some of the purge campaigns. The Hatch Act

demolished the national Roosevelt political machine as distinct from the regular Democratic organization. Yet Roosevelt was more interested in orienting the executive branch as an instrument of programmatic reform than he was in developing a national political machine, and the insulation of federal officials from party politics was not incompatible with such a task. This explains why Roosevelt, although he fought against passage of the Hatch Act, decided to sign it.

19. Richard A. Rovere, "A Man for This Age Too," *New York Times Magazine*, April 11, 1965, 118. For an account of the influence of Roosevelt and the New Deal on Johnson's presidency, see William E. Leuchtenburg, *In the Shadow of FDR: From Harry Truman to Ronald Reagan*, rev. ed. (Ithaca, N.Y.: Cornell University Press, 1985), chap. 4; and Milkis, *The President and the Parties*, chaps. 7 and 8.

20. Lyndon Baines Johnson, *The Vantage Point: Perspectives of the Presidency, 1963–1969* (New York: Holt, Rinehart and Winston, 1971), 323.

21. Theodore White, *The Making of the President, 1968* (New York: Atheneum, 1969), 107.

22. Rowland Evans and Robert Novak, "Too Late for LBJ," *Boston Globe*, December 21, 1966, 27.

23. David Broder, "Consensus Politics: End of an Experiment," *Atlantic Monthly*, October 1966, 62.

24. Doris Kearns, *Lyndon Johnson and the American Dream* (New York: New American Library, 1976), 256.

25. In a memorandum on one of the early strategy sessions that led to the Great Society, Larry O'Brien, Johnson's chief legislative aide, expressed concern about the acute political problems he anticipated would result from such an ambitious program. Memorandum, Larry O'Brien to Henry Wilson, November 24, 1964, Henry Wilson Papers, box 4, Lyndon Baines Johnson Library, Austin, Texas.

26. Interview with Horace Busby, June 25, 1987.

27. Memorandum, William Connel to Marvin Watson, August 27, 1967, Marvin Watson Files, box 31; Memorandum, Joseph Califano to the president, March 27, 1968, Office Files of the President (Dorothy Territo), box 10; both in Johnson Library.

28. Memorandum, Harry C. McPherson, Jr., and Clifford L. Alexander to the president, February 11, 1967, Office Files of Harry McPherson; Sherwin J. Markman, Oral History, by Dorothy Pierce McSweeny, tape 1, May 21, 1969, 24–36; both in Johnson Library. Many local Democrats felt threatened by the community action program with its provision for "maximum feasible participation." See Daniel P. Moynihan, *Maximum Feasible Misunderstanding* (New York: Free Press, 1970), 144–145.

29. William E. Leuchtenburg, "The Genesis of the Great Society," *Reporter*, April 21, 1966, 38.

30. Memorandum, Hayes Redmon to Bill Moyers, May 5, 1966, box 12, Office Files of Bill Moyers, Johnson Library. For an excellent book-length treatment of Johnson's personnel policy, see Richard L. Schott and Dagmar S. Hamilton, *People, Positions, and Power: The Political Appointments of Lyndon Johnson* (Chicago: University of Chicago Press, 1983).

31. Memorandum, James Rowe to John W. Macy, Jr., April 28, 1965, John Macy Papers, box 504; James H. Rowe, Oral History, by Joe B. Frantz, interview 2, September 16, 1969, 46–47; both in Johnson Library. Rowe's battles with Macy are noteworthy and ironic: as a charter member of the White House Office he performed Macy's role for the

Roosevelt administration, upholding the principle of merit against the patronage requests of the DNC chair James Farley and his successor, Ed Flynn.

32. On the importance of institutional reform, see Draft Memorandum, Horace Busby to Mr. Johnson, n.d., box 52, folder of memos to Mr. Johnson, June 1964; Busby quote is from Memorandum, Horace Busby for the president, September 21, 1965, box 51, Office Files of Horace Busby, Johnson Library.

33. Terry Moe, "The Politicized Presidency," in *The New Direction in American Politics*, ed. John E. Chubb and Paul E. Peterson (Washington, D.C.: Brookings Institution, 1985), 254.

34. Memorandum, Horace Busby to the president, April 21, 1965, and attached letter from John Macy (April 17, 1965), box 51, Office Files of Horace Busby, Johnson Library; Joseph Young, "Johnson Boost to Career People Called Strongest by a President," *Washington Post*, May 16, 1965; Eugene Patterson, "The Johnson Brand," *Atlanta Constitution*, April 30, 1965; and Raymond P. Brandt, "Johnson Inspires the Civil Service by Appointing His Top Aides from among Career Officials," *St. Louis Dispatch*, May 2, 1965. For a comprehensive treatment of Johnson's management of the bureaucracy, see James A. Anderson, "Presidential Management of the Bureaucracy and the Johnson Presidency: A Preliminary Exploration," *Congress and the President* 1 (Autumn 1984): 137–163.

35. Memorandum, Bill Moyers to the president, December 11, 1965, box 11, Office Files of Bill Moyers, Johnson Library.

36. James Rowe became quite concerned upon hearing of the task force proposal. He warned the White House staff that this might further weaken the regular party apparatus, which was "already suffering from shellshock both in Washington and around the country because of its impotent status." James Rowe, "A White Paper for the President on the 1968 Presidential Campaign," n.d., Marvin Watson Files, box 20, folder of Rowe, O'Brien, Cooke, Criswell Operation, Johnson Library.

37. Allan Otten, "The Incumbent's Edge," *Wall Street Journal*, December 28, 1967.

38. Byron E. Shafer, *Quiet Revolution: The Struggle for the Democratic Party and the Shaping of Post-Reform Politics* (New York: Russell Sage Foundation, 1983). In 1969 the Democratic National Committee, acting under the mandate from the 1968 Chicago Convention, established the Commission on Party Structure and Delegate Selection. Under the chairmanship first of Sen. George McGovern and, after 1971, of Congressman Donald Fraser, the commission developed a set of guidelines governing the state parties' procedures for selecting delegates to the national conventions. Their purpose was to weaken the prevailing party structure and to establish a more direct link between presidential candidates and the voters. The Democratic National Committee accepted all the guidelines of the McGovern-Fraser Commission and declared in the call for the 1972 convention that they constituted the standards that state Democratic parties, in qualifying and certifying delegates to the 1972 Democratic National Convention, must make "all efforts to comply with." The new rules eventually caused a majority of states to change from selecting delegates in closed councils of party regulars to electing them in direct primaries. Although the Democrats initiated these changes, many were codified in state laws that affected the Republican party almost as much. For a discussion of the long-term forces underlying the McGovern-Fraser reforms, see David B. Truman, "Party Reform, Party Atrophy, and Constitutional Change," *Political Science Quarterly* 99 (Winter 1984–1985): 637–655.

39. Memorandum, John P. Roche for the president, December 4, 1967, White House

Central Files, PL (Political Affairs) folder; Memorandum, Ben Wattenberg to the president, December 13, 1967, Marvin Watson Files, box 10; Memorandum, Ben Wattenberg to the president, March 13, 1968, Marvin Watson Files, box 11; all in Johnson Library.

40. Memorandum of conversation, April 5, 1968, White House Famous Names, box 6, Robert F. Kennedy folder, 1968 Campaign, Johnson Library.

41. Richard Nathan, *The Administrative Presidency* (New York: Wiley, 1983).

42. On Nixon's party leadership as president, see the Ripon Society and Clifford Brown, *Jaws of Victory* (Boston: Little, Brown, 1973), 226–242.

43. Nathan, *Administrative Presidency*, 43–56. Toward the end of the Johnson presidency, the administration gave attention to the need to consolidate further the president's control of the activities of the executive branch. Johnson's second task force on government organization—the Heineman task force—made many recommendations in 1967 that formed the basis of the Nixon administrative reform program. For example, it called for the regrouping of executive departments and agencies into a smaller number of "superdepartments" that would be "far more useful and much more responsive to, and representative of, Presidential perspectives and objectives than the scores of parochial department and agency heads who now share the line responsibilities of the executive branch." Johnson favored the Heineman task force's central recommendations and planned to implement some of them after his reelection in 1968; of course, Johnson's retirement came sooner than expected. Task Force on Government Organization, "The Organization and Management of the Great Society Programs," June 15, 1967, and "A Recommendation for the Future Organization of the Executive Branch," September 15, 1967, both reports located in *Outside Task Forces*, box 4, Task Force on Government Organization folder, Johnson Library. See also Peri Arnold, *Making the Managerial Presidency: Comprehensive Reorganization Planning, 1905–1980* (Princeton, N.J.: Princeton University Press, 1986), 268.

44. A. James Reichley, "The Rise of National Parties," in *The New Direction in American Politics*, 191–195. By the end of the 1980s, Reichley was much less hopeful that the emergent national parties were well suited to perform the parties' historic function of mobilizing public support for political values and substantive government approaches and policies. See his richly detailed study, *The Life of the Parties: A History of American Political Parties* (New York: Free Press, 1992), esp. chaps. 18–21.

45. Rhodes Cook, "Reagan Nurtures His Adopted Party to Strength," *Congressional Quarterly Weekly Report*, September 28, 1985, 1927–1930; David S. Broder, "A Party Leader Who Works at It," *Boston Globe*, October 21, 1985, 14; and personal interview with Mitchell Daniels, assistant to the president for political and governmental affairs, June 5, 1986.

46. Thomas E. Cavanaugh and James L. Sundquist, "The New Two-Party System," in *The New Direction in American Politics*.

47. As the minority report of the congressional committees investigating the Iran-contra affair acknowledged, "President Reagan gave his subordinates strong, clear and consistent guidance about the basic thrust of the policies he wanted them to pursue toward Nicaragua. There is some question and dispute about *precisely* the level at which he chose to follow the operational details. There is no doubt, however, . . . [that] the President set the U.S. policy toward Nicaragua, with few if any ambiguities, and then left subordinates more or less free to implement it." *Report of the Congressional Committees Investigating the Iran-Contra Affair*, 100th Cong., 1st sess., House Report 100-433, Senate Report 100-216 (Washington, D.C.: U.S. Government Printing Office, 1987), 501 (emphasis in original).

48. Interview with Sen. Richard Lugar, August 7, 1987.

49. Nixon transformed the Bureau of the Budget into the Office of Management and Budget by executive order in 1970, adding a cadre of presidentially appointed assistant directors for policy to stand between the OMB director and the bureau's civil servants. Consequently, the budget office both attained additional policy responsibility and became more responsive to the president. In the Reagan administration, the OMB was given a central role in remaking regulatory policy. See Richard A. Harris and Sidney M. Milkis, *The Politics of Regulatory Change: A Tale of Two Agencies* (New York: Oxford University Press, 1989).

50. Sidney Blumenthal, *The Rise of the Counter-Establishment: From Conservative Ideology to Political Power* (New York: Times Books), 9.

51. Interview with William E. Brock, August 12, 1987.

52. Benjamin Ginsberg and Martin Shefter, *Politics by Other Means: The Declining Importance of Elections in America* (New York: Basic Books, 1990).

53. On election day Bush won the support of at least 80 percent of the voters who approved of Reagan's performance, while losing the votes of the 40 percent of those who disapproved of Reagan by a margin of nine to one. Michael Nelson, "Constitutional Aspects of the Elections," in *The Elections of 1988*, ed. Michael Nelson (Washington, D.C.: CQ Press, 1989), 192.

54. Ibid., 195.

55. Jeffrey A. Eisenach is quoted in Burt Solomon, "Bush's Zeal for Partisan Duties Tempered by His Bipartisan Style," *National Journal*, October 28, 1989, 2651.

56. Solomon, "Bush's Zeal," 2651.

57. On the budget battles of 1990, see Barbara Sinclair, "Bush and the 101st Congress," in *The Bush Presidency: First Appraisals*, ed. Colin Campbell and Bert Rockman (Chatham, N.J.: Chatham House, 1991), 174–183.

58. Harold F. Bass, "George Bush: Party Leader" (Paper presented at the annual meeting of the American Political Science Association, Washington, D.C., August 29–September 1, 1991), 10–11.

59. Burt Solomon, "In Atwater's Absence, Sununu Is Bush's Top Political Advisor," *National Journal*, June 23, 1990, 1544–1555.

60. John J. Pitney, Jr., letter to the author, August 12, 1991.

61. The Democrats added 1 seat in the Senate, strengthening their majority to 56 to 44, and 8 seats to their already lopsided advantage in the House, yielding an advantage of 268 to 167. The losses were mild by historical standards; indeed, some Republicans argued that by losing only 8 seats in the House and 1 in the Senate, their party fared rather well in the midterm campaign. But this argument ignored the fact that the GOP was starting from a very low base in the legislature and that it suffered very disappointing defeats in the Florida and Texas gubernatorial races. James A. Barnes, "Back to Square One," *National Journal*, November 10, 1990, 2704–2709.

62. On the institutional conflicts and partisan estrangement that characterized the final two years of the Bush presidency, see Milkis, *The President and the Parties*, chap. 11.

63. The term "extraordinary isolation" is Woodrow Wilson's. See *Constitutional Government in the United States*, 69.

64. William Schneider, "A Loud Vote for Change," *National Journal*, November 7, 1992, 2544.

65. See, for example, Theodore J. Lowi, "The Party Crasher," *New York Times Magazine*, August 23, 1992, 28, 33.

66. Alan Brinkley, "Roots," *New Republic*, July 27, 1992.

67. William Clinton, "The New Covenant: Responsibility and Rebuilding the American Community" (Speech delivered at Georgetown University, Washington, D.C., October 23, 1991).

68. Similar ideas and attendant policy proposals are spelled out in detail in Will Marshall and Martin Schramm, eds., *Mandate for Change* (New York: Berkeley Books, 1993).

69. On President Clinton's use of executive orders, his attempt to carry out policy "with the stroke of a pen," see Thomas Friedman, "Ready or Not Clinton Is Rattling the Country," *Washington Post*, January 31, 1993, IV 1. Candidate Clinton's promise to focus on the economy like a "laser" is quoted in Ann Devroy and Ruth Marcus, "President Clinton's First Hundred Days: Ambitious Agenda and Interruptions Frustrate Efforts to Maintain Focus," *Washington Post*, April 29, 1993, A1.

70. Douglas Jehl, "Rejoicing Is Muted for the President in Budget Victory," *New York Times*, August 8, 1993, 1, 23; David Shribman, "Budget Battle a Hollow One for President," *Boston Globe*, August 8, 1993, 1, 24.

71. William Clinton, Address before a Joint Session of Congress on Administration Goals, printed in *Weekly Compilation of Presidential Documents*, February 17, 1993, 215–224; Jill Zuckerman, "Pared Funding Speeds Passage of National Service," *Congressional Quarterly Weekly Report*, August 7, 1993, 2160–2161.

72. Indeed, during the early days of his presidency, Clinton sought to identify with his party's leadership in Congress and the national committee—partly, one suspects, to avoid the political isolation from which Carter had suffered. Whereas Carter kept party leaders in Congress and the national committee at arm's length, Clinton sought both to embrace and to empower the national organization. The White House lobbying efforts on Capitol Hill focused almost exclusively on the Democratic caucus; and the administration relied heavily on the Democratic National Committee to marshal public support for its domestic programs. Interviews with David Wilhelm, chairman, Democratic National Committee, October 18, 1993, and Craig Smith, political director, Democratic National Committee, October 19, 1993; Rhodes Cook, "DNC under Wilhelm Seeking a New Role," *Congressional Quarterly Weekly Report*, March 13, 1993, 634.

73. Al From and Will Marshall, "The Road to Realignment: Democrats and the Perot Voters," in *The Road to Realignment: Democrats and the Perot Voters* (Washington, D.C.: Democratic Leadership Council, 1993), 1-3–1-5.

74. David Shribman, "A New Brand of D.C. Politics," *Boston Globe*, November 18, 1993, 15; Gwen Ifill, "56 Long Days of Coordinated Persuasion," *New York Times*, November 19, 1993, A27.

75. Address to Congress on Health Care Plan, printed in *Congressional Quarterly Weekly Report*, September 25, 1993, 2582–2586; Robin Toner, "Alliance to Buy Health Care: Bureaucrat or Public Servant?" *New York Times*, December 5, 1993, I 38.

Part V   Presidents and Government

14 The Institutional Presidency

John P. Burke

Not until 1857 did Congress appropriate funds for a White House staff—one clerk. More than a half-century later President Woodrow Wilson had only seven full-time aides. Growth in the size of the White House staff began in earnest during the presidency of Franklin D. Roosevelt and, with occassional lapses, the growth has yet to abate. The major challenge for presidents—not just for Roosevelt and his Democrat successors, such as Bill Clinton, but also for conservative Republicans like Ronald Reagan and George Bush—has been to keep pace with an ever-expanding bureaucracy. Ironically, John P. Burke argues, the size and complexity of the modern presidential staff have caused the White House itself to take on "the character of a bureaucratic organization." Presidents, with varying success, have adopted a number of strategies to make good use of their staffs, which Burke chronicles.

Analysis of the workings of the White House staff, both by those who have served on it and by scholars, has a peculiar if not schizophrenic quality. For some, the staff system is simply a reflection of the personality, style, and managerial skills of the incumbent president. Richard Neustadt notes, for example, that "the great growth in staff since 1936 is an undoubted help" to a president, but "it is not sufficient to gesture toward the 'institutionalized presidency.' ... A president is helped by what he gets into *his* mind." According to H. R. Haldeman, Richard M. Nixon's chief of staff, the staff system must "fit that president's method of working. ... You must build a new office of the president for each president, and it must evolve as that president evolves in office."[1]

Others, in contrast, emphasize characteristics of the presidency that seem to endure from administration to administration. Herbert Stein holds a view different from that of Haldeman, with whom he served in the Nixon White House: "a certain organization is passed down from one administration to another; it is not organized anew every time." Hugh Heclo sees a "deep structure" at work "that a president can change slowly if it all." This structure, Heclo explains, "is the raw, exposed ganglion of government where immense lines of force come together in ways that no single person can control. The total effect is to program the modern president."[2]

Both of these perspectives have some merit. Presidents do seem to leave their imprint—for better or for worse—on the office. The formal and hierarchical arrangements of the Dwight D. Eisenhower, Richard M. Nixon, and Ronald Reagan presidencies and the more collegial, informal, and ad hoc patterns in the John F. Kennedy, Lyndon B. Johnson, and Bill Clinton White Houses can be linked to the organizational preferences and "work ways" of each of these chief executives. But the very large White House staff, composed now of some 2,000 employees in significant policy-making positions, serves as an organizational context that can—just as in any bureaucracy—set limits on what a president can do and sometimes thwart even the best of presidential intentions. For the skillful president, the White House staff is like very hard clay that can be molded with great effort, patience, and understanding; for the less skilled it can become a hard rock, if not a brick wall, that can resist presidential management and control.

A full analysis of how presidents have succeeded or failed at this "organizational artistry" would require a detailed account of the presidential staff system that has evolved since the late 1930s and a close examination of the efforts of each of the presidents from Franklin D. Roosevelt through Bill Clinton to organize and manage the institutional presidency. In what follows, I outline only part of this larger project: some of the institutional characteristics of the modern presidency and the managerial challenge with which it confronts incumbent presidents.[3]

One point that surely deserves mention at the outset is how odd the need for organizational leadership would have seemed to presidents in the nineteenth and early twentieth centuries. Thomas Jefferson served in office with only one messenger and one secretary. Sixty years later, in the administration of Ulysses S. Grant, the size of the staff had grown to three. By 1900 the staff consisted of a private secretary (now formally titled "secretary to the president"), two assistant secretaries, two executive clerks, a stenographer, three lower-level clerks, and four other office personnel. Under Warren G. Harding the size of the staff grew to thirty-one, but most staff members were clerical. Herbert Hoover managed to persuade Congress to approve two more secretaries to the president, one of whom he assigned the job of press aide.

It was common practice for early presidents to hire family members and other relatives as their secretaries, an indication that their few staff members functioned as personal aides and factotums rather than as substantive policy advisers. John Quincy Adams, Andrew Jackson, John Tyler, Abraham Lincoln, and Ulysses S. Grant all engaged their sons as private secretaries. George Washington, James K. Polk, and James Buchanan employed their nephews. James Monroe employed his younger brother and two sons-in-law. Zachary Taylor hired his brother-in-law.

Early presidents also paid the salaries of their small staffs out of their own pockets. Not until 1857 did Congress appropriate money ($2,500) for a presidential clerk—one. As recently as the Coolidge presidency the entire budget for the White House staff, including office expenses, was less than $80,000.[4] In 1994 the corresponding figure for the Executive Office of the President was more than $225 million.

As demands on the presidency mounted, more help was needed. Grappling with the Great Depression of the 1930s, Franklin D. Roosevelt's solution was to "muddle through." Early in his administration he experimented with a form of cabinet government but quickly became dissatisfied with its members' parochial perspectives, in-fighting, and tendency to leak information to the press— problems that would be encountered by many of Roosevelt's successors who also took office thinking that the cabinet would play a central role in their policy making. Roosevelt then moved to a series of coordinating bodies that included relevant cabinet officers and the heads of the new agencies that were created as part of his New Deal. Another of FDR's managerial strategies was to borrow staff from existing departments and agencies; staff members thus remained on their home agencies' personnel budgets while they were "detailed" to the White House. In fact, the legislative whirlwind of Roosevelt's first hundred days was the product of a loosely organized group of assistants, many of whom did not have formal positions on the White House staff. Roosevelt especially liked to use departmental assistant secretaries, because "no specific duties were required by law."[5] Two key members of his "brains trust" had appointments of this sort. Rexford Tugwell and Raymond Moley both left the faculty of Columbia University to join the new administration. Because few positions were available on the White House staff, Roosevelt made them assistant secretaries in regular cabinet-level departments—Tugwell in the Department of Agriculture, Moley at the State Department—but had them report directly to him, employing their talents as he saw fit. In Roosevelt's second term, one of his closest assistants, Thomas P. Corcoran, held the position of counsel to the Reconstruction Finance Corporation.

Other members of Roosevelt's "brains trust" did not even join him in Washington. For example, although he continued to serve as an influential adviser, Judge Sam Rosenman stayed on the New York bench, at least in the early years. What few positions Roosevelt could fill went to other longtime aides. Louis Howe was given the title of secretary to the president, and Steven Early served as press secretary, Marvin McIntyre as appointments secretary, and Marguerite "Missy" LeHand as the president's personal secretary.

Roosevelt's patchwork arrangement worked, but just barely. In an interview with a group of reporters shortly after the 1936 election, Roosevelt publicly attributed his victory to the failure of Gov. Alfred P. Landon of Kansas, his Republican opponent, to seize on the president's chief weakness. "What is your weakness?" one of the reporters asked. "Administration," replied the president.[6] Clearly something needed to be done.

In fact, Roosevelt had already taken steps to rectify his administrative problems, forming the Committee on Administrative Management, headed by Louis Brownlow. Roosevelt's creation of the Brownlow Committee was not the first presidential effort to seek administrative advice on how to make the presidency work more effectively.[7] Theodore Roosevelt's Keep Commission and William Howard Taft's Commission on Economy and Efficiency also sought to provide resources and managerial advice to the president. During Warren Harding's presidency, the Bureau of the Budget (BOB) was created to centralize and coordinate the executive branch's annual budget requests to Congress.[8] Some scholars have also claimed that Herbert Hoover is really the "father" of the institutional presidency, noting that he was the first president both to be formally authorized to hire three administrative assistants and to use them in substantial policy-making roles.[9] But it was the Brownlow Committee that most clearly and directly focused on the need for a larger, reorganized White House staff as the solution to the president's difficulties in marshaling the resources needed to respond to the ever-increasing problems that were now seen as presidential responsibilities.[10]

Concluding that "the President needs help," Brownlow and his associates proposed that in order "to deal with the greatly increased duties of executive management falling upon the president, the White House staff should be expanded."[11] After initial congressional rejection of their then-controversial proposal, the revised recommendations of the Brownlow Committee were passed by Congress in the Reorganization Act of 1939.[12] Significant increases in the staff resources available to the president also followed in the wake of the Employment Act of 1946, which created the Council of Economic Advisers, the National Security Act of 1947, which led to the development of the National Security Council, and the 1947 Hoover Commission on the Reorganization of the Executive Branch.[13] During Eisenhower's presidency, existing units within the White House Office (the core unit of the White House staff) were more clearly defined and new ones were created. Eisenhower also designated Sherman Adams as the first White House chief of staff and assigned him significant authority to oversee and coordinate the domestic policy component of the staff system.[14]

From the handful of aides that Roosevelt and his predecessors could appoint, the numbers have steadily increased in each succeeding administration. By 1953, the size of the White House Office (the unit in closest proximity to the president) was about 250. Twenty years later, it had grown to almost 500 persons. In 1977, criticizing the size of the staff as a symptom of the "imperial presidency," Jimmy Carter reduced it by 100 employees, mostly by moving them to other parts of the executive branch. By 1980, Carter's last year in office, the size of the staff had inched back up to 500, larger than that of any of his predecessors; it has remained at about that size under Ronald Reagan, George Bush, and Bill Clinton. When other administrative units under direct presidential control (the larger Executive Office of the President) are included— such as the Office of Management and Budget, the National Security Council, and the Council of Economic Advisers—the number swells to almost 2,000 appointees, operating with a budget of more than $225 million in 1994. Physically, the entire Executive Office of the President has spilled out from the East and West wings of the White House, first to occupy the Old Executive Office Building next door to the White House—once large enough to house the Departments of State, War, and Navy—and then to encompass the New Executive Office Building on the north side of Pennsylvania Avenue as well as other, smaller buildings in the vicinity.

A marked change in the character of the presidency has thus occurred. By recognizing that the American executive is an institution, a *presidency*, not merely a *president*, we can better understand the office, how it operates, what kinds of challenges it faces, and how it affects our politics.

The Institutional Presidency

If the presidency is best understood as an institution, then clearly it should embody some of the characteristics of an institution. But what do we mean by

Table 14.1. The White House Office, 1939

Secretary to the president	Stephen Early
Secretary to the president	Brig. Gen. Edwin M. Watson
Secretary to the president	Marvin H. McIntyre
Administrative assistant	William H. McReynolds
Administrative assistant	James H. Rowe, Jr.
Administrative assistant	Lauchlin Currie
Personal secretary	Marguerite A. LeHand
Executive clerk	Rudolph Forster

Source: *United States Government Manual, 1939* (Washington, D.C.: U.S. Government Printing Office, 1939).

terms like *institution, institutional,* and *institutionalization*? Our concern here is for the organizational character of the presidency—its growth in size, the complexity of its work ways, and the general way in which it resembles a large, well-organized bureaucracy.[15] More specifically, an institution is complex in what it does (its functions) and how it operates (its structure); it also is well bounded, that is, differentiated from its environment.[16]

Complex Organization

Institutions are complex: they are relatively large in size, each part performs a specialized function, and some form of central authority coordinates the parts' various contributions to the work of the whole. The first aspect of complexity—the increase in size of the institutional presidency—can easily be seen by comparing the White House staff available to President Roosevelt in 1939, before the adoption of the Brownlow Committee's recommendations for administrative reform, with the staff at work in the Clinton White House. The eight individuals that the *United States Government Manual* for 1939 lists as members of the White House staff (Table 14.1) are clearly dwarfed by the long list of staff members currently serving under President Clinton. A comparison of the Roosevelt and Clinton staffs also illustrates the second aspect of organizational complexity: increasing specialization of function. Roosevelt's aides were, by and large, generalists; they were simply called "secretary to the president" or "administrative assistant." If one were to look at the staff list of the Clinton White House, by contrast, one would find such titles as assistant to the president for communications, deputy assistant to the president for legislative affairs (Senate), special assistant to the president for agricultural trade and food assistance, deputy assistant to the president for public liaison, and associate counsel to the president. Many other units of the White House staff operate within functionally defined, specialized areas, such as national security or environmental quality. In fact, one of the primary causes of the growth of the White House staff has been the addition of these units: the Bureau of the Budget (created in 1921, transferred from the Treasury Department in 1939, and reorganized as the Office of Management and Budget in 1970), the Council of Economic Advisers (1946), the National Security Council (1947), the Office of the United States Trade Representative (1963), the Office of Policy Development (1970), the Council on Environmental Quality (1970), the Office of Science and Technology Policy (1976), the Office of Administration (1977), the National Critical Materials Council (1984), and the Office of National Drug Control Policy (1989).[17] All told, the once relatively simple tasks of the president's staff—writing speeches, handling correspondence, and orchestrating his daily schedule—have evolved into substantive duties that affect the policies the president proposes and how he deals with the steadily increasing demands placed on his office.

The final characteristic of institutional complexity is the presence of some central authority that coordinates the contributions of the institution's functional parts. For the presidency, such authority nominally resides in the president himself. But in recent administrations, coordinating authority has been especially manifest in the increasing importance of the White House chief of staff—Sherman Adams under Eisenhower; H. R. Haldeman under Nixon; Hamilton Jordan under Carter; James Baker, Donald Regan, Howard Baker, and Kenneth Duberstein under Reagan; John Sununu and Samuel Skinner under Bush; and Thomas F. "Mack" McLarty III and Leon Panetta under Clinton—many of whom have played substantive roles in policy making and in most cases have possessed day-to-day authority over the workings of the White House staff.

In fact, the centralization of authority in the role of chief of staff seems to be unavoidable, regardless of the president's own wishes. For example, Carter, at the beginning of his administration, publicly announced he wanted no chief of staff of the sort that H. R. Haldeman had been under Nixon. By the end of Carter's second year in office, however, Jordan functioned as de facto chief of staff, and in Carter's third year the appointment was made official. When Carter spoke of a national "crisis of confidence" during an ill-fated July 1979 speech, he traced the problem to the nation's moral fabric; but most observers blamed it on Carter, particularly his staff.[18] Carter, however, "solved" the crisis by firing a good chunk of his cabinet, several of whom had clashed with the White House staff. More than half the cabinet went, but almost all of Carter's staff, especially the "Georgia mafia," remained. "From now on, the Cabinet will have to clear everything with the White House," declared Stuart Eizenstat, then serving as assistant to the president for domestic affairs.[19]

During his first nine months as president, Clinton also appeared to be following this pattern of initially trying to avoid a strong chief of staff, then suffering the consequences as disorder and disarray began to pervade his White House. Like Carter, Clinton has a penchant for immersing himself in policy detail and acting as his own chief of staff. Although Clinton did designate his longtime friend Mack McLarty to serve as his first chief of staff, McLarty's role was one closer to that of a doorkeeper than an active policy maker or presidential "enforcer." By May 1993, it was clear that changes were needed. Clinton retained McLarty as chief of staff but brought in David Gergen—who had worked in the Nixon, Ford, and Reagan White Houses—as senior counselor, all-purpose adviser, and political trouble-shooter. Clinton also reassigned a number of his top aides, most notably, George Stephanopoulos. In June 1994, one year later, problems still persisted and McLarty was replaced by yet another veteran Washington insider—former congressman and current OMB director Leon Panetta.

Differentiation from Environment

The increasing complexity of the presidency and its growing reliance on expert advice have given the institution its own unique place in the policy process, differentiating it from its political environment. One way this has occurred is through increased White House control of new policy initiatives. Presidents now routinely try to shape the nation's political agenda, and the staff resources they have at their disposal increase their ability to do so. John Kennedy, Lyndon Johnson, and especially Richard Nixon, with his creation of the Domestic Council, all emphasized White House control of policy proposals, de-emphasizing the involvement of the cabinet and the bureaucracy. Carter and Reagan both began their terms of office with calls for more presidential reliance on the cabinet. They quickly found that goal to be unworkable in practice, however, and turned inward to the White House staff for policy advice. Clinton has also followed this pattern. Although one of the major initiatives of his administration—health care reform—was largely crafted by an ad hoc commission led by First Lady Hillary Rodham Clinton, most of his other efforts were mainly the work of his immediate staff. Clinton's staff also proved to be the source of many of his early gaffes and difficulties: the string of on-again, off-again nominees to be attorney general and justice of the Supreme Court, the $200 haircut on the runway of the Los Angeles airport, and the firing and unfiring of the White House travel staff.

Those outside the White House—Congress, the bureaucracy, the news media, and the public—have responded to presidential direction of the national agenda by expecting more of it. Political lobbying and influence seeking, especially by those directly involved in Washington politics, are increasingly focused on the president. American politics remains highly decentralized, incremental, and open to multiple points of access. But those seeking to influence national politics try to cultivate those who have most to do with policy proposals: the White House staff.

A second aspect of the presidency that differentiates it from the surrounding political environment is the way parts of the staff are organized explicitly to manage external relations. The press secretary and staff coordinate and in many cases control the presidential news passed on to the media.[20] Since 1953, specific staff assistants also have been assigned solely to lobby Congress on the president's behalf. Today, White House lobbying efforts are formally organized within the large, well-staffed Office of Legislative Affairs.

One interesting device that presidents have used to manage relations with the political environment has been the establishment of special channels of influence for important constituent groups. This practice began in the administration of Harry S. Truman, when David Niles became the first staff aide explicitly assigned to serve as a liaison to Jewish groups. Eisenhower hired the first black presidential assistant, E. Frederic Morrow, and added a special representative from the scientific community as well. In 1970 Nixon created the Office of Public Liaison as the organizational home within the White House staff for the increasing number of aides who served as conduits to particular groups. By the time Jimmy Carter left office in 1981, special staff members were assigned to such diverse groups as consumers, women, the elderly, Jews, Hispanics, white ethnic Catholics, Vietnam veterans, and gays, as well as such traditional constituencies as blacks, labor, and business.[21] The increasing differentiation of the presidency as a discrete entity thus complements its increasing complexity and reliance upon expertise as evidence of its status as an institution.

The Effects of an Institutional Presidency

Even if the presidency bears the marks of an institution, do its distinctly institutional characteristics—as opposed to the individual styles, practices, and idiosyncrasies of each president—matter? Despite the tremendous growth in the size of the president's staff, perhaps it remains mainly a cluster of aides and supporting personnel, with their tasks, organization, and tenure varying greatly from administration to administration, even changing within the term of a particular president. After all, both scholarly analysts and journalistic observers of the presidency have noted enormous differences between the Kennedy and Eisenhower White Houses, between Johnson and Nixon, Carter and Reagan, and even between Reagan and Bush. It is the personality, character, and individual behavior of each of these presidents that have generally attracted the attention of press and public.

Some of these observations are true, but to the extent that the institutionalized daily workings of the presidency transcend the personal ideologies, character, and idiosyncrasies of those who work within it (especially the president), it makes sense to analyze the presidency from an institutional perspective. Not only do many of the presidency's institutional characteristics affect the office, but they do so for the worse as well as for the better. Thus, the institutional presidency can have a great effect on the success or failure of a particular presidency.

External Centralization: Presidential Control of Policy Making

The creation of a large presidential staff has centralized much policy-making power within the confines of the presidency. This development has both positive and negative aspects. On the positive side, an institutional presidency that centralizes the control of policy can protect those programs that presidents wish to foster. The Washington political climate is not receptive to new political initiatives, which must compete for programmatic authority and budget allocations against older programs that are generally well established in agencies and departments, have strong allies on Capitol Hill, and enjoy a supportive clientele of special interest groups.

In creating the Office of Economic Opportunity (OEO), Lyndon Johnson, a president whose legislative skills were unsurpassed, recognized precisely this problem. The OEO was designed to be a central component of Johnson's War on Poverty. As Congress was considering the legislation to create the OEO, the departments of Commerce; Labor; and Health, Education, and Welfare all lobbied to have it administratively housed within their respective bailiwicks. Johnson, recognizing that this would subordinate the OEO to whatever other goals a department might pursue, lobbied Congress to set up the OEO so that it would report directly to the president. Johnson was especially swayed by the views of the Harvard economist John Kenneth Galbraith, who warned: "Do not bury the program in the departments. Put it in the Executive offices, where people will know what you are doing, where it can have a new staff and a fresh man as director."[22]

The centralization of power in the president's staff has not always redounded to his advantage. One of the worst effects of increasing White House control of the policy process, especially in foreign policy, has been to diminish or even exclude other sources of advice. Since the creation of the National Security Council (NSC) in 1947, presidents have increasingly relied for policy recommendations on the council's staff, especially the president's special assistant for national security. Ironically, Congress's intent in creating the NSC was to check the foreign policy power of the president by creating a deliberative body whose members (set by law) would provide an alternative source of timely advice to the president.

Except during Eisenhower's presidency, the NSC has not generally functioned as an effective deliberative body. What has developed is a large, White House-centered NSC staff, headed by a highly visible national security assistant, that often dominates the foreign policy-making process. The reasons why the NSC staff and the national security assistant come to dominate the foreign policy-making process are plain: proximity to the Oval Office, readily available staff resources, and a series of presidents whose views about decision-making processes differed from those held by Eisenhower. Beginning with McGeorge Bundy under Kennedy, and continuing with Walt W. Rostow under Johnson, Henry Kissinger under Nixon, and Zbigniew Brzezinski under Carter, most national security assistants have not only advocated their own policy views but have also eclipsed other sources of foreign policy advice, especially the secretary of state and his department.

Perhaps the best testimony to the problems created by centralized control of foreign policy by the NSC staff can be found in the memoirs of three recent secretaries of state. Cyrus Vance, who served under Carter, repeatedly battled with the president's special assistant for national security, Zbigniew Brzezinski. Vance's resignation as secretary of state, in fact, was precipitated in 1980 by the administration's ill-fated decision—from which Vance and the State Department were effectively excluded—to try to rescue the American hostages in Iran.[23]

Alexander Haig, Reagan's first secretary of state, encountered similar problems with the NSC. In his memoirs, Haig claims he had only secondhand knowledge of many of the president's decisions. In a chapter tellingly entitled

"Mr. President, I Want You to Know What's Going On Around You," Haig reports:

William Clark, in his capacity as National Security Adviser to the President, seemed to be conducting a second foreign policy, using separate channels of communications . . . bypassing the State Department altogether. Such a system was bound to produce confusion, and it soon did. There were conflicts over votes in the United Nations, differences over communications to heads of state, mixed signals to the combatants in Lebanon. Some of these, in my judgment, represented a danger to the nation.[24]

Haig's successor as secretary of state, George P. Shultz, also found himself cut out of a number of important policy decisions by the NSC staff. The most notable was the Reagan administration's secret negotiations with Iran to exchange arms for the release of American hostages in Lebanon and its covert use of the profits generated by the arms sales to fund the contra rebels in Nicaragua. The arms deal violated standing administration policy against negotiating for hostages, and the disclosure of the secret contra funds undermined congressional support for Reagan's policies in Central America. The affair not only indicated Shultz's conflicts with the NSC but was also politically damaging to President Reagan.

There have been two exceptions to the general pattern of NSC dominance in foreign policy making—one occurred during the Ford administration, the other in the Bush presidency. In both cases a reasonable balance was struck in the advisory roles of the State Department and the NSC. But the two cases are revealing about the conditions under which excessive centralization can be avoided. In both presidencies the same individual, Brent Scowcroft, served as the NSC adviser, and Scowcroft deliberately crafted his job to be a "neutral broker" of the foreign-policy-making process rather than a policy advocate. Furthermore, in both administrations the secretaries of state had extensive White House staff experience. Kissinger had served under Nixon as NSC special assistant, and for part of his tenure in the Nixon and Ford administrations he was simultaneously NSC special assistant and secretary of state. Bush's secretary of state, James Baker, had served as White House chief of staff and secretary of the treasury under Reagan.

The Clinton national security apparatus offers yet another twist: NSC special assistant Anthony Lake serving, like Scowcroft, in the role of neutral broker but with a secretary of state, Warren Christopher, who has yet to articulate a broader vision of America's foreign policy in the post-cold war world and both serving under a president who himself has more interest and experience in domestic than foreign affairs. This arrangement has generated criticisms of "policy drift" and a "foreign policy vacuum." It remains to be seen if Clinton will respond to these concerns and, if he does, whether he will centralize power in the hands of a more active NSC special assistant or find a secretary of state more interested in putting the administration's mark on its foreign policy.

Internal Centralization: Hierarchy, "Gate-Keeping," and Presidential Isolation

The general centralization of policy-making power by the White House staff has been accompanied by a centralization of power *within* the staff by one or two chief aides. This internal centralization is further evidence of the institutional character of the presidency, and it too can affect the way the institutional presidency operates, providing both opportunities and risks for a president.

On the positive side, centralization of authority within a well-organized staff system can assure clear lines of responsibility, well-demarcated duties, and orderly work ways. When presidents lack a centralized, organized staff system, the policy-making process suffers.

The travails of Franklin Roosevelt's staff well illustrate the problems that can arise from lack of effective organization. Roosevelt favored a relatively unorganized, competitive staff system, one in which the president acted as his own chief of staff. But rather than establishing regular patterns of duties and assignments and an orderly system of reporting and control, Roosevelt often gave several of his staff assistants the same assignment, in effect pitting them against each other.

Some analysts have argued that redundancy—two or more staff members doing the same thing—can benefit an organization.[25] But in Roosevelt's case, staff resources were minimal. Worse, his staff arrangements generated competitiveness, jealousy, and insecurity among his aides, none of which is conducive to sound policy advice or effective administration. Patrick Anderson writes: "Roosevelt used men, squeezed them dry, and ruthlessly discarded them. . . . The requirement [for success] was that they accept criticism without complaint, toil without credit, and accept unquestioningly Roosevelt's moods and machinations."[26]

In addition to making the staff more effective, a system in which one staff member serves as chief of staff or is at least *primus inter pares* (first among equals) is advantageous to a president for other reasons. It can protect the president's political standing, for example. A highly visible staff member with a significant amount of authority within the White House can act as a kind of lightning rod, handling politically tough assignments and deflecting political controversy from the president to him or herself.

Perhaps the best example of this useful division of labor comes from the Eisenhower presidency. Part of Eisenhower's success as president derived from a leadership style in which he projected himself as a chief of state who was above the political fray, while allowing his assistants, especially Sherman Adams, the flinty former governor of New Hampshire and Eisenhower's chief of staff, to seem like prime ministers concerned with day-to-day politics. In a 1956 *Time* magazine feature on Eisenhower's staff, Adams's scrawled "O.K., S.A." was said to be tantamount to presidential approval. Although in reality it was Eisenhower who made the decisions, Adams's reputation as the "abominable 'No!' man" helped to "preserve Eisenhower's image as a benevolent national and international leader" and protect his standing in the polls.[27]

But a well-organized, centralized staff can also work against a president. There are dangers—especially corruption and the abuse of power—in elevating one assistant to prominence and investing that person with a large amount of power. Sherman Adams proved politically embarrassing to Eisenhower when he was accused of accepting gifts from a New England textile manufacturer. Eisenhower found it personally difficult to ask his trusted aide to resign and delegated the job to Vice President Nixon. In fact, the political and personal problems Eisenhower experienced by relying on, then having to fire, Adams seem to be part of a pattern: Truman and Harry Vaughan, Johnson and Walter Jenkins, Nixon and Haldeman, Reagan and Donald Regan, and Bush and John Sununu.

Another two-edged consequence of a centralized staff system is that a highly visible assistant with a large amount of authority can act as a "gatekeeper," controlling and filtering the flow of information to and from the president. Both Jordan under Carter and Regan under Reagan were criticized for limiting access to the president and selectively screening the information and advice their presidents received. Joseph Califano, Jr., Carter's secretary of health, education, and welfare, had repeated run-ins with Jordan. While lobbying Dan Rostenkowski, the Democratic congressman from Illinois and influential chairman of the Health Subcommittee of the House Ways and Means Committee, on a hospital cost containment bill, Califano found that Rostenkowski also resented the treatment he was receiving from Jordan. "He never returns a phone call, Joe," Rostenkowski complained. "Don't feel slighted," Califano replied. "He treats you exactly as he treats most of the Cabinet."[28] In July 1979 Carter fired Califano and promoted Jordan.

Donald Regan, who succeeded James Baker as Reagan's chief of staff in 1985, acquired tremendous power in domestic policy, played a major role making important presidential appointments, and was even touted in the media as Reagan's prime minister. Immediately upon taking office, Regan flexed his political muscles by revamping the cumbersome cabinet council system, substituting instead two streamlined bodies: the Economic Policy Council and the Domestic Policy Council. Regan retained control of the two councils' agendas. According to Becky Dunlap, an aide to Attorney General Edwin Meese III, "Don Regan more than anyone else has the authority to say this issue has to be dealt with by the Cabinet council. And he does that on a regular basis." Subsequent council reports to President Reagan also flowed through Regan: "The simplified system strengthened Regan's direct control over policy, establishing him as a choke point for issues going to the President."[29]

Regan certainly was effective in centralizing power in his hands, but his attempts to exercise strong control over the policy-making process did not always serve the president's ends. In the realm of domestic policy, the tactics of Regan and his staff frequently upset House Republicans: Regan "ignored them while shaping a tax bill with [Democratic] House Ways and Means Chairman Dan Rostenkowski." President Reagan salvaged tax reform with a personal appeal to his party in Congress, "but the specter of the president traveling to Capitol Hill like a supplicant to plead for *Republican* House votes plainly raised doubts about the quality of White House staff work."[30]

In the realm of foreign affairs, Regan was the first chief of staff to play a major role in both making and implementing policy. Regan's attempts to influence foreign policy precipitated the resignation of Robert McFarlane, special assistant to the president for national security, and led to the selection of Admiral John Poindexter, a Regan ally, as his replacement. The Regan-dominated, Poindexter-led NSC soon embroiled the Reagan administration in the politically embarrassing Iran-contra affair.

Although George Bush was more personally involved in the policy process than Reagan, his management style fared little better. In foreign affairs, he tended to operate with a close-knit group of advisers, especially his trusted and longtime associate Secretary of State James Baker. Although simultaneously at the center of the decision process and avoiding "micro-management" of his decisions in the U.S. effort to depose Panamanian dictator Manuel Noriega and the Persian Gulf War, Bush appears to have been vulnerable to some of the problems Irving Janis has identified in his theory of "groupthink": a tendency for the leader to announce his preferences before the group has fully explored alternatives, exclusion of dissenting views (for example, the absence of the chairman of the Joint Chiefs of Staff, Colin Powell, from several key meetings in the early days following Iraq's invasion of Kuwait), and a certain degree of like-mindedness in the views of those who are participants.[31] Bush may have avoided any decision fiascoes, however, because of his own foreign policy expertise and experience and his ability to reach out to other world leaders in forging effective coalitions, especially during the Gulf War.

Bush clearly preferred foreign to domestic affairs, largely turning the latter over to Chief of Staff John Sununu. Early in his presidency published reports likened Bush's domestic policy style to Alexander George's theory of multiple advocacy—an approach strongly embraced by one of Bush's top domestic aides, Roger Porter.[32] However, John Sununu and the OMB director, Richard Darman, quickly asserted control over Bush's domestic policy operations, leading, according to Walter Williams, to a "domestic policy regency." Sununu and Darman, Williams observes,

operated off the top of their heads with little sound analysis and without much debate, resulting in a "policy-less," reactive domestic presidency. The two "assistant presidents" for domestic affairs spurned information and advice, were imperious and secretive, and operated with a top down style that cut off ideas from below. . . . Darman and Sununu often were rude and insulting, uninterested in the opinions of others, arrogantly full of themselves, in marked distinction to the gentlemanly president.[33]

Centralized authority of the kind Donald Regan and John Sununu practiced is clearly preferable to organizational anarchy. But as hierarchy and centralization develop within the White House staff, presidents can find themselves increasingly isolated, relying on a small, core group of advisers. If that occurs, the information the president gets will already have been selectively filtered and interpreted. Discussions and deliberations will be confined to an inner circle of like-minded advisers. Neither development is beneficial to the quality of presidential decision making and the formulation of effective policy proposals.

Bureaucratization

As the top levels of the White House staff have increased in authority and political visibility, the rest of the staff has taken on the character of a bureaucratic organization. Among its bureaucratic characteristics are complex work routines, which often stifle originality and reduce differences on policy to their lowest common denominator. Drawing on his experience in the Carter White House, Greg Schneiders complains that if one feeds "advice through the system ... what may have begun as a bold initiative comes out the other end as unrecognizable mush. The system frustrates and alienates the staff and cheats the President and the country."[34] Schneiders also notes that the frustrations of staffers do not end with the paper flow:

There are also the meetings. The incredible, interminable, boring, ever-multiplying meetings. There are staff meetings and task force meetings, trip meetings and general schedule meetings, meetings to make decisions and unmake them and to plan future meetings, where even more decisions will be made.[35]

"All of this might be more tolerable," Schneiders suggests, "if the staff could derive satisfaction vicariously from personal association with the President." But few aides have any direct contact with the president: "even many of those at the highest levels—assistants, deputy assistants, special assistants—don't see the President once a week or speak to him in any substantive way once a month."[36]

What develops as a substitute for work satisfaction or personal proximity to the president are typical patterns of organizational behavior: "bureaucratic" and "court" politics. With regard to court politics, for example, White House staff members often compete for assignments and authority that serve as a measure of their standing and prestige on the staff and ultimately with the president. Sometimes these turf battles are actually physical in character, with staff members competing for larger office space and closer proximity to central figures in the administration, especially to the president and his Oval Office in the West Wing. At the beginning of each presidential term, journalists take an intense interest in the size of staff offices and their location in relation to the president; these are taken as signs of relative power and influence by the Washington political community. Speculation continues during the president's entire term. In the Clinton White House, for example, George Stephanopoulos's appointment as a senior counselor was accompanied by reports emphasizing that his new office was one of the few with a door to the Oval Office.

Occasionally something as insignificant as a *the* can make a world of difference to a staff assistant. In 1946 President Truman appointed John Steelman as "assistant to the president." When Steelman's charter of operations was being drawn up by the Bureau of the Budget, he cleverly inserted "The" before his title, telling the budget official, "My understanding is that I am supposed to be the chief of staff of the White House." The article stayed and was printed at the top of Steelman's stationery, thereby enhancing his status in dealing with other staff members and those outside the administration. Truman continued to call him an assistant to the president, but other staff members grumbled about Steelman's self-assumed importance.[37]

As the Steelman example suggests, not only are staff members concerned about their standing within the White House, but they are also attentive to how they are perceived by outsiders. Patterns of behavior—bureaucratic politics—can develop that relate to a staff member's place in the organization: "Where one stands depends upon where one sits." Staff members often develop allies on the outside—members of the press, members of Congress, lobbyists, and other political influentials—who can aid the programs and political causes of particular parts of the institutional presidency or the personal careers of staffers. Conversely, they can also create hostility and enmity among those outside the staff who compete with them for presidential attention. One classic example of this is the "us versus them" attitude that develops between the Office of Policy Development (inside) and regular departments (outside) in domestic policy and between the NSC staff (inside) and the State Department (outside) in foreign policy. In part, such attitudes may stem from different orientations and perspectives: "Political appointees seem to want to accomplish goals quickly while careerists opt to accomplish things carefully."[38] But these attitudes may also inhere in simple bureaucratic competition and politics, generated by a complex, bureaucratic institution.

Politicization

As a response to the bureaucratization of the White House staff, presidents are increasingly politicizing the institutional presidency. That is, they are attempting to make sure that staff members heed the president's policy directives and serve his, rather than their own, political needs.

In most cases, the president's aim in politicizing the staff is understandable. The Constitution's system of shared powers deals the president a weak hand. Furthermore, a president should expect broad agreement among his aides and assistants with his political programs and policy goals. President Nixon, for example, created the Domestic Council as a discrete unit within the White House staff to serve as his principal source of policy advice on domestic affairs because he feared that the agencies and departments were staffed with unsympathetic liberal Democrats.[39]

The difficulty for a president comes in determining to what extent he should politicize his staff. Excessive politicization can limit the range of opinions among (and thus the advice from) the staff; taken to extremes, politicization may result in a phalanx of like-minded yes men.

Excessive politicization can also weaken the objectivity of the policy analysis at the president's disposal, especially if the newly politicized staff unit has a tradition of neutral competence and professionalism. As Terry Moe summarizes the argument, "Politicization is deplored for its destructive effects on institutional memory, expertise, professionalism, objectivity, communications, continuity, and other bases of organizational competence."[40]

One part of the president's staff in which politicization has been most noticeable—and the debate over politicization most charged—is the Office of Management and Budget. The same Nixon effort that created the Domestic Council also led to the reorganization of the old Bureau of the Budget into the present OMB. Although an arm of the executive branch and certainly not wholly above politics, the BOB was regarded as a place where neutral competence was paramount, "a place where the generalist ethic prevailed . . . a place where you were both a representative for the President's particular view and the top objective resource for the continuous institution of the Presidency."[41]

Under Nixon, the number of political appointees in the OMB was increased. Moreover, some functions once assigned to professionals were given to political appointees; presidentially appointed program associate directors, for example, were placed in the OMB's examining divisions.[42] The effects of these changes have been noticeable: greater staff loyalty to political appointees, less cooperation with other parts of the White House staff and with Congress, and reduced impartiality and competence in favor of ideology and partisanship. The role of the OMB in the policy process has also changed: it now gives substantive policy advice—not just objective budget estimates—and has taken an active and visible role in lobbying Congress.

The experience of the Reagan administration is particularly revealing about the risks of excessive politicization in an area—budget making—where expertise and objective analysis must complement the policy goals expressed in the president's budget proposal. Reagan relied heavily on the OMB, especially during the directorship of David Stockman, both in formulating Reaganomics and trying to get its legislative provisions passed by Congress. Stockman himself concluded—and announced that conclusion in the title of his memoirs—that the so-called Reagan revolution failed.[43] Part of Stockman's thesis was that

Reagan was done in by normal Washington politics, which is particularly averse to a budget-conscious president. But Stockman's own words reveal a politicized, deprofessionalized OMB, which may not have been able to give the president the kind of objective advice that he needed, at times, to win over his critics and political opponents:

The thing was put together so fast that it probably should have been put together differently. . . . We were doing the whole budget-cutting exercise so frenetically . . . juggling details, pushing people, and going from one session to another. . . . The defense program was just a bunch of numbers written on a piece of paper. And it didn't mesh.[44]

The politicization of the OMB cannot explain all of Stockman's difficulties. But as Stockman's account attests, Reagan and his advisers needed hard questioning, objective analysis, and criticism of the sort that the old bureau, but not the new OMB, could provide a president.

Putting the President Back In

During the last fifty years the institutional presidency has undoubtedly offered the president some of the important resources he needs to meet the complex policy tasks and expectations of his office. But as we have seen, the effects of an institutional presidency—centralization of policy making in the president's staff, hierarchy, bureaucratization, and politicization—have detracted from as well as served the president's policy goals.

Presidents are not, however, simply at the mercy of the institution. Having emphasized the institutional character of the presidency, we should not neglect the presidential character of the institution. Although the presidency is an institution, it is an intensely personal one, which can take on a different character from administration to administration, from one set of staff advisers to another. Presidents and their staffs are by no means hostage to the institution; they have often been able to benefit from the positive resources it provides while deflecting or overcoming institutional forces that detract from their goals.

The most obvious management task a president faces is the basic recognition on first being elected that the organization and staffing of the White House are matters of highest priority. All of Washington and the media wait in eager anticipation for the president-elect's announcements about who will become secretary of state or defense. However, it is early and careful study about how the president-elect will organize the White House staff—whether he will favor the more formal system of an Eisenhower, Nixon, or Reagan or the more collegial arrangement of a Kennedy, Johnson, or Carter—and select the persons who will work for him that will make or break his presidency.

Clinton's difficulties during his first year as president can be attributed in great measure to a failure, during the transition period before he took office, to understand what it takes to create an effective staff system. According to one report, "Though it had studied the operations of every other major government agency, [the transition team] assigned no one to study the workings of the White House."[45] This failure was "an insane decision," according to one senior Clinton aide. "We knew more about FEMA [Federal Emergency Management Agency] and the Tuna Commission than we did about the White House. We arrived not knowing what was there, had never worked together, had never worked in these positions."[46]

Clinton's appointment of top aides exhibits another pattern of which presidents need to be wary: the tendency to offer staff positions to longtime political loyalists and campaign workers. As one Clinton aide noted, "unable to shift from a campaign mode, it [the Clinton transition team] made staffing decisions with an eye to rewarding loyal campaign workers instead of considering the broader task of governing."[47] Presidents surely need assistants who are personally loyal to him and share his deeply held political views, but presidents also need aides who are adept in Washington politics or possess substantive expertise in a particular policy area. Too many friends from Little Rock, Sacramento, or rural Georgia can doom a presidency very quickly.

Beyond striking a good balance between loyalty, on the one hand, and Washington experience and policy expertise, on the other, presidents must also be aware of the strengths and, especially, the weaknesses of the various ways of organizing the staff members they have selected. For example, in order to reduce some of the negative effects of relying on a large-scale White House staff, Eisenhower complemented his use of the formal machinery of the NSC and Adams's office with informal channels of advice. In foreign affairs, he turned not just to his trusted secretary of state, John Foster Dulles, but also to a network of friends with political knowledge and experience, such as Gen. Alfred M. Gruenther, the supreme allied commander in Europe. Eisenhower also held regular meetings with his cabinet and with congressional leaders to inform them of his actions, to garner their support, and to hear their views and opinions.[48]

When dealing with his staff, Eisenhower encouraged his aides to air their disagreements and doubts and to be candid and straightforward in their comments. He especially emphasized the need to avoid expressing views that simply reflected departmental or other bureaucratic interests. Herbert Brownell, his attorney general from 1953 until 1957, recalls that Eisenhower "time after time" would tell his cabinet members, "You are not supposed to represent your department, your home state, or anything else. You are *my* advisers. I want you to speak freely and, more than that, I would like to have you reflect and comment on what other members of the cabinet say."[49] Minutes of Eisenhower's NSC meetings reveal a president who was exposed to the policy divisions within his staff and who engaged in lively discussions with John Foster Dulles, Richard Nixon, Harold Stassen, Henry Cabot Lodge, and others. But Eisenhower was also careful to reserve the ultimate power of decision for himself; although they had a voice in the process, neither the NSC nor Adams decided for the president.

Kennedy dismantled most of the national security staff that had existed under Eisenhower, preferring instead to use smaller, more informal and collegial decision-making forums. Kennedy's abandonment of more formal procedures may have been unwise, but his experience with the collegial Ex-Com (his executive committee of top foreign policy advisers) offers lessons about how presidents can work effectively with informal patterns of advice seeking and giving. In April 1961, Kennedy's advisers performed poorly, leading him into an ill-conceived, poorly planned, hastily decided, and badly executed invasion of Cuba—the Bay of Pigs disaster. In the aftermath of that fiasco, Kennedy commissioned a study to find out what had gone wrong; on the basis of its findings, he reorganized his decision-making procedures—including major changes in the Central Intelligence Agency (CIA)—and explored the faults in his own leadership style. By the time of the Cuban missile crisis in October 1962, Kennedy and his advisers had become an effective decision-making group. Information was readily at hand, the assumptions and implications of policy options were probed, pressures that could lead to a false group consensus were avoided, and Kennedy himself deliberately did not disclose his own policy preferences—sometimes absenting himself from meetings—in order to facilitate candid discussions and to head off a premature decision.

In addition to developing a suitable leadership style, a president can also take steps to deal with the bureaucratic tendencies that can crop up in his staff. Kennedy's New Frontier agenda, for example, included a number of unbureaucratic programs, such as the Peace Corps; his personal style generated loyalty and trust. Eisenhower lacked the youthful vigor of his successor, but his broad organizational experience made him a good judge of character with a sure instinct for what and how much he could delegate to subordinates and how best to organize and use their respective talents. As with members of his cabinet,

Eisenhower emphasized to his staff aides that they worked for him, not for the NSC, Adams, or others.

Finally, although the tendencies toward centralization of policy-making power within the White House and politicization of the advisory process have been powerful, all presidents have the capacity to choose how they will act and react within a complex political context populated by other powerful political institutions, processes, and participants. Too much politicization weakens any special claims of expertise, experience, and general institutional primacy that the president might make in a particular policy area. Too much centralization eclipses the role of other political actors in a system that is geared to share, rather than exclude, domains of power; it may also set in motion a powerful antipresidential reaction.

Presidents would be well advised not to neglect the observation about presidential success that Richard Neustadt made more than thirty years ago: "Presidential power is the power to persuade."[50] But what presidents also need to know is that the character and intended audience of that persuasion must be tailored, not just to the requirements of legislative bargaining and enhancing popular support, but to the institutional character of the presidency itself.

Notes

1. Richard E. Neustadt, *Presidential Power: The Politics of Leadership* (New York: Wiley, 1960), 122–123 (emphasis in original). H. R. Haldeman, quoted in *The Nixon Presidency: Twenty-two Intimate Perspectives*, ed. Kenneth W. Thompson (Lanham, Md.: University Press of America, 1987), 84.

2. Herbert Stein, quoted in Thompson, *The Nixon Presidency*, 168. Hugh Heclo, "The Changing Presidential Office," in *Politics and the Oval Office*, ed. Arnold Meltsner (San Francisco: Institute for Contemporary Studies, 1981), 165.

3. For a fuller account see John P. Burke, *The Institutional Presidency* (Baltimore: Johns Hopkins University Press, 1993).

4. Stephen J. Wayne, *The Legislative Presidency* (New York: Harper and Row, 1978), 30.

5. Patrick Anderson, *The President's Men* (New York: Doubleday, 1969), 29.

6. Quoted in Louis Brownlow, *A Passion for Anonymity: The Autobiography of Louis Brownlow*, vol. 2 (Chicago: University of Chicago Press, 1958), 392.

7. For fuller discussion of earlier efforts see Peri Arnold, *Making the Managerial Presidency: Comprehensive Reorganization Planning, 1905–1980* (Princeton, N.J.: Princeton University Press, 1986).

8. The BOB was housed in the Treasury Department rather than as part of the White House staff and during the 1920s and 1930s was generally underused as a presidential resource until it was incorporated into the Executive Office of the President as recommended by the Brownlow Committee. See Larry Berman, *The Office of Management and the Budget and the Presidency* (Princeton, N.J.: Princeton University Press, 1979), esp. 8–9.

9. See Charles Walcott and Karen Hult, "Management Science and the Great Engineer: Governing the White House during the Hoover Administration," *Presidential Studies Quarterly* 20 (1990): 557–579.

10. I use the term "larger" here to refer to the Brownlow Committee's recognition that the president needed greater staff resources and its recommendations that the Bureau of the Budget be brought over from the Treasury Department and that an Executive Office of the President be created. In its advice on increasing the size of the president's immediate staff, the committee's recommendations were rather modest: the addition of six administrative aides who would avoid the political spotlight and have a "passion for anonymity." These new positions did not so much add new members to the Roosevelt White House as provide formal positions and to some extent set out new responsibilities for the ad hoc staffing arrangement that had existed previously. It is also interesting to note that Roosevelt rejected Brownlow's recommendations that the position of a chief of staff be created and that a more hierarchical, formally organized White House be established; their implementation would await FDR's successors.

11. President's Committee on Administrative Management, *Administrative Management in the Government of the United States* (Washington, D.C.: U.S. Government Printing Office, 1937), 4.

12. The initial Brownlow Committee recommendation for reorganizing the executive branch also included controversial proposals to redefine the jurisdiction of cabinet departments, regroup autonomous and independent agencies and bureaus, and give the president virtually unchecked authority to determine and carry out the reorganization and any needed in the future. These more controversial proposals were either dropped or made more palatable in the reorganization act passed by Congress in 1939.

13. For further discussion of the Brownlow and Hoover commissions, as well as other efforts at reorganizing the presidency, see Arnold, *Making the Managerial Presidency.*

14. On the growth of the White House staff during the Eisenhower presidency, see John Hart, "Eisenhower and the Swelling of the Presidency," *Polity* 24 (1992): 673–691.

15. The reader should note that this sense of *institutional* differs from the way others have used the term. For former Kennedy aide Theodore Sorensen, for example, the word refers to what he took to be the overly formalized and structured staff organization of the Eisenhower presidency, which his boss rejected: "From the outset he [Kennedy] abandoned the notion of a collective, institutionalized presidency. He abandoned the practice of the Cabinet and the National Security Council making group decisions like corporate boards of directors" (Theodore Sorensen, *Kennedy* [New York: Bantam Books, 1966], 281). This notion of *institutional* differs from the one I use.

16. The characteristics of institutionalization are adapted, in part, from Nelson Polsby, "The Institutionalization of the U.S. House of Representatives," *American Political Science Review* 52 (1968): 144–168. On the notion of the presidency as an institution, also see Lester Seligman, "Presidential Leadership: The Inner Circle and Institutionalization," *Journal of Politics* 18 (1956): 410–426; Norman Thomas and Hans Baade, eds., *The Institutionalized Presidency* (Dobbs Ferry, N.Y.: Oceana Press, 1972); Robert S. Gilmour, "The Institutionalized Presidency: A Conceptual Clarification," in *The Presidency in Contemporary Context,* ed. Norman Thomas (New York: Dodd, Mead, 1975), 147–159; John Kessel, *The Domestic Presidency: Decision-Making in the White House* (North Scituate, Mass.: Duxbury Press, 1975); Lester Seligman, "The Presidency and Political Change," *Annals* 466 (1983): 179–192; John Kessel, "The Structures of the Carter White House," *American Journal of Political Science* 27 (1983): 431–463; John

Kessel, "The Structures of the Reagan White House," *American Journal of Political Science* 28 (1984): 231–258; Colin Campbell, *Managing the Presidency* (Pittsburgh: University of Pittsburgh Press, 1986); and Peri Arnold, "The Institutionalized Presidency and the American Regime," in *The Presidency Reconsidered*, ed. Richard Waterman (Itasca, Ill.: F. E. Peacock, 1993), 215–245.

17. Until 1977 the Office of Policy Development was named the Domestic Council.

18. See, for example, Dom Bonafede, "Carter Turns on the Drama—But Can He Lead?" *National Journal*, July 28, 1979, 1236–1240. According to Bonafede, "The Cabinet shuffle was provoked, in large measure, by the traditional rivalry between the Cabinet and the White House staff, and by the desire by Carter and his senior assistants to strengthen their grip on the federal bureaucracy." (1237)

19. Quoted in Bonafede, "Carter Turns on the Drama," 1238.

20. On White House-press relations see Michael Grossman and Martha J. Kumar, *Portraying the Presidency* (Baltimore: Johns Hopkins University Press, 1981).

21. For further discussion see Joseph Pika, "Interest Groups and the Executive: Federal Intervention," in *Interest Group Politics*, ed. Allan J. Cigler and Burdett A. Loomis (Washington, D.C.: CQ Press, 1983), 298–323.

22. Galbraith, quoted in Lyndon Johnson, *Vantage Point: Perspectives of the Presidency, 1963–69* (New York: Holt, Rinehart and Winston, 1971), 76.

23. Vance had earlier opposed the mission as poorly conceived and difficult to execute, but while Vance was on a brief weekend vacation in Florida, Carter hastily called a meeting of his top foreign policy advisers. The meeting was dominated by members of Brzezinski's staff and the military, who favored the rescue attempt. The State Department, which favored a more cautious, diplomatic solution to the hostage crisis, was represented in the meeting only by Vance's undersecretary, Warren Christopher. Christopher reported that he was isolated in his dissent: "Everyone else at the meeting supported the rescue attempt." When Vance returned to Washington on Monday morning, he was "stunned and angry that such a momentous decision had been made in his absence." After several days of "deep personal anguish," he decided to resign. Cyrus Vance, *Hard Choices: Critical Years In America's Foreign Policy* (New York: Simon and Schuster, 1983), 409–410.

24. Alexander Haig, *Caveat: Realism, Reagan, and Foreign Policy* (New York: Macmillan, 1984), 306–307.

25. Martin Landau, "Redundancy, Rationality, and the Problem of Duplication and Overlap," *Public Administration Review* 29 (1969): 346–358.

26. Patrick Anderson, *The President's Men* (Garden City, N.Y.: Anchor Books, 1969), 10.

27. Fred I. Greenstein, *The Hidden-Hand Presidency* (New York: Basic Books, 1982), 147. Adams's counterpart in the field of foreign affairs was Secretary of State John Foster Dulles.

28. Joseph A. Califano, Jr., *Governing America: An Insider's Report from the White House and the Cabinet* (New York: Simon and Schuster, 1981), 148.

29. Ronald Brownstein and Dick Kirschsten, "Cabinet Power," *National Journal*, June 28, 1986, 1589.

30. Bernard Weinraub, "How Donald Regan Runs the White House," *New York Times Magazine*, January 5, 1986, 14.

31. Irving Janis, *Groupthink: Psychological Studies of Policy Decisions and Fiascoes*, 2d ed. (Boston: Houghton Mifflin, 1982). On possible problems with Bush's small group de-

cision making in the Gulf War, see Bob Woodward, *The Commanders* (New York: Simon and Schuster, 1991); Daniel P. Franklin and Robert Shepard, "Analyzing the Bush Foreign Policy" (Paper presented at the annual meeting of the American Political Science Association, Washington, D.C., August 29–September 1, 1991); and Cecil V. Crabb, Jr., and Kevin V. Mulcahy, "The Elitist Presidency: George Bush and the Management of Operation Desert Storm," in *The Presidency Reconsidered*, ed. Richard Waterman (Itasca, Ill.: F. E. Peacock, 1993), 275–300. On problems in the Panama invasion of 1989, see John Broder and Melissa Healy, "Panama Operation Hurt by Critical Intelligence Gaps," *Los Angeles Times*, December 24, 1989, 1.

32. Michael Duffy, "Mr. Consensus," *Time*, August 21, 1989, 19. George's theory also found its way into Porter's book analyzing Gerald Ford's Economic Policy Board; see Roger Porter, *Presidential Decision Making* (Cambridge: Cambridge University Press, 1980).

33. Walter Williams, "George Bush and White House Policy Competence" (Paper presented at the annual meeting of the American Political Science Association, Chicago, September 3–6, 1992), 12–13.

34. Greg Schneiders, "My Turn: Goodbye to All That," *Newsweek*, September 24, 1979, 23.

35. Ibid.

36. Ibid.

37. Ken Hechler, *Working with Truman: A Personal Memoir of the White House Years* (New York: Putnam, 1982), 46–47.

38. Thomas P. Murphy, Donald E. Neuchterlein, and Ronald J. Stupak, *Inside the Bureaucracy: The View from the Assistant Secretary's Desk* (Boulder, Colo.: Westview Press, 1978), 181.

39. For evidence, based on a 1970 survey, supporting Nixon's view, see J. D. Aberbach and B. A. Rockman, "Clashing Beliefs within the Executive Branch: The Nixon Administration," *American Political Science Review* 70 (1976): 456–468. In data largely taken from a 1976 survey, Cole and Caputo found that Republicans were more likely to be selected to career positions during the Nixon years and that executives calling themselves Independents during that period were more likely to resemble their Republican colleagues in attitudes and values. Richard Cole and David Caputo, "Presidential Control of the Senior Civil Service: Assessing the Strategies of the Nixon Years," *American Political Science Review* 73 (1979): 399–413.

40. Terry M. Moe, "The Politicized Presidency," in *The New Direction in American Politics*, ed. John Chubb and Paul Peterson (Washington, D.C.: Brookings Institution, 1985), 235.

41. Hugh Heclo, "OMB and the Presidency: The Problem of 'Neutral Competence,'" *Public Interest* 38 (1975): 81.

42. Ibid., 85.

43. David A. Stockman, *The Triumph of Politics: Why the Reagan Revolution Failed* (New York: Harper and Row, 1986).

44. Quoted in William Greider, *The Education of David Stockman and Other Americans* (New York, Dutton, 1982), 33, 37.

45. Jack Nelson and Robert Donovan, "The Education of a President," *Los Angeles Times Sunday Magazine*, August 1, 1993, 14.

46. Quoted in Nelson and Donovan, "The Education of a President," 14.

47. Ibid.

48. On Eisenhower's "binocular" use of informal and formal patterns of advice, see Greenstein, *The Hidden-Hand Presidency*, 100–151. On his decision-making processes, see John P. Burke and Fred I. Greenstein, with Larry Berman and Richard Immerman, *How Presidents Test Reality: Decisions on Vietnam, 1954 and 1965* (New York: Russell Sage Foundation, 1989).

49. Herbert Brownell with John P. Burke, *Advising Ike: The Memoirs of Attorney General Herbert Brownell* (Lawrence: University Press of Kansas, 1993), 294.

50. Richard Neustadt, *Presidential Power.*

15 The Presidency and the Bureaucracy: The Presidential Advantage

Terry M. Moe

Separation of powers guarantees that presidents will face a fragmented bureaucracy whose centrifugalism and autonomy are protected by Congress, Terry M. Moe explains. This situation seriously limits presidential leadership and control. Yet, Moe argues, the system also endows presidents with key advantages—some arising from their unilateral powers of discretionary action, others from Congress's vulnerability to collective action problems—that allow them to shape the structure of government, gain greater control over bureaucracy, and shift the balance of power in their favor. Although they cannot hope to remove all obstacles to their leadership, presidents can make "a bad situation better." Moe illustrates his thesis with case studies on civil service reform, congressional oversight of the institutional presidency, and regulatory review.

In our system of separation of powers, it is inevitable that the president and Congress will struggle over the bureaucracy. Both have legitimate roles to play in creating and designing public agencies, staffing them, funding them, and overseeing their behavior. But what they want from them is often very different. Presidents have their own agendas, addressing the needs and aspirations of a national constituency. Legislators are driven by localism and the narrow demands of special interest groups. Both need bureaucracy to get what they want. And so they struggle.

During the nineteenth century, there was very little bureaucracy; the departments and agencies of the executive branch were few in number and small in size and scope. Presidents tended to be weak and Congress strong. But as government began actively addressing the burgeoning problems of industrial society during the early decades of this century, particularly during the New Deal, American bureaucracy grew enormously. And as the bureaucracy grew, so did the presidency, which has evolved into a complex institution whose specialized components—from the Office of Management and Budget to the National Security Council to the White House domestic policy staff to the White House appointments unit and many others—are largely devoted to providing presidents with a capacity for coherent, centralized control of the bureaucracy.[1] These developments are the defining structural features of modern American government. It is bureaucratic and presidentially led.

This is not to say that presidents somehow reign supreme over the bureaucracy. Far from it. For reasons discussed below, separation of powers virtually guarantees that they will face a fragmented bureaucracy whose centrifugalism and autonomy are protected by Congress. Under the circumstances, the best presidents can do is make a bad situation better—and it is by reference to this grim baseline that they have been successful. Rather than take an unfavorable system as a given and accept the way it stacks the political game against them, presidents have moved to restructure the system itself and, in so doing, to transform the game into one more hospitable to their leadership and control. Separation of powers is naturally brutal to presidents. But they have made it less so.

The question posed in this chapter is, How have presidents been able to do this? If Congress and the president share authority, if they are both broadly powerful, and if both want to control the bureaucracy, then why has their struggle allowed presidents to restructure the system in their own favor?

A detailed historical account would suggest that various factors have been at work. A common claim, for example, is that Congress has simply deferred to presidents, recognizing that they are better suited to provide the expertise, co-ordination, and dispatch necessary for effective government in an era of complex policy. There is surely some truth to this, especially for cases in which their interests have not been in conflict. Nonetheless, a more interesting and consequential claim is the following: even when the interests of presidents and Congress are in conflict, which is much of the time, presidents have inherent advantages in the realm of institution building that allow them, slowly but surely, to strengthen their hand in the ongoing battle with Congress for control of the bureaucracy.

This is the claim I want to argue in this chapter. The discussion is divided into two parts. In the first, I offer a perspective on how decisions about bureaucratic control are made in the American system, the relative roles that presidents and Congress play, and the forces that give rise to the presidential advantage in restructuring the system. Notable among these forces are the president's unilateral powers of discretionary action and Congress's debilitating collective action problems.

In the second part, I illustrate this argument with three cases that bear directly on the institutional balance of power: the Civil Service Reform Act of 1978, congressional oversight and funding of the institutional presidency, and presidential review of regulatory rulemaking.

Why Bureaucratic Control Is So Difficult

In a world defined by separation of powers, the bureaucracy is destined to be difficult for presidents to control.[2] Indeed, the bureaucracy is not designed for coherent, central control by the president or anyone else. In one way or another, most of it arises out of fragmented, decentralized processes of congressional politics and is slowly put together piece by piece over time. Each piece is a separately conceived and orchestrated political product, fashioned by a unique coalition of legislators and interest groups, and designed to promote a particular set of interests.

The designers of public agencies take a steadfastly myopic and parochial approach to bureaucracy. As individual actors in a fragmented system, interest groups and members of Congress are not held responsible for the performance of the system as a whole, as the president is. And they have no serious concern for broad issues of management, efficiency, and coordination, as the president does. Interest groups have their eyes on their own interests, and little else. Legislators have their eyes on their own electoral fortunes, and thus on the special (often local) interests that can bring them security and popularity. Groups and legislators need each other, and they work well together. For both, politics is not about the system. It is about the pieces, and about special interests.

What kind of pieces do they build? Specifically, how do they go about designing public agencies? In any given case, of course, a legislative coalition wants an agency that can do its bidding most effectively. But this is not simply a matter of creating structures that promote effective organization, in the usual sense. For whether the agency actually pursues coalition objectives through time, effectively or not, depends on who controls it and what they want it to do. If control falls into the "wrong" hands, all the effectiveness in the world will not help. The central political challenge a coalition faces, then, is not to build an effective organization per se, but, rather, to ensure its own control and insulate against the control of others.

To some extent, the solution is to identify the obvious opponents—an unfriendly president, say, or a powerful business group—and adopt structures that protect the agency from their influence. But the control problem actually runs much deeper than this. In fact, it is rooted in democracy and in the political uncertainty that goes along with it. Under democratic rules, a new agency is subject to control by whoever happens to hold public authority. Today's friendly authorities may be replaced by enemies tomorrow, as electoral and other shifts in political fortunes bring new players into positions of power—and give them the legal right to control the agency, and to ruin everything. In a democracy, then, the only sure way to insulate an agency against unwanted control by others is to insulate it against future authority in general, and thus against democratic accountability.

This strategy may sound pernicious, but the forms it takes are exceedingly common and widely accepted in American politics. The most direct approach is for a coalition to impose detailed formal restrictions on its agency—via decision procedures, standards, timetables, personnel rules, and the like—that tell it by law precisely what to do and how to do it, thus removing much of its behavior from ongoing democratic control. In so doing, the coalition is able to exercise its own control ex ante, embedding its interests in strategically chosen structures that essentially put the agency on autopilot, resistant to future control by others. The benefits of insulation do not come cheap: these same structures tend to bury the agency under an avalanche of formalism and undermine its effectiveness. But in a world of political uncertainty, this is a price worth paying if the agency is to be protected.

Presidents are prime targets of this strategy, even when coalitions regard the current incumbent as friendly. The reason is that all presidents, for institutional reasons, use their power in ways that are threatening to legislators and groups. Their interests are different. As national leaders with broad, heterogeneous constituencies, they think in grander terms about social problems and the public interest, and they tend to resist specialized appeals. Moreover, because they are held uniquely responsible by the public for virtually every aspect of national performance, and because their leadership and their legacies turn on effective governance, they have strong incentives to seek coherent, central control of the federal bureaucracy for themselves and their national agenda.

Legislative coalitions have ample reason to fear presidents, then, and to insulate agencies against presidential influence. All the formal restrictions mentioned above help to do that: by insulating agencies from external control in general, they help to shut out presidents. But other restrictions are aimed directly at presidents. The independent regulatory commission, for example, is a popular structural form that restricts presidential removal and managerial powers. Similarly, legislation often limits the number of presidential appointees in an agency and uses civil service and professionalism to insulate personnel from presidential direction.

Presidents have every incentive, whatever their party or agenda, to oppose these restrictions and to press for a bureaucracy they can control—and institutions that allow them to do it better. One strategy is to participate actively in the legislative process, using their political clout to push, bargain, and logroll their way toward somewhat better structures when agencies are created or reorganized. Another is to avoid the legislative process as much as possible and instead to use their executive powers to cobble together the structures they want. Both strategies, but especially the second, have been major forces animating the growth and elaboration of the institutional presidency—which represents, in structural form, a continuing effort by modern presidents to strike back and gain the upper hand.

This is how the institutional battle lines are drawn. Legislators and groups, motivated by parochial concerns, routinely go about the piecemeal construction of a bureaucracy that is buried in formalism, poorly designed for its tasks, and insulated from coherent control. Presidents, motivated to lead, find this unacceptable. They take aggressive action to modify the "congressional bureaucracy," to develop their own institutional capacity for control, and to presidentialize the system. Legislators and groups resist, presidents counter, and so it goes. The central dynamic of the American bureaucratic system derives from this tension between presidents who seek control and the legislative and group players who want to carve out and defend their own small pieces of turf.

Presidential Advantage: Discretion and Unilateral Power

This is a dynamic in which the president holds certain key advantages. In time, these advantages allow him to move the structure of the system, however haltingly and episodically, along a presidential trajectory.

The president is greatly advantaged by his position as chief executive, which gives him the right to make unilateral decisions about structure and policy. If he wants to develop his own institution, review or revise agency decisions, coordinate agency actions, make changes in agency leadership, or otherwise impose his views on government, he can simply proceed—and it is up to Congress (and the courts) to react. For reasons discussed below, Congress often finds this difficult or impossible to do, and the president wins by default. The ability to win by default is a cornerstone of the presidential advantage.

Why does the president have powers of unilateral action? Part of the answer is constitutional. The Constitution, rather than spelling out his authority as chief executive in great detail—a strategy favored by those among the framers who were most concerned with limiting the executive—remains largely silent on the nature and extent of presidential authority, especially in domestic affairs. It broadly endows the president with the "executive power" and gives him responsibility to "faithfully execute the laws" but says little else. This very ambiguity, as Richard Pious notes, "provided the opportunity for the exercise of a residuum of unenumerated power."[3] The proponents of a strong executive at the Constitutional Convention, who won out on this language, were well aware of that.

The question of what the president's formal powers really are, or ought to be, will always be controversial among legal scholars. But two things seem reasonably clear. One is that, if presidents are to perform their duties effectively under the Constitution, they must be (and in practice are) regarded as having certain legal prerogatives that allow them to do what executives do: manage, coordinate, staff, collect information, plan, reconcile conflicting values, and so on. This is what it means, in practice, to have the executive power.[4] The other is that, although the content of these prerogative powers is often unclear, presidents have been aggressive in pushing an expansive interpretation: rushing into gray areas of the law, asserting their rights, and exercising them—whether or not other actors, particularly in Congress, happened to agree.[5]

The courts, which have the authority to resolve ambiguities about the president's proper constitutional role, have not chosen to do so. Certain contours of presidential power have been clarified by major court decisions—on the removal power, for instance, and executive privilege—and justices have sometimes offered their views on the president's implied or inherent powers as chief executive.[6] But the political and historical reality is that presidents have largely defined their own constitutional role by pushing out the boundaries of their prerogatives.

There is nothing that Congress can do to eliminate the president's executive power. He is not Congress's agent. He has his own constitutional role to play and his own constitutional powers to exercise, powers that are not delegated to him by Congress and cannot be taken away. Any notion that Congress makes the laws and that the president's job is simply to execute them—to follow orders, in effect—overlooks what separation of powers is all about: the president is an authority in his own right, coequal to Congress and not subordinate to it.

Precisely because the president is chief executive, however, what he can and cannot do is also shaped by the goals and requirements of the laws he is charged with executing. And Congress has the right to be as specific as it wants in designing these laws, as well as the agencies that administer them. If it likes, it can specify policy and structure in enough detail to narrow agency discretion considerably, and with it the scope of presidential control. It can also impose requirements that explicitly qualify and limit how presidents may use their prerogative powers, as it has done, for example, in protecting members of independent commissions from removal and in mandating civil service protections.[7]

Yet these sorts of restrictions ultimately cannot contain presidential power. To begin with, presidents are powerful players in the legislative process, and they will fight for statutes that give them as much discretion as possible. In addition, the legislative authors of statutes cannot eliminate all discretion from their delegations of authority to bureaucracies and presidents, and they would not want to even if they could. Their concern, politics aside, is still the effective provision of benefits to their constituents. For problems of even moderate complexity, especially in an ever-changing world, this requires putting most aspects of policy and organization in the hands of agency professionals and allowing them to use their expert judgment to flesh out the details. Once the authority is delegated, however, it is the president and the agencies who govern, not Congress. Short of new legislation, Congress can only oversee from the outside. The president is chief executive, and the ball is in his court.

Thus, although legislators and groups may try to protect their agencies by burying them in rules and regulations, a good deal of agency discretion will remain, and presidents cannot readily be prevented from turning it to their own advantage. They are centrally and supremely positioned in the executive, they have great flexibility to act, they have a vast array of powers and mechanisms at their disposal—not to mention, of course, informal means of persuasion and influence—and they, not Congress, are the ones who are ultimately responsible for day-to-day governance. Even when Congress directly limits a presidential prerogative (the removal power, say), presidents have the flexibility simply to shift to other means of control.

In part, Congress's problem is analogous to the classic problem a board of directors faces in trying to control management in a private firm.[8] The board, representing owners, tries to impose rules and procedures to ensure that management will behave in the owners' best interests. But managers have their own interests at heart, and their expertise and day-to-day control of operations allow them to strike out on their own. Much the same is true for Congress and the president. However much Congress tries to structure things, the president can use his own institution's—and through it, the agencies'—informational and operational advantages to promote the presidential agenda.

But the corporate analogy is not quite on target. Owners have control problems even though their authority is supreme: their agents are managers whom they hire and have authority over. Congress's problem is far more severe. The president possesses all of the resources for noncompliance that the corporate manager does, but his position is far stronger because he is not Congress's agent in the scheme of government. He is an authority in his own right. Congress does not hire him, it cannot fire him, and it cannot structure his powers and incentives in any way it might like. Yet it is forced to entrust him with the execution of the laws. From a control standpoint, this is a nightmare come true.

It is also important to recognize that, although Congress can try to limit presidential prerogatives through statute, the president is greatly *empowered* through statutory law whether Congress intends it or not. Some grants of power to the president are explicit, such as the negotiation of tariffs and the oversight of mergers in the foreign trade field. But the most far-reaching additions to presidential power are implicit. When new statutes are passed, almost regardless of what they are, they increase the president's total responsibilities and give him a formal basis for extending his authoritative reach into new realms. At the same time, they add to the total discretion available for presidential control, as well as to the resources contained within the executive.

It may seem that the proliferation of statutes would tie the president up in knots as he pursues the execution of each one. But the aggregate effect is liberating. The president, as chief executive, is responsible for *all* the laws—and, inevitably, those laws turn out to be interdependent and conflicting in ways that the individual statutes themselves do not recognize. As would be true of any executive, the president's proper role is to rise above a myopic focus on each statute in isolation, to coordinate policies by taking account of their interdependence, and to resolve statutory conflicts by balancing their competing requirements. All of this affords the president substantial discretion, which he can use to impose his own priorities on government.[9]

Regulatory review is but one example. Since the presidency of Richard M. Nixon, all presidents have insisted on reviewing the proposed rules of regulatory agencies (particularly those of the Environmental Protection Agency), causing a number of important rules to be delayed, modified, or shelved.[10]

Critics in Congress have complained loudly that regulatory review prevents the agencies from single-mindedly pursuing their mandates. And they are right. Yet presidents are responsible not just for each particular statute, but for all statutes—including those that direct them to reduce inflation and unemployment, promote economic growth, conserve energy, and otherwise enhance the nation's economic well-being. Thus, presidents have a statutory (as well as a constitutional) basis for asserting their coordinating-and-balancing prerogatives in bringing these other values to bear on the regulatory agencies. What this means in political practice, of course, is that they have a legal argument for imposing presidential priorities and expanding the scope of their own discretionary action. The greater the proliferation of congressional legislation over the years, the greater the president's opportunities to find just this sort of conflict and interdependence—and to assert control.

Presidential Advantage: Congress's Collective Action Problems

Another major source of presidential advantage deserves equal emphasis. The president is a unitary actor who sits alone atop his own institution. What he says goes. In contrast, Congress is a collective institution that can make decisions only through the laborious aggregation of members' preferences. As such, it suffers from serious collective action problems that the president not only avoids but can exploit.

This crucial fact of political life is too often overlooked. Scholars and journalists tend to reify Congress, to treat it as if it were an institutional actor like the president, and to analyze their interbranch conflicts accordingly. The president and Congress are portrayed as fighting it out, head to head, over matters of institutional power and prerogative. Each is seen as defending and promoting its own institutional interests. The president wants power, Congress wants power, and they struggle for advantage.

This misconstrues things. Congress is made up of hundreds of members, each a political entrepreneur in his or her own right, each dedicated to his or her own reelection and thus to serving his or her own district or state. Although all have a common stake in the institutional power of Congress, this is a collective good that, for well-known reasons, can only weakly motivate their behavior.[11] They are trapped in a prisoner's dilemma: all might benefit if they could cooperate in defending or advancing Congress's power, but each has a strong incentive to free ride if support for the collective good is politically costly to them as individuals. Just as most citizens, absent taxation, would not voluntarily pay their shares of national defense costs, so most legislators will not flout the interests of their constituencies (and thus their own electoral interests) if that is the price of protecting congressional power. If a legislator were offered a dam or a veterans' hospital or a new highway to vote for a bill that, among other things, happened to reduce Congress's power somewhat relative to the president's, there would be little mystery as to where the stronger incentives lie.

The internal organization of Congress, especially its party leadership, imposes a modicum of order and authority on member behavior and gives the institution a certain capacity to guard its power.[12] But disabling problems still run rampant, and they are built in. Party leaders are notoriously weak—and they are weak because their "followers" want them to be. Good leadership means promoting the reelection prospects of members: by decentralizing authority, expanding their opportunities to serve special interests, and giving them the freedom to vote their constituencies' preferences.[13]

Presidents are not hobbled by these collective action problems and, supreme within their institution, can simply make authoritative decisions about what is best. Although their interests as individuals may sometimes conflict with those of the presidency as an institution—for example, if their desire for responsiveness and loyalty in an agency like the Office of Management and Budget (OMB) undercuts the presidency's long-term capacity for expertise and competence[14]— their drive for leadership almost always motivates them to promote the power of their institution. Thus, not only is the presidency a unitary institution, but there is also substantial congruence between the president's individual interests and the interests of the institution.

This sets up a basic imbalance. Presidents have both the will and the capacity to promote the power of their own institution, but individual legislators have neither and cannot be expected to promote the power of Congress as a whole in any coherent, forceful way. This means that presidents will behave imperialistically and opportunistically, but that Congress will not do the same in formulating an offensive of its own, and indeed will not even be able to mount a consistently effective defense against presidential encroachment.

Congress's situation is all the worse because its collective action problems do more than disable its own will and capacity for action. They also allow presidents to manipulate legislative behavior to their own advantage—getting members to support or at least acquiesce in the growth of presidential power. One basis for this has already been established by political scientists:[15] in any majority rule institution with diverse members, so many different majority coalitions are possible that, with the right manipulation of the agenda, outcomes can be engineered to allow virtually any alternative to win against any other. Put more simply, agenda setters can take advantage of the collective action problems inherent in majority-rule institutions to get their own way.

Presidents have at least two important kinds of agenda power. First, precisely because Congress is so fragmented, presidentially initiated legislation is the most coherent force in setting Congress's legislative agenda. The issues Congress deals with are fundamentally shaped each year by the issues presidents decide will be salient.[16] Second, presidents set Congress's agenda when they or their appointees in the bureaucracy take unilateral action to alter the status quo—by changing the direction of an agency's policy, for example. This happens all the time, and Congress is simply forced to react or acquiesce. In either case, presidents can choose their positions strategically, with an eye to the various majorities in Congress, and engineer outcomes more beneficial to the presidency than they could if dealing with a unified opponent.[17]

Presidential leverage is greatly enhanced by the maze of obstacles that stand in the way of each congressional decision. A bill must pass through subcommittees, committees, and floor votes in the House and the Senate; it must be endorsed in identical form by both houses; and it is threatened along the way by rules committees, filibusters, holds, and other roadblocks. Every veto point must be overcome if Congress is to act. Presidents, in contrast, need succeed with only one to ensure the status quo.

More generally, the transaction costs of congressional action are enormous. Not only must coalitions somehow be formed among hundreds of legislators across two houses and a variety of committees—which calls for intricate coordination, persuasion, trades, promises, and all the rest—but, owing to scarce time and resources, members must also be convinced that the issue at hand is more deserving than the hundreds of other issues competing for their attention. Party leaders and committee chairs can help, but the veto-filled process of generating legislation remains incredibly difficult and costly. And because it is, the best prediction for most issues most of the time is that Congress will take no positive action at all. Whatever members' positions on an issue, the great likelihood is that *nothing will happen.*

When presidents are able to use unilateral powers and discretion to shift the status quo, what they want most from Congress is no formal response at all—which is exactly what they are likely to get. This would be so in any event, given the multiple veto points and high transaction costs that plague congressional choice. But it is especially likely when presidents and their agents weigh into the legislative process on their own behalf—dangling rewards, threatening sanctions, directing the troops, unsticking legislative deals with side payments.[18] Presidents are especially well situated and endowed with political resources to do this. And again, blocking is fairly easy.

Whether presidents are trying to block or to push for positive legislation, the motivational asymmetry between them and Congress adds mightily to their cause. I referred to this earlier, but it is important enough to need underlining. Presidents are strongly motivated to develop an institutional capacity for controlling the bureaucracy as a whole, and, when structural issues are in question, they take the larger view. How do these structures contribute to or detract from the creation of a presidential system of control? Legislators are driven by localism and special interests, and they are little motivated by these sorts of system concerns. This basic motivational asymmetry has a great deal to do with what presidents are able to accomplish in their attempts to block or steer congressional outcomes.

On issues affecting the institutional balance of power, presidents care intensely about securing changes that promote their institutional power, while legislators typically do not. They are unlikely to oppose incremental increases in the relative power of presidents unless the issue in question directly harms the special interests of their constituents—which, if presidents play their cards right, can often be avoided. On the other hand, legislators are generally unwilling to do what is necessary to develop Congress's own capacity for strong institutional action. Not only does it often require that they put constituency concerns aside for the common good, which they have strong incentives not to do, but it also tends to call for more centralized control by party leaders and less member autonomy, which they find distinctly unattractive.

When institutional issues are at stake in legislative voting, then, presidents have a motivational advantage: they care more. This asymmetry means that they will invest more of their political clout in getting what they want. It also means that the situation is ripe for trade. Legislators may fill the airwaves with rhetoric about the dangers of presidential power, but their weak individual stakes allow them to be bought off with the kinds of particularistic benefits (and sanctions) that they really do care about. This does not mean that presidents can perform magic. If what they want requires affirmative congressional action, the obstacles are many and the probability of success is low. But their chances are still much better than they otherwise would be, absent the motivational asymmetry. And if all they want to do is block, which often is all they need, then the asymmetry can work wonders in cementing presidential *faits accomplis.*

Presidential Advantage: Three Cases

The weight of all these factors, taken together, points to a decided presidential advantage in the battle for institutional power. Presidents are unitary decision makers, they can take unilateral action in imposing their own structures, their individual interests are largely congruent with the institutional interests of the presidency, and they are dedicated to gaining control of the bureaucracy. Congress is hobbled by collective action problems, vulnerable to agenda manipulation by presidents, and populated by individuals whose interests diverge substantially from those of the institution. The result is an imbalance in the dynamic of institutional change, yielding an uneven but relentless shift toward a more presidential system.

To illustrate this argument, let us now take a brief look at three important cases in recent institutional politics, all of them involving attempts by presidents to expand their own powers at the expense of Congress. The first explores the politics of the Civil Service Reform Act of 1978, in which President Jimmy Carter sought a significant increase in presidential control over federal employees, and asks how Congress responded. The second looks at congressional oversight and funding of the institutional presidency and asks how effectively Congress has used its own powers to prevent presidents from increasing theirs. The third spotlights regulatory review, in which presidents have imposed their own rules and priorities on agency decision making, and asks what Congress has done to stop them.

Civil Service Reform

The career civil service, whose members are neither hired nor fired by presidents, is obviously a major impediment to presidential leadership. But until Jimmy Carter, no modern president had invested much effort in trying to alter the system. Civil service reform had been contemplated in broad reorganization packages, notably under Franklin D. Roosevelt (via the Brownlow Committee) and Dwight D. Eisenhower (via the second Hoover Commission), but it had never been a high priority on its own.[19] This is hardly surprising. Genuine reform calls for new legislation of the first magnitude, which is extraordinarily difficult and politically costly to achieve. With so many other ways to enhance their power through unilateral action, presidents had little incentive to pursue it.

Carter's situation was different from his predecessors', though. He oversaw a government much bigger, more bureaucratic, and more expensive than theirs.

And by the mid-1970s, in a worsening atmosphere of stagflation and energy shortages, Americans were fed up. Strong antigovernment, antitax sentiments swelled within the electorate, and politicians—including Jimmy Carter—responded with pledges of reform.[20]

It was easy to portray civil service reform as part of this broad movement for better, more effective government. But for Carter it was much more than that: it was a way to make the civil service system an arm of the presidency and thus to enhance the president's capacity for controlling the bureaucracy. The kind of reform he had in mind amounted to nothing less than a clear shift in the balance of institutional power.

In the early spring of 1978, barely a year after assuming office, Carter placed a comprehensive proposal for civil service reform before Congress. Together with Alan Campbell, the chair of the Civil Service Commission, he turned loose a small army of White House staffers, cabinet members, and OMB officials to mobilize support within Congress.[21] The proposal involved five major changes in the federal personnel system.[22] These would

1. Divide the Civil Service Commission, long a nonpartisan independent agency, into two parts. One, the Office of Personnel Management (OPM), would be headed by a single presidential appointee and would determine personnel policies for federal employees. The other, the Merit Systems Protection Board (MSPB), would be an adjudicatory agency for handling appeals and grievances.

2. Create a Senior Executive Service (SES), a flexible corps of high-level administrators (about 9,200 in number) who could be moved from job to job and would qualify for substantial merit pay.

3. Move from automatic pay raises for supervisors and managers toward performance evaluations and merit pay.

4. Substantially curtail veterans' preferences, which, since World War I, had given them the inside track for federal jobs.

5. Codify the arrangements for unionization and collective bargaining by federal employees and place responsibility for these matters in a new agency, the Federal Labor Relations Authority (FLRA).

There is nothing here to fool legislators into seeing civil service reform as a statesmanlike attempt to achieve "good government." The OPM would be an arm of the presidency and would be granted a great deal more discretion than the old Civil Service Commission—discretion that could be turned to this president's, and any future president's, advantage. There would be a large corps of senior executives (whose personal views, loyalties, and partisanship are easily identified) that the OPM could allocate at its discretion across key jobs in agencies throughout government. And these executives, as well as others not in the SES, would be subject to performance evaluations and merit pay—which would be determined, inevitably, by the discretionary judgments of the president's appointees within the OPM and the agencies.

How did Congress respond? It responded just as we would expect. Legislators simply did not care much about the balance-of-power issue, and, with a few exceptions, did not oppose this clear shift in authority and discretion to the president. Virtually all the political controversy was stimulated by the intense opposition of special interest groups—labor unions and veterans' organizations—to the provisions of the act that specifically affected them.[23]

The committees with primary jurisdiction for civil service reform were the Governmental Affairs Committee in the Senate and the Post Office and Civil Service Committee in the House. The Senate committee is not tied to any particular interest groups, because its mandate is to oversee government organization generally and because it attracts senators from various constituencies. These senators, like all politicians during the late 1970s, knew that supporting almost anything labeled "reform" would have its electoral advantages. And there were few direct effects on their constituencies to worry about. Meanwhile, Carter was pushing hard, using the resources at his disposal to win the committee over. The result was almost total support, among both Democrats and Republicans, for the core provisions of the president's bill.

Even this committee, however, was not immune to group influence. Aware of the broadly based power of veterans' groups in Congress, committee members feared a bloody floor fight that could derail the whole bill. They also may have responded to direct pressure—veterans in every state are numerous, organized, and active. In any event, the committee reported a bill that substantially weakened the offensive provision about veterans, but otherwise preserved what the president wanted.[24]

On the Senate floor, two Republicans who had opposed the bill in committee, Charles Mathias, Jr., of Maryland and Ted Stevens of Alaska, argued the dangers of politicization of the civil service by the president. This was the only serious opposition that was couched in institutional rather than interest-group terms.[25] They were appeased, however, with minor amendments that left the essence of the bill unchanged. The amended bill was then approved by the Senate by a vote of 87 to 1, hardly an indication that senators were staying up nights worrying about the balance of institutional power.[26]

In the House, there was more of a political struggle—but not over institutional issues. The House Post Office and Civil Service Committee was a friendly place for interest groups. Because of the nature of its jurisdiction, it was a high-priority setting for federal employees' unions and the politicians who sought to serve them. And they were not happy with this act.[27]

Initially, the president had attempted to buy off the opposition with provisions codifying important aspects of federal labor relations and creating the FLRA. But the unions found these concessions too weak, and not enough to compensate for the act's threatened expansions of executive discretion and merit pay, which directly eroded the kinds of rule-based protections that unions consistently demand for their members.

The federal employees' unions did not have enough support to defeat the bill in the House, but they were strong enough to cause trouble. Their fallback was to have Congressman William Clay, a Democrat from Missouri, attach an amendment that relaxed existing Hatch Act limitations on political activities by federal employees. Although this left the remaining provisions unaffected, it was something the unions desperately wanted, and it had actually passed the House the year before. Altering the Hatch Act was vehemently opposed by Republicans, however, who were generally quite supportive of Carter's original bill. Thus, Clay's amendment gave Republicans the incentive to launch strategic maneuvers of their own, leading to a complicated battle whose intricacies can be appreciated only by seasoned parliamentarians.[28]

In the end, the Clay amendment was dropped. Labor did persuade the House to attach an amendment limiting the SES to a small pilot program, but Republicans went along, knowing it would be dropped from the bill at the conference committee stage. More concretely, labor also succeeded in strengthening the provision on collective bargaining a bit. Veterans left their mark, too: the House accepted the Senate's wording, and thus retained most veterans' preferences. The resulting bill passed the House by a vote of 385 to 10.[29] As in the Senate, the House decision had nothing to do with general concerns about the balance of power. Once the interest groups were satisfied, the legislators were willing to go along.

The conference committee, with Republican support, restored the full SES program. But to mollify labor Democrats, it tacked on a two-house legislative veto to this provision alone. After five years, Congress could overturn the SES provision if both houses voted (within a prescribed sixty-day period) to do so. Aside from this change—and, of course, the victory by veterans—the bill that came out of conference was almost exactly what President Carter had requested:

an act radically transforming the civil service system by granting the president substantial new discretion and power. It passed both houses without controversy.[30]

While all this was happening, a revealing decision was being made along a separate track. The president had sought most of his changes in the civil service through new legislation, but he had asked for authority to divide the Civil Service Commission into two parts, the OPM and the MSPB, through a reorganization plan that, by law, would take effect unless vetoed by either the House or the Senate.

The reaction of legislators to this aspect of the proposal is especially telling evidence of how they approach matters of institutional power, because this Carter reorganization plan was an issue shorn of all special-interest provisions. It simply called for an up-or-down vote on whether presidents should bring personnel more fully under their control throughout the government. Did members of Congress rise up to stop this presidential power grab? Hardly. The House at least voted on the matter: a resolution to kill the president's plan was defeated, 19 to 381. The Senate did not even vote.[31]

In sum, the president cared a great deal about the issues of institutional power embedded in civil service reform, but members of Congress did not. The few political fireworks were supplied by the only special interest groups directly affected by this legislation: unions and veterans.

Congressional Oversight of the Presidency

Under our constitutional system, Congress's powers are vague at the margins too, just as the president's powers are. Although Congress has the right to make the laws, it is unclear how far it can go in making laws that undermine the president's ability to carry out his duties as chief executive. Similarly, Congress has the power of the purse, but it cannot be too draconian in denying the president funds without encroaching on his proper responsibilities.

Still, an aggressive Congress bent on defending and increasing its own power would do what presidents have done: it would push its prerogatives to the limit and use every ambiguity in the Constitution to its own advantage. If threatened, as it clearly has been, by the growing scope and reach of the institutional presidency, Congress has the formal power to reduce funding, withhold authorization, stifle appointments, and engage in aggressive oversight. Indeed, it could just as well try to nip all its problems in the bud by preventing the emergence of a powerful institutional presidency in the first place. Presidents cannot build a powerful institution with no money.

Yet Congress has done nothing of the sort. It not only has failed to act aggressively in asserting its own powers, but it has largely stood on the sidelines and allowed presidents to do what they want in building their own institution in their own way. John Hart sums it up this way:

Ever since the Executive Office of the President was established in 1939, Congress has shown a marked reluctance to enforce, let alone strengthen, its oversight of the presidential branch. Even the events of Watergate, which helped to crystalize a great deal of criticism of the White House staff, did little to increase enthusiasm for improving congressional oversight in this area. Those efforts that were made came from a handful of legislators who were never able to convince the majority of their colleagues on Capitol Hill to share their concerns with the same intensity, and, today, the presidential branch remains relatively immune from congressional scrutiny of any kind.[32]

Hart explains Congress's reticence by pointing to the norm of comity, an understanding among legislators that, in the interests of harmony between the branches, presidents should be given latitude to develop their institution as they see fit. Even if there is such a norm, however, deeper questions remain. Why would legislators find it compatible with their interests? Why would they leave presidents alone when they have the power to go after them?

The answer is rooted in Congress's collective action problems. Legislators do not care much about incremental changes in the institutional presidency unless their constituents are directly affected. There are no interest group "fire alarms" to prod them into action, no clear electoral benefits to be gained from opposing the president. Meantime, presidents care intensely, and they dedicate their resources to getting what they want.

The creation of the Office of Management and Budget, the workhorse of the institutional presidency, illustrates what Congress is up against when presidents take the offensive on purely institutional issues. The vehicle was Richard Nixon's Reorganization Plan no. 2, which sought to transform the Bureau of the Budget (BOB) into a more powerful presidential agency. Political appointees would replace careerists as heads of operating divisions; the bureau's functions in program management, coordination, and information would be expanded; and all functions vested by law in the BOB would be transferred to the president. The whole point of this plan was to give the OMB greater managerial control of the bureaucracy, and to make the OMB more responsive to the president.[33] Legislators saw this proposal for what it was, but the institutional issues were not sufficient to galvanize opposition. The Senate never even voted on a resolution of disapproval. The House did, but the Nixon forces put together a coalition of Republicans and southern Democrats to win.[34]

In time, Congress would put up more resistance. But until the early 1970s, Congress had little success in braking the institutional presidency and showed little interest in doing so. It did try to influence the kind of advice presidents received—creating the Council of Economic Advisors (CEA) and the National Security Council (NSC), for example, within the Executive Office of the President (EOP)—but this was futile as a control mechanism, since presidents can refuse to take any advice they do not want. The CEA and NSC, like all other units in the EOP, quickly became creatures of the sitting president anyway, since each president was given a free hand to organize, employ staff, assign jobs, and allocate resources.[35] Congress was largely in the dark, moreover, about exactly what presidents were doing. It did not even know how many people were employed within the White House Office, where they came from, which units of government paid their salaries, or what their jobs were. Congress was funding all this, routinely and without question. But it literally did not know what it was funding.[36]

Things changed in the early 1970s. By then Richard Nixon had transformed the BOB, dramatically increased (or so it appeared) the size and power of his White House staff, and in a variety of ways antagonized the Democrats and their interest group supporters. In response, a small number of legislators began to press for closer congressional oversight. These sorts of isolated challenges normally would not pose much of a threat. But then Watergate hit with full force, generating a public backlash against the "imperial presidency" and turning up the political heat. More and more legislators found that attacking the presidency was a popular thing to do, at least for a short while.

The most notable struggles to come out of all this had their roots in a 1972 study by the House Post Office and Civil Service Committee, which, for the first time, collected simple data documenting the growth of the presidency and the centralization of power in the White House. It decried these developments and called for more intensive efforts by Congress to amass information about the presidency and to restrict its institutional development.[37]

The next year, Congressman John Dingell, a Democrat from Michigan, tried to unhinge the presidential budget by revealing an amazing discovery: while Congress was regularly funding some 500 White House employees, a 1948 statute still in effect authorized only 6 presidential assistants and 8 secretaries! President Nixon mobilized enough support in Congress to gain authority and funding for his staff in the short term, but a permanent legislative solution obviously had to be found. His opponents, meanwhile, had been accidentally empowered beyond their wildest dreams.[38]

During the next several years, various legislators tried to engineer a bill that would both authorize a reasonably sized White House staff and provide Congress with better information and control. After a series of failed attempts, the House Post Office and Civil Service Committee came up with a bill that, with much modification, was passed into law as the White House Personnel Authorization-Employment Act of 1978. The committee's original proposal was highly threatening to the president. It imposed strict ceilings on the total number of White House staff, as well as the number of senior presidential aides and executives; it also required presidents to submit an annual report to Congress with detailed information about who works in the White House, what they do, and who pays their salaries. As we would expect, however, resisting this bill proved to be a top-priority matter for President Carter. He maneuvered House members into supporting a friendly, largely symbolic final bill: one that authorized a large White House staff and gutted the ceiling and reporting requirements.

Specifically, Carter got the House committee to remove its limit on total staff and to accept an unconstraining ceiling on senior officials. (Indeed, the "ceiling" would have allowed a fully staffed Carter White House to double its senior staff if it wanted.) He then persuaded the Senate, whose members cared even less about the issue, to reduce the reporting requirements further: instead of detailed records on individual employees, the White House would need to report only the total amounts spent on different types of staff. Information that was genuinely revealing would remain hidden, as before. In the conference committee, the Senate version prevailed, and the fully gutted bill became law. The president got his authorization. Congress got next to nothing.[39]

To date, the 1978 law has been Congress's most coherent attempt to get a grip on the institutional presidency. But legislation is not Congress's only avenue of attack. There is also its annually exercised power of the purse, which is clearly capable of eviscerating the institutional presidency if used strategically. How has Congress wielded this formidable power? It has barely put it to use. Until the 1970s, presidential budgets were lightly scrutinized and typically passed through Congress unchanged. Presidents provided almost no information about the White House and its operations, or even about the details of EOP agencies, and Congress simply appropriated whatever they said was necessary. During the 1970s, matters became more contentious, peaking during the Watergate era but never entirely subsiding thereafter.[40]

Presidents have to work a little harder for their money now. The Appropriations committees demand more information, scrutinize it more carefully, and are more critical than they used to be. But there is much less here than meets the eye. Presidents continue to get virtually everything they request, legislative rhetoric aside.[41] And the information they provide to Congress is next to useless for genuine control purposes. For the most part, their requests take the form of lump sum amounts pertaining to entire EOP units or to broad categories of employees or activities, with no information about the details of presidential organization, programs, or staffing. Even these days, then, the presidency is treated with kid gloves, and Congress remains largely in the dark about what happens inside it.

Regulatory Review

Regulatory review is often spotlighted as an issue that captures what the institutional battle between the president and Congress is all about. Presidents have imposed new procedures on regulatory agencies in a sustained attempt, stretching over a period of some twenty years, to gain control of agency rulemaking and assert presidential priorities. Meanwhile, the agencies and their legislative supporters have vigorously protested, claiming that the bureaucracy is being denied the autonomy and discretion it needs to fulfill its legislative mandates. What could better reflect the struggle for institutional power and advantage than this?

Yet regulatory review is quite different from most institutional issues in one crucial respect: it has entailed direct presidential attacks on interest groups, notably environmental groups. Thus, unlike civil service reform or congressional oversight of the presidency, whose effects are broad and general, the effects of regulatory review have been concentrated on a few powerful targets. Not surprisingly, these targets have fought back. As a result, legislators' normally weak incentives to protect Congress's institutional interests against presidential onslaughts have been bolstered, enormously so, by powerful groups demanding legislative action. Regulatory review, then, is an unusual—and, for Congress, quite fortunate—case in which interest groups are actually pressuring Congress to protect its own institutional interests.[42]

The controversy began in the early 1970s, when President Nixon instituted the Quality of Life review program under the OMB. His real target was the Environmental Protection Agency (EPA), newly created in 1970, which was devising antipollution rules that stood to cost industry billions of dollars a year at a time when the national economy—Nixon's main concern—was headed for trouble. The administration adopted procedures requiring the EPA to submit its rules for prepublication review so that other agencies (notably the Department of Commerce) could comment, economic costs could be analyzed, conflicting views could be reconciled, justifications could be required—and pressure could be applied to bring EPA rules more in line with the president's program.

During this period, however, new legislation deepened the presidency's regulatory problems. As Robert Percival notes,

Seven new regulatory agencies had been created, including EPA, OSHA [Occupational Safety and Health Administration], and the Consumer Product Safety Commission. Between 1970 and 1974, twenty-nine major regulatory statutes had been enacted and the number of pages in the Federal Register had more than doubled from 20,036 to 42,422 per year.[43]

When Gerald Ford became president in 1974, he faced a rising tide of costly regulations, along with serious inflation and energy problems that demanded action.

Ford responded by creating a more extensive system of regulatory review. The Quality of Life program was continued. In addition, with the consent of an inflation-concerned Congress, he established the Council on Wage-Price Stability (COWPS) in the EOP and ordered regulatory agencies to submit their proposed rules, along with "inflation-impact statements," to COWPS for review. The aim, once again, was to use procedure, analysis, and pressure to get regulatory agencies to recognize economic costs and modify their rules accordingly.

When Jimmy Carter, a Democrat, took office, environmental and labor groups looked forward to a relaxation that would give their agencies a freer hand. But Carter faced virtually the same problems that the Republicans Nixon and Ford had, and his response was distinctly presidential: he took even more aggressive action along the same general path. In Executive Order 12044, agencies were told to prepare "regulatory analyses" for all rules having major economic effects by rigorously evaluating their cost-effectiveness. Proposed rules would then be reviewed by the new Regulatory Analysis Review Group (RARG), made up of representatives from seventeen executive agencies, led by the OMB, COWPS, and the CEA, and staffed by economists who were committed to cost-benefit analysis.

It is clear from insider accounts that regulatory agencies—which were led, of course, by presidential appointees—responded by moderating some of their rules, at times against their own best judgment.[44] The most affected interest groups and agencies, particularly the environmentalists and the EPA, complained loudly, and members of Congress, led by Senator Edmund Muskie, a Democrat from Maine, obliged with sympathetic hearings but little else. Near the end of the Carter administration, however, the insistent pressure finally bore fruit: Carter pledged to go easier on the EPA, and RARG backed off.[45]

This was the calm before the storm. In little more than a year, Ronald Reagan took office and pushed regulatory review well beyond the bounds of his predecessors. He began quickly, appointing a Task Force on Regulatory Relief (chaired by Vice President George Bush), which promptly suspended some two hundred pending regulations and prepared a hit list of current regulations to be targeted for review. He followed up with his ground-breaking Executive Order 12291, which brought regulatory agencies under presidential control as never before.

The executive order required agencies to submit all proposed rules to the OMB's Office of Information and Regulatory Affairs (OIRA) for prepublication review, accompanied by rigorous cost-benefit analyses and evaluations of alternatives. In a departure from past practice, the OMB now allowed agencies to issue rules only when the benefits could be shown to exceed the costs; it also required them to choose among alternatives in such a way as to maximize the net benefits to society as a whole. Moreover, the OMB now asserted the right to delay proposed rules indefinitely while review was pending.[46]

The Reagan scheme imposed severe constraints on the EPA, OSHA, and other regulatory agencies.[47] Environmental groups, especially, were furious, and launched all-out attempts to persuade Congress to break the hold of regulatory review. This pressure had been building for more than ten years, as frustration with past presidents had prompted demands for a congressional counterattack. But now, with the Reagan agenda so aggressive, the groups were pulling out the stops.

How did Congress respond? It did not take on the president directly in an all-out assault—say, through major legislation that declared Executive Order 12291 null and void. Instead, its approach was piecemeal and fragmented, and it generated just what we would expect from a group-dominated institution: special interest legislation—such as the 1982 amendments to the Endangered Species Act, the 1984 amendments to the Hazardous and Solid Waste Act, and the 1986 Superfund amendments—that, through countless new restrictions, further narrowed the EPA's discretion, hobbled it with even more cumbersome administrative burdens, and, on very specific items, directed the president and the OMB not to interfere. For the most part, then, legislators and groups attacked the president by burying the EPA in more bureaucracy. As Percival describes it, "Congress has expressed its dissatisfaction with the consequences of regulatory review by adding more specific statutory controls on agencies' discretion every time it has reauthorized the environmental laws. The result has been a distinct trend toward reduced flexibility."[48]

At the same time that all this was going on, another drama was unfolding. OIRA, as it happens, was not really a Reagan invention. It had been created at the tail end of the Carter period as part of the Paperwork Reduction Act of 1980, and only later did Reagan, through an executive order, put regulatory review into its hands.[49] The problem was that as a statutory agency OIRA had to weather the budgetary process every year to get funding—and to make matters worse, its authorization was set to run out in 1983. In principle, then, OIRA was vulnerable to attack.

What happened? OIRA's opponents had a perfect chance to shoot it down in 1983, since reauthorization called for an affirmative act of Congress and they needed only to block. And in fact, the act was not reauthorized. The House went along, but the Senate did not.[50] Reagan countered by instructing OIRA to do what it had always done. But it was now acting without legislative authorization; and this meant that, merely on a parliamentary point of order, legislators could move to deny the agency funding. No authorization, no funding.

Yet opponents were not able to make this tactic work. In 1984 and 1985, OIRA was funded. In 1986, John Dingell credibly threatened to employ the point-of-order strategy, and a bargain was struck with the White House: the act would be reauthorized and OIRA would receive funding, but future agency heads would require Senate confirmation and OIRA would have to increase public disclosures about its review process.[51] These were concessions by Reagan, but not serious ones considering that, if legislative opponents really had been able to exercise power, they could have put OIRA out of business. The president clearly held the upper hand. The regulatory review system churned on, shaping and delaying regulations—and infuriating interest groups and agencies.

The Bush years witnessed more of the same. Although Bush was not as committed to regulatory review as Reagan, the basic structure of Executive Order 12291 remained in place, a less zealous OIRA continued to do its presidential job, and the interest groups continued to nibble away at their nemesis through piecemeal congressional action. Environmentalists scored an indirect success (with Bush's assistance) through the new Clean Air Act of 1990, which buried the EPA in more bureaucratic constraints, directives, and timetables.

This bill, as Jonathan Rauch puts it, "is one of the most expensive and compli-cated regulatory measures of the postwar years. It runs to almost 800 pages."[52]

They also took direct shots at OIRA. Its authority, which had been renewed in 1986, ran out again in three years, and this gave opponents yet another op-portunity to kill it. In 1990, legislators agreed to reauthorize the Paperwork Reduction Act if Bush would accept certain restrictions on OIRA's powers, among them a sixty-day deadline for reviewing rules and a requirement that it provide detailed explanations for any substantive changes in rules. These, again, were not major concessions, because they would leave the entire regulatory review apparatus in place. Although Bush was willing to go along, key Republi-can senators opposed the bill (for reasons of their own), and it was defeated.[53] The result left OIRA without authorization, and thus vulnerable to extinction. Yet the Bush (and later the Clinton) administration succeeded in getting funding for the agency every year since.

In short, OIRA's legislative opponents had everything going for them, and still they failed to stop regulatory review. They did, however, make trouble: they defeated Bush's nominee to head OIRA. The president then relied on his ex-ecutive flexibility, choosing not to submit another candidate and instead to ask an OIRA careerist to serve as acting head. He also took a look at all the prob-lems surrounding OIRA as a statutory agency and decided to change strategy, shifting major responsibility for regulatory review from OIRA to the Com-petitiveness Council, a purely presidential unit headed by Vice President Dan Quayle.[54]

The Competitiveness Council, which originally had been given a broad presidential mandate to look into issues ranging from legal reform to job training, dove quickly into regulatory review and, with staff assistance from OIRA, became an influential and controversial force. For the remainder of the Bush presidency, legislative opponents shifted their ire to the council, and went after it in the usual ways.[55] But they were never able to deny it funding; they had no basis for affecting its personnel or appointments; and they never passed legislation challenging the council's right to do what it did.[56]

When the Democrats finally took back the White House in 1993, one of the first things President Bill Clinton did was to get rid of the Competitiveness Council. This action evoked a joyous response from many legislators and in-terest groups, but it was largely symbolic—for he most assuredly did not get rid of regulatory review. Indeed, he made it clear that regulatory review is es-sential to presidential leadership and that he intends to keep it: precisely what we would expect of all presidents, whatever their partisanship. Review functions have been returned to OIRA, and procedures are being revamped to reflect the new president's agenda—by ensuring access, for example, to environmentalists, labor, and other Clinton supporters. It remains to be seen what will come of this, but the best guess is for "a fine-tuning of what's evolved over the past couple of decades," not a radical change.[57]

Overall, the story of regulatory review is more riddled with outright conflict than the others we have told. In this case, attempts by presidents to expand their institutional powers have taken the form of attacks on specific groups, and these groups have launched counterattacks. It is Congress's good fortune to have been caught in the middle, for the groups have been pressuring legislators to take actions that, coincidentally, defend the interests of Congress as an institution. This is why Congress has been more active and successful in regulatory review than in the other areas we have looked at.

Nonetheless, Congress's limited success is nothing to brag about. Regulatory review is now a routine part of the executive process. Presidents began it, built it up, and regularly exercised its powers in the face of interest group and legislative hostility. Congress did not rise up and pass major legislation to stop them, although it had the power to do so. It did not refuse to fund the review agencies, although it also had the power to do that. Instead, it succeeded only in imposing minor restrictions on regulatory review—and burying the EPA still further in bureaucracy.

Conclusion

This is not a story about presidential triumph. Separation of powers creates a governmental system that is distinctly unfriendly to presidents. It fragments authority, multiplies opposition and conflict, promotes inertia, generates a bureaucracy resistant to central control, and, in a host of other ways, produces an environment hostile to any kind of forceful, coherent leadership.

But presidents are strongly motivated to try to overcome as much of this as they can. And their best bet is not to accept a system that is stacked against them, but rather to do what they can to modify the architecture of the system itself—making it more presidential, more conducive to the leadership they strive to exercise. It is here that the story looks brighter for them. For whatever separation of powers does to frustrate their leadership, it also ensures that they will benefit from certain critical advantages over Congress in the politics of institution building and bureaucratic control. In time, they can create a friendlier system.

Some of these advantages arise from their unilateral powers of discretionary action as chief executive. These are powers that Congress does not possess and, except at the margins, cannot readily stop presidents from exercising. They give presidents tremendous flexibility in designing and developing their institutional capacity for control. They also enable presidents to take aggressive action in shifting the status quo, allowing them to win by default if Congress cannot react effectively.

Equally important advantages accrue to presidents because, as unitary decision makers, they have the good fortune to face a Congress that is inherently vulnerable to serious collective action problems. One manifestation is the motivational asymmetry: presidents care much more about institutional issues than legislators do, and they are far better able to take action. Another is that multiple veto points and high transaction costs make it extremely difficult for Congress to take decisive action at all, especially in the face of presidential opposition. This means that, when presidents use their powers of unilateral action to change the status quo, Congress often cannot do anything about it. And presidents win by default.

The case studies serve to illustrate how these presidential advantages play out in American politics. Whether we look at civil service reform, congressional oversight, or regulatory review, presidents have clearly been aggressive in building their own institutions for controlling the vast government bureaucracy. And Congress has typically been disorganized, ineffective, and even passive in response. Presidents did not always get their way in these cases, and Congress did not always fail to act. But changes in the institutional balance of power came about because presidents were pushing and shoving to occupy new institutional terrain, and Congress did not have what it took to stop them.

Inevitably, I have not been able to discuss everything that may seem relevant to these cases nor to the general theme of this chapter. Politics is complicated, and complete histories would show that many influences have been at work. Each president is different, for example, and their personalities, ideologies, and agendas surely help to explain why some of them (Reagan, say) place more emphasis on strategies of institution building and control than others (such as Bush). Similarly, divided government surely contributes to the pattern of conflict we have observed: Republican presidents are less likely than Democrats to find support for their agendas in a Democratic Congress, and they are more likely to pursue an "administrative presidency" that places a premium on bureaucratic control.[58] And then there is the familiar argument that Congress defers to presidents. This may sometimes be valid, especially for foreign policy issues that have little effect on constituency interests; but most of the time, I suspect, deference is just another way of saying that legislators do not have strong incentives to act on institutional issues.

I have also had to neglect Congress's own attempts at institution building. A more extensive analysis would examine, for example, the political origins of the Congressional Budget Office, the War Powers Act, the tremendous growth in legislative staff, and other recent developments that may seem to counterbalance the institutional presidency. Still, such an analysis would be unlikely to challenge the thesis of presidential advantage. The new congressional budgetary process is a disaster of fragmentation and irresponsibility. The War Powers Act has largely been ignored by presidents. And legislative staff members spend most of their time pursuing the parochial interests that so animate their bosses. Were the picture more fully drawn, Congress would continue to reveal that it is not nearly as well equipped to defend or promote its interests as the president is.

What does the future hold in store? Most obviously, it promises continued gains by presidents and continued movement toward a more presidential system. Although this may raise legitimate concerns among those who fear excessive presidential power (or certain presidents' agendas), on the whole it can be regarded as a healthy development. The American system has always been fragmented and decentralized, and the institutions favored by today's legislators and interest groups are cut from this same mold. Whether they intend to be or not, they are protectors of the institutional status quo. Were they to prevail consistently, they would entrench an outdated brand of centrifugal government that cannot possibly address the burgeoning problems of a modern, complex society.

What is new and different in the modern period is the presidency. Presidents are the ones who are out of step with tradition, pushing for leadership, control, responsibility, and effectiveness—and for new institutional arrangements that fly in the face of old-style practice and parochialism. They are the ones, conservatives and liberals alike, who represent the driving force for change in the structure of American government, change that is needed if government is to work at all well.

This does not mean that, over time, presidents are somehow destined to take over. It does not even mean that they will have enough authority or control to govern effectively. Separation of powers sets up too many impediments, from the legal requirements of the Constitution to the competitive dynamics of modern politics, to allow for such a one-sided shift in the institutional balance.

The most reasonable expectation is for some sort of equilibrium to be reached in future years, an equilibrium more presidential than we have now—but still a far cry from what presidents would like and what effective leadership would require.

Notes

1. Terry M. Moe, "The Politicized Presidency," in *The New Direction in American Politics*, ed. John E. Chubb and Paul E. Peterson (Washington, D.C.: Brookings Institution, 1985); John P. Burke, *The Institutional Presidency* (Baltimore: Johns Hopkins University Press, 1992).

2. For a more fully developed discussion of these issues, see Terry M. Moe, "The Politics of Structural Choice: Toward a Theory of Public Bureaucracy," in *Organization Theory: From Chester Barnard to the Present and Beyond*, ed. Oliver E. Williamson (New York: Oxford University Press, 1990). For empirical evidence on the political design of bureaucracy, see Terry M. Moe, "The Politics of Bureaucratic Structure," in *Can the Government Govern?* ed. John E. Chubb and Paul E. Peterson (Washington, D.C.: Brookings Institution, 1989).

3. Richard Pious, *The American Presidency* (New York: Basic Books, 1979), 38.

4. Harold H. Bruff, "Presidential Power and Administrative Rulemaking," *Yale Law Journal* 88 (1979): 451–508; Bruff, "Presidential Management of Agency Rulemaking," *George Washington Law Review* 57 (1989): 533–595; Lloyd N. Cutler, "The Case for Presidential Intervention in Regulatory Rulemaking by the Executive Branch," *Tulane Law Review* 56 (1982): 830–848; Peter Strauss, "The Place of Agencies in Government: Separation of Powers and the Fourth Branch," *Columbia Law Review* 84 (1984): 573–669.

5. Pious, *The American Presidency*.

6. Strauss, "The Place of Agencies in Government."

7. Louis Fisher, *The Politics of Shared Power* (Washington, D.C.: CQ Press, 1993); Strauss, "The Place of Agencies in Government."

8. Eugene Fama and Michael Jensen, "Separation of Ownership and Control," *Journal of Law and Economics* 26 (1983): 301–325.

9. Pious, *The American Presidency*; Bruff, "Presidential Power and Administrative Rulemaking"; Bruff, "Presidential Management of Agency Rulemaking"; Strauss, "The Place of Agencies in Government"; Cutler, "The Case for Presidential Intervention in Regulatory Rulemaking by the Executive Branch."

10. Robert V. Percival, "Checks without Balance: Executive Office Oversight of the Environmental Protection Agency," *Law and Contemporary Problems* 54 (1991): 127–204.

11. Mancur Olson, *The Logic of Collective Action*, 2d ed. (Cambridge: Harvard University Press, 1971).

12. Gary Cox and Mathew McCubbins, *Legislative Leviathan* (Berkeley: University of California Press, 1993).

13. David Mayhew, *Congress: The Electoral Connection* (New Haven: Yale University Press, 1974).

14. Hugh Heclo, "The OMB and the Presidency: The Problem of Neutral Competence," *Public Interest* 38 (Winter 1975): 80–98.

15. Richard D. McKelvey, "Intransitivities in Multidimensional Voting: Models and Some Implications for Agenda Control," *Journal of Economic Theory* 12 (June 1976): 472–482.

16. See John Kingdon, *Agendas, Alternatives, and Public Policies* (Boston: Little, Brown, 1984); Paul Light, *The President's Agenda* (Baltimore: Johns Hopkins University Press, 1982).

17. Thomas H. Hammond, Jeffrey S. Hill, and Gary J. Miller, "Presidents, Congress, and the 'Congressional Control of Administration' Hypothesis" (Paper presented at the annual meeting of the American Political Science Association, Washington, D.C., 1986).

18. George C. Edwards III, *Presidential Influence in Congress* (San Francisco: W. H. Freeman, 1980); Stephen J. Wayne, *The Legislative Presidency* (New York: Harper and Row, 1978).

19. Richard Polenberg, *Reorganizing Roosevelt's Government 1936–1939* (Cambridge: Harvard University Press, 1966); Peri E. Arnold, *Making the Managerial Presidency* (Princeton, N.J.: Princeton University Press, 1986).

20. Felix A. Nigro, "The Politics of Civil Service Reform," *Southern Review of Public Administration* 20 (1979): 196–239.

21. Patricia W. Ingraham, "The Civil Service Reform Act of 1978: The Design and Legislative History," in *Legislating Bureaucratic Change: The Civil Service Reform Act of 1978*, ed. Patricia W. Ingraham and Carolyn Ban (Albany: State University of New York Press, 1984); Harlan Lebo, "The Administration's All-Out Effort on Civil Service Reform," *National Journal*, May 27, 1978, 837–838.

22. Nigro, "The Politics of Civil Service Reform."

23. Arnold, *Making the Managerial Presidency*; Ann Cooper, "Carter Plan to Streamline Civil Service Moves Slowly toward Senate, House Votes," *Congressional Quarterly Weekly Report*, July 15, 1978, 1777–1784.

24. Cooper, "Carter Plan to Streamline Civil Service."

25. It may well be that their rhetoric was really just a vehicle for defending group interests. Mathias, in particular, had every reason to be keenly sensitive to what the federal employees' unions wanted, since many of their members live in his state.

26. Ann Cooper, "Carter Military Bill Veto Could Slow Senate Action on Civil Service Measure," *Congressional Quarterly Weekly Report*, August 19, 1978, 2174; Cooper, "Senate Approves Carter Civil Service Reforms," *Congressional Quarterly Weekly Report*, August 26, 1978, 2239, 2299.

27. Nigro, "The Politics of Civil Service Reform."

28. Ann Cooper, "Carter Civil Service Plan: Battered but Alive," *Congressional Quarterly Weekly Report*, July 22, 1978, 1839–1841, 1890–1894.

29. Ann Cooper, "House Civil Service Debate Slowed by Bill Opponents," *Congressional Quarterly Weekly Report*, September 9, 1978, 2441; Cooper, "Civil Service Reforms Likely This Year," *Congressional Quarterly Weekly Report*, September 16, 1978, 2458–2462.

30. Ann Cooper, "Enactment of Civil Service Reforms Nears," *Congressional Quarterly Weekly Report*, October 7, 1978, 2735–2736.

31. Ann Cooper, "Civil Service Reorganization Plan Approved," *Congressional Quarterly Weekly Report*, August 12, 1978, 2125–2127.

32. John Hart, *The Presidential Branch* (New York: Pergamon, 1987), 169.

33. Hugh Heclo, "The OMB and the Presidency; Moe, "The Politicized Presidency"; Arnold, *Making the Managerial Presidency*.

34. "Congress Accepts Four Executive Reorganization Plans," *Congressional Quarterly Almanac, 1970* (Washington, D.C.: Congressional Quarterly, 1971), 462–467.

35. Edward S. Flash, Jr., *Economic Advice and Presidential Leadership: The Council of Economic Advisers* (New York: Columbia University Press, 1965); I. M. Destler, *Presidents, Bureaucrats, and Foreign Policy* (Princeton, N.J.: Princeton University Press, 1972); Bert Rockman, "America's Department of State: Irregular and Regular Syndromes of Policymaking," *American Political Science Review* 75 (1981): 911–927.

36. Dean L. Yarwood, "Oversight of Presidential Funds by the Appropriations Committees: Learning from the Watergate Crisis," *Administration and Society* 13 (1981): 299–346.

37. House Committee on Post Office and Civil Service, *A Report on the Growth of the Executive Office of the President 1955–1973*, Committee Print 19, 92d Cong., 2d sess., 1972.

38. "Executive Office, Treasure Funds," *Congressional Quarterly Weekly Report*, August 4, 1973, 2155–2157.

39. "White House Staff," *Congressional Quarterly Almanac, 1978* (Washington, D.C.: Congressional Quarterly, 1979), 796–798; Hart, *The Presidential Branch*.

40. Yarwood, "Oversight of Presidential Funds."

41. If there is an exception, it is in the controversial (and special interest) area of regulatory review, discussed in the next section. For data on presidential budgets, see the accounts of Treasury, Post Office, and Civil Service appropriations in *Congressional Quarterly Almanac* (Washington, D.C.: Congressional Quarterly, 1970–present).

42. The basic history of regulatory review is well known. The following account relies largely on William F. West and Joseph Cooper, "The Rise of Administrative Clearance," in *The Presidency and Public Policy Making*, ed. George C. Edwards III, Steven A. Shull, and Norman C. Thomas (Pittsburgh: University of Pittsburgh Press, 1985); Elizabeth Sanders, "The Presidency and the Bureaucratic State," in *The Presidency and the Political System*, 3d ed., ed. Michael Nelson (Washington, D.C.: CQ Press, 1990), 409–442; Thomas O. McGarity, *Reinventing Rationality: The Role of Regulatory Analysis in the Federal Bureaucracy* (Cambridge: Cambridge University Press, 1991); and Percival, "Checks without Balance."

43. Percival, "Checks without Balance," 139.

44. See, for example, John Quarles, *Cleaning Up America* (New York: Houghton Mifflin, 1976).

45. Christopher C. De Muth, "Constraining Regulatory Costs—Part I: The White House Review Program," *Regulation* 4 (January/February 1980): 13–26.

46. To this already stringent set of procedures, Reagan later added Executive Order 12498, which required agencies to submit annually a program outlining all significant regulatory actions planned for the coming year so that the OMB would have plenty of time to review them without the pressure of statutory deadlines.

47. Peter M. Benda and Charles H. Levine, "Reagan and the Bureaucracy: The Bequest, the Promise, and the Legacy," in *The Reagan Legacy: Promise and Performance*, ed. Charles O. Jones (Chatham, N.J.: Chatham House, 1988).

48. Percival, "Checks without Balance," 175.

49. Benda and Levine, "Reagan and the Bureaucracy."

50. Ann Cooper, "Paperwork Reduction," *Congressional Quarterly Almanac, 1983* (Washington, D.C.: Congressional Quarterly, 1984), 590–591.

51. Ann Cooper, "OMB Regulatory Review," *Congressional Quarterly Almanac, 1986* (Washington, D.C.: Congressional Quarterly, 1987), 325.

52. Jonathan Rauch, "The Regulatory President," *National Journal*, November 30, 1991, 2902–2906.

53. Kitty Dumas, "Administration Deal Pushes Paperwork Reduction Act," *Congressional Quarterly Weekly Report*, October 27, 1990, 3602; Janet Hook, "101st Congress Leaves Behind Plenty of Laws, Criticism," *Congressional Quarterly Weekly Report*, November 3, 1990, 3699.

54. Rauch, "The Regulatory President."

55. Kirk Victor, "Quayle's Quiet Coup," *National Journal*, July 6, 1991, 1676–1680.

56. On the failed attempt to deny the council funding, see Susan Kellam, "Social Security Riders Thrown from Senate Treasury Bill," *Congressional Quarterly Weekly Report*, September 12, 1992, 2712–2713; Kellam, "Conferees Cut $200 Million, Pave Way to Approval," *Congressional Quarterly Weekly Report*, September 26, 1992, 2936.

57. Viveca Novak, "The New Regulators," *National Journal*, July 17, 1993, 1802.

58. Richard Nathan, *The Administrative Presidency* (New York: Wiley, 1983).

16 The President and Congress

Mark A. Peterson

Presidents need Congress—to ratify treaties, to confirm executive and judicial appointments, and, most important, to pass the legislation they want and sustain their vetoes of legislation they do not want. Yet presidents vary tremendously, both from each other and at different periods within their own terms of office, in their ability to persuade Congress to do their will. Mark A. Peterson argues that the best way to understand the protean relationship between the presidency and Congress is to view them as "tandem institutions." Such institutions need each other's support or acquiescence to succeed, yet may be thwarted by changing conditions of "partisanship, ideology, objective needs, technical feasibility, campaign commitments, and electoral constraints." Although most of these elements lie outside the presidency, individual presidents can make a difference. Peterson concludes by assessing the influence that each president can wield through strategy and skill.

In August 1993, just before the start of the summer recess, Congress enacted President Bill Clinton's long-term economic recovery program, as embodied in the highly controversial and intensely debated budget-reconciliation bill. The vote could not have been closer; indeed, the passing of the bill depended upon the last-second reversal of one freshman Democratic member of the House of Representatives and the constitutional power of the vice president to break tie votes in the Senate. No one on Capitol Hill or in the punditry could recall any previous president winning passage of a major legislative initiative, as had Clinton, without securing a single favorable vote in either house from a member of the opposition party. For a chief executive who was suffering the lowest levels of popular support ever recorded for a president so early in the first term, this razor-thin vote on the budget—following the earlier defeat by Republican filibuster of his short-term economic "stimulus" package—was not an auspicious beginning for his relationship with Congress. No longer could the gridlock of divided government be blamed for tensions between the executive and legislative branches, because Bill Clinton's election in November 1992 and the continued Democratic majorities in Congress had brought about unified party government for the first time in more than a decade.

Twelve years earlier a new conservative Republican president, Ronald Reagan, had engineered a critical victory for his quite different but equally controversial economic recovery program. With that success in hand, Reagan could rest. His platform was one of government retrenchment, not activism. Not so Clinton. While members of Congress spent the recess traveling to their districts and states attempting to explain their budget votes to their constituents, President Clinton was preparing the next round of his expansive legislative agenda: achieving campaign finance reform; winning ratification of the North American Free Trade Agreement (NAFTA); implementing the plan to "reinvent" government by changing the way it conducts its business; and reforming the nation's health care financing and delivery system, the largest and most complex social policy initiative ever launched by a United States president. September, the newspapers said, was to be the month for "policy wonks."

In the months ahead the president and Congress would also work through the confirmation process for Clinton's appointments to the executive branch and the judiciary and engage one another on foreign policy issues that were as momentous as they were unpredictable. The prime minister of Israel and the head of the Palestine Liberation Organization would make history by shaking hands on the south lawn of the White House; Clinton and Congress would have to settle on the proper amount of foreign aid to both parties. The Russian president, Boris Yeltsin, would use force to end the rebellion of his opponents in the parliament; Clinton and Congress would have to revisit the question of American support for the fledgling democracy. A warlord in Somalia would transform a United Nations humanitarian aid mission involving U.S. troops into an open military confrontation that cost many American lives; Clinton and Congress would debate the appropriateness of a continued U.S. armed presence. The tragic war in Bosnia and Herzegovina, and its import for America, would never be far from anyone's thinking.

The first year of the Clinton administration serves to highlight many of the central questions concerning the relationship between the president and Congress in our constitutional system. What are the myriad and diverse ways in which presidents and Congress must interact, and how do these interactions differ from one another in character and consequence? If we are concerned about presidential leadership, how might we assess, with some analytical confidence, presidential effectiveness in dealing with Congress? Can we explain the range of institutional conflict and cooperation that characterizes modern executive-legislative relations, or account for the tremendous variations in how successfully different presidents have managed their interactions with Capitol Hill?

In this chapter, I first approach these questions from the perspective of the president. I begin by describing the various ways in which presidents need one or both houses of Congress—to ratify treaties; to approve their nominees for positions in the executive and judicial branches; and to enforce the president's positions on legislation, whether that means supporting presidential initiatives, adopting the president's budget, or sustaining the president's vetoes. Taking the task of legislating to be the main activity that entangles the two branches (and the one that exhibits the greatest variation over time), I then explore different ways of evaluating presidential effectiveness. Explaining differences in effectiveness—both within single administrations and across several presidencies—leads to important questions about how much presidents can control or even influence their own legislative fates. Here I describe a vital distinction between two approaches to understanding the presidential-congressional relationship. One I call the "presidency-centered perspective," a view pervasive in scholarship, journalism, and popular impressions. The other I term the "tandem-institutions perspective," which I believe brings us closer to the realities of the institutional relationship between the two branches. Analysis from the tandem-institutions perspective reveals that although the president and Congress actually cooperate more regularly and presidents are legislatively successful more often than the conventional—that is, the presidency-centered—wisdom would allow, American chief executives possess far less influence over the legislative process than is required to meet popular expectations about presidential leadership.

When the President Needs Congress

When, on October 19, 1987, the stock market's Dow Jones industrial average suddenly and unexpectedly plummeted 508 points, all eyes turned to President Reagan for a quick and effective response.[1] Ever since the Great Depression and President Franklin Delano Roosevelt's advocacy of New Deal programs to remedy it, the president has in popular expectations borne the responsibility to ensure a healthy economy and domestic tranquility. Similarly, America's involvement in World War II and its resulting status as a nuclear superpower engendered equivalent expectations of the president in the realm of foreign policy. The Constitution, however, compels a major distinction between popular expectations of the presidency and the realities of governance. In Richard Neustadt's now classic phrase, it established a government of "separated institutions sharing powers."[2] In one sphere after another, the Constitution makes Congress the president's inescapable partner. Presidents can accomplish little of enduring value without the support or, at the very least, the acquiescence of a significant number of representatives and senators. Nor can Congress do much in the face of an antagonistic chief executive.

Presidents traditionally are afforded their greatest policy-making discretion in matters of foreign and national security policy. This has been especially true since the aftermath of World War II, when the nuclear trigger and the cold war policy of containing the Soviet Union required the kind of timely responsiveness that legislative bodies cannot offer. Even in the international arena, however, the Constitution makes it difficult for presidents to ignore Congress and achieve their desired ends. Article I, section 8, for example, grants the legislature the sole power to declare war and to raise an army. Under the terms of Article II, section 2, treaties negotiated by the president with other nations must be ratified by two-thirds of the Senate if they are to take effect. The participation of the United States in declared wars, formal alliances, strategic arms control accords with world powers like the former Soviet Union, and international trade agreements is impossible without explicit Senate approval.

As it turns out, the constitutional standard of congressional involvement has not been a consistently onerous limitation on chief executives. As the U.S. military actions in Korea, the Dominican Republic, Vietnam, Grenada, and Panama demonstrate, warfare in the modern era rarely entails declared confrontations between massed armies in the traditional sense. When Congress enacted the War Powers Resolution of 1973 over the veto of President Richard M. Nixon, it tried both to recognize this modern reality and to define a constitutional place for itself in the new context of international conflict. But Nixon and all of his successors have challenged the constitutionality of the resolution, and none has permitted it, at least in an overt fashion, to interfere with the prosecution of his national security agenda. The Persian Gulf War in 1991 may represent the single exception to presidential hegemony in modern warfare, because Congress insisted on debating and voting on a resolution authorizing the use of military force. Because the resolution passed in both houses (albeit by the slimmest margins in history for anything resembling a declaration of war), we do not know what would have happened if Congress had defeated the authorization and President George Bush had chosen to proceed with an armed assault on Iraq anyway.

If Congress's constitutional prerogatives in foreign policy are in fact meaningful, we would expect them to be most in evidence in the domain of treaty making. Unlike military engagements, treaties do not require rapid and secret action; by their very nature they permit a more deliberative decision-making process of the sort practiced in legislatures. Because of the potential social, political, economic, and domestic consequences of such agreements, they also fit with Congress's main responsibilities and capabilities. It is not surprising, therefore, that Congress has on occasion played a significant role in the exercise of the treaty power, with a clear capacity to disrupt presidential intentions. President Carter came close to having his presidency derailed when the none-too-popular Panama Canal Treaty just barely attracted the two-thirds vote required in the Senate. Later, Carter had to defer submitting to the Senate the second Strategic Arms Limitation Treaty with the Soviet Union—the discovery of a Soviet military brigade in Cuba had already prompted most senators to oppose the accord. The future of the North American Free Trade Agreement, negotiated by President Bush and promoted vigorously by President Clinton, had an uncertain future on Capitol Hill until the votes were actually taken and the president prevailed.

These compelling anecdotes aside, presidents usually have overcome potential congressional barriers to international accords. From 1953 to 1983, 931 treaties, protocols, and conventions for which Senate ratification was constitutionally required were negotiated by various administrations. Only two were rejected outright by the Senate (neither was among the 127 treaties). Another twenty-three were withdrawn by the president from Senate consideration. Taken as a whole, the ratio of actually ratified treaties, protocols, and conventions to those rejected or withdrawn in this period was 17 to 1.[3] Chief executives have also turned to greater use of executive agreements with the leaders of other countries, which do not require Senate approval.[4] During the 1970s, Sen. Walter Mondale noted, with considerable frustration, that Congress was being asked to ratify relatively inconsequential treaties on archaeological preservation, international aviation, and radio regulation while the president negotiated clandestine executive agreements committing the use of American intelligence and military forces.[5]

The Constitution also involves Congress in the president's appointment power. Presidents nominate individuals to serve in both the federal judiciary and the executive branch, but Article II, section 2, provides the Senate with the role of "advice and consent." No federal judge or justice can be seated, no political appointee to a federal agency can execute federal laws and regulations, and no ambassador-designate can represent the United States abroad without having been confirmed by a majority vote of the Senate.[6] This congressional authority does not go unused. Some senators, such as the conservative Republican Jesse Helms of North Carolina, routinely exploit the Senate's advice and consent power and its filibuster rule to thwart appointments or delay confirmation votes; their goal is to extract something in exchange. On occasion, too, the nomination of an individual to the federal bench or an executive position has prompted a moment of high drama in interbranch relations. Judge Robert Bork, nominated to the U.S. Supreme Court by President Reagan in 1987, joined the list of twenty-six previous Court nominees who failed to obtain Senate confirmation. (Eleven of them were formally rejected by the Senate.)[7] Even selections for the president's cabinet can fall victim to Senate antipathy, either by a direct vote or by strength of opposition that compels the president or the nominee to withdraw his or her name. Sen. John Tower, President Bush's unsuccessful 1989 nominee for secretary of defense, and Zoë Baird and Judge Kimba Wood, President Clinton's first two choices for attorney general, are among the memorable personnel selections that have been cast aside in the face of Senate opposition. Nominations for lower-level offices can also produce fireworks and Senate disapproval, as happened when a rising storm on Capitol Hill led Clinton painfully to withdraw the name of his friend Lani Guinier as his nominee to head the Civil Rights Division of the Justice Department.

As with treaties, however, congressional cooperation in appointments is more the rule than the exception. Presidents typically are able to name several hundred people to the federal district courts, circuit courts of appeal, and the Supreme Court. Reagan successfully appointed 385 judges, filling slightly more than half of all the positions on the federal bench. Bush followed with 187 appointments, almost a quarter of all judicial positions.[8] Clinton, with congressional support, will also be able to leave his mark on the judicial branch. Because of normal attrition and the nearly 100 vacancies that were carried over from the Bush administration, Clinton may name as many as 250 federal judges, about one-third of the judiciary, during his first term.[9] The few public battles over cabinet and subcabinet nominations also belie the usually favorable response that the Senate accords presidents when they seek to fill the roughly three thousand executive branch positions not covered by the civil service system. Taking together all the nominations that require Senate confirmation, no president from Dwight D. Eisenhower to the present has had less than 95 percent of his appointments confirmed in the year of their presentation; most have been above 98 percent.[10]

Although presidents typically choose individuals on philosophical grounds (which can divide the president and the Senate), judicial nominees, especially those for lower courts, who will be constrained by Supreme Court precedent, are evaluated mostly with regard to their established legal talents. The practice of "senatorial courtesy" also gives members of the Senate from the president's party the means to influence selections for federal district courts in their states. Because the Supreme Court is overtly involved in policy making through interpretation and precedent setting in such contentious areas as civil rights, abortion rights, and criminal justice, both presidents and the Senate pay closer attention to the ideological principles involved when a justice is to be appointed. Still, the overwhelming majority (more than 80 percent) of presidential selections for the high court have received the Senate's endorsement. Presidents are even more likely to get their way with appointments to executive agencies and departments. Members of Congress, for the most part, recognize that chief executives should be granted the opportunity to form their own administrations and choose their own teams. In addition, unlike federal judges and justices, executive positions are not lifetime posts.[11] The opposition party in Congress always has the potential to win the next presidential election and place its own political appointees in the bureaucracy.

Treaties and appointments aside, the most important arena for presidential-congressional interactions is legislating—identifying what should be on the public-policy agenda and formulating, debating, and either enacting or defeating policy proposals to address society's problems. This activity lies at the core of Congress's constitutional mandate and the modern presidency's leadership commitment, especially as it has been defined by Theodore Roosevelt and Woodrow Wilson and consummated by FDR and his successors.

Presidents now have three legislative roles. First, Article I, section 7, of the Constitution demands that the chief executive be at least *reactive* to legislation emanating from Capitol Hill. Bills passed by Congress become federal statutes if they have been signed by the president or enacted over the president's veto.[12] Most of the early presidents believed that bills should be vetoed only if they posed a direct threat to the constitutionally granted powers of the executive or the judiciary. The veto was a device for self-preservation, not policy making. President Andrew Jackson, rejecting the desire of Congress to establish a United States Bank, initiated what has become the modern norm: employing the veto to stop what the president perceives simply to be bad law.[13] Serving during periods of united-party government, John F. Kennedy, Lyndon B. Johnson, and

Jimmy Carter, taken together, used the regular veto an average of only twice per year. Eisenhower, Nixon, Reagan, and Bush, typically confronting a Congress controlled by the opposition Democrats, annually wielded the veto pen an average of 4.5, 4, 10, and 9 times, respectively.[14] In an administration that lasted just over two years, Ford sent back forty-five regular vetoes to the Democratic Congress. Presidents have also frequently exploited the threat of a veto to promote changes in legislation more to their liking.

Second, presidents must involve themselves in *mandatory* legislative business. Each year the government requires a budget to finance its activities. The budget actually is enacted in the form of any legislation that changes provisions in the internal revenue code and in thirteen separate appropriations bills. Since the implementation of the Budget and Impoundment Control Act of 1974, "reconciliation" bills have also become a regular instrument for defining important features of the federal budget. Presidents, of course, are required either to sign or veto all of these pieces of legislation. In addition, the Budget and Accounting Act of 1921 explicitly requires that the president, with the help of the Office of Management and Budget, submit to Congress a unified federal budget proposal. Before then, federal agencies had worked directly with Congress to establish their individual operating budgets.

Third, presidents can—and now do—have a more *proactive* role in legislating. Article II, section 3, of the Constitution has always specified that the president "shall from time to time give to the Congress Information of the State of the Union, and recommend to their Consideration such Measures as he shall judge necessary and expedient." Modern presidents have turned this constitutional invitation into an elaborate and routine process for transmitting to Congress all manner of initiatives, ranging from the most minor changes in existing programs to extraordinarily bold policy departures. One can hardly imagine, for example, a proposal that would affect a greater share of the economy, more interests, and a higher proportion of the population than President Clinton's health care reform plan. Presidents may not dominate Congress, but they are usually the lead player in establishing the agenda of issues that Congress will debate and consider.[15] To a significant degree, the president's agenda becomes the legislature's agenda.

Treaties, appointments, and legislation demarcate the formal domains of presidential-congressional relations. But both across domains and within them tremendous variations exist in how active presidents choose to be and how regularly they obtain congressional assent. Some presidents, for example, eschew heavily laden legislative agendas but quite willingly strike down bills that they consider inferior. Others almost drown Congress in a tide of presidential initiatives. A few presidents see a sizable majority of their proposals passed into law, while others can persuade Congress to accept but a small minority. Almost all presidents, however, enjoy far greater congressional acceptance of their treaties and appointments than of their domestic policy initiatives, which members of Congress view as lodged in their own turf. In the remainder of this chapter, I focus on the president's role as "chief legislator" in order to explore presidential effectiveness in Congress—how it varies among presidents and within single administrations, and why. Because struggles over contentious appointments and treaties involve the same kind of dynamics that characterize presidential legislative priorities, an assessment of legislative effectiveness will contribute to an understanding of all aspects of presidential-congressional relations.

Presidents as Effective Legislative Leaders

Quite frequently we hear or read reports in the media about a president's success with Congress or, instead, about a particular incumbent's difficulties with the legislative branch. What does success or failure mean in these reports? What ideas and activities are captured by considerations of a president's effectiveness as a legislative leader?

Recent studies of presidential leadership in Congress have typically relied on one of three different ways of assessing the president's influence and effectiveness on Capitol Hill. The first measure, which usually is referred to as "presidential support," involves calculating in various ways the percentage of times in a year that particular members, clusters of members, or the House or the Senate as a whole have cast recorded roll-call floor votes that support the president's publicly expressed position. From 1953 to 1984, for example, individual representatives in the House supported the president's position on an average of 55 percent of the votes; in the Senate the average was 58 percent. By focusing on the decisions and actions of individual members, the authors of these studies use presidential support scores to explain "the influence and leadership that presidents exercise to elicit congressional support for their proposals, . . . [to] provide a solid basis for inferences about the causes of congressional behavior."[16] They seek to determine the extent to which the legislator's decision to vote in support of the president's position was the result of what the president actually did to influence the vote, and the extent to which it was simply the consequence of other factors, independent of the president, that led to the same decision. In the first case the president has exercised effective leadership; in the second, the president has been irrelevant.

This method of evaluating presidential effectiveness has two limitations. It tells us little about either what Congress ultimately accomplished legislatively or whether the president's leadership had any effect on the types of public policies that were actually enacted into law. Did government action on education, transportation, or health care financing, for example, change as a result of presidential leadership? In addition, because calculations of presidential support depend on formally recorded roll-call votes on the floor of the House and Senate, they do not incorporate instances in which the president was either effective in influencing the outcome of nonrecorded (for example, voice) votes or ineffective in overcoming obstacles at the committee level that thwarted executive initiatives.

A second measure of effectiveness is more concerned with the actual consequences of congressional action. It asks, When presidents have announced public positions on legislative issues for which there were recorded roll-call votes, have their positions been victorious? What percentage of times has their side won? Presidents from the time of Eisenhower's inaugural through Reagan's first term have seen their positions prevail on 75 percent of these votes in the House and Senate.

This second way of evaluating presidential influence in Congress has several virtues. Presidents, and the public that assesses their performance, are concerned about whether or not they are able to work with Congress and produce real results. As Jon Bond and Richard Fleisher express it, "Although presidents care about and keep track of which individuals [in Congress] support them, the more important issue for the president is the collective result."[17] In addition, roll-call victories and defeats, because they may include decisions on treaties and presidential appointments, offer some indication of the president's achievements in domains other than the enactment of legislation.[18]

As with presidential support scores, however, knowing how often the president's publicly stated positions have prevailed in congressional roll-call votes leaves us with an incomplete picture of the presidential-congressional relationship. All manner of reasons explain why people vote for different presidential candidates, but prominent among them is people's perception of the candidates' ability to get things done. If presidents are to have enduring influence, they have to play an instrumental role in passing legislation that reshapes the contours of the nation's laws. Modern presidents, especially, have emphasized the formulation, presentation, and enactment of what we refer to as the president's legislative program—the compilation of proposals large and small that constitutes the chief executive's plan for addressing legislatively the nation's social, economic, and national security needs. Although Congress maintains its independence, it also finds advantages in having the president organize the legislative agenda. As one House member suggested to an official in the Eisenhower administration, "Don't expect us to start from scratch on what you people want. That's not the way we do things here. You draft the bills and we work them over."[19]

A third indicator of effectiveness in Congress is thus the frequency with which presidential legislative initiatives are actually enacted into law—either precisely as proposed by the president or in some compromised form.[20] When presidents propose legislation to expand funding for education, support urban mass transit, publicly finance health care, restrict access to guns, regulate air pollution, cut personal income taxes, or any number of other objectives, how often does Congress incorporate these programs into the body of federal law? Of perhaps greater interest, how often are presidents successful in persuading Congress to pass legislative initiatives of substantial scope and importance? In the period 1953–1984, 54 percent of domestic policy initiatives introduced by presidents were enacted, at least in substantial part. Almost 60 percent of their specific initiatives introduced as part of major bills were passed into law.[21] Consider, too, that legislative enactment is far more complicated than simply winning recorded roll-call votes on the floors of the House and Senate. Legislation has to survive several hurdles: subcommittee and committee deliberations and markups, sometimes involving several committees in both houses of Congress; action by the Rules Committee in the House; floor votes in both the House and Senate; conference committee action; and then final votes on the conference report in both chambers.

One should note briefly that the veto is another way presidents affect legislative outcomes. Presidents are considerably more successful in preventing congressional actions they dislike than in gaining congressional acceptance of the legislation they support. Chief executives from 1953 to 1984 may have seen barely more than half of their legislative programs enacted and three-quarters of their roll-call positions affirmed, but 83 percent of their regular vetoes succeeded (that is, there was either no override attempt by Congress or the override attempt failed). In this setting the demands of presidential influence are far more limited. The Constitution requires a two-thirds vote in both houses to override a veto. As President Bush demonstrated with a long string of sustained vetoes (thirty-five in a row, followed by a single override), sustaining a veto only requires holding on to a coalition of thirty-four senators (one-third of the Senate plus one)—a far simpler task than orchestrating majorities, especially the multiple majorities required to pass legislation.

Although they each tap somewhat different aspects of the presidential-congressional relationship, these three ways of assessing presidential effectiveness—presidential support, victories for presidential positions on roll-call votes, and success with presidential legislative initiatives (or success in preventing unwanted legislation proposed by others)—are obviously related to one another. Since both presidential support scores and victories on roll-call votes are determined from the same recorded votes, it is not surprising that they are highly correlated (Pierson's r equals .77 for the House, .69 for the Senate). Because enactment of presidential initiatives involves so many more steps and types of congressional action, the correlations with the other measures of influence are weaker but still meaningful (between roll-call victories and enactment, .34; between enactment and support scores in the House and Senate, .43 and .24, respectively).[22] Simply put, it is difficult for presidents either to win roll-call votes or to enact legislation if they cannot consistently gain support from a majority of the members of each house. And although many presidential initiatives are passed by voice vote or by other unrecorded methods of voting, they are often important and controversial enough to stimulate the call for a recorded roll-call vote.[23]

The variations among these indicators of presidential effectiveness also make intuitive sense. The percentage of roll-call victories will almost certainly be higher than the level of support the president enjoys among individual members of Congress. If presidents could always be assured that 51 percent of the House and Senate would support their positions on roll-call floor votes, then their side would prevail 100 percent of the time. Still, one expects the percentage of the president's program that is enacted to be lower than general levels of support, largely because successful initiatives have to win a majority in so many different subcommittee, committee, and floor settings. That is why Jimmy Carter could prevail on 77 percent of roll-call votes and enjoy average annual House and Senate support scores nearly as high as any other president (56 percent and 60 percent, respectively) but gain passage of only a third of his legislative program (Table 16.1).

As important as the overall trends in presidential legislative effectiveness may be for assessing the general influence of the presidency in the congressional domain, most people are interested in the performance of individual

Table 16.1. Three Measures of Presidential Effectiveness with Congress (percent)

President	Overall success on roll-call votes[a]	Average annual member support		Percentage of presidential initiatives enacted[b]	Percentage of Regular presidential vetoes sustained
		All votes or initiatives			
		House	Senate		
Eisenhower	71	58	58	67	94
Kennedy	85	60	59	48	100
Johnson	82	58	58	69	100
Nixon	64	55	53	46	79
Ford	58	44	53	37	57
Carter	77	56	60	33	85
Reagan (1st term)	72	49	62	54	76
Reagan (2nd term)	52	44	52	N/A	77
Bush	52	45	57	N/A	97
		Important votes or initiatives			
Eisenhower	63	52	52	80	
Kennedy	71	51	54	48	
Johnson	72	53	60	67	
Nixon	59	49	50	69	
Ford	55	44	39	33	
Carter	71	48	52	36	
Reagan (1st term)	70	48	56	56	

[a] Recorded votes on which the president took a public position and prevailed in the House and Senate combined.
[b] Domestic initiatives enacted as a result of compromise, presidential dominance, or consensus.

Sources: For overall success on all roll-call votes, *Congressional Quarterly Almanac* (Washington, D.C.: Congressional Quarterly, 1953–1992); data for overall success on "important" roll-call votes, Jon R. Bond and Richard Fleisher, *The President in the Legislative Arena* (Chicago: University of Chicago Press, 1990), table 3.3, 78. Data for the average annual percentage of support for all votes and important votes, George C. Edwards III, *At the Margins: Presidential Leadership of Congress* (New Haven: Yale University Press, 1989), table 2.2, 26–27. Data for the percentage of all and important presidential initiatives enacted, Mark A. Peterson, *Legislating Together: The White House and Capitol Hill from Eisenhower to Reagan* (Cambridge: Harvard University Press, 1990), table 7.1, 232. Data for vetoes sustained, David W. Rohde and Dennis M. Simon, "Presidential Vetoes and Congressional Response: A Study of Institutional Conflict," *American Journal of Political Science* 29 (August 1985): table 1, 399; "Vetoes Cast by President Reagan," *Congressional Quarterly Weekly Report*, November 17, 1984, 2957; "Past Performance," *Congressional Quarterly Weekly Report*, June 23, 1990, 1934; and "35 Hits and a Miss," *Congressional Quarterly Weekly Report*, October 10, 1992, 3148.

presidents. Table 16.1 presents all of these measures of effectiveness for presidents from Eisenhower to Bush.[24]

Several important characteristics of presidential effectiveness are revealed in this table. First, tremendous variation has occurred from one president to the next. Nearly seven of ten legislative initiatives introduced by Dwight Eisenhower and Lyndon Johnson were enacted into law, but neither Gerald Ford nor Jimmy

Carter could get even 40 percent of his proposals through Congress. Presidential legislative initiatives also engendered varying levels of conflict, whether or not they were successful. In a previous analysis I ascertained that nearly two-thirds of LBJ's legislative plans were met with a cooperative, rather than a confrontational, congressional response. That was true of only a quarter of Reagan's initiatives in his relatively successful first term.[25] Similar patterns of success and cooperation prevailed for presidential initiatives associated with major legislation.[26] Variations are also evident in other measures of effectiveness. Kennedy won 85 percent of the roll-call votes on which he took a position, whereas Bush was successful only half the time. With victories on 89 percent of roll-call votes as of September 14, 1993, President Bill Clinton experienced the best first-year record of any president since Eisenhower.[27] In general, then, for each measure of presidential influence a considerable range exists between the most and the least legislatively effective president—16 percentage points between Kennedy (most) and Ford, and Reagan in his second term (least), for House support, 8 points between Carter and the second-term Reagan for Senate support, 33 points between Kennedy and both Reagan (after 1986) and Bush for roll-call victories, 36 points between Johnson and Carter for enacted initiatives, and 43 points between Kennedy's and Johnson's perfect record and Ford for vetoes sustained.

Second, as the break between Reagan's first and second terms illustrates, individual presidents may experience widely divergent results during the course of their administrations. Support for Reagan was lower in the second term; he also had decidedly more trouble getting Congress to support his positions. The percentage of Reagan's roll-call victories cascaded thirty-nine points from a high of 82.4 percent in his first year (1981) to 43.5 percent in 1987. Eisenhower witnessed fluctuations in annual roll-call victories of 37 points; Johnson, 18; Nixon, 26; and Bush, 20.[28]

We are left, then, with two central puzzles in trying to understand presidential effectiveness in Congress. The first involves *similarities*. How could presidents who are so different—Eisenhower and Johnson, Ford and Carter—have such similar experiences with Congress? President Johnson, celebrated for his command of the legislative process, sent almost three hundred domestic proposals a year to Capitol Hill, whereas Eisenhower, hardly a longtime congressional hand, annually submitted just one hundred initiatives.[29] Yet their *rates* of success were nearly identical; indeed, Eisenhower did better than Johnson with major legislation. Ford and Carter, too, could hardly be more dissimilar, but one would not know it from these measures of their legislative records. The second puzzle involves the *disparities* in success rates, both across different presidencies and within single administrations. Were Ford and Carter simply inept compared with the other chief executives? Was Eisenhower, never identified as a legislative master, really that much more able than most other contemporary presidents? How could President Bush, with past experience as a member of Congress, party leader, political appointee, and vice president, prove so ineffective in handling legislative issues? As for the disparities within administrations, did, say, Reagan in the second term misplace the legislative talents that he seemed to demonstrate so effortlessly during his first years in office?

In the next section I try to explain these variations. My objectives are to determine why some presidents are more successful than others in Congress and to ascertain why some encounter less conflict and more cooperation from the legislature. Answering these questions will put us in a better position to determine the extent to which presidents have the opportunity to influence their own legislative success or must simply accept fortunes that are beyond their control.

The President as Leader or Prisoner?

Most accounts of presidential effectiveness with Congress—whether in the press or in scholarship—focus on the president. An interpretation of presidential performance from this presidency-centered perspective assumes a natural and appropriate ascendancy of the chief executive over Congress in legislative affairs, observes and bemoans what is perceived as frequent interbranch conflict, and places upon the shoulders of individual presidents the burden of achieving success or experiencing failure as a consequence of their own skills in the practice of presidential power.[30] Troubles with Congress are a sign of the president's failed leadership—amateurism, naivetée, intemperance, inconsistency, or lack of judgment. Legislative victories, in contrast, are the product of the masterful exercise of formal prerogatives and individual influence, from command of the media to sophisticated application of bargaining and arm twisting.

As appealing as this explanation may be (since it comports with our general inclination to focus on the human drama in any setting), it does not square well with the facts. From the presidency-centered perspective it is difficult to understand how very different kinds of presidents, with sharply contrasting backgrounds and styles, can enjoy comparable rates of success with Congress. The perspective also overemphasizes the importance of conflict between the president and Congress, ignoring the reality that interbranch conflict more often than not reflects a division between two contending coalitions in Congress, with one led by the president. Further, the presidency-centered perspective offers almost no means to comprehend the considerable fluctuations in legislative achievement that occur within a single presidency. Finally, not one study of presidential-congressional relations that has systematically examined many presidencies and numerous legislative events for an extended period of time has found presidential legislative skills to be the most potent explanation for variations in congressional responses to the president.[31]

To correct for the deficiencies of the presidency-centered perspective, I offer the tandem-institutions perspective in its place.[32] While recognizing that the Constitution, in Edward Corwin's famous phrase, extends to Congress and the president "an invitation to struggle" by separating the two branches, the tandem-institutions perspective emphasizes both the need that the president and members of Congress have for one another, if any of their legislative objectives are to be realized, and the tempering effect that this mutual need can generate.[33] It leaves open the possibility of both legislative conflict *and* cooperation. (Indeed, on domestic legislation submitted by presidents from 1953 to 1984, there was an even split between conflictual and cooperative responses by Congress).[34] Most important, rather than accentuating interbranch confrontation, this perspective draws our attention to a legislative arena that combines Congress and the president, an arena in which presidents attempt to build coalitions by attracting congressional allies to support their public positions and programmatic initiatives. Our concern, then, is to understand the variety of factors—institutional, political, financial, substantive, and, yes, personal—that affect such coalition building.

Take *institutional* factors. Our system of separated institutions sharing powers makes coalition building problematic. That is a constant. But other aspects of institutional design change over time and alter the imperatives of coalition formation either in favor of or against the president's intentions. For example, Congress does not show the same institutional face to every president. From 1911 to about 1970, it was dominated fairly consistently by an oligarchy of often autonomous standing committees that ran according to the dictates of powerful chairmen. Occasionally a dramatic electoral sweep, such as those produced by the elections of 1932 and 1964, would momentarily change the parameters of committee influence and congressional deliberation, but more typically, committee leaders were the essential figures in crafting winning legislative coalitions.[35] For presidents, these leaders' support could be instrumental to success;

their opposition was an all but certain signal of defeat. During the early 1970s, however, Congress—especially the House of Representatives—was institutionally transformed by a set of internal reforms that strengthened the party leaders in some respects but mostly made the place far less predictable and more difficult to manage. Power was decentralized among scores of subcommittees. A concomitant decline of the political parties as the institutional organizers of electoral politics brought many more entrepreneurial members into the now more open and fragmented legislature. At the same time, the interest group community—always attempting to gain influence over relevant issues—became larger, more differentiated, and increasingly contentious within its own ranks.

These changes, taken together, have created a legislative environment in which presidents have to muster favorable coalitions in an increasing number of venues by working with more members with fewer institutional ties to the president; in which their activities are under closer scrutiny by the media and the organized interests; and in which their opponents have the advantage of additional veto points for blocking presidential initiatives. It is not surprising, therefore, that the legislative records of Presidents Nixon, Ford, Carter, Reagan, and Bush show more signs of confrontation with Congress and fewer legislative successes than do the records of their predecessors. Even the most skillful president can do almost nothing to influence these institutional transformations, other than to find creative ways to maneuver through the new terrain.

Institutional arrangements determine the number and sequence of legislative decision making and veto points, affect the number of supporters the president needs, and help to shape the access of noncongressional allies and opponents to the legislative process. They do not determine what coalitions can actually be formed, and when. The success of the president's coalitions depends on the number of representatives and senators who are either natural supporters of the president's position (because of shared perspectives, interests, or electoral incentives) or can be persuaded to go along.

The president's coalitional base is critically affected by larger *political* dynamics in the American system. An obvious starting point, for example, is the number of seats in the House and Senate that are held by members of the president's party. Since not a single Republican voted for Clinton's budget plan in 1993, without a Democratic majority one of the president's core legislative initiatives would have gone down to defeat. Eisenhower (after 1954), Nixon, Ford, Reagan (except for the Senate from 1981 to 1986), and Bush always had to begin their coalition-building efforts knowing that their Republican party was in the minority. Even unanimous support from partisan compatriots in Congress could not guarantee success for their programs, and the potentially useful prerogatives of the House Speaker and of committee and subcommittee chairmen rested in the opposition's hands. All modern presidents have also experienced the ill effects of one of the few near-laws of American politics. In every midterm congressional election in this century, except for 1934, the president's party has lost seats in the House of Representatives. The effects of this loss are not uniform and depend on the nature of the issues being considered in Congress, but whether one is explaining presidential support, presidential victories on roll-call votes, or favorable action on the president's legislative agenda, the partisan distribution in Congress always emerges as a significant independent factor.[36]

Significant, but far from determinative. American political parties are notoriously weak compared with those in other democracies. They are largely federations of quite disparate state party organizations, lacking in resources, and deeply divided within themselves in regard to fundamental issues of public policy. Regional and racial issues have split the Democrats ever since FDR assembled the New Deal coalition of southern Democrats, northern industrial workers, members of ethnic groups, and African Americans. The efficacy of Democratic majorities in Congress has frequently been threatened by the "Conservative Coalition," a sometime voting bloc of Republicans and conservative southern Democrats. These conservatives have hampered the coalition-building efforts of Democratic presidents from FDR to Carter and, in some cases, Clinton. In contrast, along with a Republican surge in the House in the 1980 election, they gave Ronald Reagan the basis for forging a working majority in the nominally Democratic House of Representatives, leading to the passage of his major budget-cutting and tax reduction initiatives in 1981. Thus do ideological forces complicate the task of coalition building for presidents during periods when both the executive and legislative branches are controlled by the same party and open up otherwise unavailable opportunities for presidents who serve during periods of divided government.[37] Even with substantial Democratic majorities in Congress (292 to 143 in the House—nearly the same as in Johnson's Eighty-ninth Congress—and 62 to 38 in the Senate), Carter had great difficulty moving his legislative program. As already noted, Eisenhower, working with a Democratic Congress for six of his eight years in office, had a legislative success rate nearly indistinguishable from Johnson's—aided, no doubt, by Congress's fairly even division between the parties and its ideological compatibility with him.

Media accounts often note the importance of another dynamic feature of the political environment, one that can vary dramatically during a single president's term: presidential popularity, or, more precisely, the proportion of the public that approves of the president's job performance. Presidents are believed to do better with Congress when the people like them. Thus, a certain amount of surprise underlay the *Congressional Quarterly Weekly Report* headline in September 1993 that reported, "Clinton Prevails on Capitol Hill Despite Poor Showing in the Polls." Consistent with this conventional wisdom, some studies have isolated the relation between the president's standing with the public and his effectiveness in Congress.[38]

Other studies, however, have found that public approval has an extremely limited or inconsistent effect.[39] The apparent confusion has many possible explanations. First, although it is to be anticipated that a president who is way down in the polls, as Nixon was in the aftermath of the Watergate scandal,[40] will encounter a less accommodating Congress, other, more typical, variations in popular support are not enough to alter legislative politics that have already been shaped by party orientation, ideology, policy preferences, and constituency interests.[41] Second, levels of presidential job approval have to carry some meaning or relevance for members of Congress in order to affect their decision making. After the victory against Iraq in the Persian Gulf War, President Bush saw his public approval rating soar to an unprecedented height—89 percent in one Gallup poll.[42] This rating had essentially no effect, however, on how Congress reacted to Bush's domestic initiatives. Members of Congress could distinguish between public acclaim for the president's actions as commander in chief and the public's far greater reticence about his performance on the domestic (largely economic) front. Third, a popular president may be emboldened to challenge opponents in Congress too severely, leading to intensified legislative conflict rather than greater success. Although public support probably strengthens the influence of presidents with their partisan allies, members of the opposition party may react quite differently. Finally, uncertainty exists about the direction of causality. Does public support breed legislative success, or does legislative success produce favorable ratings? Probably some of each. All that we can safely conclude, then, is that truly unpopular presidents are going to have quite a challenge demonstrating the effectiveness of their legislative skills. Harry S. Truman, Richard Nixon, and Jimmy Carter faced this test more severely than other recent presidents.

Other dynamic political attributes may influence presidential interactions with Congress. Elections not only determine the partisan distribution of seats in Congress; they also convey direct signals about presidents themselves. A president who achieves a landslide victory in the popular vote is in a better position to claim, rightly or wrongly, a mandate in favor of the administration's legislative positions and programs than is a president who receives less than half the votes cast.[43] In some elections, too, the president has "coattails" that either aid the victories of some members of Congress, giving the president a claim on their loyalty, or shave points from the vote totals of winning members of the opposition, possibly raising concerns about their political futures. In 1980, for example, Ronald Reagan received a higher share of the vote than the victorious House members in nearly two hundred congressional districts. For Bill Clinton that happened in only thirteen districts.

The politics of presidential-congressional relations can also be shaped by resource availability or scarcity. When, as was the case during the Eighty-ninth Congress (1965–1966) early in the Johnson administration, the economy is humming along, revenues are flowing into the federal coffers without the imposition of higher taxes, and the federal deficit is under control, new programs can be introduced and existing ones expanded without cutting into the existing programmatic base. Legislative politics can be accommodating rather than confrontational. During times of scarcity and deficits, when presidents are grappling with the choice between budget cuts and tax increases, the executive-legislative relationship becomes far more conflictual. Witness the major congressional battles over the economic programs of Ronald Reagan in 1981 and Bill Clinton in 1993. Each won the final vote, but by slim margins and only after contentious and costly debates.[44]

Presidents cannot control the institutional setting in which they must practice leadership. That setting is largely the product of the Constitution, internal congressional decisions about the legislative rules and structure, and large-scale social forces that help shape the political party and interest group systems. Although presidents do make decisions that bear on their electoral fortunes, their popularity, the success of their party's candidates in Congress, and the health of the economy, the world is too complicated for them to be able to exercise full leverage over these political and economic conditions. If presidents could control these factors, they would always win landslide reelections, carry party majorities into Congress, keep the faith of the American public, and ensure an economy with high growth, low unemployment, low inflation, and budget surpluses. That is not exactly the record of the postwar period.

Presidents have somewhat more control of how to formulate and transmit their programmatic agendas. To be sure, even here the choices are limited by partisanship, ideology, objective needs, technical feasibility, campaign commitments, and electoral constraints. But some latitude exists for the president to set the size, scope, character, and timing of the public policy positions to be announced and the legislation to be proposed. These choices affect the president's legislative effectiveness. Programs to regulate behavior—especially of powerful and well-organized industries—are more likely to meet serious congressional resistance than are proposals to distribute benefits widely among the population, such as bridge and highway expansion. Large-scale interventions into existing policy domains will probably generate more controversy than will relatively limited excursions into areas where interests are either not threatened or poorly organized. Consider the difference between proposing comprehensive reform of the American health care system, as President Clinton has done, and the first, uncontroversial federal financial contributions toward expanding hospital construction, promoted in the 1940s. We usually think of politics creating policy, but several scholars, notably Theodore Lowi, have demonstrated that policies can generate their own politics.[45] The substance of legislative initiatives introduced by presidents will affect their effectiveness with Congress well before they have a chance to demonstrate their skills in the legislative arena. Ford and Carter, for example, grappling with unprecedented inflation, the energy crisis, and environmental concerns, submitted legislative agendas that were two to four times as regulatory in content as those of other modern presidents.[46] These programs were not recipes for consensus and legislative success. Neither president, however, could find more attractive options.

Presidents operating in a tandem-institutions setting, therefore, begin the task of coalition building buffeted by a series of forces that they do not command and may not be able to influence. To that extent presidents are more prisoners of circumstances—favorable or unfavorable—than leaders who can actively and consistently transform the parameters of politics and debate. When all of the institutional, political, economic, and policy characteristics of the legislative setting are empirically estimated and used to predict the nature of congressional responses to each president's domestic legislative initiatives, those predictions come quite close to the actual outcomes.[47] Lyndon Johnson may well have been a brilliant strategist and tactician, but the way Congress handled his legislative proposals fits closely with what one would expect, given such factors as a legislature not yet decentralized by reform, his electoral landslide, the sizable Democratic majorities in Congress, and the booming economy. It also is no surprise that Gerald Ford, an unelected president who faced huge congressional majorities of the other party, an institutionally fragmented Congress, an energy crisis, and the worst economy since the Great Depression, had troubles with Congress, even though he personally had extensive experience as a congressional leader and retained many strong friendships on both sides of the aisle. Jimmy Carter's trials and tribulations, initially unexpected for a president whose party had seemingly commanding majorities on Capitol Hill, were close to what empirical analysis would predict because of other factors, such as the decentralization of Congress and the poor performance of the economy, that affect legislative coalition building.[48]

The message for later presidents is also discouraging. Many of the institutional and economic changes that inhibited successful coalition building by Presidents Ford and Carter have endured, suggesting that the tandem-institutions baseline has shifted in the direction of greater congressional conflict and reduced effectiveness of the president as a legislative player. Even Ronald Reagan's initial legislative victories proved more the exception than the rule, and they came in the wake of extraordinary electoral events: the resounding defeat of an incumbent president and a decidedly unanticipated change in partisan control of the Senate for the first time in nearly thirty years.

Reagan's successor, George Bush, had few advantages as he entered the legislative fray. His election had no influence on the fortunes of members of Congress; indeed, his party, already in the minority, lost seats in both the House and Senate. Continuing a trend that began during the latter part of the Reagan administration, as partisanship in roll-call voting increased, support for the president among House Democrats fell to an all-time low.[49] In the meantime, federal deficits continued to climb and the economy weakened.

The challenge for President Clinton as a legislative leader is almost as daunting. Congress is still decentralized and perhaps more unpredictable than ever. Interest groups continue to proliferate, and campaign contributions from their political action committees (PACs) complicate the incentives that drive congressional behavior. Clinton entered the White House with the smallest percentage of the popular vote (43 percent) since 1912. Almost every member of Congress ran ahead of the president on the ballot. Although the Democrats retained majorities in both houses, their margin in the Senate is the smallest that any Democratic president has experienced since the days of Truman and, in the House, since the last Congress of the by-then dispirited administration of Lyndon Johnson. The current deficit situation will only worsen without determined, and intensely contentious, action to reverse it. In addition, after twelve years of Republican administrations that blocked major Democratic legislation, and having been elected on a platform of change, Clinton is in no position to restrict his legislative agenda to uncontroversial initiatives that are primed for success. No matter how skillful a president he turns out to be, the impediments to successful coalition building in this setting make any repeat of the Eisenhower, Kennedy, and Johnson years well-nigh impossible.

Can Individual Presidents Still Make a Difference?

In *Presidential Power*, first published just before the start of the Kennedy administration, Richard Neustadt spoke to the issue of how to lead effectively. When making decisions, Neustadt argued, presidents must work assiduously to protect their future power stakes, always asking themselves (since no one else can be trusted to do it for them), How will the choices I make today affect the influence that I can wield tomorrow? Such choices have consequences for what Neustadt identified as the president's currency of influence—that is, prestige among the public and reputation among Washington political and policy professionals.[50]

Some readers of Neustadt's book discerned in it an assumption that presidents are the architects of their own destiny. So simple an assessment, however, misses his main point. In a system in which separated institutions share powers (intertwining the executive not just with Congress but also with the relatively autonomous departments and agencies of the executive branch, state and local governments, and even business and other institutions in the private sector), no presidential objective can be accomplished without the support or acquiescence of other individuals with authority. And none of these other individuals quite shares the president's perspective or needs. Agreement comes only through bargaining and presidential persuasion. The starting premise of presidential leadership, therefore, is that the challenges to it are great and need to be overcome.

My analysis of a particular aspect of presidential leadership—interactions with Congress on legislative issues—has highlighted just how great that challenge can be. We cannot expect any competent individual to enter the Oval Office and automatically take command of legislative affairs, even during times of unified party government. Having said that, I must highlight two additional points. First, the circumstances surrounding congressional responses to the president are in a constant state of flux. No two presidents encounter precisely the same alignment of institutional, political, economic, and policy characteristics. Some presidents have more room to maneuver than others. The mix even changes for the same president. As analysts, and responsible citizens, we would like to know how much.

Second, the very real constraints on leadership do not mean that individual presidents do not matter and cannot influence presidential-congressional relations. For one thing, since different presidents have different agendas, and those agendas are instrumental in directing both congressional and public debate, it often matters greatly who is elected president in any particular year.[51] What Congress and the president produced together would have been quite different had Jimmy Carter been reelected in 1980 rather than being defeated by a far more conservative Ronald Reagan. Indeed, it is the complexity of our system, and all of the barriers to unified action, that place a premium on leadership. If leadership were not a difficult and demanding enterprise, if it were not needed to move the system along, it would not be in such demand.

Presidents have a variety of choices open to them that can affect their effectiveness with Congress. How they organize the Executive Office of the President, whom they appoint as senior advisers or to political positions in the federal agencies, what issues they decide to address in their legislative programs, and how much they ask of Congress—and when they ask it—can all lead to variations in legislative success.[52] Legislative initiatives of high priority to presidents from Eisenhower to Reagan, for example, were more likely to receive serious congressional attention and even to pass than issues of low priority. With priority usually comes increased effort by presidents and their administrations to get those initiatives enacted, as reflected in the frequency of presidents' public statements on behalf of their legislation. Although the precise effects of concurrent negotiations, bargains, and exchanges cannot be measured, we do know that initiatives referred to frequently by some presidents have been more likely to pass—even taking into account the institutional, political, economic, and policy environment in which congressional deliberations are embedded. I found such positive effects for Kennedy, Johnson, and Nixon, but not for Eisenhower and Reagan. And, on average, when Carter applied energy to lobbying for his initiatives, he actually appears to have had a negative effect on congressional responsiveness, a discouraging result for any leader.[53]

Particular kinds of lobbying strategies also can be important, under the right conditions. Samuel Kernell has shown the increasing importance of "going public" as a way for presidents to influence the legislative process.[54] Presidential speeches to the nation and to more focused constituencies have become a prevalent activity of the modern presidency. When presidents from Eisenhower to Reagan had the approval of more than half the electorate and went on television to discuss issues related to what the public considered to be the most important problems facing the nation, Congress reacted more favorably to the president's initiatives in those areas—both by acting on the presidents' requests and by passing more of them into law.[55]

In the end, as in the beginning, presidents need Congress. They need to be partners, if only grudgingly, in order for the nation's legislative business to be accomplished. The "tandem-institutions" partnership requires that the president engage in a constant process of legislative coalition building, a task made harder or easier, depending on the nature of the institutional environment, the configuration of political forces, the availability of economic resources, and the substantive character of the policy problems on the nation's agenda. As a result of systematic changes in institutions and resources, the challenge of presidential effectiveness in Congress is more pronounced in the 1990s than usual. The range and depth of President Clinton's legislative agenda accentuate the enormity of the challenge. Enacting health care reform, welfare reform, campaign finance reform, and the other parts of the president's legislative program will necessitate beating the odds. Although far from being the whole story, Clinton's performance as a legislative leader will tangibly affect whether or not he turns those odds to his advantage.[56]

Notes

Thanks are owed Yolanda Scott for her assistance in compiling some of the information presented in this chapter.

1. Elizabeth Wehr and John R. Cranford, "Crippled Market Spurs Budget Breakthrough," *Congressional Quarterly Weekly Report*, October 24, 1987, 2573.

2. Richard E. Neustadt, *Presidential Power and the Modern Presidents* (New York: Free Press, 1990), 29.

3. Figures are calculated from information reported in Gary King and Lyn Ragsdale, *The Elusive Executive: Discovering Statistical Patterns in the Presidency* (Washington, D.C.: CQ Press, 1988), tables 3.2 and 3.4.

4. Louis Fisher, *The Constitution between Friends* (New York: St. Martin's Press, 1978).

5. Thomas E. Cronin, *The State of the Presidency*, 2d ed. (Boston: Little, Brown, 1980), 193.

6. Presidents can and have made, however, "recess appointments" of individuals to executive positions when Congress was not in session; these individuals can formally carry out their duties until the end of the subsequent session of Congress.

7. King and Ragsdale, *The Elusive Executive*, 233–234.

8. Joan Biskupic, "Bush Lags in Appointments to the Federal Judiciary," *Congressional Quarterly Weekly Report*, January 6, 1990, 39; Holly Idelson, "Clinton's Unexpected Bequest: Judgeships Bush Did Not Fill," *Congressional Quarterly Weekly Report*, February 13, 1993, 317.

9. Idelson, "Clinton's Unexpected Bequest," 317.

10. Calculated from figures provided in King and Ragsdale, *The Elusive Executive,* table 4.14.

11. Presidents can establish an extended legacy through their appointments to the federal bench. More than twenty years after Kennedy's death, 56 percent of the judges he appointed were still serving in their positions. King and Ragsdale, *The Elusive Executive,* table 4.19.

12. Enacted legislation may also become law if the president chooses not to sign it and Congress remains in session for at least ten more days. A president can "pocket veto" a bill that passes in the last ten days of a congressional session by simply not signing it.

13. Edward S. Corwin, *The President: Office and Powers* (New York: New York University Press, 1957), 278–279.

14. Figures for Eisenhower to Carter are calculated from David W. Rohde and Dennis M. Simon, "Presidential Vetoes and Congressional Response: A Study of Institutional Conflict," *American Journal of Political Science* 29 (August 1985): table 1. The Reagan figure is from "Past Performance," *Congressional Quarterly Weekly Report,* June 23, 1990, 1934; for Bush the source is "35 Hits and a Miss," *Congressional Quarterly Weekly Report,* October 10, 1992, 3148.

15. John W. Kingdon, *Agendas, Alternatives, and Public Policies* (Boston: Little, Brown, 1984).

16. The quotation is from George C. Edwards III, *At the Margins: Presidential Leadership of Congress* (New Haven: Yale University Press, 1989), 16.

17. Jon R. Bond and Richard Fleisher, *The President in the Legislative Arena* (Chicago: University of Chicago Press, 1990), 69.

18. Ibid., 59.

19. Quoted in Stephen J. Wayne, *The Legislative Presidency* (New York: Harper and Row, 1978), 19.

20. See Mark A. Peterson, *Legislating Together: The White House and Capitol Hill from Eisenhower to Reagan* (Cambridge: Harvard University Press, 1990), chap. 3 and app. B, for a discussion of the problems associated with measures of the president's legislative program, as well as presidential support scores and other quantitative assessments of presidential action.

21. Figures are based on the analysis presented in ibid. Comparable figures for foreign policy initiatives are not available, although presidential success rates on legislation pertaining to foreign affairs may be even higher. See Aaron Wildavsky, "The Two Presidencies," *Trans-Action* 4 (December 1966); Bond and Fleisher, *The President in the Legislative Arena,* chap. 6; Edwards, *At the Margins,* chap. 4.

22. Correlations are based on the values of presidential support scores, percentage of roll-call victories, and percentage of presidential initiatives enacted, as calculated for each presidential administration from 1953 to 1984.

23. The Legislative Reorganization Act of 1970 made it easier for members to require a recorded roll-call vote in the House of Representatives. Specifically, twenty members could request a "recorded teller vote" in the "Committee of the Whole," the status under which the House conducts most of its legislative business.

24. The percentage of presidential initiatives enacted by Congress is available only for the beginning of Eisenhower's presidency through Reagan's first term. In addition, for the purposes of this chapter, "important votes or initiatives" could be calculated only for this period.

25. See Peterson, *Legislating Together,* 188–196.

26. Simple correlations between the measures calculated for all votes or initiatives and their counterparts among important votes or initiatives range from .69 to .92.

27. Steve Langdon, "Clinton Prevails on Capitol Hill Despite Poor Showing in the Polls," *Congressional Quarterly Weekly Report*, September 25, 1993, 257.

28. Based on information provided in sequential *Congressional Quarterly Almanac* (Washington, D.C.: Congressional Quarterly Inc., 1953–1992).

29. Peterson, *Legislating Together*, table C.1.

30. Myriad books and articles have been written from this perspective. The policy-making concerns of contemporary presidential-legislative interactions are explored perhaps most forcefully in Michael Mezey, *Congress, the President, and Public Policy* (Boulder, Colo.: Westview Press, 1989). For a more complete review of the presidency-centered perspective, see Peterson, *Legislating Together*. An additional useful rejoinder on the value of Congress is found in Robert J. Spitzer, *President and Congress: Executive Hegemony at the Crossroads of American Government* (New York: McGraw-Hill, 1993).

31. See, for example, Bond and Fleisher, *The President in the Legislative Arena*; Cary Covington, "Congressional Support for the President: The View from the Kennedy/ Johnson White House," *Journal of Politics* 48 (August 1986): 717–728; George C. Edwards III, *Presidential Influence in Congress* (San Francisco: Freeman, 1980); Edwards, *At the Margins*; Paul C. Light, *The President's Agenda: Domestic Policy Choice from Kennedy to Carter* (Baltimore: Johns Hopkins University Press, 1982); Paul C. Light, "Passing Nonincremental Policy: Presidential Influence in Congress, Kennedy to Carter," *Congress and the Presidency* 9 (Winter 1981–1982); Peterson, *Legislating Together*; Rohde and Simon, "Presidential Vetoes and Congressional Response"; Terry Sullivan, "The Bank Account Presidency: A New Measure and Evidence of the Temporal Path of Presidential Influence," *American Journal of Political Science* 35 (August 1991): 686–723.

32. For a complete description of this perspective, see Peterson, *Legislating Together*.

33. Corwin, *The President*, 171.

34. Peterson, *Legislating Together*, 189.

35. Bond and Fleisher, *The President in the Legislative Arena*.

36. Bond and Fleisher, *The President in the Legislative Arena*; Edwards, *At the Margins*; Light, "Passing Nonincremental Policy"; Peterson, *Legislating Together*.

37. See Bond and Fleisher, *The President in the Legislative Arena*, chap. 4; Morris Fiorina, *Divided Government* (New York: Macmillan, 1992), chap. 6; David Mayhew, *Divided We Govern: Party Control, Lawmaking, and Investigations, 1946–1990* (New Haven: Yale University Press, 1991).

38. Edwards, *At the Margins*, chap. 6; Douglas Rivers and Nancy Rose, "Passing the President's Program: Public Opinion and Presidential Influence in Congress," *American Journal of Political Science* 29 (August 1985): 397–427.

39. Bond and Fleisher, *The President in the Legislative Arena*, chap. 7; Peterson, *Legislating Together*, chap. 6; Harvey G. Zeidenstein, "Varying Relationships between Presidents' Popularity and Their Legislative Success: A Futile Search for Patterns," *Presidential Studies Quarterly* 8 (Fall 1983).

40. At the lowest point, only 24 percent of the public approved of Nixon's job performance. George H. Gallup, *The Gallup Poll: Public Opinion 1972–1975* (Wilmington, Del.: Scholarly Resources, 1978), 325.

41. Indeed, this more circumscribed role for public approval of the president is closer to the meaning Richard Neustadt originally gave to "presidential prestige" in *Presidential Power*, first published in 1960.

42. George Gallup, Jr., *The Gallup Poll: Public Opinion 1991* (Wilmington, Del.: Scholarly Resources, 1992), 67.

43. These effects are investigated in Peterson, *Legislating Together*, chaps. 4 and 6. See Edwards, *At the Margins*, chap. 8, and Robert A. Dahl, "The Myth of the Presidential Mandate," *Political Science Quarterly* 105 (Fall 1990): 355–372, for critical assessments of the role of electoral mandates.

44. These issues are explored in greater detail in Peterson, *Legislating Together*, chaps. 4 and 6.

45. Theodore J. Lowi, "American Business, Public Policy, Case Studies, and Political Theory," *World Politics* 16 (July 1964): 677–715.

46. Peterson, *Legislating Together*, 236.

47. These predictions are based on a multivariate probit analysis of congressional responses to 299 presidential initiatives introduced from 1953 to 1984, which is reported in Peterson, *Legislating Together*, chap. 7.

48. Mark A. Peterson, "Leading Our Way to Health: Entrepreneurship and Leadership in the Health Care Reform Debate" (Paper presented at the annual meeting of the American Political Science Association, Chicago, September 3–6, 1992), 16.

49. Bruce I. Oppenheimer, "Declining Presidential Success with Congress," in *The Presidency Reconsidered*, ed. Richard W. Waterman (Itasca, Ill.: F. E. Peacock, 1993), 77–78.

50. Neustadt, *Presidential Power*, chaps. 4 and 5.

51. See Kingdon, *Agendas, Alternatives, and Public Policies*, on the importance of elections and changes in who serves as president.

52. Peterson, *Legislating Together*, chap. 7.

53. Peterson, *Legislating Together*, 237. See also Light, "Passing Nonincremental Policy," and, for the limits of presidential lobbying, Edwards, *At the Margins*, chaps. 9 and 10.

54. Samuel Kernell, *Going Public: New Strategies of Presidential Leadership*, 2d ed. (Washington, D.C.: CQ Press, 1993). For a critique of Kernell's emphasis on going public instead of bargaining, see Marc A. Bodnick, "'Going Public' Reconsidered: Reagan's 1981 Tax and Budget Cuts, and Revisionist Theories of Presidential Power," *Congress and the Presidency* 17 (Spring 1990): 13–28.

55. Peterson, *Legislating Together*, 161–175.

56. See Sullivan, "The Bank Account Presidency."

17 The Presidency and the Judiciary

John Anthony Maltese

According to Article III of the Constitution, once Supreme Court justices and other federal judges are nominated by the president and confirmed by the Senate, they serve "during good Behaviour"—that is, for as long as they want to serve, barring an impeachment and conviction. Because judges are virtually immune from removal (hardly any have ever been impeached and convicted) and other forms of political pressure, the president has an important incentive to choose nominees carefully and the Senate an equal incentive to review nominations closely. These incentives have grown in recent years, both because the federal courts have become increasingly involved in matters of public policy and because the White House and the Senate have usually been controlled by different political parties. The consequence, John Anthony Maltese argues, is that presidents and senators now fight about judicial nominations the same way they fight about controversial legislation. Maltese examines the methods by which recent presidents have appealed to public opinion, lobbied the Senate, and mobilized interest groups in support of their Supreme Court nominees.

This chapter examines the president's power to influence judicial policy making through federal court appointments. Particular emphasis is placed on the strategic resources that are available to modern presidents to help secure confirmation of their judicial nominees. These resources include an unprecedented (and unrivaled) ability to communicate directly with the American people, to mobilize interest groups, and to lobby the Senate. In each of these areas, specialized White House staff units have evolved to advise presidents and implement strategic initiatives.[1]

The development and use of the president's strategic resources is closely associated with the rise of the "institutional presidency." As John P. Burke pointed out in chapter fourteen, the institutionalization of the presidency has led to the development of a large White House staff, including specialized staff units that perform highly specific functions. These include both policy-making units (charged with formulating policy) and operational units (charged with implementing policy). The institutionalization of these units has led to a White House–centered system of government in which presidents and their staff play a more important role in overseeing the formulation and implementation of policy.

Recent presidents have used policy-making units of the White House staff to screen judicial nominees and to determine the type of judges to be nominated. They have also used operational units to help secure confirmation of these nominees. Presidents use such resources because judges can have a direct influence on policy. By defining privacy rights, interpreting the First Amendment, setting guidelines for the treatment of criminal defendants, and exercising the power of judicial review in a host of other areas, the judiciary establishes public policy.

In theory, impartial judges who objectively apply the law according to established standards of interpretation should all reach the same "correct" decision in cases that come before them. In practice, judges hold different views about how to interpret legal texts. Moreover, as human beings, judges are influenced, at least in part, by their backgrounds, personal predilections, and judicial philosophies. Quite simply, different judges will reach different conclusions when confronted with the same case. Thus, presidents use the appointment process as a way to influence policy.

In a memorandum to President Richard Nixon in 1969, the White House aide Tom Charles Huston noted that judicial appointments were perhaps "the least considered aspect of Presidential power." "*In approaching the bench*," he wrote,

it is necessary to remember that the decision as to who will make the decisions affects what decisions will be made. That is, the role the judiciary will play in different historical eras depends as much on the type of men who become judges as it does on the constitutional rules which appear to [guide them].[2]

Thus, Huston urged Nixon to establish specific criteria for the type of judges to be appointed in an effort to influence judicial policy making. If the president "establishes *his* criteria and establishes *his* machinery for insuring that the criteria are met, the appointments will be *his*, in fact, as in theory."[3] In response Nixon wrote, "RN *agrees.* Have this analysis in mind when making judicial nominations."[4]

Following this reasoning, presidents since Nixon have developed numerous resources to gain more control over the judicial selection process. But just as presidents recognized the opportunity to influence policy through judicial appointments, so did other political actors. As a result, nominations, especially at the Supreme Court level, became particularly contentious. Divided government—with the White House controlled by one political party and the Senate controlled by another—contributed to that contentiousness. So, too, did the "transformative" nature of recent Supreme Court vacancies, in which single appointments had the potential to alter key voting blocs on the court.[5] Thus, a single appointment could determine the direction of future court decisions on such controversial issues as abortion. In such an atmosphere, interest groups eagerly entered the fray, waging massive lobbying and public relations campaigns for and against judicial nominees. Presidents, in turn, became particularly reliant on their own resources to mobilize public opinion, generate interest group activity, and lobby senators as a way of combating opponents of their judicial nominees.

The institutionalization of presidential resources—both for screening potential nominees and for generating support for confirmation—is a significant development of the modern presidency. It is one part of a broader effort by presidents to increase their power over the policy-making agenda of government. Of course, that power is checked in a number of ways. Most obviously, constitutional constraints limit the president's power. Thus, it is useful to begin with a brief review of the constitutional underpinnings of the appointment power.

The Scope of the Presidential Appointment Power

Supreme Court Appointments

Article II, section 2, of the Constitution gives the president the power to *nominate* Supreme Court Justices. *Appointment* comes only with "the Advice and Consent of the Senate." The clause clearly dictates that the two branches must share power but leaves the precise scope of advice and consent open to debate. Its language was a compromise between those at the Constitutional Convention of 1787 who wanted the appointment power to rest with the president and those who wanted it to rest with Congress.

The original Virginia Plan called for legislative appointment of judges by both chambers. Presidentialists, led by James Wilson, quickly opposed the provision and called for executive appointment. A variety of other plans also surfaced. James Madison, who later changed his mind, suggested that judicial appointments be made by the Senate alone; the Committee of the Whole suggested that justices of the Supreme Court be appointed by the Senate and that other federal judges be appointed by the House; and Alexander Hamilton suggested executive appointment subject to Senate approval.

The convention rejected both executive appointment and executive appointment subject to the advice and consent of the Senate on July 18. Three days later, James Madison suggested executive appointment that could be vetoed by a two-thirds vote of the Senate. That proposal also failed, and the convention finally settled on appointment by the Senate. The Committee of Detail then incorporated Senate appointment into its draft of the Constitution, but the clause faced renewed opposition from presidentialists at the end of August. Thus, the debate moved to the Committee on Postponed Matters, which substituted the compromise language that finally made its way into Article II, section 2. Staunch presidentialists, such as Wilson, opposed the compromise on the grounds that it still gave too much power to the Senate.[6]

One may reasonably assume that the ambiguities of the appointments clause were intentional, since its language was designed to accommodate competing positions and placate various interests at the convention. Ambiguity allowed for a degree of consensus that otherwise would have been impossible to achieve, by allowing delegates to cling to differing interpretations of the same constitutional language. Thus, presidentialists could argue that the advice and consent clause allowed the Senate only a minimal role—one limited, as Hamilton wrote in *The Federalist*, no. 76, to checking "a spirit of favoritism in the President" and deterring "the appointment of unfit characters."[7]

Congressionalists, on the other hand, could interpret the advice and consent clause as allowing a vigorous role for the Senate in the confirmation process. Professor James E. Gauch has noted that the congressionalists went into the compromise with the clear upper hand; their plan for Senate appointment of judges had already won the approval of the convention on July 21. Gauch argues that there is "not even a hint" that the subsequent compromise "entailed a drastically curtailed role for the Senate, except with the power to nominate." Moreover, Gauch points to the vigorous opposition of presidentialists to the compromise as a sign that "the Senate still had a meaningful role" in the process.[8]

But what exactly does a "meaningful role" entail? Does it, for example, allow the Senate to reject a nominee solely on the basis of ideology? This was an issue that the framers did not confront, but at least some early observers predicted (and sanctioned) ideologically motivated rejections.[9] In fact, the Senate rejected nominees on such grounds from the very beginning. Even George Washington seemed to admit that the Senate could reject nominees for whatever reason it wanted. In a message to a Senate committee concerning treaties and nominations, Washington wrote that just "as the President has a right to nominate without assigning reasons, so has the Senate a right to dissent without giving theirs."[10]

In practice, the amount of power exercised by the Senate has ebbed and flowed with changing political circumstances. Likewise, support for an aggressive senatorial role has come variously from both ends of the political spectrum, depending upon whose toes were being pinched at the moment. During the liberal Warren Court era of the 1950s and 1960s, many conservatives—charging the Court with unprincipled activist rulings—called for strict senatorial scrutiny of Supreme Court nominees. For example, as a private attorney in 1959, William Rehnquist wrote,

[T]he Supreme Court has assumed such a powerful role as a policy-maker in the government that the Senate must necessarily be concerned with the views of the prospective justices . . . as they relate to broad issues confronting the American people, and the role of the Court in dealing with those issues. . . . The Senate is entitled to consider those views, much as the voters do with regard to candidates for the presidency . . . or U.S. Senate.[11]

Later, when they controlled the presidency, conservatives such as Bruce Fein and William Bradford Reynolds argued for a very limited Senate role in the confirmation process, while liberals such as Laurence Tribe called for strict scrutiny of judicial nominees.[12]

Much of the current debate concerns the Senate's consent function. The Senate long ago relinquished some of its power to the president by not aggressively exercising its advice function. The Senate has almost never offered formal advice to the president about whom to nominate. (One exception was in 1874 when President Ulysses S. Grant sought the advice of Senate leaders before nominating Morrison Waite to be chief justice.) An increased advice function, however, might limit interbranch conflict during the confirmation stage of the process; the Senate would find it difficult to oppose a nominee that it had played a role in selecting. In the wake of the Clarence Thomas confirmation battle in 1991, Senator Paul Simon, a Democrat from Illinois, submitted a resolution calling for the Senate to exercise the advice portion of the advice and consent clause, but nothing came of Simon's proposal.[13]

Lower Federal Court Appointments

The Constitution does not specify how lower federal judges should be appointed. In fact, the Constitution does not even require that there be a federal judiciary below the Supreme Court, leaving it to Congress to create lower federal courts at its discretion. Congress created a system of lower federal courts in 1789, and they have existed ever since. The appointment process for lower federal court judges has always followed the process for appointing Supreme Court justices: the president nominates and the Senate confirms. However, senators have traditionally had broad power to offer advice to the president about whom to nominate for these posts—especially at the district court level. Judicial districts, in which the federal trial courts operate, fall within the boundaries of a single state. By tradition, judges for these district courts come from the state in which the district falls.

Under the practice of "senatorial courtesy," presidents relied on senators of their own political party from the state in which the vacancy occurred to suggest a nominee. Because senatorial courtesy accorded home-state senators of the president's party a virtual veto power over nominations that they disapproved, presidents were bound to clear their district court nominees with these senators.[14] As a result, presidential power to nominate district court judges was limited, with the posts being treated largely as a patronage tool of senators. The former attorney general Robert F. Kennedy once said that the practice amounted to "senatorial appointment with the advice and consent of the Senate."[15] Senatorial courtesy also applied to the appointment of judges to appellate courts but in a more diluted form because judicial circuits (in which the federal appeals courts fall) cross state lines.

In 1977 President Jimmy Carter undermined senatorial courtesy by creating, through an executive order, the Circuit Court Nominating Commission. The establishment of the nominating commission was part of an effort to institute merit selection of federal judges. Thus, the power to screen nominees for the courts of appeals and suggest whom to appoint was taken away from senators and given to the nominating commission (which was appointed by the White House).[16] In a separate executive order, President Carter urged senators to create, voluntarily, nominating commissions to advise him on the selection of district court judges. By 1979, senators from thirty-one states had complied with Carter's request to establish district court nominating commissions.[17]

When Ronald Reagan became president in 1981, he abolished Carter's commission system and seized control of the lower federal selection process by creating the President's Committee on Federal Judicial Selection. The committee was staffed by representatives from the White House and the Justice Department. It "concentrated power within—and institutionalized the role of—the White House" in the selection of federal judges.[18] Thus, President Reagan succeeded in creating the type of formal machinery for screening judicial nominees that Tom Charles Huston had urged President Nixon to create in 1969.

President Reagan also expanded the power of the Justice Department by giving its Office of Legal Policy broad responsibility for judicial selection. Previously, such responsibilities had been left to the attorney general. The reforms greatly increased the ability of the president to influence judicial policy making because it gave him greater control over the selection process. As Sheldon Goldman has written:

The screening process was systematized and, for the first time in the history of judicial selection, all leading candidates for judicial positions were brought to Washington for extensive interviewing by Justice Department personnel. If a candidate had previous judicial experience, that person's record would be carefully examined. Articles and speeches of candidates likewise were scrutinized. Arguably, the Reagan administration was engaged in the most systematic judicial philosophical screening of candidates ever seen in the nation's history.[19]

Critics charged that the new selection units were responsible for administering an ideological "litmus test" to potential nominees.[20] Fred Fielding, counselor to the president under Reagan, admitted that the reforms were designed to choose "people of a certain judicial philosophy." Attorney General Edwin Meese was even more candid, saying that Reagan's judicial appointments were designed to "institutionalize the Reagan revolution so it can't be set aside no matter what happens in future presidential elections."[21]

Of course, future presidents can appoint judges who reflect their own ideology, so presidential elections will, in time, undermine the judicial legacy of a particular president. But because federal judges have life tenure they can influence policy long after a president leaves office. Fielding called Reagan's judicial appointments his "best legacy," and Huston reminded Nixon in his memorandum that through judicial appointments a president "has the opportunity to influence the course of national affairs for a quarter of a century after he leaves office."[22] Presidents have thus treated the judicial selection process as an important vehicle for increasing their control over the policy-making process.

By the time Bill Clinton became president in 1993, his Republican predecessors Ronald Reagan and George Bush had appointed more than 60 percent of federal judgeships below the Supreme Court (389 of 645 district court judges in active service and 102 of 167 appeals court judges in active service).[23] At the Supreme Court level, Reagan and Bush had appointed six of the nine justices. Of the remaining three justices, only one—Byron White—had been appointed by a Democratic president. Just as Reagan and Bush had nominated judges who reflected their conservative ideology, Clinton began to nominate judges who reflected his more liberal ideology. In his first year alone, Clinton had the opportunity to nominate some 130 federal judges, including Justice Ruth Bader Ginsburg, who replaced the retiring Justice White.[24]

Presidential control of the federal judicial selection process was firmly in place. Institutionalized staff units continued to screen nominees and exert control over their selection. Bush retained the President's Committee on Federal Judicial Selection that Reagan had created. Clinton transferred the responsibility of that committee to the White House Counsel's Office, which worked together with the Office of Policy Development in the Justice Department to select potential nominees. But the selection of nominees is only half of the process. Securing confirmation is the work of other staff units.

Presidential Resources for Securing Confirmation

Presidential power is measured by more than just constitutional provisions. Such provisions mean little if the president cannot persuade others to follow his lead. As Richard Neustadt so succinctly put it, "presidential power is the power to persuade."[25] Thus, modern presidents have institutionalized a variety of operational units to promote their policy goals. Many of these units are used to help secure the confirmation of judicial nominees. They are most likely to be employed for Supreme Court nominees.

"Going Public"

Modern presidents are increasingly dependent on public support for the enactment of their policies. No longer does public support merely elect presidents. Now public support is a president's most visible source of political power. More than ever before, presidents and their surrogates take messages directly to the people in an attempt to mold mandates for policy initiatives. The strategy of presidential power based on such appeals is known as "going public."[26] The result is a sort of unending political campaign.[27]

Changes in the presidency have been stimulated in part by changes in the Senate. Clearly, Senate deliberation concerning Supreme Court nominees is not as shielded from public pressures as it used to be. Prior to the ratification of the Seventeenth Amendment to the Constitution in 1913, senators were chosen by state legislators. As Charles R. Epp has argued, the shift of the Senate's electoral base to a popular constituency "made possible the growing role of mass-based interest groups in confirmation politics."[28] Suddenly, senators were more directly accountable to the people and, thus, more susceptible to public opinion.

The Senate responded to demands to make their proceedings more public by opening their floor deliberations on Supreme Court nominees to the public in 1929. Until then, all discussions of Supreme Court nominations were held in executive session unless two-thirds of the Senate voted to open the proceedings—a rare occurrence.[29] The Senate Judiciary Committee was especially shielded from public view. Its proceedings were almost always closed and records were seldom kept, let alone made public. In 1881 the *New York Times* reported that the "Judiciary Committee of the Senate is the most mysterious committee in that body, and succeeds better than any other in maintaining secrecy as to its proceedings."[30] Only since 1949 has the Judiciary Committee held public hearings for all Supreme Court nominees, and only since 1955 have nominees routinely testified before the committee. The televising of hearings did not begin until 1981.

As public opinion became more important to senators, presidents increasingly relied on the tactic of "going public" in an attempt to direct that opinion. This practice is a far cry from what the framers expected. Scholars of the presidency, such as Jeffrey Tulis, remind us that until this century, popular presidential rhetoric of any kind was largely proscribed because it was thought to "manifest demagoguery, impede deliberation, and subvert the routines of republican government."[31] Although the framers felt that public consent was a requirement of republican government, they nonetheless believed that the processes of government should be insulated from the whims of public opinion.

Even after the tactic of going public became more common, presidents were unwilling to use it overtly to promote Supreme Court nominees. To do so would be an admission that they were stooping to "politics" in the appointment process. For example, when a variety of groups, including the American Federation of Labor (AFL) and the National Association for the Advancement of Colored People (NAACP), openly mobilized to defeat Herbert Hoover's nomination of John J. Parker in 1930, President Hoover felt constrained not to respond publicly—although he very much wanted to. Hoover drafted at least three versions of a public statement decrying the Senate's defeat of Parker but did not issue any of them. Later, the stormy battles about the nominations of Abe Fortas in 1968, Clement F. Haynsworth, Jr., in 1969, and G. Harrold Carswell in 1970 did not provoke any appreciable number of public statements by the president. Not until Ronald Reagan did presidents personally embrace the tactic of going public on behalf of their Supreme Court nominees and use it as a routine tool.

Before Reagan, Supreme Court nominees were lucky if the president publicly uttered their name after nominating them. Even the nomination announcement was often left to the White House press secretary or a Justice Department spokesperson. Now presidents announce their Supreme Court nominees with great fanfare and follow up on the announcement with many public statements aimed at eliciting popular support for the nominee. This practice has been standard procedure since 1987, when Reagan waged a full-scale personal campaign on behalf of his Supreme Court nominee Robert Bork. From July 1 through October 23, 1987, he made thirty-four public statements concerning Bork. Twenty of the statements were covered by the evening newscasts of the three major television networks, and two others were carried live on prime-time television.[32] It seemed that the president would use virtually any public forum to push his nominee, whether signing a proclamation for National Hispanic Heritage Week or German-American Day, speaking at an awards dinner for Minority Enterprise Development Week, or delivering remarks before groups such as the National Alliance of Business, the National Law Enforcement Council, and Concerned Women for America. Reagan's use of going public was part of his broader politicization of the judicial appointment process. Subsequent nominees have all drawn public statements of support from the president who nominated them, although President Clinton made relatively few on behalf of Ruth Bader Ginsburg in 1993—probably because her confirmation was never in any doubt (Table 17.1).

Although Reagan was the first president who made it standard procedure *personally* to go public on behalf of his nominees, earlier presidents often relied on surrogates to make their case for them. That way, the president could claim to be above the political fray. This was true as early as 1916, when President Woodrow Wilson nominated Louis Brandeis to the Supreme Court. Big business saw Brandeis as a radical who threatened its interests. Accordingly, business launched a campaign against Brandeis by alleging unprofessional conduct, an undesirable reputation, and the lack of a "judicial temperament." Although Brandeis publicly refused comment ("I have nothing to say about anything, and that goes for all time and all newspapers, including both the *Sun* and the moon"), he and the Wilson administration counterattacked with a behind-the-scenes public relations offensive of their own, using Norman Hapgood, editor of *Harper's Weekly*, to employ "aggressive publicity" on the nominee's behalf.[33]

Today, presidents routinely use surrogates to promote their judicial nominees. The institutionalization of this practice dates to 1969, when President

Table 17.1. Public Statements by Presidents Truman through Clinton Concerning Their Supreme Court Nominees

President	Nominee	No. of statements
Harry S. Truman	Harold H. Burton	0
	Fred M. Vinson	0
	Tom C. Clark	0
Dwight D. Eisenhower	Earl Warren	0
	John M. Harlan	2
	William J. Brennan, Jr.	0
	Charles E. Whittaker	0
	Potter Stewart	0
John F. Kennedy	Byron R. White	0
	Arthur J. Goldberg	0
Lyndon B. Johnson	Abe Fortas	0
	Thurgood Marshall	3
	Abe Fortas (Chief Justice)	3
	Homer Thornberry	1
Richard M. Nixon	Warren E. Burger	1
	Clement F. Haynsworth, Jr.	2
	G. Harrold Carswell	3
	Harry A. Blackmun	0
	Lewis F. Powell, Jr.	0
	William H. Rehnquist	0
Gerald R. Ford	John Paul Stevens	1
Jimmy Carter	[No nominees]	
Ronald Reagan	Sandra Day O'Connor	2
	Antonin Scalia	5
	William H. Rehnquist (Chief Justice)	4
	Robert Bork	32
	Douglas Ginsburg	3
	Anthony M. Kennedy	10
George Bush	David H. Souter	10
	Clarence Thomas	24
Bill Clinton	Ruth Bader Ginsburg	5

Note: Numbers do not indicate initial statement of nomination or statements issued upon confirmation, rejection, or withdrawal.

Nixon created a staff unit called the Office of Communications.[34] Nixon quickly used this public relations apparatus on behalf of his Supreme Court nominees. For example, the office pursued a strategy of getting the entire administration to "speak with one voice." Thus, it distributed a "fact sheet" called "The Truth about Judge Haynsworth" to members of the cabinet and other administration spokespersons in 1969. Recipients were asked to use the material to tout Haynsworth whenever possible, whether in a speech, broadcast interview, or comment to a reporter.[35] At the same time, the Office of Communications actively scheduled television appearances to support the nominee. Thus, administration officials and pro-Haynsworth senators could be found on everything from *The Tonight Show with Johnny Carson* to the Sunday morning talk shows.

Nixon also recognized the importance of local newspapers as a means of bypassing the influential "eastern establishment" media and taking messages directly to the people. When Nixon nominated Warren Burger as chief justice in 1969, the Office of Communications hired a direct mail firm and inundated some 30,000 magazine and newspaper publishers with a fact sheet about the nominee. Jeb Stuart Magruder, an aide to White House Chief of Staff H. R. Haldeman and later deputy director of the Office of Communications, wrote,

[H]undreds of editors wrote to express their thanks for this attention, and thousands of small newspapers carried more information on Burger than they otherwise would have. From a political point of view, we had to assume that this kind of publicity helped generate a favorable climate for Senate confirmation, although in Burger's case confirmation was never in doubt.[36]

A similar mailing was sent in an effort to bolster support for Haynsworth later that year.[37]

During the 1970 Carswell nomination, the White House even generated letters to be published in letters-to-the-editor columns of newspapers to demonstrate support for the nominee. The letters were written by professionals at the administration's behest, then sent around the country to Republican loyalists, who copied them and added their own signatures. Some of the letters were written by members of the White House staff, including the speechwriter Patrick Buchanan. Later, the letter-writing operation was transferred to the Republican National Committee, where it generated fifty to sixty letters a week, 15 to 20 percent of which were published.[38] Ron Baukol, a White House Fellow who was assigned to the letter-writing operation in early 1971, described the program as "a true under cover operation." He said that the cost was about $100 per letter published. The operation targeted influential publications such as the *Washington Post, New York Times, Christian Science Monitor,* and *Newsweek.* Baukol concluded that "a $100 tab for a good letter in the *Washington Post* is pretty cheap compared to what we spend on our other public efforts."[39]

The Office of Communications continues to play an active role in Supreme Court nominations. During the Bork fight in 1987, the office actively generated public statements on behalf of the nominee. Reagan's communications director, Thomas Griscom, said that promoting Bork was "a very broad based effort." Secretary of Education William Bennett and Attorney General Edwin Meese III were "very much out on the circuit," he recalled, "but you'd also try to find . . . senators who might be helpful who'd go out and talk for you."[40] According to Martha Joynt Kumar, the White House used administration officials to promote Bork through satellite interviews with local television stations—particularly in the South; through radio interviews; and through op-ed articles. During the five-week public relations offensive, Kumar reports, the Office of Communications arranged an average of fifteen radio interviews a week about Bork and published twenty op-ed articles in newspapers "under the signature of administration officials."[41]

Bork himself went public. He participated in the longest and most detailed public testimony before the judiciary committee of any Supreme Court nominee in history. In addition, he took the unusual approach of actively courting the press—starting with an hour-long interview with the *New York Times* reporter Stuart Taylor, Jr., on July 7.[42] "It was our way of humanizing him and showing he didn't have horns," according to the White House lobbyist Thomas Korologos, who added that Bork "was not to talk about anything specific as far as legal issues or cases. He was to talk about his life and times and favorite color."[43] Nonetheless, Bork's opponents were able to set the agenda. As Thomas Griscom put it, the opposition created a negative "perception" of Bork that "became a reality." Those who win in politics, Griscom noted, are those who have "the ability to control and manage the agenda—control and manage public perception."[44]

Thus, the administration of George Bush went out of its way to set the terms of the debate after the president nominated David Souter in 1990. In public statement after public statement, White House Chief of Staff John Sununu, White House Legal Counsel C. Boyden Gray, and other administration officials repeated the White House line: there should be no Senate "litmus test"—"no condition in exchange for confirmation." That line dovetailed neatly with the other point the administration was stressing: Souter's "fairness"—his judicial temperament.

A year later, the Bush White House was able to criticize Anita Hill and others for carrying out a public "high-tech lynching" of nominee Clarence Thomas and at the same time aggressively speak out on behalf of the nominee. Bush claimed that the White House had used "no litmus test" in the selection of Judge Thomas, but he accused liberal interest groups of unfairly attacking Thomas for failing their own litmus test. When such a litmus test is failed, Bush told reporters, "some groups are going to rant and rave and go after [the nominee] with anything they can bring to bear on the process."[45] At the same time, the president attempted to rouse public support for Thomas. The judge, he reminded one audience, "has tremendous support from a broad . . . cross-section of America . . . [including] overwhelming support in minority communities. . . . So when you hear about opposition to Judge Thomas from one beltway group or another, it's clear that they are simply out of touch with mainstream America."[46]

The presidential tactic of going public does not necessarily imply the sound and fury associated with the Bork fight or the Anita Hill-Clarence Thomas confrontation, nor does it necessarily detract from the decorum of the confirmation process. In fact, Bush's use of the tactic for Souter and Clinton's use of the tactic for Ginsburg may have increased the process's decorum by disarming the opposition. However it is employed, going public is now part and parcel of a Supreme Court appointment process that is ever more grounded in public opinion.

Congressional Liaison

Since the administration of Dwight D. Eisenhower, presidents have had a Congressional Liaison Office at their disposal in the White House. That office— often working with a special ad hoc unit created for each nomination—now plays an important role in the confirmation process of Supreme Court nominees. The tactics used to lobby senators often resemble those associated with bare-bones political fights.

When President Johnson nominated Abe Fortas to be chief justice in 1968, Johnson's congressional liaison unit resorted to a number of lobbying tactics. As Nigel Bowles has written, these tactics included enlisting cabinet members and other departmental officials to draw "on political capital accumulated over time with senators they had worked closely with." For example, because Senator Henry Jackson, a Democrat from the state of Washington, was a member of the Armed Services Committee and interested in defense and weapons procurement, Johnson had officials from the Defense Department lobby him on the Fortas nomination.[47]

According to Bowles, the liaison unit also "systematically organized interest groups to bring additional pressure on senators," prepared speeches and other written material for use by friendly senators, and even resorted on occasion to the leverage of patronage and politics. "Try to soften [Senator] Russell Long [a Democrat from Louisiana] on Abe Fortas," Johnson wrote. "He is interested in

Camp Polk—I'm helping him; he wanted Buffalo NY building—I helped him; I need his quiet help."[48] Despite the prodding, Long did not listen.

Similar tactics were employed by President Nixon's liaison unit. Like Johnson, Nixon supplemented the activities of the Congressional Liaison Office with those of special ad hoc units. During the Carswell nomination, the ad hoc unit included the congressional liaison director, Bryce Harlow, and the deputy attorney general, Richard Kleindienst, as co-chairs; William Rehnquist and John Dean of the Justice Department; the Republican senators Robert Dole (Kansas) and Howard Baker (Tennessee); and the White House aides Charles Colson, Herbert G. Klein, Jeb Magruder, and Lyn Nofziger. According to Magruder, the group met "at eight each morning to plan the day's pro-Carswell activities."[49] In preparation for nominations to fill the vacancies left by retiring justices Hugo Black and John Harlan in 1971, the White House aide Egil Krogh recommended to Nixon's chief domestic affairs adviser John Ehrlichman that a similar group be formed:

[T]here should be a White House unit directly charged with seeing these proceedings through. I think it will require the attention of the best people here, and an *integrated* effort is mandatory. Therefore, I think a Confirmation Committee—on a very secret basis—should be established which would meet *ad hoc* beginning right away. Members would include:

Clark MacGregor[and] Bill Timmons

Congressional Relations. They should be asked to prepare a general and then a specific congressional relations plan which would be daily updated. I would encourage this type of Congressional Relations be undertaken directly by them.

Dick Moore [and] Bill Safire

Press plan/announcements/statements. They should develop a precise plan for announcing the nominees and, working with the Congressional Relations team, work out timing. Both are very sensitive to questions of tone.

Chuck Colson

Public Support/PR. Interest group support. I think it's clear that some of the muscle—if it's necessary—will have to come through Chuck's operation. . . .

John Dean

Committee Coordinator. He knows the Hill, the confirmation business, the Court, and possesses good judgment. He should be entrusted with the daily—even the hourly—watchdog responsibility for the work of the Committee. . . .

David Young

I think one independent mind, very facile and penetrating, should be brought to bear on this. David would be excellent.[50]

As it turned out, little orchestration was needed to fill the Black and Harlan vacancies. Nonetheless, Charles Colson recalls that the Confirmation Committee did meet.[51]

Some have argued that the Reagan White House spent too little time courting senators during the Bork nomination fight in 1987.[52] According to Ethan Bronner, the former Supreme Court reporter for the *Boston Globe*, Reagan did not make any telephone calls to lobby senators to vote for Bork until September 30, 1987—"after most senators had made up their minds." "[Reagan] did not call most southern Democrats," Bronner continues. "His first meeting with Republican Senate leaders took place on the day [confirmation hearings] began, September 15." Bronner also argues that Howard Baker, the White House chief of staff and former Senate majority leader, waited too long to increase the lobbying effort. Baker "called all the southern Democrats on July 21 and 22 but did no more personal lobbying until mid-September," Bronner concludes.[53] In fact, the White House simply was not prepared for the intensity of the lobbying effort against Bork. As the communications director, Griscom, put it: "We thought it was going to be a coast job, to tell you the truth—that it was going to be easy. . . . [We had] never seen somebody run the type of effort they ran [against Bork] and we let it get away from us."[54]

Unlike Reagan, both Johnson and Nixon closely supervised the congressional lobbying efforts on behalf of their Supreme Court nominees. Nixon frequently issued orders and demanded to be kept informed of his lieutenants' activities. On March 25, 1970, William Timmons of the Congressional Liaison Office sent Nixon a memorandum outlining the office's activity on behalf of Carswell:

1. Friendly reporters are trying to get "soft" Democrats to publicly commit.

2. The "Conscience of the Senate" John Williams [R-Del.] is planning to make a public statement in support.

3. Justice Department is preparing a detailed, item by item speech for [Sen.] Bob Griffin [R-Mich.] to use to refute opponents.

4. We have duplicated favorable articles and editorials for Senate distribution each day by a different Carswell supporter.

5. Bill Rehnquist of Justice Department is spending time with the undecided and weak Senators.

6. Jeb Magruder is redoubling efforts to stimulate mail to undecided and soft Senators.

7. Chuck Colson is arranging for prominent attorneys from selected states to write key Senators.

8. Harry Dent [director of Nixon's Political Affairs Office] is having influential GOP leaders contact Republican leaners from their home states.

9. National [Republican Party] Chairman Rog Morton will personally talk to undecided and soft Republican Senators. Campaign Chairman John Tower [R-Tex.] is being asked to make a pitch to Win Prouty [R-Vt.] and Hiram Fong [R-Hawaii], both up for re-election this year.

10. Justice Department has arranged for Carswell's professional colleagues to write selected Senators.

11. Working through [Rep.] Jerry Ford [R-Mich.] we are applying House pressure on Senators [Marlow] Cook [R-Ky.], [Mark] Hatfield [R-Ore.], [Richard] Schweiker [R-Pa.], [William] Saxbe [R-Ohio], and [James] Pearson [R-Kan.].

12. Congressman Bill Brock [R-Tenn.] will keep up a running attack for [Sen. Albert] Gore [D-Tenn.] to take a public position on Carswell.

13. This office is continuing its day-to-day contacts with Members.[55]

Nixon, like Johnson, was also willing to use patronage and politics to secure votes. Examples abound. Nixon's briefing paper for a White House meeting with an undecided senator, Marlow Cook, noted that Cook had a strong interest in having a particular person appointed to the Sixth Circuit Court of Appeals, but that the Justice Department had opposed that person because of his age and poor qualifications. The briefing paper suggested that *"a promise to give [Cook] the judgeship,* if he brings it up, *might secure his vote for Carswell."* This was followed by the reminder: *"Cook's support on Wednesday is crucial."*[56] Whatever transpired at that meeting, Cook voted against Carswell. In 1986 the Reagan administration reportedly attempted a similar deal with Senator Slade Gorton, a Republican from Washington, to secure Gorton's vote for Daniel Manion—Reagan's nominee to the Seventh Circuit Court of Appeals. Gorton voted for the nominee.[57]

Nixon wooed other senators with a simple phone call, or through tactics such as an invitation to join the president at a Sunday White House church service.[58] Other tactics were more blunt. During the Haynsworth fight, for example, the political affairs director, Harry Dent, wrote the following about the activities of his office: "We are gathering together the list of favors the target Senators have been asking the Administration for—jobs, projects, grants, etc., and are trying to use this as leverage with the Senators, usually using the State Chairmen as the intermediary parties."[59]

The Congressional Liaison Office routinely provides written material to friendly senators to use on and off the Senate floor. During 1969–1970, Senator Roman Hruska, a Republican from Nebraska, was Nixon's point man for Haynsworth and Carswell. Whenever his chief opponent, Senator Birch Bayh, a Democrat from Indiana, spoke out against the nominees, the White House urged Hruska to come out swinging. The television networks often gave Hruska coverage. The strategy was part of Nixon's "attack" program in Congress. During Nixon's first month in office, H. R. Haldeman wrote that Nixon was "especially anxious . . . [to] set up a system of furnishing attack material on a daily basis to a group of key people on the Hill that Bryce Harlow will be lining up to be our first line of battle for the Administration."[60] The responsibility for writing such material ultimately came to rest with Lyn Nofziger, who joined the congressional liaison staff in July 1969.

Finally, the White House can try to bully senators through threats. Such threats can take many forms. For example, the president can threaten to make a "spite" nomination if the current nominee is rejected.[61] Reagan made such a threat during the Bork nomination and then proceeded to nominate Douglas Ginsburg to the Supreme Court. (Ginsburg—younger and less distinguished than Bork—withdrew a few days later when it was revealed that he had smoked marijuana.) Likewise, Nixon's choice of Carswell may be viewed as a spite nomination in retaliation for Haynsworth's rejection. Carswell was clearly less qualified than Haynsworth. The Senate defeated Carswell in part because of his alleged racism. As a twenty-eight-year-old candidate for the Georgia legislature in 1948, Carswell gave a speech in which he said: "I believe the segregation of the races is proper and the only practical and correct way of life. . . . I yield to no man . . . in the firm, vigorous belief in the principles of white supremacy, and I shall always be so governed."[62] After Carswell's defeat, Nixon seriously considered yet another spite nomination. According to Charles Colson, "Nixon was on the verge of appointing [Sen. Robert C.] Byrd to put the Congress on the spot."[63] Byrd was a Democrat from West Virginia. In his youth he had been a member of the Ku Klux Klan—advocating a Klan rebirth in every state of the Union as late as 1946. Although Byrd had long repudiated his Klan membership, he had filibustered the 1964 Civil Rights Act with a fourteen- hour speech that was one of the longest in Senate history. Thus, voting for Byrd after voting against Carswell would be awkward for Senate Democrats. At the same time, it would be awkward for the Senate to reject a colleague. As Colson put it, Nixon's plot was "*pure* politics. I mean, Bob Byrd wanted it. Bob Byrd was a lawyer. And the idea was, 'We'll put up somebody that the Congress can't afford to say no to.' For the sake of the Court, it's a good thing that vindictive thought didn't come to pass."[64]

Threats can also take the form of direct action against individual senators. During the Haynsworth and Carswell fights, the Nixon administration leaked derogatory stories about Birch Bayh and other Senate opponents to friendly newspapers. This was done at the instigation of the president, who was particularly furious with Bayh. In October 1969 Nixon told Haldeman that they needed "a murderer's row in [the] Senate—need to kick Bayh around."[65]

Another example of a specific attempt to threaten senators involved the Nixon administration's use of corporate campaign contributors during the Haynsworth battle. In Ohio alone, the White House enlisted some fifteen major contributors to pressure Senator Saxbe to vote for Haynsworth.[66] In like fashion, major contributors from Pennsylvania, Illinois, Tennessee, Oregon, Idaho, Kansas, Missouri, Washington, Iowa, Delaware, and Arkansas were enlisted to pressure particular senators.[67] For the most part, such threats (as well as the more overt tempting of senators with favors) were orchestrated by Nixon's Political Affairs Office rather than the Congressional Liaison Office. In the end, Nixon "froze out" Republican senators who did not support Haynsworth by ignoring them and denying them access to the White House.[68]

In short, the Congressional Liaison Office lobbies senators with threats and reassurances as part of a coordinated effort to secure Senate confirmation of Supreme Court nominees. The office works with other White House staff units to mobilize grass-roots pressure on wavering senators. These efforts include building public support for the nominee and orchestrating lobbying efforts by powerful interest groups.

Mobilizing Interest Groups

Organized interests have long been active in the judicial selection process. At the Supreme Court level they have been involved since at least 1881, when interest groups such as the National Grange and the Anti-Monopoly League lobbied senators to reject the nomination of Stanley Matthews.[69] Organized labor began to take an active interest in Supreme Court nominations in the early twentieth century. It opposed President William Howard Taft's nominations of Horace H. Lurton in 1909 and Mahlon Pitney in 1912, and—together with the NAACP—successfully blocked President Herbert Hoover's nomination of John J. Parker in 1930. Still, routine participation by a broad range of interest groups in the judicial selection process is a relatively recent phenomenon. As Gregory A. Caldeira and John R. Wright have noted, such participation was not institutionalized until the 1970s.[70]

The Senate Judiciary Committee hearings for Parker were the first in which organized interests testified about a judicial nominee. That testimony was one part of a coordinated interest group campaign to defeat Parker. President Hoover was not pleased. After Parker's defeat, Hoover wrote:

Judge Parker's confirmation was opposed by vigorous nation-wide propaganda from different groups among our citizens resulting in numbers of protests to senators from their constituents. These groups, in advancing the causes to which they are devoted, have carried the question of confirmation into the field of political issues rather than personal fitness.[71]

Today, interest groups routinely participate in the judicial selection process, and presidents actively court the support of interest groups for their nominees. Since 1970 the Office of Public Liaison has existed in the White House as an institutional mechanism for mobilizing such support. Presidential use of the office to support judicial nominees is another indication of the politicization of the process and the extent to which presidents (and special interests) are eager to use the selection process to influence public policy.

The first director of the Office of Public Liaison was Charles Colson. Colson recently described his job this way:

I was Special Counsel to the President in charge of relationships with groups outside the White House—any public interest group or any special interest group. My job was to listen to them, represent their points of view at different things that went on in government, and mobilize them to get support for the President.[72]

Colson's post was not created until the Haynsworth fight was all but over. Therefore, White House efforts to mobilize interest group support for Haynsworth were done on an ad hoc basis, largely by the Office of Political Affairs, headed by Harry Dent. In a memorandum to Attorney General John Mitchell, Dent outlined some of the things his office had done: "The following individuals and organizations were contacted either directly or indirectly by my staff. All of them have been known to favor 'conservative' causes at one time or another in the past and they were asked to use their influence to generate as much pro-Haynsworth mail as possible into the offices of target Senators." A nine-page list of contacts followed, including:

G.B. Nalley, a South Carolina lumberman who will contact key leaders of the lumber industry in other states.
Willis Cantey, a South Carolina banker who will contact bankers in other states.
Carter Poe, a South Carolina hardware dealer who will contact hardware associations in other states to get mail coming in.
Phyllis Shlafly, a conservative women's leader is starting a mail campaign. . . .
Captain Robert Orrell of Virginia. Mrs. Orrell is the Procter and Gamble heiress and has a 12,000 person mailing list.
Reed Larson, head of the Right to Work Committee is working on mail. . . .

Harold Stringer of the American Legion is helping on mail.

Roger Fleming of the American Farm Bureau . . . is helping on mail.

Darrell Coover, Vice President for Government Relations of the National Association of Independent Insurers has begun a mail campaign.

Arch Booth of the National Chamber of Commerce has pledged his support.

[Clark] Mollenhoff talked to his people and revved them up.

Paul Harvey, the radio commentator, is going to try to generate mail.[73]

Dent also encouraged state Republican organizations and other groups such as Young Republicans and Young Americans for Freedom to generate mail in support of Haynsworth.

Interest group mobilization for the rest of Nixon's Supreme Court appointments was directed by Colson. He was most active during the Carswell nomination but undertook similar efforts for Harry Blackmun, William Rehnquist, and Lewis Powell. For example, Colson's handwritten notes indicate the following activity in support of Rehnquist and Powell:

Calls: 1) Prominent attorneys, 2) Bar Association Leaders, 3) Republican Governors, 4) Party Officials, 5) friendly Editors & Broadcasters, 6) Columnists, 7) Loyalists, 8) Judges, 9) Hill. Group mobilization: 1) Chamber [of Commerce], 2) NAM [National Association of Manufacturers], 3) NAHB [National Association of Home Builders], 4) Police Chiefs, 5) firefighters, 6) VFW [Veterans of Foreign Wars]. [Pat] Buchanan with conservative groups.[74]

The Bork nomination was a watershed in terms of interest group involvement. More than 300 groups opposed Bork.[75] As Caldeira and Wright have pointed out, these groups "used a wide variety of tactics, including advertising, grass roots events, focus groups, and polling."[76] The White House responded by using its Office of Public Liaison to mobilize group support for Bork. It targeted direct mailings and helped groups place favorable editorials in states where there were crucial swing senators.[77] But the White House appeared to have been caught off guard by the groundswell of opposition to Bork and it never regained the offensive. Presidents since then have learned the lesson and have worked closely with organized interests to mount campaigns on behalf of their nominees. When George Bush nominated Clarence Thomas in 1991, conservative groups waged a campaign at the behest of the White House that tended to spend more money and be better organized than the opposition.[78]

In addition to using interest groups to help secure confirmation, presidents also use judicial appointments as a way to build support for themselves and their party among particular groups. Benjamin Ginsberg and Martin Shefter note that Republican presidents in the 1980s sought to add several constituencies to the GOP camp, including southern whites. "By concentrating on issues such as abortion, school prayer, and pornography, Republicans . . . sought to politicize the moral concerns of white southerners," wrote Ginsberg and Shefter. "Moreover, they . . . used evangelical churches, which are a prominent feature of the southern landscape, to forge institutional links between southern whites and the party." As a result, Republicans secured a strong base in the South "for the first time in the party's 135-year history."[79] The judicial nominations of Reagan and Bush clearly supported this strategy. As David O'Brien has written, Reagan defined the Justice Department's "social policy agenda largely in terms of the New Right's opposition to the rulings of the Burger Court (1969–86) on abortion, affirmative action, busing, school prayer, and the like."[80] Reagan and Bush then used their increased control over the judicial selection process to choose nominees whose judicial philosophy supported such an agenda.

Having built a base in the South, it is not surprising that Bush used a southern strategy to promote Clarence Thomas.[81] In fact, the group that spent the most money on behalf of Thomas during his confirmation battle was the Christian Coalition, a Virginia-based group founded by the fundamentalist broadcaster Pat Robertson.[82] Similarly, religious organizations such as the Moral Majority and Focus on the Family played an important role in supporting Bork in 1987.[83]

Conclusion

As we have seen, modern presidents have at their disposal a wide range of resources to generate support for their judicial nominees. The development and use of these resources is an important component of the "institutional presidency"—one in which presidents and their staff play an important role in formulating and implementing policy. In this context, presidents treat the judicial selection process as a way to influence policy, and use institutional resources to maximize their influence. However, presidents must compete with other political actors, who use their own strategic resources to oppose their nominees. Thus, presidential use of these strategic resources does not guarantee success.

In fact, five Supreme Court nominees (Abe Fortas in 1968, Clement Haynsworth in 1969, G. Harrold Carswell in 1970, Robert Bork in 1987, and Douglas Ginsburg in 1987) have failed to win confirmation since 1968.[84] Other variables that have historically put presidents in a weak position to secure confirmation played a role in these defeats. The nominations of Fortas, Bork, and Ginsburg all took place at the tail end of a presidential term—historically a bad time for presidents to make such nominations. In addition, both Nixon and Reagan faced a Senate controlled by the opposition party. As Stephen Wasby reported in 1988:

[Supreme Court] nominees have been confirmed roughly 90 percent of the time during the president's first three years in office, but less than two-thirds of later nominations have been successful. However, when there is a partisan difference between Senate and president (Nixon's situation and Reagan's after the 1986 elections), the president has had a success rate of roughly two-thirds, but the rate falls to a devastatingly low *27 percent* (four of 15) in the last year of the president's term. Independent of this matter of timing, the president's success rate is over 90 percent when his party controls the Senate, but only 42 percent when his party is in the minority.[85]

Compounding the situation were legitimate charges of conflict of interest (in the case of Fortas), legitimate concerns about qualifications (in the case of Carswell and Ginsburg), and unusual political circumstances (in the case of Haynsworth and Bork). Many liberal senators were retaliating against Haynsworth for conservative opposition to Fortas. Then, when conflict-of-interest charges surfaced against Haynsworth, some conservatives felt compelled to vote against him so as to legitimize their opposition to Fortas. With Bork, many liberals were responding to what they perceived as an attempt by the Reagan administration to pack the court with conservatives.[86] In addition, Bork's problems were compounded by his controversial writings, the fact that he would be replacing a moderate "swing vote" on the Supreme Court, and the White House's lack of preparation for such intense opposition.

It should be added that there are limits to a president's ability to influence policy through judicial appointments. Once on the bench, appointees can disappoint the president who named them by voting against him on important cases, or by embracing an ideological approach different from the one he had expected. History books are filled with the pithy quotes of presidents who were spurned by their judicial nominees. For example, betrayed by Justice Tom Clark's votes on important cases, Harry Truman called Clark's appointment his "biggest mistake." Truman had first named Clark as his attorney general and then elevated him to the Supreme Court. "I don't know what got into me," Truman later said. "He was no damn good as Attorney General, and on the

Supreme Court . . . it doesn't seem possible, but he's been even worse. He hasn't made one right decision that I can think of. . . . It's just that he's such a dumb son of a bitch."[87] The heightened screening of judicial nominees in recent years minimizes the likelihood of such "mistakes," but no one can completely predict the behavior of individuals once they sit on the Court.

The contentiousness of recent Supreme Court nominations—in which so much emphasis has been placed on the judicial philosophy of nominees—demonstrates how important the outcomes are. In this context, the president must be able to compete with other players who wish to influence the selection process. The institutionalization of the president's resources to do so is an important part of modern presidential power and a further example of presidential efforts to lead public policy.

Notes

1. These staff units include the Office of Communications, the Office of Public Liaison, and the Office of Congressional Liaison. The first two were established during the administration of Richard Nixon. The third was established during the administration of Dwight D. Eisenhower.

2. Memorandum, Tom Charles Huston to President Richard Nixon, March 25, 1969. My thanks to Professor Sheldon Goldman for giving me this copy of the memo. Another copy, which apparently included handwritten comments by President Nixon, was withdrawn from Nixon's public papers at the request of the former president.

3. Ibid., 7.

4. Memorandum, John D. Ehrlichman to Staff Secretary, March 27, 1969, with President Nixon's handwritten note, in folder "News Summaries (March 1969)," box 30, President's Office Files, Nixon Presidential Materials Project (hereafter NPMP), Alexandria, Virginia.

5. Bruce A. Ackerman, "Transformative Appointments," *Harvard Law Review* 101 (1988): 1164.

6. James E. Gauch, "The Intended Role of the Senate in Supreme Court Appointments," *University of Chicago Law Review* 56 (1989): 346–350.

7. Alexander Hamilton, James Madison, and John Jay, *The Federalist Papers,* ed. Clinton Rossiter (New York: New American Library, Mentor Books, 1961), no. 76, 457.

8. Gauch, "The Intended Role of the Senate," 354.

9. For example, Tench Cox, quoted in Gauch, "The Intended Role of the Senate," 356.

10. "Conference with a Committee of the United States Senate," August 8, 1789, in *The Papers of George Washington,* ed. W. W. Abbot (Charlottesville: University Press of Virginia, 1989), 401.

11. Quoted in U.S. Senate, *Congressional Record,* daily ed., 102d Cong., 1st sess., October 15, 1991, S14640.

12. Bruce Fein, "A Circumscribed Senate Confirmation Role," *Harvard Law Review* 102 (1989): 672; William Bradford Reynolds, "The Confirmation Process: Too Much

Advice and Too Little Consent," *Judicature* 75 (August–September 1991): 80; Laurence H. Tribe, *God Save This Honorable Court* (New York: Random House, 1985).

13. U.S. Senate, *Congressional Record*, October 15, 1991, S14639.

14. For a more thorough discussion of senatorial courtesy, see Harold W. Chase, *Federal Judges: The Appointing Process* (Minneapolis: University of Minnesota Press, 1972), 6–13.

15. Quoted in David M. O'Brien, "Background Paper," in *Judicial Roulette: Report of the Twentieth Century Fund Task Force on Judicial Selection* (New York: Priority Press, 1988), 33.

16. Larry C. Berkson and Susan B. Carbon, *The United States Circuit Judge Nominating Commission: Its Members, Procedures, and Candidates* (Chicago: American Judicature Society, 1980).

17. Alan Neff, *The United States District Judge Nominating Commissions: Their Members, Procedures, and Candidates* (Chicago: American Judicature Society, 1981).

18. O'Brien, "Background Paper," 61.

19. Sheldon Goldman, "Reagan's Judicial Legacy: Completing the Puzzle and Summing Up," *Judicature* 72 (April–May 1989): 319–320.

20. David M. O'Brien, "The Reagan Judges: His Most Enduring Legacy?" in *The Reagan Legacy*, ed. Charles O. Jones (Chatham, N.J.: Chatham House, 1988), 68; Herman Schwartz, *Packing the Courts: The Conservative Campaign to Rewrite the Constitution* (New York: Scribner, 1988).

21. Fielding and Meese quoted in O'Brien, "Background Paper," 61–62, 23–24.

22. Fielding quoted in O'Brien, "The Reagan Judges," 60; Memorandum, Huston to Nixon, March 25, 1969, 1.

23. Neil A. Lewis, "Unmaking the G.O.P. Court Legacy," *New York Times*, August 23, 1993, A10.

24. Ibid.

25. Richard Neustadt, *Presidential Power: The Politics of Leadership* (New York: Wiley, 1960).

26. Samuel Kernell, *Going Public: New Strategies of Presidential Leadership* (Washington, D.C.: CQ Press, 1986).

27. Richard Rose, *The Postmodern President: The White House Meets the World* (Chatham, N.J.: Chatham House, 1988), chap. 7.

28. Charles R. Epp, "The Brandeis and Bork Battles: A Systematic Comparison" (Paper presented at the annual meeting of the Midwest Political Science Association, Chicago, April 1991), 4.

29. Paul Freund, "Appointment of Justices: Some Historical Perspectives," *Harvard Law Review* 101 (April 1988): 1157.

30. "The Electoral Count," *New York Times*, January 30, 1881, A1.

31. Jeffrey K. Tulis, *The Rhetorical Presidency* (Princeton, N.J.: Princeton University Press, 1987), 95.

32. Based on material in the *Television News Index and Abstracts* of Vanderbilt University, Nashville, Tennessee.

33. Alpheus Thomas Mason, *Brandeis: A Free Man's Life* (New York: Viking, 1946), chaps. 30–31.

34. John Anthony Maltese, *Spin Control: The White House Office of Communications and the Management of Presidential News* (Chapel Hill: University of North Carolina Press, 1992).

35. Memorandum, Ken Cole to Jeb Stuart Magruder, October 22, 1969; Memorandum, John C. Whittaker to Members of the Cabinet and Under-Secretaries; both in folder "EX FG 51/A (10/1/69–10/31/69) (2 of 2)," box 3, White House Central Files, NPMP.

36. Jeb Stuart Magruder, *An American Life* (New York: Atheneum, 1974), 94.

37. Memorandum, Robert C. Odle to Jeb Stuart Magruder, October 28, 1969, in folder "Haynsworth (2 of 3)," box 6, Harry Dent Files, NPMP.

38. Magruder, *An American Life*, 95.

39. Memorandum, Ron Baukol to Charles Colson, April 26, 1971, in U.S. Senate, Select Committee on Presidential Campaign Activities, *Final Report*, 93d Cong., 2d sess., 1974, S. Rept. 93-981, 151.

40. Interview with Thomas Griscom, Chattanooga, Tennessee, December 5, 1988.

41. Martha Joynt Kumar, "Free Lancers and Fogmeisters: Party Control and White House Communications Activities" (Paper presented at the annual meeting of the American Political Science Association, September 1993), 19.

42. Stuart Taylor, Jr., "Bork's Evolving Views: Far from the New Deal," *New York Times*, July 8, 1987, A1.

43. Quoted in Lois Romano, "Leading the Charge on Bork," *Washington Post*, September 15, 1987, D11.

44. Griscom interview, December 5, 1988.

45. President George Bush, Exchange with Reporters, October 13, 1991, *Weekly Compilation of Presidential Documents*, 1438.

46. President George Bush, Remarks at a Kickoff Ceremony for the Eighth Annual National Night Out against Crime, August 6, 1991, *Weekly Compilation of Presidential Documents*, 1119.

47. Nigel Bowles, *The White House and Capitol Hill: The Politics of Presidential Persuasion* (Oxford: Clarendon Press, 1987), 159–160.

48. Ibid., 166–168; Johnson quoted on 166.

49. Magruder, *An American Life*, 110.

50. Memorandum, Egil "Bud" Krogh to John Ehrlichman, September 24, 1971, Supreme Court Nominations, box 17, David R. Young Files, NPMP.

51. Interview with Charles Colson, Atlanta, Georgia, July 11, 1989.

52. For example, Patrick B. McGuigan and Dawn M. Weyrich, *Ninth Justice: The Fight for Bork* (Washington, D.C.: Free Congress Research and Education Foundation, 1990), 219.

53. Ethan Bronner, *Battle for Justice: How the Bork Nomination Shook America* (New York: Norton, 1989), 200.

54. Griscom interview, December 5, 1988.

55. Memorandum, William E. Timmons to the President, March 25, 1970, in folder "[CF] FG 51/A—Supreme Court [1969–70]," box 22, White House Central Files, NPMP.

56. Memorandum, Bryce Harlow to the President, April 6, 1970, in folder "[CF] FG 51/A—Supreme Court [1969–70]," box 22, White House Central Files, NPMP (emphasis in original).

57. Herman Schwartz, *Packing the Courts: The Conservative Campaign to Rewrite the Constitution* (New York: Scribner, 1988), 107.

58. Action Items—Carswell Nomination, April 2, 1969, in folder "[CF] FG 51/A—Supreme Court [1969–70]," box 22, White House Central Files, NPMP.

59. Memorandum, Harry Dent to Ken Belieu, October 17, 1969, in folder "Haynsworth (2 of 3)," box 6, Harry Dent Files, NPMP.

60. Memorandum, H. R. Haldeman to Herbert Klein, February 9, 1969, in folder "H. R. Haldeman I (1 of 3)," box 1, Herbert Klein Files, NPMP.

61. For a discussion of spite nominations, see Peter G. Fish, "Spite Nominations to the United States Supreme Court: Herbert Hoover, Owen J. Roberts, and the Politics of Presidential Vengeance in Retrospect," *Kentucky Law Journal* 77 (1988–1989): 545.

62. Speech by G. Harrold Carswell before a meeting of the American Legion, August 2, 1948; full text reprinted in U.S. Senate, Committee on the Judiciary, *Hearings on the Nomination of George Harrold Carswell*, 91st Cong., 2d sess. (1970), 22–23.

63. Colson interview, July 11, 1989.

64. Ibid.

65. H. R. Haldeman notes, Meeting between the President and H. R. Haldeman, October 21, 1969, in folder "Haldeman Notes: July–December 1969 [October–December 1969—Part 2]," box 40, H. R. Haldeman Files, NPMP.

66. Memorandum, Jack A. Gleason to Harry Dent, October 24, 1969, in folder "Haynsworth (Brownell)," box 6, Harry Dent Files, NPMP; see also Memorandum, Jack A. Gleason to Kevin Phillips, October 15, 1969, in folder "Haynsworth (3 of 3)," box 6, Harry Dent Files, NPMP.

67. Memorandum, Jack A. Gleason to Harry Dent, October 24, 1969.

68. See Bruce Oudes, ed., *From: The President—Richard Nixon's Secret Files* (New York: Harper and Row, 1989), 69–70.

69. Scott Ainsworth and John Anthony Maltese, "Early Policy Influence of the National Grange at the Federal Level: 1878–1881" (Paper presented at the annual meeting of the Southern Political Science Association, November 1993).

70. Gregory A. Caldeira and John R. Wright, "Lobbying for Justice: The Rise of Organized Conflict in the Politics of Federal Judgeships" (Paper presented at the annual meeting of the American Political Science Association, September 1990), 2, 12.

71. Draft statement by Herbert Hoover, May 7, 1930, in folder "Judiciary—Supreme Court of the United States, Endorsements: Parker, 5/6–5/10/30," box 193, White House Central Files, Herbert Hoover Presidential Library, West Branch, Iowa.

72. Colson interview, July 11, 1989.

73. Memorandum, Harry S. Dent to the Attorney General and Bryce Harlow, October 27, 1969, in folder "Haynsworth (2 of 2)," box 34, John Ehrlichman Files, NPMP.

74. Handwritten notes, Charles Colson, no date, in folder "Supreme Court," box 115, Charles Colson Files, NPMP.

75. Caldeira and Wright, "Lobbying for Justice," 17.

76. Ibid.

77. Kumar, "Free Lancers and Fogmeisters," 19; Patrick B. McGuigan and Dawn M. Weyrich, *Ninth Justice*, 125.

78. Timothy M. Phelps and Helen Winternitz, *Capitol Games: Clarence Thomas, Anita Hill, and the Story of a Supreme Court Nomination* (New York: Hyperion, 1992), 133–136.

79. Benjamin Ginsburg and Martin Shefter, "The Presidency, Interest Groups, and Social Forces: Creating a Republican Coalition," in *The Presidency and the Political System*, 3d ed., ed. Michael Nelson (Washington, D.C.: CQ Press, 1990), 346–347.

80. O'Brien, "The Reagan Judges," 64.

81. Phelps and Winternitz, *Capitol Games*, 24.

82. Ibid., 133.

83. McGuigan and Weyrich, *Ninth Justice*, 124.

84. I include Douglas Ginsburg, even though his name had not been formally submitted to the Senate when he withdrew under fire.

85. Stephen L. Wasby, *The Supreme Court in the Federal Judicial System*, 3d ed. (Chicago: Nelson-Hall Publishers, 1988), 128.

86. Schwartz, *Packing the Courts*.

87. Quoted in David M. O'Brien, *Storm Center: The Supreme Court in American Politics*, 3d ed. (New York: Norton, 1993), 121–122.

18 The Vice Presidency:
New Opportunities, Old Constraints

Joseph A. Pika

Constitutionally, vice presidents have virtually no powers and responsibilities. Historically, they have been almost without informal influence as well. But in recent years, Joseph A. Pika argues, a new vice presidency has developed: active, influential, and endowed with ample institutional resources to take on new advisory and diplomatic assignments for the president. Hastening this transformation has been the competence of most modern vice presidents, such as Gerald R. Ford, Nelson A. Rockefeller, Walter F. Mondale, and George Bush. Bill Clinton's vice president, Al Gore, fits well into this pattern of vice presidential competence. Yet, according to Pika, the experience of Gore's predecessor, Dan Quayle, may be even more significant. Quayle's personal competence was widely doubted. Yet so great has been the transformation of the vice presidency that even he enjoyed considerable responsibility and influence in the Bush administration.

Moments before the inauguration of Bill Clinton on January 20, 1993, Albert Arnold Gore, Jr., was sworn in as the nation's forty-fifth vice president. Gore assumed an office that has undergone substantial changes since reaching its nadir in 1973 when Vice President Spiro T. Agnew was forced to resign after pleading nolo contendere to a Justice Department charge of accepting bribes. In the aftermath, Gerald Ford and then Nelson Rockefeller became the nation's first unelected vice presidents under provisions of the Twenty-fifth Amendment, which had become part of the Constitution only a few years earlier, in 1967. Ford succeeded to the presidency, choosing Rockefeller as his vice president. Rockefeller, although dropped from the Republican ticket in 1976, initiated important changes that made the vice presidency integral to the modern presidency. Serving with presidents who were receptive to their activism, Rockefeller and his successor, Walter Mondale, fostered a renaissance for the vice presidency by enlarging the possibilities and influence of an office often ridiculed even by its occupants.

Mondale was followed as vice president by George Bush. By serving for a full eight years, Bush provided considerable stability to the vice presidency and continued several of the developments pioneered by Mondale. Bush's ultimate contribution to the office, however, remains uncertain. Criticized by conservative Republicans as an overly silent partner of Ronald Reagan, Bush's behind-the-scenes role in the Iran-contra affair remained a controversial issue even in the final days of his presidency. Bush's selection of James Danforth "Dan" Quayle as his own running mate drew widespread criticism during the 1988 presidential campaign, and the doubts about Quayle's capacity for the job lingered for four full years. Even as late as July 1992, just a few weeks before the Republican National Convention, some party leaders were trying to have Quayle replaced on the national ticket.

Quayle's term as vice president presented an especially severe test for the "new vice presidency." Could the office's newfound prominence and stature survive an occupant whose credentials were so widely questioned by both the general public and political elites? To some, Quayle's elevation to the second-highest office in the land confirmed doubts as to whether the vice presidency had improved at all in recent years. As Arthur Schlesinger argues, the job may remain "a resting place for mediocrities."[1]

Vice President Gore faces higher performance expectations than did Quayle; indeed, the 1992 campaign suggested that Gore would serve as Bill Clinton's "partner." But despite its post-Agnew strengthening, the vice presidency has not fundamentally changed: its incumbent can wield only as much influence as the president allows.

Recent changes in the vice presidency have two important implications. This transformation, accomplished in a relatively brief period, provides evidence of how political institutions evolve, a process often studied in association with the presidency. Moreover, if vice presidents have become integral to the day-to-day workings of the modern presidency, we may have ended a recurring nightmare of the political system—a vice president forced to assume the complex and critical responsibilities of the presidency but largely unprepared to do so. This was the situation that confronted Vice President Harry S. Truman when he succeeded Franklin D. Roosevelt in April 1945. Roosevelt had served as president since March 1933, guiding the country during a period of economic depression and international danger; Truman had been vice president less than three months and had met with the president only ten times before being called upon to replace him. In the decades following Truman's succession, concern about instability at the top of our government was heightened by the ever-present possibility of a nuclear confrontation with the Soviet Union. Although that danger has receded, the nation is still periodically shocked by reminders of presidential mortality.

Rise of the Vice President as Policy Adviser

What is new about the vice presidency? Both journalists and academics have drawn attention to the expanded policy role that was played by Rockefeller and Mondale, a new set of responsibilities that supplemented the job's ceremonial and political activities.[2] Before agreeing to serve as vice president, Rockefeller sought and received an explicit mandate from President Ford to chair the Domestic Council, an important center of White House decision making in domestic policy since its inception in the Nixon administration. From this vantage point, Rockefeller expected to direct the nation's domestic policy agenda much as Henry Kissinger had dominated foreign policy from his position as head of the National Security Council staff. Mondale, whose role in the Carter White House expanded considerably after his first year in office, became a senior presidential adviser on a wide range of topics and oversaw the annual effort to set the administration's legislative agenda.

Both vice presidents benefited from having a large and professional staff, ready access to the Oval Office, and presidents who were receptive to their advice and involvement. As Paul Light demonstrates, the vice president's staff grew from twenty aides in 1960 to more than seventy during the Carter presidency. This expansion made it possible for the vice president to develop an independent staff structure that largely paralleled the president's, including specialists in both domestic and foreign policy and assistants for scheduling, speechwriting, congressional relations, and press relations. Thus, when Rockefeller and Mondale participated in group meetings or met with the president privately, as they both did weekly, they benefited from a substantial amount of analytic support. Mondale enjoyed additional advantages: he was only the second vice president to have an office in the West Wing of the White House amid the president's closest advisers (Agnew had briefly occupied a White House office), and he had an open invitation to attend any meeting on the president's schedule. The result for both Rockefeller and Mondale was an enlarged, more challenging position that went well beyond the job's existing responsibilities to lobby Congress, serve as an administration spokesman to the general public and important interest groups, attend ceremonial functions in the president's stead, and assist the party's candidates for office.

Previous vice presidents enjoyed only limited policy responsibilities. These were exercised through service on study commissions and interdepartmental committees that were often more symbolic gestures than genuine policy assignments. In the long history of the office, only Henry Wallace, Franklin Roosevelt's vice president from 1941 to 1945, wielded substantial authority as head of the Economic Defense Board and its successor, the Board of Economic Warfare. Rockefeller and Mondale seemed to usher in a new era. Conflict with the White House staff and Ford's shift to budget austerity prevented Rockefeller from dominating the domestic agenda as he had hoped. (A major review of domestic priorities conducted under his direction produced nineteen policy recommendations for the 1976 State of the Union address, but only six were included and those were in modified form.)[3] But Rockefeller met with greater success in other areas: he overcame extensive opposition to win presidential support for an innovative approach to the energy crisis, worked to establish the White House Office of Science and Technology Policy, and used his personal meetings with the president to promote other priorities, albeit unsuccessfully. Mondale parlayed his extensive Washington experience, contacts with the Democratic party's liberal wing, and interpersonal skills into a White House presence as a senior adviser. Overseeing the administration's agenda-setting process was a routine assignment of limited duration that freed Mondale to become a "generalist" who moved into and out of issues as he chose.

Even the most enthusiastic observers of the enhanced vice presidency of the 1970s recognized how temporary these changes might prove to be. "If the next President does not want an active Vice-President and does not want to spend time in conference with his running mate," observed Paul Light, "there is no law or constitutional provision that can compel him to do so."[4] Nonetheless, the more presidents adhere to the precedents set by Rockefeller and Mondale, the more firmly such practices become part of White House lore. Although subject to reversal by any president at any time, informal norms may begin to channel or even constrain presidential use of the vice presidency.

In fact, an impressive array of precedents has begun to accumulate, and a mechanism has developed to transmit them from one vice president to the next. Like his predecessor, George Bush enjoyed a West Wing office, had a weekly slot on the president's schedule, received the president's daily briefing on foreign policy, and could attend any meetings he wished.[5] The same held true for Dan Quayle. Moreover, an informal system continues to transmit such precedents from one administration to the next. Mondale learned about the job from Rockefeller and Hubert H. Humphrey, Lyndon B. Johnson's vice president and one of Mondale's longtime mentors. Rockefeller met with Mondale on several occasions and provided him with an extensive review of staff operations.[6] Even though Mondale consciously sought to avoid several aspects of Rockefeller's service, he could not help but draw lessons from his predecessor's experience. Bush met with Mondale during the transition period and seems to have incorporated far more of Mondale's practices.[7] Ford received advice from a variety of sources during his confirmation hearings, including a private letter of advice from Humphrey.[8]

As former vice presidents, Gerald Ford and George Bush were in an ideal position to serve as mentors to Rockefeller and Quayle, respectively. There is little indication that Ford and Rockefeller enjoyed a close personal relationship; in any event, Rockefeller, a senior Republican with far more years of executive and national political experience than Ford, would probably have been unreceptive to advice. Nonetheless, Ford drew on his own experience in the Nixon administration to foster several changes designed to achieve "broader incorporation into [White House] staff operations of the Vice President."[9] Quayle, much younger and far less experienced on the national scene than any recent vice president, acknowledged his desire to emulate Bush's vice-presidential role while developing a distinctive style of his own. It was Quayle's and the nation's good fortune that he was in a position to learn from the man who, along with Richard Nixon, served longer in the job than any other living American. Thus, an ill-defined but cumulative set of "lessons" has begun to develop, which is reinforced by academic and journalistic accounts. Al Gore has acknowledged studying those accounts and making a conscious effort to abide by their advice. He also spoke with Mondale and Quayle about their experiences in office.

Presidential and Vice-Presidential Roles

Students of the presidency customarily examine the major roles associated with the office. A similar approach to the vice presidency reveals how meager its responsibilities are and how recent is their vintage. An untold number of roles has been ascribed to the president.[10] Their origins, however, are circumscribed: the Constitution, statutes passed by Congress, or practice and precedent established by predecessors. Lists of the president's constitutional roles typically include chief diplomat, commander in chief, chief legislator, chief magistrate, and chief administrator. Roles such as economic manager and party leader can be traced to nonconstitutional sources: in these cases, the 1946 Full Employment Act and informal precedents, respectively. Although the modern era has seen a proliferation of new presidential tasks, the executive's constitutional roles have been the basis for a substantial expansion of presidential power. This is especially true in the formulation of foreign and domestic policy, in which presidents have come to take the lead. Vice-presidential roles offer a sharp contrast both in significance and origin.

Constitutional Roles

Under the Constitution, vice presidents serve as heir designate in the event of vacancy in the presidency. They also preside over the Senate, casting a vote only in the event of a tie. Far from serving as the basis for expanded influence, as in the case of the presidency, these constitutional roles have seriously inhibited the development of the job.

Many obstacles have prevented a close working relationship from forming between the president and vice president. Part of the explanation seems to lie in the constitutional design of the office: vice presidents, by their mere presence, serve to remind presidents of their own mortality. Thus, it is not surprising to find that presidents are reluctant to work closely with their designated successors. Other political leaders and the public also seem to resent vice presidents for the same reason. Following William Henry Harrison's death, John Tyler became the first vice president to succeed to the presidency; he had to overcome congressional resistance to his assuming the title of president rather than "acting president." Presidents who came to the office by vice-presidential succession have, as a group, been held in lesser regard than their predecessors by the public and historians alike.[11] Serving as vice president during a period of presidential illness has been an even more difficult experience; cabinet members and White House aides often actively communicate their resentment of the person who is most likely to prosper at their mentor's expense. Such jealousy emerged, somewhat surprisingly, in July 1985, when Ronald Reagan underwent surgery for cancer of the colon. Although Reagan had worked out an arrangement with Vice President Bush to cover the eight-hour period when he would be under general anesthetic, considerable infighting reportedly emerged between the presidential and vice-presidential staffs, so much so that Bush was forced to make a public denial of such difficulties.[12] Thus, the role of heir designate has not been an easy one.

Presiding over the Senate, a position that would seem to provide extensive opportunities for vice presidents to exercise influence, has actually been a source of weakness by making the office a "constitutional hybrid," lacking a home in either branch of government.[13] Historically, the result was that vice presidents were excluded not only from executive branch activities but also from a meaningful legislative role.[14] In the Senate, norms emerged that minimized the presiding officer's discretion in controlling business and debate. Even the vice president's power to cast tie-breaking votes has declined. John Adams cast twenty-nine tie-breakers and John C. Calhoun twenty-eight, but recent vice presidents have been less fortunate: Johnson cast none, Agnew two, Mondale one, Bush eight, and Quayle none. Al Gore cast two tie-breakers on important budget votes within weeks of each other in 1993. Vice presidents have "dwelt in a constitutional limbo somewhere between the legislative and executive branches," functioning as full-time members of neither.[15]

Two constitutional amendments have had a bearing on the vice presidency. The Twenty-fifth Amendment, ratified in 1967, established procedures for dealing with presidential disabilities and for filling vice-presidential vacancies, a timely change that provided guidelines for the selection of Ford and Rockefeller.[16] The Twelfth Amendment (1804) had a more profound effect on the office. It provided for separate Electoral College balloting for president and vice president in order to avoid a repetition of the electoral confusion in 1800. Thomas Jefferson and his party's vice-presidential nominee, Aaron Burr, received the same number of votes, which threw the election into the House of Representatives. (Under the original Constitution, all electoral votes were cast for president with the runner-up candidate becoming vice president.) Most scholars, however, regard the Twelfth Amendment as having reduced "the Vice-Presidency to an insignificant office sought only by insignificant men," an outcome correctly anticipated by some members of Congress at the time of its passage.[17] The revised selection process, together with popularly based political parties, ensured that vice-presidential nominations would be used "to add balance to the ticket, to placate a faction of the party, or to carry a swing state."[18] Vice presidents literally became "also-rans," party tagalongs of mediocre qualifications and accomplishments rather than the second most qualified candidates for president, which was probably the case with John Adams and Thomas Jefferson, the nation's first two vice presidents. Thus, the vice president's constitutional roles have actually inhibited rather than encouraged the office's institutional development.

Statutory Roles

By law, vice presidents, unlike presidents, have not been given numerous responsibilities nor the influence that goes with them. The greatest potential for influence lies in the vice president's statutory membership on the National

Security Council (NSC). But even here, the vice president's actual involvement hinges on the president's preferred style of foreign policy making. Although the NSC is available to help presidents coordinate many facets of foreign policy, its use is optional rather than mandatory. John F. Kennedy, for example, created an ad hoc group of advisers to help him resolve the Cuban missile crisis. It included some NSC members but not Vice President Johnson. Nixon side-stepped the NSC altogether (as well as Vice President Agnew) when deciding to invade Cambodia (1970), reestablish ties with mainland China (1972), and sign the Strategic Arms Limitation Treaty (SALT I) with the Soviet Union (1972). And, although Ronald Reagan used the NSC staff to conduct secret negotiations with Iran in 1985–1986, he did not work through the full council. Thus, membership on the NSC does not ensure vice-presidential access to decision making.

Practice and Precedent

Practice and precedent have by far been the most important determinants of vice-presidential roles. The development of these roles is a twentieth-century phenomenon. Some roles of the modern president can be traced to precedents established by nineteenth-century and turn-of-the-century predecessors, such as Jefferson's active leadership of Congress, James K. Polk's and Abraham Lincoln's expansion of war and emergency powers, and Theodore Roosevelt's effective use of the press to shape a national agenda. In contrast, harbingers of vice-presidential power are few and far between, making the office a distinctly recent product.

The inclusion of vice presidents in meetings of the cabinet was not actively considered until the last years of the nineteenth century. Adams was the last vice president to participate in cabinet meetings until Woodrow Wilson asked Vice President Thomas R. Marshall to preside over these sessions during the president's trip abroad to negotiate the peace treaty at Versailles. Although a few presidents relied on their vice presidents for policy advice (notably Polk, Lincoln, and William McKinley), Vice President Jefferson chose to emphasize his legislative rather than executive role, a convenient arrangement because President Adams, a political opponent, excluded him from cabinet meetings anyway. In 1896, Theodore Roosevelt, then a vice-presidential candidate, suggested that vice presidents be given a seat in the cabinet (although he never followed the practice himself when given the opportunity as president), and this idea was endorsed by both tickets in the 1920 presidential election. Calvin Coolidge, Warren G. Harding's vice president, regularly attended cabinet

Table 18.1. Foreign Trips by Recent Vice Presidents

Vice President	Number of Foreign Trips	Vice President	Number of Foreign Trips
Nixon	7	Mondale	14
Johnson	10	Bush	23[a]
Humphrey	12		18[b]
Agnew	7	Quayle	19
Ford	1	Gore	3[c]
Rockefeller	6		

[a] first term; [b] second term; [c] initial fifteen months.
Sources: Data covering Nixon through Mondale come from Joel K. Goldstein, *The Modern Vice Presidency: The Transformation of a Political Institution*, 159, © 1982 Princeton University Press. Reprinted by permission of Princeton University Press. Bush data come from "George Herbert Walker Bush: Chronology," a document issued by the White House. Quayle data come from the former vice president's records.

meetings. New practices, however, are often fragile. Charles G. Dawes, elected on the Republican ticket with Coolidge in 1924, announced even before the inauguration that he would not become part of the cabinet: to do so, argued Dawes, would limit the freedom of future presidents in selecting advisers. Herbert Hoover reinstituted the practice, and vice presidents have been routinely included in meetings of the cabinet ever since.[19]

It is not clear when vice presidents began to serve as representatives of the administration to foreign and domestic audiences. John Nance Garner, who was Franklin Roosevelt's vice president from 1933 to 1940, was the first to travel abroad in an official capacity. Until that time, vice presidents were not involved in international relations, a pattern established by Jefferson when he declined a request from Adams to visit France as the president's diplomatic representative. Henry Wallace, FDR's second vice president, was dispatched on several wartime missions, and recent vice presidents have traveled extensively as roving ambassadors, although largely to make ceremonial appearances at state funerals and inaugurations rather than to deliver diplomatically sensitive messages (Table 18.1). Domestic appearances by the vice president on the administration's behalf can be traced to Thomas Marshall, a popular speaker during his term in office who was heavily involved in Liberty Loan campaigns during World War I but does not appear to have served as a general policy spokesman for the Wilson administration. Alben W. Barkley, Truman's vice president, is credited with expanding these largely ceremonial activities into a role that has been regularly performed by more recent occupants of the office.

In addition to ceremonial appearances, today's vice presidents are called upon to carry explicit political messages to Congress and to important interest groups, but the origin of these activities is quite recent. In view of the vice president's constitutional duty to preside over the Senate, it is surprising to discover that, historically, few vice presidents have actively lobbied for congressional passage of administration proposals; even more surprisingly, several of them actively conspired with administration opponents to defeat such proposals.[20] While running as the Democrats' vice-presidential nominee in 1920, Franklin D. Roosevelt suggested that liaison with Congress was an area of potentially greater vice-presidential activity, and he later dispatched Garner on legislative assignments.[21] Garner, a former congressional party leader himself, is credited with devising the system of weekly presidential conferences with congressional leaders that have become a mainstay of legislative-executive relations. Garner also functioned as an effective New Deal lobbyist until 1937, when he asserted his independence by opposing Roosevelt's proposal to expand the Supreme Court. His relationship with Roosevelt broke down completely when the president decided to violate the precedent of serving only two terms. Garner's successors have varied widely in their efforts as congressional lobbyists, but it is instructive to note that of the twelve men who have served as vice president since Garner, nine brought congressional experience to the job.

Most of the vice presidency's activities are relatively recent developments that have been firmly translated into public expectations. Today it is practically inconceivable that a vice president would publicly oppose a president's nominee for an appointive post or openly question administration policy, steps that were not uncommon as recently as the 1930s. A critical change in the office occurred in 1940, when Roosevelt became the first presidential candidate to demand the right to select his own running mate. Party bosses, who traditionally controlled nominating conventions, had never shown concern for compatibility between the presidential and vice-presidential nominees in selecting the national ticket. As a consequence, it was the exception rather than the rule to find the members of a victorious ticket serving as a team after their election. Since 1940, however, presidential nominees have gradually won the right to stress compatibility as a criterion for vice-presidential nominations, thereby making it possible for the candidate to select someone who is expected to be an administration "lieutenant."[22] In this way, recent vice presidents have had a greater opportunity to become trusted advisers, although traditional concerns for providing geographic and ideological balance to the national ticket may still be weighed more heavily.

An Expanded Political Role

Since World War II, succession crises and electoral politics have thrust the vice presidency more frequently into the national spotlight. These events account for the office's newfound political prominence. Between 1945 and 1976 the presidency was occupied nearly half the time by three men who were originally chosen to serve as vice president. Death, assassination, and resignation played havoc with the customary obscurity of the vice presidency. Roosevelt and Kennedy died in office, and their successors, Truman and Johnson, achieved reelection to full terms of their own. Nixon's resignation from the presidency led to Ford's brief tenure. The frailty of presidents was further underscored by the medical problems of presidents Eisenhower, Johnson, and Reagan. Unsuccessful assassination attempts were made on Truman, Ford, and Reagan while they were in office. The nation went through two health scares with George Bush. In May 1991 he was briefly hospitalized with atrial fibrillation (a rapid heartbeat) caused by a thyroid condition that was subsequently controlled with medication. More dramatically, in the midst of a trip to Asia in January 1992, the president collapsed during a state dinner being given in honor of his visit to Japan. The entire incident was recorded by television cameras, although the tape of Bush vomiting into the lap of Prime Minister Kiichi Miyazawa and then fainting was not released in its entirety. The incident was diagnosed as an attack of gastroenteritis, or stomach flu, and was unrelated to his earlier ailment. Seeking to quiet undue public concern, White House spokesman Marlin Fitzwater reminded the press, "The President is human; he gets sick."[23] But that is precisely the problem. In the postwar era, only Walter Mondale was not suddenly catapulted into the national spotlight because of concern about the president's health.

During the same period, vice presidents have become more prominent figures in presidential elections. Partly because of the recent spate of unexpected transfers of power, the vice presidency has emerged as an important springboard to a party's presidential nomination. Winning the presidency, however, has not proved as easy. Until George Bush's victory in 1988, no incumbent vice president had been elected to the presidency since Martin Van Buren. Even so, the job had become an important source of candidates. Among recent vice presidents, Nixon, Humphrey, and Mondale received their party's presidential nomination, and Bush was regarded from the start as a strong contender for nomination. Of the ten men who won the Democratic presidential nomination between 1948 and 1992, four had once served as vice president, as had three of the seven Republican nominees.

Vice-presidential candidates are also receiving more attention during the general election campaign. Repeating the precedent set in 1976, televised vice-presidential debates were held in 1984, 1988, and 1992. Bill Clinton altered the traditional pattern of operating separate presidential and vice-presidential campaigns when he and Al Gore traveled together extensively in 1992. The practice began immediately after the Democratic convention with a wildly successful bus tour of eight Northeastern states. The joint appearances went so well that additional tours were conducted during the campaign and the two candidates spent a great deal of time together on the campaign trail.

Bush's Record as Vice President

George Bush was only the sixth vice president to complete a full eight years in the position.[24] His service occurred during a period when changes were being made in the resources, responsibilities, and respect accorded the office. How did Bush use these opportunities during his long tenure and what legacy did he leave to his successors? Did he sustain the trends set in motion by Rockefeller and Mondale? Were new precedents established? Answering these questions requires a review of both Bush's major activities as vice president and the questions that linger about his role in one of the Reagan administration's most controversial undertakings, the Iran-contra affair. Moreover, Bush may have altered his legacy for the vice presidency through his selection of Dan Quayle as a running mate and his oversight of Quayle's activities in office.

Perhaps the most prominent aspect of the vice presidency during Bush's service was the role of heir designate. Ronald Reagan was the oldest person ever to be sworn in as president and the oldest ever to serve in the office. Blessed with robust health, the president survived an assassination attempt and a major operation for colon cancer. Confusion about succession and disability surfaced at the time of John Hinckley's attempt on Reagan's life in March 1981. In the absence of details about the president's condition, Secretary of State Alexander Haig issued a misleading statement from the White House about who was constitutionally in charge. Reagan's closest aides hastily convened in a supply closet at the hospital to discuss how they would deal with the Twenty-fifth Amendment's provisions for presidential disability.[25] Four years later, when Reagan was put under general anesthesia, there was far less confusion; when

Reagan signed a letter at 10:40 a.m. on July 13, 1985, Bush became the first vice president since the amendment was ratified to assume the duties of acting president.[26]

By the time of Reagan's second health crisis, Bush had established his credentials as a loyal lieutenant. From the outset, he carefully emulated practices that Mondale had found helpful in establishing himself as a key member of the Carter administration. Like his predecessor, Bush occupied a White House office and a regular slot on the president's weekly schedule (lunch on Thursdays). He also sought a set of general rather than specific assignments in order to conserve his time and energy.[27] Overall, Bush pursued the sort of self-effacing strategy most vice presidents must master if they hope to gain admission to an administration's inner councils. Avoiding trouble, displaying absolute loyalty, and doing the dirty work are essential parts of the job description. These activities were especially important for Bush, who had been Reagan's principal opponent for the Republican party's 1980 presidential nomination, a competition that produced some lingering ill will. No doubt Bush came to regret having once described Reagan's tax and spending proposals as "voodoo economics."

Bush managed to project enthusiasm even in undertaking the many menial tasks assigned to vice presidents. Chairing task forces, attending state funerals, giving commencement addresses, receiving visitors, raising campaign funds, and lobbying Congress are duties that all modern vice presidents are asked to perform. In the short run, Bush established his reputation as a team player by contributing in little ways; in the long run, these activities helped him gain public exposure and prepare for the 1988 presidential campaign, which, in terms of intraparty maneuvering and pursuit of support, began shortly after Reagan took the oath of office for a second term in 1985. However, Bush's mark in the Reagan administration and his primary contribution to the lore of the vice presidency were made through his foreign policy assignments. As a former ambassador to the United Nations, chief of the American liaison office in Beijing, and director of the Central Intelligence Agency, Bush's international experience was conspicuous in a White House dominated by "outsiders"—aides largely unfamiliar with Washington. Bush won an early power struggle with Haig over who would chair the administration's group for handling international crises; he also became a roving ambassador who, during his first four years in office, managed to undertake more foreign trips than any of his predecessors.

Many of Bush's foreign trips involved relatively unimportant ceremonial tasks such as goodwill missions and attendance at state funerals and inauguration ceremonies. Yet even these activities may help to elevate a vice president's status by enabling him to share in the performance of the president's duties as chief of state, a unifying role for the nation. More concretely, such travels build a valuable network of international contacts that can form the basis for offering useful advice to the president. Firsthand knowledge of foreign problems and personalities can enhance the vice president's role as adviser. Because Bush headed the American delegations to the funerals of three Soviet leaders—Leonid I. Brezhnev, Yuri V. Andropov, and Konstantin U. Chernenko—and spoke with each leader's successor, he was able to carve out a knowledgeable role in the administration. In 1983, Bush also undertook two important trips to West European capitals; both were designed to win support from the North American Treaty Organization (NATO) countries for the American approach to strategic weapons issues, an approach that included both the proposed deployment of intermediate-range nuclear missiles and a tough stand in disarmament negotiations with the Soviet Union. Hedrick Smith of the *New York Times* dubbed the missions "public relations diplomacy" because of their intentional appeal to European public opinion.[28]

In sum, George Bush substantially continued the institutional developments begun by his two immediate predecessors. He sought to cultivate a close advisory relationship with the president and drew on his personal expertise to become an administration "player," someone whose views were sought in critical policy decisions. Direct involvement in important decisions, however, can come at a cost. For Bush, the cost was continuing controversy over his participation in the Iran-contra affair.

Echoes from the Past: Lingering Uncertainty about Bush and Iran-Contra

Serious questions were raised during the 1988 and 1992 presidential campaigns about Bush's role in the Reagan administration. George Will, a conservative critic, likened him to a "lap dog"—eager, fawning, but largely ineffectual. Democratic critics sometimes portrayed Bush as the opposite—a savvy former CIA director who had been able to cover his tracks both in purported dealings with Gen. Manuel Noriega, the now-deposed leader of Panama, and in helping to plan the guns-for-hostages deal with Iran that raised funds for the Nicaraguan contras, rebel forces seeking to overthrow their nation's Sandinista government. Reports had linked Bush with clandestine U.S. activities in Central America even before the Iran-contra revelations of November 1986.

Demands for an explanation of Bush's role in covert operations were symbolized by the taunting chant of delegates to the 1988 Democratic National Convention; in unison with Sen. Edward Kennedy, they repeatedly cried, "Where was George?" The answer has never been clearly established. Many thought the trials of Manuel Noriega, who was returned to the United States after his surrender to American troops, and figures involved in the Iran-contra affair would provide more evidence. But little hard evidence emerged.

Among his many trips as vice president, Bush visited Honduras in 1985 and allegedly delivered a message to its president that $110 million of U.S. economic and military assistance depended on Honduran support for the contras, an arrangement that possibly would have violated the spirit and letter of the congressional prohibition on U.S. government efforts to overthrow the Nicaraguan government. The allegation stemmed from several previously unavailable documents released during the trial of Oliver North in April 1989. The documents suggested that Reagan had personally approved the quid pro quo offer to Honduras and that Bush had been fully aware of the plan prior to his trip. These charges cast doubt on Bush's claims of noninvolvement.

During the next five weeks in the spring of 1989, Congress launched an investigation to determine whether the implicating documents had been intentionally withheld from the House and Senate committees that investigated the Iran-contra affair in 1987; Lee H. Hamilton, a Democrat from Indiana who had chaired the House investigating committee, called for a new investigation of Reagan and Bush's activities;[29] several of Bush's nominees for ambassadorial and administration posts who had unclear links to the Iran-contra affair (including Donald P. Gregg, the foreign policy adviser on Bush's vice-presidential staff) were subjected to rough questioning during their Senate confirmation hearings (and one was forced to withdraw to avoid such treatment); there was even talk of impeachment.

Bush remained silent in the face of mounting pressure for him to clear the air; he argued it would be inappropriate for him to comment until the North verdict was in. Nonetheless, defending statements came from two administration officials.[30] Finally, on the day of the North verdict, Bush publicly denied that his Honduran trip had in any way been a part of the White House plan. The denial was echoed in a letter to the editor by Langhorne A. Motley, former assistant secretary of state for inter-American affairs in the Reagan administration, who was the only other American to attend the Honduran meetings.[31]

By late June the excitement had died down. Congressional investigators discovered lapses in White House handling of documents but no evidence of deliberate withholding; human error was blamed for the oversight. George

Mitchell, the Senate majority leader, formally announced on June 25 that there was no reason to reopen the investigation. But questions lingered about Bush's role. Some witnesses, such as the former national security adviser Robert C. McFarlane, claimed that Bush had spoken out against shipping arms to Iran; others said he had remained silent. The lawyers for Adm. John Poindexter, McFarlane's successor, cast doubt on Bush's noninvolvement in the planning sessions, stating that their client had briefed the vice president about meetings that he had been unable to attend.

In the midst of the demands for a renewed investigation, a precedent-setting meeting took place between Bush and Vice President Quayle concerning the transfer of power that would occur under the terms of the Twenty-fifth Amendment if Bush became disabled. Mrs. Bush and several White House aides were present during the discussion of the confidential contingency plans, which were stored in the White House. The meeting was held on April 18, 1989, but was not announced until April 27. The reason, according to an unidentified source, was "to avoid a public reminder of Democratic charges during the campaign that Quayle lacked the necessary experience to become president."[32] In fact, the intent may have been precisely the opposite—to remind everyone of Quayle's possible limitations. The announcement came the day after Congressman Hamilton called for a new investigation amid the denials of Bush's involvement issued by current and former officials. In drawing attention to the meeting on disability, a powerful message was sent to the Washington community: by endangering Bush, critics were countenancing "the accession of Dan Quayle to the Presidency," a message that the journalist Elizabeth Drew reports was actively discussed among Senate Democrats and that helped convince their leader to put a halt to further investigations.[33]

The questions persisted until Bush's last week as president, when excerpts were released from a diary he began to keep on November 4, 1986, the day that the Iran-contra arrangements were made public in the United States. The diary reveals Bush's efforts to help President Reagan contain the political damage that followed. He volunteered to chair an investigation; considered drafting a speech that would have admitted that mistakes were made; and knew about a behind-the-scenes effort by one of his aides to encourage Oliver North to waive his Fifth Amendment rights against self-incrimination and absolve the president of responsibility. But the diary also shows that Bush was not included in all White House deliberations. When excluded from a crucial meeting on November 21, 1986, he confided to the diary, "I am the one guy who can give the president objective advice and I have felt a twinge as to why the hell they didn't include me, but on the other hand, you wind up not dragged into the mess."[34] Some observers discount these personal revelations and contend that Bush was still protecting himself right up to the last minute. Renewed controversy erupted when he pardoned Caspar Weinberger, the former secretary of defense, and others on Christmas Eve 1992 from any further prosecution for actions during the Iran-contra period.

Thus, a cloud continues to hang over Bush's service as vice president. Because of the job's historical insignificance, there is no tradition of deniability associated with the vice presidency (as there has been with the presidency) to protect incumbents from being implicated in illegal or immoral activities. The Bush experience did not create such a precedent, but it came close. Charges of a coverup, of course, were all the more disturbing because any political damage caused to Bush by the missing documents might have reshaped the 1988 election. In a reversal, Bush supporters cried foul when Special Prosecutor Lawrence Walsh issued an indictment of Weinberger just days before the 1992 election, an action that dominated the news during the campaign's closing days. Future vice presidents may look at Bush's service and conclude that he was able to exercise influence on even the most sensitive Reagan administration policies without suffering damage: Bush chose to be an administration player—"in the loop"—and survived. Others may regard Bush's experience as a warning about how vulnerable vice presidents really are and ask whether it may not be in their best interests to remain above the fray.

Quayle as Vice President

Bush shaped the vice presidency not only through his own service but also through the selection of Dan Quayle as his running mate in 1988 and his mentoring of Quayle as an understudy for four years. Announced to the media aboard a ship moored in the Mississippi River and greeted with widespread skepticism, the choice of Quayle was regarded as Bush's "riverboat gamble."

Bush's selection of Quayle removed, once and for all, any doubt that may have remained about a presidential candidate's freedom to select the party's vice-presidential nominee, the precedent established by Franklin Roosevelt in 1940. The reaction of Republican party officials and press observers would more appropriately be described as incredulity than surprise. (The Democrats, in contrast, were elated with what they viewed as a major campaign error.) Had the Bush-Quayle ticket lost, there may have been reconsideration by the parties of how vice-presidential candidates are selected. With victory, however, came a strengthening of the present system—even those presidential candidates seen as choosing "inferior running mates" may escape punishment at the ballot box.[35]

Questions in 1988 centered on Quayle's qualifications, and even after three years in the public eye, self-conscious efforts to improve his image, and often favorable reviews from journalists, Quayle had still not convinced either the public or Washington insiders that he belonged in the vice presidency. Quayle entered the vice presidency with fewer assets than any predecessor since Richard Nixon in 1953. Like Nixon, Quayle had moved from the House to the Senate, had received modest acclaim for limited achievements, and brought youth to the ticket. Also like Nixon, Quayle experienced a painful baptism in presidential politics. Nixon had to endure a scandal over campaign funds during the 1952 election, giving rise to the famous "Checkers" speech, which is credited with having saved his position on the ticket. The furor over Quayle's entering the National Guard at the height of the Vietnam War rather than enlisting or allowing himself to be drafted and his admission to law school despite a mediocre academic record quickly established him as a potential liability to the ticket; he virtually disappeared from major media markets during the campaign except for the single televised debate with Sen. Lloyd Bentsen, the Democrats' candidate for vice president. Bentsen delivered one of the campaign's most memorable lines in rebutting Quayle's comparison of himself with President John F. Kennedy; the line, "Senator, you're no Jack Kennedy," was delivered with withering directness. The campaign experience reportedly shook Quayle's confidence and did little to restore the public's.

Nixon and Quayle are similar in other ways. Like Nixon, Quayle chose foreign policy and national security issues as an area for special involvement. Both men can appropriately be considered representatives of the Republican party's right wing as it was constituted during their respective eras. And both experienced a challenge to their remaining on the national ticket during the president's reelection effort. Two incumbent vice presidents have been ousted from the national ticket in the modern era: Rockefeller was dropped by Ford in 1976 (replaced by Robert Dole) and Henry Wallace by FDR in 1944 (replaced by Truman). In 1952 Nixon salvaged his position on the ticket, but Eisenhower considered replacing him for the 1956 reelection effort.

Quayle confronted repeated efforts to dump him from the 1992 ticket that began remarkably early in his term and never fully disappeared. George Bush had to come to his rescue with a resounding endorsement even before a full year had passed in office. Initial criticism surfaced during the summer and fall of 1989, when apparent differences between Quayle and Secretary of State James A. Baker III about U.S.-Soviet relations fueled speculation that Baker or Jack Kemp, the secretary of housing and urban development, would replace Quayle in 1992. Rumors became so insistent that Bush finally announced "Absolutely," Quayle would be on the ticket, an unusual step so far in advance of the election.[36] But the issue remained alive. As late as July 23, 1992, the *New York Times* ran a front-page article suggesting that Quayle might be replaced on the ticket as a way to reinvigorate the campaign. This followed a strikingly successful Democratic convention, Ross Perot's unexpected withdrawal from the presidential contest, and a twenty-four-point lead by Clinton over Bush. A group of fifteen Republican senators had met with Bush and at least half had suggested the ticket change. Bush, however, reiterated his support at a photo session, and Quayle announced the next day that the issue had been resolved.[37] Thus, discontent with the vice president is not unprecedented, but emergence of an early "Dump Quayle" movement and its persistence illustrate how tenuous was Quayle's hold on the position and the extent to which Bush's judgment remained in question.

Quayle hopes to emulate Nixon in one additional respect: a triumphant return to the national spotlight as the Republican party's presidential nominee. There is no shortage of Republican contenders for 1996, and Quayle need not be in a hurry. He has five presidential elections before he is as old as Ronald Reagan was when he was first elected president. His immediate plans after returning to Indiana were to write a book on his experiences as vice president, chair a think-tank center on business competitiveness at the Hudson Institute, write a newspaper column, give speeches around the country for substantial honoraria, and head a financial services company. Richard Nixon reportedly advised him to take his time and focus on foreign policy.[38]

Unlike Nixon, Quayle served in a transformed vice presidency, and he enjoyed all the trappings that have now become commonplace symbols of the new vice presidency: an office in the West Wing of the White House, a staff of considerable size and professional ability, a regular slot on the president's weekly schedule (Thursday lunch, as was true for Bush and Reagan), and daily briefings with the national security adviser. This list now constitutes a virtual "litmus test" that observers apply to vice presidents; to violate any of these expectations would run the risk of embarrassing both the vice president and the administration. A measure of assurance is thus provided that the incumbent will become an active member of the administration. But even these resources proved insufficient to help Dan Quayle transform his public image.

Quayle's first year in office was far from the disaster some had predicted. The task he confronted was difficult: to overcome skepticism and negative impressions held by both Washington insiders and the general public. Pundits made the task no easier by making Quayle the butt of endless jokes. Blunders quickly made the rounds in Washington, although some of the best were wholly fictitious. Rep. Claudine J. Schneider, a Republican from Rhode Island, was credited with a widely reported story that had Quayle saying, "I was recently on a tour of Latin America, and the only regret I have was that I didn't study Latin harder in school so that I could converse with those people." The *Washington Post*, hardly a pro-Quayle newspaper, felt compelled to denounce the story and take the media to task in a sympathetic editorial.[39] But there was no shortage of genuine gaffes. For example, Quayle, who headed the National Space Council after its reestablishment in March 1989, seemed to suggest in one television interview that water had been found in the canals on Mars, making human exploration more feasible.[40] Quayle never lost his penchant for the newsworthy slip. He began 1992 by misspelling "potato(e)" at a grade school spelling bee and went on to engage in a much-publicized exchange with Murphy Brown, the title character on a popular television sitcom who had chosen to have a child out of wedlock. Both incidents provided new material for public mockery.

The lore that developed around the vice president makes it especially difficult to find the "real" Dan Quayle in the public record. After being charged with savaging the candidate during the election campaign, the media may have looked for the opportunity to make amends, a trend predicted by Michael Kinsley of the *New Republic*, for which he facetiously created the "Quayle revisionism contest" to recognize press reports of "newfound depths of wisdom, unexpected insights, and—extra points—growth in the job."[41] Whether deserved or not, news reports of Quayle's performance as vice president were generally favorable, culminating in early 1992 in a series of seven articles and a book written by Bob Woodward and David S. Broder, two of the *Washington Post*'s most respected reporters. The long journey back to respectability seemed to be over. But as Kevin Sack wrote in the *New York Times* on the day after Quayle reintroduced himself to the American public at the 1992 Republican convention in a carefully produced film and acceptance speech, "each time that Mr. Quayle has given the country reason to take him seriously, he has said something, done something or spelled something that instantly reversed the progress and fed the stereotype" created during the 1988 campaign.[42] Thus,

Quayle's record needs careful examination if we are to get a sense of his performance and his potential.

Quayle's Assignments

Much like his predecessor, Dan Quayle spent considerable time outside the United States. At the beginning of his fourth year in office, he had already visited forty-two countries, including eight trips to Latin America and three to Japan.[43] Some of the visits were eventful, but there is no indication that any of them involved the kind of sensitive diplomatic matters so common to Bush's vice presidency. He was reportedly blocked by Secretary of State Baker from visiting Germany or the Soviet Union during the delicate period after German reunification and the fall of communist control.

At home, Quayle, as chair of the National Space Council, helped to shape the administration's first-year space initiative. His push for a permanent return to the moon and piloted missions to Mars later produced conflicts with the head of the National Aeronautics and Space Administration (NASA), who resigned in early 1992. One congressional critic, Sen. Al Gore, complained about attempts to run NASA from the vice president's office.[44]

These criticisms were modest compared with those Quayle encountered as chairman of the Council on Competitiveness. Initially a nominal assignment, the council became the administration's principal weapon against regulations that were regarded as antibusiness and antifree market. These commitments led the council to devote particular attention to environmental regulations, such as those dealing with wetlands development. Because it was housed in the executive office, Quayle's staff considered itself immune from the usual procedures requiring public comment on proposed changes in regulatory policy, allowing them to work behind the scenes to achieve administration goals while leaving "no fingerprints." At the same time, the unwritten White House rule was for "no appeals" of council decisions to the president. The result was that Dan Quayle became "the man to see in the Bush administration for business people across the country and their Washington lobbyists."[45] One academic study of the Quayle council's operation concluded that it intervened in those regulatory cases regarded as politically advantageous to the administration and economically significant.[46]

In typical vice-presidential style, Quayle was dispatched as a trouble-shooter to Alaska in the wake of a catastrophic oil spill, to California after the 1989 San Francisco earthquake, and to Los Angeles following the 1992 riots. After announcing his intent before the 1988 inauguration to help change the Republican party's image to one of concern for minorities and the poor, Quayle spoke to conventions of the National Association for the Advancement of Colored People and the Southern Christian Leadership Conference, thereby assuming the minority liaison role that Bush had performed in the Reagan administration. More prominent throughout his term, however, was Quayle's liaison with conservative groups, such as the Christian Coalition. Like Vice President Agnew, Quayle sometimes filled the role of "rhetorical point man," speaking out in "flashy, pretentious speeches about complex matters" and going for the jugular of administration opponents.[47] This pattern was most prominent, however, during his first year in office and again during the 1992 campaign.

Initial reports indicated that Quayle expected to be a continuing presence on Capitol Hill, in line with the advice provided during the transition period by the former Senate majority leader Howard Baker.[48] Within days of his inauguration, however, Quayle's plans had come more into line with Walter Mondale's advice that he spend most of his time "downtown," concentrating on White House policy making.[49] Quayle still averaged two afternoons a week on the Hill, and the contacts he maintained there occasionally proved valuable to the administration. Not only did he lobby aggressively for NASA funding whenever it came under attack in Congress, but he also proved to be a valuable bridge to conservative Republicans when they broke with the president in October 1990 over the budget agreement Bush had negotiated with congressional Democrats.[50] Finally, Quayle spent his share of time working on party issues: he was a major fund-raiser for Republican candidates and devoted particular effort to helping candidates in state legislative races, a major target for Republican inroads.[51] Such grass-roots party activity typically has a long-run payoff for presidential aspirants, something that Richard Nixon demonstrated in 1960.

Following the Mondale or Bush Model?

Dan Quayle entered the vice presidency knowing that he needed to develop a conscious strategy to overcome the damage wrought by the 1988 election. Three goals were central: be a player, become a force in the Republican party, and generate public approval. To achieve these goals, Quayle had to reject the relative invisibility and anonymity that were hallmarks of Bush's approach to the vice presidency; a low profile, he feared, would harden rather than dispel the lingering questions and negative impressions.[52] The consensus among journalistic observers was that Quayle was modeling himself more closely on

Mondale's approach to the job than on his immediate predecessor's. Rather than settle for access to the president, Quayle was also seeking to enter policy disputes. The risk inherent in this behavior, of course, is that the vice president can lose such battles and thereby damage his standing with his only constituent, the president. Much depended, therefore, on Bush's willingness to accept Quayle's active strategy.

There was ample evidence of Quayle's assertiveness in administration policy councils. The pattern began during his first year in office when he lost a battle over the minimum wage and won one on a new deployment strategy ("brilliant pebbles") for the Strategic Defense Initiative. But policy visibility risks missteps. Quayle's hard-line public pronouncements about U.S.-Soviet relations were most problematic. Quayle called the arms control proposals of the Soviet president Mikhail Gorbachev "PR gambits" and suggested that a Soviet attempt to suppress the independence movements in the Baltic states of Latvia, Lithuania, and Estonia might produce a "negative response" from the United States.[53] Just one day after a major speech by Secretary of State Baker about how the United States could provide assistance to the Soviet internal reform program known as perestroika, Quayle seemed to set forth a completely contradictory line in emphasizing the two nations' continuing cold war. Aides, attempting to reconcile the disparate stands, later suggested that Baker was reflecting American encouragement of reform while Quayle addressed the need for continued realism.[54] A similar round of apparent contradictions emerged in early December 1989 after President Bush's trip to Malta for a summit meeting with Gorbachev. In the aftermath of the cordial discussions, Quayle continued to question the "totalitarian" Soviet government's internal reforms and criticized the Soviets' sustained aid to Cuba and Nicaragua. Woodward and Broder suggest that this was the only time Quayle displeased Bush, who was returning home when Quayle publicly expressed his doubts. Bush passed word to the vice president that the president "should be the first to interpret Soviet policy."[55] The mistake was not made again. To minimize press speculation, the White House leaked a report that Bush had approved Quayle's criticism as a means to assuage the Republican right wing, even though that explanation ran the risk of insulting the intended audience.[56]

Public Perceptions

Despite establishing himself as a player in the administration, boosting his reputation among Washington insiders, and working diligently for the Republican party, Quayle's credentials for office continued to be questioned. His standing in opinion polls never improved substantially. At the time of his inauguration, approximately 20 percent of the public viewed Quayle favorably and 25 percent unfavorably. His favorable ratings peaked in early 1992 at about one-third but declined to about 20 percent again by August. As one report concluded at the time of the Republican convention, Quayle's "approval ratings are the lowest and . . . his disapproval ratings are the highest of any Vice President in 40 years."[57]

Not surprisingly, therefore, much discussion occurred about Quayle's remaining on the ticket. A Yankelovich poll conducted for CNN and *Time* magazine in July 1992 found that, when asked, "Who do you think is more qualified to be President—Quayle or Senator Albert Gore of Tennessee?" 63 percent said Gore and 21 percent Quayle. A Gallup poll, also taken in July, found that 48 percent of the public favored Bush's choosing someone other than Quayle for the ticket; 41 percent said to keep him. Even among Republicans, 37 percent said Bush should replace Quayle.[58] Jack Germond and Jules Witcover stressed the possible consequences of inaction: "in a cliff-hanger, Bush could pay for the casual decision he made four years ago and can't bring himself to undo now."[59]

Despite these doubts, Quayle's performance in the 1992 campaign was a distinct improvement over that in 1988. For many months his efforts seemed to provide the only spark for what most observers regarded as a lackluster, confused Bush campaign. Quayle was extremely active at the convention, making twenty appearances (Bush made four). Marilyn Quayle was given a prominent role in prime time, a first for a vice president's wife. Quayle's acceptance speech suffered from his typically poor delivery, but he displayed a new skill he had developed for turning personal negatives into positives, as in the following: "For more than a month the media have been telling us that Bill Clinton and Al Gore are 'moderates.' Well, if they're moderates, I'm a world champion speller." Quayle was given more prominent campaign assignments than in 1988, and his spirited performance in the vice-presidential debate seemed to renew hope among the faithful and even rekindle some fire in Bush. Most commentators had expected Gore to overshadow Quayle. But the confrontation was judged a draw, with both participants lowering the level of public discourse in their determination to be aggressive. On the whole, the campaign probably helped Quayle's image even though it did not return him to office.

Learning on the Job versus Being Prepared

Quayle was never able to excite public enthusiasm and confidence. The most thoughtful commentaries published during his first year in office posed a vital question: How much would Quayle grow in the job?[60] The book-length study by the political scientist Richard Fenno of the vice president's Senate career offered an intriguing picture of Quayle's ability to master a new political role, the very task that now confronted him in the vice presidency and that would confront him again if he were forced to assume the presidency.

Fenno left unchallenged the claim that Quayle was a poor representative but argued that he became a credible senator through a process of political maturing. Several especially noteworthy personal characteristics emerged in Fenno's portrait: a competitive and determined nature, an emphasis on coalition building and interpersonal relations more than mastery of substance or rhetoric, open-mindedness, and considerable ambition combined with a strategic approach to career building.

Did these qualities evidence themselves during Quayle's term as vice president? Woodward and Broder's conclusion was cautious: although "a more complex and resourceful politician than the comic-strip caricature that emerged during the 1988 campaign," Quayle remains "a man of average gifts and modest vision."[61] Quayle surrounded himself with an impressive staff, some of whom came with Bush's blessing but others whom Quayle assembled on his own.[62] Quayle's strategic career building was much in evidence, as was his need for involvement and results. His major test in the vice presidency came in the first year while Bush was flying to Malta for the summit with Gorbachev. A coup attempt in the Philippines prompted the government of President Corazon Aquino to request military support from the United States. Quayle presided over deliberations in the White House Situation Room, spoke twice with the Philippine president, and recommended to Bush that U.S. fighter jets fly over rebel bases. He was judged by most to have done a creditable job.

A more fundamental question for those concerned with the vagaries of presidential succession is whether it was wise for the nation to be saddled with a vice president who had to learn so much on the job. No one enters the office fully prepared, but minimizing the amount of required learning surely seems desirable. Recent history suggests that vice presidents have a high probability of becoming president and all too often are forced to do so unexpectedly. The country, it follows, is better off from the outset with a clearly competent leader than one who is largely unproved and untrusted.

Gore: Early Indications

Al Gore was one of six finalists for the Democratic vice-presidential nomination who were identified prior to the Democratic convention by a Clinton-appointed committee headed by Warren Christopher, a lawyer and Clinton's eventual secretary of state. The six reportedly included four other senators and a member of the House: Bob Graham (Florida), Robert "Bob" Kerrey (Nebraska), John D. Rockefeller IV (West Virginia), Harris Wofford (Pennsylvania), and Congressman Lee Hamilton (Indiana). Clinton interviewed the contenders and was especially impressed during a three-hour session with Gore in late June. Since both men were southerners, baby boomers, career politicians, and party moderates, the media presented the selection as a bold departure from traditional "ticket balancing" calculations. In a year when Ross Perot's candidacy had challenged "politics as usual," Clinton's choice of Gore appeared to be a bold move by a candidate who was sufficiently secure in his own abilities to select someone of presidential caliber as a running mate. The contrast with the Bush/Quayle ticket seemed sharp.[63]

In fact, Gore contributed substantially to the Democratic ticket. Having two southerners on the ballot strengthened the party's appeal to southern and border state voters whose support was critical for a Democratic victory. Clinton and Gore's youth (they formed the youngest successful ticket in major party history) emphasized the theme of generational change, a prominent message in the fall campaign. Their shared moderation protected the Democrats from undergoing a repeat of 1988, when their presidential nominee was portrayed as a liberal. As the selection list illustrates, Clinton sought an "insider" as running mate to offset his own lack of Washington and foreign policy experience. Moreover, Gore's personal qualities helped Clinton overcome some of the character flaws that were revealed during the presidential primaries. Gore was strong on family values, had served in Vietnam, and was regarded as a straight shooter in contrast to Clinton's image as "Slick Willy." Gore was also a favorite of environmentalists and Jewish groups, vital voter blocs in California, New York, and many urban areas. Finally, Gore had been through a presidential campaign in 1988, when he unsuccessfully sought the nomination, a source of valuable experience and a guarantee that his record had been closely scrutinized.

The party's liberal wing was initially concerned about Gore's selection but gradually accepted it. Jesse Jackson, an original critic, was later quoted as saying, "This time around they have a vice president who cannot spell 'potato' and our candidate can spell 'chlorofluorocarbon' [and] 'antidisestablishmentarianism' at the same time."[64] The candidates and their wives campaigned extensively together, further underlining the ticket's novelty. The initial six-day, 1,200-mile bus trip through eight states caught the imagination of the media and the public as the two young, attractive couples traveled the countryside, obviously relishing the excitement. It was a brilliant means to transmit images central to the campaign—generational change, action, and movement.

Clinton promised that his relationship with Gore in office would be a "full partnership," something that skeptics have pointed out is unlikely in view of the presidency's constitutional indivisibility.[65] One journalistic account, published on the eve of the inauguration, referred to Gore as "The Incredible Shrinking Vice President," but it merely documented the inevitable: presidents will decisively overshadow their vice presidents. For example, at Clinton's postelection press conference, Gore joined the president-elect on the stage but was given no opportunity to speak.[66] Comedians quickly picked up on his rigid, silent stance.

Instead of focusing on Gore, media attention quickly shifted to Hillary Rodham Clinton. As one Republican lobbyist quipped, "Al Gore hasn't yet realized there is going to be a co-Presidency, but he's not going to be part of the co."[67] Studies of media coverage found that during the period January through March 1993, Hillary logged fifty-two minutes on network evening newscasts and Gore only four. *USA Today* mentioned Hillary 197 times to Gore's 70; in the *Washington Post* the gap was 282 to 111.[68] Certainly, Gore's role will be different in an administration in which the president's wife receives important, substantive assignments like reforming health care. But as William Safire sagely noted, "Bill Clinton is the first President in American history to entrust the top power positions in his administration to two people he cannot fire: the First Lady and the Vice President."[69]

Even if Mrs. Clinton has overshadowed him, Gore has emerged as an important, general purpose adviser during Clinton's first year in office. He is included in the small group that reviews drafts of major presidential speeches, receives copies of presidential pollster Stanley Greenberg's strategy memos, and is linked to important White House policy-making structures through members of his staff. For example, Gore's national security aide is a member of the main working group on foreign policy (the deputies' committee) and his long-time Senate chief of staff was named second deputy to the White House chief of staff in May 1993. Gore reportedly was involved in formulating the administration's economic plan, its legislative strategy, and its policy on Bosnia.[70] Moreover, Gore remained close by the president's side during his first eleven months in office, traveling abroad only once. He made two additional foreign trips in December 1993, a brief visit to Mexico and a longer journey to Germany, Russia, and the central Asian states that were formerly part of the Soviet Union. The later trips coincided with Gore's emergence as a more visible spokesperson on foreign policy issues.

In addition to his general advisory activities, Gore has been given several specific assignments and continues to pursue policy areas of special interest. He chaired the National Performance Review Commission, an effort to "reinvent" government by consolidating functions, changing personnel processes, and modernizing government work with the application of new technologies. The commission's recommendations, developed during a six-month period, were announced in September 1993, with Gore playing a leading role in publicizing the major initiatives, which included proposed cuts in federal jobs, eight hundred suggestions on how to improve efficiency, and a proposal for the federal government to shift to a two-year budget cycle. He also was charged with coordinating administration deliberations on revising immigration policy, an early initiative that was given greater urgency during the summer. In addition, Gore is heavily involved in the administration's redesign of the regulatory review process. The Council on Competitiveness, Quayle's foothold on regulatory review, was dismantled on the administration's first full day in office.[71]

Since becoming vice president, Gore has been actively engaged in environmental and technology issues, areas of special interest while he served in Congress. Two of his former aides have landed critical environmental positions in the administration. Carol M. Browner heads the Environmental Protection Agency and Kathleen McGinty serves as head of the White House Office on Environmental Policy. The vice president's recommendation that the United States adopt a stronger position on global warming than that of other Western nations was accepted by the president. But Gore also got burned on a promise he made during and immediately after the campaign that a hazardous waste incinerator plant in East Liverpool, Ohio, would not be allowed to come on line. The Bush administration approved a test of the facility in January 1993 and a federal appeals court ruled that operations could commence.

Like his predecessor, Gore has a special interest in space and technology issues, having chaired a related subcommittee in the Senate. He played a leading role in launching the administration's technology initiative, which relies heavily on research partnerships between government and industry. He is especially interested in redesigning computer information systems and has championed proposals to link libraries, health facilities, and schools with national information databases.

Like all modern vice presidents, Gore has done his share of liaison work. He has addressed conventions of Jewish groups, the National Association for the Advancement of Colored People (NAACP), and environmental groups. He toured flood-devastated areas of Missouri and Illinois during the summer of 1993. He also has worked with Congress, using his vice-presidential office on Capitol Hill as a base for lobbying legislators. He placed calls to members on important administration votes. His most dramatic moments came on June 25, 1993, and August 6, 1993, when he cast the tie-breaking votes on the Senate version of the budget reconciliation plan and on the conference committee report on the budget for fiscal year 1994. During the June showdown, Gore presided over much of the eighteen hours of debate as Republican amendments were defeated, often by close votes. Gore's most important contribution to the administration's first-year legislative record came on the evening of November 9, 1993, during a ninety-minute debate with Ross Perot on the merits of NAFTA, the North American Free Trade Agreement. Televised nationally on the *Larry King Live* show, where Perot began his quest for the presidency in 1992, Gore's performance may have done even more to reduce Perot's public standing than to boost NAFTA, which won approval from both the House and the Senate during the following week. Perot, who had waged a national campaign against the trade pact, appeared irascible and petty in responding to a series of questions that Gore posed about Perot's own business interests in Mexico and how the anti-NAFTA campaign was financed. Subsequent polls revealed Gore to be the consensus winner and Perot's image to have been damaged, an outcome that made it easier for undecided legislators to support what many observers regarded as the president's most significant congressional victory of the year.

Gore oversees a staff of sixty-six and a budget of $3.1 million, evidence of how the new vice presidency persists. He has pursued a strategy most like that of Walter Mondale, the last Democratic vice president: demonstrate your value to the president and the administration by performing helpful tasks, providing advice based on years of Washington experience, and working to advance the president's program. No doubt Gore, like all of his recent predecessors, hopes that this loyalty eventually will pay off in a presidential bid of his own.

Conclusion

George Bush and Dan Quayle passed on to Al Gore a vice presidency that has been substantially strengthened. Bush's selection of Quayle posed a test to the institutional changes that had transformed the office in recent years. At one level, providing extensive vice-presidential staff assistance has made the office less sensitive to the personal abilities and limitations of each occupant and should lead to more consistent performance. By drawing on the vice presidency's enhanced reputation for influence, including access to the president, a relatively weak incumbent may also be able to develop a record of accomplishment. But the relationship between office and occupant is interactive. Just as institutional resources may prove beneficial to the individual, personal limitations may be detrimental to the office. The new vice presidency survived an occupant who failed to convince the public of his competence and who provoked major portions of the Washington establishment to plot his political demise.

As with the modern presidency, as successive incumbents fill the new vice presidency, a growing body of precedent should expand the office's possibilities. But unlike presidents, vice presidents are accountable to an elected superior and must gear their own activities toward satisfying the president. Only then can they become significant players in Washington.

Notes

1. Arthur M. Schlesinger, Jr., *The Cycles of American History* (Boston: Houghton Mifflin, 1986), 341.

2. Joel K. Goldstein, *The Modern American Vice Presidency: The Transformation of a Political Institution* (Princeton, N.J.: Princeton University Press, 1982), draws a distinction between institutional and political duties performed by vice presidents (134–135). Paul Light, *Vice-Presidential Power: Advice and Influence in the White House* (Baltimore: Johns Hopkins University Press, 1984), divides the job into ceremonial, political, and policy activities (chap. 2). For other general discussions of the vice presidency, see Thomas E. Cronin, "Rethinking the Vice-Presidency," in *Rethinking the Presidency*, ed. Thomas E. Cronin (Boston: Little, Brown, 1982), for a twelve-part job description (326–327); Michael Nelson, *A Heartbeat Away* (New York: Priority Press, 1988); and Michael Turner, *The Vice President as Policy Maker: Rockefeller in the Ford White House* (Westport, Conn.: Greenwood, 1982). See also Michael Nelson, "Office of the Vice President," in *Guide to the Presidency*, ed. Michael Nelson (Washington, D.C.: CQ Press, 1989), 911–917, which largely parallels the treatment in this chapter.

3. Turner, *The Vice President as Policy Maker*, 85 and 210 n91.

4. Light, *Vice-Presidential Power*, 1–2.

5. Ibid., 265.

6. Letter, Rockefeller to Mondale, December 10, 1976, folder "Transition-Rockefeller (4)," box 22, Cannon Papers, Gerald R. Ford Library, Ann Arbor, Mich.

7. Light, *Vice-Presidential Power*, 248–249.

8. Humphrey had good cause to alert Ford to the tentative nature of authority delegated by the president. As he wrote to Ford, "the President can give you assignments and trust you with authority—grant you some power as he sees fit. Likewise he can remove the authority and power at his will. I used to call this Humphrey's law—'He who giveth can taketh away and often does.'" Letter, Humphrey to Ford, October 30, 1973, Ford Vice-Presidential Papers, box 242, Ford Library.

9. Memorandum, John Marsh to President, December 20, 1974, folder "President 12/74–2/75," box 87, John Marsh Files, Ford Library.

10. For a discussion and critique of the focus on presidential roles, see David L. Paletz, "Perspectives on the Presidency," in *The Institutionalized Presidency*, ed. Norman Thomas and Hans Baade (Dobbs Ferry, N.Y.: Oceana, 1972).

11. Steven J. Jarding, "Historical Assessments of Succession Presidents," *Extensions* (Carl Albert Congressional Research and Studies Center), Fall 1985, 14–15. Jarding found that "succession presidents cannot overcome the martyred image of their predecessors" and that this judgment endures among historians (15).

12. *New York Times*, July 24, August 16, and September 26, 1985.

13. The term *constitutional hybrid* is used by John D. Feerick, *From Falling Hands: The Story of Presidential Succession* (New York: Fordham University Press, 1965), ix; and by Cronin, "Rethinking the Vice-Presidency," 329.

14. Lyndon Johnson was the first vice president to have an office in the presidential compound, in this case in the Old Executive Office Building. With the provision of office space in the West Wing, Vice Presidents Mondale and Bush actually enjoyed three prestigious office locations because they retained quarters in the Capitol, as well.

15. Donald Young, *American Roulette: The History and Dilemma of the Vice Presidency* (New York: Viking, 1979), 3–4.

16. The Twenty-fifth Amendment provides that the vice president shall serve as acting president when a presidential disability is declared either by the president or by the vice president and a majority of the cabinet. It also provides that a vacancy in the vice presidency can be filled by presidential appointment, with the consent of both houses of Congress.

17. Quote from Young, *American Roulette*, 21. Congressional reaction is reported by Feerick, *From Falling Hands*, 73–74.

18. Goldstein, *The Modern American Vice Presidency*, 48. Also see Danny M. Adkison, "The Electoral Significance of the Vice Presidency," *Presidential Studies Quarterly* 12 (Summer 1982): 330–336.

19. Young, *American Roulette*, 123, 156–157.

20. This was especially true of vice presidents Burr, Calhoun, and Charles Fairbanks.

21. FDR's suggestions appeared in an article published in the *Saturday Evening Post* during October 1920. See the discussion in Feerick, *From Falling Hands*, 182.

22. Vice-presidential nominees were selected by the conventions of both parties in 1948 and by the Democratic convention in 1952 and 1956.

23. *New York Times*, January 9, 1992, A1, 8, 9.

24. John Adams and Daniel D. Tompkins served for two full terms under George Washington and James Monroe, respectively. In the twentieth century there were three

two-term vice presidents prior to Bush: Thomas R. Marshall (Woodrow Wilson), John Nance Garner (Franklin D. Roosevelt), and Richard M. Nixon (Dwight D. Eisenhower). Two other vice presidents served nearly two terms but died (George Clinton) or resigned (John C. Calhoun) before completing their service.

25. Laurence I. Barrett, *Gambling with History: Reagan in the White House* (New York: Penguin, 1984), 114–115; and *New York Times*, June 12, 1983.

26. Although the transfer of power was smooth, there was tension between the Bush and Reagan staffs. Donald Regan, Reagan's chief of staff at the time of the surgery, may have sought to keep Bush out of Washington and out of the national limelight. Bush is reported to have maintained a deferential attitude toward Nancy Reagan, who proved to be extremely assertive during the president's recovery. *Washington Post National Weekly Edition*, August 5, 1985.

27. *New York Times*, January 21, 1981, II 3.

28. Ibid., January 30, 1983, IV 3.

29. *Washington Post*, April 27, 1989, A1.

30. Michael Kozak of the State Department announced that the Honduran aid plan had been scuttled in the face of departmental objections, although a later clarification suggested that the plan may have been implemented after all. John Sununu, Bush's White House chief of staff, said Bush had informed him that no quid pro quo discussion had been held with the Honduran president, although at least one of the new documents suggested that it had. *Washington Post*, April 25, 1989, A11, and June 2, 1989, A6; *Washington Post*, May 1, 1989, A1.

31. *Washington Post*, May 5, 1989, A26.

32. Ibid., April 28, 1989, A1.

33. Elizabeth Drew, *New Yorker*, August 28, 1989, 82.

34. Quoted in *Washington Post National Weekly Edition*, January 25–31, 1993, 31.

35. Many commentators severely questioned Quayle's qualifications, and polls indicated that the public entertained serious doubts as well. This suggests that formal changes in rules and procedures may well be the only way to deal with the problem. For the alternative perspective see Michael Nelson, *A Heartbeat Away* (New York: Priority Press, 1988), 60.

36. For speculation about Quayle's position see R. W. Apple, *New York Times*, April 20, 1989, B12, and the series of columns by Jack Anderson and Dale Van Atta in the *Washington Post*, October 12, 1989, DC11; November 1, 1989, D15; and November 4, 1989, MD16. Bush's announcement came in an interview with the *Dallas Morning News* published November 5, 1989.

37. *New York Times*, July 23, 1992, A1.

38. *Philadelphia Inquirer*, May 30, 1993, A1; *Washington Post National Weekly Edition*, August 16–22, 1993, 14.

39. *Washington Post*, June 1, 1989, A24; also see "Topics of the Times," *New York Times*, June 8, 1989, A30.

40. The interview was on Cable News Network (CNN) on August 11, 1989. See *Washington Post*, September 1, 1989, A25.

41. As quoted by Jeffrey A. Frank, *Washington Post*, January 22, 1989, D5. Also see "Notebook," *New Republic*, May 1, 1989, 11–12, where the contest is described as "examples of journalists finding wholly unexpected depth and maturity in the vice president."

42. *New York Times*, August 21, 1992, A11.

43. *Washington Post*, January 8, 1992, A1.

44. *National Journal*, February 22, 1992, 456–457.

45. *Washington Post*, January 9, 1992, A16.

46. Kent E. Portney and Jeffrey M. Berry, "Centralizing Regulatory Control and Interest Group Access: The Quayle Council on Competitiveness" (Paper presented at the annual meeting of the American Political Science Association, Washington, D.C., September 2–5, 1993).

47. On "Agnewism" see Edwin M. Yoder, *Washington Post*, February 3, 1989, A25.

48. *Los Angeles Times*, January 6, 1989, A8.

49. Ibid., January 25, 1989, A10.

50. *National Journal*, February 1, 1992, 265; *Washington Post*, January 8, 1992, A16.

51. *Christian Science Monitor*, October 31, 1989, 1.

52. As Quayle's chief of staff put it, "We had to move before the clay hardened." Laurence I. Barrett, "Dan Quayle's Salvage Strategy," *Time*, June 26, 1989, 22. For other articles that discuss the Quayle strategy see *Wall Street Journal*, December 15, 1989, A14; *New York Times*, April 24, 1989, A14; *Washington Post*, March 28, 1989, A1; and Fred Barnes, "Danny Gets His Gun," *New Republic*, June 26, 1989, 10.

53. Rowland Evans and Robert Novak, "The Kremlin vs. Quayle," *Washington Post*, September 20, 1989, A25.

54. *Washington Post*, October 19, 1989, A24; *New York Times*, October 20, 1989, A14, and October 30, 1989, A18.

55. *Washington Post*, January 8, 1992, A14.

56. *New York Times*, December 8, 1989, A18, and December 12, 1989, A25.

57. Ibid., August 20, 1992, A20.

58. *National Journal*, August 8, 1992, 1862.

59. Ibid., August 1, 1992, 1801.

60. Dom Bonafede, "Review Essay: The Last American Viceroyalty: Dan Quayle and the Vice Presidency," *Congress and the Presidency* 16, no. 1 (Spring 1989): 57–66; Maureen Dowd, "The Education of Dan Quayle," *New York Times Magazine*, June 25, 1989, 18ff.; Richard F. Fenno, Jr., *The Making of a Senator: Dan Quayle* (Washington, D.C.: CQ Press, 1989).

61. *Washington Post*, January 12, 1992, A1.

62. See the discussion in Dowd, "Education of Dan Quayle"; Barnes, "Danny Gets His Gun."

63. *New York Times*, July 10, 1992, A1; *Philadelphia Inquirer*, July 10, 1992, A12.

64. *Philadelphia Inquirer*, July 19, 1992, C6.

65. Michael Nelson, "Vice President Gore: Not Second Fiddle," *Baltimore Sun*, August 1, 1993, C5.

66. Michael Kelly and Maureen Dowd, "The Company He Keeps," *New York Times Magazine*, January 17, 1993, 25.

67. Quoted in Kelly and Dowd.

68. *National Journal*, April 24, 1993, 1005.

69. William Safire, "Who's Got Clout," *New York Times Magazine*, June 10, 1993, 27.

70. *Washington Post National Weekly Edition*, March 15–21, 1993, and March 22–28, 1993, 12; *National Journal*, July 10, 1993, 1750.

71. *National Journal*, January 30, 1993, 297; July 17, 1993, 1802.

Part VI   Presidents and Policy Making

19 Divided Government and Policy Making: Negotiating the Laws

Paul J. Quirk and Bruce Nesmith

Although the election of Bill Clinton and a Democratic Congress in 1992 restored united party government to Washington, the normal situation in recent years has been divided government—specifically, a Republican in the White House and the Democrats in control of one or both houses of Congress. A large and confusing literature has developed in political science in answer to the question: Is public policy making different when the same political party controls both elected branches from what it is when control is divided between different parties? James Sundquist is among those who say yes; David Mayhew and others say no. By looking at the relationship between the president and Congress through the lenses of negotiation theory, Paul J. Quirk and Bruce Nesmith demonstrate that each group of scholars is correct in describing some circumstances and incorrect in describing others. Their main contribution in this chapter is to specify what those circumstances are.

The voting public often delivers a split verdict in national elections, handing control of the presidency and Congress to different political parties. This did not occur in 1992, when the voters installed Democrat Bill Clinton as president while keeping Democratic majorities in the Senate and the House of Representatives. But divided party control of the executive and legislative branches prevailed for twenty-eight of the forty years from 1953 to 1992. Owing either to good luck or to some significant electoral advantage, Republicans won most of the presidential elections in that era.[1] The Democrats dominated congressional elections. Barring a major electoral realignment, divided control may be a recurring feature of American government for years to come.

No consensus has emerged on what difference it makes whether control of government is unified or divided. Many commentators view divided government with alarm. In an influential essay, James Sundquist pointed out that divided government flies in the face of long-standing conventional wisdom about how American government is able to work—namely, that potentially excessive conflict between Congress and an independently elected president is overcome by the ties of a common party affiliation. Lacking these ties, he argued, divided government is prone to stalemate, incoherence, and irresponsibility.[2] By the end of George Bush's presidency, this view was widely accepted. In the 1992 campaign, both Clinton and Bush blamed divided government for causing "gridlock." And most of the voters who were questioned in the election-day exit poll said they preferred unified party control.[3]

Other commentators, however, come to the defense of divided government. They point out that divided control offers protection against the potential abuses of an "imperial presidency." They also deny that partisan differences necessarily prevent cooperation between the president and Congress.[4] At the most sanguine extreme, the political scientist David Mayhew claims that divided control makes little difference to government performance.[5]

In this chapter we attempt to cast some new light on the consequences of divided government by taking a closer look at relevant theoretical issues. We interpret the legislative process as a negotiation between the president and Congress. In doing so, we take into account both the policy and electoral dimensions of party competition. And we consider how the nature of that competition turns on the issues at stake.

The State of the Debate

Both the critics and the defenders of divided government have been prone to make sweeping claims.[6] Critics argue that divided control creates three fundamental obstacles to effective government.[7] First, the president and an opposite-party Congress have clashing views on national policy. Second, because the president and an opposite-party congressional majority each want to prevent the other from gaining credit with the voters, they have strong incentives to oppose each other's legislative initiatives. In a sense, opposing the president is the other party's job in a two-party system. Finally, because each party controls only part of the policy-making machinery, neither party can be held accountable by the voters for results. For all these reasons, the critics conclude, divided government is indecisive, incompetent, and irresponsible.

In support of this view, the critics point out that the most sweeping changes in national policy have been accomplished mainly under unified government—especially when strong presidents, such as Woodrow Wilson, Franklin Roosevelt, and Lyndon Johnson, have had a large same-party majority in Congress. In contrast, critics associate divided control with disastrous failures—such as the massive budget deficits and the incoherent policy toward Nicaragua during the administrations of Ronald Reagan and George Bush.

Defenders of divided government reject this critique. In a major empirical study, David Mayhew identified 267 important laws that were enacted by Congress between 1946 and 1990. He was able to show that these laws were passed with almost equal frequency under the two forms of party control.[8] Mayhew also notes many examples of incoherent or irresponsible policy making under unified control and points out that, apart from the singular experience of the 1980s, divided government has not produced larger budget deficits. In short, Mayhew concludes, divided party control makes no important difference to the performance of government.

The debate is far from over. It is clear that the critics' worst fears about divided government are not supported by the evidence. Yet the view that it makes no difference is hardly plausible.[9] Whether the president and the majority in Congress have compatible ideological and electoral goals or conflicting ones almost certainly matters somehow. The question is how. Does divided government lead to deadlock, or just cause some friction and delay? Does it change legislative politics or outcomes in other ways? Does divided party control have any advantages? How do its effects depend on the nature of the issues?

Presidential-Congressional Negotiation

The legislative process is fundamentally a *negotiation* between the president and Congress. It has the three features of any negotiation.[10] First, the president and Congress are interdependent in the sense that each can affect the other's interests. Apart from rare instances (Congress may override a president's veto), neither branch can achieve legislative goals unless Congress passes a bill and the president signs it.

Of course, Congress is a complex institution, with 535 members and no single set of interests. Broadly speaking, however, Congress's behavior in negotiations with the president reflects the decisions of those members whose policy preferences are near the center of congressional opinion on the major issues in dispute. On a civil rights bill, the president must deal primarily with the civil rights moderates; on defense spending, with the defense moderates; and so on. The reason is that these members will cast the pivotal votes.[11] Who these pivotal members are varies according to party politics and the nature of the issue. In a legislative debate with a clear-cut division between the parties, the pivotal members are in the majority party—in the post–New Deal era, usually the

Democrats. On an issue that cuts across party lines, they include both Democrats and Republicans.[12]

Second, the president and Congress are generally in "mixed-interest conflict." That is, they have both conflicting interests (something to fight about) and complementary ones (a basis for reaching agreement). These interests may concern policy goals, electoral goals, or both. For example, President Bush and the Democratic Congress both favored an increase in the minimum wage, but Bush favored a small increase and Congress wanted a large one. President Richard M. Nixon and the congressional Democrats both wanted to pass a strong clean-air bill; but each side wanted to claim the credit for introducing the stronger measure.

Third, the president and Congress communicate with each other to seek agreement. Formally, the legislative process is very simple: Congress passes a bill, then the president either signs it or vetoes it (subject to Congress's power to override the veto). In view of this, some theorists have argued that Congress sets the agenda for the president and therefore has a major strategic advantage over him in the legislative process.[13] In reality, however, the roles of each branch are quite symmetrical. The president and Congress both make offers and counteroffers, implicitly or explicitly, throughout the long process of enacting a law. And each side can demand concessions by threatening to block action. Moreover, they do not merely exchange offers: they also clarify their interests, evaluate alternatives, and often invent new solutions.[14] If successful, they reach an agreement and carry it out by enacting a bill.

Properties of Negotiation

To understand how the president and Congress interact in the legislative process, one must understand negotiation. Two general properties of negotiation are especially important.[15]

Bargaining Power. First, the actors in a negotiation have greater or lesser bargaining power. There is usually a range of potential outcomes—a "zone of agreement"—that both sides prefer to the status quo. They have conflicting preferences among those outcomes. And their relative success—which side gets the better deal—reflects their bargaining power. For the most part, each actor's bargaining power arises from its "best alternative to a negotiated agreement," that is, how it will fare in the absence of an agreement.[16] Whoever can walk away from the bargaining table more easily will take away more of the gains from an agreement.

The relative power of the president and Congress depends, therefore, on how badly each wants to end a dispute and enact a bill. Suppose that a Democratic Congress wants a large spending increase for domestic programs but a Republican president wants only a small one. Because the president is thus more satisfied than Congress with current spending, other things being equal, he can insist on a smaller increase. Congress may have the upper hand, however, if it can embarrass the president by attacking his position, or if inaction will hurt the president politically, such as by prolonging a recession. If the president and Congress are both committed to action, the balance of power is fairly equal. For example, because they both want to avoid the disruption of failing to pass an appropriations bill, they have comparable power on discretionary spending, even if one side is more satisfied with the status quo than the other.

The relative success of competing negotiators also depends on bargaining skill. For example, if the president can make accurate judgments about how far he can push Congress, he can win more favorable terms in negotiations than if his judgments are off the mark.

Bounded Efficiency. Second, negotiation has a bounded and variable capability to produce efficient outcomes. That is, negotiation can overcome conflicts and produce agreements that take advantage of opportunities for mutual gain; yet this capability has limits and varies considerably from one negotiation to another.

Negotiation is efficient, in this sense, because the participants can exchange information about their interests, undertake joint deliberations, and make binding commitments to a course of action. Exploiting this capability, the president and Congress can use a variety of methods to resolve their conflicts and achieve action. They can work out a compromise on issues where they have conflicting goals in order to forge an agreement that serves their common goals. For example, they may compromise on the shape of a tax cut to pass an economic stimulus measure they both want. They can look for improved solutions to policy problems, with less need for sacrifice of objectives by either branch. To some degree, a divided-control president and Congress can even negotiate the electoral effects of legislative action. The president may promise to share credit with the opposition party, perhaps by inviting its leaders to the bill-signing ceremony. In some cases, the president and Congress may adjust the division of a bill's benefits between their respective party constituencies to compensate for other electoral effects that would otherwise hinder agreement. For example, if passing a tax cut will tend to help a Republican president, a Democratic congressional majority may demand that its constituency groups get the larger share of the cuts. In sum, negotiation can overcome even serious conflict to permit action on common interests. That is what negotiation is for.

The efficiency of negotiation is bounded and variable, however, because conflicting interests cause friction. Negotiators compete for larger shares. They become angry, fear to appear weak, or are deterred from cooperating by constituencies that do not recognize the advantages of doing so. Even with important common interests at stake, therefore, negotiators may fail to agree. Or they may settle for a "lowest-common-denominator" agreement—one that requires only the easiest concessions but fails to exploit the available opportunities for mutual gain. All these barriers to cooperation may be important in legislative negotiations between the president and Congress.

Circumstances and Cooperation. Thus the success of negotiation varies enormously—from highly efficient achievement of mutual gains to utter failure to resolve conflict constructively. In general, the ability to cooperate depends on several factors. First, the more prominent the negotiators' conflicting interests are, compared with their complementary interests, the greater is the friction between them and the poorer the prospects for cooperation.[17] Simply put, the more they have to disagree about, and the less they have to gain by reaching agreement, the more likely they will fight. For example, a Republican president and a Democratic Congress may negotiate constructively to avert an impending calamity, such as the threatened insolvency of the Social Security system in the early 1980s; but they may have great difficulty resolving a long-term problem like the federal budget deficit.

In some cases, negotiators may fail to perceive their common interests. For example, because the Republicans had coopted the issue of "crime in the streets," the Democrats for many years generally failed to recognize the importance of controlling crime for black and low-income constituents. Although President Clinton has tried to correct this error, it worked against bipartisan cooperation on the crime issue for decades.[18]

Second, negotiations may go through cycles of conflict and cooperation. Tough negotiating tactics sometimes elicit even tougher responses, leading to a spiral of increasing hostility. (This is why negotiations are sometimes suspended for a "cooling off period.") On the other hand, a cooperative gesture may induce a cooperative reply, causing a de-escalation of conflict. A divided-control president and Congress may go through some periods of partisan rancor and posturing and other periods of effective cooperation.

Third, negotiators may have only fragile commitments to goals that reflect their sense of responsibility as opposed to their tangible self-interest. If they can work out a mutually acceptable sharing of the burdens, negotiators may make large sacrifices for the sake of such goals; if not, they may abandon them entirely. Partly for this reason, the president and Congress sometimes act in a remarkably high-minded and principled manner—for example, passing an unpopular treaty to cede control of the Panama Canal—and other times completely cave in to political pressure.[19]

Fourth, the success of negotiators in resolving conflict, like their bargaining power, also depends on their skills and strategies. An effective negotiator can defuse tensions and discover opportunities for mutual gain.[20] Political leaders have varying degrees of such skill. Perhaps more important, they also have different political strategies. House Minority Leader Robert Michel, a Republican from Illinois, usually wanted to deal with the Democrats to accomplish something. But his equally skillful successor, Newt Gingrich, a Republican from Georgia, has often picked fights to define party differences for the voters.

Other circumstances also matter. Agreement is easier if there is a "focal solution"—a prominent potential outcome, like a fifty-fifty split. Budget negotiators have often adopted the focal solution of deriving deficit reductions from equal amounts of spending cuts and tax increases.[21] Agreement is also more likely if the terms can be reliably enforced. Democratic and Republican leaders can monitor an agreement that each party will provide a certain number of votes to pass a bill. If either party reneges, it suffers embarrassment. But the leaders cannot monitor an agreement not to attack each other's position. The Democrats might like to promise a Republican president that if he proposes a tax increase, they will not attack him for it in the next campaign. But with hundreds of Democrats making thousands of statements all around the country throughout the campaign, both sides know that such a promise is unenforceable.

In the end, negotiations have an element of intrinsic unpredictability.[22] Skilled negotiators disguise their strategies to avoid being at a disadvantage. As a result, some negotiations fail because the participants misperceive each others' intentions. Other negotiations surprise everyone by succeeding.

Legislative Performance under Unified and Divided Government

How, then, does divided government affect negotiation between the president and Congress? Although it has no systematic bearing on most of the conditions that affect cooperation, divided government does increase the relative prominence of conflicting interests between the two branches. It should sometimes make cooperation more difficult. Yet the increased conflict is by no means consistently important.

To begin with, divided party control leads to policy disagreement between the president and Congress, but only in certain circumstances. Democrats and Republicans have quite consistent differences on what we will call *ideological* issues—those, ranging from civil rights to environmental regulation to taxes on the wealthy, on which liberals and conservatives differ. A divided-control president and Congress will often be at odds on these issues.[23]

Nevertheless, they also will often see eye-to-eye. Even on ideological issues, the two parties will respond similarly to a major change in the balance of political pressures and policy demands.[24] Both Democrats and Republicans will want to do something, for example, in response to a widespread alarm about pollution. In such cases, a Republican president and a Democratic Congress will have common goals for legislative action—even though they may disagree on exactly how far to go.

Moreover, many policy issues cut across the liberal-conservative cleavage, either eliciting a broad consensus among politicians or causing divisions within both ideological groupings. For our purposes, there are two types of such *cross-cutting* issues, as we call them. On ordinary or *constituency-driven* cross-cutting issues, the president and Congress largely respond to public or interest group demands, which are not sorted along ideological lines. Such issues include immigration, disaster relief, the deregulation of certain industries, and support for Israel, among others. On *autonomy* issues, policy makers must choose whether to respond to constituency demands or to act autonomously, on the basis of a shared conception of the public interest. In the view of many commentators, the ability to resist narrow, uninformed, or shortsighted demands is crucial to effective governance.[25] Such issues may include foreign aid, trade policy, and the reduction of budget deficits, among others. Because both sorts of cross-cutting issue are relatively free of partisan conflict about policy, divided control does not automatically lead to increased conflict between the president and Congress.

A complication arises, however, when cross-cutting issues are linked with ideological ones in the same piece of legislation. For example, a decision whether to reduce the budget deficit (a cross-cutting, autonomy issue) cannot be separated from ideological conflicts about spending and taxes. In such a case, a divided-control president and Congress may agree on the cross-cutting issue; but to take action, they will have to negotiate their conflicting interests on the ideological issue.

In much the same way as with policy conflict, divided control leads to inter-branch electoral conflict, but only in certain respects. At the collective level, party electoral competition is zero-sum: if the Republicans pick up support as a party, the Democrats lose it. This is why Sundquist argues that a congressional opposition party almost inevitably will try to defeat the president's initiatives.[26]

But two features of the situation help get around this difficulty. One is that, as noted above, partisan effects are negotiable. If Democrats and Republicans both must act, they can work out a deal that avoids harm to either party. For example, if the president needs opposition-party support to pass a popular public works bill, he can agree to share the credit with opposition leaders; or he can adjust the bill's provisions to do more for their constituencies. In short, he can make cooperating worth their while.[27]

The second and more important consideration is that the zero-sum conflict is between the parties' collective electoral interests, not the president and opposition-party members as individuals. After all, they do not run for reelection against each other; they all run against their own challengers. If the president and opposition members have compatible constituency interests on a given issue, they can all strengthen their individual reelection prospects by supporting the same measure.[28] For example, congressional Democrats were happy to share credit with President Reagan for the 1986 Tax Reform Act.[29] Indeed, because American politicians notoriously look out for themselves more than their parties, they can readily cooperate across party lines.

Issues and Performance

How divided-party control affects legislative negotiation is complex and varies with the nature of the policy conflict. Consider the three kinds of issues we have discussed.

Ideological issues. Because of the ideological difference between the parties—the Democrats' liberalism and the Republicans' conservatism—the effects of divided government are especially pronounced on ideological issues. Yet, the amount of conflict depends on the circumstances.

In fact, the bogeyman divided-government-induced gridlock appears only under rather special conditions—namely, when the political pressures and policy demands on an issue do not change very much.[30] In such a period, a divided-control president and Congress typically want to move in opposite directions. Even if both then become slightly more liberal or slightly more conservative in response to a change in demands, they may still disagree about the direction of change, resulting in deadlock. For example, a modest uptick in public support for a social program will not generate support for expansion from a Republican president who thinks the program is already too large. In contrast, a unified-control president and Congress will take policy where they want it. If a change then occurs in the political demands, they can respond together, producing action.

This difference in responses has been apparent in the politics of welfare. Public attitudes toward welfare have gone through three shifts in recent decades: an increase in support reaching a high point in the early 1970s; a rightward turn from the mid-1970s to the early 1980s; then a rebound toward more liberal views. The fluctuations were relatively mild, however, with the proportion saying that "too much" was being spent on welfare ranging between 40 and 60 percent.[31] As expected, divided government has dampened the response to these modest shifts in political demand.

Despite the rising popular support during the divided-government presidencies of Richard Nixon and Gerald Ford, welfare spending did not increase significantly (except for automatic increases to meet the growth of the eligible population).[32] Ignoring this rather modest trend in opinion, both presidents took a hard line on welfare. By the beginning of the unified-Democratic administration of Jimmy Carter, the public was getting more impatient with welfare recipients, and neither branch wanted much change. The House in 1979 passed a bill setting an income floor for welfare families, but the Senate killed it.

The rightward shift on welfare after 1975 produced action during Ronald Reagan's first year, 1981, in a brief period of "quasi-unified" party control. (The Republicans controlled the presidency and the Senate; despite a nominal Democratic majority in the House, the Republicans and conservative Democrats formed a working majority that largely controlled that body too.) This quasi-unified Republican government was able to act on welfare. Reagan's initiatives, embodied in the Omnibus Budget and Reconciliation Act of 1981, dropped 400,000 families from the welfare rolls and reduced benefits to 300,000 others, mainly by eliminating Aid to Families with Dependent Children (AFDC) allowances for the working poor.

The Democrats recaptured genuine control of the House in the 1982 elections, beginning ten years of clear-cut divided control. About the same time, the public mood shifted again, becoming somewhat more liberal during the rest of the 1980s. But the Republican presidents again were not swept away by the moderately more generous public mood, and divided government did not respond to it.

When the demands on an issue change dramatically, however, the presence of divided government may not make much of a difference. In the face of sufficiently powerful demands, a divided-control president and Congress will both see which way the wind is blowing and set their sails accordingly. They may fight over political credit or disagree about exactly how far to go, but because such demands create an important shared interest in action they are usually able to reach agreement.

Clearly, divided party control made little difference in the legislative response to the consumer and environmental movement of the 1960s and 1970s. The unified-control Johnson presidency yielded major legislation on fair packaging and labeling, meat and poultry inspection, wilderness protection, highway beautification, automobile emissions, and water quality. But the divided-control Nixon presidency went even further, producing several landmark laws on consumer and environmental matters: the Consumer Product Safety Act of 1974, the Magnuson-Moss Act of 1974, the National Environmental Policy Act of 1969, the Clean Air Act of 1970, and the Water Pollution Control Act of 1972, among others. As Mayhew pointed out, the strong public sentiment on these issues made the difference between unified and divided control virtually irrelevant.[33]

By the same token, divided control has not kept the president and Congress from reacting to sea changes in the political demand for defense spending. As the United States withdrew from Vietnam and improved its relations with the Soviet Union and China from 1969 to the mid-1970s, Americans who favored reductions in military spending outnumbered those favoring increases by at least three to one. The divided-control Nixon and Ford administrations as well as the unified-control Carter administration cut defense spending, in relation to domestic spending, every year from 1969 to 1977. Disillusionment with détente in the mid-1970s brought increased support for defense spending. After the Soviet Union invaded Afghanistan, respondents in a 1980 poll favored defense increases over cuts by five to one.[34] The result was eight straight real increases in defense spending—under unified Democratic control (Carter, 1978–1980), quasi-unified Republican control (Reagan, 1981), and divided control (Reagan, 1982–1985). The late 1980s brought yet another broad shift. With the Soviet Union in eclipse, public sentiment went back to the parsimonious mood of the early 1970s. The divided governments under Reagan and Bush allowed real defense spending to drop substantially.

The expectation that unified and divided government will respond similarly to major changes in political demand largely accounts for the central finding of Mayhew's study—that the two situations produced about the same number of important laws. For the most part, these laws are the result of major changes in political demand.

One effect of divided control concerns not *whether* government can act on ideological issues, but rather *what kind* of action it takes. Because the president and Congress both have bargaining power, divided control requires compromise between the parties and leads to ideologically moderate outcomes. This effect has been apparent, for example, in how tax bills have treated different income groups. Not surprisingly, unified governments of either party have imposed new taxes primarily on the constituency groups of the other party: Democrats "soak the rich," whereas Republicans collect more from lower- and middle-income groups. In contrast, divided governments have kept the distribution of the tax burden roughly constant. The quasi-unified Republican government of Reagan's first year passed a huge tax cut, with the benefits heavily slanted toward wealthier citizens. Based on supply-side economics, the 1981 law reduced the top personal income tax rate by 20 percent, cut the capital gains rate by 8 percent, tripled exemptions for estate and gift taxes, and permitted the accelerated depreciation of business investments.[35]

Recession and the 1982 congressional elections ended the de facto conservative control of the House, and the divided government of the rest of the Reagan-Bush era was more evenhanded. The Tax Equity and Fiscal Responsibility Act of 1982, the first of a series of tax increases aimed at reducing budget deficits, was a balanced package. New rules for the alternative minimum tax and the sale of corporate tax benefits extracted revenues from the wealthy. Increased excise taxes for cigarettes and telephones mostly affected lower-income persons.[36] In the same manner, the 1990 budget agreement raised taxes in several ways but took close to the same percentages of total revenues from most income groups as before the bill.[37]

After the 1992 election, the unified-Democratic Clinton presidency brought back partisan tax policy, imposing a hefty tax increase primarily on upper-income groups. The Clinton tax program raised the top personal rate by 5 percent, with an additional 10 percent surtax on incomes over $250,000. It also raised the alternative minimum tax and took more from well-to-do retirees. The only major provision that hit all income groups was a modest boost in the gasoline tax, accounting for just one-eighth of the new revenue.[38]

Cross-Cutting Issues. Divided control should matter much less on constituency-driven cross-cutting issues, which cut across the liberal-conservative cleavage. Because Democrats and Republicans are not at odds on these issues, a president and Congress of opposite parties are just as likely as those of the same party to agree on them. Although their partisan rivalry for political credit may obstruct action in some cases, they can usually negotiate around that rivalry. The main difficulty for divided government occurs when cross-cutting issues are linked to ideological ones on which the parties are indeed at odds.

Apart from some maneuvering for credit, therefore, divided government should not cause much trouble on cross-cutting issues that are not tied to ideological disputes. It has not done so, for example, on efforts to cut back wasteful agricultural subsidies or anticompetitive regulatory programs—reforms supported by consumer-oriented liberals, free-market conservatives, and academic policy analysts and opposed by the affected industries and their employees.[39] Dramatic reforms of anticompetitive regulation in transportation, financial services, and other industries were initiated in the abbreviated divided-control Ford administration and adopted soon afterward in the unified-control Carter administration.

Although reforming agricultural subsidies has been tougher, progress has actually been more rapid under divided government than unified government. The Republican Nixon administration worked with the Democratic Congress to pass a 1970 law that trimmed subsidized acreage, lowered price supports, and limited payments to individual farmers.[40] They collaborated again on a 1973 law that abolished "parity," the practice of basing farm support on 1910–1913 prices.[41] Both Carter's unified Democratic administration and Reagan's 1981 quasi-unified Republican administration made few changes. But the Reagan and Bush divided governments resumed the attack with a 1985 law that scaled down farm loan programs and lowered target prices and a 1990 law that took 15 percent of farmland out of the commodity support system.

How much trouble comes when a divided president and Congress have to deal with a cross-cutting issue and an ideological one in the same legislation depends, among other things, on the relative salience of the two issues. If the cross-cutting issue is clearly the more salient, the president and Congress should be able to cut a deal. For example, they will not quibble very long over who should pay the increased taxes to fund a military response in a genuine national-security crisis.

They may not have equal influence in these negotiations. As we have mentioned, a divided president and Congress may adjust a bill's ideological tendency, such as its division of burdens or benefits between each party's constituencies, to compensate for other partisan effects. Because the president automatically gets the largest share of the praise or blame for anything that happens, action on a constituency-driven cross-cutting issue will tend to benefit the president's party. Thus, he may have to go more than halfway with the congressional majority to attract its support.

On the other hand, if they are more focused and committed on the ideological issue, a divided-control president and Congress may get bogged down in trench warfare. If that happens, their shared interests on the cross-cutting issue may come to nothing. This has occurred, for example, when the abortion issue has figured prominently in debate over government health programs.

The dynamics of linked cross-cutting and ideological conflicts have been apparent in how the president and Congress have dealt with economic recessions. If an economic slump is severe, and if neither inflation nor an oversized budget deficit militates against fiscal action, the parties have a strong cross-cutting interest in adopting a stimulus package. If a downturn is mild or other conditions stand in the way of fiscal action, that interest is weaker. In either case, the parties will also have ideological conflicts about the mix of tax cuts and spending increases in such a package.

Presidents Nixon and Ford both faced lagging economies in periods of manageable budget deficits and moderate inflation; their and Congress's cross-cutting interest in fiscal action was quite strong.[42] As we would expect, divided government posed no major obstacle to such action. In each case, the president and Congress fought a partisan battle over how to respond but eventually passed a substantial stimulus bill. As we would also expect, in view of the president's political stake in a healthy economy, the Democrats got much of what they wanted in these measures: In the 1971 agreement with Nixon, they successfully demanded increases in domestic spending and public works projects, along with their long-sought wage and price controls (which Nixon ordered unilaterally). In the deal with Ford four years later, they won a larger stimulus than Republicans wanted and blocked Republican demands to link tax cuts with spending limits. For their part, both Nixon and Ford enjoyed a strengthened economy in time to help with their reelection bids.

In the two recessions of the 1980s, troublesome inflation or massive deficits made fiscal stimulus hard to justify economically; the cross-cutting interest in stimulation was, therefore, virtually nonexistent. Both Carter's unified government and Reagan's divided government were stymied. With inflation running as high as 18 percent in 1980, Carter urged Congress to focus on cutting the budget to fight inflation rather than stimulating the economy.[43] In the severe recession of 1982–1983, in the Reagan era, it was the combination of an unprecedented peacetime federal budget deficit and Republican opposition to spending increases and "make-work jobs" that precluded action.[44] Reagan pleaded with the public to "stay the course" while the government waited out the recession.

Divided government appeared to make a real difference only in the in-between case of the mild but prolonged economic slump during the last two years of the Bush administration. Only an ambivalent, slowly emerging cross-cutting interest existed in fiscal action. In this circumstance, the parties could not easily resolve their ideological differences, and divided control led to stalemate. Especially in the early stages of the recession in 1991, most economists cautioned against a deficit-increasing fiscal stimulus, and both parties were internally divided on the issue. Through most of the year, President Bush and significant Republican and Democratic factions in Congress opposed any such action. As the slump dragged on, both the president and the Democrats gradually came around to favoring a stimulus measure, at least in principle. But they had serious ideological conflicts about specific tax cuts and spending increases, and neither party was sufficiently committed to a bill to make major concessions on those issues. In March 1992, the Democrats pushed a highly partisan stimulus measure through Congress. Bush vetoed it. No serious negotiations were undertaken before Congress recessed for the election campaign.[45]

Autonomy Issues. The effects of unified or divided control are hardest to figure out on autonomy issues, those issues on which policy makers try to overcome popular or interest-group pressure and act responsibly according to their own view of the public interest. Each form of control has both advantages and disadvantages, and the overall balance is far from obvious.

Suppose, for example, that both parties see a need to cut entitlement spending or to increase aid to post-communist Russia—actions that have little or no political constituency and are sure to offend large parts of the electorate. As critics have often pointed out, divided control creates two kinds of obstacles to such action. First, the president and Congress will each want the other to take the lion's share of the responsibility. Each has an incentive to lie back and wait for the other to act first. Second, they will fight about any linked ideological issues that may be at stake, such as how much to cut middle-class as opposed to low-income entitlements. Preoccupied with such tensions, the president and Congress may neglect their shared goal of acting responsibly.

On the other hand, divided government also defuses the electoral risks of autonomous action. Because both parties must eventually get on board for any bill to pass, they share the blame for saying no to powerful constituencies. A divided-control president and Congress can act autonomously, therefore, without requiring either party to pay dearly in loss of support.[46] Moreover, with votes coming from both parties, their leaders can tolerate numerous defections by individual members of Congress and still assemble a winning coalition. In particular, they can allow many of the politically vulnerable members of each party to play it safe and vote against the leadership position.

With unified control, the situation is just the reverse. A same-party president and Congress will not do battle over ideological issues or try to outmaneuver each other to avoid blame. But they will have no protection from the potentially adverse electoral consequences of acting autonomously. As the boxer Joe Louis might have said (if he had addressed this subject), a party that controls both branches can run from responsibility by caving in to political pressure; but if it chooses to act autonomously, it can't hide from the voters.

In view of the lack of any clear-cut advantage for either unified or divided control, the president and Congress seem likely to have roughly the same ability to act autonomously in each situation. As we have mentioned, for example, divided government does not lead to larger budget deficits. To be sure, from 1946 to 1988 the average annual deficit was much larger under divided government ($65 billion) than under unified control ($16 billion). But the difference results almost entirely from the massive deficits of the Reagan years. Take away the peculiar experience of those years—presumably the result of other causes—and the average deficits under unified and divided control are just about the same.[47]

Moreover, the president and Congress have succeeded in cutting deficits under both forms of party control. Significant cuts were made during both recent periods of unified Democratic control. President Carter pushed tight, deficit-reducing budgets through Congress in both 1979 and 1980, although his budget-balancing aspirations were defeated by a sinking economy.[48] President Clinton carried out a promise of his 1992 campaign by enacting a deficit-reduction plan with substantial spending cuts and upper-income tax increases. With Republicans solidly opposed, the Clinton plan passed by narrow margins in both the House and the Senate, and only after numerous concessions to Democratic members. But it still promised to reduce the deficit by $490 billion over five years.

Similar deficit reductions have occurred under divided government, even during the high-deficit years of the Reagan and Bush administrations. In 1969

President Nixon and the Democratic Congress agreed on expenditure ceilings that allowed Nixon to make specific spending cuts. The arrangement broke down after three years, however, because the Democrats lost patience with Nixon's severe treatment of liberal programs.[49] During the Reagan presidency, Senate Republicans took the initiative on deficit reduction, mediating between the White House and congressional Democrats. A 1982 package strengthened tax enforcement, repealed business deductions, and cut spending by $17 billion; a 1984 measure pared away a smaller chunk of the deficit. The Senate Republicans tried again in 1985, but Reagan and the Democrats struck a deal to pass a looser budget. In 1990, after Bush had recanted a 1988 campaign pledge not to raise taxes, a deficit-cutting bipartisan budget was soundly defeated on the House floor. Despite the inauspicious beginning, however, a revised bipartisan bill was enacted that raised taxes, cut spending, and reduced the deficit by about one-quarter.[50]

Even if divided party control has little or no overall effect on the ability of the president and Congress to act autonomously, it may change the dynamics of autonomy issues in another way: the performance of divided government may be more volatile. On the one hand, a divided-control president and Congress can in effect conspire with each other to override popular or interest group demands and largely avoid the risk of either party's losing electoral support. On the other hand, they can become so embroiled in partisan and ideological warfare that they essentially abandon their shared interest in acting responsibly.

Which response actually occurs depends on the complex and somewhat unpredictable dynamics of negotiation, with its potential for upward and downward spirals of conflict. A dramatic episode of escalating conflict occurred in the divided-control Nixon presidency. As we have mentioned, the Democratic Congress in 1972 reacted against Nixon's cuts in domestic programs by refusing to pass a new spending ceiling. Responding aggressively, Nixon tried to enforce a ceiling of his own by vetoing popular legislation, pocket vetoing appropriations bills, and impounding funds that had been appropriated.[51] Congress turned up the heat even further, taking the president to court to undo his impoundments and passing new statutory restrictions on the president's discretion in carrying out the budget. In some degree, the acrimonious dispute may even have strengthened Congress's disposition to impeach and remove Nixon during the Watergate affair.

A somewhat similar escalation of partisan conflict probably contributed to the deficits during the Reagan and Bush years. Tired of the electoral burden of the Republicans' traditional austere economics, Reagan in 1980 pushed a massive tax reduction, throwing aside any genuine concern for the fiscal conse-quences.[52] The Democrats, angered by Reagan's strategy and unwilling to bear the burden of fiscal responsibility alone, mounted a vehement defense of do-mestic spending. With intermittent exceptions, both sides stood their ground and mostly ignored the deficit for the entire decade.

Of course, a president and Congress of the same party will also vary in their willingness to act autonomously. But their ability to do so will not depend on volatile interparty negotiations.

As with constituency-driven cross-cutting issues, a divided president and Congress may find ways to balance out the gains and losses for the two parties on autonomy issues. But in this case, other things being equal, enacting a bill that runs against public opinion or rejects interest group demands will be more costly to the president's party than to the congressional majority. As compen-sation, the president should do relatively well on any ideological issues in the dispute.

In deficit reductions under divided-party control, for example, presidents have managed to keep their own party's constituency groups from bearing the brunt of the burden. In exchange for taking on the politically painful task of enforcing expenditure limits that had been set by the Democratic Congress, Nixon was able to favor his own spending priorities until Congress discontin-ued the arrangement in 1972. In the deficit-cutting packages of 1982 and 1984, Reagan succeeded in preserving his defense increases and limiting tax increases to the closing of certain business loopholes.[53]

The budget agreement of 1990 was the kind of exception that demonstrates the rule. When rank-and-file congressional Republicans killed a bipartisan summit agreement on the House floor, they put President Bush under intense political pressure to come up with a new agreement—pressure that only in-creased after the 1991 fiscal year began without a budget. Bush's need for a speedy resolution turned around the partisan stakes and strengthened the Democrats in the negotiations. When the dust cleared, the final budget con-tained an increase in personal income tax rates for wealthy individuals and other sweeteners for the congressional majority.[54]

The Question of Reform

Reformers have suggested various means to ensure, or at least make it more likely, that the same political party ends up in control of both the presidency and Congress. Their proposals range from eliminating midterm congressional elections, to giving the president's party bonus seats in Congress, to mandating a straight party vote for the offices of president, vice president, senator, and representative.[55]

None of these reforms has ever had widespread support. During the current interlude of unified Democratic control, they are off the political radar screen. But dissatisfaction with "gridlock" and blame of divided government reached new heights during the 1992 campaign. And if the Republicans win back the presidency, such proposals may soon be seriously debated. Thus we must ask, Is the chronic tendency toward divided control of the presidency and Congress a serious malady of American government, one for which reformers should indeed seek a cure?

Judging by our theoretical analysis and casual evidence, probably not. Contrary to the clean-bill-of-health view issued by Mayhew, we conclude that divided government does have fairly significant costs in reduced efficiency and responsiveness. But contrary to Sundquist's grim assessment, we argue that those costs are inherently limited and balanced by compensating advantages.

A divided-control president and Congress will sometimes have completely incompatible policy objectives, resulting in deadlock. But this should generally occur only on ideologically salient issues—and even then, only in the absence of broad consensus on the desired direction of change. If a Republican president wants to cut social programs and a Democratic Congress wants to expand them, nothing will happen. But this conflict will usually reflect a corresponding division in public and elite opinion. When such a division exists, deadlock is arguably appropriate; it does not count as a cost.

Allegations to the contrary notwithstanding, divided control probably has no significant, overall effect on the ability of the president and Congress to act autonomously in the face of misguided or narrowly based political demands. Divided government may be stymied by partisan and ideological squabbling between the branches; but unified government may be paralyzed by the majority party's fear of giving the opposition an issue to exploit in the next election. Of course too much governmental autonomy would be dangerous. But there is evidently little difference, in this respect, between the two forms of control.

The real costs of divided party control lie elsewhere. In many cases, a president and Congress of different parties will have a hard time reaching agreement and taking action even though they share a common interest, both substantively and politically, in policy change. Their competing electoral interests, or especially their conflicting ideological preferences, get in the way. For example, the president and Congress may both want to stimulate a sluggish economy; but they may fail to agree on a bill because the president wants a tax cut and the congressional majority wants new public works spending. They may both want to strengthen civil rights policy but be unable to agree on how far to go. The possibility that bipartisan, perhaps widely shared policy objectives will not be served because of partisan conflict on other matters is the principal cost of divided government.

That divided government imposes this cost is not a damning indictment, however, for two reasons. First, negotiation limits the damage. In general, the more important the bipartisan policy interests that are at stake, the more readily the president and Congress can overcome their conflicts and reach agreement. Just as labor negotiations usually avoid extremely costly prolonged strikes, legislative negotiations usually avoid extremely costly policy stalemate. Divided government will block action in certain cases when the perceived need to act is neither clear-cut nor urgent. The prototype of this situation is the 1991–1992 economic slump: because neither party was fully convinced of the need for a fiscal stimulus package, they would not compromise to achieve one.

Second, the losses from destructive partisan conflict are balanced by what is arguably an important advantage. Divided party control of the presidency and Congress ensures that both liberal and conservative views are influential and that the policies adopted are ideologically moderate. In an important sense, these middle-of-the-road policies are more in tune with the public's wishes than the one-sided outcomes that either party would impose if left to its own devices. In short, under divided government we put up with a great deal of partisan bickering, and with a more modest amount of genuine failure to act on common interests, in order to avoid the excesses that may lie at either end of the political spectrum.

Notes

We are grateful to Stella Herriges Quirk for providing helpful editing without pecuniary compensation.

1. For an assessment of the supposed Republican advantage in the Electoral College, see Michael Nelson, "Constitutional Aspects of the Elections," in *The Elections of 1988*, ed. Michael Nelson (Washington, D.C.: CQ Press, 1989), 192–195.

2. James L. Sundquist, "Needed: A Political Theory for a New Era of Coalition Government in the United States," *Political Science Quarterly* 103 (Winter 1988–1989): 613–635.

3. Voter Research and Surveys, *General Election Poll*, November 3, 1992.

4. Roger H. Davidson, "Invitation to Struggle: An Overview of Legislative-Executive Relations," *Annals of the American Academy of Political and Social Science* 499 (September 1988): 9–21.

5. David R. Mayhew, *Divided We Govern: Party Control, Lawmaking, and Investigations, 1946–1990* (New Haven: Yale University Press, 1991).

6. For a useful set of essays on the debate, see James A. Thurber, ed., *Divided Democracy* (Washington, D.C.: CQ Press, 1991). For a critical commentary, see Morris P. Fiorina, *Divided Government* (New York: Macmillan, 1992), chap. 6.

7. See especially Sundquist, "Needed: A New Political Theory." For additional critical views, see Michael L. Mezey, "The Legislature, the Executive, and Public Policy: The Futile Quest for Congressional Power," in *Divided Democracy*, chap. 6; and the essays in Gary W. Cox and Samuel Kernell, eds., *The Politics of Divided Government* (Boulder, Colo.: Westview Press, 1991).

8. Mayhew found a slightly greater frequency of important laws under unified government. But he argued that his measure understated the policy change under divided government because Reagan's 1981 tax and budget measures, representing a sweeping reorientation of federal policy, were embodied in just two laws (*Divided We Govern*, chap. 4).

9. The existing empirical evidence is by no means definitive. See Fiorina, *Divided Government*, chap. 6. Among the difficulties, the number of important laws is a limited indicator of government performance. Nor has anyone measured the demand for policy change in different periods.

In any case, Mayhew's historical record is too short for reliable inferences. Although his decision to study the post–World War II era was reasonable, one or two highly productive or unproductive presidencies could change the average performance of unified or divided government significantly for such a period. Some authors have taken a long-term perspective or used evidence from the American states. See James E. Alt and Charles Stewart, "Parties and the Deficit: Some Historical Evidence" (Paper presented at the National Bureau of Economic Research Conference on Political Economics, February 2–3, 1990); and James E. Alt and Robert C. Lowry, "Divided Government and Budget Deficits: Evidence from the States," Harvard University, Cambridge, 1993.

Mayhew offers a cogent theoretical discussion to support his empirical findings. In our view, however, he is more successful in explaining why the difference in performance between unified and divided government may be obscured by other forces (what he calls "constancy" and "alternative variation") than in arguing that the difference does not exist at all (owing to "compensation"). See Mayhew, *Divided We Govern*, chaps. 5–6.

10. Paul J. Quirk, "The Cooperative Resolution of Policy Conflict," *American Political Science Review* 83 (September 1989): 905–921; cf. Thomas C. Schelling, *The Strategy of Conflict* (Cambridge: Harvard University Press, 1980). Two collections of essays provide a good overview of the contemporary literature on negotiation: H. Peyton Young, ed., *Negotiation Analysis* (Ann Arbor: University of Michigan Press, 1991); J. William Breslin and Jeffrey Z. Rubin, *Negotiation Theory and Practice* (Cambridge: Program on Negotiation at Harvard Law School, 1991).

11. We rely here on a loose form of median-voter theory. For an accessible introduction to this theory and the larger body of spatial theory, see Gerald Strom, *The Logic of Lawmaking: A Spatial Theory Approach* (Baltimore: Johns Hopkins University Press, 1991). We refer to moderate members (in the plural), instead of the single median mem-

ber, for several reasons: to reflect the uncertainties of the legislative process; to avoid the implication that the president can negotiate with a single pivotal member (and perhaps win his or her support with a side payment); and to allow for the possibility that the group of moderate members is bipartisan.

Our analysis ignores the structures and procedures of Congress (committees, leadership positions, the filibuster, and so on) and the complexities of coalition building. We do not argue that it is a full account of congressional behavior, but only that it provides the best simple understanding of Congress's positions in negotiations with the president. For a defense of the median-voter perspective in interpreting Congress, see Keith Krehbiel, *Information and Legislative Organization* (Ann Arbor: University of Michigan Press, 1992).

Because median-voter theory does not apply straightforwardly to legislative decisions with more than one major dimension, our assumption is somewhat more shaky in those cases. Very roughly, we assume that members whose preferences are near the median on any of the major dimensions are especially influential.

12. For convenience we will refer to actions or positions of Congress, the congressional majority, or the majority party, depending on the context; but the reasoning will always concern the policy and electoral interests of the median members.

13. D. Roderick Kiewiet and Mathew D. McCubbins, "Presidential Influence on Appropriations Decisions," *American Journal of Political Science* 32 (1988): 713–736.

14. Howard Raiffa, *The Art and Science of Negotiation* (Cambridge: Harvard University Press, 1982).

15. Our perspective on negotiation is influenced partly by rational-choice analyses but also by social-psychological theories and by the large practical literature on conflict resolution. See Steven J. Brams, *Negotiation Games: Applying Game Theory to Bargaining and Arbitration* (New York: Routledge, 1990); Dean G. Pruitt, *Negotiation Behavior* (New York: Academic Press, 1981); J. Z. Rubin and B. R. Brown, *The Social Psychology of Bargaining and Negotiation* (New York: Academic Press, 1975); R. Fisher and W. Ury, *Getting to YES: Negotiating Agreement without Giving In* (Boston: Houghton-Mifflin, 1981); Susan L. Carpenter and W. J. D. Kennedy, *Managing Public Disputes* (San Francisco: Jossey-Bass, 1988). For an attempt to apply a conflict-resolution perspective in a general analysis of public policy making, see Quirk, "The Cooperative Resolution of Policy Conflict."

Our treatment of the negotiation perspective is a new synthesis of the broad themes of the negotiation literature.

16. The phrase was introduced in Fisher and Ury, *Getting to YES.*

17. This is Robert Axelrod's notion of "conflict-of-interest." We avoid his term, however, because of its misleading connotations of financial impropriety. Robert Axelrod, *Conflict of Interest: A Theory of Divergent Goals, With Applications to Politics* (Chicago: Markham, 1970).

18. James Q. Wilson, *Thinking about Crime* (New York: Basic Books, 1975).

19. This variability is also stressed, but explained differently, in R. Douglas Arnold, *The Logic of Congressional Action* (New Haven: Yale University Press, 1990).

20. This is a major theme of practical literature about negotiation. See Fisher and Ury, *Getting to YES*; Raiffa, *The Art and Science of Negotiation*; and I. William Zartman and Maureen R. Berman, *The Practical Negotiator* (New Haven: Yale University Press, 1982).

21. Paul Light, *Artful Work: The Politics of Social Security Reform* (New York: Random House, 1985); John Gilmour, "Summits and Stalemates: Bipartisan Negotiations in the

Postreform Era," in *The Postreform Congress*, ed. Roger H. Davidson (New York: St. Martin's Press, 1991), chap. 12.

22. See Otomar J. Bartos, "How Predictable Are Negotiations?" in *The 50% Solution*, ed. I. William Zartman (New Haven: Yale University Press, 1983), 485–509. Also see Oran Young, ed., *Formal Theories of Negotiation* (Urbana: University of Illinois Press, 1975), especially the editor's introductory essays.

23. Some of our reasoning appeals to a casual and implicit spatial analysis of negotiation games. Other aspects of our argument would not lend themselves to a spatial representation.

24. We assume that the two parties maintain a fairly constant distance from each other on any given ideological issue but that they move in the same direction in response to unidirectional changes in public opinion, interest group demands, or objective policy conditions (such as poverty rates or evidence of environmental hazards).

25. Eric Nordlinger, *On the Autonomy of the Democratic State* (Cambridge: Harvard University Press, 1982); Peter B. Evans, Dietrich Rueschmeyer, and Theda Skocpol, eds., *Bringing the State Back In* (New York: Cambridge University Press, 1985); Kent Weaver and Bert Rockman, *Do Institutions Matter?* (Washington, D.C.: Brookings Institution, 1993).

26. Sundquist, "Needed: A New Theory."

27. Roughly speaking, he will have to reduce the opposition party's political costs of passing his bill enough that opposition members would prefer to accept that collective cost rather than take the risk, individually, of being blamed for obstructing it.

28. Mayhew makes a similar point about individual electoral incentives in *Divided We Govern*, 102–103.

29. Timothy J. Conlon, Margaret T. Wrightson, and David R. Beam, *Taxing Choices: The Politics of Tax Reform* (Washington, D.C.: CQ Press, 1990).

30. Roughly, the condition required for divided government to produce deadlock is that fluctuations in the parties' positions must be smaller than the difference between them.

31. Richard G. Niemi, John Mueller, and Tom W. Smith, *Trends in Public Opinion: A Compendium of Survey Data* (New York: Greenwood, 1989), 89.

32. Our account of changes in welfare policy is based largely on James T. Patterson, *America's Struggle against Poverty* (Cambridge: Harvard University Press, 1986), 192–207, 212–214.

33. Mayhew, *Divided We Govern*, 58–60, 85–86.

34. Niemi, Mueller, and Smith, *Trends in Public Opinion*, 87.

35. Howard E. Shuman, *Politics and the Budget: The Struggle between the President and Congress*, 3d ed. (Englewood Cliffs, N.J.: Prentice-Hall, 1992), 129–131.

36. Karen W. Arenson, "Ramifications of Tax Law Affect Many," *New York Times*, August 23, 1982, D7. Lower-income people spend a larger share of their incomes on cigarettes and telephones.

37. Shuman, *Politics and the Budget*, 328–329.

38. David S. Cloud, "New Levies on Gas and the Rich Would Yield $240 Billion," *Congressional Quarterly Weekly Report*, August 7, 1993, 2132–2133.

39. Martha Derthick and Paul J. Quirk, *The Politics of Deregulation* (Washington, D.C.: Brookings Institution, 1985).

40. "1970 Agricultural Act Cleared after 16-Month Debate," in *Congressional Quarterly Almanac, 1970* (Washington, D.C.: Congressional Quarterly, 1971), 634–636.

41. Willard W. Cochrane and Mary E. Ryan, *American Farm Policy, 1948–1973* (Minneapolis: University of Minnesota Press, 1976), 69, 83.

42. "Bold Moves on Economy by Nixon Administration," in *Congressional Quarterly Almanac, 1971* (Washington, D.C.: Congressional Quarterly, 1972), 58; Herbert Stein, *Presidential Economics: The Making of Economic Policy from Roosevelt to Reagan and Beyond* (New York: Simon and Schuster, 1984), 215.

43. "Carter Seeks 'Prudent' 1981 Spending Plan," in *Congressional Quarterly Almanac, 1980* (Washington, D.C.: Congressional Quarterly, 1981), 131–132.

44. Stein, *Presidential Economics*, 276.

45. Paul J. Quirk and Bruce Nesmith, "Explaining Deadlock: Domestic Policymaking in the Bush Presidency," in *New Perspectives on American Politics*, ed. Lawrence C. Dodd and Calvin Jillson (Washington, D.C.: CQ Press, 1994), 200–201.

46. See Weaver and Rockman, *Do Institutions Matter?* 451–452.

47. Fiorina points out in *Divided Government*, 94–95, that congressional Democrats restrained Reagan's tax cuts and defense buildup and that even many Republicans opposed his cuts in domestic spending. Thus, he suggests, a unified Republican government during the early 1980s might have enacted even larger tax cuts and defense increases, accomplished no greater spending cuts, and therefore produced even larger budget deficits.

48. "Budget and Appropriations," in *Congressional Quarterly Almanac, 1979* (Washington, D.C.: Congressional Quarterly, 1980), 172.

49. John B. Gilmour, *Reconcilable Differences: Congress, the Budget Process, and the Deficit* (Berkeley: University of California Press, 1990), 46–47.

50. Paul J. Quirk, "Domestic Policy: Divided Government and Cooperative Presidential Leadership," in *The Bush Presidency: First Appraisals*, ed. Colin Campbell and Bert A. Rockman (Chatham, N.J.: Chatham House, 1991), 69–92.

51. Gilmour, *Reconcilable Differences*, 46–49.

52. Stein, *Presidential Economics*, chap. 7.

53. Dennis S. Ippolito, *Uncertain Legacies: Federal Budget Policy from Roosevelt through Reagan* (Charlottesville: University Press of Virginia, 1990), 70.

54. Daniel A. Franklin, *Making Ends Meet: Congressional Budgeting in the Age of Deficits* (Washington, D.C.: CQ Press, 1993), 88.

55. For a thorough discussion of these and other proposals to strengthen the linkage between the president and Congress, see James L. Sundquist, *Constitutional Reform and Effective Government* (Washington, D.C.: Brookings Institution, 1986), chap. 4.

20 The Presidency and the World: Adjusting to the Post–Cold War Era

Bartholomew H. Sparrow

The recent victory of the United States and its allies against the Soviet Union in the cold war has left more questions than answers in its wake, especially concerning the U.S. role as the only superpower in the world. Bartholomew H. Sparrow identifies and addresses several of these questions, with particular attention to the Clinton administration's early actions in foreign policy. Specifically: What moral responsibilities does the United States have in the post–cold war world? What are the appropriate roles of the president and Congress in foreign policy making? How should agencies of foreign policy such as the State Department, the Defense Department, and the Central Intelligence Agency be organized to meet their new challenges? What old policies should be abandoned or modified and what new ones adopted? Sparrow concludes that only the president "has the nationally representative electorate, the political and informational resources, and the leadership capability" to provide answers to these questions.

The United States is at a historical juncture—the end of the cold war era and the beginning of another, undefined era. No longer does the fight against communism dominate U.S. foreign policy and the institutions of government. But the United States lacks a doctrine analogous to the Monroe Doctrine of the 1820s or to the Truman Doctrine of the late 1940s that spells out its new, post–cold war foreign policy. In the absence of a clear and present danger from the Soviet Union, U.S. foreign policy is in disarray—as events in Bosnia, Somalia, Haiti, and North Korea make apparent.

The shock waves from the fundamental shift in the global order are forcing changes in U.S. foreign policy that span four dimensions: (1) the American mission in the world; (2) the respective roles of the president and Congress in making foreign policy; (3) the mission, size, and configuration of the government organizations that enact American foreign policy; and (4) the actual foreign policies of the United States. Assessing these four dimensions of foreign policy making is indispensable to an account of the relation between the presidency and the world. The definition of a grand strategy requires particular organizational capabilities and specific policies, just as the processes of making foreign policy—and therefore its legitimacy—affect the stability of and support for U.S. foreign relations. Similarly, changes in policy or organization would be nonsensical in the absence of a defined grand strategy.

It falls to the president as head of state, commander in chief of the armed forces, chief executive of the federal government, and principal legislator to redefine and restructure U.S. foreign policy. No other political actor has the nationally representative electorate, the political and informational resources, and the leadership capability to chart a new course in foreign policy.[1] The Clinton administration has begun to act on several of these fronts, although much adjustment of foreign policy remains to be done.

The four dimensions are each discussed in turn in the sections below. Each section includes a sketch of the pressures and challenges facing the president in foreign policy, a discussion of the extent to which the Clinton presidency is moving ahead on each front, and a survey of the questions and issues yet to be addressed in the face of the changing international system.

Moral Leadership

An International Mission

The central issue facing the presidency is the articulation of an international mission: what is America's grand strategy as it enters the twenty-first century?[2] With the end of the cold war the United States is, for the first time, in a position to define its national interests (and thus its international interests) in positive and proactive terms. Although the United States has had other moments of historical redefinition, all prior "rendezvous with destiny" were moments of reaction.[3] The War of Independence established the United States as the land of religious freedom and economic opportunity, distinct from England and the European continent. President Lincoln and the Civil War determined that the United States was to be a union as opposed to a confederation of states— the South would be prevented from seceding. The notable exception was the economic, strategic, and moral internationalism of the late nineteenth and early twentieth centuries, culminating in Woodrow Wilson's international liberalism of the Treaty of Versailles.

But with the collapse of international trade, the breakdown of the international system of payments, and the global economic depression in the 1930s, and then the outbreak of World War II, the explosion of the atomic bomb, and the postwar expansion of U.S. trade and investment in the 1940s and 1950s, American interests (and thus grand strategy) became ineluctably global. Yet they stayed essentially defensive: President Franklin D. Roosevelt and President Harry Truman made the United States a beacon of political and economic freedom in contrast to the totalitarian governments of Nazi Germany and the Soviet Union. The creation of such postwar institutions as the Marshall Plan, the North Atlantic Treaty Organization, the Inter-American Treaty, the Alliance for Progress, the security treaties with Japan and with Australia and New Zealand, and the Mutual Defense Treaties with South Korea and the Philippines was based on American opposition to and fear of the Soviet Union. Only when U.S. military and financial interventions could assist in the fight against communism did the political and economic rights and the living conditions of people in other countries matter. Hence the United States supported—at various times, to various lengths, and in varying degrees—undemocratic and despotic regimes in the Philippines, Indonesia, South Vietnam, South Korea, Iran, Iraq, South Africa, Zaire, Morocco, Brazil, Argentina, Panama, El Salvador, Chile, and elsewhere.

President Bush's "new world order," despite the promise of the phrase, did little to redefine American foreign policy.[4] For all the political success of the Bush administration's characterization of the Gulf War as a mission to mete out justice, protect the innocent, and establish a precedent against international aggression, the crux of the "new world order" was nothing more than the realpolitik of the U.S. government's interest in vanquishing the Iraqi military.[5] The Bush administration's response to the invasion of Kuwait on August 2, 1990, was unaccompanied by serious diplomatic pressure either before the invasion or in the weeks and months afterward; it personalized the U.S.-Iraqi relationship; and it issued ultimatums rather than giving economic sanctions time to work. This was no new world order but a punitive mission to force Iraq's retreat from Kuwait, to protect oil supplies, and to balance the alignment of military forces in the Middle East.

The U.S. government took up the policeman's nightstick once more when the Bush administration decided to intervene militarily in Somalia in December 1992, a humanitarian mission that the Clinton administration inherited. Although the U.S. military action was part of an international effort, American troops did much of the fighting and dying. President Clinton proceeded to announce a doubling of troop levels and an increase in material support for the U.S. forces in Somalia on October 7, 1993, even as he simultaneously pledged to withdraw U.S. forces by March 31, 1994. They were withdrawn.

Common to U.S. policy toward Somalia and Iraq (as well as to the former Yugoslavia, where the U.S. government has become part of a unilateral United Nations [UN] effort) has been its defensive character. The U.S. government responded to crises, rather than prevented or preempted them from emerging. The presence of international bogeymen—Lt. Gen. Raoul Cedras of Haiti, Gen. Mohammed Farrah Aidid of Somalia, Slobodan Milosevic of Serbia, and Saddam Hussein of Iraq, following in the footsteps of Manuel Noriega, the Ayatollah Khomeini, Muammar Khadafi, Idi Amin, Fidel Castro, and others—marked a further continuity with the cold war era.[6]

Although the defensive character of American foreign policy marks a continuation of the earlier cold war policy, the orderliness of the containment of communism has been replaced by an ad hoc quality in U.S. foreign policy, which seems to be guided by presidential or public whims rather than by deliberation or consistent logic. Consider the 180-degree turnaround between the conciliatory conversation of the U.S. diplomat April Glaspie with Saddam Hussein in late July 1990 and the statement by President Bush on August 4, 1990, that Iraq's invasion of Kuwait would not stand. Consider the public's reaction to the television pictures of starving Somali children in late 1992, which lured the Bush administration into Somalia, and then the response to the pictures of a captured American pilot and of an American body being dragged through the streets of Mogadishu in the fall of 1993: polls revealed that about 60 percent of Americans wanted the United States to get out of Somalia, and Congress proceeded to pressure the Clinton administration to withdraw the U.S. troops. Consider, too, the influence that television pictures and news reports have had on public opinion and the inconsistent messages being sent to the former Yugoslavia and to China.[7]

The danger of ad hoc foreign policy is that it causes confusion both at home and abroad. The secretary of defense was utterly browbeaten by members of Congress who wanted to know why the United States was in Somalia at all, for instance,[8] and the deputy secretary of state had already been forced to resign. Some suspect that the difference between the willingness of the U.S. government to intervene in Somalia and its caution in doing something about the horrors in Bosnia is merely the tractability of desert warfare as opposed to the difficulty of combat in mountainous and forested terrain. Confusion and miscalculation about U.S. intentions have already led to Iraq's invasion of Kuwait—confusion and miscalculation that come at a cost to American soldiers and taxpayers, not to mention the lives and livelihoods of others around the world.

In sum, the absence of a formidable opponent has led the United States to question its international identity. When President Truman spoke of the different ways of life of the United States and the Soviet Union, he painted a contrast that was able to guide American foreign policy for the next four decades. But the very absence of a single, obvious enemy now makes things far less clear and considerably more difficult for the United States. Neither Bush nor Clinton has so far been able to come up with a coherent, positive foreign policy mission, even though the world looks to the United States and to its president for direction. Issues of trade, nuclear proliferation, arms sales, hunger and population, international terrorism, the environment, and regional balances will not rest. The United States has to lead, as Colin Powell, Paul Kennedy, Joseph Nye, and Michael Mandelbaum, among others, well recognize.[9] But a new purpose for the United States awaits articulation.

The Clinton Administration's Foreign Policy

The Clinton administration began to try to articulate a vision of U.S. foreign policy in the fall of 1993. In September, National Security Adviser Anthony Lake described a policy of "enlargement," a U.S. commitment to enlarge the family of democratic governments and market economies by facilitating political and economic reform in nations such as Russia, Haiti, and Nigeria. U.S. foreign policy would have four priorities in this new vision: first, to strengthen the existing major market economies—namely, Japan, Germany, and France; second, to help democracies and markets expand in areas where the United States still has security interests, such as eastern Europe and the former Soviet Union; third, to minimize the ability of "states outside the circle of democracy and markets to threaten" the enlargement of democratic and market-oriented states; and fourth, to decide where to intervene on matters of human rights.[10] The enlargement doctrine is consistent with the prodemocratic foreign policy that Clinton enunciated during his presidential campaign, which "avoided calling for a democratic crusade" and put "a premium on political and economic means, not military."[11]

Under the enlargement policy, the United States would neither ignore the condition of the major market economies nor forget that force will sometimes be needed to deal with states that threaten democratic governments and market economies. Lake's statement promised to offer a positive, general framework for understanding the role of the United States in the world.

Questions of Enlargement

Yet the new enlargement doctrine prompts more questions than it answers about the adjustment of U.S. foreign policy to the post-cold war world:

Is the first priority—strengthening the major market economies—consistent with "enlargement"—or more in keeping with "consolidation"? Consider that the further opening of the major market economies to foreign goods threatens the standard of living of those who live in these countries, especially farmers and low-wage workers. Politics is typically short term. How, then, is it possible to sustain the economic and political stability of the major market economies and simultaneously to open markets to the commodities and products of the four-fifths of the world that is poor?[12]

Does strengthening the core nations require institutional reform among the Group of Seven (G-7)?[13] If the major market economies of the G-7 are unable to agree about how to strengthen themselves or restart global growth, can the United States proceed to its other priorities?

To what extent will the United States use or rely on multinational actions to achieve its goals? The U.S. ambassador to the United Nations, Madeleine Albright, told Congress that the United States would insist on tough requirements for the creation of any United Nations peacekeeping force. These requirements include establishing that a real threat exists to international peace and security; specifying the objectives and defining the scope of the mission; determining if a cease-fire is in place and if the parties agree to the presence of a UN force; seeing if the necessary financial and human resources for accomplishing the mission are available; and identifying an end point to UN participation.[14] President Clinton also stressed the need for a viable, defined, and responsible UN peacekeeping capacity in a speech to the United Nations in September 1993. Both the president and his UN ambassador suggested that there were situations in which U.S. interests could be furthered through multilateral and, especially, UN efforts, as in the UN Security Council's vote before the Korean War, the UN resolutions supporting U.S. objectives in the Persian Gulf conflict, and George Bush's success in getting other powers—European, Asian, and Middle Eastern—to assist with or otherwise contribute to the war against Iraq.

No doubt the more difficult issue for international cooperation is trade. Here, the new administration was able to get the North American Free Trade Agreement (NAFTA) through Congress in November 1993 and has completed the Uruguay round of the General Agreement on Tariffs and Trade (GATT). Serious issues remain, however. Not only do the exact terms of the GATT, agreed to in Geneva, remain to be spelled out, but the uncertainty about trade relations with Japan and China continues, as do the unsettled conflicts among nations (especially between rich and poor ones) over such issues as the environment, intellectual property, service industries, and continued agricultural subsidies. On these issues, as in the next (and ninth) round of the GATT, the White House has the task of persuading American voters and the U.S. Senate that its trade-offs between protection and openness, and between political and economic considerations, are both coherent and correct.

Another set of issues concerns American security interests. Why is the enlargement of democracy and market economies one of America's "security interests" in the former Soviet Union and eastern Europe? Do these areas matter more than other American security interests (such as in Israel and the Middle East, Latin America, South Korea, and Taiwan and the Far East) because of the size of their armed forces and their nuclear arsenals? What are the minimum criteria for U.S. intervention in these areas?

What happens when American allies are themselves not democratic, or when further democratization may actually threaten U.S. interests? Which has priority, creating markets or creating democratic governments? As former defense (and energy) secretary James Schlesinger notes, the United States has consistently supported the nondemocratic government of Saudi Arabia and has abstained from insisting on more democracy in Kuwait. Schlesinger also points out the danger that further democratization could pose to Egypt (and thus to northern Africa and southwestern Asia). It is also unclear that the United States can do anything to shape China's internal political or economic policies.[15] Does the Clinton administration's enlargement doctrine constitute a comprehensive indictment of previous American foreign policy, analogous to President Carter's human rights agenda—or is it simply naive?

What should the United States do in the former third and fourth worlds (what economist Robert Heilbroner calls "the rest of the world"), where human rights violations and human tragedies are everyday occurrences? In his speech to the United Nations, President Clinton suggested that the condition of nondemocratic, poor countries was a matter of grave concern. During the past decade, 1.5 million children have died as a result of wars, he noted, and 40 million children have died from wholly preventable diseases. Clinton emphasized the importance of investing in vaccines and potable water. The juxtaposition of the president's remarks to the United Nations and Lake's speech implies that the Clinton administration intends to use the UN to address the human rights and human welfare issues that are not mentioned in the enlargement doctrine. The same logic would presumably apply to nuclear proliferation and the control of biological weapons (also missing from Lake's speech but featured in Clinton's UN address)—namely, that the administration intends to act multilaterally and not go at them alone.

What classifies a state as lying outside the "circle of democracy and markets"—the "backlash states"—when many market-oriented states are undemocratic and when all governments interfere to some extent in their domestic economies? North Korea may be an obvious pariah, but it is less obvious what U.S. policy should be toward, say, Cuba, or Sudan. Moreover, situations like those in Somalia, Bosnia, and Haiti in the early 1990s are unlikely to be exceptions or aberrations under the new international system, but precedents and precursors.[16]

Finally, what of America's own interests? The Clinton administration's enlargement doctrine does not explicitly address what action the U.S. government would take to protect the level of wealth and the quality of life of present day and future Americans. Would acting in the national interest demand tight restrictions on immigration, the stockpiling of vital, imported raw materials and manufactured goods, and the lessening of American dependence on foreign oil in the intermediate and long terms? "Enlargement" does not say.

Filling the vacuum created by the lack of a redefined U.S. foreign policy, however, has been leadership of a different sort: the dissemination of cynicism, consumerism, and callousness by the mass media, commercial advertising, and popular music. When "hedonism, self-gratification, and consumption are the essential definitions of the meaning of the 'good life,'" Zbigniew Brzezinski and others point out, Western liberalism reveals itself to the world as "hypocritical and empty." If the United States is to be respected globally as a political model and moral authority, it has to regain its own moral consciousness. At the heart of a new vision of the world must lie "a clear sense of America's moral self-worth," as Henry Nau notes.[17]

The United States can and should be explicit about gross human rights violations in other countries, for example, and can encourage more open government in the form of freer political debate and fair elections. Human rights are not chits to be traded off for economic advantage or smooth political relations; they go beyond political and economic liberties. As Charles William Maynes points out in writing about Bosnia, "unless we can encourage a perception that the West cares about how others treat Serbs as much as it cares about how Serbs treat others, any peacekeeping force will be seen as biased—and as a target of attack."[18] The importance of a fair and conscientious foreign policy can hardly be overemphasized.

Yet moral leadership need not mean coercive intervention in the pursuit of human rights, as many fear. Distinguishing moral leadership from a program of global policework is the integrity of U.S. foreign policy, integrity in two senses. One is the recognition that the United States has severe political and economic problems of its own. The U.S. government is in no position to infringe on the sovereignty of other nations for the furtherance of political and economic rights in view of the condition of its own cities, crime rate, educational system, and wage differences between the economically advantaged and the economically disadvantaged. If U.S. policy is to limit conventional weapons sales by other countries, say, the Czech Republic, the Republic of Slovakia, and China, then the U.S. government must first look to its own weapons exports.[19] A politics of meaning begins at home, with the integration of domestic and foreign policy.[20] The best leadership is rooted in example.[21]

As attractive as it may be to think the United States can end the horrors of a Bosnia or Haiti, such activism is belied by the triple conceit that the United States knows what is good for other nation-states, that it can successfully impose order on them, and that its intervention will have the intended effects. The view that the "best hope for safety" in these abnormal times is "American strength and will—the strength and will to lead a unipolar world, unashamedly laying down the rules of world order and being prepared to enforce them" is right about leadership but wrong about the rest.[22] An overestimation of American effectiveness kept the United States in Vietnam and Southeast Asia, and it was an arrogance of power that has more recently ensnared the U.S. government. An example is President Bush's justification for intervening in Somalia: sending in American forces was a "humanitarian mission" in "the finest tradition of service"; it was "God's work."[23] The U.S. government is not God.

The second aspect of integrity that blunts the sword of moral leadership is the conceptualization and implementation of a foreign policy that is consistent among all foreign policy organizations and consistent from diplomatic word to economic action to military deed. "When force is used deftly—in smooth coordination with diplomatic and economic policy—bullets may never have to fly," argues Gen. Colin Powell.[24] If the government is to restrict immigration to United States, for example, then it needs to pursue policies, whether independently or multilaterally, that remedy the causes of emigration. Similarly, if the U.S. government is to restrict the production of chemical weapons and stop nuclear proliferation abroad, then its policies need to promote the stability of a state or a region so as to reduce the demand for arms and obviate the need to sell chemical or nuclear weapons. No one in the American political system is better equipped than the president to articulate a new, more moral mission of U.S. international relations.

Constitutional Balance in Foreign Policy Making

A second issue concerning the presidency and the world, perhaps as important as the first, is apparent from the Gulf War, the action taken in Somalia, U.S. policy toward the former Yugoslavia, and the promotion of free trade—namely, the unsettled relationship between the presidency and Congress. The consultation and cooperation between the branches of government that succeeded during the late 1940s in forging the Marshall Plan, unifying the armed services, and establishing the other institutions of the cold war has largely disappeared in recent decades. The White House is wary and suspicious of Congress; Congress is wary and suspicious of the White House.

Although the battle between the executive and legislative branches dates from the earliest days of the republic—at least since President Thomas Jefferson sent the navy to suppress the Barbary Pirates in 1805—the conflict had more serious consequences during the cold war because the United States was a superpower. The actions of Presidents John F. Kennedy, Lyndon B. Johnson, and Richard M. Nixon in Vietnam and Southeast Asia to circumvent Congress marked the emergence of the "imperial presidency." Congress responded by passing the War Powers Resolution of 1973 (which imposed consulting and reporting requirements and a sixty-day time limit on the president's commitment of U.S. troops overseas without explicit congressional authorization), the Hughes-Ryan amendment of 1974 (which amended an appropriations bill by imposing certain reporting requirements on the Central Intelligence Agency [CIA] as a prerequisite to its expenditure of appropriated funds), and other oversight measures. Congress's increased intervention in the making of foreign policy led, in turn, to expanded covert operations by the administration of Ronald Reagan in the 1980s and to the Iran-contra affair.

The end of the cold war did not end the institutional struggle over foreign policy making. Although the congressional debate on whether or not to send troops to Saudi Arabia after Iraq's invasion of Kuwait appeared to smooth out executive-legislative relations, both the subsequent revelations about the Bush administration's funding and support for Iraq until almost the moment of the invasion and the lack of closure to the Iran-contra affair suggest the continuing tension between the two branches.

The cost of the ongoing struggle between Congress and the presidency has been an inconsistent and, in the instances when the White House has attempted to escape congressional control, an illegitimate foreign policy. Consider the rapidly changing U.S. policies of recent decades toward Iran, Iraq, Panama, and

(South) Vietnam. The fact that Presidents Reagan and Bush left office under the foreign policy clouds of the Iran-contra and Iraq affairs, respectively, suggests the corrosive effects that this institutional struggle has had on public trust in the government: both matters were products of the go-it-alone foreign policy presidency.

Yet the courts have discouraged balanced decision making and, instead, have deferred to the executive branch. Harold Koh sees the principles of constitutional government as divided between the doctrine in *United States v. Curtiss-Wright Export Co.* (executive prerogative) and in *Youngstown Sheet and Tube Co. v. Sawyer* (the sharing of foreign policy making powers between the executive and legislative branches). He argues that although *Youngstown* (1952) came after *Curtiss-Wright* (1936), "executive practice has recently gained undue predominance as a source of customary constitutional law in the area of foreign affairs." The Supreme Court has "uncritically support[ed] the executive" in recent decades, even though the Court's tendency to minimize judicial review of presidential foreign policy making has little foundation in the Constitution. With the Warren E. Burger and William H. Rehnquist courts both upholding the *Curtiss-Wright* doctrine, Koh finds it no surprise that Oliver North relied on *Curtiss-Wright* to justify his actions in dealing arms for the release of hostages.[25]

Koh concludes grimly that

under virtually every scenario, the president wins. If the executive branch possesses statutory or constitutional authority to act and Congress acquiesces, the president wins. If Congress does not acquiesce in the president's act, but lacks the political will either to cut off appropriations or to pass an objecting statute and override a veto, the president again wins. If a member of Congress or a private individual sues to challenge the president's actions, the judiciary will likely refuse to hear that challenge on the ground that the plaintiff lacks standing; the defendant is immune; the question is political, not ripe, or moot; or that relief is inappropriate.[26]

The result is that Congress has rarely challenged the president.

Instead, Congress has used its powers to micromanage the executive branch's conduct of foreign policy. For example, the intelligence community is overseen by forty-five staff members of the Senate Intelligence Committee, who are often left without guidelines or clear instructions from their Senate bosses. As a result, oversight tends to focus on trivial matters or pet projects while more serious issues and the vast majority of programs go unexamined.

Change is in the wind, however. Presidential persuasion (rather than fiat or secrecy) has long been the rule in domestic politics. The increased intertwining of trade, monetary policy, and technology on the national and international levels and the new participation of the news media and nongovernmental groups in forming public opinion will extend this practice to foreign policy making. Without the unifying threat of the bipolar world and with the interrelationship of domestic and foreign policies, Congress can no longer avoid playing a larger role in foreign policy making.[27] Thus far, there has been little progress in finding a new postwar relationship between the president and Congress. If anything, the Bush and Clinton administrations have tried to continue the cold war superiority of the executive branch. Yet an effective foreign policy demands congressional support. There can be no successful redefinition or reorganization of U.S. foreign policy without presidential leadership and Congress's cooperation.

Structural Changes

A third set of issues confronting the American presidency is the reorganization of the executive departments and agencies of the cold war. As the U.S. Department of State and the Carnegie Endowment for International Peace observe in recent reports, the transformation in the international system demands accompanying changes in the organizations that enact foreign policy. The departments and agencies that make American foreign policy face an international system in which issues of trade, economic competitiveness, the environment, drugs, and disease have taken on increasing importance; conversely, military and intelligence operations are being scaled down and reoriented to the more diverse and complex threats facing the United States.[28] These organizations of foreign policy now must transform their reigning ideas and standard operating procedures.

The State Department, National Security Council, and National Economic Council

In several instances the Clinton administration has begun to adjust the making of foreign policy to the new post–cold war requirements. The Clinton administration has consolidated some offices in the White House proper and has created others. The Bush administration had fourteen staff offices reporting to the president; the Clinton administration has twelve, with six of the twelve, including the newly created National Economic Council (NEC) and Domestic Policy Council, grouped as "Policy Development."[29] The Clinton administration initiated a major structural innovation by forming the National

Economic Council on January 25, 1993, as an economic counterpart to the National Security Council (NSC). The NEC was set up to coordinate economic issues and "to pull together the enormous number of departments and agencies that have an interest in trade." One of the NEC's main tasks is to coordinate trade policies with the relevant agency and departmental personnel. The NSC and the NEC share economic staff, divided into trade and investment issues and G-7 issues. Working with the NEC are the two interagency trade policy making groups, the Trade Policy Staff Committee and the Trade Policy Review Group.[30]

Secretary of State Warren Christopher announced the reorganization of the State Department on February 5, 1993. A new undersecretaryship has been created for global affairs, and the five undersecretaries, together with the secretary's deputy, are to be the principal advisers to the secretary; they also serve in the direct chain of command under the secretary. In addition, the State Department created three new bureaus: the Bureau of Democracy, Human Rights, and Labor; the Bureau of Narcotics, Terrorism, and Crime; and the Bureau of Population, Refugees, and Migration. An Office of Secretary of State was created as well, and an ambassador at large and a special adviser to the secretary were appointed for the newly independent states of the former Soviet Union. Furthermore, the State Department consolidated operations by getting rid of about 40 percent of the deputy assistant secretaries and their equivalents.[31] Most of the changes followed directly from State 2000, the State Department's comprehensive report of December 1992, which specified many of the changes needed during the next half decade in the administration of U.S. foreign policy.[32]

The State Department has also begun to implement its "reinvention of government" (as requested by the Clinton administration) by setting up a ten-person team to "identify ways the Department can better serve the public and make more effective use of resources."[33] In short, the State Department, the NSC, and the NEC appear to be adjusting to the post–cold war world.

The Military

The much larger defense establishment faces a greater challenge: it must adjust the size and the configuration of the military to respond to regional conflicts, rather than to fight a European land war against the Soviet Union.[34] So far, the Clinton administration has attempted to steer a middle course between unilaterally disarming in the interest of economy and keeping the existing military capability in order to maximize U.S. security and global influence. On the one hand, if the United States is to be able to act effectively when military action is necessary and if it is to continue to deter hostile actions by others, then it clearly must retain a modicum of personnel, weapons, inventory, and forward bases; uncertainties the world over, especially in Russia and southwestern Asia, preclude unilateral disarmament.[35] On the other hand, significant reductions in the military are now possible in the wake of the cold war. Under the Clinton administration's "win-hold-win" strategy, the United States would be prepared to fight two regional wars at the same time (perhaps one war in the Middle East and another in Korea), winning one and holding the line in the other until the victorious forces from the first conflict could enter the second.

The "win-hold-win" scenario allows for cuts in the armed forces beyond those proposed by the Bush administration. The Clinton administration would reduce the army's 14 active divisions to 10 and its 6 reserve divisions to 5 by 1999. (There were 18 active divisions in 1990.) It would cut the navy's 13 carrier groups to 11 (16 carrier groups were afloat in 1990). The air force would be reduced from 16 active fighter wings (20 in 1990) to 13 and from 12 reserve fighter wings (12 in 1990) to 7. The number of active marines would be trimmed from 182,000 troops to 174,000.[36]

The military will go ahead with the development of the F-22 fighter jet (manufactured by Lockheed), the navy's F-18E/F fighter plane (McDonnell-Douglas), the Commanche scout helicopter (Boeing and Sikorsky), the Apache/Long Bow helicopter (McDonnell-Douglas), and the Seawolf submarine (General Dynamics' Electric Boat Division). This procurement plan will preserve core technologies (and companies) so that they will be available for future contingencies. Furthermore, the budget for the Strategic Defense Initiative, "Star Wars," will be reduced from nearly $40 billion in fiscal 1995 to $20 billion by 1999.[37] In the absence of a single, overwhelming opponent, American forces are to focus on capabilities (the "Base force"), rather than threats.[38]

In the task of cutting the size of the military, two dimensions of foreign policy come prominently into play. First, an integrated American foreign policy allows for greater economy and efficiency, since it is clearly more cost-effective to solve disputes diplomatically or through the carrots and sticks of economic sanctions and international assistance than by force. War is a last resort—Clausewitz's politics by other means—and not an end in itself. The Clinton administration has referred to this principle as "preventive diplomacy" and has developed a list of problems and areas of the world where it might be useful.[39] Second, cooperation between the president and Congress is critical: only if foreign policy is articulated by the president and Congress and the public is persuaded of the stakes that the United States has in its foreign policies will there be the necessary popular and financial support for an effective military establishment.

The analogies that some Clinton critics draw between the present military cutbacks and the draconian cutbacks after World War II or the severe reduction of military readiness after World War I are misleading.[40] Now, unlike after World War II, no analogous Soviet Union waits in the wings; moreover, the United States was far weaker in the post–World War II period than it is at present—or will be in the foreseeable future. The line drawn between adequate military protection and competing demands for resources is fundamentally a political question of acceptable risk. Defense is a budgetary issue—even for a comparatively wealthy United States.

The Clinton administration has also begun to reorganize the military. The Office of the Secretary of Defense is creating undersecretaries for "Economic and Environmental Security," for "Democracy and Human Rights," and for "Nuclear Security and Counter Proliferation." The general counsel and the public and legislative affairs personnel are to function in the manner of an executive staff to the head of a large corporation, with only four, rather than twenty-four, undersecretaries reporting to the secretary of defense. Troubling in this reorganization is that the new undersecretaryships created by the Pentagon are in areas that have traditionally been the province of the State Department. Will the overlap between the Pentagon and State Department bespeak a "deep collaboration" or the introduction of "creative tension?"[41]

The Defense Department itself has taken steps to reorganize. Forces in the continental United States will be under one person, the commander in chief of the Atlantic Command. The new command will prepare soldiers for new roles, such as humanitarian missions and disaster relief.[42] The capabilities of each of the services will be employed jointly rather than separately. The reorganization of the Atlantic Command constitutes a promising first step in the necessary reform of the institutions that were established in the early years of the cold war, when the armed services were allowed to divide weapons systems, military missions, and procurement among themselves. The internationally transformed and fiscally austere conditions of the present bring these issues once more into question.

The irony of the cold war is that as the military prepared to fight an extensive ground war in central Europe, the actual uses of force in Korea, Vietnam, Panama, Grenada, and Kuwait involved at once extensive combinations and a limited commitment of ground, sea, and air forces. Future wars, too, will likely be quick, limited, joint operations. Following the logic of the new Atlantic Command and that of the reorganized staffs of the NSC and NEC on trade issues—that is, the logic of sharing staff resources—the staff, material, training, and even command of the three services could be combined. Put differently, if airplanes, ships, mechanized armor, and infantry are but instruments for the U.S. government to use in executing a mission, and if future wars will involve the concurrent deployment of these forces, then the divided administration and resources of the army, navy, air force, and marines have to be consolidated. Although reorganizing the military on an interservice or nonservice basis would represent a drastic departure from existing practice, the communications, mobility, and strategy of modern warfare are themselves radically different from what they were as recently as the 1970s.[43]

The Intelligence Community

The post–cold war world demands "the most sweeping changes in the modern intelligence apparatus of the government since the Central Intelligence Agency was erected by the National Security Act of 1947," argues Sen. David Boren, a Democrat from Oklahoma. "If the intelligence community fails to make these changes, it will become an expensive and irrelevant dinosaur."[44] Like the military, the intelligence community faces both a reduction in scale ("rightsizing") and a reorganization.

Consider the intelligence failures of the Gulf War: intelligence concerning Iraqi troops massing on the Kuwaiti border was either not coordinated or not presented in a sufficiently convincing manner to President Bush (the photographic evidence existed); intelligence misconstrued the intent and capability of Iraqi forces, even miscounting the number of Iraqi troops in and near Kuwait by hundreds of thousands; intelligence mistook a camouflaged milk formula plant outside Baghdad for a biological weapons facility, thus leading to its destruction and a public relations coup for Saddam Hussein; intelligence failed to anticipate the threat posed by the mobile Scud missile launchers; and intelligence was never able to catch up with Saddam Hussein.

Despite the end of the cold war, only $1.3 billion was cut from the $29 billion intelligence budget for fiscal 1994, leaving it about the same as in fiscal 1993. The CIA receives about $3 billion, with the remainder of the budget going to the Defense Intelligence Agency (DIA); army, navy, air force, and marine intelligence; the National Security Agency (NSA); the National Reconnaissance Office (NRO); and the intelligence bureaus of the Justice, Energy, State, and Treasury departments.[45]

Yet more could be cut from the intelligence budget. Additional cuts could be made by reducing the number of spy satellites (more information is picked up by the $4 billion worth of "big-eared" satellites than can be transcribed), by curtailing and reforming the collection of tactical intelligence (the United States spends $11 billion a year for the DIA and the intelligence units of the military services to track military movements and monitor defense installations on a minute-by-minute basis), and by cutting back the number of spies and analysts.[46]

As for reorganizing the existing intelligence community, the director of Central Intelligence (DCI), James Woolsey, and Secretary of Defense Les Aspin chartered the DCI-SecDef Joint Security Commission to investigate the role of intelligence in the post–cold war world. Each member of the committee was a present or former military or intelligence official, however, with the exception of the commission chair, Jeffrey Smith, a former staff member for Sen. Sam Nunn of Georgia.[47] A task force formed in the Information Security Oversight Office was then instructed, in April 1993, to reevaluate President Reagan's Executive Order 12356 (which put severe restrictions on the release of classified information). Committees within the task force were charged with addressing oversight, access and dissemination, safeguards, classification standards (including excessive classification and the duration of classification), and declassification. But the task force was composed entirely of government officials who already dealt with classified documents: representatives from domestic organizations such as the Treasury Department, Federal Bureau of Investigation, National Archives, Federal Emergency Management Agency, Department of Transportation, and Nuclear Regulatory Commission, and from foreign policy organizations such as the DIA, navy, coast guard, army, air force, and CIA.

A preliminary account of the proposed changes confirmed the intuition that only incremental changes would emerge from committees composed of the same persons who have been minding the shop all along. Agencies still would be required to systematically review classified documents older than twenty-five years; government officials would not be required to consider the public's need to know when they decide whether to classify documents; and the forty-year "maximum life span" for classified information would be higher than the thirty-year period set under President Nixon and the twenty-year period set under President Carter. More promising is the proposed creation of a government-wide database of declassified documents, the imposition of penalties for the abuse of classification, and the elimination of the presumption that any national security information is classified. Nonetheless, the reality of the draft proposal is at odds with the commission's sweeping mandate and even with the proposal's own ambition to balance "the need to protect critically sensitive information with the public's need to know."[48]

The intelligence community has also reduced in number and relocated analysts formerly working on Soviet and Eastern European matters, and it has increased the number of analysts studying economics and trade. A twelfth officer has been added to the National Intelligence Council, which is responsible for releasing the community's assessments of the world, with a portfolio of environmental, human rights, and other global matters.[49] There has also been a major shake-up of the NRO: signal intelligence satellites are now managed by the air force, photo reconnaissance by the CIA, and ocean-monitoring satellites by the navy.[50]

Yet the post–cold war world requires a reorganization and redirection of the intelligence community beyond what the Clinton administration has accomplished to date. The lack of control over the intelligence community by the DCI remains a severe problem. The director does not appoint the heads of the DIA or the NSA. Neither does the director control the funds and programs of the DIA, the service intelligence agencies, the NSA, or the NRO—each of them a member of the intelligence community for which the director of intelligence is responsible. Without funding and staffing authority, the director cannot direct the community or reasonably be held accountable for its performance by the president and Congress. If intelligence resources are to be reduced, the director of intelligence must have more discretion over personnel appointments and the allocation of resources.

Efficiency is another issue: there are too many producers of intelligence and not enough coordination of their products. The NSA; the army, navy, and air force intelligence; the NRO; the DIA; the State Department's own Intelligence and Research Bureau; the CIA; the NSC staff; and other agencies (including the FBI) produce intelligence, but much of it duplicates the work of others. Ten or more studies may be made of the same topic, all of them little read. Although redundancy offers clear advantages in intelligence (it provides multiple channels of information under conditions in which the lack of adequate intelligence could be disastrous),[51] more intelligence is not always better intelligence. Rather, the less the intelligence community produces and the better coordinated and verified its product, the greater the chance that the product will be used by its consumers, especially its final consumer, the president.

Another problem with the efficiency of the intelligence community is the lack of feedback that it receives. Uncertainty is omnipresent in the community about what the consumers of intelligence want and what they need. Intelligence producers seldom know how their products are being used. Absent clear directives from the administration, the intelligence community becomes driven by its tasks (that is, by its organizational divisions of labor and its technologies) and by its employees (that is, by personal and agency politics), rather than by its mission. Yet even the clearest directives and specifications of presidential needs will have little effect without adequate feedback from the consumers of intelligence to the producers.

A further difficulty faced by the intelligence community is its lack of credibility. The failures of the CIA and other intelligence agencies to anticipate events have been serious: the invasion of Czechoslovakia in 1968 by the Soviet Union under its premier Leonid Brezhnev; the timing of the Tet offensive in Vietnam (also in 1968); Egypt's Yom Kippur attack on Israel in 1973; and the fall of the shah of Iran in 1979.[52] Most recently, John Lehman, navy secretary under President Reagan, has written that the intelligence community's performance in the Persian Gulf conflict "adds fuel to the growing controversy about the gross incompetence of the vast American intelligence bureaucracy." The intelligence product "was largely useless" and "on vital questions of battle and strategic assessments it was downright wrong."[53] Although the actual successes and failures of American intelligence will not be known for many years, the apparent failures are cause enough for concern.

Reports from former CIA analysts that intelligence has repeatedly been shaped to support certain policies have further damaged the community's credibility. William Casey and Robert Gates are said to have used false claims of Soviet support for the Nicaraguan government to justify aid to Nicaragua's contras, to have slanted analysis about the extent of Soviet influence and the moderating influences in Iran to justify the arms sales to Iran, and to have prevented analysts from warning policy makers about the collapse of the Soviet Union and its retreat from the third world.[54] Yet President Clinton's director of intelligence is not only an old hand from the cold war security team but also one who supported President Bush's nomination of Robert Gates as DCI.

An additional problem of the intelligence community is the danger posed by pervasive secrecy: even though democratic government depends on the widespread availability of accurate and adequate political information, information of potential importance is routinely withheld from the public and Congress alike. According to the General Accounting Office, there are "several thousand" special access programs, and hundreds of unauthorized "black" programs (financed by funds either not contained in or hidden in the official budget) dating from the 1980s; civilian control of these programs "has eroded to the point of meaninglessness."[55] Not only are the technical specifications of black projects kept secret, but so are the projects themselves. The absence of accountability, of a check on government, is disturbingly undemocratic. Indicatively, when the Commonwealth of Independent States (the former Soviet Union) asked the United States government for help in establishing intelligence operations in a democratic society, its questions—How do we keep control of intelligence agencies? How do we check the agencies? What are the lessons you have learned?—received few answers.

In short, the intelligence community's large and inefficient organization, as well as its lack of credibility and its overuse of secrecy, pose a danger to the executive branch's command of foreign policy. Remedying the situation need not mean placing the CIA in the State Department or Pentagon or in consolidating the entire intelligence community. A clear need still exists for different sorts of intelligence (human, signal, and image) and for multiple channels of access to and analysis of raw data. But the low state of the intelligence community does suggest that the veil of secrecy hanging over it needs to be lifted, and that the intelligence mission needs to be thoroughly reappraised. Many who have worked with classified materials admit that only a small portion of the information that is withheld from the public is vital to national security.[56]

Conclusion

In its *Memorandum to the President-Elect*, the Carnegie Endowment argued that the U.S. government had to adapt to the transformed policy agenda of the post–cold war era, and that organizing the government required, "first and foremost, organizing the Presidency." It challenged the Clinton presidency to formulate strategy and policy in ways that "cut across established bureaucratic boundaries." The new administration followed much of the memorandum's advice: it established the NEC and the Domestic Policy Council, reorganized the State Department, increased U.S. involvement in and support for the United Nations, and set up task forces to review the role of intelligence and secrecy.[57]

Yet much reorganization remains to be done. If, "to make the government work effectively, it is essential to break down the bureaucratic walls still separating increasingly interrelated issues," then the planning, operations, and administration of the army, navy, air force, and marine corps could be shared among services or even combined. Similarly, serious reevaluation, reorientation, and consolidation of the intelligence community is still wanting; plenty of walls are left to break down.[58] As the head of the federal government and as its chief administrator, the president has the responsibility to initiate changes that are capable of restoring trust in the organizations and processes that safeguard democratic government. But the consolidation or realignment of the organizations of government—especially in the less-visible defense and intelligence sectors—has to be accompanied by an articulation of America's new role in the world.

Foreign Policies and Domestic Politics

A fourth aspect of American foreign policy in the new international system concerns the reorientation of the actual U.S. policies, or sets of policies. As chief legislator, the president is best equipped to promulgate new policies. In addition to the fundamentally important international trade and peacekeeping discussed above, policies in four areas appear especially important.

The Former Soviet Union

The stakes that the United States has in the former Soviet Union are enormous. Russia's stability is vital to Asian and European stability, as is that of all fifteen republics.[59] Unfortunately, it is unclear what the best policies for helping the former U.S.S.R. are, especially as it continues to experience political and economic crises.[60] Consider Russian president Boris Yeltsin's suspension in fall 1993 of the legislature, the Communist party, and the Supreme Constitutional Court. Consider also the civil war in Georgia, the fighting in Moldova, the war between Armenia and Azerbaijan, and the civil war in Tajikistan. Consider, finally, that Russia suffered 25 percent inflation *per month* in 1992 and in the first nine months of 1993 and that its gross domestic product declined by 20 percent in 1992 and 11 percent in the first nine months of 1993. Were Russia to begin to restructure its economy and allow inefficient state industries to fail, living conditions could become much worse in the near future. It may be that policies to expand market forces and to create and support democratic institutions in Russia are mutually inconsistent, or that the pursuit of any one of these policies will exacerbate an already volatile situation.

Nonetheless, it is in the interest of the United States to do what it can to help Russia and the other republics of the former Soviet Union, both for preventive reasons (so that there will not be chaos, a military coup, a return to one-party government, or a threat to U.S. security) and for the prospect of future returns. Although U.S. trade is eight times greater with China than Russia, Russia has an educated citizenry and a national income that in 1992 was seven times greater than China's. A privatized, growing Russian economy would mean "thousands of jobs and billions in trade for the U.S," as former president Richard Nixon observed.[61]

What seems clearly *not* in the interest of the U.S. government is to become tied to a particular ruler, as President Bush was to Gorbachev and as President Clinton is to Yeltsin. Such ties are especially risky if the Russian leader is unwilling to compromise with his opponents and is uncommitted to democratic practices. The advantage to the U.S. government of offering early, vocal support to the winning side of a governmental crisis surely must be tempered by the risks of alienating the Russian people and future power holders and of encouraging repressive, undemocratic government.[62]

Global Issues

Another set of issues that the end of the cold war brought into focus concerns the desperate political, economic, population, health, and environmental problems of the states of northern Africa, southwestern Asia, Sub-Saharan Africa, Oceania, and Latin America. Expressions of nationalism, the problems of immigrant and refugee populations, and political turmoil do not conveniently confine themselves within national boundaries; rather, they spill over to other states. International terrorism, population growth and immigration, the depletion of the ozone layer and global warming, and AIDS all pose severe threats to the U.S. government and the American people.[63] Where these spillover problems have been sufficiently severe, the United States has responded with force. Yet, as seen in Somalia, Haiti, Panama, El Salvador, and elsewhere, direct U.S. military intervention or military assistance to existing regimes is usually expensive and ineffective. Military intervention is damage control—a response to broken institutions—not a cure.

Despite the end of the cold war, however, U.S. aid policies have changed little, with almost half of American aid going to just two nations: Egypt and Israel. Nor has the United States increased its munificence: last year, the United States gave 0.2 percent of its national income ($11.7 billion) in foreign aid. Among developing countries, the richest 40 percent receive more than twice as much aid per capita as the poorest 40 percent.[64] Here is where the contributions of multinational and UN agencies would be valuable. Here, too, the integrity of foreign policy is crucial: if the U.S. government is to turn people away from its borders, interdict drug smugglers, and use force as a last resort, then U.S.

foreign policy has to grapple with the immense problems that face most developing nations.

Petroleum

Oil was one of the justifications for the Gulf War; indeed, accessible imported oil is crucial to the American standard of living. But the United States has yet to reduce its exposure to threats against its oil supplies. At a price of $20 to $25 per barrel, oil alone will increase the annual U.S. trade deficit by $70 billion to $95 billion by 1995—about the *entire* trade deficit for 1991.[65] Steps to reduce oil imports are crucial if the United States is to avoid another oil crisis.

Choices do exist. Because the Middle East supplies only 32 percent of the world's oil and the region is divided among several major producers, the United States need not be dependent on Saudi Arabia or any other state. Russia will produce more oil in the future as its fields are developed, as Western companies invest, and as its technology is upgraded. Natural gas is an increasingly competitive alternative for nontransportation uses of petroleum, and its use can be expanded accordingly. Moreover, there is much that the United States can do to alter its demand for foreign-supplied petroleum: make further domestic exploration more feasible; raise taxes on the sale of gasoline and diesel fuel at the pump; mandate higher fuel efficiency in cars and trucks; and provide incentives to get gas-guzzling (and more polluting) older vehicles off the road. In fact, the United States has the power of the Organization of Petroleum Exporting Countries (OPEC) in reverse: as the world's largest buyer of petroleum, it has the power to reduce oil prices by reducing its own consumption.[66]

Domestic Politics

Domestic social and economic conditions cannot be kept separate from the presence of the United States in the world.[67] Issues of education, the infrastructure (roads, bridges, sewers, and communication lines), the cities, and crime matter. Concerns over energy, the federal deficit, and the trade deficit not only carry a greater weight in the post–cold war world, but the lack of progress currently being made on these issues threatens the security of the United States as a free society able to maintain its fundamental institutions and values. Unfortunately, the American electorate and the U.S. government have yet to confront these problems directly.[68] A world of increased economic competition demands more active leadership by national officials to reduce the budget deficit and meliorate the pathological conditions that exist in the nation's urban and many of its suburban areas. Without domestic political reform, the specter of congressional term limits will grow. But the imposition of term limits would only lessen congressional expertise, strengthen the executive branch at the expense of the legislative branch, and enhance the importance of the nonelected, semipermanent congressional staff. Once more, the president has to educate and consult with the public and with Congress about the goals and priorities of American national interests and, hence, foreign policy.

Conclusions

Just as the Roosevelt and Truman administrations were instrumental in setting up the International Monetary Fund and the International Bank for Reconstruction and Development in the Bretton Woods accords of 1944, creating the United Nations in 1945, and establishing national and international institutions to carry on the cold war in the middle and late 1940s, so is the administration of President Clinton—or its successor—in a position to make necessary changes for the 1990s and beyond. The end of the cold war and the erosion of the bipolar world system will affect U.S. foreign policy across the board, from its stated mission to the process of policy making, to the organizations that enact it, to the policies themselves.

The Bush administration spoke of a "new world order," but it did little to adjust the presidency to the post–cold war world. No doctrine was offered in the place of anticommunism; no reappraisal of presidential-congressional relations took place; no redesign or reconfiguration was made of the organizations that conduct U.S. foreign policy; and no comprehensive set of policies was developed for dealing with the former Soviet Union, developing states, American dependence on foreign oil, or domestic problems. Bush had reasons for staying the course—the very suddenness of the collapse of the Soviet Union and its Eastern European satellites, and the Gulf War—but the result is that it has been left to the Clinton administration to reorient the presidency for the post–cold war world.

Where the Clinton administration is heading is still unclear. Clinton's actions on Somalia, the former Yugoslavia, Haiti, and the republics of the former Soviet Union suggest an ad hoc and defensive foreign policy, without overarching vision. On the other hand, the pronunciation of the enlargement doctrine, the formation of the National Economic Council, the limited reorganizations of the State and Defense departments, the establishment of committees to reappraise the intelligence community and the use of secrecy, and the NAFTA victory suggest that the Clinton administration recognizes the need to reevaluate American foreign policy. For all the criticism that Clinton has received on foreign policy, the president and his advisers may yet recognize the rare opportunities of the present.

In addition to the international pressures on the presidency, two other factors point to the urgency of presidential action. One is the American people's loss of respect for their government; almost three-quarters of Americans do not trust the government to do what is right.[69] Although the widespread dissatisfaction with government is largely the product of domestic political issues such as the budget deficit, the savings and loan crisis, and health care, foreign policy is also implicated. Consider the news that the Pentagon systematically inflated the Soviet threat during the cold war, misled the public about the ability of the B-1 bomber to attack the Soviet Union without detection, exaggerated the ability of the B-2 Stealth bomber to penetrate Soviet air defenses, and misrepresented the comparative advantages of U.S. and Soviet submarines (underestimating the capacities of the former, overstating those of the latter).[70] Consider, further, the reports that the Star Wars tests were rigged and the results falsified in order to deceive the Soviet government (and consequently, the U.S. Congress). This pattern of official deception has contaminated respect for the U.S. government, the conduct of U.S. foreign policy, and the presidency.

Another reason for prompt presidential action to establish a comprehensive new foreign policy—one able to span ideas, organizations, and policies—is that troubling patterns are already starting to emerge in existing policy. One is the seemingly ad hoc intervention of American forces in trouble spots around the world. Such policework by the United States or multinational forces is short-sighted and unsustainable in the absence of criteria that specify clear objectives and contingencies and unless the policework is duly complemented by appropriate diplomatic, economic, and humanitarian policies.

A second disturbing pattern is the continuing search for enemies. Japan, China, and Islam have all been suggested as new, major threats to American security. To be sure, good political, economic, and strategic reasons exist for taking seriously the actual or potential conflicts between the United States and a number of non-Western states.[71] But in view of the success of Western culture, the U.S. model of government and civil society, and U.S. power, the government does itself and international liberalism a disservice by reacting so fearfully to its real or imagined enemies and by responding so heavy-handedly to its critics.[72] Indeed, the fact that most serious threats facing the United States have varied over the last three years—from Japan, to Iraq, to North Korea—

suggests the shallowness and impermanence of these very threats, to be contrasted with the danger posed by the Soviet Union in the cold war era and by Germany during the late nineteenth and early twentieth centuries. The Clinton presidency and Congress can now, with the end of the cold war, afford to be both more confident and more introspective. Why is the United States so disliked in some quarters? Are U.S. foreign policies having the effects intended? What aspects of U.S. foreign policy need to be rethought or redesigned? The marvel of liberal democracy is that it contains within it the processes for changing how a nation-state relates to the world.

At no time since its founding has the United States been in such a flexible position in its relationships with the rest of the world. The United States is at a critical time in its history, a time when it is able to define itself on terms that it chooses. That the Clinton administration is struggling to come to grips with the post–cold war world should not be a surprise. But it would be ironic if the president, Congress, and the public were unable to recognize and take advantage of the opportunity that the United States has won through its own strategic, political, and economic successes of the cold war. The initiative in foreign policy necessarily lies with the president. Only the president is in a position to revive the moral leadership of the United States; meliorate the institutional relations between the executive and legislative branches; lead in redefining, consolidating, and reorganizing the agencies that conduct U.S. foreign policy; and propose new foreign policies.

Notes

The author thanks Camille Busette, Scott Parrish, Elspeth D. Rostow, Walt W. Rostow, and Michael Nelson for their contributions to an earlier draft of this chapter.

1. See, for example, Richard Rose, *The Postmodern President*, 2d ed. (Chatham, N.J.: Chatham House, 1991). This is not to deny the parallels and continuities of the present era with that of the cold war: the control of the Atlantic and Pacific oceans, expansion of U.S. businesses abroad, and limiting the proliferation of nuclear weapons.

2. Numerous articles have been written on the need for the Clinton administration to articulate a foreign policy. See, for example, Leon Sigal, "The Last Cold War Election," *Foreign Affairs* 71 (Winter 1992/1993): 1–15; David C. Hendrickson, "The End of History: American Security, the National Purpose, and the New World Order," in *Rethinking America's Security: Beyond Cold War to New World Order*, ed. Graham Allison and Gregory F. Treverton (New York: Norton, 1992); Gregory F. Treverton and Barbara A. Bicksler, "Conclusion: Getting from Here to Where?" in *Rethinking America's Security*; Carla Ann Robbins, "A Failure to Define Foreign Policy Plans Is Dogging Clinton," *Wall Street Journal*, August 25, 1993; Robert L. Bartley, "The Case for Optimism," *Foreign Affairs* 72 (September/October 1993): 15–18; "How American Sees the World" and "Otherwise Engaged," *Economist*, October 30–November 5, 1993.

3. The former chairman of the Joint Chiefs of Staff, Gen. Colin Powell, notes that the present, like the Revolution, the Civil War, and World War II, marks a "rendezvous with destiny" (Colin Powell, "U.S. Forces: Challenges Ahead," *Foreign Affairs* 71 [Winter 1992/1993]: 32–45). For a different periodization of "Big Changes" based on electoral realignments, see Michael Vlahos, "Culture and Foreign Policy," *Foreign Policy*, no. 82 (Spring 1991): 59–78. Also see Ernest R. May, "National Security in America's History," in *Rethinking America's Security*.

4. For an assessment of the Bush administration, see Terry L. Deibel, "Bush's Foreign Policy: Mastery and Inaction," *Foreign Policy* (Fall 1991): 3–23.

5. Lawrence Freedman and Efraim Karsh, *The Gulf Conflict 1990–1991* (Princeton, N.J.: Princeton University Press, 1993); Hedrick Smith, ed., *The Media and the Gulf War* (Washington, D.C.: Foreign Policy Institute of the School of Advanced International Studies, Johns Hopkins University, 1992); Jean Edward Smith, *George Bush's War* (New York: Holt, 1992); David Hendrickson, "The End of American History," in *Rethinking America's Security*.

6. See, for example, Aleksa Djilas, "A Profile of Slobodan Milosevic," *Foreign Affairs* 72 (Summer 1993): 81–96; Madeleine K. Albright, "Yes, There Is a Reason to Be in Somalia," *New York Times*, August 10, 1993.

7. See George F. Kennan, "Somalia, Through a Glass Darkly," *New York Times*, September 30, 1993. Also see Robert J. Donovan and Ray Scherer, *Unsilent Revolution: Television News and American Public Life* (Cambridge: Cambridge University Press, 1992).

8. Thomas E. Ricks, "Defense Secretary Aspin Draws Heaviest Fire as Criticism Mounts over U.S. Role in Somalia," *Wall Street Journal*, October 8, 1993; Sidney Blumenthal, "Why Are We in Somalia?" *New Yorker*, October 25, 1993.

9. Joseph Nye, *Bound to Lead* (New York: Basic Books, 1990); Paul Kennedy, *The Rise and Fall of the Great Powers* (New York: Vintage Books, 1989); Michael Mandelbaum, "Like It or Not, We Must Lead," *New York Times*, June 9, 1993; U.S. Department of State Management Task Force, *State 2000: A New Model for Managing Foreign Affairs* (Washington, D.C.: U.S. Department of State, 1992; hereafter cited as *State 2000*).

Contrary to the conventional reading of *The Rise and Fall of the Great Powers*, Kennedy does not say that the United States must decline, only that there is a pattern in the British and the Soviet cases that applies to the United States. Kennedy recognizes that the United States can slow and even arrest its decline; his book is a call to arms, not a claim of inevitability.

10. *New York Times*, September 23, 1993.

11. Sigal, "The Last Cold War Election," 8.

12. See Thomas C. Schelling, "The Global Dimension," in *Rethinking America's Security*, 196–210.

13. G. John Ikenberry, "Salvaging the G-7," *Foreign Affairs* 72 (Spring 1993): 132–139.

14. Elaine Scoliano, "Nunn Says He Wants Exit Strategy If U.S. Troops Are Sent to Bosnia," *New York Times*, September 24, 1993.

15. James Schlesinger, "Quest for a Post–Cold War Foreign Policy," *Foreign Affairs* 72 (1992/1993): 20–21.

16. Carnegie Endowment and Institute for International Economics Commission on Government Renewal, *Memorandum to the President-Elect: Harnessing Process to Purpose* (Washington, D.C.: Carnegie Endowment for International Peace, 1992), 16.

17. Zbigniew Brzezinski, "Weak Ramparts of the Permissive West," *New Perspectives Quarterly* 10 (Summer 1993): 4–9; Henry R. Nau, "The Moral Argument for U.S.

Leadership," *Wall Street Journal*, August 26, 1993; "The Reluctant Sheriff," *Economist*, June 19, 1993; Hans Mark, "The Only Superpower" (Paper delivered at a Symposium on "Efficient Defense for the 1990s," George Washington University, December 10, 1991).

18. Charles William Maynes, "Learning the Hard Way in Bosnia," *New York Times*, May 26, 1993.

19. The State Department's comprehensive plan for reorganizing and remaking American foreign policy also mentions the place of integrity. See *State 2000*, 3. On the need for the United States to look to its own arms sales, see A. M. Rosenthal, "So Where's the Catch," *New York Times*, September 28, 1993.

20. See Alan Tonelson, "Superpower without a Sword," *Foreign Affairs* 72 (Summer 1993): 166–180, for a similar argument on a defense strategy that protects and complements domestic vitality, rather than directly projects American force abroad. Also see Sigal, "The Last Cold War Election," 9; and the subsection "Domestic Politics" in the text below.

21. Brzezinski, "Weak Ramparts of the Permissive West," 4–9; Ted Galen Carpenter, "The New World Disorder," 37–39.

22. Charles Krauthammer, "The Unipolar Moment," in *Rethinking America's Security*, 306.

23. Blumenthal, "Why Are We in Somalia?" 53.

24. Powell, "U.S. Forces," 39.

25. Harold Hongju Koh, *The National Security Constitution* (New Haven: Yale University Press, 1990), 158, 137.

26. Ibid., 148.

27. See Sigal, "The Last Cold War Election," 9; Treverton and Bicksler, "Conclusion," 425–426.

28. See *State 2000*; Carnegie Endowment, *Memorandum to the President-Elect*.

29. Tom Shoop, "The Facilitator," *Government Executive*, May 1993, 13. The Clinton administration has also taken steps to integrate economic and, in particular, trade issues into the foreign policy organizations, with the secretary of the treasury, Lloyd Bentsen; the head of the National Economic Council, Robert Rubin; and UN Ambassador Albright all being placed on the National Security Council. The chief of staff, Mack McLarty, and the attorney general, Janet Reno, also regularly attend NSC meetings.

30. Members on the NEC include Robert Rubin as chair, Vice President Albert Gore, Treasury Secretary Lloyd Bentsen, Commerce Secretary Ronald Brown, Labor Secretary Robert Reich, Office of Management and Budget Director Leon Panetta, and the chair of the Council of Economic Advisors, Laura Tyson.

National Security Adviser Lake, who was an aide to former national security adviser and secretary of state Henry Kissinger and a protégé of former secretary of state Cyrus Vance, has initiated weekly lunches with Secretary of State Christopher, Secretary of Defense Les Aspin, and the director of the CIA, James Woolsey. Lake does not seek to dominate foreign policy, as did several of his predecessors. Rubin, for his part, is said to be a natural conciliator who sees the NEC's role as one of neutrality and impartiality. Consistent with this image of collegiality and collaboration, the NEC's meetings are often compared to graduate seminars rather than board meetings.

31. Warren Christopher, "A Message for All State Department Employees," Memorandum, February 5, 1993.

32. See *State 2000*; David D. Newsom, "The Clinton Administration and the Foreign Service," *Foreign Service Journal* 70 (April 1993); and Anne Stevenson-Yang, "Teamwork," *Foreign Service Journal* 70 (April 1993).

33. "Reinventing Government," Statement by Richard Boucher, U.S. Department of State, Office of the Spokesman, May 14, 1993; Secretary of State Warren Christopher, "To All State Employees," Memorandum, May 14, 1993. Also see the State Department's transcript of "Press Q's and A's" on the time frame and details of the Reinventing Government effort.

34. See Thomas L. Friedman, "Cold War without End," *New York Times Magazine*, August 22, 1993.

35. See Paul D. Wolfowitz, "The New Defense Strategy," in *Rethinking America's Security*. Also see Mandelbaum, "Like It or Not," on the advantages of U.S. forces in Europe and the Pacific: the forces of no other state can similarly reassure the regional powers.

36. Michael A. Gordon, "Military Plan Would Cut Forces but Have Them Ready for Two Wars," *New York Times*, September 2, 1993.

37. Eric Schmitt, "Pentagon Is Ready with a Plan for a Leaner, Versatile Military," *New York Times*, June 11, 1993.

38. Powell, "U.S. Forces," 41–44.

39. "Towards a Clinton Doctrine," *Economist*, July 17, 1993, Editorial.

40. Brent Scowcroft, "Who Can Harness History? Only the U.S.," *New York Times*, July 2, 1993; Robert M. Gates, "No Time to Disarm," *Wall Street Journal*, August 23, 1993.

41. R. Jeffrey Smith, "Defense Policy Posts Restructured," *Washington Post*, January 28, 1993.

42. Susanne M. Schafer, "U.S.-based Soldiers to Report to Single Commander," *Austin American-Statesman*, September 30, 1993.

43. See Treverton and Bicksler, "Conclusion," 423–424. Treverton and Bicksler note that "now is the time to think about radical change in the way America does its national security business," although possibly not the time to implement radical change.

44. David L. Boren, "The Intelligence Community: How Crucial?" *Foreign Affairs* 71 (Summer 1992): 52–62. Also see Douglas Jehl, "The New Challenges for the C.I.A. Are Open Secrets," *New York Times*, May 9, 1993.

45. Douglas Jehl, "Defying Warnings, Congress Prepares to Cut Spy Budget," *New York Times*, June 18, 1993; Tim Weiner, "C.I.A. Is Rebuffed on Spying Budget," *New York Times*, July 17, 1993. The director of intelligence argued for more money, of course.

46. "Spooked Over Intelligence Cuts," *New York Times*, March 18, 1993, Editorial.

47. The fact that all but one member of the commission were government insiders ran contrary to the Carnegie Endowment's advice that President Clinton use outside political appointees as well as selected members of the president's Foreign Intelligence Advisory Board for the reassessment of the role of intelligence in the post–cold war world (*Memorandum to the President-Elect*).

48. Steven Aftergood and Tom Blanton, "Secrets and More Secrets," *New York Times*, September 30, 1993.

49. Jehl, "The New Challenges for the C.I.A."

50. Tim Weiner, "C.I.A. Fights Plan to Cut Its Budget," *New York Times*, July 16, 1993.

51. See Jonathan Bendor, *Parallel Systems: Redundancy in Government* (Berkeley: University of California Press, 1985).

52. Melvin A. Goodman, "Oldthink at the C.I.A.?" *New York Times*, January 7, 1993; Jerel Rosati, *The Politics of United States Foreign Policy* (New York: Holt, Rinehart and Winston, 1993).

53. John Lehman, "The Gulf War in Review," *Wall Street Journal*, October 12, 1993.

54. Rosati, *The Politics of United States Foreign Policy*.

55. Tim Weiner, *Blank Check* (New York: Warner Books, 1991), 10–11.

56. Arthur Goldberg, the former Supreme Court justice and ambassador to the United Nations, testified during the Vietnam War that in his experience, "75 percent of documents should never have been classified in the first place; another 15 percent quickly outlived the need for secrecy; and only about 10 percent genuinely required restricted access" (Koh, *The National Security Constitution*, 200–201). Richard Garwin, who helped to build the hydrogen bomb and has been a defense consultant, calls the black programs "profoundly undemocratic." According to Garwin, most black programs exist to "avert criticism and evaluation" (quoted in Weiner, *Blank Check*, 17).

One way to allow for feedback is to bring in other government, private, and academic experts on a permanent basis. The National Intelligence Council, although currently dominated by the CIA, could serve as an intergovernmental think tank. Crucial to the success of this group would be a clear separation of government and private-sector experts from CIA operations in order to free the experts of the taint of covert operations. Or, Congress could be reintegrated into the making of foreign policy. Koh recommends completely rewriting the National Security Act of 1947 into the "National Security Reform Act," which would, among other proposed reforms, establish a legal adviser and staff on foreign and international law in Congress, equalize each branch's access to sensitive information, create a consultative group of members of Congress to meet with the president and his advisers on emergency or sensitive issues, and strengthen the Intelligence Oversight Board.

57. Carnegie Endowment, *Memorandum to the President-Elect*. The memorandum did speak of reorganizing the military, but only in relation to cooperation with the United Nations.

58. Ibid., 2.

59. Graham Allison and Robert Blackwill, "The Grand Bargain: The West and the Future of the Soviet Union," in *Rethinking America's Security*; Mandelbaum, "Like It or Not." Also see Richard Nixon, "Clinton's Greatest Challenge," *New York Times*, March 5, 1993.

60. See Walter Laqueur, "Russian Nationalism—A Turn to the Right," *Foreign Affairs* 71 (Winter 1992/1993): 103–116.

61. Nixon, "Clinton's Greatest Challenge." Nixon remarked that Russia should be treated as a proud, struggling friend, not as a begging former enemy; the Communist party was the enemy, not the Russian people.

62. See, for example, Douglas Jehl, "U.S. Officials Are Cheered by Rout of Yeltsin Foes," *New York Times*, October 6, 1993; and George Melloan, "Yeltsin Triumphs, but Some Bills Will Come Due," *Wall Street Journal*, September 27, 1993.

63. Thomas C. Schelling, "The Global Dimension," in *Rethinking America's Security*. Also see Joseph J. Romm and Amory B. Lovins, "Fueling a Competitive Economy," *Foreign Affairs* 71 (Winter 1992/1993): 46–62; Michael Teitelbaum, "The Population Threat," *Foreign Affairs* 71 (Winter 1992/1993): 63–78.

64. "While the Rich World Talks," *Economist*, July 10, 1993, Editorial.

65. Peter G. Petersen, with James Sebenius, "The Primacy of the Domestic Agenda," in *Rethinking America's Security*.

66. Ibid., 70–74.

67. See Sigal, "The Last Cold War Election."

68. Petersen, "The Primacy of the Domestic Agenda." Also see Michael Borrus and John Zysman, "Industrial Competitiveness and National Security," in *Rethinking America's Security*. Borrus and Zysman make the point that American security depends on the health of its international competitiveness in trade, technology, and finance.

69. In a 1990 National Election Studies survey, 72.5 percent of respondents felt that the government could not be trusted either almost all or most of the time, 68.5 percent felt that the government wasted "a lot" (rather than "not very much" or "some"), and 75 percent felt that the government is run by a "few big interests" rather than "for the benefit of all the people" (Warren Miller, Donald Kinder, and Steven Rosenstone, *The American National Election Studies*, vol. 1 [Ann Arbor, Mich.: Interuniversity Consortium for Political and Social Research, 1992]).

70. "Pentagon Pinocchios," *New York Times*, July 2, 1993, Editorial. In "The Primacy of the Domestic Agenda," Petersen also notes the widespread cynicism of government and its corrosive effects on national government (83–85).

71. For the best-known thesis about the dangers posed by non-Western states, see Samuel P. Huntington, "The Clash of Civilizations?" *Foreign Affairs* 72 (Summer 1993): 22–49; and Huntington, "The Islamic-Confucian Connection," *New Perspectives Quarterly* 10 (Summer 1993): 21. See Judith Miller, "The Challenge of Radical Islam," *Foreign Affairs* 72 (Spring 1993): 43–56, for complementary concerns.

Opposing arguments include: Leon T. Hadar, "What Green Peril?" *Foreign Affairs* 72 (Spring 1993): 27–42 (green referring to the color of Islam); Fouad Ajami, "The Summoning," *Foreign Affairs* 72 (September/October 1993): 2–9; Akbar S. Ahmed, "Media Mongols at the Gates of Baghdad," *New Perspectives Quarterly* 10 (Summer 1993): 10–18; Hassan Al-Turabi, "The Islamic Awakening's New Wave," *New Perspectives Quarterly* 10 (Summer 1993): 42–45; and Kishore Mahbubani, "The Dangers of Decadence," *Foreign Affairs* 72 (September/October 1993): 10–14.

72. Bartley, "The Case for Optimism."

Index

Reagan, Ronald and, 49, 244, 281, 315, 331, 376n
Reagan administration, 11, 81, 186, 361, 363, 392, 564
"second constitution" and, 115
Iran hostage incident, 79, 259, 314, 391, 405n
Iraq, 564, 565, 570
Israel
Camp David accords, 16, 162
Clinton, Bill and, 441
Egyptian Yom Kippur attack, 573
Palestine Liberation Organization, 441
political parties, 76, 77
U.S. aid to, 576
Italy, 80

Jackson, Andrew, 3, 4, 33
election of 1828, 128, 129
election of 1832, 132, 134
governmental and banking reform, 159, 165
personality, 134
as president, 126–128, 130–134, 137, 139, 164, 383
vetoes, 446
Jackson, Henry, 481
Jackson, Jesse, 228, 270n, 521–522
Janis, Irving, 184, 396
Japan, 321–322
atomic bomb, 202
government system, 62, 73
political parties, 80
political process, 71, 73
Jay, John, 92, 201. *See also* The Federalist
Jefferson, Thomas, 97
media and, 315
as president, 33, 164, 382, 503, 564
psychological attributes, 206, 209
ranking as president, 126
as vice president, 502, 504, 564
Jenkins, Walter, 394
Jensen, Richard, 333
Johnson, Lyndon B.
civil rights, 147, 279, 355
Congress and, 452–453, 460, 463, 564
election of 1964, 20
Great Society, 6, 115, 152, 302, 313, 354–358
health of, 506
image of, 53
media and, 311
personality and psychology, 7, 173, 206, 208, 209, 210, 214
political parties and, 348, 349, 354–358
as president, 9, 50, 331, 376n, 382, 388, 394, 460
public view of, 21
Supreme Court nominations, 483
vetoes, 446–447

as vice president, 147, 502
Vietnam War, 173, 203, 206, 210, 315, 331
War on Poverty, 50, 390
Johnson administration
government organization, 376n
judiciary and, 481–482
legislation, 541
Office of Economic Opportunity, 390–391
White House functions, 50
White House staff, 394
Joint Chiefs of Staff, 38, 57, 340
Jordon, Hamilton, 48, 69, 387, 394, 395
Journalists. *See also* Media; White House Press Office
Clinton, Bill, 291–292
critical reporting, 319
daily newspapers, 212
"instant analysis," 303–304
"pack journalism," 317
presidency and, 9–14, 24, 41, 42, 303–304, 312, 319
presidential narratives, 312–315
reporting standards, 310–312
role of, 275–276
White House staff and, 397
Judiciary, U.S. *See also* Federal courts; Supreme Court
appointments, confirmations, and nominations, 469, 470–491
Constitution and, 102, 105, 107
foreign policy, 565
patronage, 473, 484
political parties and, 341–342
presidency and, 413, 468–491
screening of candidates, 474

Kansas-Nebraska Act, 156, 157, 164
Katz, Elihu, 274
Kavanagh, Dennis, 73
Keep Commission, 384
Kelley, Stanley, 154
Kelso, Frank, 339
Kemp, Jack F., 180, 191, 514
Kemp-Roth tax bill, 180–181
Kennedy, Edward M.
Bush, George and, 510
Carter, Jimmy and, 161, 166, 269n
Kennedy, John F.
assassination, 16, 21, 203, 506
Bay of Pigs invasion, 37, 42, 184, 402
civil rights, 146–151, 281
Congress and, 452t, 453, 463, 564
Cuban missile crisis, 37, 79, 281, 402
image of, 37, 281
judicial system, 465n
media and, 279, 280, 281, 319
New Frontier, 145, 279, 281, 313, 402
personality and psychology, 206, 277, 279–281

Republican National Committee (RNC), 360, 364, 365, 479
Republican Party. *See also* Conservatives and conservatism
  budget issues, 341, 365, 548
  under Bush, George, 363–366, 548
  civil rights, 149, 150
  Civil Service Reform Act of 1978, 423
  Congress and, 20, 270n
  election of 1824, 128
  election of 1932, 128
  election of 1938, 136
  election of 1988, 363
  election of 1990, 365–366, 377n
  election of 1992, 267, 270n
  entrenchment in government, 338–341
  family values, 261
  filibusters, 335
  following the assassination of Lincoln, Abraham, 129
  health care reform, 325
  historians, 5
  military and, 338–340, 341
  modernization of, 360
  motor voter act, 335
  under Nixon, Richard M., 348, 349, 358–359
  nominations and elections, 226, 331
  North American Free Trade Agreement, 370
  Quayle, Dan and, 517
  under Reagan, Ronald, 360–363, 547
  Regan, Donald and, 395
  role of political parties, 349
  Southern, 146, 488–489
  taxation, 365
Research. *See also* Political science; Presidency
  National Election Studies, 232, 254, 255
  perspectives, content, and methods, 30–32, 208–209, 212, 448–450
  presidential campaigns, 236
  presidential imagery, 35–37
  presidential leadership, 448–449, 454–455, 458
  psychological, 208, 216
  voting, 232–233
Reynolds, William Bradford, 472
Ridgeway, Matthew, 53
RNC. *See* Republican National Committee
Robertson, Pat, 252, 489
Rockefeller, John D., IV, 521
Rockefeller, Nelson, 496, 498, 499–500, 513
Rockman, Bert, 22
Rollins, Ed, 366
Roosevelt, Franklin D., 3, 126. *See also* New Deal
  civil rights, 146
  Congress and, 19, 135, 350–351

Court-packing controversy, 352
  death of, 497, 506
  election of 1932, 128–129
  media and, 351, 352
  personality and psychology, 134, 172–173, 206, 209–210
  political parties and, 348–354
  as president, 115, 125, 126–128, 134–137, 164, 165, 166, 173, 279, 312, 383, 393
  selection of vice president, 505
  Supreme Court and, 134–136
  as vice presidential candidate, 505
Roosevelt administration, 383–385
  cabinet, 383
  foreign policies, 557
  reforms, 136–137, 348–354, 373n–374n, 384, 386, 403n, 404n, 420
  White House staff, 383, 386, 393
Roosevelt, Theodore, 32, 279, 301–302, 303, 313, 384, 446, 503
Rose, Richard, 66
Rosenbaum, David, 266
Rosenman, Sam, 384
Rossiter, Clinton
  American Presidency, The, 5, 80
  importance of the presidency, 16–17
  politics and the presidency, 81
Rostenkowski, Dan, 394–395
Rostow, Walt W., 391
Roth, William V., Jr., 180
Rozell, Mark, 317
Rowe, James, 356
Rubin, Robert, 582n
Rumsfeld, Donald, 47–48
Russia, 191, 441, 575, 577. *See also* Yeltsin, Boris

Sack, Kevin, 515
Safire, William, 305, 482, 522
Salant, Richard, 218
Salinger, Pierre, 280–281, 329n
SALT. *See* Strategic Arms Limitation Treaty
Sasso, John, 258
Satellites, 571, 572
Saudi Arabia, 561
Saxbe, William, 484, 486
Scandinavia, 62, 73. *See also individual countries*
Schattschneider, E. E., 333
Schlesinger, Arthur M., Jr.
  Roosevelt, Franklin D., 173
  view of presidents, 6, 9
  view of vice presidents, 497
Schlesinger, Arthur M., Sr., 3, 4, 5–6
Schlesinger, James, 182, 561
Schmidt, Helmut, 78
Schneider, Claudine J., 515
Schneider, Greg, 397
Schwarzkopf, Norman, 288
Schweiker, Richard, 484

White House Office, 40, 353, 355–356, 362, 385, 386, 426
White House Office of Congressional Liaison, 481–482, 483, 484–485, 486, 491n
White House Office of Public Liaison, 87n, 487, 488, 491n
White House Office of Science and Technology Policy, 499
White House Office on Environmental Policy, 523
White House Personnel Authorization-Employment Act of 1978, 427
White House Press Office. *See also* Journalists; Media
  coverage, 11–14
  cynicism of, 9–14
  daily briefing, 10
  negotiations with press corps, 299–302, 318
  press secretaries, 318, 329n
  role of, 11, 12, 13, 39, 304
  status of, 10–11
  Stephanopoulos, George, 293, 319
White House staff. *See also* National Security Council; Presidency
  budget, 383
  bureaucratization and politicization of, 396–400, 402–403
  Bush administration, 365, 395–396, 480–481
  Carter administration, 183, 385, 388, 394–395
  chief of staff, 48, 55, 184, 185, 387–388, 393–396
  Clinton administration, 192–193, 293, 382, 388–389, 401
  Eisenhower administration, 382, 385, 394, 401–403
  growth and size of, 7, 40, 50, 67, 81, 381, 382, 384–387, 389, 425–427, 468
  Johnson administration, 356, 382, 388
  Kennedy administration, 388, 402, 404n
  leaks by, 13, 54–55, 70
  media and, 299–305
  Nixon administration, 382, 388, 479, 485–486
  organization of, 47–48, 389–398
  policy making by, 391–393, 468–469
  presidents and, 381–383, 393–396, 400–403, 404n

Reagan administration, 183, 185, 382, 388, 395, 479–480
  role of, 67, 81, 384, 387, 389, 468–469
  Roosevelt administration, 382, 383–384, 393, 404n
  Supreme Court nominations, 479–481
White House travel office, 193, 292, 298, 388
Whitewater. *See* Clinton, Bill
Wilder, L. Douglas, 237
Will, George, 509
Williams, John, 483
Williams, Walter, 396
Willkie, Wendell, 71
Wills, Gary, 115
Wilmot, David, 144
Wilmot Proviso, 144
Wilson, Harold, 66, 83
Wilson, James, 100, 470, 471
Wilson, Woodrow, 3, 29, 126
  Brandeis, Louis and, 477
  Congressional Government, 104
  Constitutional Government in the United States, 104
  League of Nations, 206
  personality and psychology, 206, 209, 214
  political parties and, 372n
  as president, 129, 237, 303, 313, 350, 351, 503
  theories of, 32, 92, 104–114, 301–302, 350, 373n, 446
Witcover, Jules, 519
Wofford, Harris, 252, 521
Wolfe, Christopher, 104
Women's issues
  homosexuals in the military, 339
  nomination democracy, 227
  sexual harassment, 339, 342, 343
  Supreme Court, 475
Wood, Kimba, 342, 445
Woodward, Bob, 515, 518, 520
Woolsey, James, 571, 582n
Wright, Jim, 345
Wright, John R., 486, 488

Yankelovich polls, 519
Yeltsin, Boris, 307, 441, 575
Yeutter, Clayton, 365
Young, David, 482
Young Americans for Freedom, 488
Young Republicans, 488
Youngstown Sheet and Tube Co. v. Sawyer, 565